SIXTH EDITION

Terrorism and Homeland Security

Jonathan R. White

Grand Valley State University

WADSWORTH
CENGAGE Learning™

Australia • Brazil • Japan • Korea • Mexico • Singapore • Spain • United Kingdom • United States

WADSWORTH
CENGAGE Learning™

Terrorism and Homeland Security,
Sixth Edition
Jonathan R. White

Senior Acquisitions Editor, Criminal Justice:
 Carolyn Henderson Meier

Development Editors: Rebecca Johnson,
 Shelley Murphy

Assistant Editor: Beth Rodio

Editorial Assistant: Jill Nowlin

Technology Project Manager:
 Lauren Keyes

Marketing Manager: Terra Schultz

Marketing Assistant: Ileana Shevlin

Marketing Communications Manager:
 Tami Strang

Project Manager, Editorial Production:
 Jennie Redwitz

Creative Director: Rob Hugel

Art Director: Vernon Boes

Print Buyer: Linda Hsu

Permissions Editor: Bob Kauser

Production Service: Jamie Armstrong,
 Newgen–Austin

Text Designer: Lisa Devenish

Photo Researcher: Kim Adams Fox

Copy Editor: Mary Ann Short

Illustrator: Newgen

Cover Designer: Dustin York,
 Yvo Riezebos Design

Cover Image: Habib Khan/Getty Images

Compositor: Newgen

> For product information and technology assistance,
> contact us at
> **Cengage Learning Academic Resource Center,**
> **1-800-423-0563**
>
> For permission to use material from this text or product,
> submit all requests online at
> **www.cengage.com/permissions.**
> Further permissions questions can be e-mailed to
> **permissionrequest@cengage.com.**

Library of Congress Control Number: 2007938836
ISBN-13: 978-0-534-62448-4
ISBN-10: 0-534-62448-0

Wadsworth Cengage Learning
10 Davis Drive
Belmont, CA 94002-3098
USA

Cengage Learning products are represented in Canada by Nelson Education, Ltd.

For your course and learning solutions, visit
academic.cengage.com.
Purchase any of our products at your local college store
or at our preferred online store **www.ichapters.com.**

Photo Credits: Part Openers, pages 1, 2, 3, 4. 1, 117, 215, 391: © Veer/Getty Images. **Page 2:** AP Photo/Mark Mobley. **22:** AP Photo/Amit Bhardwaj. **44:** AP Photo/Ben Curtis, File. **73:** AP Photo/Ahn Young-joon. **97:** AP Photo/Luis Tejido/EFE. **118:** Bridgeman-Giraudon/Art Resource, NY. **140:** AP Photo/Adam Butler. **161:** Susana Gonzalez/AFP/Getty Images. **184:** AP Photo/Mohammed Zaatari. **216:** AP Photo/Nasser Ishtayeh. **247:** AP Photo/B. K. Bangash. **279:** AP Photo/Gemunu Amarasinghe. **316:** AP Photo/Alexander Zemlianichenko. **346:** Time Life Pictures/Getty Images. **392:** AP Photo/Mark Mobley. **429:** AP Photo/Eric Gay. **458:** Photo by Chip Somodevilla/Getty Images.

Printed in the United States of America
1 2 3 4 5 6 7 12 11 10 09 08

Dedicated to:

Doug Bodrero
President, Commissioner, Sheriff, and Friend

About the Author

Jonathan White is Professor of Criminal Justice at Grand Valley State University, Grand Rapids, Michigan, and a Senior Research Associate for the Institute for Intergovernmental Research, Tallahassee, Florida. He holds a Ph.D. in Criminal Justice and Criminology from Michigan State University and a Master of Divinity from Western Theological Seminary. He teaches classes on religious terrorism for the Department of Justice, Bureau of Justice Assistance, State and Local Anti-Terrorism Training (SLATT) program, and at the FBI Academy in Quantico, Virginia. He has also worked with several foreign police agencies and the United States Department of State Anti-Terrorism Assistance program.

Brief Contents

v

Contents

Chapter 12   Africa, Asia, and the Pacific Rim / 279

Preface

This is a book written to introduce criminal justice and other social science students to the field of terrorism. It is designed for students in law enforcement, security, and military studies who have little or no understanding of the world of terrorism, and those readers who want to understand terrorism as a social phenomenon. It is also written for students and practitioners who are charged (or will be charged) with security operations. This revision is based on requests and comments from scholars and practitioners in the field. It incorporates several new features designed to enhance student comprehension with two recurring themes. First, the major purpose of the book is to provide basic knowledge for further understanding. Second, this book focuses on the prevention of terrorism.

Issues in terrorism are emotionally charged. Therefore, the information is presented from various positions. While it is written for those who will counter terrorism, the purpose is to explain various points of view without taking sides. This is true whether examining issues like the Israel-Palestine conflict or the controversy surrounding the Patriot Act. Hopefully, the text presents enough information to allow students to make informed decisions and to engage in critical thinking. The topics are designed to increase classroom discussions, individual reflection, and student research.

New Features

There are several new or enhanced features in this edition:

• **Reorganization**   The Sixth Edition has been reorganized into four sections to move students from complex introductory issues through to efforts to prevent terrorism. The first part deals with theoretical and criminological issues. The second part brings detailed historical discussions of the birth and evolution of terrorism movements in various parts of the world. Part III deals with contemporary international and domestic terrorism, and the final part focuses on issues surrounding the prevention of terrorism through homeland security.

• **Enhanced History**   Contemporary terrorism is not practiced in a vacuum. Modern terrorism grew from the French Revolution into today's international religious-inspired violence. An entire section of the book is devoted to the historical explanation of the transformation of terrorism over the past two centuries.

• **Expanded Geographical Discussions** The new edition includes new areas of focus such as the Horn of Africa, Central Asia, the Pacific Rim, and the Indian subcontinent. It also has a section on homegrown terrorism.

• **Running Glossary** Since many concepts and key points are new to students, a running glossary on the side of each page further explains key terms used in the text. This is designed to improve student comprehension.

• **Summary Questions** The major sections of each chapter are followed by summary questions. These questions are designed to help students recall what they have read and to develop broad themes that relate the major issues to one another.

• **Essay Questions** Each chapter closes with three essay questions to relate the major themes of each chapter to each other and to push students toward critical thought. Students are asked to consider various positions, to choose their own approach, and to cite evidence to support their positions.

• **Focus on Intelligence** Terrorism frequently blurs the line between law enforcement and national security intelligence. New chapter sections in Part IV deal with law enforcement intelligence systems, fusion centers, and national security intelligence. Each discussion is enhanced with diagrams and flow charts.

• **Civil Liberties** The prevention of terrorism involves intelligence gathering and criminal investigation. These issues can threaten civil liberties, and an entire chapter of the new edition focuses on civil liberties from various perspectives.

• **New Maps and Graphics** Several professors have requested more maps and new graphic summaries of information. These have been added to the Sixth Edition.

• **Another Point of View** Many issues in terrorism and homeland security go beyond a two-sided debate. Therefore, sidebars labeled "Another Point of View" appear in many chapters. These sidebars introduce controversial opinions and alternative understandings of social processes.

• **Updated Information** Terrorism is perpetually in transition. The material in the Sixth Edition is updated to reflect the latest information in international and domestic terrorist activity.

Supplements

A number of pedagogic supplements are provided by Wadsworth to help instructors use *Terrorism and Homeland Security*, Sixth Edition, in their courses and to aid students in preparing for exams. Supplements are available to qualified adopters. Please consult your local sales representative for details.

For the Instructor

Instructor's Resource Manual with Test Bank

Fully updated and revised, the *Instructor's Resource Manual with Test Bank* for this edition includes learning objectives, detailed chapter outlines, key terms and figures, class discussion exercises, lecture suggestions, and a complete test bank. Reviewed and revised by Criminal Justice instructors, the Test Bank provides hundreds of test items, including multiple choice, true/false, fill-in-the-blank, and essay questions. Our Instructor Approved seal, which appears on the front cover, is our assurance that you are working with an assessment and grading resource of the highest caliber. Each chapter's test bank contains approximately 80 multiple-choice, true-false, fill-in-the-blank, and essay questions, which are coded according to difficulty level, and which include a full answer key.

Lesson Plans

New to this edition of *Terrorism and Homeland Security*, the instructor-created Lesson Plans bring accessible, masterful suggestions to every lesson. The Lesson Plans include a sample syllabus, learning objectives, lecture notes, discussion topics, in-class activities, tips for classroom presentation of chapter material, a detailed lecture outline, and assignments for each chapter.

eBank PowerPoint Slides

These handy Microsoft® PowerPoint® presentations will save you time in preparing engaging lectures and presentations for your course.

InfoTrac® College Edition

NOT SOLD SEPARATELY. Now available, free four-month access to InfoTrac College Edition's online database of more than 18 million reliable, full-length articles from 5,000 academic journals and periodicals (including *The New York Times, Science, Forbes*, and *USA Today*). Access includes InfoMarks—stable URLs that can be linked to articles, journals, and searches. InfoMarks allow you to use a simple copy and paste technique to create instant and continually updated online readers, content services, bibliographies, electronic "reserve" readings, and current topic sites. In addition, ask about other InfoTrac College Edition resources available, including InfoMarks print and Online Readers with readings, activities, and exercises hand-selected to work with the text. And to help students use the research they gather, their free four-month subscription to InfoTrac College Edition includes access to InfoWrite, a complete set of online critical thinking and paper writing tools. (Certain restrictions may apply. For additional information, please consult your local Wadsworth representative.)

Classroom Activities for Criminal Justice

This valuable booklet, available to adopters of any Wadsworth criminal justice text, offers instructors the best of the best in criminal justice classroom activities. Containing both tried-and-true favorites and exciting new projects, its activities are drawn from across the spectrum of criminal justice subjects, including introduction to criminal justice, criminology, corrections, criminal law, policing, and juvenile justice, and can be customized to fit any course. Novice and seasoned instructors alike will find it a powerful tool to stimulate classroom engagement.

For the Student

Current Perspectives: Readings from InfoTrac® College Edition

These readers, designed to give students a closer look at special topics in criminal justice, include free access to InfoTrac College Edition. The timely articles are selected by experts in each topic from within InfoTrac College Edition. They are available free when bundled with the text.

Terrorism and Homeland Security 0-495-12994-1

Cyber Crime 0-495-00722-6

Juvenile Justice 0-495-12995-X

Crisis Management and National Emergency Response 0-495-12996-8

Racial Profiling 0-495-10383-7

New Technologies and Criminal Justice 0-495-10384-5

White-Collar Crime 0-495-10385-3

Terrorism: An Interdisciplinary Perspective, Third Edition

This provocative booklet includes a background to terrorism, the history of Middle Eastern terrorism, the intersection of religion and terrorism, the role of globalization, and domestic responses and repercussions. Also available online.

Handbook of Selected Supreme Court Cases for Criminal Justice

This supplementary handbook covers almost 40 landmark cases, each of which includes a full case citation, an introduction, a summary from WestLaw, excerpts from the case, and the decision. The updated edition includes *Hamdi v. Rumsfeld, Roper v. Simmons, Ring v. Arizona, Atkins v. Virginia, Illinois v. Caballes*, and much more.

Careers in Criminal Justice 3.0 Interactive CD-ROM

Help your students find the criminal justice careers that are right for them. This CD includes 58 job descriptions, self-assessments, career worksheets, and web links to help your students find careers of interest. Includes video interviews with criminal justice professionals.

Guide to Careers in Criminal Justice

This handy guide gives students information on a wide variety of career paths, including requirements, salaries, training, contact information for key agencies, and employment outlooks.

Writing and Communicating for Criminal Justice

This book contains articles on writing skills, along with basic grammar review and a survey of verbal communication on the job, that will give students an introduction to academic, professional, and research writing in criminal justice. The voices of professionals who have used these techniques on the job will help students see the relevance of these skills to their future careers.

Careers Website

The Careers in Criminal Justice Website provides students with extensive career profiling information and self-assessment testing, and is designed to help them investigate and focus on the criminal justice career choices that are right for them. With links and tools to assist students in finding a professional position, this new version includes ten new Career Profiles and four new Video Interviews, bringing the total number of careers covered to 64.

Acknowledgments

Many people assisted by listening to concepts, critiquing ideas, or reading manuscripts. Special thanks go to: Dr. David Carter, Michigan State University; Dr. Richard Holden, Director of SLATT; Dr. Robert Taylor, University of North Texas; Dr. Brent Smith, University of Arkansas; Dr. Randy Borum, University of South Florida; Dr. Richard Ward and Dr. Sean Hill, Sam Houston State University; Mr. D. Douglas Bodrero, President of IIR; Mr. Richard Marquise, FBI retired; and the reviewers of the manuscript of this text:

Lee Ayers-Schlosser, Southern Oregon University

Damon D. Camp, Georgia State University

Robert Castelli, Iona College

James Jengeleski, Shippensburg University

John Neiswender, Curry College

Kathleen Sweet, Purdue University

Your ideas improved the product. The faults are mine, the improvements belong to you.

The editorial staff at Wadsworth was wonderful. Thanks go to Rebecca Johnson, Shelley Murphy, and Carolyn Henderson Meier.

Disclaimer

Much of the work for this book was completed while I was working with the State and Local Anti-Terrorism Training (SLATT) program. SLATT is a Bureau of Justice Assistance (BJA) program managed by the Institute of Intergovernmental Research (IIR) and the Federal Bureau of Investigation (FBI). The material in this book does not necessarily represent the positions of BJA, IIR, the FBI, or any entity of the Department of Justice.

© Veer/Getty Images

A BASIC INTRODUCTION TO TERRORISM

Terrorism Defined

AP Photo/Mark Mobley

Terrorism is difficult to define. Environmental extremists pled guilty to arson and criminal conspiracy for starting this blaze. Extremists call such actions "activism," but governmental authorities call it "ecoterrorism."

Learning Objectives

After reading this chapter, you should be able to

- Explain why the term *terrorism* is pejorative.
- List and define some of the contexts of terrorism.
- Discuss the range of definitions of terrorism.
- Explain the strengths and weaknesses of typologies of terrorism.

- Describe various approaches to developing typologies of terrorism.
- Summarize terrorism within a tactical typology.
- Outline the four major types of modern terrorism.
- Summarize various views about the metaphor "war on terrorism."

Y ou have probably heard and may have used the word *terrorism*. When you did, you had an image in your mind. When other people use the word they have their own images, or meanings, for the term. This creates a problem. Nobody has been able to produce an exact definition. As a result, *terrorism* means different things to different people. To make matters worse, the nature of terrorism has changed over the course of history. Violent activity called *terrorism* at one point in time is called *war, liberation,* or *crime* in another period of history. The media have influenced and helped shape our definition of terrorism. Religion has come to play an important part in some forms of terrorism in the past few years. This chapter introduces methods for understanding terrorism and some of the types of modern terrorism.

The Pejorative Meaning of Terrorism

Now matter how it is defined, terrorism is a **pejorative term**. It is beamed into our homes through television screens, it assaults us in newspapers and magazines, and it sometimes touches our lives in a more direct manner. People do not worry about the definition of terrorism at such times. They simply feel terror when they see the violence. Sometimes it seems as though the event itself defines terrorism. For example, when a bomb destroys a passenger plane, it might be called terrorism, but when military forces shoot down a civilian aircraft, it is said to be an unfortunate mistake. The United States may launch missiles at a suspected terrorist base and claim it is defending national interests. Yet it may condemn another country for doing the same thing in another part of the world. Dual standards and contradictions lead to confusion any time the term *terrorism* is employed.

The term *terrorism* has spawned heated debate. Instead of agreeing on the definition of terrorism, social scientists, policy makers, lawyers, and security specialists often argue about the meaning of the term. H. H. A. Cooper (1976, 1977b, 1978, 2001) first approached the problem by stating there is "a problem in the problem definition." We can agree that terrorism is a problem, but we cannot agree on what terrorism is.

More recently, Alex Schmid (1992) points to the central issue. Terrorism is not a physical entity that has dimensions to be measured, weighed, and analyzed. It is a **social construct**; that is, terrorism is defined by different people within vacillating social and political realities. The definition of any social construct changes with the social reality of

pejorative term
A term that is loaded with negative and derogatory meanings.

social construct
The way people view reality. Groups construct a framework around a concept, defining various aspects of their lives through the meanings they attribute to the construct.

the group providing the definition. The social construction of reality can be nebulous, or it can be threatening when one group imposes its version of reality on another.

The definition is not only produced from various social constructs but also developed through the application of political power. How the term is defined has consequences—life and death consequences. A person is politically and socially degraded when labeled a terrorist, and the same thing happens when an organization is called a terrorist group. Routine crimes assume greater social importance when they are described as terrorism, and political movements can be hampered when their followers are believed to be terrorists. Governments gain power when their enemies are called terrorists, and citizens lose freedom in the name of greater security when the threat of terrorism appears. The political nature of the definition implies that any attempt to provide a common definition will be filled with debates about the use of power.

Two examples illustrate this process. The official Federal Bureau of Investigation (FBI) definition of terrorism separates domestic and international terrorism. The FBI (2002) states, "Domestic terrorism refers to activities that involve acts dangerous to human life that are a violation of the criminal laws of the United States or of any state; appear to be intended to intimidate or coerce a civilian population; to influence the policy of a government by mass destruction, assassination, or kidnapping; and occur primarily within the territorial jurisdiction of the United States." It further says, "International terrorism involves violent acts or acts dangerous to human life that are a violation of the criminal laws of the United States or any state, or that would be a criminal violation if committed within the jurisdiction of the United States or any state."

According to the FBI, "Terrorist acts are intended to intimidate or coerce a civilian population; influence the policy of a government by intimidation or coercion; or affect the conduct of a government by mass destruction, assassination or kidnapping and occur primarily outside the territorial jurisdiction of the United States or transcend national boundaries in terms of the means by which they are accomplished, the persons they appear intended to intimidate or coerce, or the locale in which their perpetrators operate or seek asylum." The purpose of this definition is straightforward. The FBI is part of a vast criminal justice apparatus charged with maintaining legal and political order. Since the attacks of September 11, 2001, it has also been charged with the prevention of terrorism. Anything that threatens social and political order and is within the realm of these definitions is terrorism. The FBI's social construction of reality defines terrorism as a matter of criminal behavior.

Yet other people are concerned about the way the United States defines terrorism. For example, some in the Muslim world believe that the values of Islam are threatened by the materialism of the West. The social construction of reality from this perspective is quite different from that of the FBI. Foreign ministers from Islamic countries met in Kuala Lumpur at the beginning of the U.S. "war on terrorism," and they issued a statement about the definition of terrorism (Organization of the Islamic Conference, 2002).

The foreign ministers condemned terrorism conducted in the name of religion, and they denounced unprovoked attacks on civilians. They went on to say that oppressed people had a right to revolt against an occupying power and that such a revolution constituted military action, not terrorism. The statement specifically focused on Palestine, claiming the right of Muslims to reject Israeli rule. Three years later the secretary-general of the Organization of the Islamic Conference reiterated the Kuala Lumpur Declaration with a blistering defense of the right of oppressed people to revolt. He also called on the secretary-general of the United Nations to enforce various UN resolutions on terrorism and human rights. The enemies of Islam, he said, were violating the letter of the law by linking Islam to terrorism.

The pejorative nature of definitions of terrorism is illustrated by comparing the FBI approach with that of the Islamic foreign ministers. Both groups seek to use legalistic definitions and both condemn attacks on civilians for political purposes. Yet the FBI and the Organization of the Islamic Conference come to radically different conclusions about terrorism. For example, Hezbollah, a Shiite military group and political party based in southern Lebanon, is nothing more than a terrorist group to the FBI. The Organization of the Islamic Conference, however, views Hezbollah as a legitimate revolutionary force defending the rights of oppressed people. It wants the United Nations to enforce resolutions against Israel for its attacks on Hezbollah. This debate is fostered by two differing pejorative definitions of the same term.

Further confusion arises when people intertwine the terms *terror* and *terrorism*. The object of military force, for example, is to strike terror into the heart of the enemy. Systematic terror has been a basic weapon in conflicts throughout history. Some people argue that there is no difference between military force and terrorism. Many members of the antinuclear movement have extended this argument by claiming that maintaining ready-to-use nuclear weapons is an extension of terrorism. Others use the same logic when claiming that street gangs and criminals terrorize neighborhoods. Thinking that anything that creates terror is terrorism makes the scope of potential definitions limitless.

One of the primary reasons terrorism is difficult to define is that the meaning changes within social and historical contexts. This is not to suggest that "one person's terrorist is another person's freedom fighter," but it does suggest the meaning fluctuates. Change in the meaning occurs because terrorism is not a solid entity. Like crime, it is socially defined, and the meaning changes with social change.

Self-Check

- *What factors make* terrorism *a pejorative term?*
- *What is the relationship between the definition of terrorism and political power?*
- *Why is there a "problem with the problem definition"?*

The Context of Definitions

Common definitions of terrorism are worth reviewing (see Another Perspective: Official Definitions of Terrorism), but it is more important to understand that definitions of terrorism may not be helpful. The definition always appears in the social construct surrounding its interpretation. The definition of terrorism changes with social and historical circumstances. Akin to Supreme Court Justice Potter Stewart's definition of pornography, we do not know how to define terrorism, but we know what it is when we see it. The **social context** surrounding the term *terrorism* influences how it is defined. Consider these social contexts that follow.

social context

The historical, political, and criminological circumstances at a given point in time. The social context affects the way terrorism is defined.

Historical Circumstances

The meaning of terrorism has changed over time. It is almost impossible to talk about terrorism without discussing the historical context of the terrorist campaign. Modern terrorism originated from the French Revolution (1789–1799). It was used as a term to describe the actions of the French government. By 1848 the meaning of the term had changed. It was employed to describe violent revolutionaries who revolted against governments. By the end of the 1800s and the early 1900s, terrorism was used to describe the violent activities of several groups, including labor organizations, anarchists, nationalistic groups revolting against foreign powers, and ultranationalistic political organizations.

After World War II (1939–1945), the meaning of terrorism changed again. As people revolted against European domination of the world, nationalistic groups were viewed as terrorist groups. From about 1964 to the early 1980s, the term *terrorism* was also applied to the actions of violent left-wing groups, as well as those of nationalists. In the mid-1980s, the meaning changed again. In the United States, some of the violent activity of hate groups was defined as terrorism. Internationally, terrorism was viewed as subnational warfare. Terrorists were sponsored by rogue regimes.

As the millennium turned, the definitions of terrorism changed yet again. Today *terrorism* also refers to large groups who are independent from a state, violent religious fanatics, and violent groups that terrorize for a particular cause such as the environment. It is important to realize that any definition is influenced by the historical context of terrorism.

Official Definitions of Terrorism

State Department   From Title 22 of *U.S. Code* section 2656f(d): "The term 'terrorism' means premeditated, politically motivated violence perpetrated against noncombatant targets by subnational groups or clandestine agents, usually intended to influence an audience. The term 'international terrorism' means terrorism involving citizens or the territory of more than one country. The term 'terrorist group' means any group practicing, or that has significant subgroups that practice, international terrorism."

Source: U.S. Department of State, 1999.

FBI   Terrorism is "the unlawful use of force or violence against persons or property to intimidate or coerce a government, the civilian population, or any segment thereof, in furtherance of political or social objectives." The FBI further describes terrorism as either domestic or international, depending on the origin, base, and objectives of the terrorist organization.

Source: FBI, 1999.

Vice President's Task Force   "Terrorism is the unlawful use or threat of violence against persons or property to further political or social objectives. It is usually intended to intimidate or coerce a government, individuals or groups, or to modify their behavior or politics."

Source: Vice President's Task Force, 1986.

United Nations   "A TERRORIST is any person who, acting independently of the specific recognition of a country, or as a single person, or as part of a group not recognized as an official part or division of a nation, acts to destroy or to injure civilians or destroy or damage property belonging to civilians or to governments in order to effect some political goal. TERRORISM is the act of destroying or injuring civilian lives or the act of destroying or damaging civilian or government property without the expressly chartered permission of a specific government, thus, by individuals or groups acting independently or governments on their own accord and belief, in the attempt to effect some political goal."

Source: Pedhahzur, 2004.

Defense Department   "Terrorism is the unlawful use or threatened use of force or violence against individuals or property to coerce or intimidate governments or societies, often to achieve political, religious, or ideological objectives."

Source: http://www.periscope.usni.com/demo/terms/t0000282.html; site now discontinued.

Defense Intelligence Agency   "Terrorism is premeditated, political violence perpetrated against noncombatant targets by subnational groups or clandestine state agents, usually to influence an audience."

Source: http://www.periscope.usni.com/demo/terms/t0000282.html; site now discontinued.

War and Violence

The meaning of *terrorism* fluctuates with type of war. In times of conventional war, armies use commando tactics that look very much like terrorism. In the American Civil War, the federal army unleashed Major John Anderson to destroy Confederate railroads. The Confederates captured Anderson and accused him of being a spy, but he remained a hero in the North. He did not wear a uniform, and he did not fight by the accepted norm. Armies routinely use such tactics in times of war and never define their actions as terrorism.

In guerrilla war, guerrillas use terrorist tactics against their enemies and may terrorize enemies and their supporters into submission. In total war, air forces may destroy entire cities with fire. The Luftwaffe, the German air force, did so at Stalingrad in 1942, and the British and American air forces did the same at Dresden in 1945. Neither side believed it was practicing terrorism. Although it is possible to cite many other examples and endless contradictions, you should realize that the definition of terrorism changes with the nature of conflict. The term *terrorism* is more likely to be employed to describe violent activity that explodes during a peaceful period.

The insurrection in Iraq after the 2003 U.S. invasion illustrates the complexities introduced by conflict. When the postinvasion conflict began, individual American soldiers were assassinated by underground Iraqi units led mainly by former Baathists in Saddam Hussein's regime. Violence soon grew and so did the number of players and victims. Individual religious zealots from foreign countries came to fight the American-led coalition. They soon targeted every foreigner in Iraq, including humanitarian aid workers and UN personnel. Eventually, they began targeting Iraqis. Religious sects formed militias and began attacking one another. Nationalists were drawn to the Baathist insurgency and violence grew. In November 2006 President George W. Bush blamed the violence on terrorism caused by al Qaeda instigators. Former secretary of state Colin Powell disagreed, claiming that Iraq was in the middle of a civil war. The line between terrorism and insurrection was a broad band at best.

Political Power

The definition of terrorism depends on political power. Governments can increase their power when they label opponents as terrorists. Citizens seem willing to accept more abuses of governmental power when a counterterrorist campaign is in progress. "Terrorists" do not enjoy the same humanitarian privileges as "people." In the public mind, illegal arrest and sometimes even torture and murder are acceptable methods for dealing with terrorists. Labeling can have deadly results.

For example, the United States detained several individuals associated with radical Islamic movements after its offensive in Afghanistan in late 2001. The people were given a variety of names, such as "combatants," "fighters," "Islamofascists," and other paramilitary terms. They were housed in a special prison established at Guantánamo Bay in Cuba so that they would not have the protection of the U.S. Constitution. The American government justified this by labeling the people "terrorists."

Repression

Closely related to the issue of power is the concept of **repression**. Some governments routinely use terrorism to keep their citizens in line. Such repression can sometimes be seen in the political structure of the country as leaders use secret police forces to maintain power. Joseph Stalin (1879–1953) ruled the Soviet Union from 1924 to 1953 through terror, and Saddam Hussein ruled Iraq by similar methods. Latin America has witnessed several rulers who maintained power through repression, many times with help from the United States. Repression can also develop outside formal political structures. This is called **extrajuridical repression**. It refers to repressive groups who terrorize others into certain forms of behavior. Political repression is a form of terrorism, but people seldom refer to this form of violence when defining terrorism.

repression
Governmental actions that suppress freedom.

extrajuridical repression
Violent repression outside the norms of criminal law. It can be used by governments, vigilantes, criminals, terrorists, or any group to enforce rules that violate criminal law. A death squad, for example, is a form of extrajuridical repression.

Media Coverage

Journalists and television reporters frequently use *terrorism* to define political violence. However, there is no consistent standard guiding them in the application of the definition. Many times they employ the term to attract attention to a story. *Terrorism*, when used by the media, is relatively meaningless but extremely powerful. Chapter 4 will examine the impact of the media in detail.

Crime

On the surface it would seem that criminals and terrorists represent two different types of violent behavior. Some analysts would agree, but confusion remains. A presidential commission on criminal justice stated that it was necessary to look at the motivation of a criminal act to determine whether it was a terrorist action (Cooper, 1976). When a crime is politically motivated, the commission says it is terrorism. The problem with this approach is that a crime is a crime no matter what motivation lies behind the action. Except in times of conflict or governmental repression, all terrorism involves criminal activity. Nearly thirty years after the presidential commission's report, the FBI (2005) still files most political crimes under the heading of terrorism in its Uniform Crime Report.

Religion

In recent years, religion has played a more significant role in the process of terrorism. This is fully examined in Chapter 2, but for now it is important to understand that extreme religious beliefs provide a context for defining terrorism. Religious violence centers on three sources (White, 2000). First, some religious groups feel they must purify the world for a new epoch. This can be defined as **violent eschatology**. Second, some groups feel they are chosen by a higher power, which allows them to

violent eschatology
When a group believes it must wage war to purify the earth before the return of a deity.

destroy other people in the cause of righteousness. This type of attitude can lead to violent intolerance and religious war. Finally, other people may become so consumed by a particular cause that they create a surrogate religion and take violent action to advance their beliefs. Ecological terrorists serve as an example of this type of religious terrorism.

Specific Forms of Terrorism

Sometimes the term *terrorism* is defined within a specific context. A detailed look at weapons of mass destruction is presented later in this book under the heading of *technological terrorism*. Another specific form of terrorism refers to computer attacks, viruses, or destruction of an information infrastructure. This is called *cyberterrorism* (see Chapter 5). Finally, drug organizations frequently use terrorist tactics, and some terrorist organizations sell drugs to support their political activities. Some analysts use the term *narco-terrorism* to describe this type of violence (see Chapter 3). Others use terms like *ecoterrorism*, *nuclear terrorism*, or *agriterrorism*. William Dyson (2004, pp. 22–40) argues that such distinctions do not represent separate forms of terrorism. Rather, they simply reflect the political focus of a particular group.

Self-Check

- *Why do the contexts of social definitions change?*
- *Describe the problem with developing a definition that would remain constant in changing contexts.*
- *List and describe the contexts that surround definitions of terrorism.*

▼ A Range of Definitions

simple definition

A definition of terrorism that involves three parts: (1) use of force, (2) against innocent people, (3) for political purposes.

The myriad definitions of terrorism have an astonishing range. Walter Laqueur (1987, 1999) stands at one end of the spectrum with a **simple definition**. He says terrorism constitutes the illegitimate use of force to achieve a political objective by targeting innocent people. He adds that attempts to move beyond the simple definition are fruitless because the term is so controversial. Volumes can be written on the definition of terrorism, Laqueur (1987) writes in a footnote, but they will not add one iota to our understanding of the topic. Laqueur promotes a simple definition because the meaning of terrorism changes constantly as social contexts change.

But definitions hardly stop with pragmatic simplicity. Germany, the United Kingdom, and Spain outlawed terrorism more than a decade ago, and America has examined the idea of a legal definition (Mullendore and White, 1996). The beauty of legal definitions is that they give governments specific crimes that can be used to take action against terrorist activities. Beyond that, they are quite useless because they account for neither the social nor the political nature of terrorism. More important, they can be misused. Violence is the result of complex social factors that range beyond narrow legal limitations and foreign policy restrictions. Political violence often occurs during the struggle for legitimacy. For example, American patriots fought the British before the United States government was recognized.

Legal definitions also contain internal contradictions. Under the legal guidelines of the United States, for example, some groups can be labeled as terrorists, whereas other groups engaged in the same activities may be described as legitimate revolutionaries. In addition, governments friendly to the United States in Latin America have committed some of the worst atrocities in the history of the world in the name of counterterrorism. Ironically, some Latin American revolutionaries who oppose our repressive friends espouse the rights expressed in the U.S. Declaration of Independence and Constitution, yet we refer to them as terrorists. Legal definitions are frequently shortsighted.

Alex Schmid (Schmid and Jongman, 2005, pp. 1–38, 70–111) stands at the other end of the spectrum as he tries to synthesize various positions in an **academic consensus definition** (see Expanding the Concept: Schmid's Consensus Definition). He concludes there is no true or correct definition because terrorism is an abstract concept with no real presence. A single definition cannot possibly account for all the potential uses of the term. Still, Schmid says, leading definitions have some common elements and most definitions have two characteristics: someone is terrorized and the meaning of the term is derived from terrorists' targets and victims. Schmid also offers a conglomerated definition of terrorism. His empirical analysis finds twenty-two elements common to most definitions, and he develops a definition containing thirteen of those elements. Schmid sees terrorism as a method of combat in which the victims serve as symbolic targets. Violent actors are able to produce a chronic state of fear by using violence outside the realm of normative behavior. Schmid (1992) also suggests that the definition is closely related to the group searching for meaning. Academics look for a foundation to guide research, and the media uses multiple definitions as it engages in a larger public debate. Governments search for legalistic meanings to counter terrorism, and terrorists search for meanings to justify their actions.

Both sides of the definitional spectrum have been criticized. Schmid and Jongman (2005, p. 3) find that one expert was wholly dissatisfied with Laqueur's definition. The respondent to their questionnaire on definitions stated that by not defining the subject, Laqueur wrote a book on terrorism with no focus. Ami Pedhahzur (2004) says that although Schmid's consensus definition has been used by many experts in the field, it remains too vague. They especially emphasize that the consensus definition fails to include the psychological effects of terrorism on victims and the target audience.

There is a middle ground. Thomas Badey (2003) states that the definitional problem caused by terrorism must be resolved. He claims that nations are hampered by an inability to define and criminalize terror-

academic consensus definition
A complex definition based on the work of Alex Schmid. It combines common elements of the definitions used by the leading scholars in the field of terrorism.

EXPANDING THE CONCEPT

Schmid's Consensus Definition

Schmid's academic consensus definition is cited by the United Nations:

> Terrorism is an anxiety-inspiring method of repeated violent action,
> employed by (semi-) clandestine individual, group or state actors, for
> idiosyncratic, criminal or political reasons, whereby—in contrast to
> assassination—the direct targets of violence are not the main targets.
> The immediate human victims of violence are generally chosen ran-
> domly (targets of opportunity) or selectively (representative or sym-
> bolic targets) from a target population, and serve as message genera-
> tors. Threat- and violence-based communication processes between
> terrorist (organization), (imperiled) victims, and main targets are used
> to manipulate the main target (audience(s)), turning it into a target
> of terror, a target of demands, or a target of attention, depending on
> whether intimidation, coercion, or propaganda is primarily sought.

Source: http://www.unodc.org/unodc/terrorism_definitions.html.

ism, but he points to an alternative route. Badey looks at the U.S. State
Department definition of terrorism, and he concludes that although the
definition is not perfect, it divides international terrorism into functional areas. These areas can serve to guide international responses.
Governments must look at the intent and motivation of terrorists, and
they need to consider whether the event can be repeated. It is important
to examine the terrorists themselves to determine whether they work
with state support or if they exist outside the boundaries of government.
Finally, Badey says, it is necessary to consider the effects of terrorism. By
dividing the problem into functional areas, Badey argues, governments
can develop a pragmatic response. This is better than living with the dilemma posed by too much simplicity or complexity.

Self-Check

- *What are the strengths and weaknesses of simple definitions?*
- *How do legal definitions differ from other approaches to defining terrorism?*
- *Does the consensus definition solve or complicate the definitional problem?*

typology
Classification of an issue
by looking at different
types. Because this text is
designed for those studying
criminal justice and related
security functions, terrorism
will be examined by looking
at the different types of
tactical behavior.

▼Typologies of Terrorism

A **typology** is a classification system, and there are as many typologies
of terrorism as there are definitions. Models, classification systems, and
typologies, however, offer an alternative to definitions, and they have

several advantages. First, the broad scope of the problem can be presented. Terrorism is composed of a variety of activities, not a singly defined action. A typology captures the range of terrorist activities better than most definitions. Second, the scope of the problem allows the level of the problem to be introduced. Terrorism can be local, national, or international in occurrence. A typology helps identify what *kind* of terrorism is to be examined. Third, when the level of terrorism is identified, the level of response can be determined. Finally, by focusing on types of violence and the social meanings of tactics, typologies avoid the heated debates about the meaning of terrorism.

For example, this book is written for criminal justice students and security professionals in law enforcement, private corporations, and the military. Therefore, terrorism is explained from a tactical perspective, or as you will read later, a tactical typology. In addition, this text classifies types of terrorist ideologies and geographical locations. These become typologies, or ways of looking at terrorism, for security specialists and criminal justice students.

Typologies do not solve all of the problems faced when trying to define terrorism, and they do not solve all the definitional dilemmas. First, the process of terrorism is in a constant state of change. Models, taxonomies, and typologies describe only patterns among events. They are generalizations that describe extremely unstable environments. Typologies may increase our understanding of terrorism, but each terrorist incident must be understood in its specific social, historical, and political circumstances (see P. Butler, 2002; Borum, 2004, pp. 20–21; Schmid and Jongman, 2005, pp. 39–59).

Another weakness of typologies involves the distortion of reality. After developing a model, some people, including scholars, try to fit particular forms of terrorism into it. They alter what they see so that it will blend with their typology. This has been especially true regarding Latin America. Governments, journalists, teachers, and revolutionaries developed ideological typologies for Latin America and then bent reality to fit their political views. Changing events to fit a pattern can completely distort reality. When this happens, researchers see only what they want to see. In addition, typologies hide details. They produce patterns, not specifics, even when they are correctly applied (see Flemming, Stohl, and Schmid, 1988, pp. 153–195; Schmid and Jongman, 2005, pp. 39–40).

With these strengths and weaknesses in mind, several researchers have attempted to approach terrorism through typologies. Some of the early typologies attempted to classify terrorism by the way terrorists behaved (Hacker, 1976; Post, 1984). These typologies have spawned a discussion of behavioral profiling, a topic discussed in the next chapter. Others have focused the use of social or political power (Sageman, 2004, pp. 130–133, 137–173; Schmid and Jongman, 2005, pp. 56–57). Others use typologies based on criminal law and law enforcement (Vasilenko, 2004). Unfortunately, like the definitional dilemma, there are a multitude of different typologies.

Alex Schmid and Albert Jongman (2005, pp. 39–59) have a comprehensive discussion of typologies based in the social sciences. They find that some typologies are based on individual actors who represent political states or nonstate entities. They also summarize a variety of typologies based on the distribution of political power. Other typologies seek to measure multifaceted impacts of terrorism based on the social structures involved in terrorism and counterterrorism, and still other typologies examine the purpose of terrorism. Despite the multiplicity of typologies, Schmid and Jongman conclude, they do not help us understand terrorism because they are based on different definitions. To solve the problem, they argue that it is best to see terrorism within the context of political expression. They offer a typology based on the idea that terrorism, whether by the state or by insurgent groups, is a method of political communication.

Law enforcement typologies tend to focus on either the classification of the political motivation for terrorist activity or the geographical location of the terrorist incident. Laurence Miller (2006) summarizes these approaches as they evolved from the 1960s and 1970s. The first FBI typologies focused on personality types. The FBI classified terrorists in terms of their leadership capabilities, their willingness to follow a leader, and their ideological commitment to a cause. Miller argues that some of these approaches are still effective. The Secret Service typology, for example, is based on assessing the practical requirements of protecting dignitaries. It casts five types of terrorists: crusaders, political terrorists, anarchists, religious fanatics, and criminals. The Secret Service uses this typology to project what type of attack may be launched and to organize intelligence.

Self-Check

- *What is a typology?*
- *How do typologies differ from definitions?*
- *Do typologies solve definitional problems?*

Toward a Tactical Typology of Terrorism

Although it is not an optimistic thought, one simple assumption will help you understand terrorism. Humans live in a constant state of conflict. Indeed, it is impossible to have a human social organization without conflict. Even in the most peaceful community, social organization is maintained because the controlling group can force people to join the organization and force members to obey the organization's rules. The amount of force is subject to limitation, but the ability to coerce is real. Therefore, social organizations are never truly at peace; they are

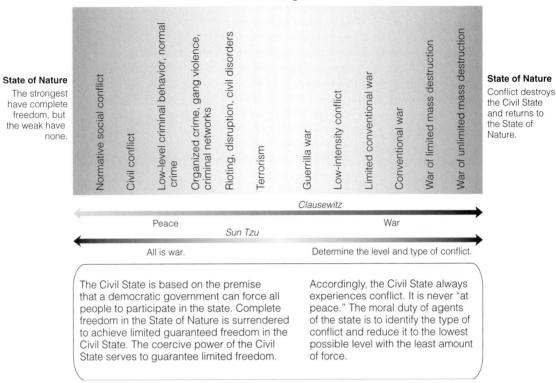

The Civil State: Guarantees the strong and the weak limited freedom.

State of Nature
The strongest have complete freedom, but the weak have none.

Normative social conflict

Civil conflict

Low-level criminal behavior, normal crime

Organized crime, gang violence, criminal networks

Rioting, disruption, civil disorders

Terrorism

Guerrilla war

Low-intensity conflict

Limited conventional war

Conventional war

War of limited mass destruction

War of unlimited mass destruction

State of Nature
Conflict destroys the Civil State and returns to the State of Nature.

Clausewitz

Peace   War

Sun Tzu

All is war.   Determine the level and type of conflict.

The Civil State is based on the premise that a democratic government can force all people to participate in the state. Complete freedom in the State of Nature is surrendered to achieve limited guaranteed freedom in the Civil State. The coercive power of the Civil State serves to guarantee limited freedom.

Accordingly, the Civil State always experiences conflict. It is never "at peace." The moral duty of agents of the state is to identify the type of conflict and reduce it to the lowest possible level with the least amount of force.

Figure 1.1
A Spectrum of Conflict

always at war. The amount and level of conflict varies, but conflict is normative.

If you accept this assumption, you will be able to understand terrorism. To illustrate this, consider a concept developed by the U.S. Army in the early 1970s. After the Vietnam War, the army realized its mission was changing and it had to be prepared to fight many different styles of war. Conflict could range from low-level brushfire wars to nuclear devastation, and the meaning of *war* was nebulous at best. To clarify this situation, the U.S. Army spoke of a **spectrum of conflict**. The spectrum was a continuum that ranged from low-intensity conflict to full-scale war (Figure 1.1). This scale probably more correctly reflects the human condition than the belief that we can be either at war or at peace. It also helps us understand terrorism.

Because humans live in a perpetual state of conflict and conflict management, civil coercive power has a place on the spectrum of conflict. Even before conflict rises to a military level, civil authorities routinely face challenges that must be met by implied or direct force. At the low-

spectrum of conflict
A system developed by the U.S. Army to define low-intensity conflict, mid-level wars, and wars of mass destruction. This text expands the definition to include many levels of social conflict far beneath traditional definitions of war.

ANOTHER PERSPECTIVE

Noam Chomsky Examines Terrorism and Morality

Noam Chomsky (2002) approaches terrorism with two critical questions: He asks How should terrorism be defined? What is the proper response to it? He says that the problem of defining terrorism is complex, but there are many straightforward governmental responses. Almost all of these definitions cast terrorism within a moral framework; that is, terrorism becomes a criminal act where innocents are victimized. These circumstances require a government to act. Yet the response frequently evokes a paradox. Governments define terrorist acts as immoral, but they tend to respond by acting outside the bounds of morality. They justify their actions by citing the original immoral act of a terrorist group.

Chomsky finds this approach unacceptable. The same moral framework that allows a society to define an illegal act as terrorism requires that the response to terror be conducted within the bounds of morality. Terrorism, Chomsky says, is something "they" do to "us," and it is never about what "we" do to "them." Citing just-war doctrine, Chomsky says the response to terrorism cannot be terrorism. A moral truism states that any illegal activity is immoral no matter how a state wishes to justify its response to an event.

The definition of terrorism provides a moral constant. For example, if an official definition states that terrorism is the use of violence against innocent people to change political behavior, a state is morally obligated to live within the bounds of this definition. It cannot use violence against innocents to force its political will. If terrorism is a crime, the response to it must not be criminal if the response is to be morally legitimate. The contradiction comes, Chomsky concludes, because the United States operates within a moral definition of terrorism only when its own interests are served. As a result, oppression, violence, and illegal actions are rarely defined as terrorism when they are condoned by the United States or its allies.

est level of organization, informal norms and mores enforce compliance, and if they fail, stronger coercive force is applied. In modern Western society, this may be civil or criminal law, whereas a more passive social group might use expulsion or shunning. Regardless, social groups always have the potential to exhibit coercive force to enforce behavior.

Terrorism is a form of violent civil disobedience, and it can be placed on a spectrum of conflict. At the most basic governmental level, the state faces low-level challenges with ordinary crime. Challenges increase with escalation to group violence, then rioting and wider disorders, and finally terrorism. At this point, military options may be employed as the continuum moves to guerrilla war, low-level war, conventional war, technological war, wars of ecological destruction, and wars of obliteration.

Ethicists may correctly argue that we must always move to minimize conflict by using the least amount of force, but morality is not the issue here. For another view, see Another Perspective: Noam Chomsky Examines Terrorism and Morality. What you should be able to see from the simple model is that terrorism is simply a form of conflict among social organizations that accept conflict as normal. There is nothing mystical

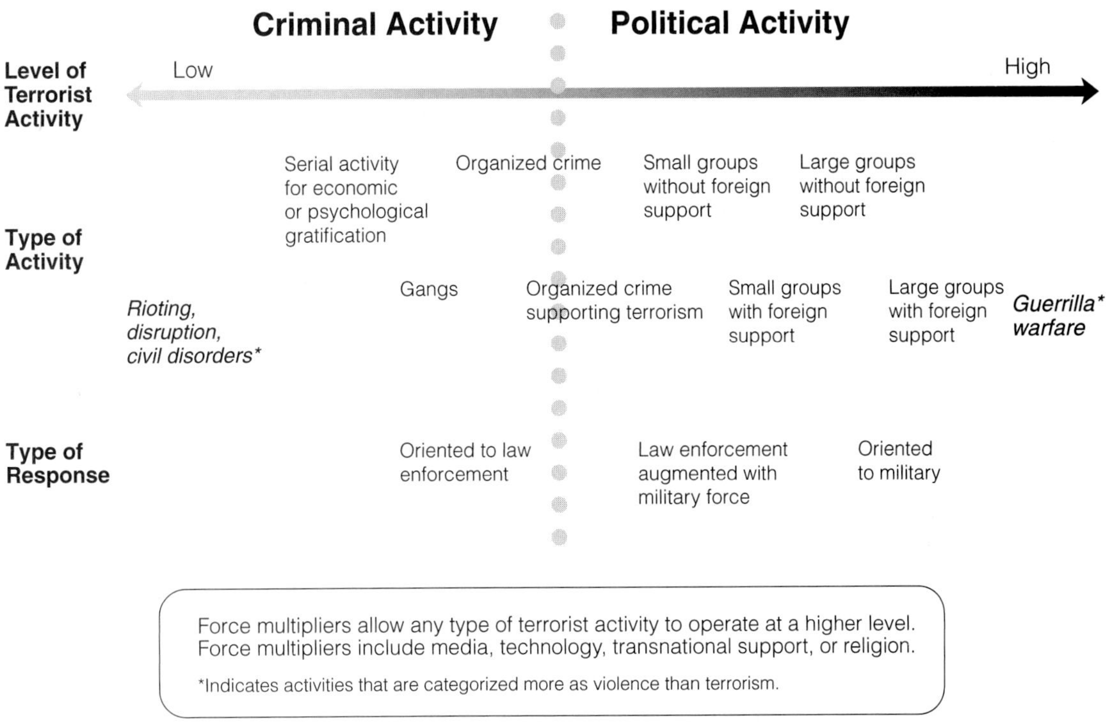

Criminal Activity ● **Political Activity**

Level of Terrorist Activity	Low					High

Type of Activity		Serial activity for economic or psychological gratification	Organized crime	Small groups without foreign support	Large groups without foreign support	
		Gangs	Organized crime supporting terrorism	Small groups with foreign support	Large groups with foreign support	*Guerrilla* warfare
	*Rioting, disruption, civil disorders**					

Type of Response		Oriented to law enforcement		Law enforcement augmented with military force	Oriented to military	

> Force multipliers allow any type of terrorist activity to operate at a higher level. Force multipliers include media, technology, transnational support, or religion.
>
> *Indicates activities that are categorized more as violence than terrorism.

Figure 1.2

A Tactical Typology of Terrorism

about terrorism. It is simply a form of conflict that comes between civil disorders and guerrilla warfare on the spectrum. As a form of conflict, its tactics can be modeled.

Over the past few years, I have used a typology to train military and police personnel in counterterrorism (Figure 1.2). It does not solve any definitional problems, but police and military officers have told me that it has helped them conceptualize their counterterrorist mission. This tactical typology may help you understand the issues involved in responding to terrorism.

The three parallel lines in the model in Figure 1.2 symbolize three different measures that roughly correlate with each other. The first measure shows the level of activity. It is fairly simple to grasp: incidents on the low end equal low activity, whereas the high end represents increasing rates of violence. The second line represents the type of activity. The line itself indicates the size of the terrorist group. On the extreme left, directly correlated with low activity on the activity continuum, is a single individual. Size increases as you move to the right. This brings the first rule of thumb. In terrorism the level of activity is generally correlated with the size of the group. Generally, the larger the group, the greater its potential for terrorist violence. This is true unless a group's force is strengthened by enhancing its striking power. This is a tactical concept known as a force multiplier (see Chapter 5).

Notice that the second line is divided by a nebulous border separating criminal and political terrorism. This border is intentionally open because terrorists are free to move between the criminal and political boundaries. The openness is designed to illustrate the movement of political violence. Some criminal groups can become so large that they may act like terrorist groups. Small terrorist groups can become so focused on crime that they become nothing more than criminal gangs. Examples of these types of groups appear underneath the line.

The final spectrum illustrates the type of response. Most criminal terrorism and a good share of political terrorism is a law enforcement responsibility. This means that when nonpolice units assist police agencies as part of a security force, they must think as the police do. For example, deadly force is always the last alternative in police operations. Additionally, legal procedures and an emphasis on individual rights guide each phase of a law enforcement response and investigation. The courts may allow certain amounts of latitude in procedures, such as internment in Northern Ireland, in the interest of public safety.

As you move across the spectrum, however, response actions become more militaristic. Although deadly force remains the final option, law enforcement personnel must think of themselves as a team, much as the military does. Teamwork, however, does not imply an ability to operate outside legal norms. Despite the necessity to develop certain military tactics or employ the direct help of the military, democracies cannot and should not tolerate activities outside the law. For example, police and military units of some countries have formed secret death squads, claiming terrorists have become too strong. If legal norms are violated, security forces can become little more than terrorists themselves.

This is one of the reasons for controversy in America's battle with terrorism. The government has defended tactics such as detaining suspects without trial, turning suspects over to countries where torture is used, using so-called aggressive interrogation techniques, and maintaining secret prisons. The government argues that the situation is so critical that these extra measures are necessary. Critics claim that the government is acting outside the law (see Tennet, 2007).

The tactical typology illustrates two important aspects of counterterrorism. First, it shows that terrorism is primarily a problem for law enforcement and the justice system. It is augmented by intelligence activities and military force, and sometimes, such as in Afghanistan, military forces must take the lead. Even then, however, they work to bring stability and capture those who act outside the law. Second, terrorists have acted outside the law. The Fourth Amendment of the U.S. Constitution allows the government to use the amount of force necessary to stop terrorist violence. The same amendment, however, does not allow the government to violate the law (see Sageman, 2004; Scheuer, 2006).

Self-Check

- *What is a tactical typology?*
- *How does a tactical typology differ from a definition?*
- *Why might law enforcement, military, and intelligence personnel want a tactical typology?*

Defining the "War on Terrorism"

In the past few years some officials in the United States have defined terrorism by rhetorically declaring war on it. Shortly after the attacks of September 11, 2001, President George W. Bush addressed the nation, stating that America and its allies were in a war with terrorism. Despite the Constitution having no provision for declaring war on a concept, federal and local bureaucracies have embraced the metaphor of war for combating terrorism. The American military even uses an acronym for it: GWOT, the Global War on Terrorism.

Many people accept the idea of a war on terrorism, even though the term *terrorism* remains undefined. Thomas Friedman (2004), a columnist for the *New York Times*, believes the United States is at war with terrorism. Friedman calls the fighting after September 11 democracy's third great struggle against totalitarianism in the past one hundred years. The first came against the Nazis (1939–1945), and the next struggle involved the West against the East during the cold war (1945–1991). Today's enemy, Friedman says, is militant groups who hate America more than they love life.

Stephen Blank (2003) of the U.S. Army War College also accepts the metaphor of war. Like Friedman, he believes that this new war differs from conflicts of the past. Blank contends that America's best weapon is to assist legitimate governments faced with armed insurgencies. Terrorism is caused by different radical groups driven by localized economic, social, and political pressures. They can be countered, Blank says, "by providing military assistance to legitimate governments and pressuring repressive governments to reform."

Ariel Cohen (2003) also believes the United States is in a war with terrorism. Examining central Asia, Cohen believes the United States must project military power in the face of terrorist threats. He argues that it is necessary to position military forces in central Asia so that they may be used in Afghanistan and elsewhere. He warns, however, that American military forces should not associate with repressive governments (see Another Perspective: State Repression). Fiona Hill (2003) of the Brookings Institution agrees. To conduct the war on terrorism, she says, it is necessary to identify militant groups and select the proper tactics that will destroy them. Cohen and Hill see no problem with a war on terrorism as long as political leaders understand that the war will require innovative weapons.

State Repression

Edward Herman (1983) says terrorism should be defined in terms of state repression. During the cold war the United States supported several Latin American dictatorships because the dictatorships were anticommunist. These governments, with some of the worst human rights records in history, routinely jailed, tortured, and executed political opponents. The United States not only ignored the repression but funded the activities and trained the repressive military and police forces. When the amount of human suffering from these dictatorships is compared to violence caused in insurgent terrorism, the pain caused by modern terrorism shrinks to insignificance. The "real terror network," Herman argues, is found in repressive government. University of Virginia sociologist Donald Black (2004) summarizes the paradox evident in Herman's earlier work. Counterterrorism, he says, is more violent than terrorism.

Not surprisingly, the federal government claims the United States is at war with terrorism. In an official statement on the second anniversary of September 11, the White House (2003) lumped domestic and international terrorists together, stating that the central front of the struggle was in Iraq. The weapons America would use in the war on terrorism would be the Homeland Security Act of 2002 and the USA Patriot Act of 2001, the press release stated.

Michael Howard (2002) has not been so quick to join the bandwagon. He believes that terrorism is an emergency situation best handled by intelligence and law enforcement services. Military forces may be used, but they serve as reinforcements for law enforcement or as special operations units for intelligence organizations. Counterterrorist work is sometimes a matter for criminal courts and is at other times best left to ruthless secret actions of intelligence units. Counterterrorism involves tedious investigations and information-gathering operations. When counterterrorism is called a war, it evokes images of battles, sophisticated weapons, and lightning strikes against a well-defined enemy. This is not the nature of terrorism, nor does it indicate the methods used to combat it.

Self-Check

- *Why would the government declare war on terrorism?*
- *Why do some analysts have problems with referring to counterterrorism as a war?*
- *In what other ways might the war on terrorism be described?*

SUMMARY

- The term *terrorism* is pejorative because it evokes a variety of politically charged responses. The way terrorism is defined often has life or death consequences.

- Terrorism is defined within social and political contexts. This is the primary reason that no single definition of terrorism will ever be successful.
- In terms of contextual definitions, the meaning of terrorism is influenced by history, conflict, political power, political repression, mass media, crime, and the specific form that terrorism takes.
- Myriad definitions cover a wide spectrum of varying meanings. Some analysts opt for complicated approaches, such as Schmid's academic consensus definition, whereas others, like Laqueur, choose simplicity.
- Some scholars turn to typologies in an effort to solve the definitional dilemma. Typologies are often based on behavior, activities, ideological orientation, or political and social classification.
- Although it does not solve debates about definitions or typologies, a tactical typology of terrorism helps to explain the problems faced by security forces.

KEY TERMS

pejorative term (p. 3)
social construct (p. 3)
social context (p. 6)
repression (p. 9)
extrajuridical repression
    (p. 9)

violent eschatology (p. 9)
simple definition (p. 10)
academic consensus definition
    (p. 11)
typology (p. 12)
spectrum of conflict (p. 15)

WRITING ASSIGNMENTS

1. Given the pejorative nature of definitions of terrorism, develop a definition of terrorism based on the information provided in this chapter. Explain the elements that are included in your definition and the issues that you have chosen to leave undefined. Develop a typology based on your definition. How does your typology enhance your definition?
2. The United States has declared war on terrorism. How does this affect our understanding of terrorism? Does it cast the definition of terrorism in a moral framework? Do the United States and other democratic governments operate within legal and moral guidelines as they fight this war?
3. Some members of the U.S. government maintain that terrorists can be treated differently from enemy soldiers or suspects accused of violating criminal law. Do you agree?

Conceptualizing Terrorism: Criminological, Political, and Religious Underpinnings

AP Photo/Amit Bhardwaj

Very few criminals are terrorists, but all terrorists commit crimes. Bombing is the most frequent terrorist activity. In this image firefighters respond to a bus bombing in Jammu, India.

Learning Objectives

After reading this chapter, you should be able to

- Compare and contrast efforts to explain the social organization of terrorist groups by using meaning and structural frameworks.

- Cite a practical method for analyzing a terrorist organization by using a meaning framework.

- Summarize a practical method for analyzing a terrorist organization by using

a structural framework involving networks.

- Describe terrorism as a religious process.

- Define and describe the "clash of civilizations."

- Compare social science explanations of religious terrorism with the approach by theologians.

- Describe the differences between terrorist and criminal behavior.

■ Contrast and compare early and more recent views on the justification of terrorist violence.

■ Develop arguments for and against social science's ability to profile terrorist behavior.

Terrorism is a social process. It involves groups of people forming associations, defining social realities, and taking actions based on the meanings given to those realities. Unlike many other social processes, terrorism is violent and it is conducted in situations where violence is not expected. Terrorism is also a psychological process. Individuals take actions within associations, applying an individualized interpretation of reality and reacting to environmental stimuli and motivators. Terrorism is also a political process. It is violent political activity designed to force particular interpretations of reality on others. Finally, since the last part of the twentieth century, terrorism has often been a religious process. When terrorism becomes holy, the social, psychological, and political aspects of terrorism are a form of sacred expression in the minds of terrorists.

Terrorism as a Social Process: Two Frameworks

The last chapter introduced the idea of a social construct. Many social scientists explain behavior as a group process taking place inside a social construct or as a multilevel mixture of constructs operating within the same time frame. This methodology has been used by modern historians when they seek to understand the dimensions of interpreting an event. Analysis of group behavior is the favorite domain of sociology and criminology, and many of their techniques are used in political science, social psychology, and other disciplines in social science. Although there are many approaches to the study of social explanations of group behavior, two schools of thought dominate the scholarly literature on terrorism. One group tends to focus on the meaning of activity, and the other school looks at the structure of action. Both approaches enrich efforts to explain terrorism from a vantage point emphasizing security, and they can be moved from theory to practical application.

The Meaning Framework

Many social scientists study group behavior by looking at the **meaning** of actions. The German tradition of sociology was very important in the search for social meaning, and some social scientists study behavior as if they are looking at scenes in a play or movie. Others came to see the study of life as drama filled and driven by meaning (see Goffman, 1959; Schutz, 1967; Manning, 1976, pp. 21–37; Kahan, 1997; Roberts, 1999).

meaning
The subjective interpretation people give to events or physical objects. Meanings are developed by individuals and groups, and different meanings can be attributed to the same event or physical object because the definitions are always influenced by interpretation. Social scientists in this tradition believe that meanings cause actions.

meaning framework
The social construct providing definitional boundaries for a particular social meaning.

Social scientists who study group and individual behavior this way believe the way we interpret the world motivates the actions we take.

When this method is used to study terrorist organizations, it can be called a **meaning framework**. Theories about terrorism in the meaning framework focus on the interpretation individuals and groups give to the actions of others as well as their own actions. Researchers also examine the circumstances in which the subjects define their roles. Mark Juergensmeyer (2000, pp. 216–229) uses this approach to study the impact of religion on terrorism. Violent religious movements and the organizational structures they create are rooted in the ways certain groups of people view reality.

Juergensmeyer sees the clash between modern values and traditional culture as one of the reasons for terrorism. Religious terrorists look at the modern world and reject it. This world is evil in the meaning framework of religious terrorists, and they refuse to accept the boundaries of the secular modern world.

Religion will be discussed more fully later in the chapter; in the meantime, the point here is that Juergensmeyer's methodology is based on the study of meaning. He approaches several militants from differing religious traditions around the world. After extensive interviews, he categorizes their discussions to find commonalities. The findings are based on the meanings his subjects attach to modernity. In Juergensmeyer's research, terrorism is created by the meanings subjects attach to social situations. This produces a common pattern in religious terrorist organizations. If Juergensmeyer is correct, groups form as like-minded individuals gather to reject modernity, select a course of action, and violently embrace their interpretation of tradition.

Historians often use this methodology. Bernard Lewis (2002) examines the rise and demise of the Ottoman Turks, the last great Islamic empire, in the face of Western expansion and colonialism. He argues that trouble between Islam and Western modernity can be attributed to the meanings each group attributes to historical change. Middle Eastern Muslims tend to search for a lost ideal, whereas the West embraces modernity. If this thesis is applied to the formation of terrorist groups, one would expect to find militant organizations forming within parts of the Islamic world based on the rejection of Western ideals. Indeed, many other researchers have come to this conclusion (see R. Wright, 1986, 1989; Armstrong, 2000b, pp. 32–60; Rubin and Rubin, 2002, pp. 3–6; Lewis, 2003a). They maintain that some militant Islamic groups reject the beliefs of the West.

Samuel Huntington (1993, 1996) makes the same argument about cultural perceptions, and Thomas P. M. Barnett (2004) advances a similar point when examining economic competition in the modern world. Huntington believes that a new political order emerged at the end of the cold war, and future conflicts will take place between the world's major civilizations (see Table 2.1). Barnett believes the world is divided in three economic groupings, and conflict will be based on the distribution

Memorize

Table 2.1   Huntington's View of Civilizations

Western	United States, Canada, Western Europe, Australia
Confucian	China, parts of Siberia, Southeast Asia
Japanese	Japan
Islamic	Middle East, Turkey, Southwest Asia, parts of Southeast Asia, North Africa, Balkans
Hindu	India
Slavic-Orthodox	Russia and Eastern Europe
Latin American	Mexico, Central and South America
African	Africa

Source: Huntington, 1996.

of wealth. Both political scientists argue that the social meanings groups of people give to the world explain political behavior.

The point here is not to critique social scientists who use meaning frameworks but to demonstrate that some sociologists, historians, economic analysts, and political scientists embrace a similar assumption. Social action is based on social meaning. When applied to terrorism, terrorist organizations are the result of subjective meanings, and any strategy designed to confront and destabilize terrorist organizations must include an aggressive effort to introduce alternative meaning frameworks.

The discussion so far has been limited to academics, but it can be taken away from college campuses. Malcolm Nance (2003, pp. 47–59), probably inadvertently, advances a **theory of action** while dealing with the practical aspects of counterterrorism in *The Terrorist Recognition Handbook*. In Nance's analysis, terrorists take action out of an ideological desire for social change. He implies that all terrorists are not happy with the state of the world, and they are motivated to change it.

theory of action
A social science theory that assumes human beings take action based on the subjective meanings they attribute to social settings.

Nance makes no effort at all to discuss any type of social science theory, yet his entire practical guide assumes that terrorism results from the meanings terrorists apply to the modern world. This assumption is the foundation of his discussion of the rise of anticolonialism, trouble in the Middle East, state-sponsored terrorism from Libya in the 1980s and 1990s and North Korea, and all aspects of domestic and international terrorism. Tactically, counterterrorism involves specific steps to prevent violence and deconstruct terrorist groups. Strategically, it involves countering ideas with alternative interpretations of reality. Nance is a veteran of the American intelligence community with no seeming interest in social theory, but his step-by-step manual is grounded in the meaning framework.

The Structural Framework

Another social science tradition seeks to avoid subjective meanings when examining events. This methodology maintains that human societies need to accomplish certain functions, so they create organizations to do them. Organizations develop according to the needs of a society or any group of people. Such organizations take predictable actions, or func-

Actual Location

structural framework

The idea that social constructs are based on systems that provide order. The systems are social structures that accomplish functions necessary to survive. Human activity occurs to accomplish the functions required to maintain the social structure of the system.

structure

The manner in which a group is organized and its purpose. Social scientists from this tradition feel that a group's structure and purpose cause it to act. They also believe that groups are created for specific functions.

social geometry

As used by Donald Black, the social space occupied by a structure and the direction it moves.

netwar

One network fighting another network.

nodes

In counterterrorist or netwar discussions, the points in a system where critical components are stored or transferred. The importance of a node is determined by its relationship to the network.

tions (Parsons, 1951; Martindale, 1965; Schmaus, 1999; Tetlock, 2002). Approaches to understanding terrorist behavior by looking at the way organizations function can be called a **structural framework**.

Donald Black (2004) approaches terrorism from this vantage point. Black argues that explaining terrorist behavior is no different than explaining any other aspect of human action. Groups do not organize and take action based on the meanings people attribute to the world. All groups, including terrorist organizations, take action because they belong to a **structure** that operates for a specific purpose. Black calls this **social geometry**. Groups take actions based on their relationships with other groups. Terrorist groups move to strike governments, and governments have structures that strike back. Groups are not violent, Black says. The structures that contain them may be.

Black thinks many analysts do not understand terrorism because they search for social and political meanings to find the root causes of conflict. Scholars are often particularly weak in their understanding of terrorism because they focus their attention on descriptions of violent groups and individuals. The structure and movement of groups explain terrorism. Terrorism develops when a group with inferior power moves against a superior group, inducing mass civilian casualties.

Terrorism was rare in the past because geography would not allow it to develop. For example, people exploited by a European colonial power in 1870 had no ability to strike Europe and kill massive numbers of civilians. Modern technology has changed this situation by shrinking distance and providing weapons. Black sees the process of terrorism as violent self-help, and terrorists organize in quasi-military units fighting outside the norms of war and criminal law.

Black's methodology is a radical approach to the study of organizational structures, but many researchers use a structural methodology when examining terrorism. Vito Latora and Massimo Marchioni (2004) believe terrorist organizations are complex systems that can be modeled mathematically and projected by computer simulations. Meaning frameworks have little to do with understanding terrorist behavior from this standpoint. According to their thesis, terrorist organizations are structured in the same manner as communication and transportation systems. This means they are composed of networks that move in patterns—for example, telephone lines or highways—to particular critical points, or nodes.

Latora and Marchiori's position reflects a new theory in modern warfare called **netwar** (see Arquilla and Ronfeldt, 1996). According to this theory subnational criminal, terrorist, or revolutionary groups organize themselves in a network of smaller logistical structures, groups, or command posts. Any point where information, weapons, or personnel are gathered or exchanged is called a **node**, and the node is the critical target for counterterrorist operations. Latora and Marchiori argue that once an organization is modeled as a network, the nodes will appear as movement is monitored. If the node is destroyed, the network is disrupted.

Figure 2.1
Traffic Pattern as a Network

The traffic pattern on the highway is akin to a network, and the crucial intersections, merge ramps, and expanded traffic lanes are nodes.

To understand this approach to terrorist organizations, consider the traffic pattern in a major city. If you monitor cars moving through the city at rush hour, you will soon find critical points where traffic must keep flowing or the city will become locked in a traffic jam. The traffic pattern on the highway is akin to a network, and the crucial intersections, merge ramps, and expanded traffic lanes are nodes (see Figure 2.1). If vehicles begin clogging at a node, traffic slows or comes to a standstill at many points in the network. Notice how this differs from organizational models based on meaning. In the netwar metaphor, a vehicle does not take action based upon the meaning it attributes to the network. When the network is disrupted, the vehicle cannot operate effectively.

Researchers at Sam Houston State University in Huntsville, Texas, use a structural model to track terrorist organizations throughout the world (Ward and Hill, 2002). Avoiding a meaning framework, they have identified more than 500 violent groups engaged in subnational violence. Using public information, they have created a database that tracks twenty-one types of events with a multiplicity of variables. The structures emerging from their research are defined by the events and variables. The effort results in a comprehensive picture of terrorist violence.

Self-Check

- *In what way is terrorism a social process?*
- *Describe the differences between meaning approaches and functional approaches when examining terrorism.*
- *Compare and contrast examples of meaning approaches and functional approaches.*

Terrorism as a Religious Process: Anthropological and Sociological Approaches

According to Marxist theories, conventional wisdom of modern societies, and some schools of science, modernization should lead to the decline of religious identification (see Dawkins, 1998; and Wilson, 1999). Ironically, the opposite trend seems to be true. Tanja Ellingsen (2005) says two primary reasons account for the continued influence of religion. First, religion has always been an important factor in the history of humanity. There is no reason to believe that it will fade as technology grows. Second, modernization tends to break down communities, families, and social orientation. People seek a deeper meaning to their lives. After conducting an empirical study of the influence of religion on terrorist violence, Ellingsen says the world is not witnessing a resurgence of fundamentalism; rather, people have had deep religious feelings all along. Religion continues to hold sway in people's lives, and she argues that her findings demonstrate that its impact on terrorism is more important than political and economic factors.

Susanna Pearce (2005) uses an empirical analysis of religion to examine social science, theological, and historical analyses of religion and terrorism. She believes that strong religious beliefs increase not only the likelihood of religious conflict but also the intensity of fighting. Violence results when sacred traditions are threatened, and the cosmic consequences of failure mean that victory is the only option available to the faithful. **Eschatology** plays a major role because messianic warriors in the end-time correct the heresies of the past and fight for the ideal divine order of a deity. Pearce believes that empirical findings demonstrate that terrorism is partially a religious process.

eschatology

(pronounced es-**ka**-taw-low-gee) A Greek word used to indicate the theological end of time. In Judaism and Christianity it refers to God bringing creation to an end. In some Shiite Islamic sects and among Christians who literalize biblical eschatological literature, believers contend that Jesus will return to lead a final battle against evil. Other major religions also have end-time theology.

Anthropologist Marvin Harris (1991, pp. 437–453) believes human beings have experienced two types of religions: killing and nonkilling religions. Killing religions developed during the food-gathering cycles of preagrarian and early agricultural societies, and they were premised on a deity helping the community in times of crisis. In the killing religions, gods slaughtered enemies. Harris says these beliefs gave way to the nonkilling religions because the older, killing religions did not, in fact, protect early villages from the ravages of war and natural disasters. The nonkilling religions embraced enemies and developed elaborate theologies to justify violence as a last resort. The nonkilling religions appeared in order to try to transcend everyday experience. Harris says the irony of the human experience is that nonkilling transcendence is often transformed into a militant ideology designed to protect a state or some other social group by this rationalizing of the use of violence as a last resort. Why does this happen?

Jessica Stern (2003b) answers the question by stating that people around the world are returning to their religious roots as a means to escape the complexity of modern life. People have too many choices, she says. All the choices bring confusion, and most people want to escape confusion. Returning to old, established patterns of earlier generations, frequently the truths of their traditional religions, people confused by modern complexity seek to ground their lives. Unfortunately, old truths in one society may collide with the truths of another society. This is especially so when one group believes it is under attack. When mythological truths compete, violence often results.

People use stories to explain deep truth beyond the immediate world, and terrorist groups build their own mythologies to justify their actions through a story. Stern believes stories change the nature of terrorist organizations, and they help to produce different group organizations and styles. Some organizations center on rigid structures. Other groups grow when insecure people gather around a strong personality. Some groups are informal, and everybody in the group has a leadership function. Some loners loosely affiliate with a group but tend to act on their own. Criminals flock to other associations. Stern says the most successful groups operate with a variety of different styles of subgroups.

Individuals come to a group, according to Stern, because they believe they have been called to the story of an entire people. They join a cosmic struggle, a holy cause. New recruits each take a separate path to terrorism, but they are usually motivated by the organization's sacred story. Most sacred stories emphasize self-sacrifice and even death. As a result, many new terrorists seek a path of martyrdom, sometimes facing grave dangers and other times intentionally committing suicide to destroy cosmic enemies. Another path involves developing some type of specialty, and many are motivated to become mighty warriors. Thinking of ancient heroic stories like those about the mythic Greek Hercules illustrates Stern's point. Hercules was half human and half god, and he had strength far beyond that of any mortal. Upon his death, Zeus, the king of the gods, placed Hercules in the heavens as a constellation. This type of myth serves as a model for the ultimate warrior. In a similar way, stories about warriors who sacrifice themselves can be used to justify self-sacrifice or suicide.

Many times people become disillusioned with leaders who fail to live up to mythical standards, and they leave the group but remain sympathetic to the cause. Stern says those who become leaders originally join a group because they believe in the myth, but after a time the lifestyle produces the need for professional behavior, and the group must face professionalization of the leadership, that is, the emergence of a professional terrorist. In other words, the power of the myth becomes less important and the day-to-day job of terrorism grows. Terror for the sake of terror becomes a way of life, and peace threatens the leader's livelihood.

To maintain the power formally given by the sacred story, leaders develop internal enforcement mechanisms. Rewards are given and withheld to encourage correct behavior within the group. When ideology breaks down, leaders may find themselves in alliances with enemies. At this point, the behavioral patterns of religious terrorists cease to matter. They eventually become long-term professional leaders who know only one kind of work. They are professional terrorists for sale to the highest bidder.

Stern also believes that religion helps to produce the "lone wolf avenger," a person striking out with an ideology but no group. An individual lone-wolf avenger needs to find some type of justification for his or her actions, and religion provides the perfect path. Stern says lone-wolf avengers have a special, narcissistic relationship with their deities. In essence, they create a god in their own image. They become the ultimate loners, and Stern demonstrates that they are the most difficult type of terrorist to deter or detain.

Mark Juergensmeyer (1988, 2000) spent many years examining the issues surrounding religious terrorism. Believers must identify with a deity and think they are participating in a struggle to change history. And this struggle must be a cosmic struggle; that is, the outcome of the struggle will lead to a new relationship between good and evil. When they feel the struggle has reached the critical stage, violence may be endorsed and terrorism may result. The call to violence, Juergensmeyer argues, is a call to purify the world in a holy war that eliminates the nonbeliever and the incorrect interpreters of tradition. The lines of battle are clear and positions cannot be compromised. Such a war allows only one way of thinking: those people who do not stand with the holy warrior are evil. If the holy warrior falls in a losing cause, the warrior becomes a martyr for hope. If the warrior is successful, it is a victory for the deity. The holy terrorist is victorious either by killing the enemy or dying in the struggle (see Another Perspective: Religion and Ideology).

Self-Check

- *Why would some social scientists examine terrorism from a religious perspective?*
- *What role do sacred stories and narrative play in religious violence?*
- *What theological steps are involved in religious terrorism?*

Criminological Views of Terrorism: Crime for a Cause

There are two branches of criminology in the practical world of criminal justice. When using the word *criminology* in an academic setting, images of psychological and sociological theories appear in the minds of researchers and teachers. This is classic criminology, tracing its origins to Cesare Beccaria and using the most modern theories of individual and group behavior. When the word is mentioned in a law enforcement agency, another image appears. Practical criminology focuses on the common actions of lawbreakers. Police officers are not as concerned with theories of criminality as they are with the practical aspects of

Religion and Ideology

David Rapoport believes that religion has influenced terrorism because of eschatological expectations. Belief in end-of-the-age theology and the coming of a deity serves to justify violent behavior. Although this seems to separate religious and political terrorists, Rapoport argues that both sets of behavior are similar. Political ideology plays the same role for political terrorists as eschatology does for religious ones. There is little difference in behavior between secular and religious terrorists, and both types of terrorists are intensely dedicated to a cause. Ideology and eschatology differ, but the behavioral outcome is similar.

Source: Rapoport, 1984.

criminal behavior. They want to know what criminals do so that they may deter them from committing a crime or catch them after the crime is committed.

The purpose here is to consider this second use of *criminology*, the applied actions in crime prevention and apprehension. This consideration is important because, although terrorists commit crimes as they struggle for a cause, they differ from ordinary street criminals. Terrorists have organizational structures, belief systems, and motivational values that separate them from ordinary criminals. Law enforcement personnel must recognize the differences between typical criminal behavior and terrorist activity if they want to prevent crime and apprehend criminals. Law enforcement officials are frequently the first governmental agents on the scene of a terrorist incident. If they fail to recognize that the scene may be something more than an ordinary crime, they may well miss the point of the investigation. For example, should malicious destruction of property always be classified as a simple misdemeanor or a felony? If someone unlawfully enters a farm, destroys cages, and frees the animals, is this simply malicious destruction? Many law enforcement officers would answer yes, but consider the Animal Liberation Front (ALF). In instructions to members and sympathizers, the ALF advocates the systematic destruction of farms that produce fur for clothing. Their web page gives potential recruits tactics for the most effective destruction of mink farms (www.nocompromise.org/alf/alf.html). If a deputy sheriff or state trooper happens on such an attack, it will probably be classified as malicious destruction of property even though it may well be part of a larger operation.

To counter such tendencies in law enforcement, the FBI has created localized terrorism task forces—Joint Terrorism Task Forces (JTTFs)—around the country. In theory, this allows the FBI to coordinate law enforcement resources in the face of domestic terrorism and to expand investigations. Internationally, the FBI also provides investigative resources when Americans are victimized by terrorism in other countries. Yet the fact remains that individual patrol officers are usually the first

EXPANDING THE CONCEPT

Terrorists and Ordinary Criminals

Terrorists behave differently from ordinary criminals. Consider the following:

1. Criminals are unfocused. Terrorists focus their actions toward a goal.

2. Criminals may live in a criminal underworld, but they are not devoted to crime as a philosophy. Terrorists are dedicated to a cause.

3. Criminals will make deals to avoid punishment. Terrorists rarely cooperate with officials because they do not wish to betray their cause.

4. Criminals usually run when confronted with force. Terrorists tend to attack.

5. Criminals strike when the opportunity to do so is present. Terrorists strike against symbols after careful planning.

6. Criminals rarely train for crime. Terrorists prepare for and rehearse their operations.

Source: Bodrero, 2002.

people to arrive on the scene of a terrorist incident. They must recognize the traits of terrorism to begin the investigation. Terrorist investigations do not follow the pattern of most criminal investigations because terrorists seldom behave like normative street criminals.

D. Douglas Bodrero, the former commissioner for the Department of Public Safety in Utah and former member of the International Association of Chiefs of Police Committee on Terrorism, offers a comparative analysis between terrorist behavior and that of ordinary criminals (see Expanding the Concept: Terrorists and Ordinary Criminals). Bodrero (2002) argues that typical criminals are opportunistic. This means that criminals tend to be impulsive. Most street criminals do not plan their crimes extensively, and they react to easy opportunities on the spur of the moment. Criminals are usually uncommitted to a cause. Even career criminals do not believe in crime as an ideology or religion. Crime is just a method for obtaining goods. Because of this lifestyle, criminals tend to be self-centered and undisciplined. Except for a small proportion of career criminals, ordinary street criminals are untrained. Their goal is to obtain cash or goods and get away.

Bodrero and most police officers base crime prevention and apprehension strategies on these assumptions about street criminals for one simple reason. They work. By protecting (or hardening) targets, denying opportunity, and conducting aggressive patrol, many ordinary street crimes like burglary can be suppressed (W. Harris, 1998). In addition, making police an extension of the community can reduce crimes that seem to defy suppression, such as domestic violence (Trojanowicz et al., 1998). By using criminal intelligence files to keep track of known felons, criminal associations, and crime patterns, police suppress criminal activity. Police search for hangouts of local criminals, they know their friends and family, and they maintain sources of information about suspicious activity. These procedures not only serve as the basis of community policing but also are the essence of criminal investigation.

Bodrero (2002) says terrorist behavior differs from standard patterns of criminal behavior because terrorists are highly motivated and loyal to a particular cause. Whereas ordinary criminals are opportunistic, terrorists are focused. They may select targets of opportunity, but the target has a symbolic value. Terrorists use crime to make a symbolic statement about a political cause.

If criminals are uncommitted and self-centered, terrorists find strength in a cause and the ideology or religion behind the cause. They are supported by an organization and sent on a mission. They are team oriented even when they act as individuals. For example, suicide bombers do not act alone; their preparation involves team work. Being part of something greater than themselves becomes the basis for action. Even in the case of lone wolves, the ideology is all consuming. They might act alone, but deep-seated beliefs cause loners to feel that their actions are part of the vanguard of a movement. Terrorism is an organizational process whether support is real or implied through ideology (Schweitzer, 2000; Khashan, 2003; Kaplan, Mintz, Mishal, and Samban, 2005; Azam, 2005).

Ideology and religion are not limited to suicide bombers; they also influence individuals who will become terrorists for a single event. For example, Buford Furrow entered a Jewish day care center in August 1999 and began shooting people. He was a lone wolf, or what is called a "berserker." He had no extensive logistical network or support organization. Yet Furrow was consumed by an ideology of hate and a religion that demonized Jews. He was not an uncommitted opportunistic criminal acting alone. He was an agent of an ideology on a divine mission. Again, as Bodrero (2002) indicates, this is not the pattern of typical criminals. Bodrero says that criminals are undisciplined, untrained, and oriented toward escape. Terrorists are exactly the opposite. They have prepared for their mission, they are willing to take risks, and they are attack oriented. Lone wolves might be untrained, but they are prepared and attack oriented.

The significance of Bodrero's argument can be measured in the investigative response to terrorism. When investigating a crime, police officers can take advantage of the behavioral characteristics of typical criminals. The most hardened criminals will usually act in their own self-interest, and they will make deals to receive a lesser sentence. When searching for a fleeing felon, law enforcement officers find it productive to question known associates and keep family and friends under surveillance. These tactics do not work in countering terrorism. Law enforcement, military, and security officials need to focus on ideology, group and individual behavior, and sharing information over broad geographical regions to successfully investigate terrorism.

Self-Check

- *Why do some researchers say there is no criminology of terrorism?*
- *What are the differences between terrorists and criminals?*
- *Could terrorists avoid criminal behavior? Why or why not?*

The Process of Moral Justification

Every person who uses force must seek to justify it. As the amount of force increases, the need to justify it becomes greater. Deadly force demands the greatest amount of justification. When a person threatens to kill or does kill another person, he or she must feel it was right to do so. Executioners employed by the state cannot stop to cross-examine themselves if they want to do the job.

When a person engages in violent activity on the state's behalf, the government unveils its most sacred symbols and rituals to reward the person. Warriors need such rewards. Terrorists have the same need for social approval, but they rarely obtain it because their actions are not sanctioned by the governments they attack. They are routinely condemned by the population at large. Even when citizens approve of the cause associated with terrorism, they are reluctant to embrace and endorse the methods of mayhem. Terrorists must, therefore, look outside normative social channels to gain approval for their acts.

The terrorist group becomes the primary source of social reality for individual terrorists. It provides social recognition and reinforcement for its members. Like soldiers, who undergo a similar bonding process during basic training, potential terrorists join groups for varied reasons: they may be sympathetic to the cause or they may simply be social misfits. The terrorist group reshapes identities and provides a ticket to social acceptance.

For social acceptance to work, however, the terrorist group must be isolated from mainstream society. Richard Cloward and Lloyd Ohlin's (1960) study of American urban youth gangs provides an analogy. The gang is a self-referential group in a world gone awry. By rejecting the norms of the urban environment, the gang is free to create its own norms. Israel's experience with Arab suicide bombers has shown that terrorists go through the same process. A terrorist must be isolated before beginning a mission, interacting only with others who are directly involved in the mission. During this period, the terrorist is constantly indoctrinated in the importance of the mission and reminded that the goal is more important than human life. Suicidal terrorists are often housed together so that they can continue reinforcing each other. Like gang members, terrorists must enter a world of their own reality.

Early Studies on Group Reinforcement and Isolation

In one of the early studies of terrorism, Paul Wilkinson (1974, pp. 23–25) says terrorist groups reinforce individual loyalty through the process of justification. They may argue that terrorism is a just revenge for social evils or that it is a lesser evil than the exercise of governmental power. Terrorism is also often justified as being the only course of action available. Regardless of the argument used, Wilkinson demonstrates, the terrorist group must develop its own parameters of ethical normalcy and go through a process of moral justification.

As the literature on terrorism developed, Jerrold Post (1987) began to compare the process of justification with the group dynamics inside terrorist organizations. Post's research was designed to measure the effects of retaliation on terrorist groups. Some politicians have argued that terrorists can be stopped only when they know they will be repaid harshly for every act of violence. This is a politically popular deterrence argument, similar to one criminological school's insistence that swift and sure punishment deters crime. Post is not convinced such an argument is applicable to modern terrorism.

Post believes there is no single terrorist personality but that terrorists do follow similar behavioral patterns. The most important pattern has to do with group and individual acceptance. Terrorist groups are very much like criminal groups in having been rejected by mainstream society. The group becomes the only source of social reward because of its members' isolation. Terrorists reinforce one another. Post says this pattern holds true across cultures.

The individuals who are attracted to terrorist groups are as much outcasts as the organizations they seek to join. According to Post, terrorists are usually people who have been rejected by mainstream society and who fall in with like-minded individuals. This observation not only explains group reinforcement in terrorist organizations but also demonstrates the reason terrorist groups remain isolated. Individual members find rewards only within the group, so the desire to remain isolated is reinforced. Post believes this results in an us-against-them mentality.

The constant reinforcement of antisocial behavior in terrorist groups produces conforming behavior inside the organizations, although strong leaders may not conform and may splinter the group. When mainstream society is rejected, the individual's only hope of social acceptance lies in the group that rewards behavior. If the group rewards antisocial behavior, the fanatic is further motivated to attack the norm. According to Post, the rejection of external authority results in the acceptance of internal authority because behavior must be reinforced somewhere.

This set of dynamics is applicable to any group rejecting social norms. For example, a young religious person who joins a fundamentalist denomination might well experience the same set of dynamics. The person will be encouraged to reject the norm and turn to the new way of life within the denomination. The initiate can spurn outside behavioral reinforcement and norms because the group provides its own set of incentives. Religious conversion in this sense is psychologically similar to accepting the values of any deviant group.

Yet religious conversion does not usually lead to terrorism. In fact, it almost never does. Post says the key point for conversion in terrorist organizations is when the group shifts from violent rhetoric to action. Once the group engages in criminal activity, a distinct split with society occurs. The crimes required by terrorism become the final gestures of social rebellion. Crime both reinforces group isolation and increases the risk of leaving the group. In Post's analysis, criminal activity marks the true beginning of a terrorist group.

Recent Studies on the Justification of Violence: Multiple Factors

More recent research suggests that the approaches used by Wilkinson and Post were correct. Randy Borum (2004) says that researchers have come to the conclusion that there is no standard rationale for justifying behavior. He says it is profitable to distinguish three different phases of self-justification: reasons for joining, reasons for remaining, and reasons for leaving the group. The rationale for each decision constantly changes, and individuals are motivated by a variety of factors. Borum concludes that the decision to join, remain in, or leave a terrorist group cannot be summarized with a set of psychological factors; rather, it is a process beginning when a potential terrorist believes that social and political conditions are not morally correct. Justification is a process involving the constant assessment of morality. Individuals gravitate to violence in an attempt to achieve social equity, and if equity is not achieved, they blame the group in control. Violence can be justified in the face of evil power.

Jeff Victoroff (2005) agrees that a multiplicity of factors is used to justify violence, but he does not believe current research to be comprehensive. There are multiple theories and suggestions, he writes, but there are few empirical studies of the motivational factors that support terrorist violence. He says that an examination of peer-reviewed publications finds more theories than empirical analyses. Given the weakness of empirical evidence, Victoroff offers a few tentative conclusions. First, terrorism is caused by a variety of social and psychological factors, including biological predispositions toward violence. The factors have yet to be identified, but it is not impossible to do so. Second, terrorists operate and justify violence because they emotionally attach themselves to an ideology, they cannot tolerate moral ambiguity, and they have the capacity to suppress instinctive and learned moral limitations on behavior. Finally, there is a need to study the impact of leadership on group behavior. Terrorists must justify violent behavior, but Victoroff argues that we do not yet know all the ways they do it. He urges social scientists to test these conclusions, arguing that terrorism requires more empirical research. Scientific inquiry should be interdisciplinary, and it must involve direct study of terrorists, according to Victoroff.

H. H. A. Cooper (2001) develops a new twist in the justification of terrorism by looking at the problems caused by overexposure. Cooper believes that the public has become jaded with the constant bombardment of news about terrorism. The television-viewing audience has come to see death and destruction in terrorist events as a normal part of the story. This may force terrorists to do something extraordinary, and they might seek to increase the drama and body count to recapture public attention. In short, Cooper says, terrorists would justify more destruction because it is required for televised drama. Presciently, Cooper penned this prediction shortly before the 9/11 attacks.

Research by Brock Blomberg, Gregory Hess, and Akila Weerapana (2004) suggests that economic factors also play a role in justifying terrorist violence. Because many modern terrorists come from middle-class backgrounds and some have more education than average citizens, some researchers conclude that poverty and terrorism are not related. But meeting Victoroff's demand for more empirical research, Blomberg, Hess, and Weerapana believe they disprove this. After examining terrorism in 127 countries from 1968 to 1991, they conclude that terrorist groups form because they are not happy with the economic status quo. Researchers have missed the point. The individual socioeconomic position of a single terrorist is less important than economic welfare and opportunity at large. Terrorists exhibit a collective frustration about poverty, whether they are impoverished or not, and believe violence is justified to redress denial of economic opportunity. Increased access to economic activity decreases the level of violence, and in contrast, decreased opportunities in high-income countries increase the probability of terrorism.

Regardless of the cause, justification is reinforced when the ties that hold a group together are strong. Jessica Stern (2003b, pp. 159–160) believes that several factors must be in place for group cohesion to be effective. First, the group must identify an enemy and create an us-against-them atmosphere in daily life. Second, the group must have "a story," an almost mythological element, that inspires and guides its membership. Third, the group needs its own language, or symbolic words, to demonize the enemy.

Chip Berlet and Matthew Lyons (2000, pp. 323–344) complement Stern's research in this area. They say that groups first look for conspiracies and then blame (or scapegoat) a particular group for the conspiracy. Eventually, they demonize the scapegoats for being the primary cause of social injustice. Stern concludes (2003b, p. 157) that leaders must be able to inspire members to action and constantly search for more demonized enemies. Terrorists and their leaders reinforce each other in the process.

Self-Check

- *Why do people seek to justify violence?*
- *What did early researchers of terrorism find out about justification?*
- *How does more recent research support or discredit earlier research findings?*

Classification Systems: Can the Terrorist Personality Be Profiled?

Frederick Hacker (1976) introduced a general theory of individual terrorist behavior, and others followed. As research increased, the typical terrorist was thought to be a young, unmarried, middle-class male with some university training and an understanding of left-wing political philosophy (Russell and Miller, 1983, pp. 33–41). Unfortunately, this described millions of people, most of whom were not terrorists. Continued study failed to enhance the profile of a typical terrorist, causing Andrew Silke (2001) to lament that researchers still know very little about terrorism. This leads to a debate on the merits of profiling behavior.

Many law enforcement agencies, including the Behavioral Science Unit in the FBI, have attempted to develop practical models for profiling terrorists based on individual psychological characteristics. They employ a variety of techniques and have become more sophisticated in using behavioral science against many forms of criminality (Turvey, Tamlyn, and Chisum, 1999). Agencies also attempt to assess the level of potential threats, and violent political extremists usually represent the most dangerous threat.

A practical example of such classification systems comes from the United Kingdom. Police officials there make practical decisions based on profiles of terrorists and the classification of each incident. When faced with an act of terrorism, the local ranking police official makes an assessment of the event. If it is classified as a criminal activity or the result of a mentally deranged individual, the local police commander handles the incident. If the commander deems the action to be the result of political terrorism, the central government is informed, and the incident is handled on the prime minister's level. In addition, if the level of the threat is sufficiently high, the matter may be referred to the national government.

Although such profiling has practical applications in law enforcement, the larger question remains: is it possible to profile the terrorist personality? The question has spawned a heated debate. One side claims that profiles cannot be developed because terrorism changes with historical events. The other school believes profiles can be developed, but they must measure a variety of factors.

Rejecting Terrorist Profiles

Walter Laqueur (1999, pp. 79–104) says that no one can develop a composite picture of a terrorist because no such terrorist exists. Terrorism fluctuates over time, Laqueur argues, and the profile of the terrorist changes with circumstances. There can be no terrorist mosaic because there are different types of terrorism. Laqueur says we can be sure that most terrorists are young, but their actions and psychological makeup vary according to social and cultural conditions.

Laqueur (1999) believes other group characteristics can be discerned through the type of movement. Nationalistic and separatist groups are aggressive, and their actions are painted in horrible violence. Such violence may or may not be the result of psychological inadequacies. In democracies, Laqueur says, terrorists tend to be elitists. Nationalistic movements produce terrorists from the lower classes, but religious terrorists come from all classes. Individual and group profiles are the result of political and social conditions.

In the final analysis, Laqueur believes it is impossible to profile a terrorist personality because terrorism is not the subject of criminology. In the past, he says, perfectly normal individuals have opted to engage in terrorism as a rational political statement. Terrorism is a political phenomenon different from ordinary crime or psychopathology.

Several researchers agree with Laqueur. Randy Borum (2004, p. 37) states that there is no single terrorist personality and that terrorists represent a variety of physical types. He further states that the word *profiling* has so many different meanings that it has become virtually useless. Furthermore, if terrorist groups learn that members are being profiled, they select an operative who does not match the profile. If terrorist prevention rests on profiling, Borum concludes, it is doomed to failure.

Proponents of the impossibility of profiling also look at specific types of terrorism and terrorist groups. Robert Pape (2003) finds that suicide bombers come from several varying backgrounds and there is no single description of them. Marc Sageman (2004, pp. 66, 81–91) finds that the social process of becoming a terrorist may have a pattern, but there is no pattern of psychological disorders (see Another Perspective: Using a Group to Profile). Rohan Gunaratna (2002) states that al Qaeda operatives came from several countries and had differing ethnic backgrounds. With so many variables, critics believe that profiling is impossible.

Proposing a Multivariate Profile

Jeffrey Ian Ross (1999, pp. 169–192) offers an alternative view. Rather than attempting to delineate an individual profile, Ross says it may be possible to conceptualize terrorism in a model that combines social structure with group psychology. He believes such a model is necessary for policy makers to develop better counterterrorist responses.

Ross believes five interconnected processes are involved in terrorism: joining the group, forming the activity, remaining in the campaign,

ANOTHER PERSPECTIVE

Using a Group to Profile

Marc Sageman changes the entire debate on profiling behavior by shifting the unit of analysis to the group rather than the individual and engaging in empirical study. Rather than looking for a social or psychological factor that would remain constant in changing social space and time, Sageman began looking at radicalized members of al Qaeda. Using public sources and the biographies of 172 militants, he found a common behavioral pattern in al Qaeda. The terrorists were almost exclusively male and were radicalized in the West. Most of the men were mentally stable, and they came from middle-class—sometimes wealthy—families. They had no history of violence, and few of them had arrest records. There is no evidence to show that they were recruited by a sinister network or that they were brainwashed by militant ideology. Future al Qaeda members were lost and lonely. They joined with a small group of other isolated men and began the path to radicalization. In a sense, members of the group fell in love with each other, and radical ideology or religion played only a minor role in their decisions. Group loyalty was their most important factor. Radicalization came when members of a group tried to outdo each other in zeal for al Qaeda. According to Sageman, each group was "a bunch of guys." He finds psychological parallels in the world of religious revival and cults. Sageman, who comes from both the medical and intelligence worlds, finds it is possible to create profiles. The unit of analysis should be a particular group, not terrorists in general.

Source: Sageman, 2004.

leading the organization, and engaging in acts of terrorism. He says many analysts have attempted to explain terrorism based on these concepts, but they fall short because there is no model of terrorism. Rather than simply trying to profile the typical terrorist, Ross tries to explain how social and psychological processes produce terrorism. The model offers a great deal of promise.

Two factors are involved in the rise of terrorism at any point in history. The first centers around social structure. Structural factors include the way a society is organized, its political and economic systems, its historical and cultural conditions, the number of grievances citizens have and their mechanisms for addressing grievances, the availability of weapons, and the effectiveness of counterterrorist forces. Ross says that modernization, democracy, and social unrest create the structural conditions that facilitate terrorism. In Ross's analysis, urban areas produce the greatest potential for unrest and the greatest availability of weapons. When governments fail to address social pressures in such areas, the likelihood of terrorism increases. When counterterrorist intervention fails, the amount of terrorism is likely to increase.

Ross believes structural factors interact with the psychological makeup of potentially violent people to produce terrorism. He says several schools of psychology can be used to explain violence, but none is adequate to explain terrorism. As a result, he identifies five psychological and other factors involved in the development of terrorism: facilitating traits, frustration/narcissism-aggression, associational drives, learning opportunities, and cost-benefit calculations.

Psychological factors change constantly and interact with each other. Facilitating traits include fear, anger, depression, guilt, antisocial behavior, a strong ego, the need for excitement, and a feeling of being lost. Ross says the more of these traits a person exhibits, the more likely that the person will engage in terrorism. Frustration/narcissism-aggression means that a person has suffered a blow to the ego and reacts hostilely. Frustration refers to aggression channeled toward another person or symbol. Ross believes that high frustration may result in terrorist acts. This, in turn, interacts with structural factors to cause more violence. Associational drives are developed in group settings. Ross believes that when potential terrorists perceive benefits from particular groups, they tend to join those groups. Once inside, violent behavior is likely to increase because the group's acts of terror reinforce it. The existence of groups that engage in acts of terrorism create an environment for teaching terrorism to others. As learning opportunities increase, Ross says, the amount of terrorism increases. Finally, violence takes place after a cost-benefit analysis. In other words, terrorists evaluate whether the cost of an attack is worth the result.

Although not a typical profile of a terrorist personality, Ross's ideas explain the transformation of terrorism across history and provide social and psychological indicators of terrorism. Ross believes certain psychological factors interact with social factors to create a climate conducive to terrorism. Laqueur (1999) says a profile cannot be obtained because terrorism is a political activity, but Ross counters by demonstrating both political and psychological factors.

Self-Check

- *Do patterns of behavior exist in terrorist groups?*
- *If yes, how could this be used to develop a profile of terrorist behavior?*
- *If no, why is it difficult or impossible to profile terrorist behavior?*

SUMMARY

- Terrorism is a social process that takes place within meaning frameworks. One of the methods used to study the process involves focusing on the interpretations that people attribute to actions. Another way to examine the social process of terrorism is to examine the social organization, or structure, of terrorism.
- The methods social scientists use to examine terrorism from meaning and structural frameworks are frequently applied to the practical world of security operations.

- Recently, several terrorist groups seem to be motivated by religious duty. One group of analysts believes the world is witnessing a surge in religious violence.
- Samuel Huntington argues that conflict after the cold war is defined by clashes among the world's eight major civilizations. Each civilization is defined by culture, and religion is the primary force shaping culture.
- Social scientists approach religious terrorism by looking at structures or meanings. Theologians tend to compare militant with peaceful religious traditions. One prominent theological approach focuses on the literalization of sacred stories.
- The behavior of criminals and terrorists differs. Criminals tend to be unfocused and not dedicated to a cause. Terrorists are focused and dedicated. Some analysts believe that religious terrorists are more dedicated than political terrorists.
- All people, including terrorists, must feel they are justified in their behavior. Socially, terrorists are justified by the use of group reinforcement, ideology, and symbols.
- Some scholars believe that terrorist behavior cannot be profiled because it fluctuates with historical, political, and social circumstances. Others believe that profiles are possible, if social factors are matched to a behavioral profile.

KEY TERMS

meaning (p. 23)
meaning framework (p. 24)
theory of action (p. 25)
structural framework (p. 26)
structure (p. 26)

social geometry (p. 26)
netwar (p. 26)
nodes (p. 26)
eschatology (p. 28)

WRITING ASSIGNMENTS

1. Social scientists use the term *methodology* to describe the way they look at issues. Two of the main methodologies discussed in this chapter focused on meanings and structures. Imagine that you are watching a terrorist event unfold on television. The experts on television explain the way this terrorist group views the world. How would this affect the attack? Another expert cites social structures around the terrorist group, such as the state of the economy, religious organizations, and families. Does this change the way the attack is viewed? Are meanings and structures separate or can both approaches be used to explain the attack?

2. Consider the following scenarios. In the first, an infantry unit from an invading army attacks through a city to take an objective, a bus station in the town's center. The second scenario involves a revo-

lutionary group in the same city. In this scene the group sets off a bomb in the bus station to protest economic injustice in the city. Both incidents kill 100 civilians. Is there a difference between these two actions? How might the soldiers justify their actions? What justifications might the revolutionary group use?

3. R. Scott Appleby (2000) argues that in-depth theological education might keep people in peaceful religious traditions from following militants. Argue for or against his position. Consider the authority figures who would be charged with setting the agenda for education. What obstacles would they face? Could they deal with differing interpretations of sacred stories?

The Organization and Financing of Terrorism

AP Photo/Ben Curtis/File

An underground economy is used to finance terrorist groups, and some analysts believe this includes illegal diamond trading in Africa. The 9/11 Commission found no such evidence to support this. Here, a legal diamond dealer in Sierra Leone weighs a gem taken from a local mine.

Learning Objectives

After reading this chapter, you should be able to

■ Trace the transformation of terrorist organizations from cells to networks.

■ Explain the problems of managing any terrorist organization.

■ Describe the impact of an organization's size and structure on the length of a terrorist campaign.

■ Explain how analysts developed an understanding of the importance of financing.

■ Outline competing views about using financial weapons against terrorists.

■ Describe some of the illegal sources of income for terrorist groups.

■ Explain the use of underground networks in financing terrorism.

- Describe legitimate methods used to raise funds for terrorist groups.
- Explain the hawala system.
- Outline the development of the "new economy of terrorism."
- Summarize both sides of the debate over narco-terrorism.

Terrorism changes constantly, as do other forms of conflict, but the same structural principles apply to successful terrorist groups as to any other organization. Labor must be divided in particular ways, and each subunit must complete its assigned specialty to complement the work of other units. Even though its goals are more difficult to accomplish because the work must be completed with extreme secrecy, a terrorist group must be organized and managed for success. In addition, terrorism must be financed. Some terrorist groups fund themselves through crime, others have a state sponsor, and more recently, networked organizations have developed a mix of legitimate and illegal methods of funding. The networks also represent a radical change in organization. This chapter explores changing organizational and financial structures.

Changing Dynamics and Structures

The invention of dynamite was one of the two most important developments in the history of modern terrorism. It gave small groups of violent people a powerful tool. The other development dealt with the deployment of power, that is, the formation of tactical groups. Terrorists must organize in the same manner as any other rational human group, and they have to operate in secret. The first organizations were created in Ireland in the early 1900s during the struggle for independence. Michael Collins, leader of the Irish Republican Army (IRA), studied revolutionary tactics from the eighteenth and nineteenth centuries and developed a method of isolating small units of terrorists. He called the small units **cells**. Each cell had its own mission, and it operated without knowledge of other cells in the area. This method of organization reemerged after World War II, and it dominated the structure of terrorism until the 1990s. At that time many large terrorist groups developed more dynamic methods of organization.

Late Twentieth-Century Cells

James Fraser, a former counterterrorist specialist in the U.S. Army, discusses the organization of terrorist groups by analyzing two factors: the structure of the organization and its support. According to Fraser and Ian Fulton (1984, pp. 7–9), terrorist groups are necessarily designed

cell
The basic unit of a traditional terrorist organization. Groups of cells form columns. Members in cells seldom know one another. In more recent terrorist structures, *cell* describes a tactical group dispatched by the network for selected operations.

Figure 3.1

A Pyramid Organization

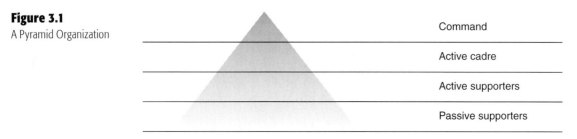

Command

Active cadre

Active supporters

Passive supporters

pyramid

An illustration of the way terrorists organize themselves into hierarchies. It is an analogy showing a large base of support culminating in a small group of terrorists at the top.

to hide their operations from security forces, and so analysis is difficult. Still, certain organizational principles are common to all terrorist groups. Groups employ variations of command-and-control structures, but they are frequently organized in the same pattern no matter what causes they endorse.

The typical organization is arranged in a **pyramid** (Figure 3.1). It takes many more people to support terrorist operations than to carry them out; therefore, the majority of people who work in terrorist organizations serve to keep terrorists in the field. The most common job in terrorist groups is support, not combat. According to Fraser and Fulton, the hierarchical structure of terrorist groups is divided into four levels. The smallest group, at the top of the pyramid, is responsible for command. As in military circles, leadership makes policy and plans and provides general direction. Other researchers have often pointed out that the command structure is not as effective as in legitimate organizations because of the demand for secrecy. The command structure in a terrorist organization is not free to communicate openly with its membership; therefore, it cannot exercise day-to-day operational control.

active cadre

A military term that describes the people actually carrying out terrorist activity in an organizational hierarchy. The active cadre refers to the small terrorist group at the second level of a pyramid, under the command level.

The second level of Fraser and Fulton's hierarchy is the **active cadre**, or the people responsible for carrying out the mission of the organization. Depending on the organization's size, each terrorist in the cadre may have one or more specialties. Other terrorists support each specialty, but the active cadre is the striking arm of the terrorist group. After the command structure, the cadre of active terrorists is the smallest organization in most terrorist structures.

Under the active cadre is the second largest and the most important level of a terrorist organization: the active supporters. These people are critical to terrorist campaigns. Any group can carry out a bombing or kidnapping, but maintaining a campaign of bombings and kidnappings takes support. Active supporters keep the terrorists in the field. They maintain communication channels, provide safe houses, gather intelligence, and ensure that all other logistical needs are met. This is the largest internal group in the organization.

The last and largest category is the organization's passive supporters. This group is extremely difficult to identify and characterize because passive supporters do not readily join terrorist groups; they simply represent a favorable element of the political climate. When a terrorist group can muster political support, it will have a relatively large number

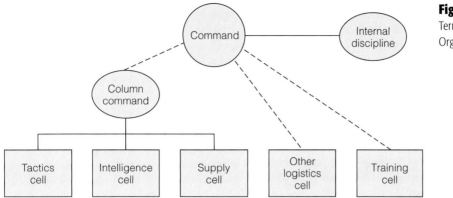

Figure 3.2
Terrorist Group
Organization

of passive supporters. When its cause alienates the mainstream, passive support dwindles. Passive support complements active support.

Most terrorist groups number fewer than fifty people as active supporters, cadre, and command and are incapable of mounting a long-term campaign. Under the command of only a few people, the group is divided according to specific tasks. Intelligence sections are responsible for assessing targets and planning operations. Support sections provide the means necessary to carry out an assault, and the tactical units are responsible for the actual terrorist action.

Larger groups are guided by the same organizational principles, but they have major subunits capable of carrying out extensive operations. In particularly large groups, subunits have the ability to act autonomously. Large groups have the tactical units and the support sections to conduct terrorist campaigns.

Anthony Burton (1976, pp. 70–72) describes the basic structure of subunits. Terrorist organizations have two primary types of subunits: the cell and the **column**. The cell is the most basic. Composed of four to six people, the cell usually has a specialty; it may be a tactical unit or an intelligence section. In some organizations, the duties of tactical cells vary with the assignment. Other cells are designed to support the operations (Figure 3.2).

Groups of cells create columns, which are semiautonomous conglomerations of cells with a variety of specialties and a single command structure. As combat units, columns have questionable effectiveness. They are too cumbersome to be used in major operations, and the secrecy demanded by terrorism prevents effective intercolumn cooperation. Their primary function is combat support because elements in a column can be arranged to support the tactical operations of cells.

Although both Fraser and Fulton's work and Burton's analyses appear to be dated, the structures they outlined are still applicable to terrorist groups. Patrick Seale (1992) finds the same type of structure when examining the Abu Nidal group, which was sponsored by many states in the Middle East and Europe. Reuven Paz (2000) sees similarities with

column
Groups of cells in a terrorist or guerrilla organization.

Figure 3.3

The Umbrella Organization

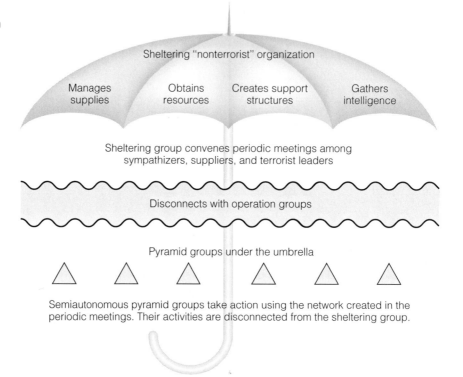

Sheltering "nonterrorist" organization

Manages supplies

Obtains resources

Creates support structures

Gathers intelligence

Sheltering group convenes periodic meetings among sympathizers, suppliers, and terrorist leaders

Disconnects with operation groups

Pyramid groups under the umbrella

Semiautonomous pyramid groups take action using the network created in the periodic meetings. Their activities are disconnected from the sheltering group.

the organization of the Islamic resistance movement Hamas. Religious terrorists, such as Aum Shinrikyo in Japan, also copy the group model (Brackett, 1996). The only terrorists who do not follow typical organizational models are individual terrorists who operate without a group.

Newer Models: Umbrella Organizations and Modern Piracy

Around 1982, new types of organizational styles developed from the pyramid, and organizational transformations continue today. The first change came with the birth of the **umbrella** organization (Figure 3.3). In this style of organization, several small pyramids gather under a sheltering group that manages supplies, obtains resources, creates support structures, and gathers intelligence. The umbrella organization does not become directly involved with terrorism, claiming to be a legitimate organization representing a political cause. The sheltering group convenes periodic meetings with sympathizers, suppliers, and terrorist leaders, thus allowing terrorists to resupply, select targets, and plan. The sheltering umbrella disassociates its activities from violence, casting a blind eye when the semiautonomous pyramid groups take action.

The actions of Unionists and Republicans in Northern Ireland illustrate the operation of the umbrella. Both sides maintain legitimate political organizations to campaign either for continued relations with the United Kingdom or unity with the Republic of Ireland. Paul Dixon

umbrella

A group that shelters, supports, and inspires smaller terrorist groups. The RAND Corporation refers to this as a hub.

(2004) argues that much political activity is conducted as a public drama to hide other activities. A number of researchers claim that violent paramilitary groups have operated under the umbrella of legitimate organizations for decades, while the respective political party—the umbrella—continually denies any connection to terrorist violence (see Hastings, 1970, pp. 40–56; Winchester, 1974, pp. 171–180; Lee, 1983, pp. 59–97; Dunn and Morgan, 1995).

Gal Luft and Anne Korin (2004) worry that such practices may soon take place on the high seas. Arguing that most people incorrectly assume that piracy is an activity of the past, they note that incidents have doubled in the past decade. Today's pirates are armed with global positioning systems, satellite phones, machine guns, rockets, and grenades. Most of them currently work for organized crime syndicates, but Luft and Korin warn that international terrorists could take note of the recent rise and success of piracy. If their thesis is correct, organized crime provides an ideal model for terrorists: a seemingly legitimate business (the sheltering organization) provides cover for pirates (the pyramid organization) while denying all connection with illegal activities. Today's piracy is already conducted under an umbrella. In reality, the legitimate business is the front for an organized crime group. The business group, in turn, denies any affiliation with crime, and it shelters the pirate groups operating under its shield. Terrorists need merely to copy the model.

Researchers from the RAND Corporation (Arquilla, Ronfeldt, and Zanini, 1999) identify several other types of new organizational styles that emerged in the 1990s. **Virtual organizations** are created through computer and information networks. **Chain organizations** involve small groups linked by some type of communication and whose members periodically cooperate. A hub organization has a centralized group with semiautonomous groups supported in other regions. Centralized hubs developed to manage or support individual cells, and they operate much like umbrella groups. The most important new style of organization identified in Arquilla, Ronfeldt, and Zanini's and other research is the terrorist network.

The network's structure can range from the simple to complex (Arquilla and Ronfeldt, 1996, 2001; Arquilla, Ronfeldt, and Zanini, 1999; Sageman, 2004, pp. 137–174). A complex all-channel network is composed of groups, logistical systems, and overlapping relationships among groups, individuals, and technology. The second concept in the network is the node. A node can refer to any critical function in the network, and this can range from a group to support systems, such as a bomb-making factory or a cybercafé. The network is a series of nodes held together with communication.

The RAND approach reveals the structure of **networks**. They involve terrorist, extremist, criminal, and disruptive-activist groups. The key to networks, according to this approach, is their ability to operate in a technological setting. Operations are characterized by the dual nature of the network. Violence takes place on two levels: organized small groups and

virtual organizations

Associations that develop through communication, financial, and ideological links. Like a network, a virtual organization has no central leadership.

chain organizations

Temporary associations of diverse groups. Groups in a chain come together for a particular operation and disband after it is over.

networks

Organizations of groups, supplies, weapons, and any structure that supports an operation. Much like a traffic system or the World Wide Web, networks do not have central leadership, and they operate under a variety of rules.

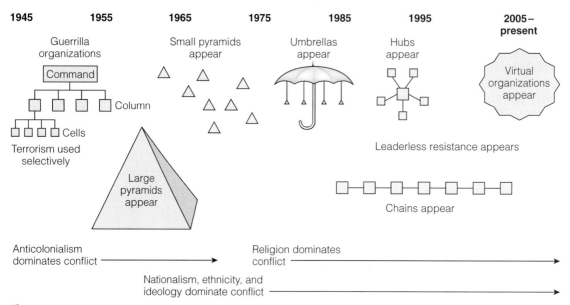

Figure 3.4
Timeline of Organizational Styles

disruptive violence from demonstrations. Another characteristic is the structure of the group. It is not a traditional hierarchy; it is a network. Members can be quickly assembled although they operate from diverse locations, and group structures are temporary. They are designed to fit a particular situation. They appear seemingly from nowhere, strike, and return to obscurity. RAND refers to this as the ability to swarm.

Marc Sageman (2004, pp. 171–173) states that networks are frequently composed of groups of friends. In jihadist organizations, for example, isolated individuals rediscover their religious past and join others who have had the same experience. It is the beginning of deep bonding, which Sageman calls a love affair. This is a friendship network arising from a religious revival, but if the group is exposed to and accepts a militant philosophy, it can become militarized.

The network cannot enter the jihad at this point, however, because it is not connected to a jihadist network. Although the group can take action on its own, its striking power is limited. The group reaches greater lethality if it can become attached to the ideological jihadist network. The jihadist movement is a concept, held together by communications among various groups. If the group is successful in making contact and joining a militant network, it will become a node linked to other groups in a larger network. Violent action is not the result of centralized decision making or leadership. It comes out of the synergistic relationships inside the node as individuals express love for fellow group members by exhibiting increased radicalization. Nodes also interact with other nodes, forming temporary alliances for particular operations. Figure 3.4 shows a timeline of organizational styles.

Self-Check

- *Describe the structure of terrorist cells immediately after World War II.*
- *What changes in organizational styles influenced the ways terrorists organized themselves?*
- *What is a terror network?*

Managing Terrorist Organizations

Whether groups organize in a traditional pyramid, an umbrella, a hub, or even a virtual organization, it is possible to chart the structure of even the most secretive groups. Any student could probably make a fairly accurate diagram of most terrorist groups after taking an Introduction to Management class. Terrorist leaders face operational problems and seek to solve them with the same strategies taught in such a management class. Terrorist leaders also have special organizational problems.

The first problem is the need for secrecy. This dominates the operational aspects of terrorism and leads to a variety of problems that open organizations do not encounter. Ironically, although secrecy is the greatest strength of the terrorist organization, it also is the basis of its greatest weakness. Terrorism demands secrecy, and secrecy prevents effective communication. Sometimes a terrorist group's work is so secret that even the members do not know what they are doing.

Because the necessity for secrecy is so great in any style of terrorist organization, subgroups are usually allowed a relatively high degree of autonomy. Terrorism is a decentralized affair, and the larger the group, the greater the degree of decentralization. This is not the most desirable kind of organization, but it is an operational necessity. Terrorists know a centralized structure is easily infiltrated and destroyed by security forces. One well-placed informant can destroy an entire organization.

Decentralization offers relative security: very few people know many other members of the organization. This approach affords great protection but difficult administration. The organization of the Provisional IRA can be used to illustrate the problem. The IRA is organized like most large terrorist groups. It is governed by a supreme council whose members are drawn from IRA battalion or column commanders. Column commanders are responsible for a number of cells, which in the IRA are frequently called by military names such as platoons, squadrons, and companies. The command of the IRA, however, has problems that emanate from secrecy and decentralization.

On paper, the organizational chart looks extremely logical. In practice, that logic is modified by the need for each unit to be protected from discovery. This means members of various cells and columns usually have no idea who the other members of the IRA are and what they are doing. They get their orders from one person, and that person supposedly represents the Supreme Council. This paves the way for potential splintering or, at the least, misunderstandings. It is easy to see why the IRA is difficult to manage.

To prevent factionalism and excessive autonomy, terrorist commanders turn to internal discipline for control. In essence, what commanders continually threaten to do is terrorize the terrorist organization. However, internal discipline can become a major factor in the demise of a terrorist organization. There are two opposing dynamics at work, one pulling for cohesion and cooperation through fear and the other pulling for autonomy through decentralization and secrecy. Sometimes, attempts at discipline backfire. For example, when leaders try to punish errant members by assassination, they may find themselves the target of disgruntled followers. As a result, large terrorist organizations frequently find themselves splitting.

Another problem of terrorist management is that of gaining immediate tactical support for operations. As Fraser and Fulton (1984) suggest, the most important element of a terrorist campaign is the number and structure of active supporters. Without active supporters, launching a campaign is impossible. Although the press has frequently portrayed terrorist leaders as secretive plotters controlling hidden armies of true believers, in reality terrorist leadership must exert itself to develop and maintain active support. The majority of time is spent creating networks of active supporters, not launching headline-grabbing operations.

Marc Sageman (2004, pp. 171–173) believes that operations are managed by the social organization of networks. Examining militant Salafi structures associated with the al Qaeda movement, Sageman finds four major clusters, or nodes, connected by a central staff cluster. Friendships and social relations form the communication and managerial nexus of the organization. These relations are enhanced by cliques within the group. Al Qaeda and its affiliates thrive because command is decentralized in the network. The one exception is Jamaat Islamiyya, a militant religious group in Indonesia still organized around the concept of cellular hierarchy. Hierarchies are more difficult to manage because power is concentrated. Therefore, they are more vulnerable to counterterrorist techniques.

Self-Check

- *What problems do terrorist leaders face?*
- *How are these problems similar to ones managers in any organization face?*
- *What special problems separate terrorist organizations from other groups?*

▼ Group Size and Length of Campaign

Regardless of the behavioral aspects of terrorist organizations, the size of a group affects its ability to operate over time. Large groups last longer than small ones. Ted Robert Gurr (1988a, pp. 23–50) conducted an empirical analysis of terrorist groups operating in the ideological revolutionary period of the twentieth century. He was one of the first researchers to discuss the relationship between a group's size and its effectiveness. As ideological groups grew in the West, many analysts associated an organization's staying power with state sponsorship. Groups that had sponsors survived, and independent groups fell apart or were destroyed (Livingstone and Arnold, 1986, pp. 1–10). In the 1990s it became popular to speak of failed states, regions of lawlessness where criminal and terrorist organizations could thrive (Napoleoni, 2003, pp. 11–28). Today, it is also important to consider the religious and ideological factors that hold international networks together (Scheuer, 2006, pp. 65–68).

Gurr's analysis of group size demonstrates that larger groups are more effective than smaller groups over time, although most terrorist actions involve only a few people who generate more noise than injury. He finds that, despite the popular belief that political revolutionaries dominate terrorist groups, the majority of successful groups embrace other doctrines, such as nationalism. Gurr concludes that terrorist violence has diverse causes and many remain unidentified. No matter what the cause, however, most terrorist campaigns end within eighteen months of the initial outburst of violence.

Terrorism is short-lived because it seldom generates support. A terrorist campaign promises the greatest opportunity for success, but political revolutionary and radical groups do not have the popular appeal needed to gain support for their activities. As a result, many terrorist activities remain isolated and do not grow into a campaign. Terrorists seldom offer serious challenges to authority. Gurr believes large groups became large because they embraced popular political issues. Only a few groups have been able to adopt popular positions since 1945.

Vittorfranco Pisano (1987, pp. 24–31) illustrates the importance of group size with an analysis of terrorism in Italy from 1975 to 1985. There were a tremendous number of terrorist actions in Italy during the 10 years of Pisano's study, and a relatively large number of groups were responsible for the attacks. The reason for the plethora of groups, according to Pisano, was that most terrorist organizations were not capable of mounting a long-term campaign against the government. They could strike only a few times before their resources ran out or they were captured. Large Italian terrorist groups took advantage of this situation, using many different names in an attempt to confuse authorities. Yet investigators came to realize that only large groups were involved in sustained actions. Everyone else became "single-incident" terrorists; that is, they could mount only one operation.

Christopher Hewitt (1984) reflects Gurr's position by stating that small groups do not have the resources to damage an opponent over an extended time: they cannot launch a campaign. He believes terrorist campaigns are more important than isolated acts of terrorism because they demand extensive logistical networks. Hewitt argues terrorist campaigns became important after World War II for two primary reasons. First, the campaigns of large terrorist organizations accounted for the majority of terrorism around the world. Small, isolated terrorist organizations failed to match the extent of activities of their larger counterparts. Second, large terrorist organizations have prompted governments to employ macropolicies. Large terrorist organizations can actually bring about a change in governmental political response because they represent a problem far beyond the means of local law enforcement. Therefore, large groups represent political threats.

Yet extremists rarely attract a political base—except among other extremists. In general, people do not readily flock to small terrorist organizations. Large groups like the Basque Nation and Liberty (ETA; a revolutionary terrorist group in northern Spain and southern France) and the IRA have gained support because their causes are so popular among their **reference groups**. Their methods may be extreme, but their political appeal has a broad base. Many small groups recognize this and attempt to follow the examples of the larger groups. By rhetorically abandoning their extremist positions and taking on a more popular political cause, small groups hope to broaden their appeal.

Neil Livingstone (Livingstone and Arnold, 1986) was one of the first analysts to discuss state sponsorship. Describing terrorism as "warfare on the cheap," Livingstone found that a nation could support a terrorist group, giving the group the ability to wage a terrorist campaign. In other words, state support automatically created a large group. Hezbollah serves as an example of a state-supported group. Hezbollah began as a political movement inside revolutionary Iran. In 1982, after Israel invaded Lebanon, Hezbollah moved to the Bekaa Valley in Lebanon. The group not only grew, it became a potent military and political power in Lebanese politics. The source of its strength is direct support from Iran (see Hiro, 1987; R. Wright, 1986, 1989; Harik, 2004).

Hezbollah also illustrates the importance of a failed state. Lebanon went through a debilitating civil war from 1975 to 1990. Several local militias, including Hezbollah, gained power in different areas of the country. Some of these militant groups became so strong that the Lebanese government could do little to control them, and the most successful group was Hezbollah. It developed its own military wing, fought Israel, provided social and educational services to Shiites in southern Lebanon, and formed its own economic system. Using local support and continued financial backing from Iran, Hezbollah emerged as a strong, semiautonomous structure far beyond the control of the Lebanese government (Harik, 2004). Israel launched a monthlong war against Hezbollah in the summer of 2006, claiming that it was not at war with Lebanon, and many observers feel that Israel lost the war. Hezbollah not only has state sponsorship but has evolved in a country where the national government could not control internal affairs. Hezbollah's size is partially due to its growth in a failed state.

Despite the experience with terrorism from roughly 1965 to 1990, it would be a mistake to assume that group size is the result only of inter-

reference group

The primary group whose values with which individuals or other groups identify. It is an idealized group of peers that serve as a model for behavior.

nal political appeal, state sponsorship, and failed states. Michael Scheuer (2006, pp. 20–23) believes that if these approaches are applied to Islamic militants, it will be impossible to understand both the organizational characteristics and the growth of al Qaeda and related groups. Numbers of jihadist groups are large, but for a differing reason. Militant Islamic theology is popular with tens of millions—Scheuer says maybe hundreds of millions—of Muslims throughout the world. This theology is responsible for the size of the group. Previous movements took place inside an organization where a group of managers exercised some type of control. Although some operations are controlled by a leadership group, the jihadist movement is loosely structured. Its size is due to religious inspiration, not sponsorship or control. Scheuer's argument goes back to Marc Sageman's (2004) findings. In jihadist terrorism the size of the network is more important than the size of a single group.

Self-Check

- *Describe Gurr's research on campaigns.*
- *Why are elements of these findings still applicable?*
- *Speculate about the power of networks in terms of findings about older organizations.*

Financing Modern Terrorism

The seventeenth-century Hapsburg general Raimondo Montecuccoli once said a nation needed three things to make war: money, money, and more money. This saying is applicable to terrorism: terrorists need money to run an operation. Spontaneous violence can occur without planning or resources, but organized political violence requires financial backing. It takes money to fund organizations and resources to support operations. Some new forms of terrorism even require salaries to pay professional terrorists. The families of suicide bombers receive compensation in the Middle East, and other terrorist organizations have found they can take advantage of existing criminal networks to raise money.

As mentioned in Chapter 2, Donald Black (2004) suggests that modern terrorism has developed because travel time between potential terrorists and their targets has been reduced. This concept is especially applicable to financing. Several hundred years ago European nations financed most governmental activity by physically transferring precious metals like gold and silver from one place to another. The rise of currency and modern banking replaced this system, and electronic transfers and rapid communication systems revolutionized the financial world. The distance between two parties in an economic transaction is insignificant. This applies to parties that operate within and outside the boundaries of the law. It is also applicable to terrorism.

When modern terrorism began to emerge after World War II, security forces frequently concentrated on investigative measures, military force, and tactics to counter terrorism. Financing was often overlooked. One of the works that changed this line of thinking came from James Adams (1986), who at that time was the defense correspondent for the *Times* of London. The most effective method for stopping terrorism, Adams argued, was to stop the flow of money. Terrorism is relatively cheap, but it still requires resources. If governments cut off the flow of funds, terrorists would find it difficult or impossible to operate. Although it seemed to be an unconventional approach at the time, today Adam's thesis is accepted as common wisdom.

Capone discovery

A term used by James Adams to explain the Irish Republican Army's entry into organized crime.

Adams focused on banking and organized crime to demonstrate his point. The Palestine Liberation Organization (PLO) ran its own bank, Adams said, and the IRA made a **Capone discovery**, in which it developed an organized crime network to finance operations. Other researchers found that methods of terrorist financing had changed over time. Many terrorist organizations began using petty crime, money laundering, and transfer of illegal contraband to finance operations (Hinnen, 2004). Harvey Kushner and Benjamin Jacobson (1998) found terrorists using illegal grocery coupons to raise funds. Other investigators have found legal businesses laundering millions of dollars for terrorist organizations (Navias, 2002).

The awareness of the importance of financing began to evolve slowly. This was partly because of an inherent contradiction in the cost of a single terrorist event in contrast to the cost of a campaign. Stated simply, a terrorist operation does not cost a lot of money, but the overall budget for a campaign is quite high. The *Economist* (2003) reports that terrorism is cost effective in terms of the causalities and destruction terrorist events cause. Events like the 1995 Oklahoma City bombing or the multiple bomb attacks on trains in Madrid in 2004 cost only a few thousand dollars. Yet, as Neil Livingstone and David Halevy (1988) explain, it takes a lot of cash to run a terrorist group for any time. For example, 9/11 was inexpensive, but holding al Qaeda together cost several thousand dollars per month (L. Wright, 2006, pp. 168–169). After Adams raised the issue, investigators and analysts began looking at the larger picture—the maintenance of a terrorist group. Tracing money is a tactic in an investigation, but it becomes a strategy in a counterterrorist campaign.

There is a debate about whether a financial strategy can be effective. Martin Navias (2002) argues that the major strategy of counterterrorism should be waging "financial warfare" with financial weapons. His suggested methodology is an expansion, using modern means, of Adams's thesis charging governments to stop the flow of funds. The National Strategy for Combating Terrorism (2006, p. 7) endorses this approach and targets two areas: the source of financing and the mechanisms to transfer money. Financial approaches take the position that campaigns are expensive, so attacks on terrorist financing should reduce incidents of terrorism. Critics argue this approach is too simple. It assumes that terrorists will act only in the legal formalized economy. In reality, terrorists participate in underground criminal networks that are relatively immune to financial regulations. So-called financial warfare will not be effective because terrorists do not respond to formal controls (Basile, 2004).

Regardless of academic or governmental policy debates, law enforcement agencies have successfully used **forensic accounting** for many years. Techniques have been employed against organized crime groups, drug networks, and corporations defrauding investors. It is the favorite tool of the Criminal Investigation Division of the Internal Revenue Service (IRS), and crime analysts in many agencies believe the maxim "follow the money." This is hardly "financial warfare"; it is a good investigative technique that can be applied to a single terrorist incident or a large terrorist organization. John Cassara (2006) argues that America has stalled in its efforts to fight terrorism because law enforcement agencies have not used sufficient forensic accounting tools. It is possible to track terrorists through money laundering, cash purchases, banking accounts, and stock and business investments. Cassara also argues that tracking money can create a better intelligence: criminal intelligence and national security intelligence. Mapping the financial activities of suspected groups and individuals gives intelligence a comprehensive focus. Forensic accounting can be used to solve crime and to gain information.

forensic accounting
An investigative tool used to track money used in illegal activities. It can be used in any crime involving the exchange, storage, or conversion of fiscal resources.

Self-Check

- *How does terrorism intersect with organized crime?*
- *Can any organization or network make a Capone discovery?*
- *How does the idea of "following money" help investigators?*

Funding: Sources and Networks

It is easier to approach this debate if it is seen from several levels. Financing terrorism is not a single proposition. It involves multiple layers of organizations and activities operating in a variety of ways. Three major categories help explain the structure of financing. The first element deals with the unlawful raising and distribution of funds. It is necessary to examine the illegal sources of income and the underground networks used to disburse the funds. Terrorists also use another source of income, the formal regulated economy. Therefore, it is necessary to examine activities that appear to be legitimate. The third category has little to do with financing but has much to do with financial effectiveness. Some analysts propose using financial weapons against terrorists, and some terrorists have learned that economic targeting is a technological force multiplier. In other words, it is also necessary to consider the ways terrorists can turn the tables and use the costs of terrorism as a weapon.

As Adams's early study indicated, terrorists need money. In the past two decades the links between criminal networks and terrorist organizations have increased all over the globe. Middle Eastern terrorists engage in smuggling and document fraud. Document fraud raises money for terrorist organizations and provides terrorists with false identification. In central Asia terrorist organizations trade illegal arms, launder money, and distribute drugs. Latin American terrorism is tied to drug production and public corruption. In the United States domestic terrorists engage in fraud schemes and robberies to finance political violence (Mili, 2006).

Criminal Methods of Funding and Distribution

expropriation
A term used by Carlos Marighella for armed robbery.

Raising money for illegal operations is nothing new. The Brazilian terrorist-philosopher Carlos Marighella argued that "urban warfare" begins with a campaign of **expropriation**; that is, robbery (1969, 1971; see also Burton, 1976). Terrorists around the world use a variety of criminal methods to raise funds. Violent activities involve kidnapping, extortion, and robbery. Less violent methods include fraud, larceny, smuggling, dealing in contraband, forgery, and counterfeiting (Nance, 2003). Investigation of such activities follows standard law enforcement procedures with one major exception. The key to a successful counterterrorist investigation focuses on motivation. Criminals steal for self-gratification, but terrorists steal for a cause (Bodrero, 2002). If investigators discover motivating factors beyond immediate gratification, it may be indicative of an effort to raise funds for terrorism (Dyson, 2001, pp. 41–44: Ehrenfeld, 2003, pp. 77–78; Navarro, 2005, pp. 80–82).

Counterfeiting and fraud are common weapons of the American extremist right. Mark Pitcavage (1999a) points out that the extremist right loves to engage in counterfeiting and fraud. They are especially good at defrauding their own Christian compatriots. In one scheme (Pitcavage, 1999b, 1999c), a patriot claimed that the U.S. government went bankrupt after abandoning the gold standard in 1933. The patriot, however, found out about the bankruptcy and sued the government for issuing Federal Reserve notes. The Supreme Court sympathized with the patriot and awarded him $600 trillion in gold. Delta Force went abroad to gather the world's gold to pay off the debt, and now every American was entitled to $20 million to $40 million. All a person had to do to file a claim was to give the patriot $300.

Domestic extremists are not the only violent fanatics who raise funds in the United States; international terrorists also engage in fraudulent activities in America. From approximately 1981 to 1986 the Abu Nidal Organization engaged in different criminal activities in Tennessee and the St. Louis metropolitan area to generate funds (E. Harris, 1995). Hezbollah ran cigarettes from North Carolina to Michigan and used some of the profits to fund operations in Lebanon (*United States of America v. Mohamad Youseff Hammoud, et al.*, 2002). There are a variety of schemes across the country utilizing baby formula. American baby formula is treasured throughout the world because of its nutritional value. Terrorists sometimes steal formula and use illegal distribution networks to raise money (Clayton, 2005). In Cincinnati, law enforcement officers broke a ring of convenience stores that were selling stolen goods to finance terrorist organizations (Coolidge and Prendergast, 2003). Police in Dearborn, Michigan, arrested two men for making false identification papers for Middle Eastern groups (U.S. Immigration and Customs Enforcement, 2005).

The Internet has become a tool for fraud. Terrorists use online activity in identity theft and gaining access to bank and credit card accounts. They also sell items at Internet auctions. Security fraud is another method of raising funds. For example, a group might buy a large amount of stock in a company that is fairly inactive. They then fill the Web with stories of new products, new technology, or some other item that will cause the company's stock to increase. As the stock value increases, terrorists sell the stock at an inflated price even though the company had no real increase in value. Before the stock drops back to its normal level, the terrorists make a huge profit. This process is known as "pump and dump," and it is frequently used by dishonest stock speculators and other criminals (Hinnen, 2004).

In addition to the IRA's Capone discovery, terrorists use extortion and protection rackets to raise money. Terrorist organizations force legitimate businesses or other people to make payoffs to avoid being attacked. Loretta Napoleoni (2003, pp. 27–28) reports that the Shining Path of Peru taxed farmers for protection. Rebels and death squads in Colombia did the same thing. Zachary Abuza (2003b) says similar tactics are used in Southeast Asia. In essence, Abuza concludes, terrorists use the same fund-raising techniques that criminals have used for years in addition to their unique methods of gathering money.

Examples of illegal fund-raising could extend to all forms of crime. At the heart of illegal activity is fund-raising. Terrorists have learned that crime can pay. Traditional crimes, especially large embezzlement schemes in the global economy, represent a source of income for small groups as well as large organizations (Labeviere, 2000, pp. 54–55; Napoleoni, 2003, pp. 203–205; D. Kaplan, 2005). After raising these funds, terrorists frequently expend them in underground networks to support operations.

Underground Networks and Organized Crime

David Carter (2004) points to an important characteristic of terrorist organizations. When terrorists move goods, people, weapons, money, or contraband, they must do so in underground networks. It is not possible to build a network overnight; they develop only through long-term trust. This means, Carter concludes, that terrorists use existing criminal networks for logistics, including financing activities. The FBI estimates the underground economy produces $500 billion per year. An underground economy requires secret institutions, and terrorists have found various enterprises for hiding money (Maier, 2003). Rachel Ehrenfeld

(2003, pp. 10–30) says that terrorists run banks and create phony companies to launder or hide their funds. They also engage in secret transactions and form alliances with organized crime.

Frederich Schneider (2002) says the underground economy and its ties to crime are so important to terrorists because all the transactions remain hidden. Organized criminal and smuggling networks have long had the means of hiding money through seemingly legal transactions. Terrorists take advantage of these networks. Schneider believes that terrorism has become a big business. Terrorists not only move funds but also smuggle stolen goods and contraband. As mentioned earlier, document fraud and forgery are money-raising activities. The *Wall Street Journal* (Simpson, Crawford, and Johnson, 2004) reports that European police agencies uncovered a lucrative underground railroad running from central Asia through Europe in the spring of 2004. Ansar al Islam, a group formed by ethnic Kurds, and al Tawhid, an allied group headed by Abu Musab al Zarqawi until his death in 2006, generate phony documents and sell them to immigrants. They use forged passports to move their operatives through Europe and move contraband through the same avenues. These efforts help to keep Ansar al Islam and al Tawhid operational.

Terrorism is linked to organized crime throughout the world, and in some cases it is almost impossible to distinguish between terrorist and criminal activity. Tamara Makarenko (2002) says that Russian organized-crime groups trade weapons for drugs in Colombia. She also finds that both terrorists and criminals take advantage of political instability in regions like central Asia and the **Triborder region** in South America (around the common border of Argentina, Brazil, and Paraguay; Figure 3.5). In the Middle East and Southeast Asia, terrorists and criminals kidnap for profit. She believes that terrorist and criminal organizations have grown into global enterprises.

The **globalization** of crime and terrorism has created opportunities for vast profits in the diamond trade. African diamonds, or "conflict diamonds," are obtained illegally and sold in an underground network. According to Global Witness (2003), a British human rights organization, al Qaeda spent ten years moving into unregulated diamond trading in western Africa. In the early 1990s it infiltrated legitimate trading centers to establish a base. After success in mainstream trading, al Qaeda slowly and quietly switched from legitimate trading centers to underground criminal networks. Then, taking advantage of weak governments and regulations in Africa, it established its own international trading network. The new system allowed al Qaeda and allied jihadist groups to make tremendous profits while providing a ready-made network to hide and launder money. It should be noted that the 9/11 Commission (2004, p. 171) examined claims about al Qaeda's involvement in the diamond trade, and it came to a different conclusion. The commission found no evidence that diamonds were used to support al Qaeda. Global Witness disagrees and believes it has presented evidence of al Qaeda's activities.

Triborder region
The area where Brazil, Paraguay, and Argentina join. The major city is Cuidad del Este.

globalization
A common global economic network ideally uniting the world with production and international trade. Proponents believe it will create wealth. Critics believe it creates corporate wealth and increases distance between the rich and poor.

Figure 3.5
The Triborder Region

The Triborder region is the area in South America where Paraguay, Brazil, and Argentina have a common border. Quite a bit of criminal activity takes place in the region, and the Paraguayan city Ciudad del Este is particularly known for its lawlessness. The region is also home to more than 20,000 Middle Eastern immigrants. Hamas, Hezbollah, and other terrorist groups have been known to frequent the area.

Self-Check

- *Describe common methods of fund-raising.*
- *How do underground networks assist investigators?*
- *What avenues are available for fund-raising?*

Legal Sources of Funding: Charities

Terrorists do not limit their financial activities to underworld networks and illegal revenue sources. Many groups engage in legitimate business activities to raise and distribute money (Navias, 2002). Activities include soliciting contributions, operating businesses, running nongovernmental organizations (NGOs), creating charities, using wire transfers, forming or using banks, and using the hawala system (described in the next section). Terrorists are able to use these systems because participants are unaware that terrorists are involved or because governments have poor oversight and monitoring practices (National Strategy, 2006).

According to several researchers (S. A. Emerson, 2002, pp. 183–219; Ehrenfeld, 2003, pp. 21–22; Napoleoni, 2003, pp. 111–179) charities have been involved in funding terrorism. Data from national and international law enforcement sources agree with these findings (Scott-Joynt, 2003; Isikoff and Hosenball, 2004; U.S. Department of State, 2004b). Many people who contribute to charities do not know they are supporting terrorist organizations. Others believe the efforts they are supporting are not terrorist operations but legitimate military operations. Zachary Abuza (2003b, p. 93) writes that terrorists often set up a phony charity or skim the proceeds from legitimate organizations. Either way, charitable funds are frequently diverted to terrorist groups.

Two examples of charitable organizations that support terrorism are the Benevolence International Fund (BIF) and the al Rashid Trust. BIF formed in the United States in 1993 and received tax-exempt status from the IRS. It was able to raise millions of dollars in the next few years to support radical Islamic causes. The leader of BIF was arrested for supporting a terrorist organization and he pleaded to a lesser included offense in 2003. The al Rashid Trust formed in Pakistan and solicited donations through the Internet. It claimed neither radical philosophies nor militancy, and it listed a vast array of humanitarian accomplishments. Intelligence analysis revealed that the al Rashid Trust was a front organization for the Taliban in Afghanistan. A presidential order subsequently froze its U.S. assets (Hinnen, 2004).

Charities are difficult to investigate for several reasons. First, they can be formed overseas and established in states with weak financial regulations. Second, they may be state supported. Third, they may hide the true purpose of their operations, such as the al Rashid Trust. Fourth, they may be covered or supported by a legitimate business that is not aware of the actual purpose of the charity. Finally, if established by a terrorist group, a charitable front is difficult to infiltrate (Higgins, 2006).

Nontraceable Funding: The Hawala System

hawala system

A system of exchanging money based on trust relationships between money dealers. A chit, or promissory note, is exchanged between two hawaladars, and it is as valuable as cash or other traded commodities because the trust between the two parties guarantees its value.

Many international terrorist groups move money through an ancient trading network called the **hawala system**. The system originated several hundred years ago in China under the name of Feng Chin, or "flying money." Today it is primarily based in Pakistan and India, but there are hawala dealers around the world. It is a legitimate means of transferring money without using money or moving funds across international borders, although it may violate currency transfer regulations in some countries. It is a network based on long-term trust relationships and the knowledge that each dealer is impeccably reliable for all debts (see Expanding the Concept: Advantages of the Hawala System).

Several hundred years ago central Asian merchants were frequently robbed of the gold and silver they carried in caravans to pay for goods. They developed a system of noncash exchange as a result. Rather than carrying money, caravan leaders would visit merchants and pay for goods with a promissory note. When the caravan reached its destination, the leader sold goods and the distributors would pay the caravan leader with promissory notes. The leader returned home, presented the note, and the local chit dealer paid the debt. The system worked because the

EXPANDING THE CONCEPT

Advantages of the Hawala System

- Money moves with no record
- Money crosses international borders with ease
- It is based on trust, and long-term trusting relationships are in place
- Money can easily be bartered for contraband
- No tax records exist

dealers honored the promises. As long as people trusted each other, each chit was worth silver or gold, and merchants, caravan leaders, and others could travel without money. The hawala system is one version of this ancient practice (Schramm and Taube, 2002; Sharma, 2006).

Today's hawala system works much as the old system did (Figure 3.6). Imagine that Asadullah Kahn lives and works in Los Angeles. He is an American citizen, but his parents live in Peshawar, Pakistan. Asadullah wishes to assist his parents, so he regularly sends them money. It is difficult, however, to get funds into Pakistan, and it is even more difficult to move them across the North-West Frontier Province to Peshawar. Postal service is frequently unavailable and even parcel services can take months to deliver a package. Therefore, Asadullah goes to a local jewelry store because he knows the owner is a *hawaladar*, a hawala dealer. Asadullah gives the hawaladar $500 and tells him that he wants it delivered to his parents. The hawaladar subtracts a small fee, usually 1 or 2 percent, and sends word to a hawaladar in Peshawar that Asadullah sends his parents the balance. Asadullah's parents visit the Peshawar hawaladar and he pays them the promised money. No money actually moved from Los Angeles to Peshawar, but Asadullah's parents received nearly $500. The system works because the hawaladars in Peshawar and Los Angeles implicitly trust each other. They know the debt will be honored (see U.S. Department of the Treasury, 2003).

Change the imaginary scenario a bit and the impact on terrorism can be demonstrated. In the revised situation imagine that Asadullah is not a hard-working son seeking to support his parents but an operative for the Lashkar-e-Taiba, a Kashmiri terrorist group. Asif, Asadullah's contact in Peshawar, needs $500 to buy AK-47s. After raising funds in the United States, Asadullah visits the hawaladar, hands over $500, and asks the hawaladar to get the money to Asif. The Peshawar hawaladar gives Asif the money, not knowing its use. Asif buys the weapons and delivers them to contacts in the Lashkar-e-Taiba. There is no record of the transaction, and no way to trace the flow of funds. The hawala system was not established to support terrorism, but it hides transactions in the modern world of international banking (Sharma, 2006).

Figure 3.6

The Hawala System

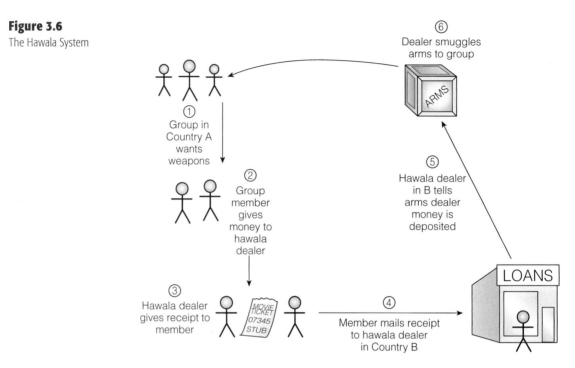

① Group in Country A wants weapons

② Group member gives money to hawala dealer

③ Hawala dealer gives receipt to member

④ Member mails receipt to hawala dealer in Country B

⑤ Hawala dealer in B tells arms dealer money is deposited

⑥ Dealer smuggles arms to group

ARMS

LOANS

MOVIE TICKET 07345 STUB

Legitimate Business Operations

Sometimes terrorists fund activities through legitimate businesses or localized marketing of specialized products. Osama bin Laden set up several local businesses in Sudan in 1992 after being exiled from Saudi Arabia. Some analysts believe he used profits to fund terrorists, but others argue it simply kept al Qaeda functional (L. Wright, 2006, pp. 168–169). At least one analyst believes he is able to operate partly by keeping legitimate businesses open (Basile, 2004). According to FBI officials, European Islamic extremists finance terrorism through a variety of legitimate businesses. One group ran a car-repair shop, and a group in Germany ran a used-car dealership. One person who recruited some of the 9/11 hijackers raised money as a stockbroker (Levitt, 2002).

Domestic violent political extremists use small markets to raise cash. Some violent right-wing extremists sell videos, propaganda, and firearms at gun shows. Posse Comitatus members gathered at a hotel in Grand Rapids, Michigan, with a front room filled with students studying Christian Identity, a white-supremacist religion, and a back area filled with items for sale. The objects ranged from "secret books" of the Bible to primary source material that "proved" space aliens had colonized the earth for white people. One of the vendors stated that she regularly traveled the lecture and gun-show circuits to sell these items. A founding member of the militia movement lectured and sold videotapes on militia propaganda, and another opened his store for special deals after maneuvers (White, 1997). Other extremist groups market on the Internet (see

Imperial Knights of the Ku Klux Klan, 2007). The extremist right benefits from small-business marketing.

Self-Check

- *What legitimate methods do terrorists use to raise funds?*
- *Why is it difficult to investigate these methods?*
- *Describe the hawala system.*

◢ A Macroeconomic Theory of the New Terrorist Economy

The financial aspects of terrorism have influenced the changing nature of the international economy. After the collapse of the former Soviet Union in 1991, the United States became the world's only superpower. Promoting an economic system that emphasized international production, trade, and consumption, American economic policies focused on reducing the trade barriers between nation-states. Some countries prospered under the international philosophy, called globalization or the global economy, but other countries grew weaker and poorer. Globalization is based on the belief that international trade barriers should be removed so that commerce and industry can develop in an international free market. Terrorism took hold in some of the areas left behind in the rush toward globalization, and this changed the nature of terrorist financing (see Barber, 1996, pp. 48–49).

Loretta Napoleoni (2003) examines this process while formulating a new theory about the financing of terrorism. Agreeing with Adams's early findings and other studies that found links between organized crime networks and terrorism, Napoleoni goes far beyond a summary of the immediate circumstances. In *Modern Jihad* she argues that terrorism has evolved as an economic entity. The fall of the Soviet Union and subsequent globalization have produced what she calls the **new economy of terrorism**. Napoleoni says that the origins of the new economy of terrorism grew from the cold war (1945–1991). As Bruce Hoffman (1998, pp. 43–65) says, colonial revolts began at the end of World War II (1939–1945). Napoleoni (2003, pp. 11–28) sees this as the beginning of a macroeconomic shift. Western nations began to use underground methods to fund their struggles in the colonies, and revolutionaries sought their own sources of money. The origins of the new economy of terrorism can be traced to anticolonial revolts.

To demonstrate the birth of this new economy, Napoleoni turns to France. After World War II, when France was still a colonial power in charge of many foreign countries, nationalists revolted against French rule all over the world. In Vietnam the revolutionary nationalists were called the Vietminh after their leader Ho Chi Minh. Although they had communist backing, the Vietminh needed money. They muscled their

new economy of terrorism
A term used by Loretta Napoleoni to describe the evolution of terrorist financing from the beginning strategies of the cold war to the present. Economic support and antiterrorist policies interact to form the new economy.

way into opium production, sold the drugs, and used the profits to keep their guerrillas in the field.

Ironically, France tried the same concept. When the war against the Vietminh became politically unpopular, the French government found it difficult to finance military operations. Napoleoni says the French took over opium profits and used them to finance the war. As a result, drug trafficking became one of the primary methods governments used to finance activities during the cold war.

Napoleoni says that as the cold war developed, the Soviet Union and the United States fought each other by proxy; that is, they did not fight each other directly. The Soviets used allies to attack countries loyal to the United States, and the United States used its friends to attack Soviet-backed countries. Napoleoni believes that modern terrorist groups evolved from these surrogate conflicts, and they looked for ways to become independent from both superpowers. The desire for autonomy led terrorist groups to join criminals in an underground economy.

Napoleoni cites several examples to support this idea. She says a radical Marxist group in Peru, the Shining Path, turned to the drug trade in northern Peru, regulating drug production to fund their activities. The Popular Armed Forces of Colombia (FARC) went a step further and joined the Colombian drug trade. Militant Palestinians went in another direction, using robbery and extortion to raise funds. The IRA started diverting funds from American charities before turning to organized crime. Napoleoni says these sources of financing fueled most of the terrorist activities of the 1970s and early 1980s.

The ETA changed the structure of terrorist finance. Instead of seeking links to an underground economy, the ETA tried to gain control of the economy. They forced Spanish businesses out of the Basque areas of northern Spain and weakened the entire state. The Basque region became a **failed state**, a place where Spain could no longer exert power. When this happened, the ETA established an illegitimate economy in a **shell state**. It paid salaries to terrorists, provided for the families of fallen members, and even ran a pension system for retired terrorists. The ETA was successful because the Spanish economy failed in the Basque region, leaving the area in a hopeless political mess. The ETA was strong enough to assert stability.

The new terrorist economy can be understood from the example of the ETA. Napoleoni believes that globalization has created pockets in the world where failed or weak states are left to govern with little economic and political power. Terrorists and criminal groups grow in such places, running their own underground economies and providing some form of political stability because they are strong enough to resist the state. Illegitimate groups form a shell state, an organization that acts as a government in a place where the government is not strong enough to act.

As globalization increased, according to Napoleoni, it not only created economic vacuums where shell states could form but also fueled the growth of a global underground economy. In other words, it provided

failed state

An area outside a government's control. Failed states operate under differing warlords, criminal groups, or competing governments.

shell state

A political situation where a government nominally controls its own state but where large regions are either anarchic or under the control of others. A government is unable to enforce law or provide for other forms of social order in a shell state.

illegal trade routes for drugs, arms smugglers, contraband dealers, and human traffic. Terrorist groups funded themselves through these activities, and they could not exist without them.

Napoleoni believes that modern terrorism is an international force supported by groups in shell states that continually change both their organizational structures and political goals to maintain income from an international underground economy. They hide their economic views with religious rhetoric or patriotic slogans, but their most important objective is to raise funds. Without funding, a terrorist group cannot exist. The prime goal of a group, then, is to maintain its finances. Napoleoni concludes that powerful groups even become strong enough to invest in legitimate markets, and in some instances they move so much money that they affect the global economy.

Complementing Napoleoni's work is a model developed by Mario Ferrero (2002), who argues that modern radical Islamic groups use violent activity as a means of providing economic stability. Jihadist groups cannot keep outsiders away or fire slackers for being unproductive. Numerous recruits flock to training camps and meetings, including people who are less than totally motivated. The slackers threaten stability by using a group's limited resources. To control this, jihadists increase rhetoric and violence to drive all but the most loyal members away from the group. This leaves enough resources to support the true believers.

If these macroeconomic theories of terrorism are correct, they have meaning for the nature of counterterrorism. Many criminologists believe that crime can be reduced when potentially deviant groups have a vested interest in the economic structure of society. Macroeconomic theory suggests that counterterrorism policies should be aimed at providing the world's people with economic stability, opportunity, and participation in the mainstream economy (see Barnett, 2004, p. 49). Economic policies to counter terrorism would involve supporting states in danger of failure, providing opportunities for people to participate and benefit from economic systems, and eliminating underground economic networks. When a state fails and a terrorist group creates its own shell state, the group has no incentive to participate in legitimate economic enterprises. As Benjamin Barber (1996, p. 299) says, when economic globalization threatens the ability of ordinary people to meet their needs, they will find other ways to survive. Indeed, this reflects Napoleoni's thesis. Poverty does not cause terrorism, but economic and political failures may result in a shell state where terrorism can be organized and funded.

Self-Check

- *What is a macroeconomic theory?*
- *How does it apply to terrorism?*
- *What political assumptions must be made to see the logic of a macroeconomic theory?*

The Narco-terrorism Debate

narco-terrorism

A controversial term that links drugs to terrorism in one of two ways. Either drug profits are used to finance terrorism or drug gangs use terrorism to control production and distribution networks.

One of the heated issues surrounding the discussion of terrorist financing is the relationship between terrorism and drugs. The term **narco-terrorism** refers to terrorists using either terrorist tactics to support drug operations or drug-trade profits to finance terrorism. Rachel Ehrenfeld championed the idea of narco-terrorism in her early works, and she recently expanded on the idea (Ehrenfeld, 2003). According to her research, terrorists are involved in the international production and distribution of drugs; indeed, she believes, the narcotics trade is one of their primary sources of money. The U.S. government tends to accept this position, but it is nonetheless extremely controversial.

The Link between Drugs and Terrorism

Steven Casteel (2003), an executive with the Drug Enforcement Administration (DEA), told a U.S. Senate committee that terrorism and the drug trade are intertwined. Organized criminals, smugglers, and drug dealers naturally linked with terrorist groups, he says, because all these organizations move in the same circles. As does Napoleoni, he believes that globalization has intensified this relationship. He says that the relationship between drugs and terrorism has been in place throughout history.

David Adams (2003), reporting for the *St. Petersburg Times,* says that Hezbollah and Hamas use the Latin American drug trade to raise funds. He writes that U.S. military units have tracked their activities in South America, and the military is concerned about the large amount of money involved. According to the U.S. Central Command, hundreds of millions of dollars have been raised in Latin America. The military's prime concerns are the Triborder region, the Venezuelan island of Margarita, and the areas controlled by FARC in Colombia. The DEA agrees with this assessment. An official from the U.S. Department of State puts it succinctly: whether it is from Latin America or elsewhere, terrorist groups are financed through drugs. This is demonstrable, not debatable (J. P. Walter, 2002).

Other nations also believe that terrorism and drugs are linked. The French Ministry of Defense issued a report stating that drugs are the primary currency used to finance international terrorism. The French government points to the Shining Path and FARC to show the influence of cocaine. The Ministry of Defense claims that radical Islamic groups get most of their money through the drug trade in central and Southeast Asia. Afghanistan is the primary source of heroin in Europe, and the profits from these drug sales fund all international Islamic terrorist groups (Chouvy, 2004). Officials in India believe that Lashkar-e-Taiba and al Qaeda smuggled drugs and other contraband through Africa, central Asia, and eastern Europe (*Times of India,* 2003). According to many in the Indian government, militant Islamic groups are funded by the drug trade.

Joshua Krasna (1997) takes the argument to another level. He says that if people are willing to expand the definition of national security beyond the framework of military defense, drugs pose a security problem. Defining security as social safety, Krasna says that the drug trade threatens political and economic stability while disrupting society. The drug trade limits the ability of legitimate governments and increases the power of insurgent and terrorist groups. Terrorists, for their part, use drugs not only to exploit the social safety of their enemies but also to fund terrorist activities.

Narco-terrorism: Another View

Not everyone accepts the link between drugs and terrorism. Some people argue that terrorists may use drugs as a source of income, but they also use several other illegal activities to raise money. Selling drugs is only one method, and the drug problem is not caused by terrorism. Other people believe that the use of the term *narco-terrorism* is an attempt to take political advantage of the fear of terrorism. If drugs and terrorism come to mean the same thing, it will be easier to take actions against drug dealers. Critics believe that combining the drug problem with terrorism confuses two different issues.

The 9/11 Commission (2004, pp. 171–172) dismisses the idea that drugs were linked to al Qaeda's attack on New York and Washington, D.C. There is no evidence, the commission writes, that indicates bin Laden used underground drug networks or narcotics trafficking to support the September 11 attacks. The Taliban used narcotics trafficking to support Afghanistan, but bin Laden used a network of donors based in Saudi Arabia and the Gulf States.

In the same article in which he explains narco-terrorism, David Adams (2003) acknowledges critics. He points to skepticism about the military and DEA assessment of Latin America. Many critics believe these organizations have overstated the problem. Other people point to misunderstandings. Terrorists are not necessarily linked to the drug trade even when they appear to be involved with drugs. Many Arabs live in the Triborder region, and they support Hamas and Hezbollah. Just because drug traders flourish in this region does not mean that either the Arabs or the terrorist groups are associated with drugs.

David Kaplan (2003) says the financing of militant Islamic groups has very little to do with the drug trade. Based on a five-month study for *U.S. News and World Report*, Kaplan blames Saudi Arabia for funding the spread of an intolerant form of Islam. Violent intolerance, he says, spawned the rise of terrorist groups, and the sect most sympathetic to an intolerant version of Islam comes from Saudi Arabia. Charities are responsible for the bulk of terrorist financing, he believes, and the money funds radical mosques, militant schools, and Islamic centers that support the jihad movement. Saudi money can be traced to violence in Algeria, Bosnia, Kashmir, the West Bank, Gaza, Indonesia, Somalia, and Chechnya. The spread of militant Islam is not about drugs.

Pierre-Arnaud Chouvy (2004) does not agree with the position of the French military. He argues that the term *narco-terrorism* is too vague to describe either drug traffickers or terrorists, and it does not help address either problem. The problem with drugs involves supply and demand. Western Europe and North America provide ready markets for drug use. Typical Afghan farmers fight to survive. They produce opium, the base for heroin, because it is a cash crop. Western Europe has the demand, Chouvy says, and Afghanistan has the supply. Opium production has nothing to do with terrorism. Narco-terrorism is a convenient term for the French government to use, appealing to public emotions and giving the police more power.

Civil libertarians are especially critical of attempts to link terrorism and drugs (TalkLeft, 2003). Agreeing with Chouvy, civil libertarians see the attempt to link narcotics and terrorism as a ploy by states. If terrorism were to disappear, the drug trade would remain. But if governments link drugs with terrorism, they can reinvent the meaning of crime. Drug dealers will become terrorists, and a frightened public will grant the government expanded powers to combat drugs. In addition, courts more readily grant search warrants and wiretaps against terrorists. Civil libertarians often believe governments want to define drug pushers as narco-terrorist kingpins in an effort to increase their own power.

Michael Scheuer (2006, pp. 42–44) takes the middle ground in the debate over narco-terrorism. In an examination of Osama bin Laden, Scheuer writes that the analyses of al Qaeda's use of heroin to finance the jihad range from believable to fantastic accounts. Some reports of the narcotics connection are true, some are simply asserted without evidence, and a great deal of propaganda is obviously false. The narcotics trade in Afghanistan makes billions of dollars. It would be naïve, Scheuer concludes, to assume that bin Laden has not been able to take advantage of some of those funds.

Self-Check

- *Define the two elements of narco-terrorism.*
- *What arguments support the idea?*
- *Why do some analysts reject the idea of narco-terrorism?*

SUMMARY

- When terrorism emerged after World War II most groups tended to follow the hierarchical model of Michael Collins's IRA. By the 1990s some groups still followed that model, but many loose terrorist networks were forming.
- Whether a hierarchy or a network, groups still require management. Hierarchical groups use cell structures and top-down management.

Small groups in networks are much more autonomous. Management, communications, supply maintenance, and all other administrative functions are hampered by the need for secrecy.

- Large groups or networks are more effective than smaller ones outside a network.
- Analysts slowly developed an appreciation of the importance of terrorist financing. Today it is commonly assumed that good counterterrorist policy involves strategic efforts to deny fiscal resources to terrorists.
- One group of analysts and scholars believes that a financial strategy against terrorism will reduce violence. Another group argues that this approach is too simple because terrorists operate in an underground economy immune from formal governmental sanctions.
- The relation between terrorism and economic systems is multifaceted. One way to approach the complexity is to look at illegal funding and networks and legal methods of participating in the economy.
- Terrorists raise money through traditional criminal methods and exchange resources in underground networks. The key difference between traditional crime and terrorism in this realm is motivation.
- Terrorists also raise money through legal operations. They divert funds to support terrorist operations. Charities and business operations are the most frequent legal activities.
- The hawala system is based on an old method merchants used to exchange money without risking transport of actual cash. Today, some terrorists use this system to fund operations.
- The macroeconomic theory of terrorism is based on the premise that terrorist groups create shell states within failed states. They finance operations using methods from the cold war.
- The idea of narco-terrorism is controversial. Proponents believe that terrorists use drugs to finance operations; opponents argue that governments use the term to increase their own power.

KEY TERMS

cell (p. 45)
pyramid (p. 46)
active cadre (p. 46)
column (p. 47)
umbrella (p. 48)
virtual organizations (p. 49)
chain organizations (p. 49)
networks (p. 49)
reference group (p. 54)
Capone discovery (p. 56)

forensic accounting (p. 57)
expropriation (p. 58)
Triborder region (p. 60)
globalization (p. 60)
hawala system (p. 62)
new economy of terrorism (p. 65)
failed state (p. 66)
shell state (p. 66)
narco-terrorism (p. 68)

WRITING ASSIGNMENTS

1. Trace the organizational shifts in modern terrorism from hierarchies to networks. Where is the strength in the hierarchy located? What shift do networks bring to managerial issues?

2. When most people think of terrorist financing, they picture the means by which terrorists raise, move, and spend money. Summarize the methods terrorists use to do this. Do financing methods present both offensive and defensive meanings for security planning and operations?

3. Compare and contrast the debate about narco-terrorism within the context of Napoleoni's summary of the new terrorist economy. If Napoleoni's thesis is removed from the debate, does it impact the meaning of narco-terrorism?

Terrorism and the Media

4

AP Photo/Ahn Young-joon

Koreans gather around a television screen to listen to a North Korean defector's political statement. All media multiply the impact of events, whether it is political news, terrorism, or any form of violence.

Learning Objectives

After reading this chapter you should be able to

- Discuss the role of the media in constructing social reality.
- Discuss terrorism as a method of communication.
- Summarize popular media misconceptions.
- Explain the tension between security forces and the media.

- Describe how the media can be viewed as a weapon.
- Explain news frames and their impact on reporting terrorism.
- Describe the relationship between terrorism and television.
- Describe the effects of growing international media and the Internet on terrorism.

- Discuss issues surrounding objective reporting.
- Define the contagion effect.
- Debate the issues of freedom of the press and censorship.

If disseminating information is the purpose of television, radio, and print news media, drama is the means for attracting viewers, listeners, and readers. Sponsors like drama too because it means that more people consume their advertising. Terrorism, in the words of one of the early scholars who focused on the subject, is made for TV drama, and radio and newspapers also cover it. Reporting perspectives have increased as new outlets for media opened in the non-Western world in the past two decades. These organizations not only cover the drama but add differing interpretations and flavors to their stories. Nothing has revolutionized the flow of information more than the Internet, which also arrived on the scene in the last two decades. Websites report news from hundreds if not thousands of perspectives, and the World Wide Web serves as a source for propaganda and communication. An Algerian terrorist once said he would rather kill one victim in front of a news camera than one hundred in the desert where the world would not see them. His point should be noted: Modern terrorism is a media phenomenon.

The Media and the Social Construction of Images

Terrorism involves symbolic communication usually aimed at an audience far beyond the immediate victims of violence. Alex Schmid and Albert Jongman (2005, p. 21) write that terrorism is a message generator, a method of communicating an event. Nancy Snow (2006) points out that terrorism is such an effective communication device that governments respond by trying to send their own messages through the media. Communication develops in three primary manners. The first, and most obvious, involves the reporting of terrorist events. Media exposure magnifies events, campaigns, and causes, and both terrorists and governments attempt to manipulate reports so that they are portrayed in a favorable light. This is especially true with television, but it is applicable to all news reporting. In the second, the media plays a major role in creating the social definition of terrorism. It can, for example, globalize a local event or personalize a global event on a local level. In the third, the World Wide Web has become a conduit for propaganda and communication. In any form, terrorism sends a message.

Some scenes have become all too familiar. A hooded member of Black September stands on a hotel balcony in Olympic Village. Elsewhere, a hijacker forces an airplane pilot to stick his head out the cockpit window while the hijacker fires a pistol into the air. On the Internet, a fanatic stands behind a blindfolded and rope-bound hostage, reading a religious proclamation claiming the innocent hostage represents evil. After the proclamation, the terrorist kicks his hostage to the floor, pulls out a long knife, and slowly beheads the hostage while crying out, "God is great!" Scenes like this played out time and time again on television, on the Internet, on radio talk shows, and in newspaper stories and pictures.

Popular Media Misconceptions

Everybody in the public eye wants to use the media to its advantage, and interest groups, including governments and terrorists, compete for favorable labels and images. Daya Thussu (2006) states that the United States' perspective of terrorism has dominated the international media since 9/11. This is due to the media's ability to create and sustain the social image of terrorism. Thussu refers to this power as mythmaking, and the myths circulated by television news shape the worldview of those who watch. Such myths and misconceptions are presented far beyond the West, and they have defined social reality after 9/11 in many parts of the world. If social constructs are created by collective definitions, the power of the media helps to define the boundaries of those constructs.

According to Thussu, the media's presentation of terrorism is dominated by several simplified stories presented and re-presented on twenty-four-hour cable news networks. This type of reporting leads viewers to believe that terrorism is the result of Islamic radicalism, and it results in other falsehoods and misconceptions in the minds of viewers. Viewers are encouraged to accept a few isolated, simple facts about complicated issues and to accept misappropriated labels. Every event is portrayed in a moralistic tone.

Islam suffers from cable news simplifications. Viewers are encouraged to believe that radicalism defines Islam and that all Muslims believe exactly the same thing. There is no difference between Hezbollah, Hamas, and al Qaeda. In fact, the religious radicals have replaced the Soviet Union as a cold war rival to the West, and the only way they can be confronted is to respond with military force. Not only is Islam defined by radicals but reports gradually demonize the entire religion. When Muslims appear, they are described with negative labels, such as "radical cleric," "violent Wahhabi," or "Islamic militant."

Other myths become subtly assumed as the larger image takes shape, and they are not limited to religion. When reporting on terrorism in general, the media exaggerates the threat of weapons of mass destruction. They also use simple catchphrases or accept the simplifications that politicians use to popularize a point. Phrases like "broken borders" and "war on terrorism" create images that become reality after they are used again and again. Thussu (2006), critical of American counterterrorist policy, feels media myths distort the issues surrounding terrorism.

Tension between Security Forces and the Media

Although some scholars believe the media favors governments, police and security forces frequently find themselves at odds with this media power. On the one hand, they compete for favorable media coverage. On the other hand, governments exhibit strong disdain for the press because media social constructions often run counter to governmental objectives and policies. Paul Wilkinson (1997) argues that governments seek to harness the power of the media for social control. For example, in hostage situations security forces are responsible for the fate of the victims. Reporters often do not focus on the security mission of such incidents because they are under tremendous pressure to be first with the story, and they have their own agendas when reporting the story. As a result, Wilkinson concludes, law enforcement and military goals often conflict with the goals of the reporters.

Whereas Thussu concludes that the social meanings created by news segments favor governmental policy, security forces come to the opposite conclusion. Within everyday police or military operations it is not uncommon to hear many statements criticizing the media. Chiefs of police and military commanders generally do not respect or trust media figures and reporters, and their attitudes are reflected by line personnel. Specialized command units are often created in police agencies to portray a favorable image to reporters, and U.S. military forces include public relations units when they go to war.

Police and security forces officially represent the social order, and they are charged with maintaining governmental authority. They see themselves as servants of the public interest in the United States and other Western democracies. Additionally, they believe they make decisions for the public good. They perceive themselves to be the forceful extension of democracy. They think reporters are only trying to gather sensationalistic stories. Scholars like Douglas Keller (2006) think this may be somewhat ironic because media reporting generally favors security forces.

Police and military forces frequently try to take advantage of the media's ability to define social reality. For example, in the 2003 invasion of Iraq, the Pentagon invited print and electronic journalists to join combat units. They were known as embedded reporters. The military assumed that this would lead to better control of news reports. The results were partially realized. When compared to free coverage during the 1991 Gulf War to oust Iraq from Kuwait and the subsequent enforcement of no-fly zones in northern and southern Iraq from 1991 to 2003, reports submitted by embedded journalists to their editors were more favorable to American military units. After editing, however, published reports did not exhibit more favorable general coverage (Pfau et al., 2004).

The Media as a Weapon

The late Richard Clutterbuck once concluded that the media was similar to a loaded gun lying in the street. The first person to pick it up got to choose how to use it. Governments see the media as that loaded gun. If they pick it up, such as by embedding reporters, they can use it to their benefit. Police executives and military officers are frequently trained in media manipulation. They want to make skillful use of the weapon when they pick it up.

Terrorists also recognize the power of the media as a weapon. Ayman al Zawahiri, a leader of al Qaeda, views the media as one of the tools in al Qaeda's arsenal. First, any attack, especially if it is sensational, can dramatize the struggle. Major attacks draw major media coverage, and although the reports are not favorable among the enemy audience, they play well with sympathizers to al Qaeda. Second, Zawahiri can turn to his own media relations group. When he ran Egyptian Islamic Jihad, Zawahiri relied on a suborganization devoted to public relations; after joining al Qaeda, Zawahiri continues to rely on one. Third, Zawahiri uses his own writings to justify terrorism. He writes books and pamphlets, playing on sympathies for Muslims victimized throughout the world. Finally, along with other jihadists, he uses the Internet (Aboul-Enein, 2004).

Counterterrorist researchers from the Combating Terrorism Center at West Point find that literature from violent extremists frequently reveals important information about their organizations and strategies (Brachman and McCants, 2006). Steven Corman and Jill Schiefelbein (2006), from Arizona State University, examine literature from militant Islamic groups to determine their media strategies. Their analysis shows that jihadists are keenly aware of the media's ability to influence the social construction of reality. Jihadist texts reveal three media strategies. First, they seek legitimacy for their movement, especially wanting to justify acts of violence to other Muslims. Second, they want to spread their message and increase sympathy for their militant interpretation of religion. Third, their opponents, both the West and Muslims with a different interpretation of Islam, are targeted for intimidation.

Self-Check

- *How do media outlets construct an image?*
- *Describe the tension between security forces and the media.*
- *How can the media be turned into a weapon?*

News Frames and Presentations

Although communication scholars debate the definition, David Levin (2003) says reporting patterns are packaged in segments called **news frames**. The purpose of a news frame is to assemble words and pictures to create a pattern surrounding an event. The news becomes a symbolic representation of an event in which the audience is allowed to participate from a distance. Television and other media spin the event so that it can be translated into the understanding of popular culture. They use

news frames
Visual, audible, or written packages used to present the news. Communication scholars do not agree on a single definition, but news frames generally refer to the presentation of the news story. They contain a method for beginning and ending the story, and they convey the importance of characters and actions as the story is told.

rhetoric and popular images to set the agenda, and drama becomes the hook to attract an audience.

News frames form the basis for communicating symbols. Karim Karim (2001, pp. 18–19) says the news frame creates a narrative for understanding a deadly drama. Characters are introduced, heroes and villains are defined, and victims of violence become the suffering innocents. The people who produce the frame provide their interpretation to the audience. Because the news frame takes place within the dominant political context of the producers, it is not necessary to expend a great amount of energy on propaganda. The audience has been indoctrinated by journalists and mainstream reporters who present governmental officials as protectors and terrorists as villains. The news frame provides the "correct" symbolism for the consumer.

Simon Cottle (2006) believes that news frames help "mediatize" the presentation of terrorism; that is, it shapes the way an event is communicated. The news frame is used by all media, but it is especially applicable to television. The news frame, although intentionally used, is one of the least understood aspects of broadcast journalism because its complexity goes unnoticed. Discussions of news frames usually focus on a specific story or they involve reducing ideas to common elements. Actually, Cottle says, selecting from among the different styles of news frames presents an issue in a particular fashion. The classic approach for television is the **reporting frame**. It is usually short and designed to provide the latest information. Although facts and figures are presented, the story fails to focus on context or background. It is superficial and alters reality into violent actions and reactions, and the underlying causes of conflict are ignored.

reporting frame
The simplest form of a news frame. It is a quick, fact-driven report that summarizes the latest information about a story. It does not need to contain a beginning or an end, and it assumes that the consumer understands the context of the facts.

Types of Frames

Other frames complement the reporting frame, according to Cottle. A dominant frame presents a story from a single point of view. An authority figure or institution defines the story in this type of frame. Closely related is the conflict frame, which presents a story frame with two views, each side having experts or witnesses to support a position. A contention frame summarizes a variety of views, and investigative frames champion the role of the press as the protectors of democracy. Cottle identifies other frames designed to serve the community, enhance collective decision making, and enrich social understanding of an event (see Expanding the Concept: Communication Frames). Frames can also campaign for a single interpretation of an event or provide in-depth coverage beyond the shallowness of a reporting frame. Finally, Cottle says, television news presents a mythic frame, which reinforces deeply held values. This frame is frequently used to depict those people who have sacrificed their lives for a cause. The combination of all these communication frames complicates the presentation of the news on terrorism.

EXPANDING THE CONCEPT

Communication Frames

Simon Cottle (2006) says that news frames are complex because they are composed of a variety of communication frames. Terrorism is reported within the following types of frames:

- Reporting frames: superficial, short, and laced with facts
- Dominant frames: one authority's view
- Contest frames: two sides, with experts
- Contention frames: a variety of positions
- Investigation frames: exposing corrupt or illegal behavior
- Campaigning frames: the broadcaster's opinion
- Reportage frames: in-depth coverage with background
- Community service frames: information for viewers
- Collective interest frames: reinforce common values
- Cultural recognition frames: a group's values and norms (can be used for the opposing group to avoid "us" versus "them")
- Mythic tales frames: hero stories

Source: Cottle, 2006.

Ambiguous Stories and News Frames

News frames give the story a structured meaning, but sometimes a story defies structure. The frame is centered on getting viewers' attention, presenting information, and revealing the results. What happens when the results are inconclusive? Frank Durham (1998) answers this question by looking at the crash of TWA Flight 800, a passenger airliner that exploded over the Atlantic Ocean shortly after taking off from JFK Airport in New York City in 1996. Durham believes the news frame works when a report is based on sources with definitive explanations of an event. There were no solid answers in the TWA crash, however, and no authority could emerge with a definitive story on the crash. Durham tracked reporting in 668 stories from the *New York Times* for one year following the explosion. Dominant news frames emerged, but all were proved incorrect.

Durham concludes that ambiguity destroys the ability to create a sustainable news frame. Reporters covering TWA 800 expected to find facts that would reveal a logical cause. They looked to terrorism, a missile strike, and finally mechanical error. In the first months following the crash, neither facts nor logical conclusions pointed to an answer. As a result, Durham says, the *New York Times* could not produce a news frame for the story.

Durham's conclusion might have an interesting effect on understanding terrorism. If terrorism is reported in well-defined news frames, both the media and the consumer will assume that there is a political beginning, a violent process, and a logical end. If there is ambiguity about the story, however, the method by which reporters gather the story and present it becomes the story because there is no logical conclusion. Currently, most media outlets report terrorist events within the logic of a well-defined frame (see Althaus, 2002). When violence is ambiguous and continual, the frame loses meaning, and terrorism is reported as an endless cycle of violence. As Leon Uris (1977, p. 815) writes in *Trinity*, a novel about Anglo-Irish conflict in Ulster, there is no future in Ireland, just the cycles of the past. Circles may not be amenable to news frames.

Beating the War Drum

Regardless, the news frame is a powerful instrument. It gives the media outlet covering an event the power to define it. Douglas Kellner (2002) knows that terrorism attracts attention, but he is critical of America's typical news frame. After September 11, Kellner says, American television presented only one news frame, patterning the attack as a clash of civilizations and suggesting that only a military response would stop future attacks. The militants behind the strike responded in the same manner with diatribes filled with simplistic anti-Americanisms, and American and international news frames defined their reports of al Qaeda within the boundaries of militancy.

Rather than examine the complexity of the issues, Kellner says, television beat the war drum and called in a variety of terrorism experts who reflected the single view. Radio was even worse, engaging in sensationalistic propaganda. The process did not stop with news reporting. One national network broadcast patriot war movies after several days of news coverage. Whether **postmodern** or not, news frames simplified the cause and pointed to one logical solution, war. A military solution may well have been the proper answer to 9/11, but news frames presented no other option.

Terrorism and Television

Benjamin Barber (1996, pp. 76–83) analyzes the problems of news frames and popular images on television in *Jihad vs. McWorld*. The title suggests that he is examining the world of the jihadists, but he is looking at global economic inequities and the resulting ideologies that drive people into different systems. Instead of moving people to discuss problem solutions, Barber believes, the media flourishes on one overriding factor: entertainment. He humorously calls the twenty-four-hour news networks the infotainment telesector.

The infotainment telesector is not geared for depth; it is designed to create revenue. "News" becomes banter between a news anchor and guest, and debates evolve into shouting matches between controversial representatives. Issues are rarely discussed. Hosts perpetually interrupt

postmodern
Describing the belief that modernism has ended. Some events are inexplicable, and some organizations and actions are naturally and socially chaotic and defy explanation. A postmodern news frame leaves the consumer thinking there are many possible conclusions.

their guests or provide answers to their own questions. Coverage of many shows is driven by a pleasing personality who either lacks intellectual depth or does an excellent job hiding it. Morning news shows are full of interviewers who discover issues obvious to the rest of the world and who shake their heads in wonderment when common knowledge is revealed.

These contexts of the infotainment telesector and the desire to beat the other networks have a negative effect on homeland security. Documents are leaked, confidential plans are unveiled, and vulnerabilities are exposed. Terrorism becomes more horrific to create better drama. News film is constantly replayed, giving the illusion that attacks are repeated time and time again. News hosts spend time interviewing reporters from the field who speculate on the facts surrounding an event. This leads to a dilemma for policy makers. Freedom of the press is guaranteed in the First Amendment to the Constitution, but television coverage frequently becomes part of the story it is covering.

Over the years several studies have pointed to the close relationship between terrorism and television. H. H. A. Cooper (1977a) was one of the first analysts to point to the issues explaining that terrorist acts were made-for-TV dramas. Abraham Miller (1982) published one of the first books on the subject pointing out that television brought terrorist events into our homes. More recently, Yassen Zassoursky (2002) says that television and the Internet give terrorists an immediate international audience. Gadt Wolfsfeld (2001) says acts have become so graphic and sensational that they grab media attention. In one of the best standard-setting studies, Alex Schmid and Jany deGraaf (1982) say that the relationship between terrorism and the media is so powerful that Western democracies may need to take drastic actions and even implement censorship.

David Levin (2003) says the purpose of television news coverage is to keep the audience primed with emotion and excitement. This means the next exciting event is always just around the corner. Of course, the report will come after a series of commercials, and it will include a breathtaking on-the-scene interview with the reporter covering the story. Terrorism is perfect for this scenario because it is so dramatic, but the story need not be about terrorism. Any drama will do.

The drama pattern is designed to keep the viewer tuned to the station. The attention-getting theme is the essence of the drama. On-the-scene reporters send reports back to the anchor, who calmly sits at the desk gathering information, sometimes asking urgent questions to clarify issues for the audience. The pattern, like the message, remains constant. The hidden meaning of the report intimates that the station has crucial information on "breaking news" and members of the audience need to know it. The anchor is the authority figure who is able to process information for the viewers. Reporters are the researchers sending the latest information back from the scene. The overriding message of the drama is "stay tuned." It is the drama pattern of Greek tragedy, and it works for television whether covering the weather, terrorism, election

EXPANDING THE CONCEPT

TV Drama Patterns

What makes a good news drama?

Change: The situation is changing and the outcome is unknown.

Information: The latest and breaking news about the situation is on *this* station.

Stay tuned: You must keep watching; the best is coming.

Expertise: Only this station is qualified to explain the situation.

On-the-scene reports: Reporters are there telling you what is happening, even when they do not know.

Control: The anchor controls the information from the studio, giving you a vicarious feeling of control.

Participation: You are allowed to vicariously participate in the event.

Money: The station breaks away to sponsors but promises even more drama after the commercial.

results, or *Football Night in America* (see Expanding the Concept: TV Drama Patterns).

Control of the drama pattern has been held in a Western monopoly until recently. New networks such as al Jazeera and al Arabia have challenged the West's, especially the American, hold on international news. If there is an effect from twenty-four-hour cable news slanted toward a particular interpretation, new national perspectives influence it (Gilboa, 2005). In addition, localized networks present other perspectives and definitions of terrorism. Judith Harik (2004, pp. 160–161, 189) points out that Hezbollah has learned to do this by projecting a positive image on Lebanese national television. She says Hezbollah took advantage of al Manar television, Lebanon's network, as the Israelis withdrew from Lebanon and again during the al Asqa Intifada.

Al Manar television presented a sympathetic view of the al Asqa uprising, and Hezbollah was quick to take advantage of al Manar's twenty-four-hour coverage. The method of reporting was the key to success. The news was interspersed with inspirational religious messages. Hezbollah was able to get al Manar to focus on Hezbollah's role in the intifada and to run programs on its former glories. In an effort to demoralize the Israelis, al Manar broadcast pictures of Israeli casualties and ended with the question Who will be next?

Power came in the form of visual images. Harik believes al Manar television helped to elevate Hezbollah to heroic status. She cites one example whose effect swept through Lebanon. Faced with heavy fighting in a West Bank village, Israeli forces withdrew. The Israeli Defense Forces (IDF), using Israeli mass media, denied it had abandoned the village. Al Manar presented another view. When the Israelis withdrew, Hezbollah fighters entered the village along with Palestinian mujahideen. Hezbollah raised its flag over the village, and someone took a picture. As the IDF was denying it had retreated, al Manar showed the village with the Hezbollah flag flying high overhead. Hezbollah achieved a media victory.

The growth of media outlets and competing perspectives has had a huge impact on the way the United States is viewed around the world, and this impact extends to perceptions of terrorism and America's foreign policy. For example, the Middle East Forum (2004) makes note of a television program dealing with the Clinton administration's embargo on Iraq during the 1990s. It showed U.S. secretary of state Madeleine Albright being asked if Iraqi citizens suffered under the embargo. She admitted they did. She also said that children were affected, but the costs were worth it. The Forum points out that this statement from the program was played once in the United States, and most Americans agreed with it, wanting to keep weapons of mass destruction out of Saddam Hussein's grasp. The same statement played dozens of times in the Middle East, where it was commonly believed that hundreds of thousands of Iraqi children were starving to death. The Forum concludes that one television program changed the way many Arabs view the United States.

Self-Check

- *What is a news frame?*
- *How are news frames used to cover terrorism?*
- *Describe the relationship between terrorism and television.*

The Internet and Terrorism

The Internet impacts news coverage of all events and often exceeds the ability of the established media to report an event. It is also used to present terrorism. As discussed in Chapter 3, this applies to financing, but it is also used in communication, propaganda and reporting, recruiting and training, and as a tactical weapon. Either side can directly control information or hack into opponents' websites. Both sides can data mine and gather intelligence. The Internet can be a weapon, and either side may use it effectively. Terrorists have learned to use it on several levels.

Todd Hinnen (2004) says the Internet is used most frequently as a communication device, and sending unsecure e-mail is the most common usage for terrorists. Unsecure e-mail is easy to penetrate, and evidence from it is frequently used in criminal prosecutions. Hinnen cites charges against a Colombian terrorist group for arms trafficking based on evidence gathered from e-mail. Terrorists, aware of the dangers of unsecure e-mail, use a variety of methods to hide communications. One way, Hinnen writes, is to give an e-mail account's password to several members of a group. A member can draft a message, but never send it. Other members log on, read the draft, and then delete it after all have viewed it. Because the message is never sent, there is no e-mail record. A second method involves setting up a secure website, such as terroristgroup.com, with its own e-mail server. All members of a terrorist group would receive an address, such as Jsmith@ terroristgroup.com. If e-mail stays exclusively within the secure site, it is difficult to intercept or trace.

Terrorists understand the power of the Internet. They run their own websites, and they sometimes hack into existing sites to broadcast propaganda videos. Yassen Zassoursky (2002) says these abilities enhance the power of terrorist groups, and he believes that the Internet's communication capabilities allow terrorist groups an opportunity to attack the global community. Sonia Liff and Anne Sofie Laegren (2003) reinforce Zassoursky's thesis by pointing to Internet cafés. They say that cybercafés enhance the Internet's striking power because they make communication untraceable.

Steganography is frequently said to be one of the Internet's greatest vulnerabilities to criminal and terrorist communication. The process refers to embedding hidden information in a picture, message, or another piece of information. The process is not new. A Roman general once shaved the head of a slave, had a secret message tattooed on the slave's head, and waited for the slave's hair to grow back. When the message was covered, he sent the slave to the recipient with instructions to shave the slave's head (Lau, 2003). Obviously, the Internet presents faster possibilities for communication, and it does not present the risk of permanently displaying the message if the messenger goes bald! A steganographic message can be encrypted, placed in plain text in a hidden file, or sent on a covert channel (Westphal, 2003). There are numerous potential methods to use steganography in terrorism. It could be used to hide communications, steal information from security forces or an organization within the critical infrastructure, or provide opportunities for electronic attack (Wingate, 2006).

There are two positions on the steganographic threat to the United States. Stephan Lau (2003) says one position claims that steganography is used by terrorist groups to communicate and launch cyberattacks. After 9/11, for example, media reports claimed al Qaeda was hiding information in steganographic images. Some believe that it will be used in denial-of-service attacks or to deface websites. Lau takes the other position, claiming that fear of steganography is the stuff of urban legends. Although steganography programs are readily available and difficult to detect or prevent with security hardware, statistical analysis programs of data contained in any Internet transmission readily reveal irregularities and the location of a hidden image. Entrepreneurs are marketing these programs to corporations and governments, but Lau believes the threat is not in the hidden image. He says there is no evidence to show the use of steganography by terrorists. The real threat, Lau argues, is the American government's enhanced ability to decipher private communications based on threat that does not exist.

In the areas of propaganda, reporting, and public relations, the Internet has been a boon. It allows terrorist groups to present messages and portray images that will not appear in mainstream media. Paul Wilkinson (1997) says terrorists have always used any medium for communication. In the past it ranged from tavern gossip to handbills. Building on this logic it is logical to assume the Internet serves the same purpose only it literally operates at the speed of light. Major groups run websites to present alternative views. For example, the Liberation Tigers of

As Sahaab versus al Hurra

Al Qaeda's media campaign has proved difficult for the United States to counteract. Al Qaeda's underground video network, known as As Sahaab, wages an effective propaganda campaign using the Internet. Evan Kohlmann (2005), an NBC terrorism analyst, explains the process. Local camera operators film studio sequences of a propaganda statement or live-action footage of mujahideen along the Pakistan-Afghanistan border. The footage is edited on a computer, dubbed or subtitled, and handed over to an Internet group called al Fajir, which posts links to the clip in Arab chat forums. Ironically, most of these forums are hosted in North America. Television networks pick up the broadcasts. Western networks heavily edit them, but on networks like al Jazeera they sometimes appear as a full-length broadcast, according to the Discovery Times Channel (2005). In its own media offensive, the United States launched al Hurra, an Arabic-language twenty-four-hour satellite station, in early 2004. The results have been disappointing. One prominent Arab writer called the $62 million project the American *Pravda*, after the Communist news organization in the former Soviet Union (Cochrane, 2004). The Discovery Times Channel agreed, stating most Arabic-speaking viewers distrust the news produced by al Hurra. In essence, a few thousand dollars invested in webcams, PCs, and video software have made more impact than a multimillion dollar television enterprise. The United States has yet to capitalize on the Internet for spreading propaganda.

Sources: Kohlmann, 2005; Discovery Times Channel, 2005; Cochrane, 2004.

Tamil Eelam (LTTE) runs a news service called EelamWeb (http://www.eelamweb.com). Violent single issue groups use the web for propaganda as well (see Expanding the Concept: As Sahaab versus al Hurra).

The Internet can also be used for recruiting and training. Abdul Bakier (2006b) finds Salafi-jihadists using websites and e-mail to make training manuals available. The World Wide Web has become more important as growing numbers of females join the Salafi movement. One blogger, who identified herself as the mother of Osama, claims the Internet gives women the opportunity to become *mujahidat* (female holy warriors). Bakier finds some sites specifically aimed at recruiting or retaining females. Other sites encourage suicide bombings. Discussion groups examine tactics and provide basic weapons orientation, and some militant scholars provide in-depth theological apologies to justify religious violence. One site has an entire first-aid course to deal with battlefield wounds. Bakier finds more and more groups using recruiting sites.

The Internet is also used in target selection, reconnaissance, and sometimes as a tool to support an attack. Maps, satellite imagery, and diagrams provide ready-made intelligence sources. Stephen Ulph (2006a) sees terrorists increasingly using Internet searches to find economic targets. He believes this trend is notable because terrorists across the globe can unite and research a particular target in a matter of minutes. He also finds terrorist groups attracted to data mining. One terrorist training manual points out that it is possible to gather enough information on enemy targets simply by using the Internet. Ulph (2006b) also sees the Internet as a potential weapon. Terrorists want to take hacker warfare to their enemies. Groups post methods to steal passwords and instructions for breaking into secure areas. There are instructions on systems and denial-of-service attacks, too. As a logistical tool, the Internet can also be used to assemble people for a violent action. Clearly, the Internet has become a weapon in many arsenals.

Self-Check

- *How do terrorists use the Internet to communicate?*
- *What is the value of Internet propaganda?*
- *Is the Internet a potential weapon for terrorism? Why or why not?*

Issues in the Media

Because the media is so powerful, many of the issues surrounding reporting and communication are hotly debated. For example, Fox News claims to be "fair and balanced." Critics maintain it is not, but supporters believe it presents objective reports. National Public Radio (NPR) reporting is debated in the same manner, except critics believe NPR has a liberal bias. Such debates are not solved easily, and the arguments favoring one side or the other are frequently full of opinions instead of hard evidence. Before leaving the discussion of the media, it would be helpful to review some of these issues.

Liberal and Conservative Biases in Terrorism Reporting?

Most mainstream media claim objectivity when presenting information about terrorism. They know governments and terrorists are trying to manipulate news stories, so they seek an ideal—objectivity. Many reporters believe it is their job simply to tell the truth. They seek to be fair and balanced, as Fox News claims to be. These assumptions are naïve, according to former CBS employee Bernard Goldberg (2003, pp. 103–114). All news comes with a slant, and reporters are expected to create news frames reflecting their outlet's orientation. For people outside the newsroom, the debate is intense. At one end of the spectrum, critics claim the media has a liberal bias. Critics fume, claiming the print and electronic media are inherently anti-Western and anti-American (see Bozell, 2005; Anderson, 2005). These critics claim reporters are sympathizing with terrorism at worst or undermining the government at best.

Media Ownership

Edward Herman (1999) focuses on the social construction of reality and political bias when examining the media, but not from the perspective of most critics. The bias is economic, he says, and it is dominated by multinational corporations. The American media is part of a vast propaganda machine promoting the values and goals of business corporations. He conducts case studies examining advertising, ownership, and content to demonstrate the point. Stories affecting corporate profits are manipulated in a positive way. Dictators are portrayed as moderate or benign when they favor corporate investments and profits, even as the same leaders repress or massacre their own citizens. Newspapers use catchphrases such as "free trade," "third world elections," and other simplifications to hide the powerful economic forces behind political action. The political bias is neither liberal nor anti-American; it is based in market orientation.

Pundits and other nonscholars attack this position. They claim that the media has been taken over by conservatives. Talk show hosts and guests banter about pseudofacts, reinforcing right-wing ideology. Guests are invited on programs only to be bombarded with conservative ranting. Critics claim the news media is dominated by bullies and hatemongers who seek to silence any voice but their own. Reporting on terrorism cannot be objective from such a format—it is designed to create fear and limit individual freedom (see Anderson, 2005; Willis, 2005).

Is there bias in the coverage of terrorism? Some scholars think so, but it is much more subtle and complicated than the writers of popular diatribes believe. Rather than joining the debate by measuring the amount of conservatism or liberalism in news content, Daniel Sutter (2001) analyzes the economic aspects of news production. He asks, What incentives would generate a bias and why would a profit-making entity risk losing an audience? One of Sutter's answers comes in the form of an analogy. Suppose the public is composed of 600 television news viewers who are liberal, moderate, or conservative. By statistical distribution 300 viewers would fall in the middle, or moderate, category. The remaining 300 would divide equally between liberals and conservatives. A news organization, as a profit-making entity, has the incentive to attract the largest possible audience. If the news moved either to the right or left, it would be threatened with the loss of mainstream viewers. Sutter sees no incentive for a liberal or conservative bias. Or does it have a bias that is neither liberal nor conservative? See Another Perspective: Media Ownership.

There is a caveat in his logic, Sutter admits, because some media organization owners would be willing to sacrifice profit to stand for a political position. In addition, some journalists will insert their own feelings into a story even when these feelings do not reflect the owner's position. These factors are countered by trends in the profit-driven media. First, if the entire media were to exhibit a bias, one owner would need to have a monopoly on all media outlets. One company can afford to take a position, Sutter says, but the entire industry will not. Second, journalism is a profession. Work is reviewed and approved by editors and reviewed by colleagues. Individual bias is readily identified, but each journalist or reporter thinks and presents news separately. This process prevents an overall bias in the industry. Third, as news organizations expand, there will be pressures for bias to develop special audiences among liberals and conservatives. Yet the media will remain market driven, and the entire industry will not take up the biases of a limited, specialized audience. Finally, news organizations are increasingly led by boards and groups of owners driven by the desire to make money. They do not have the incentive to introduce bias that disaffects their mainstream viewers.

David Baron (2004) takes a different approach, suggesting that bias appears on two levels: the individual discretion of the reporter collecting information for a story and the public's desire to watch or read the most captivating story. Small portions of a reporter's individual bias may slip into the story, but the corporation presenting the news will limit it. The business wants the largest amount of viewers, hence revenue, it can attract, so it keeps reporters focused on captivating issues. The organization also wants to tailor the report to the beliefs and values of the audience. Therefore, there is very little incentive for bias. The one exception deals with reporters' salaries. Less objective news appealing to a specialized, politically biased audience can mean lower overall wages for reporters. Baron says the logic is that lower quality equals less pay, and lower wages translate into higher profits. There is a risk in this process, however, because bias may lower consumption, resulting in less income and lower profits. Corporations want to avoid risk and will keep major biases out of their stories.

Tim Groseclose and Jeffrey Milyo (2005) come to a different conclusion, stating that the American media has a liberal bias. Using multiple variables, Groseclose and Milyo selected differing media outlets, including newspapers, magazines, and television and radio news shows, to study. They limited their study to only news items, eliminating editorials, commentaries, book reviews, and other opinion pieces from their study. They then selected think tanks and research organizations used to provide information, guidance, and evaluation for governmental programs and policies. Next, they divided Congress into liberal and conservative members, and counted the numbers of times liberals and conservatives cited a think tank. Finally, they compared the number of times each selected news source cited the same think tank and compared this to the Congressional numbers. They concluded that the news media cited the think tanks referenced by liberal members of Congress more than conservative ones. Groseclose and Milyo conclude that the American news media has a strong liberal bias.

Fouzi Slisli (2000) is not concerned with a liberal or conservative orientation; instead, he focuses on the use of pejorative labels. He believes adjectives introduce bias into the news. Citing sensationalism and failure to conduct in-depth reporting, Slisli says American media is full

---

ANOTHER PERSPECTIVE

Stereotypes and Media Reports

Are American television reports on terrorism objective? Fouzi Slisli (2000) gives a blunt NO! Citing sensationalism and failure to conduct in-depth reporting, Slisli says the American media are full of oversimplifications and stereotypes. Large groups of people are portrayed without depth in American television, and there are few attempts to explain complex social realities. Terms such as *fundamentalist, radical cleric,* and *terrorist* are bantered about by reporters who either fail to understand issues or sensationalize their reports.

Source: Slisli, 2000.

---

of oversimplifications and stereotypes (see Another Perspective: Stereotypes and Media Reports). The media plays to the lowest level of understanding among its viewers. Large groups of people are classified in news reports with no intention of examining complexities. False categories are created to further simplify issues. Terms like *fanatic, fundamentalist, radical cleric,* and *terrorist* are bandied about by reporters who either fail to understand issues or sensationalize their reports.

David Levin (2003) examines reporting of peace processes, intimating it has the problems of simplification, the ability of the audience to understand complexities, and a network's desire to attract an audience. The news is aimed at particular audiences, and different organizations approach audiences in a variety of ways. Information and education stations approach the news differently than twenty-four-hour cable news networks that focus on entertainment and emotions. It is difficult to explain sufficiently well the nature of the conflict, the various political positions, internal fighting within governments and terrorist organizations, and other issues surrounding attempts to bring peace to areas such as Sri Lanka, the Basque region of Spain, Israel and Palestine, and Ireland. Many people prefer simplicity and entertainment. Thus many news programs and some networks search for an unreflective audience, playing to the most susceptible members of the audience. Some producers even attempt to find a supermarket-tabloid audience by searching for the lowest common denominator among them, people who want to be spoon-fed and entertained. These shows exploit emotions, favor sensation over facts, fail to examine issues in depth, and place entertainment value above information.

Information networks approach the same issues with different objectives. They seek to educate their audiences. Their shows are thoroughly researched and focused on the complexity of information. Their purpose is to inform, and they seek an audience that wants to reflect, criticize, and analyze. They will introduce the intricacies of competing interpretations of information and accept ambiguity as normal. When trying to bring peace to an area plagued by political violence and terrorism, subtlety and complexity are the norms.

Miniter's Media Myths

Richard Miniter says that popular images, conservative and liberal views, and urban legends are popularized through the media. Many of these media-based "truths" cannot stand the test of investigation. A selection of myths follows.

The Myth	The Truth
In an e-mail, Lt. Col. Oliver North allegedly warned Senator Al Gore about Osama bin Laden.	North was testifying to another senator about Abu Nidal, a Middle Eastern terrorist.
Former–Soviet Union backpack nuclear devices have been stolen by al Qaeda.	The weapons appear to be secure and are more difficult to steal than popularly believed.
Jihadists are most likely to infiltrate from Mexico.	Canadian media has little respect for the abilities of Canadian police and intelligence services, and jihadist sympathizers operate a strong lobby in Canada. Miniter says the evidence indicates that jihadists will come from the north.
Conservative media personalities argue that political correctness keeps us from targeting via racial profiles terrorists who travel by air. If we could use racial profiles, we could identify terrorists.	Racial profiling does nothing to single out terrorists from ethnic groups. Comparing air travelers with a comprehensive terrorist knowledge base would work, but civil libertarians, both liberal and conservative, prevent that.
Liberal media personalities claim that the defense contracting company Halliburton made tremendous profits in Iraq.	Halliburton has showed little profit from Iraq, both for investors and conspiracy theorists.
A popular Internet and Arab-media myth states that Israeli intelligence warned Jews to avoid the World Trade Center on September 11, 2001.	Although the exact number is unknown, hundreds of Jews died in the 9/11 attack, including five Israelis.

Miniter believes that all media serve as a source of disinformation. The primary reasons are sloppy reporting, editors who fail to check facts, and rumors that are accepted as truth. People gravitate to belief in conspiracies as a result.

Miniter says that the American government can help stop disinformation by making its reports readily available and by releasing the entire transcripts of officials' interviews before items are reported in the news.

Source: Miniter, 2005.

Richard Miniter (2005) shifts the argument to accuracy. He states that the media used to have a conservative bias, and now it has tilted toward liberalism. This is not the problem, however. The issue for the media is that it is spreading incorrect information about terrorism. He identifies twenty-two misconceptions about terrorism accepted as truth by most newspapers, magazines, and broadcasters. The myths come from a variety of sources, including honest mistakes in reporting, American and foreign government disinformation, and contrived leaks. Although the myths are accepted by much of the media and the public, they obfuscate terrorism because they are untrue (see Another Perspective: Miniter's Media Myths). Miniter is an investigative journalist, and he cites many credible sources. Other investigative journalists citing other credible sources disagree with some of his findings (for example see Gordon and Trainor, 2006; Ricks, 2006).

There is another type of conservatism beyond popular and classical political science definitions. Some institutions provide social stability and conserve the status quo of social structure (see Manning, 1976, pp. 102–103). The media may be playing this role far beyond exhibiting a liberal or conservative bias. Todd Fraley and Elli Roushanzamir (2006) say the current conditions of subnational and supranational violence are shifting and distorting all media presentations of violence, including terrorism. They sadly conclude the mass media is spreading more propaganda than news in a world dominated by media corporations. The flow and amount of information, however, could serve to raise the awareness of news consumers, creating a new **critical media consciousness**.

News consumers need to develop analytic abilities that look beyond the news frame and examine the issues behind terrorism and other political events. If they do so, Fraley and Roushanzamir believe, political freedom will expand throughout the world. If consumers remain at the current level of understanding, corporations will continue to remain in charge of mass media outlets, and emerging subnational and supranational groups, such as multinational terrorist organizations, will fight for control of emerging media. If the established media only stabilizes existing social order, it will result in polarization with other forms of media such as the Internet. The conflict between the forms of media may well be the next battleground for terrorism.

The Contagion Effect

Some analysts are not as concerned about the content of press coverage as they are about its role in spreading terrorist violence. Does the coverage of terrorism inspire more violence? In other words, does it cause contagion? The topic has been researched for a number of years. Media images produce some types of behavior, but the effects are not totally clear.

Several years ago Allan Mazur (1982) studied bomb threats in the nuclear industry. His study compared bomb threats against nuclear power plants with the amount of press coverage the plants received. He

critical media consciousness
The public's understanding of the media and the way stories are presented. A critically conscious audience would not simply accept a story presented in a news frame. It would look for the motives for telling the story, how the story affected social constructs and actions, and hidden details that would cause the story to be told another way.

began by noting that news reports of suicides increase the actual number of suicides, and he wondered whether he might find a similar pattern in the nuclear industry. He found the number of threats proportionately matched the number of news stories. When coverage increased, bomb threats increased. Conversely, when coverage decreased, bomb threats decreased.

One of the first criminal justice scholars to study media contagion was M. Cherif Bassiouni (1981), and he felt that media coverage had several contagious effects. He found that media reports promoted fear and magnified threats. This caused fear to spread. The media also influenced the way terrorists select their targets; to spread violence, terrorists selected targets for maximum publicity. From this standpoint, terrorism was contagious: media-reported terrorism caused more terrorism.

If Bassiouni was correct, it meant that images influenced behavior. A few years later research suggested that media images produced emotional behavior, but not in ways that were completely predictable. When exposed to violent images, some people felt immediate sympathy for the victims. They responded with facial grimaces and body movements. As other images were presented, viewers reported that they felt their level of anxiety and emotion increase. At that point, several different things happened. Some people became angry, but others simply turned away (Tamborini, Stiff, and Heidl, 1990). Images influenced behavior, but they did not seem to cause violent behavior contagiously.

More recent research indicates that the effects of media exposure are even more complex. Many researchers believe that the fear generated by media reporting is contagious (Altheide, 2006). When the anthrax attacks that followed the suicide bombers of September 11 were first reported, anxiety soared. As time went on, however, even when the story was extensively reported, anxiety levels were reduced (Berger, Johnson, and Lee, 2003). In addition, news reports did not seem to cause further anthrax attacks. Other findings demonstrate that media reports might inspire a person to engage in terrorism, but so do stories from friends and families (Weatherston and Moran, 2003).

There may be a contagious relationship between a terrorist event and the level of violence in later events. On March 11, 2004, terrorists set off a series of bombs on commuter trains in Madrid. The attack was intended to kill as many people as possible in a spectacular fashion. Ana Lisa Tota (2005) believes this type of attack is a side effect of mass media reporting. International terrorists have come to understand that their attacks must be spectacular to achieve international coverage. In this sense, the level of violence is contagious.

Some researchers believe that if a contagion effect exists, it might be used to counter terrorism. For example, after a terrorist attack, security forces on the scene restoring order could lead to further order. Steven Chermak and Alexander Weiss (2006) approach the issue in a study of the impact of media reports on community policing. They find that both the police and the media agree on the merits of community policing,

ANOTHER PERSPECTIVE

Wilkinson's Analysis of the Media

Paul Wilkinson argues that terrorists must communicate their efforts and they use the media to do so. He concludes the following about the relationship between the media and terrorists:

- Terrorists and the media have an interdependent relationship.
- Terrorist groups have an underground communication system, but they need the mainstream media to spread their messages.
- Mass media serve as a psychological weapon by creating fear and anxiety.
- Terrorists may trap the media into spreading their message.
- The media may inadvertently shift blame for an incident from terrorists to victims or governments.
- Governments benefit when media sources portray the savage cruelty of terrorist groups.

Source: Wilkinson, 1997.

and law enforcement officials feel they have a good relationship with reporters in this area. Yet Chermak and Weiss found low reporting about the benefits of community policing.

Censorship Debates

Paul Wilkinson (1997) believes that governments face three choices when it comes to maintaining freedom of the press and combating terrorism. A popular position is to assume a laissez-faire attitude. This hands-off approach assumes that market forces will determine the norms. A second choice is censorship. In this case a governmental agency would have veto power over news reports. A final choice is to let the press regulate itself. Wilkinson says that many times reporters would not behave in an irresponsible manner if they knew what they could do to avoid serving terrorists. He notes that governments and security forces seldom provide direction for news organizations (see Another Perspective: Wilkinson's Analysis of the Media).

The arguments about censorship are heated and deal with core issues in democracy. At the center of the debate is the right to free speech and the essential question Does free speech allow media access to information? The media answers in the affirmative, claiming that the public has a right to know. Critics respond that free speech does not imply unlimited access to information. There is a right to speak; there is no right to know. In another sense, the censorship debate also focuses on truth or factual information. Because terrorists and governments understand that media images are important in terrorism, they both spend great amounts of energy trying to manipulate the media (Shpiro, 2002). Regardless, when a democratic government openly censors information, democracy is threatened. Manipulating the media and withholding information are very different from governmental control of the press.

Looking at actions shortly after the United States started its war on terrorism, Doris Graber (2003) summarizes both sides of the argument. She argues that freedom of the press is crucial during times of national crisis, but that is when the media is most vulnerable. She believes that people who seek increased censorship do so by developing strategic arguments based on sloganeering and knowledge of select audiences. These efforts are attempts to manipulate people into supporting censorship by using verbal tactics to make arguments that it seems illogical to disagree with. Officials in the Bush administration augmented this process by withholding information and encouraging lower-ranking officials to do the same thing. The Democrats supported this policy up to the 2002 elections.

Graber says several arguments were used to encourage censorship. The first was national security, a powerful excuse used in times of emergency. According to this position, information must be controlled to ensure the survival of the state. Another position was to claim that the public wanted the information withheld. Democratic senator Joseph Lieberman voiced his support for controlling information, claiming the American people overwhelmingly supported governmental efforts. According to this logic, America was fighting a new type of war and some form of censorship was required. The other arguments asked Americans to behave patriotically. Ultimately, governmental officials claimed they were asking for restraints, not censorship.

Freedom of Information (FOI) Act

A law ensuring access to governmental records.

According to Graber, mainly journalists presented the anticensorship view. They cited a variety of governmental mistakes and misdeeds all hidden under the rubric of national security. They condemned governmental officials who fought against the **Freedom of Information (FOI) Act**. They also argued that the terrorism was essentially a war of information. Instead of trying to silence sources, the government should focus efforts on getting out the facts. Finally, every governmental clampdown cast officials in a bad light. The anticensorship camp reserved its harshest criticism for media outlets that decided to self-censor as a governmental service.

Graber concludes that arguments for and against censorship in times of crisis are as old as warfare. They will not be resolved in the current struggle with terrorism. She also offers her own opinion. The United States is fighting for freedom and democracy, and only an informed public is capable of successfully defending liberty. Editors, she argues, should hold back information to protect citizens and security forces, but those decisions belong to the media, not the government.

Self-Check

- *Describe issues that affect the way reporters approach terrorism.*
- *Can terrorism be contagious? Why or why not?*
- *What might happen if news about terrorism is censored?*

SUMMARY

- Terrorism is a method of symbolic communication. Terrorists and security forces use a variety of media to spread messages about events, actions, and political causes.
- News frames shape stories about terrorism. They set the stage for the story, introduce the characters, give a narrative of the action, and either provide a conclusion or lead consumers to a variety of conclusions.
- Because many news consumers experience an event only through the media, all forms of media play an important role in the social construction of reality. They provide information for a construct.
- Members of the media and security forces often seem to be at odds when responding to terrorist events. Security forces want to restore the scene, investigate, and eliminate terrorism. Media sources want to tell the story, and they function in a highly competitive environment. Sensationalistic drama increases the attraction of the story to readers and viewers.
- Television and terrorism are closely related. Terrorists feed television's need for drama, and television gives terrorists a means of communication.
- International influences on the media have eliminated the West's monopoly on news programming and information dissemination. The Internet operates across borders with impunity, and new twenty-four-hour satellite stations broadcast from non-Western countries, providing their own news frames and interpretations of terrorist events.
- Heated debates rage over whether the media exhibits a liberal or conservative bias. Some analysts are more concerned with pejorative phraseology than accuracy.
- The Internet gives terrorist organizations access to audiences apart from the mainstream media's. They use it for propaganda, communication, recruiting, training, planning, and intelligence gathering.
- Debates about censorship are always present in times of national crisis. Supporters of censorship argue that national security demands it. Opponents argue that censorship is used to hide governmental mistakes and that the public must have information to make informed decisions.

KEY TERMS

news frames (p. 77)
reporting frame (p. 78)
postmodern (p. 80)

critical media consciousness
  (p. 91)
Freedom of Information (FOI) Act
  (p. 94)

WRITING ASSIGNMENTS

1. Can terrorism be considered a form of political communication? If yes, what are terrorists trying to convey? Discuss the issues that impact the effectiveness of their efforts. If no, what is the purpose of terrorism? How do arguments about censorship fit into your answer?

2. Humans are storytellers, whether told around campfires, in sagas, or in modern films. How does the news media frame stories of terrorism? What factors influence the manner of telling the story? How do stories change when certain details are either included or excluded? What images need to be included to convince an audience that it is a story about terrorism?

3. Imagine that you are the producer of the local news in a midsize American city. Would you select stories to please your audience, the station's owners and investors, or your advertisers? How would this affect the way you directed reporters to cover stories of terrorism? Would you favor providing information over entertainment if it decreased ratings? Would you self-censor information to protect your viewers?

Tactics and Force Multipliers

5

Women grieve after hearing that a kidnap victim had been murdered by the ETA in the Basque region of Spain. The tactics of terrorism usually involve simple crimes, but terrorists increase the impact by using force multipliers.

AP Photo/Luis Tejido/EFE

Learning Objectives

After reading this chapter, you should be able to

- Summarize the tactics of modern terrorism.
- List and describe four force multipliers.
- Define the types of threats posed by cyberterrorism.
- Explain the effects of biological weapons.
- Describe the effects of chemical and radiological WMD.

- Discuss the role of the media as a force multiplier.
- Summarize transnational economic targeting in the tourist, energy, and transportation industries.
- Explain the logic of suicide terrorism.
- Summarize a theory of religious suicide bombing.

Before moving into the history of terrorism, it is necessary to examine the tactics of terrorism. Terrorist tactics are simple, but their impact can be multiplied. A force multiplier is anything that increases the striking power of a terrorist group. Technology, especially development of weapons of mass destruction (WMD), has made modern terrorism deadlier than terrorism in ages past. Computers and cybersystems can be used as both a weapon or the target of infrastructure attacks, although some analysts argue that attacks on information technology constitute a separate form of terrorism. As discussed in the previous chapter, the media is viewed as a weapon; as such, they can multiply the power of an attack. Terrorists have come to understand that they are more powerful when they threaten international economic stability. They frequently use transnational connections to increase the power of a strike on economic targets. Suicide bombing was reintroduced to the world by religious terrorists, but it has been copied by secular terrorist groups because of its ability to multiply the force of an attack. These force multipliers deserve further consideration.

six tactics of terrorism
As defined by Brian Jenkins, (1) bombing, (2) hijacking, (3) arson, (4) assault, (5) kidnapping, and (6) hostagetaking.

force multiplier
A method of increasing striking power without increasing the number of combat troops in a military unit. Terrorists have four force multipliers: (1) technology to enhance weapons or attacks on technological facilities, (2) transnational support, (3) media coverage, and (4) religious fanaticism.

The Tactics of Terrorism and Multiplying Force

Although it is difficult to define terrorism, it is not difficult to summarize terrorist tactics. To begin, Ian Lesser (1999, pp. 8–10) suggests that terrorism is defined by a situation, and it changes with each new situation. If he is correct, then terrorism can be seen as a method of fighting. Tactics change in terrorism just like they change in war. Groups change structures and goals, and terrorists learn from the past and their previous successes and mistakes. Terrorists change tactics continually. This means security forces must be willing to change the way they respond to terrorists.

Brian Jenkins (1984, 2004a, 2004b) says there are **six tactics of terrorism**: bombing, hijacking, arson, assault, kidnapping, and hostagetaking. Recently, the arsenal of terrorism has grown to include threats from weapons of mass destruction (WMD), but the public does not clearly understand the threat. Technology has also modified bombing to include virtual attacks through computer systems (B. Jenkins, 1987; Brackett, 1996, p. 45; J. White, 1986, 2000; Parachini, 2003).

Jenkins says the six tactics can be enhanced by **force multipliers**. In military terms, a force multiplier increases striking power without in-

Force Multipliers

Transnational support increases the ability of terrorist groups to move and hide.

Technology allows a small group to launch a deadly attack.

Media coverage can make a minor group appear to be politically important.

Religion transcends normative political and social boundaries, increasing violence and decreasing opportunities for negotiation.

creasing the strength of a unit. Terrorists routinely use force multipliers because they add to their aura. All political terrorists want to give the illusion that they can fight on a higher, more powerful level.

Four force multipliers give terrorists more striking power (see Another Perspective: Force Multipliers). Technology can enhance a terrorist group's ability to strike (Ketcham and McGeorge, 1986, pp. 25–33; Bunker, 1998). Cyberterrorism and potential WMD attacks are examples of technological force multipliers. Daniel Benjamin and Steven Simon (2002, pp. 365–382) demonstrate that media coverage and interpretation of terrorist events often serve as force multipliers. One incident can be converted into a "campaign" as electronic media scrambles to break the latest news. Jeffrey Goldberg's (2002) research on the Triborder region in South America demonstrates that transnational support networks multiply the striking power of terrorists. A frightening new force multiplier has been the introduction of religious fanaticism in terrorist activities (B. Hoffman 1995; Laqueur, 1999; Juergensmeyer, 1988, 2000; Stern, 2003b; von Hippel, 2002). The introduction of religion has introduced suicide attacks into the arsenals of terrorism.

Although terrorist tactics change through time, the most common weapon of terrorism has been and is still the bomb. In 1848 anarchists talked about the **philosophy of the bomb**, meaning that the only way to communicate with the social order was to destroy it. In the late 1800s, militants used bombs to attack governments and businesses, culminating in a bombing campaign in 1919. The Irish Republican Army (IRA) found the bomb to be their most important weapon after 1969, and by 1985 the organization was deploying extremely sophisticated ones (Garrison, 2004). Groups in the Middle East, Sri Lanka, and eventually throughout the world found that bombs could be delivered by suicide attackers (Pape, 2003). Hijackers first used bombs to take over planes, and then, on September 11, 2001, terrorists turned civilian airliners into bombs (see Expanding the Concept: The Most Common Tactic of Terrorism). In the campaign against the U.S. military in Iraq after 2003, suicide bombings and roadside bombs became the weapons of choice (Ricks, 2006, p. 118).

Terrorists tend to increase their effectiveness in bombing by applying improved explosive technology to their weapons just as conven-

philosophy of the bomb
A phrase used by anarchists around 1848. It means that social order can be changed only through violent upheaval. Bombs were the first technological force multiplier.

EXPANDING THE CONCEPT

The Most Common Tactic of Terrorism

Although terrorist tactics change through time, the most common weapon of terrorism has been and is still the bomb. In 1848 anarchists talked about the "philosophy of the bomb," meaning that the only way to communicate with the social order was to destroy it. In the late 1800s, militants used bombs to attack governments and businesses. The Irish Republican Army (IRA) found the bomb to be their most important weapon after 1969, and by 1985 the organization was deploying extremely sophisticated ones. Groups in the Middle East, Sri Lanka, and eventually throughout the world found that bombs could be delivered by suicide attackers. Hijackers first used bombs to take over planes, and then, on September 11, 2001, terrorists turned civilian airliners into bombs.

tional military forces constantly improve the killing power of their munitions. In 2004 *New Scientist* reported that Middle Eastern terrorist groups were working on two types of military-style weapons called mini-nukes. One type of bomb is designed to spread fuel in the air and then ignite it. A **thermobaric bomb** actually explodes the air in the blast area. One analyst speculated that a terrorist bomb placed in a Tunisian synagogue in 2002 used this technology (Hambling, 2004). The purpose of this technological force multiplier is to kill more people. It should also be noted that military forces use both types of mini-nukes.

thermobaric bomb

A two-stage bomb. The first stage spreads either a fuel cloud or finely ground powder through the air. The explosive material mixes with the oxygen present in the atmosphere. The second stage denotes the explosive material, which explodes in all directions in a series of shock waves. The cloud can penetrate a number of barriers. A person breathing the material explodes from the inside out when the material is ignited.

Although the tactics are simple, they always represent a variation on a theme. Force multipliers enhance destructive power, whereas innovation is used to achieve shock and surprise. Again, this is nothing more than the tactics used by conventional military forces, but they are used outside the rules of a war with front lines and a beginning and an end. This explains why terrorism is different from war, even though terrorists and military forces sometimes use the same tactics. Donald Black (2004) points out that terrorism lacks the gaming quality of war. Terrorist tactics, though simple, create terrorism because they are designed to attack civilians and symbolic targets exclusively. The only purpose of a terrorist attack is to send a message of chaos and destruction to a larger audience. In fact, the victims most often do not constitute the real target; they are killed merely to send a message. In some ways, therefore, the tactics of terrorism actually serve as a de facto method for providing a definition.

Self-Check

- *Describe the basic tactics of terrorism.*
- *Define and describe force multipliers.*
- *How do force multipliers affect the tactics of terrorism?*

▼ Technology

Terrorism is influenced by technology. Some analysts believe that when the technological impact is so great that it turns a tactic or weapon into a strategy, it is possible to look at the resulting activity as a specific type of terrorism (see Pape 2003, 2005). Others believe that this technique confuses the issue and that types of terrorism refer only to tools any terrorist group could use (see Dyson, 2004). Striking a balance between these two positions, this section will examine four types of terrorism that are potentially powerful enough to transform the nature of terrorism. As stated earlier, these types may be only different weapons used in terrorist attacks, but special types of terrorism have become so individualized they deserve a separate review.

Cyberterrorism

Cyberterrorism refers to the use of computers to attack technological targets or physical attacks on computer networks. The National Conference of State Legislatures (2003) defines cyberterrorism as the use of information technology by terrorists to promote a political agenda. Barry Collin (2004), who coined the term in the early 1990s, believes it involves disrupting points where the virtual, electronic realm of computer networks and programs intersects with the physical world. Miami attorney Mark Grossman (1999) argues that the threat of cyberterrorism is real and international legal systems are not prepared to deal with it. Cyberterrorism is computer hacking with a body count, according to Grossman. The Council on Foreign Relations (2004) defines cyberterrorism by the ways terrorists might use computers and information networks. There are targets for cyberterrorism: computers, computer networks, and information storage and retrieval systems. Terrorists differ from hackers, the council argues, because their purpose is to launch a systematic attack for political purposes. The most common tactic to date has been the defacement of websites.

There are many potential targets for cyberterrorists. Yael Shahar (1997) envisions scenarios where a computer virus—a program that typically copies itself and moves through a computer system to disrupt a computer or computer network—is implanted in an enemy's computer. He predicts the use of "logic bombs," or snippets of program code that lie dormant for years until they are instructed to overwhelm a computer system. Shahar also believes that bogus computer chips can be sold to sabotage an enemy's computer network. Trojan horses, or malicious programs that seem to be harmless, can contain malevolent code that can destroy a system, and "back doors" in computer systems can allow terrorists to enter systems thought to be secure. Furthermore, Shahar believes that conventional attacks, such as overloading an electrical system, threaten computer security.

Cyberterrorism is an attractive low-risk strategy. Michael Whine (1999) agrees with Shahar's conclusions, claiming that computer technology is attractive to terrorists for several reasons. Computers allow terrorist groups to remain connected, providing a means for covert discussions and anonymity. Computer networks are also much less expensive and work intensive than the secretive infrastructures necessary to maintain terrorist groups. Bowers and Keys (1998) believe cyberterrorism appears to be a threat because of the nature of modern society. More and more, modern Western society needs information and the flow of information to function, so cyberterrorists threaten to interrupt or confuse that flow of information. This leads Tiffany Danitz and Warren Strobel (1999) to remind policy makers that violent political activists also use the Internet as a command-and-control mechanism. They say there is no doubt that computers are vulnerable to crime, and terrorists do use and will continue to use them.

Some research points to attacks that have already occurred rather than focusing on potential targets. A group from the Center for Strategic and International Studies (2004) examined attacks on America's cybersystems. Chaired by a former director of the FBI and Central Intelligence Agency (CIA), William Webster, the group states that there has been a sharp rise in such attacks, with the Internet providing the vehicle for launching most of the strikes. His group was especially concerned with documented attacks on the National Security Agency, the Pentagon, and a nuclear weapons laboratory. Operations were disrupted in all of these cases.

WMD: Biological Agents

Terrorism by WMD presents a potential strategic scenario and even served as the United States' excuse for invading Iraq in 2003. Biological weapons have been used for centuries. Modern arsenals contain **bacterial weapons** and **viral weapons**, with microbes cultured and refined, or weaponized, to increase their ability to kill. When people are victims of a bacterial attack, antibiotics may be an effective treatment. Antibiotics are not usually effective against viruses, however, although some vaccines issued before the use of viral weapons are effective (see Hinton, 1999; Young and Collier, 2002). Because bacterial agents are susceptible to antibiotics, nations with bacterial weapons programs have created strains of bacterial microbes resistant to such drugs. Viral agents are produced in the same manner, and they are usually more powerful than bacterial agents. Biological agents are difficult to control but relatively easy to produce. Terrorists may find them to be effective weapons.

There are four types of biological agents: (1) natural poisons, or toxins that occur without human modification, (2) viruses, (3) bacteria, and (4) plagues. The Centers for Disease Control and Prevention (CDC) classifies the most threatening agents as smallpox, anthrax, plague, botulism, tularemia, and hemorrhagic fever. Michael Osterholm and John Schwartz (2000, pp. 14–23) summarize the effect of each. Smallpox is a deadly, contagious virus. Many people were vaccinated against smallpox in their childhood, but these old vaccinations are no longer effective against the disease. Anthrax is a noncontagious bacterial infection, and plague is transmitted by insects. Botulism is a kind of foodborne illness, and other bacteria can be modified to serve as weapons. Hemorrhagic fevers are caused by viruses. One of the most widely known hemorrhagic fevers is the Ebola virus.

America has experienced two notable biological attacks since 1980. The first modern use of biological terrorism in the United States was en-

bacterial weapons

Enhanced forms of bacteria that may be countered by antibiotics.

viral weapons

Enhanced forms of viruses. The virus is "hardened" so that it can live for long periods and enhanced for deadlier effects.

gineered in 1984 by followers of a religious group in Oregon. The group spread bacteria in area salad bars in attempt to sicken voters during a local election. Their intent was to elect their religious followers to local office (Miller, Engelberg, and Broad, 2001). Hundreds of people suffered food poisoning as a result.

The second attack involved anthrax and came in the wake of 9/11. It began in Florida when two tabloid workers were infected by anthrax through the mail. One of the victims died. In the following days anthrax appeared again as NBC *Nightly News* received spores in the mail. The situation grew worse in October. The office of Senate majority leader Thomas Daschle received its regular mail delivery after lunch on Friday, October 12. Fortunately, staff members were in a class that afternoon, learning how to recognize suspicious packages. When staffers returned to work on Monday, they opened Friday's mail and someone noticed a white powdery substance in a letter. Alerted by information from Friday's class, the staffer took immediate action, perhaps saving many lives. The powder contained anthrax spores, and although there were no fatalities, legislative offices were closed in Washington, D.C., for several weeks. Mysteriously, other people died on the East Coast with no explanation of how the anthrax was spreading (Parker, 2002; Schoof and Fields, 2002).

WMD: Chemical and Radiological Weapons

The massive power and heat from atomic bombs place nuclear weapons in a class of their own, but chemical and radiological attacks are basically similar. Radiological poisoning and "dirty" radioactive devices are forms of chemical alterations. Chemicals are usually easier to deliver than biological weapons, and they are fast acting. Radiological devices act more slowly than most chemicals, but their poison lasts longer and they can be spread like chemicals. Radioactive materials are also more resistant to heat than chemicals, so bombs or other heat-producing devices can be used to scatter them.

There are four types of chemical agents: nerve agents, blood agents, choking agents, and blistering agents (Table 5.1). Nerve agents enter the body through ingestion, respiration, or contact. Blood and choking agents are usually absorbed through the respiratory system, and blistering agents burn skin and internal tissue upon contact (Organization for the Prohibition of Chemical Weapons, 2000). Radiological weapons would produce short-term burns and long-term contamination and health problems. Radiological poisoning takes place when a contaminated material comes in contact with any source that conducts radiation. The contacted material, such as food, water, or metal, becomes a contaminated object that could poison humans. Small contaminated pieces of matter can also become a means of spreading radiation through the air (U.S. Congress, Office of Technology Assessment, 1995).

Chemicals present an attractive weapon for terrorists because they are easy to control and, unlike biological weapons, the users can avoid

Table 5.1   Chemical and Radiological Agents and Their Effects

Agent	Common Entry	Effect
Nerve	Food, water, air, skin contact	Convulsions, flood of body fluids
Blistering	Skin contact, air	Burns, choking, respiratory failure
Blood/Choking	Breathing, skin contact	Failure of body functions
Radiological	Food, air, water	Burns, long-term skin contact illness

Sources: Organization for the Prohibition of Chemical Weapons, 2000; U.S. Congress, Office of Technology Assessment, 1995.

the area they attack. Nonetheless, chemical weapons present three problems. First, terrorists must have a delivery mechanism; that is, they need some way to spread the chemical. Second, it takes a lot of chemicals to present a threat. Finally, weather patterns, air, and water can neutralize a chemical threat. Chemical weapons are most effective when used in a confined space.

Because of these difficulties, many experts believe that terrorists will use chemicals or radioactive material in a dirty bomb. This means that a conventional explosive would be used to spread a chemical or radioactive agent around a large area. This technique has one major drawback: the heat produced by the explosion may destroy the chemicals attached to the bomb. This does not happen in the case of radiation; therefore, most dirty-bomb scenarios are based on the premise that a radiological agent will be used with a conventional explosive.

One of the most fearful types of radiological WMD is nuclear weapons. A stolen nuclear bomb or atomic weapon conjures the worst images of mass destruction. If nuclear terrorism happens, authorities will most likely respond with military support. The United States has plans for dealing with a nuclear disaster; military forces have the monopoly on knowledge in this area.

Reuters (2-8-04) reports that nuclear weapons are available on the black market from sources in the former Soviet Union. Jason Burke (1-18-04) says terrorists have placed instructions online for building a nuclear device. Nonetheless, it is still difficult to obtain and detonate nuclear weapons. It is much easier for terrorists to use a conventional weapon to spread either chemicals or radioactive material than for them to build a nuclear weapon.

James David Ballard (2003) looks at the problem of nuclear terrorism another way. Congress has designated a site in Nevada as the repository for all the radioactive waste from America's nuclear power plants, and all this material must be shipped across the country. Ballard wonders what would happen if terrorists seized some of this material? He points out that nuclear waste is a ready-made dirty bomb.

Self-Check

- *How does technology impact terrorism?*
- *Describe the ways cyberterrorists might operate.*
- *Describe the effectiveness of differing types of WMD.*

The Media as a Force Multiplier

Governments benefit when media sources portray the savage cruelty of terrorist groups. As images of carnage and distraught victims are beamed into their homes, viewers are frequently sickened by the suffering and destruction. Security forces, symbols of sanity in a world turned upside down, assume the role of heroes whether the report is favorable or not. They are trying to restore order. Terrorists, however, also benefit from coverage. Constant reporting makes small groups seem important, and when attacks are shown over and over again, the striking power of a group is magnified. Both governments and terrorists see the media as a force multiplier.

Every group involved in a terrorist conflict tries to manipulate images, seeking to use the media as a force multiplier. Paul Wilkinson (1997) says terrorists try to multiply force through communication. This gives terrorists and the media an interdependent relationship. Terrorists use their own underground systems, but they seek to send messages through mainstream media because it serves as a better psychological weapon. Their goal, then, is to trap the media into spreading their message in the hope that blame for an incident shifts from terrorists to victims or governments. If the process is successful, terrorism is no longer criminal; it becomes legitimate violence for a respectable political position.

According to Brigitte Nacos (2000), most terrorist groups have objectives beyond publicity, and public attention is not the only goal of terrorism. Groups want recognition of their causes, grievances, and demands. She concludes that the media is an important tool in the undertaking, and that new forms of communication exacerbate the spread of information. Terrorists will try to portray respectability in all media. Nacos's analysis leads to another conclusion. If terrorists are seeking legitimacy and they use the media as one of their tools, projection of an image is crucial. For terrorists, as well as their opponents, the crucial image is victory. Whether the image is conveyed by print, television, radio, or Internet, respect comes with success. To paraphrase Sun Tzu, the worst way to defeat a city is to surround and attack it. The best measure of victory is to make the city believe it is defeated. This gives all media a special role in terrorism. When it portrays victory, it multiplies force.

Gadt Wolfsfeld (2001) says that media victories are crucial for terrorism. In the al Asqa Intifada both sides tried to use the media, and Wolfsfeld believes there are lessons to be learned from this experience.

He says that struggles for the way a battle is reported are as important as combat on the battlefield. Neither side wants to be portrayed as the aggressor. The Palestinians know that sensational television coverage presents one of their best chances to receive outside intervention, leaving Israel to practice damage control. Both sides have structures to capture media attention and present their respective views.

Wolfsfeld also believes the media is the primary tool for demonizing the enemy, and the most powerful tool is the way television reports casualties. Both sides use the same pattern. Each side compassionately presents its own casualties and describes how they got their injuries in horrific terms, whereas the other side's killed and wounded are described as statistics. Although radio and print media are important, television takes center stage because it can show bloody images. The worst images are shown many times over on the twenty-four-hour networks.

The media makes conflict worse in a subtle way, Wolfsfeld believes, because drama dwindles when news organizations report peace efforts. Most reports about peace efforts are stories of the breakdowns. When an explosion threatens peace talks or terrorists behead a hostage after fighting has ended, television, radio, and newspaper reporters flood the world with gruesome stories. Negotiations during civil unrest are not dramatic, Wolfsfeld notes, but explosions and machine gun fire are riveting. The only time peace becomes dramatic is when major treaties are signed by heads of state. Unfortunately, violence is more frequent.

All forms of media can be used to multiply force, and the Internet is one of the most important force multipliers easily available to terrorists. Natalya Kransoboka (2002) says that research shows that the electorate in most countries is gravitating to online reporting and discussion. Many people think the Internet will make countries more democratic, but other media analysts believe it will have the same impact as traditional news sources. Kransoboka says that empirical evidence presents a different conclusion. The Internet does not have an overwhelming impact in democratic countries, but it is a powerful tool for opposition forces in authoritarian regimes.

Kransoboka says the Internet is gaining the attention of security forces. When the media is heavily controlled, online communication brings the only measure of freedom, and it is emerging as a major source of information. By extending Kransoboka's logic, it would seem that when two sides engage one another, they would see the Internet as a tool for propaganda. Indeed, Kransoboka concludes, this is exactly what happens under authoritarian regimes. Governments try to control the Internet for their own purposes. They see its potential as a weapon for opposition and revolution.

Cinema presents another venue for both assisting terrorism and distorting issues. Medhi Semati (2002) says that movies create popular images of propaganda. The American image of a terrorist is generally a cinematic picture, but terrorists use the same medium in other parts of the world to project their own image. Fouzi Slisli (2000) says that any such image is grounded in simplicity and cultural stereotypes. In the final analysis, movies are responsible for strong emotional projections. Unlike the news, they can be completely grounded in fiction. Mock documentaries even give the illusion that a propaganda film is an objective news analysis (see Expanding the Concept: Fighting for the Media).

No matter what the means of communication, the mass media is part of terrorism. Gadt Wolfsfeld (2001) concludes that it is necessary to accept that both the media and security forces will fight to control media images and that bias in the media is totally misunderstood. When searching for political bias, Wolfsfeld says, slanted news is taken for granted given the orientation of the station, press, or theater. The actual bias comes from the media's endless quest for sensational violence. The mass media compete for the most dramatic, bloody imagery. He does not hold the media responsible for terrorism but concludes that it is part of the story. Wolfsfeld wryly says gladiators keep one eye on the opponent and one eye on the crowd.

> **EXPANDING THE CONCEPT**
>
> ## Fighting for the Media
>
> Terrorists and security forces battle for media control by
>
> ■ Creating organizations to place stories in a good light
>
> ■ Demonizing their enemies
>
> ■ Creating the best images for the media
>
> ■ Appearing to support peace proposals
>
> *Source*: Wolfsfeld, 2001.

Self-Check

- *How do the media enhance terrorism?*
- *What are the ways to responsibly cover terrorism?*
- *Why do terrorists and governments want to be portrayed favorably?*

Economic Targeting and Transnational Attacks

Terrorists may use transnational support or transnational operations as a force multiplier. As the world moves closer to a global economy, terrorists have found that striking transnational economic targets increases the effectiveness of operations. If governments run counterterrorist operations against underground networks and sources, terrorists turn the tables by striking the economic system. Some systems are tied closely to the international economy, and they present tempting targets to terrorists. Three types of transnational attacks can be used to illustrate the issue: tourism, energy, and shipping.

Tourism

On the evening of October 12, 2002, several hundred people were gathered in a resort area of Bali in Indonesia. Many of the people were tourists in a nightclub, and most of the tourists were Australians. According to one of the investigators from the Australian Federal Police, who asked to remain anonymous, Indonesians were quietly advised to leave the area around the bar in the late evening. Shortly before midnight, a firebomb went off inside the bar, trapping the patrons. A second bomb ignited the exterior. Within minutes more than 200 people had been killed. The perpetrators called themselves Jamaat Islamiyya, and they vowed to strike Indonesia's tourist industry again. They would target hotels and resort areas. Leaders in Jamaat Islamiyya had multiple motives for targeting tourists. They wanted to create fear among foreigners and resented the presence of outsiders in Muslim lands. They also felt that it was a method of directly striking the West. One of the leaders claimed that as long as Western troops were in Afghanistan and Iraq, his group would continue killing Westerners in Indonesia. The leaders also felt that they were targeting economic interests (Abuza, 2006b).

There is a relationship between terrorism and tourism, but it is not simple. Terrorism does not seem to have an impact on domestic travel. Terrorism most frequently affects international travelers. If a host country has had widespread media attention to a terrorist event, tourism may drop from selected areas (Sonmez and Graefe, 1998). The impact of terrorism on tourism is not always clear. Some researchers have found that low-level terrorism gradually reduces tourism over a period of time and sudden, vicious attacks have an immediate negative impact (Drakos and Kutan, 2003). Other researchers believe that the frequency of violence is more important than the severity of terrorist attacks (Pizam and Fleischer, 2002). Regardless of mixed findings, one aspect is clear. Terrorism against tourists has a negative economic impact. Attacks on tourists have economic consequences.

Energy

The economic relationship between energy and terrorism is clearer than the impact on tourism, and terrorists have a vested interest in disrupting oil and gas production. Fossil fuels present tempting targets for two reasons: they represent the power and strength of the industrialized world, and strikes against oil refineries or transfer facilities have an economic impact on the West. Iraq serves as an example. U.S. forces invaded Iraq in the spring of 2003. An insurgency grew during the summer, and it was in full swing by November. The primary economic target of the insurgents was oil production. From June 2003 to February 2006 there were 298 attacks against oil-production facilities. The economic impact from the 26 percent reduction in oil production was devastating. The attacks resulted in $6.25 billion in lost revenue for 2005 (Daly, 2006a).

Al Qaeda noticed the impact of the oil attacks in Iraq. In January 2006 Osama bin Laden broke a fourteen-month silence to announce that the war against the United States would not be limited to Iraq. Saudi Arabia was the tempting target. Bin Laden considers Saudi Arabia as nothing more than an American colony. Oil production represents 40 percent of the country's gross domestic product (Daly, 2006a).

Al Qaeda in the Arabian Peninsula, an offshoot of the original al Qaeda, began targeting Saudi oil facilities in 2003 with a varied strategy. They sought to destroy production facilities; destroy transfer systems such as pipelines, storage facilities, and shipping; and target individual oil workers, especially foreigners. In an Internet posting a spokesperson for al Qaeda said the Saudi attacks were designed to destroy the Saudi economy and create an energy crisis in the West. He also mentioned that attacking energy sources brought a good deal of press coverage (Bakier, 2006b). The lessons of Iraq have not been lost on al Qaeda.

The International Crisis Group (2006b) reports that Pakistan is experiencing a similar problem in the Balochistan province, which produces 45 percent of the country's natural gas. At issue are the tribal divisions inside Pakistan and the energy produced in Balochistan. The Pashtun tribe controls the central government in Islamabad, and it exploits the natural gas resources in Balochistan to support ethnic Pashtuns. But Balochistan's major fields lie in the Bugti tribal area, and the Bugtis resent and resist Pashtun incursion into their native land. This has led to sharp fighting and a guerrilla war. John Daly (2006b) points out that the situation has become more complicated because of the resurgence of the Taliban along the Afghan-Pakistan border. Some Bugtis, who previously had few ethnic or political links with the Taliban, have allied with the exiled Afghan Taliban as well as al Qaeda members who fled Afghanistan in the wake of the October 2001 American offensive. Daly says the Taliban believes that the most effective way to destroy the Pakistan government is to attack economic targets. Attacks on gas facilities, which cripple gas production and are force multipliers, started in 2003.

J. Bowyer Bell (1975) refers to **endemic terrorism** as a form of violence that occurs in Africa where arbitrary national boundaries have been drawn without regard to ethnic and tribal divisions. These areas breed all forms of tribal and ethnic conflicts, including terrorism. The Niger Delta is one of the largest oil-producing areas outside the Middle East, and it is beset with endemic terrorism (Cilliers, 2003). Oil plays crucial roles in violence that has killed hundreds of thousands in the past decade. First, it is used to fund endemic terrorism and corrupt governments. Second, it becomes a target of those who cannot control production. Finally, oil companies investing in the area have a greater incentive to focus on security than the debilitating poverty engulfing the region (International Crisis Group, 2006a).

Oil in the Niger Delta represents a different opportunity for economic attack. It simultaneously funds terrorists and other violent groups while serving as a target for terrorism. In addition, dilapidated storage facilities and pipelines have become an ecological disaster for the impoverished local residents. The result is an environment that encourages subnational violence and that might serve as a base for international terrorism. Jakkie Cilliers (2003) notes that the energy environment in Africa represents an interesting paradox. According to Cilliers, if poverty,

endemic terrorism
Terrorism that exists inside a political entity. For example, European colonialists created the nation of Rwanda by combining the lands of two tribes that literally hate one another. The two tribes fight to eliminate one another. This is endemic to political violence in Rwanda.

endemic terrorism, and criminalized politics are not addressed by the industrial world, areas like the Niger Delta will evolve in two directions. They will become the base for the emergence of new international terrorist groups, providing excellent resources for training and eluding detection. At the same time, the energy resources in the delta provide a target-rich environment for terrorists.

Transportation

Transportation systems also present a tempting economic target because they produce mass casualties with minimal effort. Another benefit for terrorists trying to strike economic targets is that the costs of protecting transportation are staggering. Transportation is a major concern of homeland security, and it will be discussed in the last section of the text. We restrict our discussion here to examination of an economic attack on transportation as a force multiplier. Such attacks are quite effective.

After the September 11 attacks the federal government immediately budgeted $4.8 billion to protect the aviation industry. In addition, it created a new federal agency, the Transportation Security Administration, with 30,000 employees (Hobijn, 2002). The shipping industry is also affected by security costs. Indonesia, Malaysia, and Singapore have joined to protest insurance premiums on ships traveling through the Strait of Malacca. Rates have soared because insurance companies believe terrorist groups might start cooperating with pirates (Raymond, 2006). Critics of homeland-security policies, such as Stephen Flynn (2002, 2004a, 2004b), argue that ports remain unsecured because of the costs associated with increased protection. Although all of these examples represent policy issues, the economic impact is clear. Attacks on aviation, shipping, and transportation facilities increase the cost of security. If terrorists wish to increase the economic impact of an attack, the transportation industry presents a tempting target.

Self-Check

- *What is economic targeting?*
- *Describe the targets and methods of economic targeting.*
- *Why are attacks on energy and transportation targets force multipliers?*

Suicide Attacks and Religion

Sacrifice in times of conflict is nothing new, and sometimes warriors are sent on missions where they know their lives will be lost. At other times in history people intentionally sacrifice their lives for a greater cause. Diego Gambetta (2005) tracks incidents of suicide tactics and attacks since World War II. His edited volume develops three types of suicide attacks: (1) suicide in warfare, (2) suicide for a principle without killing others, and (3) suicidal terrorism. Several scholars note that a suicide attack is not a method chosen simply to end one's life. The social and psychological appeal is not suicide; it is a freely given sacrifice in the form of **altruistic suicide**. Suicide terrorists may be fatalistic, they may be psychologically duped, or they may be wealthy with a bright future. One thing they have in common, however, is that they frequently believe they are sacrificing their lives for a greater good (Padahzur and Perlier, 2003; Pape, 2003, 2005, pp. 171–195).

Although common logic sometimes dismisses suicide terrorists as psychologically unstable and early studies suggested that suicide bombers were young frustrated males, data suggest that neither is true (Howard, 2004). Robert Pape (2003, 2005) presents an extensive empirical analysis of suicide terrorist attacks from 1980 to 2001, and he concludes that the attackers are so diverse it may not be possible to find a single profile.

Instead of searching for social or psychological factors, Pape suggests that suicide terrorism be considered as a strategic tool. It is popular because it works, and although suicide attacks began as a form of religious violence, secular groups use the strategy because it is so effective. Suicide terrorism, Pape argues, gives a small group the power to coerce large governments. Suicide terrorists tend to be more lethal than those carrying out other types of attacks, they strike greater fear in the target audience, and each attack hints at future horrific violence. It is a strategy designed to multiply expectations of political victory.

Studies by many scholars and terrorism analysts confirm Pape's findings. More recently, B. Raman (11-22-03, 12-3-04) says terrorists favor suicide attacks because they are so intimidating. He points out that suicide bombers can penetrate secure targets with a good chance of success. Audrey Cronin (2003, pp. 9–11) gives several reasons for the popularity of suicide attacks. They generate high casualties as well as publicity for the attacking group. The nature of the attack strikes fear into an enemy, and the attacks are effective against superior forces and weapons. Suicide bombers give terrorist groups maximal control over the attack.

A Theory of Suicide Terrorism

Robert Pape (2005) takes his empirical study of suicide bombing beyond a simple description of how it happens and offers a **theory of suicide terrorism**. He believes three factors must be in place before a suicide terror campaign can take place. First, a nationalistic or ethnic group must be resisting the occupation of a foreign power. Second, the foreign power must have a democratic government whose voters will not routinely allow the indiscriminate slaughter and total repression of the people in the occupied area. Finally, there must be a difference in the religions of the occupying power and the people living under occupation. This is a key point for the theory. Such terrorism does not happen when the occupied and occupier share a single religion; it is caused by differences between two religions.

Pape (2005, pp. 127–128) says that it is difficult to test this theory because there are so many differing factors, but he argues that it might be

altruistic suicide
The willingness of individuals to sacrifice their lives to benefit their primary reference group such as a family, military unit, ethnic group, or country. It may involve going on suicide missions in combat, self-sacrifice without killing others, or self-sacrifice and killing others.

theory of suicide terrorism
A theory developed by Robert Pape that states that a group of people occupied by a democratic power are likely to engage in suicide attacks when there are differences between the religions of the group and the democratic power, and the occupied religious community supports altruistic suicide.

possible to test it by focusing on the evidence from case studies. He does so by looking at the Israeli occupation of the Shiite areas of Lebanon, the Sinhalese (Buddhist) control of the Tamil (Hindu) region of Sri Lanka, the fighting between Sunni Kurds and Sunni Turks in eastern Turkey, and the Indian (Hindu) struggle with the occupied Sikhs.

The popular conception in Lebanon is that suicide operations are grounded in Islamic extremism; that is, militant Islamic theology causes suicide terrorism. His examination of bombings casts doubt on this conclusion. Of the forty-one suicide attacks Pape studied, only eight involved the suicide of Islamic militants. Twenty-seven were conducted by communists who followed no religion, and the remaining three were carried out by Christians. Although Iran supports Hezbollah, the group that first employed suicide attacks, terrorism is homegrown in Lebanon. Bombers come from local communities where self-sacrifice is glorified by religious leaders (Pape, 2005, pp. 128–139).

Sri Lanka presents an interesting scenario because the Hindu Tamil area has been occupied by two powers, native Buddhist Sinhalese and primarily Hindu Indian soldiers. Again, the popular theory of suicide terrorism in Sri Lanka is that the Black Tigers, the suicide organization within the Liberation Tigers of Tamil Eelam (LTTE), brainwashes its bombers. The LTTE Black Tigers have conducted more suicide bombings than any other group, and they have assassinated two political leaders: an Indian prime minister and a president of Sri Lanka. Yet when the Hindu Indian soldiers were stationed in Sri Lanka from 1987 to 1990, suicide bombings stopped (Pape, 2005, pp. 139–154).

Pape attributes the cessation of suicide bombings during the Indian occupation to the differences between the Sinhalese Buddhists and Tamil Hindus. The Tamils believe their existence is threatened by the dominant Sinhalese government, and many of their religious leaders have demonized the Buddhists. Extremist Buddhists respond by dismissing Hinduism. This difference, Pape believes, is the primary cause of suicide terrorism on Sri Lanka. He does note that there are exceptions. The Hindu prime minister of India was assassinated by the Black Tigers in 1991 when it appeared that Indian forces might return to Sri Lanka. Pape says that he is not proposing a rule that cannot be broken but pointing to a trend.

This logic may also apply to Pape's ideas about democracy. For example, the Russians (Orthodox Christians) occupy Chechnya, which is populated by Sunnis with a strong Sufi influence. The Russians believe Chechnya is a Russian state, but Chechens believe they are an independent country. Although Russia has experienced the birth of some forms of democracy, the central Russian government has revoked many resulting democratic reforms. The Chechens have used suicide operations, including massive suicide attacks. Again, Pape is probably not insisting that the occupying power must be a full democracy, he is pointing to a trend. He evidence suggests trends exist.

The Kurdistan Workers Party (PKK) in eastern Turkey conducted fourteen suicide attacks from 1996 to 1999, and they were unique. They were the least deadly attacks in the course of modern suicide bombing, killing an average of two people per incident. They started when the popular leader of the PKK called for them, and they stopped at his command. More interestingly, they were conducted by long-term members of the group, and they were not followed by more attacks. Pape believes the reason the attacks were never popularized is that the Sunni Kurd community identified with Sunni Turks. Pape (2005, pp. 162–167) found the same trend in the Indian province of Punjab.

Models for Suicide Bombing

There is a debate about modeling attacks. Rohan Gunaratna (2000) suggests it may be possible to model some precursors of suicide bombings. After examining suicide attacks between 1983 and 2000, Gunaratna sees three things that all attacks have in common: secrecy, reconnaissance, and rehearsal. He believes that local groups operate in secret to prepare the bomber and the target area. Because locals can blend in with the surroundings, they provide supplies and information. They also conduct the initial scouting or reconnaissance of the target. A support group far away from the target can rehearse the attack in secrecy; the better the rehearsal, the greater the chance of success. The bomber usually conducts the final reconnaissance during the operation, but he or she can detonate the bomb in case of discovery. These factors could serve as the basis for a model.

Another school of thought suggests that models may exist, but there are so many factors that a single set of precursors cannot exist. Audrey Cronin (2003, pp. 6–8) believes different styles of bombings emerge from different places. The Hamas model, patterned after the actions of Hezbollah, involves a professional group to plan and execute the attack and a support group to prepare the attacker. For many years researchers believed this was the only model for suicide bombing (Institute for Counter-Terrorism, 2001).

Cronin finds, however, that different models emerged over time. The LTTE trained suicide bombers from an early age. The PKK leadership coerced victims to take part in suicide bombings. The September 11 suicide attacks defied the previous models, and bombings in Chechnya represent a different combination of social and psychological factors. There is no single model for suicide bombing.

Self-Check

- *Why is suicide used as a weapon?*
- *What do empirical studies suggest about suicide terrorism?*
- *How might suicide terrorism be stopped?*

SUMMARY

- Tactically, terrorism has basic forms. These include bombing, arson, hijacking, assault, kidnapping, and taking hostages.
- Terrorists use force multipliers to increase their attacking power. Force multipliers include technology, transnational support, media coverage, and religious fanaticism.
- Technology can enhance striking power when it is employed as a weapon or it becomes the target of an attack. Any form of technology may be used. Common forms include cyberterrorism, biological agents, and chemical and radiological weapons.
- Terrorists use the media as a weapon for enhancing the power of attacks, using it to broadcast a political message, gaining publicity for a violent political movement, and providing respectability for their cause.
- The force of terrorism can be multiplied by the selection of transnational economic targets. Tourism, energy, and transportation present excellent opportunities for increasing the economic impact of an attack.
- Religious fanaticism has become a force multiplier and is illustrated by the rebirth of altruistic suicide.
- Pape's theory of suicide terrorism is based on examining religious differences when a democracy occupies a foreign country or the enclave of an ethnic group. Local religious leaders must create a climate where martyrdom is supported.
- It is difficult to model suicide terrorism because there is no single group or individual profile of suicide attackers. Different groups use different methods, and suicide bombers come from a variety of backgrounds.

KEY TERMS

six tactics of terrorism (p. 98)
force multiplier (p. 98)
philosophy of the bomb (p. 99)
thermobaric bomb (p. 100)
bacterial weapons (p. 102)

viral weapons (p. 102)
endemic terrorism (p. 109)
altruistic suicide (p. 111)
theory of suicide terrorism
 (p. 111)

WRITING ASSIGNMENTS

1. How are force multipliers used to increase the amount of violence in a terrorist act? How might this impact an audience's reaction to an event?
2. Terrorists can enhance striking power by using force multipliers, but they can also combine different multipliers to further increase force.

Explain how the media might be used to increase the power of economic targeting. How might other force multipliers interact with one another?

3. Pape states that the theory of religious differences in suicide attacks is not a hard and fast rule. This text also discussed the possibility that an occupying force need not always come from a democratic country. Do these two exceptions invalidate Pape's theory of suicide terrorism?

PART II

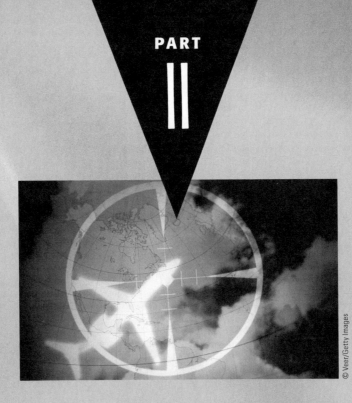

© Veer/Getty Images

THE HISTORY AND DEVELOPMENT OF TERRORISM

6 The Beginnings of Modern Terrorism

Bridgeman-Giraudon/Art Resource, NY

The word "terrorism" was coined during the French Revolution—it was used to describe the actions of the revolutionary French government. During the nineteenth century governments increasingly used the term to describe political dissidents.

Learning Objectives

After reading this chapter, you should be able to

- Define the Enlightenment and describe its impact on radical social change.
- Compare and contrast the American and French Revolutions.
- Summarize the Reign of Terror in France.
- Explain how the meaning of terrorism shifted from descriptions of governmental actions to the actions of governmental opponents.

- Summarize the impact of the 1848 revolutions on Western governments.
- Summarize the role of nineteenth-century anarchists and their influence on revolutionary and nationalistic terrorism.
- Identify the proponents of violent revolutionary change among nineteenth-century anarchists.
- Summarize the debate about the differences between old and new terrorism.

- Summarize the history of Russian revolutionary organizations from the Peoples' Will to the Bolshevik Revolution.

- Describe how the Russian Revolution influenced Western concepts of extremism and terrorism.

errorism did not begin in a vacuum. Many Americans became acutely aware of modern terrorism after the first World Trade Center bombing in 1993 and the bombing of the federal building in Oklahoma City in 1995. Yet modern terrorism began decades, even centuries, before these events. Modern terrorism, at least from the Western perspective, grew from the French Revolution (1789–1799), and the word was originally used to describe the actions of a government, not a band of revolutionaries. Terrorism developed throughout the nineteenth century, changing forms and ideology. As Walter Laqueur observes, the meaning always changed with the flow of historical circumstances, and different times gave different meanings to terms like *terrorism*, *socialism*, and *anarchism*. This chapter traces the origins of Western terrorism from the Enlightenment to Red Terror Russia.

Social Revolution and the Enlightenment

There is a danger when a label is applied to a specific time period; it leads to the assumption that all people living in the period were aware that they were experiencing historical change. For example, the people of the European Middle Ages did not think they were living in the Middle Ages, just as samurai of the Tokugawa (1603–1868) shogunate did not think they were living in feudal Japan. In contrast, many Western people living in the eighteenth century believed it was a time of historic change. Historians often call the eighteenth century the Age of Reason or the **Enlightenment**. Jonathan Israel (2001, pp. 23–29) says there is reason to use the title *Enlightenment* even though the age was full of contradictions, inconsistencies, and political turmoil. Europe had been exhausted by the carnage of the **Thirty Years' War** (1618–1648). To preserve peace, several rulers agreed to tolerate different sects of Christianity within the same realm. During the Enlightenment, theology, Israel says, lost its monopoly on providing answers to all human questions. This gave rise to science and a new age of discovery. The deductive logic of the former age was gradually replaced by empirical observation. The late 1600s and early 1700s proved to be an enlightening time.

Europe and America experienced tremendous economic, political, and social changes. Many people, especially intellectuals and the middle class, dared to question the assumptions of the past. They used the term

Enlightenment
An eighteenth-century intellectual movement following the Scientific Revolution. Also called the Age of Reason, the Enlightenment was characterized by rational thought and the belief that all activities could be explained.

Thirty Years' War
A war beginning as a dispute between Protestants and Roman Catholics in Prague and eventually pitting the north of Europe against the south. The war was savage and devastated the German states. France ended the war by leaving the Catholic alliance to fight against Austria. At the end of the war, Lutherans (and eventually Calvinists) and Roman Catholics agreed to tolerate each other's faith.

enlightenment to describe this time. Dorinda Outram (1995, p. 31) says *enlightenment* meant many things in the 1700s, and one of the definitions involved changes in the approach to political power. Before the Enlightenment, a large segment of the European population was tied to a class of nobles, and smaller groups of people were part of emerging trade and professional classes or free farmers. During the Enlightenment, many Europeans began to question how they were governed, and they sought to increase the political power of the lower classes. Questioning differed around Europe. For example, Christopher Clark (2006, pp. 163–174) points out that Prussian farmers, despite the modern stereotype of Prussian militarism, limited the power of nobles to demand their services in the Enlightenment. They worked for greater autonomy, refusing to serve when nobles were abusive. James Melton (2001, p. 45–46) demonstrates that evolving legal authority in England began to limit the power of the monarch, and the French questioned the authority of their king even more directly. The forces of change during the Enlightenment brought a new way of thinking about citizenship. Ordinary people came to believe the state existed to protect everybody, not just the nobles. The nobles and other people who held power were frightened by this type of thinking.

The Enlightenment was an international intellectual movement. Although diverse in political opinions, the philosophers of the Age of Reason produced a common idea about government. They believed that governments should exist to protect individual rights and that the best form of government was democracy. The philosophers argued that citizens had rights, and governments' duty was to protect those rights. Common people were to control the government by a social contract, or constitution, that spelled out the rights of citizens and limited governmental power. The Enlightenment brought an increased demand for democracy. Such thinking produced tension between the ruling class and the governed, and some of the tension spilled into violence.

The American Revolution, 1775–1783

Americans living in British North America believed Great Britain was evolving toward a government that would protect rights and property. Yet many American colonists also believed these basic rights were denied to Americans. By 1775 American talk of democracy moved from intellectual circles to the streets and eventually to the battlefields. The war began in April 1775 when colonists clashed with British soldiers in Lexington, Massachusetts, and again a few hours later in Concord. The British launched an offensive in Boston to stop the rebellion, but the Continental Congress formed an army. The Second Continental Congress declared independence from Britain on July 4, 1776. The British tried to fight on several fronts at the same time. Although they were frequently successful, American forces remained in the field. The Continental government formed important alliances with France, Spain, and the Netherlands. In October 1781 a major British force surrendered at Yorktown, Virginia. The British army evacuated most of its troops in 1782, and Great Britain and the United States signed a peace treaty in 1783.

The American Revolution was important in Europe, but it was viewed primarily as a "conservative" revolution. Theodore Draper (1996) sums up current thinking about the Revolutionary War. Great Britain had been quite happy to grant local autonomy to several regions of the American colonies. They were responsible for civil functions, law enforcement, and local affairs. Individual states held quite a bit of power. Great Britain cared little about the day-to-day administration and would have found it difficult to manage had it chosen to do so. Draper believes that a simple understanding between Britain and the Colonies emerged. Americans were to assist in the maintenance of the empire, serve as loyal subjects, and contribute to military ventures when needed.

By the mid-1700s America's economic and population expansion threatened Britain. As it tried to exert control, Draper argues, Britain faced an increasing number of people who wanted the democratic rights of English citizens. The desire for independence came late in the war, and it was not supported by the majority of Americans. In 1783 the locus of power moved from London to Philadelphia, and most American leaders (with notable exceptions, such as Thomas Jefferson) perceived the United States to be a British-style democracy without Britain. The birth of the United States was an evolutionary process, but when seen within the context of traditional European power struggles, it was viewed as both a defeat for Great Britain and the formation of an Enlightenment democracy.

The revolution did bring about a profound change, even though it was conservative. It *was* like Great Britain without a monarchy. Democracy was no longer an idea inside the debate circles of Enlightenment philosophers; Americans created a republic based on a representative democracy. It did not change the class structure, but it was a democracy. That idea set the imaginations of some Europeans on fire.

The Enlightenment and the birth of democracy gave rise to two paradoxes. The first deals with the relationship between democracy and terrorism. F. Gregory Gause III (2005) points to a variety of studies about this relationship, and he comes to a depressing conclusion. Terrorist attacks occur more frequently in democracies than in countries with any other form of government. Citing State Department statistics for between 2000 and 2003, Gause finds that out of nearly 530 attacks, almost 390 occurred in countries practicing full or limited democracy. The democracy factor would come into play in the nineteenth century and continue into the twentieth (see Another Perspective: Terror and Democracy). The second paradox appeared much more rapidly. Partially inspired by America's revolution and directly motivated by class inequity and the Enlightenment, French revolutionaries poured into the streets of Paris in 1789. Their actions brought a new meaning to the word *terrorism*.

Terror and Democracy

Many terrorism analysts believe that terrorists need democratic states to function. Totalitarian states, they argue, make it impossible to engage in covert activities. Terrorists need freedom of speech, freedom of thought, and freedom of action. Jenny Hocking takes the opposite view. In reaction to a terrorist attack in Bali, Indonesia, in 2002, the Australian government followed the path of the United States, Hocking says. Political rights have been trampled in the name of the war on terrorism. A counterterrorist network invades civil liberties in Australia, and the Australian Intelligence Security Service has been given permission to pry into the lives of law-abiding citizens. Terrorism is a threat, but overreaction also threatens democracies. The internment of terrorist suspects without charge or trial is a greater threat than terrorism.

Source: Hocking, 2004.

The French Revolution, 1789–1799

The French Revolution was based on the same enlightened principles of the American Revolution, but it took a very different and much more deadly tone. During the 1700s, French merchants and manufacturers were able to accumulate vast wealth from business profits, but they were not adequately represented in the feudal hierarchy of the French ruling class. Nobles and the clergy paid no taxes, but workers, the new middle class, and the poor did. In 1789 King Louis XVI called an Assembly of Notables of the **Estates General**, because only the Assembly had the authority to raise taxes. Unfortunately for Louis, the Estates General gave way to a National Assembly, and the new legislative body revolted. The revolt took a more radical turn when the National Assembly dissolved and formed an assembly to create a new government in 1791. The monarchies of Europe declared war on France, and the king tried to flee. He was captured and eventually executed. The radical revolution continued. A **National Convention** was elected in 1792, and it appointed a **Committee of Public Safety** in 1793. Controlled by radicals, the Committee of Public Safety executed thousands of nobles and clergy as France managed to stave off invading monarchies. Executions spread from Paris to the countryside. A new government formed in 1795, but France remained in political and economic chaos. In 1799 a middle-class general, Napoleon Bonaparte, returned from a disastrous expedition in Egypt and took over the government, ending the revolution. The French Revolution had been extremely bloody and was the first revolution in the modern sense of the word.

The American Revolution transferred power from the British upper classes to American upper classes. In France power was transferred *between* classes. If America represented a long-term evolutionary process toward democracy, France represented a radical shift in power structures. Not only did European governments take notice but the nobles and their upper-class supporters feared for their way of life and their

Estates General
An assembly in prerevolutionary France consisting of all but the lowest class. The Estates General had not been called since 1614, but Louis XVI assembled them in 1789 in response to demands from the Assembly of Notables who had been called to address the financial problems of France. Radical elements in the Estates General revolted, and the disruption led to the French Revolution.

National Convention
Elected in 1792, it broke from the Estates General and called for a constitutional assembly. The Convention served as the major legislative body of France until it was replaced by the Directory in 1795.

very lives. They mobilized their armies to stop the French, subjecting Europe to war for twenty years.

The Reign of Terror

The term *terrorism* appeared during this period. Edmund Burke, a noted British political philosopher of the eighteenth century, used the word to describe the situation in revolutionary Paris. He referred to the violence as the **Reign of Terror**, and he used the word *terrorism* to describe the actions of the new government. Members and associates of the Committee of Public Safety were called terrorists by French nobles, their families, and sympathizers. From 1794 to 1795 the French government conducted 17,000 legal executions. Some scholars estimate there were 23,000 additional illegal executions (Tilly, 2004). Class violence ripped through France as middle- and working-class revolutionaries tore power from the hands of the social elite and the state-sponsored Roman Catholic Church. But as the government consolidated power, the would-be democracy gave way to Napoleon Bonaparte and military authoritarianism. Hundreds of thousands more would die.

Guerrillas and the Spanish Peninsula

In the Napoleonic Wars the meaning of *terrorism* started to undergo a subtle transformation. Napoleon invaded **Spain in 1807**, and his army would face a type of threat that it had not experienced up to that point. Small bands of Spanish partisans began to attack French troops. Frequently armed and supported by the British army, the partisans attacked the French in unconventional manners. They could not gather and face a French corps on a battlefield, but they could murder off-duty soldiers, attack supply columns, and engage in hit-and-run tactics. The Spanish called the partisans patriots, but the French referred to them as terrorists. The meaning of terrorism shifted away from governmental repression and seemed to apply to those who resisted governments. This definitional transformation would continue throughout the nineteenth century (Tamas, 2001).

Self-Check

- *How did the Enlightenment revolutions differ in France and the United States?*
- *Why did the French Revolution have a major impact on terrorism?*
- *How did the meaning of terrorism change from the French Revolution to the Napoleonic Wars?*

▼ 1848 and the Radical Democrats

The reason the meaning of terrorism changed in Western minds was essentially because of the nature of European violence in the 1800s. The French Revolution did not bring democracy; it brought Napoleon. The

Committee of Public Safety

Assembled by Maximilien Robespierre (1758–1794) to conduct the war against invading monarchal powers, and it evolved into the executive body of France. The Committee of Public Safety initiated the Reign of Terror.

Reign of Terror

The name given to the repressive period in France 1794–1795. The revolutionary government accused thousands of French nobles and clergy of plotting to restore the monarchy. Executions began in Paris and spread through the countryside. Large mobs attacked and terrorized nobles in rural areas. Summary executions without trial were quite common.

Spain in 1807

The Peninsula War (1808–1814), which began when Spanish and French forces divided Portugal in 1807. Napoleon, whose army entered Spain in 1807, attempted to use his forces to capture the Spanish throne in 1808. British forces under Sir Arthur Wellesley, later Duke of Wellington, joined Spanish forces loyal to the king of Spain and Spanish partisans to fight the French.

radical democrats

Those who tried to bring democracy to all classes. They sought a more equitable distribution of wealth throughout all economic classes, believing that concentrated wealth and class inequities prevented societies from becoming truly democratic.

socialists

Radical democrats who sought wealth equality in capitalist societies. Some socialists sought governmental guarantees of living standards. Others believed that the state should control industry and divide profits among all members of society. Others believed that people would form cooperative relationships on their own with no need of a government.

communists

Socialists who believe in a strong centralized economy controlled by a strong central government. Their ideas were summarized in *The Communist Manifesto*, written by Karl Marx and Friedrich Engels in 1848.

anarchists

Those in the nineteenth century who advocated the creation of cooperative societies without centralized governments. There were many forms of anarchy. In the popular understanding of the late nineteenth and

Napoleonic Wars continued until 1815, and a new international order emerged. Although democracy continued to grow in the United States and the United Kingdom, royalists reasserted their power in the rest of Europe. Under the surface, however, democratic ideas continued to grow. The ideas led to further political struggles and demands for freedom.

The democrats of the early 1800s were not united. Most of them believed in middle-class democracy, and they were reluctant to take to the streets if a legislative process was available. They believed they could create constitutional monarchies and evolve into a system of democracy as the United States had done. The main objective of most European middle-class democrats from approximately 1815 to 1848 was to obtain constitutions to ensure liberty. Several of the German states began writing constitutions, but they were thwarted by monarchal forces and decisively defeated in 1848–49. Austrian and Russian monarchs simply controlled all governmental processes. In the wake of failure, disgruntled democrats began to speak of nonlegislative avenues for change.

Radical democrats demanded immediate and drastic change. They not only were interested in developing constitutions but wanted to distribute evenly the wealth created by trade and manufacturing. Many **socialists**, including a group of socialists called **communists**, argued for centralized control of the economy. **Anarchists**, sometime allies and sometime foes of the socialists, sought to reduce or to eliminate centralized government. The wealthy owners of industry, known as capitalists, were politically powerful, and many people from the middle class prospered when capitalist enterprises expanded. They opposed all forms of socialism and anarchy. Radical democrats felt the capitalists were little better than the royalists. They wanted all people to be equal, and they argued that democracy should be based not only on freedom but also on economic equality. This meant the class structure and distribution of wealth also had to be reorganized. This frightened the newly emergent capitalist and middle classes in the same way the French Revolution had scared European royalty. The radical democrats called for class revolution.

The revolution came in 1848. The conservative system established by governments after the Napoleonic Wars was antidemocratic. As constitutional movements failed in many countries, people grew restless. Parisians took to the streets in February 1848, and they overthrew the government. Many people in other European capitals followed suit, and by autumn almost every major European country had experienced unrest or revolution. In some cases, such as Berlin in Prussia, the army came to restore order. In other cases, such as France, a new republic was proclaimed. The middle class saw some gains, but most workers did not.

Governmental control was slowly restored in Europe between 1848 and 1849, but new class awareness and unrest emerged. The 1848 revolutions fostered working-class distaste for the distribution of wealth and power. George Woodcock (2004, p. 81) says the 1789 French Revolution ushered in a new class structure, but it also resulted in a new economic system, capitalism, and a centralized state. The conservative system after

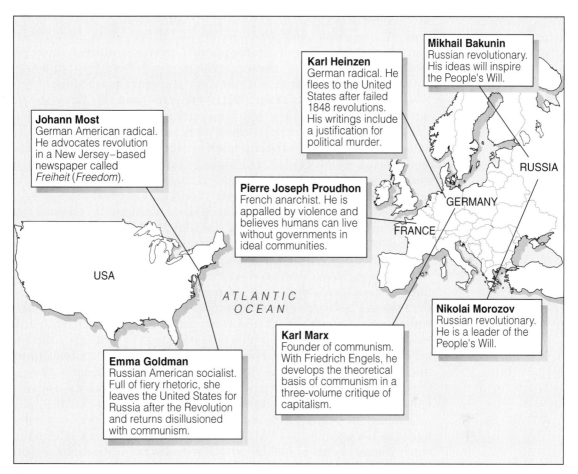

Mikhail Bakunin
Russian revolutionary.
His ideas will inspire
the People's Will.

Karl Heinzen
German radical. He
flees to the United
States after failed
1848 revolutions.
His writings include
a justification for
political murder.

Johann Most
German American radical.
He advocates revolution
in a New Jersey–based
newspaper called
Freiheit (*Freedom*).

RUSSIA

GERMANY

Pierre Joseph Proudhon
French anarchist. He is
appalled by violence and
believes humans can live
without governments in
ideal communities.

FRANCE

USA

ATLANTIC
OCEAN

Nikolai Morozov
Russian revolutionary.
He is a leader of the
People's Will.

Karl Marx
Founder of communism.
With Friedrich Engels, he
develops the theoretical
basis of communism in a
three-volume critique of
capitalism.

Emma Goldman
Russian American socialist.
Full of fiery rhetoric, she
leaves the United States for
Russia after the Revolution
and returns disillusioned
with communism.

Figure 6.1
Anarchists and Socialists

1815 tried to restrain the middle class as a new group of wealthy capitalists displaced nobility. In 1848 radical democrats revolted but failed to
change the system. Craig Calhoun (1989) adds that the 1848 street revolutions demonstrated that common people were aware of economic tensions, even if they were not able to change the social structure. In this
sense, the issues of 1848 were an extension of the class revolution of 1789.
The rebels were defeated in the street, and they moved underground.

early twentieth centuries,
anarchists were seen as
violent socialist revolutionaries. Antiglobalists calling
themselves anarchists have
little resemblance to their
earlier counterparts.

Socialists

Three strains of radical democrats coalesced after the failed revolutions
of 1848: communists, socialists, and anarchists (Figure 6.1). Socialists
wanted to completely democratize society and assume control of industrial production. They believed that a strong state would ensure that
profits from industry were distributed in an egalitarian manner. Communism represented a particular form of socialism, and it advocated a

strong centralized government, the elimination of all classes except the working class, and a complete state monopoly over all forms of industrial and agricultural production. Socialists and communists agreed that wealth was not a private matter. It belonged to all workers. Although many socialists embraced communism, communists denounced socialists who failed to advocate for strong state controls. Many socialists emphasized democracy over the centralized power of communism (see Levin, 2003). The radical democrats believed political power should be held in common. Their concept of socialism was especially popular among some groups of displaced workers. Unfortunately, the upper and middle classes frequently believed terrorism and socialism were the same thing (A. Roberts, 2002).

One of the chief spokespersons and intellectuals in the socialist camp was the founder of communism, Karl Marx (1818–1883). He finished a PhD in philosophy in 1841 and moved to Paris shortly thereafter. He met Friedrich Engels and formed a lifelong friendship. He outlined theories of socialism in several writings, including a three-volume critique of capitalism. Marx believed that social structure is arranged by the material circumstances surrounding existence. Humans shape the environment through work and even produce more than they need. Marx referred to this extra production as *surplus*. In medieval societies, nobles controlled the surplus production of peasants, but control shifted to capitalists with the end of the Middle Ages. Marx and Engels claimed the capitalist economic system exploited the lower classes for the benefit of others. He called for a change in the system.

Despite the many labels applied to him and the derogatory statements of his enemies, Karl Marx was not a terrorist. Marx referred to "revolutionary" change, but he never clarified what he meant by revolution. Further, he did not advocate political bombing and assassination. In fact, on most occasions he publicly condemned it. He believed socialism was to be a reflection of democracy, not violence. A massive seizure of power by the general population might be justified, but individual acts of murder were not.

The process of democratization was slow, however, and some of the radical democrats began to feel violent revolution was the only possible course of action. A few radical democrats went underground, choosing subversive violence as a means to challenge authority. They became popularly known as terrorists because they hoped to achieve social revolution by terrorizing the capitalist class and its supporters.

Anarchists

Anarchists shared many ideas about the egalitarian nature of society with the socialists, but they disagreed on the function of the state. The term *anarchy* was not new. It originated several hundred years earlier when Greek philosophers spoke of eliminating governments, but the nineteenth-century anarchists were also concerned with the distribution of wealth. This frightened the upper classes, which already associated socialism with terrorism. Pierre Joseph Proudhon (1809–1865) was one of the advocates of modern anarchism. His political activities eventually landed him in a French prison, but Proudhon was not a man of violence. He called for the extension of democracy to all classes, to be accomplished through the elimination of property and government. Property was to be commonly held, and families living in extended communes were to replace centralized government.

Proudhon disagreed with Karl Marx and other socialists about the role of government. Most socialists saw centralized government as a necessary evil. As the democrats did, the socialists believed government had to exist to protect the individual rights of citizens. Communists took the role of the state further, insisting on a strong central government. Proudhon, on the other hand, believed all government was evil. Proudhon had revolutionary ideals, but he was a man of peace. He believed that anarchy would develop peacefully as people learned about the structure of governments and the capitalist economy. Not all of Proudhon's disciples were of the same peaceful bent. They came to see themselves as revolutionaries, and they would have growing influence on terrorism in the second half of the nineteenth century.

Violent Anarchism

Despite the rhetoric, both the socialists and anarchists engaged in more talk than action after the 1848 revolutions. Both groups debated the efficacy and morality of violence, and most of the people who called for revolution spoke of mass action, not individual violence. Walter Laqueur (1999, p. 12) says the socialists and anarchists rejected terrorism on practical and theoretical grounds. Practically, terrorism could not promise strategic success, and many of the revolutionary theorists rejected violence in general. Marxists and anarchists favored strikes, demonstrations, and other mass actions.

Richard Jensen (2004) also believes that the initial calls in history for revolution cannot be associated with terrorism. Even though socialists and anarchists disagreed about the path for creating a new society, they avoided violence. Those who advocated violence usually did so only rhetorically. But this changed in the 1880s as anarchists began assassinating heads of state. The media sensationalized anarchist events, leading people to conclude that anarchism was a vast international conspiracy of terror. By 1880 the press and politicians had collapsed all forms of socialism into the generic term *anarchism*, and anarchists were deemed terrorists in popular opinion.

How did this change occur? Richard Jensen says several factors merged to create a culture of terrorism among some members of the anarchist movement. He outlines some of the reasons, and other researchers have identified a number of factors (Laqueur and Alexander, 1987; Laqueur, 1999; Epstein, 2001; Woodcock, 2004; Clutterbuck, 2004; Grob-Fitzgibbon, 2004). The combined ideas reveal a pattern in the transformation of some anarchists from rhetoric to violence.

The first cause for transformation can be found in the growing numbers of people attracted to the movement. Proudhon rejected violence, but new followers brought conflicting ideas. As debates grew more intense, no single view seemed to define either socialism or anarchism. Sometimes the debates caused splits inside the movement and various camps formed. The anarchist movement contained a variety of political viewpoints, and some schools of thought favored violence over peaceful social change.

Economic change also influenced the anarchist movement. As wealth shifted to capitalists in the early and mid-nineteenth century, new entrepreneurs consolidated economic power in the last decades of the 1800s. This fostered new alliances and realignment with middle-class political parties. Proudhon and other anarchists spoke of an evolution toward communal socialism, but the new political structure effectively blocked peaceful change. Middle classes, the **bourgeois**, dominated the political scene in western Europe and America, and their interests tended to coincide with the interests of capitalists.

Economic consolidation was accompanied by social stress. Labor movements attempted to foster an international relationship among workers from all countries. Hundreds of anarchists flocked to Paris, voicing their approval of the labor movement. As some anarchists turned to violence, journalists and politicians viewed all forms of labor violence as a manifestation of an international anarchist conspiracy against capitalism. In central and eastern Europe, police cracked down on revolutionary activity, creating a two-fold cycle. Each repressive measure sent more revolutionaries to the west, where violent activities continued, and anarchist violence intensified in central and eastern Europe to retaliate for governmental crackdowns.

Nationalistic factors also influenced the growth and spread of violence after 1880. Although many people viewed anarchism as an international conspiracy, it emerged differently in each country. Spanish anarchism involved artisans and skilled workers who were displaced by economic shifts. They had difficulty attracting urban workers to their movement because the living standards of industrial wage earners actually increased. Italian anarchism was tied to internal struggles for national unification, and French anarchists were inevitably caught up in the Franco-Prussian War of 1870 to 1871. Germany and Austria witnessed the growth of internal police to protect the **Hohenzollerns** and **Hapsburgs**, and the remainder of central and eastern Europe saw increased political repression. Despite—or maybe because of—repression, Russia gave birth to a revolutionary anarchist group. The United States and the United Kingdom experienced increased rhetoric, labor violence, and social unrest. The common factor in all countries was murder. Anarchists championed political assassination.

The importance of assassination cannot be overemphasized. It was propaganda by deed, the ultimate expression, as Alex Schmid (Schmid and Jongman, 2005, pp. 21–25) called it, of political frustration. Violent

bourgeois

The middle class. *Bourgeoisie* (plural) in Marxist terminology refers to tradespeople, merchants, artisans and other nonpeasants excluded from the upper classes in medieval Europe. Marx called the European democracies after the French Revolution bourgeois governments, and he advocated a democracy dominated by workers.

Hohenzollern

The ruling family of Brandenburg and Prussia that ruled a united Germany from 1871–1914.

Hapsburg

The ruling family of Austria (1282–1918), the Austro-Hungarian Empire (1437–1918), and the Holy Roman Empire (1282–1806). Another branch of the family ruled in Spain (1516–1700). Reference here is to the Austrian royal family.

anarchists wanted to send the message that no industrialist was safe and that the capitalist order would crumble under the philosophy of the bomb. Governments, journalists, and the population in general believed the message, supporting overactive measures against anything that remotely resembled left-wing violence. This trend would last well into the twentieth century. In addition, assassinations were not simply abstractions. Police officials, politicians, royal leaders, and presidents were killed by anarchists from Russia to the United States from 1880 to 1900.

The final factor influencing the adoption of violent action was the invention of dynamite. Alfred Noble blended explosive material with chemicals, cotton, and refined clay to produce an explosive twenty times more powerful than black powder. To be sure, the power of dynamite was often overestimated. One anarchist claimed that ten pounds of it could sink a battleship. But dynamite gave an individual or small group a psychological edge. For the first time in history, a small group had a technological force multiplier that allowed it to launch a major attack. Rhetoric gave birth to propaganda by the deed, but dynamite fostered the philosophy of the bomb.

Rhetoric, Internal Debates, and Action

By 1880 various groups of left-wing revolutionaries came to be known as anarchists in the popular mind. This was partially due to simplification and sensationalism in the press, but it also resulted from internal debates in the socialist movements. The debate began when Marx separated from Proudhon. Marx believed Proudhon's advocacy of cooperative, nonauthoritarian communities was an unachievable utopian ideal. Marx called for worker control of industry and a strong, centralized state dictatorship. This initial split resulted in further fragmentation in the left-wing movement and the eventual endorsement of violence.

Peter Prokoptin (1842–1921), a Russian prince turned anarchist, continued to advocate for an evolutionary pattern. George Woodcock (2004) says Prokoptin and other nonviolent anarchists saw themselves as part of a tradition dating back to prehistory. Prokoptin believed humanity existed between two competing tendencies: cooperation and authoritarianism. Cooperation involved mutual aid and altruistic humanitarianism. Prokoptin called it the creative spirit of the masses. It is evidenced in the emergence of tribes, villages, and trade guilds; all created, according to Prokoptin, without legislation. Authoritarianism competed with the cooperative tendency. Humans tended to arrange themselves in hierarchies and give authority to their leaders. Prokoptin stated sarcastically that this tendency began with witch doctors and rainmakers and ended with military bands. Woodcock says Prokoptin believed every period in human history was dominated by the tension between cooperative anarchy and authoritarianism. He rhetorically called for revolution, but abhorred violence. The forces of history worked against the interests of every centralized government, and Prokoptin believed that human cooperation would dominate the final period of human existence.

Mikhail Bakunin (1814–1876) rejected Prokoptin's nonviolent anarchy, calling for "propaganda by the deed." Barbara Epstein (2001) says Bakunin vehemently disagreed with advocates of peaceful change. Revolutionaries could not use the state as an instrument of emancipation because it was inherently oppressive. The state must be destroyed, and its destruction would come when masses of people recognized they were being exploited by the state. Anarchists could not attach themselves to an authoritarian structure in the way Marxists and some socialists did. He encouraged bombings and individual assassinations as a means of awakening the masses to reality. After spending ten years in prison following the 1848 revolutions, Bakunin championed Proudhon's ideas of international revolution, according to Richard Jensen (2004).

The trend changed. Karl Heinzen (1809–1880), a radical German democrat who embraced anarchy, came to the United States after the 1848 revolutions failed in Europe. Benjamin Grob-Fitzgibbon (2004) believes that Heinzen sat at a pivotal point, where modern terrorism can be directly related to the past. Grob-Fitzgibbon criticizes theories that state terrorism was linked to the anarchists and other radical democrats. They were assassins at worst, he argues, not the forerunners of modern terrorism, with its indiscriminate killing. Heinzen was different because he advocated political murder—murder that could be arbitrarily distributed through society. Walter Laqueur (1999, p. 13) believes Heinzen's theories were relatively insignificant until Johann Most (1846–1906) published Heinzen's writings in a radical newspaper, *Freiheit* (*Freedom*), in New Jersey. Most, a German born in Augsburg, immigrated to the United States in the late 1800s. Like Heinzen, he did not believe capitalist societies would change peacefully. He advocated terrorism in *Freiheit* and called for violent action, the best form of propaganda. The philosophy of the bomb was the method for communicating such propaganda, according to Most. Grob-Fitzgibbon believes this represents the beginning of modern terrorism. Laqueur (1999, pp. 11–12) agrees.

Heinzen and Most represent an important transition in the history of Western terrorism. Terrorism began with a group of radical revolutionaries conducting mass executions in the name of the French government. There was a subtle shift in meaning as Spanish partisans terrorized French troops with irregular tactics after the 1807 French invasion of Spain, and the meaning changed further as anarchists, socialists, and communists were labeled terrorists. Despite the label, nineteenth-century anarchists were not terrorists (see Laqueur and Alexander, 1987; Laqueur, 1999, p. 13; Grob-Fitzgibbon, 2004). In a Canadian television interview cited by Grob-Fitzgibbon (2004), David Rapoport, a noted authority on the development of modern terrorism, argued that the anarchists of the nineteenth century were a far cry from modern terrorists. When the anarchists engaged in violence, it was targeted toward either a specific person or group. It did not involve striking innocent people who had little to do with a cause.

Outdated History?

Michael Schreuer, former director of the CIA's bin Laden unit, believes the focus on history is often misplaced. There are two types of terrorist experts, he contends, retired governmental and military officials and informed commentators. The last group is made up of academics and journalists. Scheuer believes these people are far from experts because not only do they fail to understand history but they are stuck in a time frame. Media consciousness about terrorism developed and grew in the 1970s. Two issues dominated terrorism, the cold war and violence around Israel and Palestine. Expertise about terrorism came from studying both the emergence of theory, with its roots in the West, and the anticolonial movements associated with the early part of the cold war. Terrorism was a historical phenomenon, an outcome of confrontations growing from the influence of Western history. Ideological groups such as the Baader-Meinhof Gang or the Red Brigades came from political battlefields. Nationalistic groups such as the Puerto Rican Armed Forces of National Liberation (FALN) or the Basque Nation and Liberty (ETA) were motivated by patriotism, but they also centered on leftist agendas. The anti-Western attitude of Palestinian groups like Hezbollah and the Abu Nidal Organization was tinged with a left-wing philosophy and a style of operation similar to their counterparts in ideological and nationalistic movements. Western expertise was honed over two decades, from 1970 to 1990, Scheuer says, and it has very little to do with terrorism today.

Jihadist terrorism comes from a different tradition. It does not rely on political and theoretical developments in the West, and although jihadists frequently embrace the cause of the Palestinians, they do not seek to establish an independent Palestinian state or replace a destroyed Israel with a new Arab country. They come from a religious tradition dating from the twelfth century on the Western calendar, and they operate in a manner far different from terrorist groups in the late twentieth century. Expertise on the old-style groups is not applicable to the jihadists, Scheuer concludes. So-called terrorism experts are outdated. They are stuck in the past and examine modern terrorism through a perspective "yellowed with age."

Source: Scheuer, 2006, pp. 20–23.

Selective and nonselective destruction became the dichotomy between "old" and "new" terrorism in the late 1980s and early 1990s. Walter Laqueur (1987, p. 91) argues that modern terrorists are more ruthless than their historical counterparts were. Not only does Laqueur believe the terrorism of historical terrorists was mainly rhetorical but he also points out that anarchists were extremely selective about their targets. He cites one case in which an anarchist refused to toss a bomb at a Russian official because he was afraid he would injure innocent bystanders. Laqueur notes that this sensitivity is hardly typical of modern-day terrorists. He says modern terrorism has been typified by indiscriminate violence and the intentional targeting of the civilian population. Modern terrorists strike at governments by killing their citizens: They strike airliners, buses, and other targets containing innocent noncombatants with no vested interest in the outcome of a political struggle. Modern terrorists engage in the sensationalized murder of innocents and come from another tradition (Scheuer, 2006; see Another Perspective: Outdated History?).

Grob-Fitzgibbon (2004) and Jensen (2004) offer competing evidence for this view. They point to Heinzen and Most as progenitors of mass terrorism. They argue that Sergey Nechaev (1847–1882), a Russian anarchist who even murdered a fellow revolutionary, was absolutely ruthless. He cared for no innocent victims, and his purpose was to kill. Laqueur admits that some of the anarchists were violent, but still draws a distinction. Nechaev and others advocated murder, but they did not conduct attacks that resulted in massive innocent casualties. In this sense, new terrorism—as practiced in the late twentieth century—differs from the old terrorism of the nineteenth century.

Isabelle Duyvesteyn (2004) says the debate between old and new terrorism involves a false dichotomy. She believes that modern terrorism is directly related to past practices. If there is a new terrorism, she argues, it needs to be confirmed by rigorous testing and the presentation of evidence. No such evidence has been produced. The label "new" should be applied only on the basis of historical research, and it is necessary to conceive of terrorism in the same rational form across time if comparisons are to be made. In other words, to differentiate between old and new terrorism, the term must have the same meaning in 1848 as it does today. Using the labels "old" and "new," she concludes, does nothing to clarify contemporary problems.

Anarchism and Nationalism

If the 1800s witnessed the growth of anarchism, it also saw the growth of nationalism in the West. As anarchists called for an end to government, nationalistic organizations demanded the right to self-government. Many nationalists adopted the tactics of the anarchists to fight the foreign powers occupying their lands. Nationalistic groups throughout Europe turned to the philosophy of the bomb, and nationalist terrorists began to follow the pattern set by the violent anarchists.

Nationalistic groups did not view themselves as terrorists. They believed anarchists were fighting for ideas. Nationalists believed they were fighting for their countries. Anarchists were socially isolated, but nationalists could hope for the possibility of greater support. Governments labeled them terrorists, but nationalists saw themselves as unconventional soldiers in a national cause. Nationalists believed they were fighting patriotic wars. They adopted only the tactics of the anarchists, not their ideology.

The nationalistic Irish Republican Army (IRA) grew from this period. Unlike anarchists, the IRA did not reject the notion of governmental control; rather, the IRA wanted to nationalize it. The IRA believed Ireland was entitled to self-government. Their weakness relative to the government's power caused them to use the terrorist tactics fostered by the anarchists. In the twentieth century, other nationalistic groups in Europe followed the example of the IRA. (See Chapter 7 for the development of terrorism in the IRA.)

Even though two distinct positions had emerged, it is not possible to completely separate nineteenth-century anarchism and nationalism. Grant Wardlaw (1982, pp. 18–24) sees a historical continuation from anarchism to nationalistic terrorism. Richard Rubenstein (1987, pp. 122–125) makes this point by looking at contemporary anarchist and nationalistic groups. Rubenstein says the stages terrorists must go through to employ violence are similar for both types of terrorism. The moral justification for anarchist and nationalistic terrorism is essentially the same.

J. Bowyer Bell (1976) gives an excellent example of the links between the anarchist and nationalistic traditions by examining the IRA. Since 1916 the IRA has been inundated with socialist revolutionaries and nationalists who reject some aspects of socialism. Even though the two sides have frequently been at odds, both groups are heir to the same tradition. Modern nationalistic terrorism has its roots in anarchism. Both traditions formed the framework of modern European terrorism.

Terrorism in the modern sense came from violent anarchists in the late 1800s. The anarchists were based in western Europe, but they carried their campaign to other parts of the world. The most successful actions took place in Russia before the 1905 and 1917 revolutions. Anarchist groups assassinated several Russian officials, including the czar. Anarchism also spread to the United States. In America it took the form of labor violence, and American anarchists, usually immigrants from Europe, saw themselves linked to organized labor. The anarchist movement in America did not gain as much strength as the movement in Europe, and American anarchists were generally relegated to industrial areas. Right-wing extremism was not part of the anarchist movement, but by the mid-twentieth century, right-wing groups began to imitate tactics of violent anarchists.

Lindsay Clutterbuck (2004) states that most analysts believe modern terrorism derived from the blend of anarchism and nationalism in Russia after the assassination of Czar Alexander II in 1881. She argues that the major influence came from early twentieth-century Ireland. Both issues will be examined here. This chapter ends with a discussion of revolutionary Russia, and Chapter 7 contains a summary of violence in Ireland.

A Contemporary Analogy?

It is not possible to transport the values and attitudes of one period of history into another, but it is possible to examine current events through historical analogy. Before moving to revolutions in Russia, one footnote should be considered. The nineteenth-century anarchists caused a panic, and their activities were sensationalized by the press. Richard Jensen (2004) says the fear caused by dynamite and random explosions had a negative psychological effect on Europeans and Americans. People feared anarchism, and they believed that anarchists were involved in an international conspiracy designed to topple Western governments. Shortly after the turn of the twentieth century in the United States, Jensen notes, Theodore Roosevelt claimed that every aspect of national policy sank to insignificance when compared to the suppression of anarchy.

Yet the anarchists failed, and it was due neither to police nor to other governmental action. Barbara Epstein (2001) says they attempted to ally with the labor movement, but labor leaders could not support random violence. George Woodcock (2004) adds the anarchists were simply out of touch with the forces of history. They lived at a time when state power and industrialization were centralizing. He believes that anarchism was not revolutionary; it was a reaction to economic consolidation and the centralized state. He notes that anarchism was strongest where industrialization was weakest.

If Woodcock is correct, industrialized states ironically feared anarchism more than agrarian states. As anarchism and labor violence grew from 1880 in the United States, fear of anarchism increased. Several events such as the assassination of President McKinley in 1901, the Russian Revolution of 1917, and the Boston police strike and Red Scare of 1919 alarmed many Americans. As fear increased, attorney general A. Mitchell Palmer, known as the "Fighting Quaker," took extraconstitutional measures in the name of defending liberty from the anarchists. In doing so, he repressed radicals and violated the civil liberties of several Americans. To be sure, anarchist violence was a threat. In addition to random violence, radicals conducted a bombing campaign in 1919, but this hardly threatened to topple the United States government. Most historians believe that Palmer overreacted (see Cole, 2003). It might be wise to wonder, in the wake of 9/11, whether there are contemporary parallels of overreaction.

Self-Check

- *Describe the various schools of revolutionary thought in the mid-nineteenth century.*
- *Why did governments refer to these movements as terrorism?*
- *How did these revolutionaries differ from the Enlightenment revolutionaries?*

Joseph Stalin
The dictator who succeeded Lenin. Stalin solidified communist control of Russia through a secret-police organization. He purged the government of all suspected opponents in the 1930s, killing thousands of people.

Terrorism and Revolution in Russia: 1881–1921

The historiography of the Russian Revolution and the fighting that took place afterward has changed drastically since the collapse of the Soviet Union. Histories written during the cold war tended to be either pro- or anticommunist. As documents and archives became available to Western writers in the past few years, views of Russia changed and new histories and biographies emerged. Sheila Fitzpatrick (2001) views the revolution from a perspective that begins with revolt and ends several years after the rise of communism as **Joseph Stalin** (1878–1953) purged and executed his enemies in the 1930s. Robert Service (1995) concludes a three-volume biography of **Vladimir Lenin** (1870–1924) with a picture of a ruthless man who forged policy by force of will. Service's Lenin is a man who was not interested in power for its own sake and who genuinely wanted to create a better socialist state. Confrontations forced him to compromise in the end. Katerina Clark (1998) presents the tremendous culture shifts from 1913 to 1931 by focusing on St. Petersburg from late czarist times until Stalin consolidated power. Christopher Read (1996) divides his view into two periods: the collapse of czarist Russia and the building of the new socialist order. Service (2005) brings another perspective, completely rewriting the history of Russia from the fall of the czar to the rise of Vladimir Putin.

At the time of the revolution, however, the West viewed the communist state with horror. They equated communism with anarchism and revolution. The reason is that class revolution became a reality in Russia, and the West feared Russia would export revolution through terrorism. Late-nineteenth-century Russia differed significantly from the other great powers of Europe. Class distinctions between nobles and peasants were virtually the same as they had been before the French Revolution, and Russian peasants were beset by poverty. Industry had come to some of Russia's cities, but Russia's economic and governmental systems were not adequate to handle the changes. Czar Alexander II (ruled 1855 to 1881) vowed to make changes in the system. When he attempted to do so, he found himself in the midst of revolutionary terrorism.

The Peoples' Will

Three groups in Russia after 1850 felt they could reform and modernize the Russian state, but they disagreed about the ways to do it. One group, whose views Czar Alexander shared, wanted to modernize Russia from the top down. Another group, the intellectuals, wanted Russia to become a liberal Western democracy. Violent anarchists took another path. They believed Russian problems could be settled through revolution. Narodnaya Voyla (the Peoples' Will) advocated violent socialist revolution. When it launched a campaign of revolutionary terrorism in the 1870s, it faced confrontation with conservative elements such as the church, police, and military. Members of the Peoples' Will came to believe it was necessary to terrorize these conservative organizations into submission.

The motivations behind the Peoples' Will evolved out of Russian revolutionary thought. According to Laqueur (1999, pp. 15–16), the philosophy of anarchist terrorism in Russia was embodied by Mikhail Bakunin and Sergey Nechaev. Their revolutionary thought developed separately, before they met each other in the 1860s, when they formed an intellectual union. Both spoke of revolt against the czar, and both endorsed violence as the means to do it. Yet even in the nation that would experience a violent anarchist campaign and eventually a communist revolution, Bakunin and Nechaev basically stuck to rhetoric.

Vladimir Lenin

The Russian revolutionary who helped lead a revolution in February 1917 and who led a second revolution in October, bringing the communists to power. Lenin led the communists in a civil war and set up a dictatorship to enforce communist rule in Russia.

Although they were ideologically linked to anarchism in western Europe, they were distinct from their Western supporters. Russian anarchists were writing for a general population in the hope of sparking a democratic revolution. Laqueur says their significance was their influence on later revolutionaries and the violence and assassinations those later revolutionaries committed. They were not radical revolutionaries in Laqueur's view.

Sheila Fitzpatrick (2001, pp. 19–21) presents a different view. Russian economic progress dominated the last part of the nineteenth and early part of the twentieth centuries. The problem came in the attitudes of peasants and industrial workers. According to Marx, agrarian peasants did not have enough motivation to join the **proletariat** in revolution, but Fitzpatrick says Russia was different. Revolutionary sympathy was high among the peasantry, giving them a closer relationship with many urban workers. Revolutionary rhetoric and writings had touched the lower classes, but Russian economic prosperity had not. The lower classes were receptive to revolution, although as Christopher Read (1996, p. 294) illustrates, no single theme dominated the revolutionaries until it was imposed by the state under Lenin.

proletariat

A Marxist term to describe the working class.

Regardless of the debate, the writings of the Russians were powerful. Nechaev (reprint 1987, pp. 68–71) laid down the principles of revolution in the "Catechism of the Revolutionary." His spirit has been reflected in writings of the late twentieth century. Rubenstein compared the "Catechism" to Carlos Marighella's *The Minimanual of the Urban Guerrilla* and found no essential differences. Both Laqueur and Rubenstein believe that Nechaev's influence lives on. Bakunin (1866, pp. 65–68) believed the Russian government had been established on thievery. In "Revolution, Terrorism, Banditry" he argued that the only method of breaking the state's hold on power was revolt. Such rhetoric did not endear Nechaev and Bakunin to the czar, but it did make them popular with later revolutionaries. Laqueur (1999) concludes that such revolutionary pronouncements correctly belong with Russian expressionist literature, not terrorist philosophy.

These philosophies guided the Peoples' Will. They murdered the police chief of Moscow and went on a campaign of bombing and murder. In May 1881 they succeeded in striking their ultimate target; they killed Czar Alexander II. Ironically, this brought about their downfall. The Peoples' Will was eliminated, Alexander III (ruled 1881 to 1894) ended all attempts at reform, and revolutionaries went underground. Nicholas II (ruled 1894 to 1917), who succeeded Alexander III, was a man who would be toppled by revolutionary forces.

Czar Nicholas and the Revolutions of 1905 and 1917

Nicholas faced his first revolution in 1905, after his army lost a war to Japan. In addition to losing the war, Russia was consumed with economic problems and bureaucratic inefficiency. A group of unemployed workers began demonstrations in St. Petersburg, and some enlisted men in the Russian navy mutinied. Their actions were brutally suppressed, feeding the spirit of revolution that burned below the surface. Russian revolutionaries needed another national disaster to create the atmosphere for revolution. It came in 1914, when Russia entered World War I (1914–1918).

By 1917 the Russian people were tired of their economic woes and their czar. In February, a general strike in St. Petersburg turned into a revolution. Unlike 1905, the Russian army joined the workers, and a new Russian government was formed. They envisioned a period of capitalist economic expansion that would save the beleaguered Russian economy. **Workers Councils (or Soviets)** were established in major Russian cities.

The primary mistake of the February revolutionaries, called **Mensheviks**, was that they kept Russia in the war, unpopular with the Russian people. This had two immediate ramifications. It created unrest at home, and it inspired the Germans to seek a way to remove Russia from World War I. The Germans found their answer in Vladimir Ilyich Lenin. He promised to take Russia out of the war if the Germans would help him to power. After the German High Command assisted Lenin in gaining control of the **Bolsheviks** (communist revolutionaries who opposed the Mensheviks), Lenin orchestrated a second revolution in October 1917 and removed Russia from the war.

Lenin and Trotsky

The Russian Revolution utilized terrorism in a new manner, and this had an impact on the way people viewed terrorism in the twentieth century. Lenin and one of his lieutenants, **Leon Trotsky** (1879–1940), believed terrorism should be used as an instrument for overthrowing middle-class, or bourgeois, governments. Once power was achieved, Lenin and Trotsky advocated terrorism as a means of controlling internal enemies and a method for coping with international strife. Russia was very weak after the Revolution. It faced foreign intervention and was torn by civil war. By threatening to export terrorism, Lenin and Trotsky hoped to keep their enemies, primarily western Europe and the United States, at bay.

With their threat, Lenin and Trotsky placed the fear of communist revolution in the minds of many people in the West. To some, terrorism and communism became synonymous. Though the Russians and later the Soviets were never very good at carrying insurrection to other lands, Western leaders began to fear that communist terrorists were on the verge of toppling democratic governments. Despite Lenin and his successor, Joseph Stalin, having the most success with another form of terror, murdering their own people, fear of communist insurrection lasted well into the twentieth century, and some people still fear it. Even as the Soviet Union tottered into devolution, Western analysts still saw terrorism through the lens of Western-Soviet confrontation (see Livingstone and Arnold, 1986; Sterling, 1986). Former CIA analyst Michael

Workers Councils (or Soviets)
The lowest-level legislative body in the Soviet Union following the October Revolution. *Soviet* is the Russian word for "council."

Mensheviks
Russian socialists who allied with the Bolsheviks in the February 1917 Revolution to overthrow the czarist government.

Bolsheviks
Russian revolutionaries led by Lenin. The Bolsheviks overthrew the revolutionary government of Russia in October 1917, and Lenin established communist control in the newly formed Soviet Union.

Leon Trotsky
A Russian revolutionary who led foreign affairs in Stalin's government and later became the commander of the Red Army. He espoused terrorism as a means for spreading revolution. He was thrown out of the Communist Party for opposing Stalin and assassinated by communist agents in Mexico City in 1940.

Scheuer (2006, pp. 20–23) believes this hinders the ability to comprehend terrorism today.

In fairness to analysts of the cold war, Lenin's victory and subsequent writings have inspired terrorists from 1917 to the present. Although communist terrorism was not part of an orchestrated conspiracy, it did influence behavior. Some terrorists scoured the works of Lenin and Trotsky, as well as other Russian revolutionaries, to formulate theories, tactics, and ideologies. Although not a simple conspiracy of evil, this influence was real and remains today.

Self-Check

- *How did revolutionary thought develop in czarist Russia?*
- *Describe the two revolutions under Nicholas II.*
- *How did Lenin and Trotsky influence the direction of revolutionary thought?*

SUMMARY

- The Enlightenment of the 1700s served as the final intellectual catalyst to set the stage for Western democracy. The irony of democracy is that revolutionary terrorism tends to increase under democracy's freedom.
- The American Revolution resulted in the transfer of political power from London to Philadelphia. It was a conservative revolution in the sense that power moved from the males of the British upper classes to the males of the American upper classes.
- The French Revolution was a radical revolt. Middle and lower classes fought the upper classes for power.
- The modern use of *terrorism* comes from the actions of the French revolutionary government from 1794–1795. The government's execution of opponents was known as the Reign of Terror. The meaning of *terrorism* subtly shifted when the French called Spanish partisans terrorists. It changed again in the mid-nineteenth century when governments began describing revolutionaries as terrorists.
- In 1848 most major European capitals experienced forms of revolution. Although the revolutionaries were unsuccessful, Western governments began to fear socialists, communists, and anarchists. Many politicians, journalists, industrial leaders, and members of the middle class believed all forms of socialism to be symptomatic of violent revolution.
- Many anarchists and socialists abhorred violence, and their calls for revolution were rhetorical. Others developed the philosophy of the bomb and propaganda by deed. This has prompted a scholastic debate. Some scholars believe there are differences between the methods of

nineteenth-century and modern terrorists. Others see indiscriminate terrorism as the direct result of earlier practices.

- Nationalist terrorists were influenced and inspired by the ideological terrorists of the nineteenth century.
- The Russian Revolution has been viewed in a new light since the collapse of the Soviet Union. It inspired revolutionaries and terrorists in the twentieth century and probably continues to inspire them today. The West feared communist expansion of the Revolution through terrorism, and the rhetoric of the early revolutionaries encouraged the West in this fear.

KEY TERMS

Enlightenment (p. 119)

Thirty Years' War (p. 119)

Estates General (p. 122)

National Convention (p. 122)

Committee of Public Safety
  (p. 123)

Reign of Terror (p. 123)

Spain in 1807 (p. 123)

radical democrats (p. 124)

socialists (p. 124)

communists (p. 124)

anarchists (p. 124)

bourgeois (p. 128)

Hohenzollern (p. 128)

Hapsburg (p. 128)

Joseph Stalin (p. 134)

Vladimir Lenin (p. 135)

proletariat (p. 136)

Workers Councils (or Soviets)
  (p. 137)

Mensheviks (p. 137)

Bolsheviks (p. 137)

Leon Trotsky (p. 137)

WRITING ASSIGNMENTS

1. Using the material in this chapter, describe the emergence and transformation of the term *terrorism*. Explain the use of state terror by revolutionary governments in France and Russia. Explain why the United States government was established without mass executions.

2. Democracy and terrorism seem to be related. Describe that relationship. Do you agree with the statements in this chapter about democracy? Can democracy be threatened by overemphasizing the fear of terrorism? Is there a parallel between the American reaction to anarchist violence in the late nineteenth and early twentieth centuries with governmental reaction today?

3. Using the Russian Revolution and the theories of Proudhon and Prokoptin, explain the difference between anarchism and communism.

7

The Irish Troubles

AP Photo/Adam Butler

One of the distinguishing characteristics of terrorism is that violent extremists will not accept rational compromise. In Ireland both Unionist and Republican terrorists have taken violent action at times when the majority of people are seeking peace.

Learning Objectives

After reading this chapter, you should be able to

■ Describe the influence of Viking invasions on Ireland and the importance of Brian Boru.

■ Explain the Norman approach to Ireland.

■ Describe the importance of the Reformation on Ireland.

■ Summarize English policy toward Ireland from the Plantation of Ulster to the Act of Union.

■ Outline the emergence of republicanism and home rule.

■ Describe the 1916 Easter Rising.

■ Summarize the Black and Tan War and the emergence of the Free State.

- Define "selective terrorism" as used by Michael Collins.
- Explain the transformation of republicanism in the twentieth century.
- Explain the impact of British policy on Irish terrorism from 1969 to 1985.
- Describe the forms of Unionist terrorism from 1969 to 1985.

As terrorism grew in Russia because of anarchists, the Peoples' Will, and the October Revolution, a similar type of terrorist campaign began to appear in the United Kingdom. Irish Republicans, long angered by the colonial rule of England, incorporated the latest terrorist techniques in their campaign of revolution. The Irish developed nationalistic terrorism, and the Irish Republican Army set the stage for modern terrorism. Nationalism in Ireland involves the struggle for ethnic identity and an internal Christian religious conflict. Modern terrorism is associated with the 1916 Easter Rising, the Black and Tan War of 1919 to 1921, and the resurgent Irish Republican Army of 1956 and 1969. The struggle for Irish independence is a major theme of Irish history that began long before Patrick Pearse entered the Dublin post office in 1916 and bestowed a name, the Irish Republican Army, on the resistance to British occupation. Terrorism in Ireland is the product of a long, long story.

Vikings, Normans, and English Settlements, 800–1600

In August 1969, the British army was ordered to increase its presence in Northern Ireland in an effort to quell a series of riots. Although the British army had maintained bases in Northern Ireland for a while, rioting in Londonderry and Belfast was suddenly far beyond the control of local police and the handful of British regular soldiers stationed in the area. On August 18, 1969, British army reinforcements began arriving, hoping to avoid a long-term conflict. Their hopes were in vain. The British army would soon become embroiled in a new outbreak of a war that had spanned centuries.

The Vikings

Ireland has not been completely ruled by the Irish since a series of Viking incursions in 800 C.E. Giovanni Costigan (1980) writes that Irish culture originated with Celtic invasions from Britain three centuries before Christ. The Irish settled in tribal groups, and government was maintained through kinship and clans. No Celtic ruler or political authority ever united Ireland as a single entity. Thomas Cahill (2003) points out that the tribal period before and after the Viking invasions was crucial to the history of the West. The Irish were Christianized and brought a special, mystic spirituality to Christianity. Their devotion to the church, tradition of saints, and blend of Celtic mysticism not only created a special blend of spirituality but resulted in a deep attachment to the land and people. Religion would eventually unite with nationalism and patriotism in Ireland. In probably the most definitive work on Irish spirituality, Michael Herren and Shirley Brown (2002) argue that, despite the stereotype of strong orthodox ties with Rome, Celtic Christianity embraced several unique concepts, such as a belief in cosmic unity and deep mysticism.

Many scholars believe that Irish Christianity had an immense influence on the definition of culture and self-understanding (O Corrain, 2000; Curtis, 2000, pp. 16–18, orig. 1936; Herren and Brown, 2002). In traditional lore the Irish were introduced to Christianity by St. Patrick in 432 C.E., and they became some of the most fervent converts in the world. The medieval church played a large role in uniting Ireland, but the traditional Gaelic tribal groups still remained separate. They submitted to a central religion, not a central political system. The relations among Gaelic tribes became important when Viking raiders began to attack Ireland in about AD 800. The divided Irish were dominated by their Viking rulers, and the Norsemen used Ireland as a trading base and center of commerce. The Vikings built several Irish cities, including Dublin.

The Vikings did not create a unified state, and various alliances of Irish tribes skirmished with the invaders for 300 years. Viking rule of Ireland was challenged in 1014, when a tribal chieftain, Brian Boru (circa 940–1014), was declared High King of Ireland. He led a united tribal army against the Vikings and defeated them at Clontarf. Fate ruled against the Irish, however. At the end of the battle as King Brian knelt in prayer, he was assassinated along with his grandson. Under Brian Boru, Ireland might have united under central rule. Without him, there was no high king to unite the tribes. Dreams of a united Ireland crumbled after Clontarf.

The Normans

Katherine Simms (2000) points out that Ireland presented a tempting target for another invader soon after the Vikings were expelled. The Normans were especially attracted to the fortifications offered by Irish cities and the agricultural wealth of the interior. Costigan (1980) believes this paved the way for a gradual Norman invasion of Ireland. The Normans were the descendants of William the Conqueror (1027–1087) and had ambitions for extending their domains. With the Irish divided and the Viking influence limited, Normans began to stake out territorial claims on the island with the permission of the Norman king. The Normans were particularly successful in Ireland because they used new methods of warfare. By 1172, the Norman king of England had assumed the rule of Ireland.

The Normans and the Irish struggled in a way that was not reflective of modern fighting. The Normans could not maintain the field force necessary to control the Irish peasants, and the Irish did not have the technology that would allow them to attack smaller Norman forces barricaded in castles. Therefore, the Normans built castles to control Irish cities, and Irish peasants generally dominated rural areas. This situation continued until the sixteenth century.

Simms argues that despite Norman dominance the Irish maintained cultural and religious traditions. Robert W. White (1993, pp. 13–14) agrees. The Irish and English fought each other for dominance, but the Irish maintained their tribal and clan structure. More importantly, Irish nobles held their hereditary lands. Irish chieftains were relatively autonomous after Clontarf. This ended in 1601 after the English defeated Irish forces at Kinsale. Irish nobles fled for mainland Europe, and the English took their lands. For the next eighty years Scottish and English settlers laid claim to Ireland, and peasants were shoved aside in the name of colonization.

Self-Check

- *How did the Viking incursions shape Ireland?*
- *What changes came after the Normans established cities in Ireland?*

The Reformation and Ireland

The Protestant Reformation of the 1500s had a tremendous impact on Ireland. Wanting to free himself from the ecclesiastical shackles of Rome, the English king Henry VIII (1491–1547) created the independent Church of England. He followed up by creating a similar church in Ireland, but the Irish Catholics could not stomach this move. They began to rebel against the English king, and the troubles created by the Reformation have literally continued into the twenty-first century in Ireland.

The problems of the early Reformation were magnified by Henry's daughter Elizabeth (1533–1603). Not content with merely ruling Ireland, Elizabeth I carved out the most prosperous agrarian section and gave it to her subjects to colonize: this resulted in the creation of the **Plantation of Ulster**. English and Scottish Protestants eventually settled there, displacing many of the original Irish inhabitants. The Plantation of Ulster created an ethnic division in Ireland fueled by religious differences and animosities.

Historian Brendan Bradshaw (1978) explains the problem. The Reformation, a religious movement rejecting some Roman Catholic doctrine and leading to the establishment of the Protestant churches, took root in several places in Europe, such as northern German states and much of England and Scotland. This was not the case in Ireland. As the English and Scots settled Ireland, displacing native nobility and peasants, they came as colonial masters accompanied by the Anglican, Presbyterian,

Plantation of Ulster
The area of Northern Ireland selected by English monarchs for colonization in the seventeenth century. Irish peasants were displaced by Scottish and English settlers. The Irish were primarily Catholic and the settlers were mostly Protestant. The settlement was named Ulster because it encompassed the old Irish tribal area of Ulster.

and Congregational Churches. Although the Church of Ireland was nationalized in the Anglican Communion, Roman Catholic priests and peasants rejected it. Protestants, in the eyes of the colonized, were English and Scottish invaders. They were not Irish. As settlers were replaced by third and fourth generations, they considered themselves Irish, but they were distinctively Protestant. As a result, the national conflict between the Irish and English-Scots became a religious conflict. The native Irish embraced Catholicism but the newly settled invaders clung to Protestantism.

The Plantation of Ulster, Oliver Cromwell, and the Battle of the Boyne

Costigan (1980) believes the 1600s in Ireland were dominated by three major issues. First, the Plantation of Ulster was expanded, and Irish peasants were systematically displaced. Many of them perished. John Darby (1995) points out that the Ulster was unique in the sense that rather than simply colonizing an area, the Scots and English settlers drove away the Irish. The Plantation of Ulster introduced a foreign invader who spoke a different language, brought different customs, and worshipped in a different manner. It was conquest, not colonization.

The second issue dominating the 1600s came when the English Civil War (1642–1651) spilled over to Ireland. Oliver Cromwell (1599–1658) came to Ireland to quell a revolt, stop Catholic attacks on Protestants, and destroy English Catholic royalists who had allied with the local population. Cromwell landed in Dublin in 1649 and marched north to strike an English royalist and Catholic garrison at Drogheda. His actions would be remembered for centuries. Cromwell stormed the city and massacred the defenders and inhabitants. It was the first of many slaughters. His troops killed thousands of Irish Catholics in the next three years, and Cromwell thanked God for granting him the opportunity to rid the world of them, according to Costigan (1980). Cromwell's name still stirs vehement emotions in Ireland (see Another Perspective: Cromwell in Drogheda).

The third issue of the 1600s also involved Catholic and Protestant struggles, and the conflict is still celebrated in ceremonies today. From 1689 to 1691, James II (1633–1701), the Catholic Pretender to the British throne, used Ireland as a base from which to revolt against William of Orange (1650–1702), the English king. In August 1689, Irish Protestant skilled workers, called "Apprentice Boys," were relieved by the English after defending Derry, renamed Londonderry by the English, through a long siege by the Pretender. The following year William defeated James at the Battle of the Boyne River.

The revolt was over, but the Protestants were now forever in the camp of the House of Orange. The Protestants have flaunted these victories in the face of the Catholics since 1690. Each year they gather to militantly celebrate the Battle of the Boyne and the Apprentice Boys

Cromwell in Drogheda

A statue of the Lord Protector Oliver Cromwell stands outside the parliamentary chambers of Westminster in London. To many people in the United Kingdom, Cromwell stands as a hero, a military genius who transformed the army and elevated parliament in the face of the monarchy. Cromwell's New Model Army successfully defeated the royalist forces in the English Civil War, and the statue attests to his greatness. When English Catholics brought Ireland into the fray, Cromwell was furious. He landed with 3,000 troops and a desire to put the Catholic rebels to the sword. In September 1649 Cromwell's troops arrived at Drogheda. Ship cannons bombarded the city from its harbor, and Cromwell trained his siege guns at a point on the wall. When the wall broke, Cromwell's troops attacked. Thrown back twice, Cromwell personally led the third assault. He gave orders that no quarter should be given. As Cromwell's troops swept through the city, royalist soldiers and officers were killed without mercy. Priests and nuns were also targeted for murder. When a group of citizens hid in a cathedral, Cromwell's troops set it afire. Cromwell believed he was acting in God's name, seeking vengeance against Catholics who had murdered Protestants in a 1641 uprising. Military historians John Keegan and Andrew Wheatcroft do not justify the action, but they say it was no worse than what most armies did according to the standards of the time. Cromwell is a hero in the eyes of many. Most Irish people do not hold that opinion.

Source: Keegan and Wheatcroft, 1976.

with parades and demonstrations. It fuels the fire of hatred in Northern Ireland and demonstrates the division between Protestants and Catholics. In fact, the current troubles started in 1969, when riots broke out in Londonderry and Belfast following the annual Apprentice Boys parade. Today, Protestants assemble in Orange Lodges, so named for the Battle of the Boyne and William of Orange.

Republican Revolutionaries

The 1700s and early 1800s were characterized by waves of revolt, starvation, and emigration. Irish nationalists rose to challenge English rule, but they were always soundly defeated. Each generation seemed to bring a new series of martyrs willing to give their lives in the struggle against the English. The late eighteenth century also witnessed another trend in Ireland, the willingness of many Protestants and Catholics to join in the cause for independence. In 1791 two groups formed in Belfast and Dublin. They called themselves the **Society of United Irishmen** and members came from both Catholic and Protestant Churches (see Cronin, 1984; Foster, 2001, pp. 134–172).

Among the best-known leaders of the United Irishmen was Theobald Wolfe Tone (1763–1798), a member of the Church of Ireland (the Protestant Anglican Communion). Wolfe Tone's writing fanned the flames of the Society of United Irishmen. He demanded autonomy, the end of a

Society of United Irishmen
An organization formed in Dublin with a second chapter in Belfast in 1791 that united both Protestants and Catholics. The purpose of the movement was to free Ireland from British rule. The society demanded Catholic emancipation (equal rights for Catholics and Protestants), the end of British rule, and a free Irish parliament.

harsh legal system known as the Penal Laws, and complete freedom for Catholics. Wolfe Tone argued that Irish independence was more important than religious differences, and several prominent Protestants and Catholics agreed with him. Wolfe Tone drew the wrath of Britain and he fled Ireland, eventually arriving in Paris. In 1798 Ireland revolted from British rule, and Wolfe Tone sailed from France to Ireland with 15,000 French troops. The French were unable to land, however, and when Wolfe Tone returned in a second expedition, he was captured and sentenced to death by the British. Rather than accept hanging—he had requested a firing squad on the basis of his status as a French officer—he committed suicide. Britain formed the United Kingdom of Great Britain and Ireland in 1801 through the Act of Union to further solidify their hold on Ireland.

The Potato Famine

The struggle for republicanism accompanied one of the saddest periods in Irish history. Displaced from the land, Irish peasants were poor and susceptible to economic and agricultural fluctuations. Historian Cecil Woodham-Smith (1962) documents that Ireland had undergone a series of famines in the 1840s, as potato crops failed. In 1845 the crop failed again, and agricultural production among the peasants came to a standstill until 1848. As thousands of Irish starved, wealthy farms in the North exported other crops for cash.

The 1845–1848 famine devastated Ireland. Its effects were felt primarily among the poor, especially among the Irish Catholics. In an era in which other industrialized nations were experiencing a tremendous rise in population, Ireland's census dropped by 25 percent. As famine and disease took their toll, thousands of Irish people emigrated to other parts of the world. During this period, Unionists in the North consolidated their hold on Ulster.

Home Rule

home rule
The dominant issue in Irish politics from the mid-1800s until independence. Advocates of home rule wanted to establish a parliament (*Dáil* in Gaelic) in Dublin that would be independent from the British parliament in Westminster. Some advocates of home rule were willing to swear allegiance to the United Kingdom. Others demanded complete autonomy.

Efforts for liberation continued in the eighteenth century. Daniel O'Connell (1775–1847) emerged as a popular political leader for Irish nationalism and Catholic emancipation. The majority of Irish were against the Act of Union, even though the law gave Ireland a voice in the British parliament. O'Connell used the voice peacefully and championed independence. Charles Stewart Parnell (1846–1891), a Protestant, and John Redmond (1856–1918), a Catholic, united many Irish people around a legislative drive for independence, known as **home rule**. People who backed leaders like Parnell and Redmond demanded a second parliament in Ireland free from direct control of the British government in Westminster. Under home rule, Ireland would remain part of the United Kingdom and citizens would swear allegiance to the British monarchy. They would exercise autonomy through their own legislative body and prime minister (see Bew, 1999; Foster, 1989, pp. 400–415).

Most Protestants did not embrace the idea of home rule. Settlers in the North, who had been in Ireland for 200 years, were afraid of Catholics in the south. If home rule were to pass, they reasoned, they would lose their privileged status in the North, a status they felt they had worked to achieve. They wanted to remain united with the British and wanted direct rule from Westminster. These Unionists had strong allies in the British military and among conservative politicians. The majority of Ireland was Catholic, but the Irish Protestant Unionists outnumbered the Catholics two to one in the northern counties of Ulster. They slowly began to militarize their Orange organizations.

The Catholics and Protestants who favored home rule dominated the south. Most of them felt that home rule would come through negotiation. Others wanted to take the issue a step further. Instead of maintaining a relationship with Great Britain, some Republicans wanted complete autonomy. They feared the Unionists and felt that the slow pace of home rule would not be effective. They formed many movements, such as Young Ireland, the Fenian Military (named for the mythical Irish hero Finn McCool), and the Irish Revolutionary Brotherhood. They attacked British police and military targets in Ireland. They also attacked Irish Unionists in the North. The Unionists responded by excluding Catholic workers from skilled industrial jobs and by drawing closer to British authorities, especially the military. Violence eventually moved over the Irish Sea to Britain itself. The British responded by exiling Republicans rather than executing them for fear of creating martyrs. The violent Republicans continued activities from places like the United States, Canada, Australia, and New Zealand (see Foster, 1989, pp. 345–400; McElrath, 2000, pp. 7–15).

Another aspect of the evolving conflict needs to be emphasized. By the nineteenth century, both the Unionists and the Republicans were fully Irish. This means neither side had transplanted settlers from another country, and the Catholics and the Protestants—despite all political differences—identified themselves as citizens of the Emerald Isle. Unionist Protestants in the North had lived in Ireland for generations, and they were as Irish as their Catholic counterparts. The Unionists were able to call on Britain for help, but the struggle in Ireland began to take on the earmarks of an intra-Irish conflict. Irish Unionists, usually Protestant, dominated the North, and Irish Republicans, primarily Catholics, controlled the rest of Ireland (Figure 7.1).

Self-Check

- *Why did the Reformation affect English colonization of Ireland?*
- *Explain the birth of Irish republicanism in terms of Roman Catholicism and Protestantism.*
- *How could Protestants and Roman Catholics unite in the name of home rule?*

Figure 7.1
Ireland

The Early Irish Republican Army

By the twentieth century, the struggle in Ireland had become a matter of the divisions between Unionists and Republicans. A host of other conflicts were associated with this confrontation, but the main one was the Unionist-Republican struggle. The unionists often had the upper hand because they could call on support from the British-sponsored police and military forces. The Republicans had no such luxury, and they searched for an alternative.

Costigan (1980) believes that the Republican military solution came when the Irish Republican Brotherhood (IRB) formed in the 1850s. Support came from exiles and emigrants around the world. Irish Catholics had emigrated from their homeland to America, Australia, Canada, and New Zealand, but they never forgot the people they left behind. Irish immigrants in New York City created the Fenian Brotherhood as a financial relief organization for relatives in the old country. After the

American Civil War, some Irish soldiers returning from the U.S. Army decided to take the struggle for emancipation back to Ireland. Rationalizing that they had fought to free the slaves, they believed they should continue the struggle and free Ireland. They sponsored a failed revolt in 1867, and others launched a dynamite campaign in London a decade and a half later. Although the IRB pledged to work peacefully with Parnell, it gradually evolved into a revolutionary organization.

J. Bowyer Bell (1974) has written the definitive treatise on the origins and development of the Irish Republican Army (IRA). He states it began with a campaign of violence sponsored by the IRB in the late 1800s. Spurred on by increased Irish nationalistic feeling in the homeland and the hope of home rule, the IRB waged a campaign of bombing and assassination from 1870 until 1916. Its primary targets were Unionists and British forces supporting the Unionist cause. Among their greatest adversaries was the British-backed police force in Ireland, the **Royal Irish Constabulary (RIC)**.

The activities of the IRB frightened Irish citizens who wanted to remain united with Great Britain. For the most part, these Irish people were Protestant and middle class, and they lived in the North. They gravitated toward their trade unions and social organizations, among them the Orange Lodges, to counter growing IRB sympathy and power. They enjoyed the sympathy of the British army's officer corps. They also controlled the RIC.

The Fenians of the IRB remained undaunted by Unionist sentiment. Although Irish Unionists seemed in control, the IRB had two trumps. First, IRB leadership was dominated by men who believed each generation had to produce warriors who would fight for independence. Some of these leaders, as well as their followers, were quite willing to be martyred to keep republicanism alive. In addition, the IRB had an organization. It not only served as a threat to British power but also provided the basis for the resurgence of Irish culture.

Royal Irish Constabulary (RIC)

The police force established by the United Kingdom in Ireland. It was modeled after the London Metropolitan Police, but it represented British interests. After the Free State formed, the RIC became the RUC, Royal Ulster Constabulary. In turn, the RUC gave way to the Police Service of Northern Ireland (PSNI) as part of Irish and British attempts to bring peace to Northern Ireland after 1995.

Self-Check

- *Identify the factors that gave birth to Republican militancy.*
- *How did the Irish Republican Brotherhood evolve toward militancy?*
- *Might different British policies have achieved harmony between the United Kingdom and Ireland?*

The Easter Rising

At the turn of the century, no person embodied Irish culture more than Patrick Pearse (1879–1916). The headmaster of an Irish school, Pearse was an inspirational romantic. He could move crowds to patriotism and inspire resistance to British policies. He was a hero among Irish Americans, and they sent hundreds of thousands of dollars to support his

Supreme Council

The command center of several Republican terrorist organizations, including the Irish Republican Army, the Official Irish Republican Army, and the Provisional Irish Republican Army. The name was transposed from the Irish Republican Brotherhood.

cause. He told young Irish boys and girls about their heritage, he taught them Gaelic, and he inspired them to be militantly proud of being Irish. He was also a member of the **Supreme Council** of the IRB. When the possibility of home rule was defeated in the British parliament, Republican eyes turned to Pearse.

By 1916 the situation in Ireland had changed. The British had promised home rule to Ireland when World War I (1914–1918) came to an end. Whereas most people in Ireland believed the British, Unionists and Republicans secretly armed for a civil war between the North and South. They believed a fight was inevitable if the British granted home rule, and each side was determined to dominate the government of a newly independent Ireland. Some forces were not willing to wait for home rule.

With British attention focused on Germany, leaders of the IRB believed it was time for a strike against the Unionists and their British supporters. At Easter in 1916, Patrick Pearse and James Connolly (1868–1916) led a revolt in Dublin. Pearse felt the revolt was doomed from the start but believed it necessary to sacrifice his life to keep the Republican spirit alive. Connolly was a more pragmatic socialist who fought because he believed a coming civil war was inevitable.

The Rising

The 1916 Easter Rising enjoyed local success because it surprised everyone. Pearse and Connolly took over several key points in Dublin with a few thousand armed followers. From the halls of the General Post Office, Pearse announced that the revolutionaries had formed an Irish republic and asked the Irish to follow him. The British, outraged by this treachery, in their view, in the midst of a larger war, sent troops to Dublin. The city was engulfed in a week of heavy fighting.

Whereas Pearse and Connolly came to start a popular revolution, the British came to fight a war. In a few days, Dublin was devastated by British artillery. Pearse recognized the futility of the situation and asked for terms. Bell (1974) points out the interesting way Pearse chose to approach the British: he sent a message using a new title, commanding general of the Irish Republican Army, to the general in charge of British forces. The IRB had transformed itself into an army: the IRA.

The Collapse of the Rising

If Connolly and Pearse hoped to be greeted as liberators, they had greatly misjudged the mood of Ireland. Popular opinion favored home rule, but many Irish people believed it would come without a fight, Britain granting it at the end of the war. Paul Bew (1999) says that the republican Sinn Fein party had not captured the public's imagination. Had the British played to Irish sympathy, they might have stopped violent republicanism. Their actions, however, virtually empowered Sinn Fein. The British handed down several dozen death sentences for the Easter Rising. Hundreds more people received lengthy prison sentences. Pearse became an Irish legend. Standing in front of a firing squad, he gave an impassioned plea for Irish independence. Connolly, who had been badly wounded, was tied to a chair and placed before a firing squad. Public sympathy shifted to the rebels.

Two important people managed to escape the purge. Eamon de Valera (1882–1975) received a prison sentence instead of death because of questions about his nationality. He had been born in New York City and brought to Ireland at an early age. Michael Collins (1890–1922), in a cell where prisoners slated for execution were being segregated from those selected for internment, walked to the other side of the cell and found himself among the internment group. It saved his life. De Valera would emerge as a revolutionary and political leader, and Collins became the leader of the Irish Republican Army.

Self-Check

- *Was the Easter Rising inevitable?*
- *How would British military officers view the Easter Rising in the middle of World War I?*
- *Could a more moderate response to the Easter Rising have prevented further violence?*

The Black and Tan War (1920–1921)

Sinn Fein, the political party of Irish republicanism, continued its activities in spite of the failure of the Easter Rising. When World War I ended, many of the Republicans were released. There were several moderates in Ireland, represented by the Parliamentary Party, and they sought to reopen the issue of home rule. They believed that this was the only nonviolent way to approach the Irish question. Bew (1999) says that the moderates were also willing to cede the northern province, Ulster, to the Protestants who wished to remain united with Great Britain. If the Protestants were forced into a united Ireland, they reasoned, violence would continue.

Bew believes Sinn Fein took advantage of the moderate position and championed the cause of a united Ireland. The ideologues of republicanism expressed themselves in extremist terms. They not only rejected home rule but demanded a complete free state devoid of any British participation in Irish politics. For Sinn Fein anything but a united Ireland was out of the question. The British government also vacillated. Conservatives, especially the military officer corps, were reluctant to abandon the North either to home rule or an independent Ireland, whereas others sought to solve the Irish problem with some sort of home rule. Bew argues that Sinn Fein moved into the arena by discrediting the Parliamentary Party. Moderation fell to the wayside as extreme republicanism increased.

Sinn Fein

The political party of Republicans. Critics claim it represents terrorists. Republicans say it represents their political interests. Despite the debate, Sinn Fein historically has close connections with extremism and violence.

Selective Terror

Michael Collins was appalled by the amateur tactics of the Easter Rising. Revolution, he believed, could be successful, but it would not develop from a popular uprising. It needed to be systematic, organized, and ruthless. After being released from prison in a general amnesty, Collins studied the tactics of the Russian Peoples' Will and the writings of earlier anarchists and terrorists. Collins developed a strategy called "selective terrorism." Devising a plan that would later influence terrorists as diverse as those in the proto-Israeli group Irgun Zvai Leumi and Ernesto "Che" Guevara's communist revolutionaries in Cuba, Collins reasoned that indiscriminate terror was of no value. Random or large-scale attacks would alienate public opinion. Conversely, launching an attack and waiting for the population to spontaneously rise to rebellion was equally futile. To be effective, terrorism had to selectively and ruthlessly target security forces and their symbols of authority.

After months of planning, recruiting, and organizing, Collins launched a new form of the IRA. He began by gathering intelligence, learning the internal workings of British police headquarters, and obtaining a list of intelligence officers. The first attacks were devastating. Using the information from the extensive preparation, Collins's men ambushed off-duty police and intelligence officers and murdered them. He then began attacking police stations. IRA terrorists would emerge from a crowded sidewalk, throw bombs and shoot police officers, then melt back into a crowd before authorities could respond. A master of strategy, Collins continued a campaign of terror against Unionists and the RIC.

The British responded by sending a hastily recruited military force, called the Black and Tans because of their mismatched uniforms, and Ireland became the scene of a dreadful war. Both sides accused the other of atrocities, but murder and mayhem were the tactics of each. The conflict became popularly known as the Tan War or the Black and Tan War.

Separation and Independence

Meanwhile, home rule had not been forgotten by more moderate groups. Politicians in Britain and Ireland sought to bring an end to the violence by formulating the steps to grant Irish independence. The main stumbling block was the North. Protestant Unionists were afraid of being abandoned by the British. In 1921 the situation was temporarily solved by a treaty between Britain and Ireland. Under the terms of the treaty, Ireland would be granted independence and the northern section around Ulster would remain under British protection until it could peacefully be integrated into Ireland. Southern Ireland became the **Free State**—the Republic of Ireland. The majority of people in Ireland accepted the treaty. Michael Collins also accepted the treaty, but the IRA did not.

When the treaty between Ireland and Britain was ratified in 1921, a civil war broke out in the newly formed republic. Michael Collins led the Irish Army, while his former colleague Eamon de Valera took the

Free State

The name given to the newly formed Republic of Ireland after Irish independence in the Tan War.

helm of the IRA. The IRA fought Irish governmental forces, claiming that Irish independence had to extend to all Irish people. They rejected British control of the North. De Valera campaigned against his former colleagues and eventually orchestrated the murder of Michael Collins.

For their part, the British wanted nothing to do with the civil war in the southern areas. They tightened their hold on Northern Ireland and bolstered its strength with a new police force, the Royal Ulster Constabulary (RUC). The northern Unionists were delighted when the British established a semiautonomous government in Northern Ireland and gave it special powers to combat the IRA. The Unionists used this power to gain control of Northern Ireland and lock themselves into the British orbit. Ireland became a divided country (see Foster, 1989, pp. 431–465; Laffan, 1999).

Self-Check

- *How did Michael Collins's strategy differ from Patrick Pearse's?*
- *What is the meaning of "selective terror" and how did Collins employ it?*
- *The Black and Tan War led to partial independence and future violence. Why?*

Trends in the IRA through 1985

In 1927 de Valera was elected prime minister of the Republic of Ireland. Although he passed several anti-British measures, he was soon at odds with the IRA. Two important trends emerged. Bell (1974) records the first by pointing to the split in IRA ranks. By the 1930s, some members of the IRA wanted to follow the lead of their political party, Sinn Fein. They felt the IRA should express itself through peaceful political idealism. They believed they should begin working for a united socialist Ireland in the spirit of James Connolly.

Another group of IRA members rejected this philosophy. They believed the purpose of the IRA was to fight for republicanism. They would never be at peace with the British or the unionists until Northern Ireland was united with the south. They vowed to carry on the fight. They broke with the de Valera government and formed a provisional wing of the IRA in the 1930s. The Provisional IRA vowed to keep up the fight, and de Valera turned on them. Robert White (1993, p. 26) says the IRA was active from 1939 to 1944 in England. They launched an ineffective terrorist campaign in Northern Ireland from 1956 to 1962, when they fell out of favor with Irish Republicans.

J. Bowyer Bell believes the reason for IRA impotence can be found in the second generation of **Provisionals**. Wanting to follow in the footsteps of their forebears, the Provisionals began to wage a campaign against the RUC in Northern Ireland in the late 1950s. They established support bases in the republic and slipped across the border for terrorist

Provisionals

The nickname for members of the Provisional Irish Republican Army. They are also known as Provos. The name applies to several different Republican paramilitary terrorist groups.

activities. Although the Provisionals initially enjoyed support among Republican enclaves in the North, most Irish people, Unionists and Republicans alike, were appalled by IRA violence. Even the Official IRA—the segment embracing a socialist ideology—criticized the military attacks of the Provisionals. Faced with a lack of public support, the Provisional IRA called off its offensive in the North. By 1962 almost all of its activities had ceased. Some Provisionals joined the civil rights movement; others rejoined former colleagues in the Official wing. Most members, however, remained in a secret infrastructure and hoping events would restore their ranks and prestige.

Just when it seemed the Provisional IRA was defunct, a Catholic civil rights campaign engulfed Northern Ireland in 1969. The failure of the civil rights movement in Northern Ireland can be directly linked to modern Irish terrorism and the rebirth of the IRA. Alfred McClung Lee (1983, pp. 59–97) notes that the economic situation in Northern Ireland favored the Protestant Unionists. From 1922 to 1969, the government in Northern Ireland systematically reduced the civil rights of Catholics living in the North. During the same period, the economic power of the Unionists increased. When Catholics demanded the same rights as Protestants in 1969, demonstrations grew violent. The British army was called in to support the RUC.

Failed Civil Rights

According to Lee (1983, pp. 59–97), the political and economic conditions in Northern Ireland provided the rationale for a major civil rights movement among the Catholics. Although the movement had Republican overtones, it was primarily aimed at achieving adequate housing and education among Ulster's Catholic population in an attempt to improve economic growth. The civil rights movement was supported by both Protestants and Catholics, but the actions of the Northern Ireland government began to polarize the issue. Increasingly the confrontation became recognized as a Unionist-Republican one, and the old battle lines between Protestants and Catholics were redrawn. By 1969 the civil rights movement and the reaction to it had become violent.

The IRA had not been dormant throughout the civil rights movement, but it had failed to play a major role. For the most part, the leaders of the civil rights movement were peaceful Republicans. The IRA could not entice the civil rights leaders to join it in a guerrilla war, and it had virtually destroyed itself in an earlier campaign against the government of Northern Ireland. In 1969 the Provisional IRA was popular in song and legend, but it held little sway in day-to-day Irish politics. Some type of miracle would be needed to rejuvenate the IRA.

Repression on the part of the Northern government was the answer to IRA prayers. The government in Northern Ireland reacted with a heavy hand against the civil rights workers and demonstrators. Max Hastings (1970, pp. 40–56) writes that peaceful attempts to work for equal rights were stymied by Northern Irish militancy. Catholics were not allowed to demonstrate for better housing and education; if they attempted to do so, they were attacked by the RUC and its reserve force, known as B-Specials. At the same time no attempts were made to stop Protestant demonstrations. The Catholics believed the RUC and B-Specials were in league with the other anti-Catholic Unionists in the North.

Issues intensified in the summer of 1969. Civil rights demonstrators planned a long, peaceful march from Londonderry to Belfast, but they were gassed and beaten by the RUC and B-Specials. On August 15, 1969, the Protestants assembled for their traditional Apprentice Boys celebration. Just a few days before, the RUC had enthusiastically attacked Catholic demonstrators, but on August 15, 1969, it welcomed the Protestant Apprentice Boys with open arms. The Catholics were not surprised: many B-Specials had taken off their reservist uniforms to don orange sashes and march with the Protestants.

Protestant marchers in Londonderry and Belfast armed themselves with gasoline bombs, rocks, and sticks. They not only wished to celebrate the seventeenth-century victory in Derry, but they were also thrilled by the recent dispersal of the civil rights marchers and hoped to reinforce their political status by bombarding Catholic neighborhoods as they marched by. When the Protestants began taunting Catholics, violence broke out. By nightfall, Belfast and Londonderry were in flames. Three days later, Britain sent the British army in as a peacekeeping force. The British army became the miracle the IRA so desperately needed.

The Army and Overreaction

According to most analysts and observers, the early policies and tactics of the British army played an important role in the rebirth of the IRA. In an article on military policy, J. Bowyer Bell (1976, pp. 65–88) criticizes the British army for its initial response. He says the British army came to Ulster with little or no appreciation of the historical circumstances behind the conflict. According to Bell, when the army arrived in 1969, its commanders believed they were in the midst of a colonial war. They evaluated the situation and concluded there were two "tribes." One tribe flew the Irish tricolor and spoke with deep-seated hatred of the British. The other tribe flew the Union Jack and claimed to be ultrapatriotic subjects of the British Empire. It seemed logical to ally with friends who identified themselves as subjects.

Bell believes this policy was a fatal flaw. Far from being a conflict to preserve British influence in a colony, the struggle in Northern Ireland was a fight between two groups of Irish citizens. Neither side was "British," no matter what their slogans and banners claimed. The British army should have become the peaceful, neutral force, but it mistakenly allied itself with one of the extremist positions in the conflict. That mistake became the answer to IRA prayers.

Bell argues that the reaction of Republican Catholics fully demonstrates the mistake the British army made. The Unionists greeted the army with open arms, but this was to be expected. Historically, the British army had rallied to the Unionist cause. Surprisingly, however, the Republicans also welcomed the British army. They believed that the RUC and B-Specials were the instruments of their repression and that the British army would not continue those restrictive measures. It was not the British army of the past. In Republican eyes, it was a peacekeeping force. The Republicans believed the British army would protect them from the Unionists and the police.

Such beliefs were short-lived. As the British army made its presence felt in Ulster, Republicans and Catholics were subjected to the increasing oppression of British army measures. Catholic neighborhoods were surrounded and gassed by military forces searching for subversives, and the soldiers began working as a direct extension of the RUC. Londonderry and Belfast were military targets, and rebels fighting against the government were to be subdued. As confrontations became more deadly, Republican support for the British army vanished.

Feeling oppressed by all sides, Catholics and Republicans looked for help. They found it, partly, in the form of the IRA. The Officials and Provisionals were still split during the 1969 riots, and the IRA was generally an impotent organization. But the IRA pushed its internal squabbles aside, and the Officials and Provisionals focused on their new common enemy, the British army. The new IRA policy emphasized the elimination of British soldiers from Irish soil and brushed aside internal political differences (see Hamilton, 1971; R. White, 1989; 1993, pp. 74–88).

The British army found itself in the middle of a conflict it had hoped to forestall. Alienated nationalists offered support for the growing ranks of the IRA. Each time the British army overreacted, as it tended to do when faced with civil disobedience, the Republican cause was strengthened. IRA ranks grew from a few dozen to nearly 2,000, and members adopted an elaborate justification of violence. As IRA ranks grew, Unionists watched with horror. When crackdowns by British army patrols and incidents of alleged torture by intelligence services increased the ranks of the IRA, Unionist paramilitary organizations grew in response. The British army also began taking action against Unionist organizations and then truly found itself in the midst of a terrorist conflict (see Moss, 1972, pp. 16–18; Winchester, 1974, pp. 171–180; Munck, 1992; R. White, 1993, pp. 26–28, 64–99, 130–133; Kuusisto, 2001; Alonso, 2001).

In 1972 the British government issued a report on the violence in Northern Ireland. Headed by Leslie Scarman (1972), the investigation concluded that tensions inside the community were so great, once they had been unleashed, that little could be done to alleviate them. The policies of the police and the British army had done much to set those hostile forces in motion. The report concluded that normative democracy could not return until the people in Northern Ireland had faith in all governmental institutions, including the security forces. The report indicated that a legal method was needed to resolve the violence.

Robert White (1989, 1993) explains violence in Northern Ireland as a group process. Socially constructed meanings evolved in three ways:

(1) small-group interpretation within the IRA, (2) general interpretation of activities by the Catholic population, and (3) meanings assigned from the interaction between the small and large groups. IRA operatives were recruited by different patterns, and each recruiting style affected tactics, such as bombings, shootings, or hunger strikes. When the people of Northern Ireland, at least the Catholic minority, felt repressed by the British, it legitimized IRA violence. The IRA could not move without popular support. In addition, popular support came when peaceful actions appeared to produce no results. Finally, as the IRA in the republic and in Ulster grew closer together, they also identified with the Republicans of Ulster. The British were, and remain, outsiders to Republicans.

Self-Check

- *How did republicanism relate to the Catholic civil rights movement of the 1960s?*
- *Did the evolution of the IRA contribute to this relationship?*
- *Would different military reactions to the riots in Belfast and Londonderry change or eliminate violent republicanism?*

Unionist Violence

Although most Irish terrorism is associated with the IRA and its radical splinter groups, it is not proper to conclude that all Irish terrorism is the result of Republican violence. Unionist organizations also have a long history of terrorism. They represent the Unionist and Loyalist side of terrorism. Historically, it has appeared in three forms: (1) state repression, (2) vengeance, and (3) revolutionary violence for political change. Repression developed because the Unionists held power throughout most of modern Irish history. Vengeance came as Loyalist organizations struck back at Republicans. Finally, some Unionist activity has been directed at the British or other authorities. This happens when extreme Unionists feel the government is abandoning the Unionist cause (see Elbe, 2000; Wright and Bryett, 2000, pp. 63–66; Bruce, 2001).

Before the 1916 Easter Rising, Unionists feared Irish independence. If home rule were granted, they planned to go to war with the south to gain the independence of the north. They created the Ulster Volunteer Force (UVF) as a result. As long as the British remained, however, Unionists had little need of subversive groups. They controlled the events in Ireland through the police and military. For example, the IRB began importing arms before World War I. Unionists, fearful of Catholic Republican power, decided to arm themselves too. Although the British government had forbidden importing arms, police officers turned a blind eye as thousands of illegal arms were smuggled one night into the Orange Lodges. The British army also condoned the smuggling by confining soldiers to their barracks while the arms were distributed.

The Unionist position also enjoyed the backing of the military in other ways. Before World War I, it appeared home rule would be passed by the British parliament. To influence the vote, British officers began to resign their commissions en masse, forcing a crisis in government. The United Kingdom was on the verge of war with Germany; it could hardly fight without the leadership of its officer corps. Home rule was withdrawn, and Ireland remained under British control.

Things changed after the Tan War and the creation of the Republic of Ireland. Although de Valera waged war against his old colleagues, the IRA still brought terrorism to the North. Some Unionist groups formed terrorist enclaves of their own to terrorize the Republicans.

At this point, Unionist terrorism focused on retribution. When Republicans struck, the Unionists hit back. After the IRA was reborn in the 1969 violence, Orange organizations watched in fear. When IRA bombings and assassinations began, the Unionist terrorists targeted Republican leaders, especially outspoken civil rights advocates. Unionist terrorism has never matched Republican terrorism simply because Unionists were able to use official organizations to repress Catholics in Northern Ireland.

Seamus Dunn and Valerie Morgan (1995) argue that this attitude may change. In 1985 the United Kingdom and the Republic of Ireland signed a peace accord regarding the governance of Northern Ireland. Known as the **Anglo-Irish Peace Accord**, the agreement seeks to bring an end to terrorism by establishing a joint system of government for the troubled area. Dunn and Morgan believe many Protestant groups feel betrayed by this agreement. They surmise such groups may resort to violence if they feel they have no voice in the political system.

The governments in Ireland and the United Kingdom worked to give each side a voice, hoping to avoid violence. On Good Friday 1998 Britain and Ireland signed the **Belfast Agreement**, which called for independent human rights investigations, compensation for the victims of violence, and decommissioning of paramilitary groups (Northern Ireland Office, 2007). The IRA announced the end of its campaign in July 2005 and handed over its weapons in September of the same year. The Royal Ulster Constabulary was re-created as the Police Service of Northern Ireland, and both governments worked to keep peace among Protestants and Catholics.

Not everyone was happy with the agreement. Some Republicans were not willing to accept the provisions of the Good Friday Agreement. They did not trust the British government, and radicals supporting the IRA criticized the surrender of weapons. On the Unionist side, many people felt betrayed by the United Kingdom. They believed that they were losing their ability to participate in the political system and that Britain completely discounted their loyalty (BBC, 2005c). Economic prosperity may influence both Unionists and Republicans to accept the agreement. The Republic of Ireland is experiencing population growth and an expanding economy. If everyone in the North has an opportunity to

Anglo-Irish Peace Accord

An agreement signed in 1985 that was the beginning of a long-term attempt to stop terrorist violence in Northern Ireland by devising a system of political autonomy and protecting the rights of all citizens. Extremist Republicans rejected the accord because it did not unite Northern Ireland and the south. Unionists rejected it because it compromised with moderate Republicans.

Belfast Agreement

Also known as the Good Friday Agreement, an agreement signed in April 1998 that revamped criminal justice services, established shared government in Northern Ireland, called for the early release of prisoners involved in paramilitary organizations, and created a Commission on Human Rights and Equity. Its provisions led to the decommissioning of paramilitary organizations.

participate in the growing prosperity, old antagonisms may become less violent. Current trends suggest this may be happening.

> ### Self-Check
>
> - *Identify the differences between Unionist and Republican violence.*
> - *Was Irish terrorism the result of religion, politics, or a combination of both?*
> - *Did Unionist violence compare to the type of terrorism waged by groups like the Irish Republican Army?*

SUMMARY

- Viking invaders came to Ireland around 800 C.E. They built many cities, and Irish tribes fought groups of Vikings for 300 years. Brian Boru, High King of Ireland, defeated the Vikings, but his assassination prevented all the tribes from uniting under a strong monarchy.
- Norman invaders came to Ireland shortly after the defeat of the Vikings. They could not gain control of the countryside but did hold fortified areas. Their presence eventually led to English occupation.
- The religious split from the Reformation resulted in a nationalistic split in Ireland. Protestants were mostly British and Catholicism dominated among the native-born Irish.
- Three events dominated Irish history in the 1600s: (1) the creation of the Plantation of Ulster, (2) Oliver Cromwell's military actions, and (3) the defeat of Irish Catholics supporting James II by Protestants supported by William of Orange. The Plantation of Ulster displaced native Irish people with Scots and English settlers. Cromwell's army wreaked havoc after English Catholic royalists tried to use Ireland as a base in the last years of the English Civil War. British control of Ireland was solidified after the defeat of James II on the Boyne River.
- Theobald Wolfe Tone and the United Irishmen attempted to gain independence in 1797 with the help of France. After the revolt failed, Britain passed the Act of Union in 1800 and formed the United Kingdom of Great Britain and Ireland in 1801.
- Several Irish politicians championed Catholic rights and independence. Charles Stewart Parnell and John Redmond peacefully sought home rule from their elected positions.
- The 1916 Easter Rising failed, but the British overreacted. This caused public sympathy to shift toward revolutionary activity.
- The Black and Tan War, so named because of the uniforms the British wore, pitted Republicans against the British and RUC. Michael Collins emerged as a master planner who used selective terrorism to wear down the British.
- The peace treaty at the end of the Tan War separated the northern counties of Ulster from the Free State. The IRA rejected the treaty and went to war with Ireland.

- The IRA fought to place Ulster under Irish control from 1939–1944 and 1956–1962. It was ineffective. After the civil rights movement of 1969 erupted in violence, British tactics alienated the Catholics of the North. The IRA grew and was able to wage a campaign of terrorism up to and after the 1985 Anglo-Irish Peace Accord.
- Unionist terror has come in three forms: (1) repression, (2) vengeance, and (3) revolutionary violence.

KEY TERMS

Plantation of Ulster (p. 143)

Society of United Irishmen
  (p. 145)

home rule (p. 146)

Royal Irish Constabulary (p. 149)

Supreme Council (p. 150)

Sinn Fein (p. 151)

Free State (p. 152)

Provisionals (p. 153)

Anglo-Irish Peace Accord (p. 158)

Belfast Agreement (p. 158)

WRITING ASSIGNMENTS

1. If some of the historians cited in this chapter are correct, Ireland had a deep mystical religious tradition that was incorporated into Christianity. The Vikings came to Ireland with a completely different religion, but some Irish tribes allied with them. Is this evidence of a religious war? How does this compare with the different sects of Christianity clashing in Ulster in the 1600s? Use Cromwell and William of Orange in the explanation.
2. Compare and contrast the risings led by Theobald Wolfe Tone and Patrick Pearse. Were both events destined to fail? Why was Michael Collins successful in the Tan War? Are his actions more reflective of Pearse or Wolfe Tone?
3. Explain the rise of the IRA after 1969. What factors allowed its rejuvenation? How did Unionist paramilitary groups respond to the IRA?

8

Latin American Influences on Terrorism

Susana Gonzalez/AFP/Getty Images

Latin America has had a tremendous influence on the development of modern terrorism. It has provided theoretical models of revolution, and several modern groups learned to structure organizations by studying terrorism in the region.

Learning Objectives

After completing this chapter, you should be able to

- Discuss the theory of urban terrorism as described by Marighella.
- Summarize the relationship between terrorism and guerrilla warfare.
- Outline the campaign of the Tupamaros in Uruguay.
- Describe the influence of the Tupamaros on terrorism in other parts of the world.
- Describe the urban philosophy of the Tupamaros.
- Summarize the Tupamaro terrorist tactics.
- Outline the organizational structure of the Tupamaros.

I nternational terrorism is historically connected. Each region's terrorism developed along specific lines in the last fifty years of the twentieth century, but the lines were interwoven. Terrorism in one part of the world drew on other terrorist movements: Michael Collins studied Russian theories of revolution, and Middle Eastern terrorists began to follow the pattern of Collins. After a series of anticolonial revolts from 1945 to 1964, another set of ideas dominated the world of terrorism. These theories were spawned by Carlos Marighella and Ernesto "Che" Guevara and put into practice by a Uruguayan terrorist group called the Tupamaros. This Latin American influence has been felt throughout the world of terrorism for the past fifty years (Figure 8.1).

Frantz Fanon
(1925–1961) A writer, psychiatrist, and revolutionary theorist. He was also one of the most influential philosophers in the awareness of colonialism. Fanon grew up in the French colony Martinique in the Caribbean, and he became acutely aware of racism and colonialism in experiences there. He joined the French Army in World War II, and won one of France's highest military decorations. After the war he studied psychiatry. Believing that mental illness was a result of imperialism, Fanon campaigned against racism and colonialism. He supported Algerian rebels in their struggle with France and advocated for violent revolution. He died of leukemia, but his ideas influenced anticolonial revolutionaries for decades.

Toward a Theory of Urban Terrorism

The first wave of modern terrorism appeared in Africa and Asia after 1945. For the next twenty years, nationalistic rebellions broke out against Western colonial powers in struggles for independence. Some of the movements involved long guerrilla wars, whereas others involved terrorism. Some rebels, especially those in Latin America, equated economic revolution with national revolution, giving birth to ideological terrorism. Whether motivated by nationalism or ideology, the practice of modern terrorism began to gravitate toward one of two models: urban terrorism or guerrilla warfare.

Frantz Fanon

The model for modern urban terrorism was intellectually championed by **Frantz Fanon** (1925–1961). Born on Martinique in 1925, Fanon studied medicine in France and became a psychiatrist. When Algeria revolted from French rule in 1954, Fanon was sent to Algiers, the capital of Algeria, to work in a mental hospital. His experiences there caused him to side with the rebels. Fanon believed the pressures caused by exploitative imperialism were the primary causes for mental illness in Algeria. He produced two works, *The Wretched of the Earth* (1982) and *A Dying Colonialism* (1965), as a result of his Algerian experiences. He died of cancer in 1961, a year before the Algerian War ended, unable to play a leading role in revolutions; his thought, however, was strongly imprinted on Africa, Asia, and Latin America (see University of Singapore, 2007).

In *The Wretched of the Earth*, Fanon indicts colonial powers and calls on all the colonized to practice terrorism. He writes that Western powers have dehumanized non-Western people by destroying their cultures

Figure 8.1
Central and South America

and replacing them with Western values. Even when Westerners are not present, they are represented by a native middle class that embraces Western values and turns its back on the general population. Native culture is forgotten by the middle class as native intellectualism is replaced by Western traditions. The masses end up suffering a perpetual identity crisis: to succeed, they are forced to deny their heritage. Fanon argues the natives can follow only one course of action. He calls them to revolution.

To be sure, Fanon was no Gandhi. His only argument was for violent revolt, including guerrilla warfare and acts of terrorism. He claimed decolonization was destined to be a violent process because it involved replacing one group of powerful people with another group. No group would willingly surrender power. Therefore, according to Fanon, achieving freedom was inherently violent. Political action and peaceful efforts toward change were useless. Only when oppressed people recognized that violence was their only alternative would they be assured of victory. Fanon saw guerrilla warfare and individual acts of terrorism as tools of revolution. Guerrilla war was the initial method of revolt because third-world revolutionaries could not mount direct, conventional campaigns at the beginning of their struggles. Fanon's concept of guerrilla warfare was based in rural revolution, but urban terrorism would become the major weapon rendering colonial administration impotent.

Mao Zedong

(1893–1976) Also known as Mao Tse Tung, the leader of the Chinese Communist Party. He seized power in a revolution in 1949 and ruled China until his death in 1976.

Terrorism was to be limited to specific acts. Fanon argued that terrorism should not be used against the native population in general. As had communist Chinese revolutionary leader **Mao Zedong** (1893–1976), he believed it would alienate supporters. Instead, he proposed two targets for terrorism: white settlers and the native middle class. The purpose of terrorism was to terrorize Westerners and their lackeys into submission. Individual murders, bombings, and mutilations would force the white settlers to leave the country and frighten the native middle class away from their colonial masters. Brutality would be the example. It would bring on governmental repression, but this would only cause more natives to flock to the terrorist cause.

Fanon's ideas flourished in Latin America (Figure 8.1). Beginning in Brazil, some revolutionaries believed cities would be the focus of Latin American revolution, and they embraced Fanon's idea of urban terrorism. They felt a revolutionary could create the context for an impromptu general uprising through the use of spontaneous violence. Directly reflecting Fanon, these revolutionaries believed terrorism could communicate with the people and infuse them with the spirit of revolt. The foremost proponent of this idea in Latin America was **Carlos Marighella** (1911–1969; see O'Connor, 2006).

Carlos Marighella

(1911–1969) A Brazilian communist legislator and a revolutionary theorist. Marighella popularized urban terrorism as a method for ending repression and eliminating U.S. domination of Latin America. He was killed in a police ambush in São Paulo in 1969.

Carlos Marighella

Marighella was a Brazilian legislator, a leader of the nationalistic communist party, and eventually a fiery revolutionary terrorist. He was killed by Brazilian police in an ambush in São Paulo in 1969. In two major works, *For the Liberation of Brazil* (1971) and *The Minimanual of the Urban Guerrilla* (1969), Marighella designed practical guides for terrorism. These books have had more influence on recent revolutionary terrorism than any other set of theories. Marighella wanted to move violence from the countryside to the city, and although his call to terrorism was politically motivated, his model was apolitical. He designed a method for organizing a campaign of terror that, for the past forty years, has been employed by groups ranging across the political spectrum—from the Japanese Red Army to the Freemen of Montana.

Marighella believed the basis of revolution was violence. Violence need not be structured, and efforts among groups need not be coordinated. Violence created a situation in which revolution could flourish.

Any type of violence was acceptable because it contributed a general feeling of panic and frustration among the ruling classes and their protectors. Marighella's most original concept was that all violence could be urban-based and controlled by a small group of urban guerrillas. This concept of revolution spread from Brazil throughout the world.

The hierarchy of Marighella has been replaced by uncoordinated activities in many groups, but Marighella might have been satisfied by this. His four-stage model did not require coordination. **Urban terrorism** was to begin with two distinct phases, one designed to bring about actual violence, and the other designed to give that violence meaning. The violent portion of the revolution was to be a confederate campaign employing armed revolutionary cells to carry out the most deplorable acts of violence. Targets were to have symbolic significance, and although violence was designed to be frightening, its logic would remain clear with regard to the overall revolution. That is, those who supported the revolution need not fear terrorist violence (see Moss, 1972, pp. 70–72; Marighella, 1969; Smith and Damphousse, 2002, pp. 6–13).

The terror campaign was to be accompanied by a psychological offensive to provide peripheral support for terrorists. The psychological offensive would not only join students and workers in low-level challenges to governmental authority but also be used to create a network of safe houses, logistical stores, and medical units. In essence, the supporting activities would carry out standard military-support functions.

A campaign of revolutionary terrorism in an urban setting could be used to destabilize governmental power. A psychological assault would convince the government and the people that the status quo no longer held. They would come to feel that the terrorists were in control. When this situation developed, Marighella believed, the government would be forced to show its true colors. With its authority challenged and the economic stability of the elite eroded, the government would be forced to declare some form of martial law. This would not be a defeat for terrorism but rather exactly what the terrorists and their supporters wanted. Governmental repression was the goal of terrorism at this stage.

This view might appear to be contradictory at first glance, but there was a method to Marighella's madness. Marighella believed the public supported governmental policies because they did not realize the repressive nature of the state. The terrorist campaign would force the government to reveal itself, thereby alienating the public. With no place to turn, the public would turn to the terrorists, and the terrorists would be waiting with open arms. As the ranks of the urban guerrillas grew with the rush of public support, Marighella believed, the revolutionaries would gradually abandon their terrorist campaign. Their efforts would focus more and more on the construction of a general urban army, an army that could seize key governmental control points on cue. When the urban army had reached sufficient strength, all its forces would be launched in a general strike.

urban terrorism

A four-stage process described by Carlos Marighella: (1) unorganized violence accompanied by passive disruption, (2) governmental repression to stop violence, (3) massive uprising in response to repression, and (4) toppling of government.

Marighella's theory has only one weakness: it does not work. Even so, several terrorist groups have used it to organize murder throughout the world, unfortunately. Marighella writes that the purpose of the urban guerrilla is to shoot. Any form of urban violence is desirable because a violent atmosphere creates the political environment needed for success. Terrorism could be used to create that environment, and terrorism could be employed with minimal organization. Therefore, terrorism is to be the primary strategy of the urban guerrilla.

The *Minimanual of the Urban Guerrilla*

Marighella (1969) outlines the basic structure needed for an urban terrorist group in the *Minimanual of the Urban Guerrilla*. The main operational group of a terrorist organization should be the firing group. Composed of four to five terrorists each, several firing groups are needed to construct a terrorist organization. They can join as needed to concentrate their power, but their small size ensures both mobility and secrecy. For Marighella, the firing group is the basic weapon of the urban guerrilla.

In a single theory, Marighella provides the justification for violence and the organizational structure a small group needs to begin killing. Unlike Fanon, Marighella endorsed violence for the sake of violence. Another model of revolution emerged from Latin America that had a different structure. Emanating directly from the Cuban Revolution, this model calls for a more rational approach to violence.

Self-Check

- *What is urban terrorism?*
- *How do Fanon's theories relate to Marighella's?*
- *How does the* Minimanual *prepare urban groups for terrorism?*

▼ Guerrilla War and a Rural Model of Terrorism

Cuban Revolution
The guerrilla revolution led by Fidel Castro. Castro initially failed in 1956 and left for Mexico after a brief prison sentence. He returned with a small group of guerrillas and built a large guerrilla army. He overthrew the Cuban government in 1959, embracing communism shortly after taking power.

Guerrilla war is an age-old process. Several nationalistic rebellions after World War II were based on guerrilla war, but the **Cuban Revolution** in 1956 captured the minds of left-wing ideologues. They came to view guerrilla war as a statement of revolution against capitalist powers. As with terrorism, guerrilla revolutionaries produced their own theories and models (see Wickham-Crowley, 1992, pp. 51–59).

The Cuban Revolution

The Cuban Revolution did not create guerrilla warfare, but it popularized it throughout the world. Despite only one other guerrilla movement succeeding in overthrowing an established government, the Nicaraguan Sandinistas in 1979, guerrilla war is the preferred method of fighting

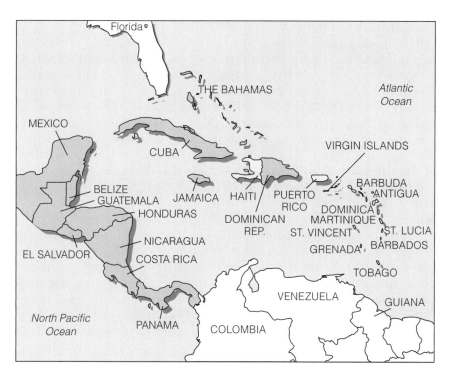

Figure 8.2
Central America and the Caribbean

among Latin American revolutionaries (Figure 8.2). Unlike the model for urban terrorism, the guerrilla model began with a successful structure then moved toward a theory (see March, 2005; O'Connor, 2006).

The process began in the hills of Cuba. The Cuban revolutionary leader Fidel Castro tried to seize power in 1956, but he was soundly defeated. Retreating to the rural regions of Cuba, he surrounded himself with a ragtag group of revolutionaries, including a friend, **Ernesto "Che" Guevara** (1928–1967). Guevara was born in Argentina in 1928. After earning a medical degree at the University of Buenos Aires, he turned his attention from medicine to the plight of the poor. He believed poverty and repression were problems that transcended nationalism and revolution was the only means of challenging authority. He served the communist regime of Guatemala in 1954 but fled to Mexico City when communists were purged from the government. There he met Castro.

Guevara immediately impressed Castro, and the two worked together to oust the Cuban military dictator Fulgencio Batista (1901–1973). After failing to seize power in 1956, Castro began to meet secretly with rural partisans. Castro organized a command-and-support structure, enlisted partisans, and formed regional guerrilla forces. As Castro's strength grew, he moved to more conventional methods of warfare and triumphantly entered Havana in 1959. Throughout the campaign, Guevara had been at Castro's side.

Ernesto "Che" Guevara
(1928–1967) Fidel Castro's assistant and guerrilla warfare theorist. Guevara advocated guerrilla revolutions throughout Latin America after success in the Cuban Revolution. He was killed in Bolivia in 1967 when trying to form a guerrilla army.

Guevara: On Guerrilla Warfare

Inflamed with revolutionary passion, Guevara completed a work on guerrilla warfare shortly after Castro took power. Far from theoretical, it can be deemed a how-we-did-it guide. Translated copies of Guevara's *Reminiscences of the Cuban Revolutionary War* appeared in the United States as early as 1961, but the book did not enjoy mass distribution until the end of the decade. It describes both Guevara's evolution toward Marxism and the revolutionary process in Cuba, and it details the structure and strategy of Castro's forces, as well as the guiding philosophy of the **Cuban guerrilla war**. Guevara also outlines the revolutionaries' methods of operation and principles of engagement. With the advantage of hindsight, it makes a stirring description of how victory was achieved.

Cuban guerrilla war

A three-step process as described by Che Guevara: (1) revolutionaries join the indigenous population to form guerrilla *foco*, as Guevara called them, (2) small forces form columns and control rural areas, and (3) columns unite for a conventional offensive to overthrow government.

Guerrilla revolutions based on the Cuban experience are typified by three phases, each one designed to progress from and complement the previous one. Guevara-style revolution begins with isolated groups. In phase two, the isolated groups merge into guerrilla columns. The final phase brings columns together in a conventional army. The goal of the strategy is to develop a conventional fighting force, or at least a force that renders the conventional opponent impotent. Although Guevara's work focused specifically on the Cuban experience, it had two important effects. In Latin America and to revolutionaries there in particular, Guevara became an icon. In addition, guerrillas throughout the world studied the guide and copied the tactics used during the revolution (see Burton, 1976, p. 70; J. K. Clark, 1988; Asprey, 2002, pp. 698–710; Taber, 2002, pp. 25–37).

Terrorism plays a limited role in Guevara's guerrilla framework. Although Guevara's focus was on the countryside, he saw the need for small urban terrorist groups to wage a campaign of support. These actions, however, are to be extremely selective; their purpose is to keep governmental forces off balance, terrorizing them in their "safe" areas, never letting them relax. The main purpose of terrorism is to strike at the government's logistical network; the secondary purpose is to demoralize the government. Terrorism is a commando-type tactic.

Debray: Expanding Guerrilla Warfare

The theory of guerrilla war came after the appearance of Guevara's work, and it was popularized by a French socialist named Regis Debray. In *Revolution in the Revolution?* Debray (1967) summarizes his concept of Latin American politics. He writes that the region has one dominating issue: poverty. Poverty threads through the entire fabric of Latin American life and entwines divergent cultures and peoples in a common knot of misery. Poverty is responsible for the imbalance in the class structure, as the wealthy cannot be maintained without the poverty of the masses. Debray sees only one recourse: The class structure must be changed and wealth redistributed. Because the wealthy will never give up their power, revolution is the only method of change.

Debray's prime target was the United States. Although the United States does not maintain a direct colonial empire as did the countries of Fanon's focus, it does hold sway over Latin America through economic imperialism. Behind every power in the south stands the United States. Debray holds the United States responsible for maintaining the inequitable class structure, and he shares the common Marxist belief that North American wealth caused Latin American poverty. It is quite logical, therefore, to target the United States.

As did Fanon, Debray continually talks of revolution. He sees little need for terrorism, however, and he minimizes the role of urban centers in a revolt. Debray believes revolution is essentially an affair for poor peasants and it can begin only in a rural setting with regional guerrilla forces. Terrorism has no payoff. At best, it is neutral, and at worst, it alienates peasants needed for guerrilla support. According to Debray, for a revolution to work, it must begin with guerrillas fighting for justice and end with a united conventional force. Terrorism will not accomplish this objective.

Self-Check

- *Are there similarities between Marighella's ideas and Guevara's?*
- *Explain the Cuban revolutionary model.*
- *What are the differences between rural and urban guerrillas?*

A Brief History of the Tupamaros: 1963–1972

In the early 1960s, a group of revolutionaries called the Tupamaros surfaced in Uruguay (Figure 8.3). Unlike their predecessors in the Cuban Revolution, the Tupamaros spurned the countryside to favor an urban environment. City sidewalks and asphalt became their battleground. A decade later, their tactics would inspire revolutionaries around the world, and terrorist groups would imitate the methods of the Uruguayan revolutionaries. The Tupamaros epitomized urban terrorism.

Politics in Uruguay

In the years immediately after World War II, Uruguay appeared to be a model Latin American government. Democratic principles and freedoms were the accepted basis of Uruguay's political structures. Democratic rule was complemented by a sound economy and an exemplary educational system. Although it could not be described as a land of wealth, by the early 1950s Uruguay could be called a land of promise. All factors seemed to point to peace and prosperity.

Unfortunately, Uruguay's promise started to fade in 1954. The export economy that had proved so prosperous for the country began to crumble. Falling prices on exported goods brought inflation and unemployment, and economic dissatisfaction grew. By 1959 many workers and

Figure 8.3

Uruguay

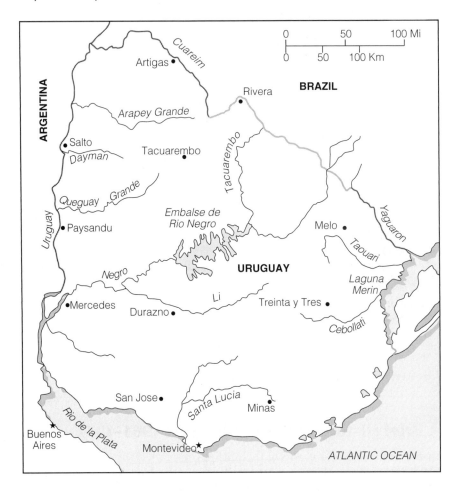

members of the middle class faced a bleak future. Uruguay had undergone a devastating economic reversal, and workers were restless.

In the northern section of Uruguay, sugar workers were particularly hard hit. Sugar exports had decreased in the 1950s, and sugar workers suffered all of Uruguay's economic woes. As a result, the workers took steps to form a national union. Several militant radicals injected themselves into the union movement, and when the sugar workers organized in 1959, the militants dominated the union and called for confrontation with the government.

By 1962 the union organizers believed they should move their organization from the rural north to Montevideo, the capital, to make its presence felt. Moderates joined militants in a united front and headed south. Even though their rhetoric was violent, union members felt an appearance in Montevideo would not only draw attention to their cause but also help legitimize it.

Their logic seemed sound. Uruguay was predominantly rural, and most of the population lived in Montevideo, a metropolis of 1.25 million people. Demographically, the capital offered the promise of recognition. Unfortunately for the union, they did not achieve the type of recognition they were seeking. Far from viewing the marchers as a legitimate labor movement, the government considered them potential revolutionaries.

The sugar workers clashed with police, and several union members were arrested. One of those taken to jail was a young law student named **Raul Sendic** (1926–1989). Disillusioned with law school and his prospects for the future, Sendic had joined the sugar workers. Sendic remained in jail until 1963. When he emerged, he had a plan for revolution.

Raul Sendic: Waiting for the Guerrilla

Sendic had not seen the brighter side of Uruguayan life in prison. The stark realities of Uruguay's now-shaky political system were evident, as torture and mistreatment of prisoners were common experiences. If the population could not be kept content by a sound economy, it had to be subdued by fear. Democracy and freedoms faded as Uruguay's economic woes increased. Sendic described the repression he saw in "Waiting for the Guerrilla," in which he called for revolt in Montevideo.

After Sendic was released from jail, several young radicals gravitated toward him. María Gilio (1972) paints a sympathetic picture of Sendic's early followers. According to Gilio, these young people were primarily interested in reforming the government and creating economic opportunities. Although they had once believed they could attain these goals through democratic action, the current repression in Uruguay ruled out any response except violence. Gilio believed the group of people who surrounded Sendic were humanist idealists who wanted to bring Uruguay under direct control of the people.

Others did not hold this opinion of Sendic and his compatriots. Arturo Porzecanski (1973) provides a more objective view of the group's next move. Sendic's group felt excluded from participation in the political system, and Sendic believed violence was the only appropriate tool to change the political order. In 1963 Sendic and his followers raided the Swiss Hunting Club outside Montevideo. The raid was the first step in arming the group, and the first step in revolution.

The Urban Philosophy

According to Porzecanski, the group was not willing to move outside Montevideo to begin a guerrilla war for several reasons. First, the group was not large enough to begin a guerrilla campaign because it represented radical middle-class students. Mainstream workers and labor activists had moved away from the militants' position before the march on Montevideo. Second, the countryside of Uruguay did not readily lend itself to a guerrilla war because unrest grew from the urban center of Uruguay. Third, the peasants were unwilling to provide popular support for guerrilla forces. Finally, Montevideo was the nerve center of Uruguay. All of these factors caused the small group to believe that it could better fight within the city.

Raul Sendic

(1926–1989) A Uruguayan revolutionary leader. Sendic founded the National Liberation Movement (MLN), popularly known as the Tupamaros. Following governmental repression in 1973, he fled the country. Sendic died in Paris in 1989.

In 1963 the group adopted its official name, the National Liberation Movement (MLN). But as they began to develop a revolutionary ideology and a structure for violent revolt, the group searched for a name that would identify them with the people, one with more popular appeal than *MLN*. According to Christopher Dobson and Ronald Payne (1982, p. 206), the MLN adapted the name of the heroic Inca chieftain Tupac Amaru, killed in a revolt against the Spaniards 200 years earlier. Arturo Porzecanski notes this story but also suggests the group may have taken its name from a South American bird. In any case, Sendic's followers called themselves the Tupamaros.

By 1965 their ranks had grown to fifty followers, and they were building a network of sympathizers in the city. Instead of following the prescribed method of Latin American revolution based on a rural guerrilla operation, the Tupamaros organized to do battle inside the city, following the recent guidelines of Carlos Marighella. Terrorism would become the prime strategy for assaulting the enemy. The Tupamaros, unlike Castro, were not interested in building a conventional military force to strike at the government.

Porzecanski estimates the Tupamaros had expanded to nearly 3,000 members by 1970. Expansion brought an extremely decentralized command structure and the evolution of a grand strategy intended to result in national socialism. The Tupamaros claimed this program would allow the government to nationalize and equitably distribute economic resources. The Tupamaros were more interested in redistributing the wealth of Uruguay than establishing a socialist government. Rather than risk alienating the population with abstract Marxist rhetoric, they wanted to create an economy that would offer opportunities to Montevideo's working class. As they expanded, the Tupamaros constantly stressed that they were trying to foster a working-class revolution, in an effort to attract a following.

Despite their willingness to expound a national socialist propaganda, the Tupamaros never developed an elaborate philosophical base; they were more interested in action. Ross Butler (1976, pp. 53–59) describes the growth of the terrorist group by tracking their tactics. He says they engaged in inconsequential activities in the early stages of their development. From 1964 to 1968, they concentrated on gathering arms and financial backing. After 1968, however, their tactics changed, and according to Butler, the government found it necessary to take them seriously.

Following the Marighella Model

In 1968 the Tupamaros launched a massive campaign of decentralized terrorism. They were able to challenge governmental authority because their movement was growing. A series of bank robberies had financed their operations, and now, armed with the power to strike, the Tupamaros sought to paralyze the government in Montevideo. They believed, as had Carlos Marighella in Brazil, that the government would increasingly turn to repression as a means of defense and the people would be forced to join the revolution.

The government was quick to respond but found there was very little it could do. The Tupamaros held all the cards. They struck when and where they wanted and generally made the government's security forces look foolish. They kidnapped high-ranking officials from the Uruguayan government, and the police could do little to find the victims.

Kidnapping became so successful that the Tupamaros took to kidnapping foreign diplomats. They seemed able to choose their victims and strike their targets at will. Frustrated, the police turned to an old Latin American tactic. They began torturing suspected Tupamaros.

Torturing prisoners served several purposes. First, it provided a ready source of information. In fact, the Tupamaros were destroyed primarily through massive arrests based on information gleaned from interrogations. Second, torture was believed to serve as a deterrent to other would-be revolutionaries. Although this torture was always unofficial, most potential governmental opponents knew what lay in store for them if they were caught.

The methods of torture were brutal. Gilio (1972, pp. 141–172) describes in detail the police and military torture of suspected Tupamaros. Even when prisoners finally provided information, they continued to be tortured routinely until they were either killed or released. Torture became a standard police tactic. A. J. Langguth (1978) devotes most of his work to the torture commonplace in Uruguay and Brazil. The torturers viewed themselves as professionals who were simply carrying out a job for the government. Rapes, beatings, and murders were common by torturers, and the police refined the art of torture to keep victims in pain as long as possible. According to Langguth, some suspects were tortured over a period of months or even years.

In the midst of revolution and torture, the Tupamaros accused the United States of supporting the brutal Uruguayan government. Their internal revolt thus adopted the rhetoric of an anti-imperialist revolution, which increased their popular support. The Tupamaros established several combat and support columns in Montevideo, and by 1970, they began to reach the zenith of their power. Porzecanski says they almost achieved a duality of power. That is, the Tupamaros were so strong that they seemed to share power equally with the government.

Their success was short-lived, however. Although they waged an effective campaign of terrorism, they were never able to capture the hearts of the working class. Most of Montevideo's workers viewed the Tupamaros as privileged students with no real interest in the working class. In addition, the level of their violence was truly appalling.

During terrorist operations, numerous people were routinely murdered. The eventual murder of a kidnapped American police official disgusted the workers, even though they had no great love for the United States. Tupamaro tactics alienated their potential supporters. In the end, violence spelled doom for the Tupamaros. By bringing chaos to the capital, they succeeded in unleashing the full wrath of the government. In addition, the Tupamaros had overestimated their strength. In 1971 they joined a left-wing coalition of parties and ran for office. According to Ronald MacDonald (1972, pp. 24–45), this was a fatal mistake. The Tupamaros had alienated potential electoral support through their terrorist campaign, and the left-wing coalition was soundly defeated in national elections.

The electoral defeat was not the only bad news for the Tupamaros. The election brought a right-wing government to power, and the new military government openly advocated and approved of repression. A brutal counterterrorist campaign followed. Far from being alienated by this, the workers of Montevideo applauded the new government's actions, even when it declared martial law in 1972. Armed with expanded powers, the government began to round up all leftists in 1972. For all practical purposes, the Tupamaros were finished. Their violence helped bring about a revolution, but not the type they had intended.

Self-Check

- *What political and economic factors gave rise to revolutionary thought in Uruguay?*
- *How did the Tupamaros envision urban revolution?*
- *Does the Tupamaro experience have any relevance today?*

The Influence of the Tupamaros

Terrorism analysts of the 1980s and early 1990s saw the influence of the Tupamaros in Europe and the United States. Peter Waldmann (1986, p. 259) believes that in terms of striking power, organization, and the ability to control a city, no group has ever surpassed the Tupamaros. They epitomized the terrorist role. As such, they served as a model for urban terrorist groups in the two decades after their demise. As the champions of revolutionary terrorism, the Tupamaros were copied around the world, especially by groups in the United States and western Europe. Many American left-wing groups from 1967 to 1990 modeled themselves after the Tupamaros. In western Europe, their structure and tactics were mimicked by such groups as the Red Army Faction and Direct Action. The Red Brigades split their activities among different cities, but they essentially copied the model of the Tupamaros.

The tactics and organization of the Tupamaros have also been copied by right-wing groups. In the United States, right-wing extremist organizations have advocated the use of Tupamaro-type tactics. Many revolutionary manuals and proposed terrorist organizations are based on Tupamaro experiences. In the right-wing novel *The Turner Diaries* (MacDonald, 1980), Earl Turner joins a terrorist group similar to the Tupamaros in

Washington, D.C. The author describes the mythical right-wing revolution in terms of Carlos Marighella and the Tupamaros. The right does not give credit to the left, but it does follow its example.

The Tupamaros embodied the Marighella philosophy of revolution, initiating an urban campaign without much thought to structure, strategy, or organization. Although both Marighella and the Tupamaros believed the people would flock to the revolutionaries when governmental repression was employed, the opposite was true. The people endorsed repression.

When the Tupamaros roamed the streets, people were afraid. Banks were robbed, officials were kidnapped, and people were murdered. Daily fear was a reality, so much so that the government was provoked into action. Adopting the terrorist group's methods, the government turned to murder and torture to eradicate the Tupamaros. This may have been the most frightening aspect of the experience: revolutionary terrorism served to justify repressionist terrorism.

Cold War or Urban Philosophy?

A group of four jihadists attacked the American embassy in Syria on September 12, 2006. Attempting to employ a technique used by al Qaeda in Saudi Arabia, the assailants used two stolen cars loaded with explosives. At 10:00 a.m. one of the cars approached the front of the embassy, and three men exited it throwing hand grenades and firing weapons. Their car caught fire when shots from security forces detonated a bomb inside the vehicle. A second car with pipe bombs approached the rear of the embassy, but the driver fled when he heard shooting from the front. All four assailants and a member of the Syrian security force were killed. No group claimed responsibility for the attack, but the Syrian government placed blame on Jund al Sham, a Syrian group associated with one of the leaders of the Iraq insurgency (U.S. Department of State, Overseas Security Advisory Council, 2006). Some highly respected terrorism analysts believe this type of attack has signaled a new type of terrorism, and all types of domestic and international groups are following new organizational patterns. The rules the West learned during the cold war are no longer applicable (see Scheuer, 2006, pp. 20–21; Barkun, 1997b).

Why Study the Tupamaros?

William Dyson (2004) argues that, although some terrorist structures change and suicide bombing has become more common, the strategic and tactical practices of terrorists remain constant. In addition, the jihadist movement represents only one form of terrorism in the modern world. Several groups still follow the model of the Tupamaros. The fact that the Tupamaros created an urban movement is important in terms of the group's impact on violence in Latin America, but it also has a bearing on the way terrorist methods have developed in Europe and the United States. Historically, Latin American terrorism had been a product of rural peasant revolt. The Tupamaros offered an alternative to this tradition by making the city a battleground. They demonstrated to Western groups the impact that a few violent true believers could have on the rational routines of urban life. The urban setting provided the Tupamaros with endless opportunities.

Their revolutionary philosophy was also indicative of their pragmatism. Rather than accepting a standard line of Marxist dogma, the Tupamaros were willing to use national socialism as their political base; this demonstrated just how much they could compromise. According to one of their propaganda statements, they argued for a nationalized economy with guaranteed employment and social security. The export economy would remain intact, but profits would be shared among the people. Although this view hardly represents Marxism, the Tupamaros were willing to take such a stand to attract a working-class following. Socialism under national control was popular in Montevideo.

The tactics of the Tupamaros reflected the same pragmatism. Because the physical situation of Uruguay was not suitable for guerrilla war, the Tupamaros turned to the city. Just as they modified socialism to suit the political situation, they forged new, flexible, and pragmatic tactics for a new environment. The Tupamaros used the concepts of Marighella in other ways as well. The basic unit of the revolution had become Marighella's firing group. Tupamaro-style terrorism involved extremely small units engaging in individual acts of violence. Such action meshed well with Marighella's concept of a decentralized command structure, as well as his belief that any form of violence supported the revolution. Tupamaro violence did not need to be coordinated; it needed only to engender fear. In a war against social order, tactics and targets were modified to meet the circumstances.

The police replaced the army as the primary enemy, and financial institutions took the place of military targets. The urban war was a battle to gain resources and a psychological edge over security forces. The foliage and cover of the jungle countryside was replaced with the mass of humanity in the city. Guerrillas hid behind trees; the urban terrorists hid among people. They were protected by congestion, mobility, and the bureaucratic rigidity of the enemy. The Tupamaros were able to appear as average citizens until the moment they struck. When the battle was over, they simply melted back into the crowd (Waldmann, 1986, p. 260). This tactic is similar to Michael Collins's use of selective terrorism in the Black and Tan War.

To accomplish these tactics successfully, the Tupamaros were forced to develop specific actions. Communication links inside the city assumed supreme importance, along with transportation. To assure these links, the terrorists had to master criminal activity. They communicated and traveled by means of an illegal network. They developed logistical support systems and safe houses to avoid confrontations with potential enemies. They traveled with false identification and collected their own intelligence from sympathizers. For all practical purposes, the Tupamaros became a secret army.

Tupamaro Tactics

Although many observers note the Tupamaros spent little time discussing their grand strategy, the group did operate under some broad assumptions. The Tupamaros knew their principles, like other extremist groups', would have to be modified to win general support. The grand strategy centered on winning support from the middle and working classes. Because of the state of the economy and the lack of opportunity for educated people, the Tupamaros began their campaign with a good deal of sympathy in the middle class. Almost without exception, Tupamaro actions were taken in the name of the working class (see Expanding the Concept: Tupamaro Tactics).

EXPANDING THE CONCEPT

Tupamaro Tactics

- Assassination
- Bank robbery
- Kidnapping
- Propaganda
- Bombing
- Internal discipline
- Infiltration of security forces
- Temporary control of urban areas
- Redistribution of expropriated goods to the poor

The Tupamaros realized they could not achieve popular support without the proper political circumstances. They believed they could obtain power only at a critical juncture, when the political, social, and economic conditions were conducive to revolution. They called this juncture the **coyuntura**, and they aimed all revolutionary activities at this point.

coyuntura
As used by Raul Sendic, the historical point where a series of ideas come together and force change.

John Wolf (1981, p. 82) says the Tupamaros saw violence as the only method to bring about social change. The coyuntura would never appear unless the people were incited to revolution. Terrorist violence was to be random and frequent, but it was only a prelude to a general attack. When the conditions were set, when the coyuntura arrived, organized popular revolution would replace terrorism.

Arturo Porzecanski (1973, p. 21) says the coyuntura was to give rise to the *salto*, or the general strike for power. The purpose of urban terrorism was to keep the idea of the coyuntura alive. The salto, however, was a separate move. Urban terrorism would be replaced by an organized people's army during the salto. The stages of the coyuntura and the salto reflected the ideology of Marighella.

The coyuntura concept was maintained through terrorist tactics. Ross Butler (1976, p. 54) writes that Tupamaro tactics changed according to their ability to attract a following. Until 1968, Butler says, the Tupamaros focused on low-level activities: arson, propaganda, and exposing public corruption. Porzecanski (1973, pp. 40–45) argues that all of their tactics were designed to make the group self-sufficient. The tactics gave the Tupamaros logistical support and allowed them to operate without support from foreign countries. Their terrorist activities were complemented by a transportation and intelligence network provided by supporters.

Bank Robbery

As the ranks of the Tupamaros grew, they became more daring. In 1969 they shifted to bank robbery, and in 1970 they staged a $6 million robbery of a Montevideo bank (Butler, 1976, p. 54). Bank robberies fell into the category of Marighella's concept of "expropriation." That is, the purpose of robbery was to finance the terrorist organization. The Tupamaros used bank robbery as their primary tactic in waging an urban guerrilla war. The banks became both symbolic and logistical targets, and the robberies upset Uruguayan society. Using a network of industrial, police, and military sympathizers, the Tupamaros mastered daring daylight robberies.

Kidnapping

Kidnapping also produced logistical support (through ransom) and it had propaganda value. There was as much drama in kidnapping as there was in robbery. The Tupamaros began by kidnapping local officials from Montevideo, but they found they could cause more disruption by taking foreigners.

On July 31, 1970, Dan Mitrione, an American police adviser assigned to assist the Uruguayan government, was kidnapped on his way to work. As he was being driven away, a gun pressed against his leg accidentally discharged. The incident and the wound caused international headlines. Mitrione's case was especially newsworthy because he had a wife and many children awaiting his return in Indiana (Langguth, 1978). Mitrione's story ended tragically. On August 10, 1970, his body was found on the streets of Montevideo. His hands had been bound, and he had two bullets through the back of his head. A Tupamaro message next to the body said he had been tried by a people's court, found guilty, and executed.

The Tupamaros kidnapped another foreign victim on January 8, 1971. Geoffrey Jackson, the British ambassador to Uruguay, was taken and held for eight months. When it became apparent the British government would pay no ransom for Jackson, the Tupamaros discussed executing him. Instead, they released him in a gesture of goodwill, hoping to offset the working-class backlash that had followed Mitrione's murder. Jackson's account of the ordeal can be found in his book, *People's Prison* (1972; also published as *Surviving the Long Night*).

Releasing Jackson was not out of character for the Tupamaros, even though they were known for their violence. They continually tried to maintain a Robin Hood image in their effort to win working-class support. One of their most noted actions in this role was the formation of the "hunger commandos." One Christmas Eve, this unit hijacked a shipment of groceries and distributed them among Montevideo's poor. These tactics were later copied by the Symbionese Liberation Army (SLA) in California when they demanded food distribution to the poor in return for the release of a kidnap victim.

Richard Clutterbuck (1975, p. 36) claims the Robin Hood tactics gained attention but failed to work. Food distribution and appeals to the working class could not neutralize violence and murder. Clutterbuck says that by 1972 the Robin Hood tactics had clearly backfired, helping form the backlash that led to the destruction of the Tupamaros. The working-class people of Montevideo saw the do-good activities as too little coming too late. Even Tupamaro humanitarian gestures were viewed with contempt because of the concurrent, violent terrorist campaign (Figure 8.4).

Figure 8.4
Tupamaro Symbol

As Clutterbuck implies, the effectiveness of all Tupamaro tactics must ultimately be evaluated by the final result. In terms of increasing support, the tactics were initially successful, but they failed in the long run. From 1965 to 1970, the ranks of the Tupamaros increased dramatically. By 1970, however, the excessive violence of the Tupamaros had had a negative impact. It alienated the middle and working classes and eventually caused many leftists to return to a nonviolent communist party. According to Waldmann (1986, pp. 275–276), the major mistake of the Tupamaros was that they alienated their supporters.

Tactics must also be evaluated according to the response of the enemy. Again, the Tupamaros enjoyed initial success but failed to maintain momentum. At first, Uruguay's political authorities were completely confused in their dealings with the Tupamaros. They were frustrated at every turn, as the kidnapping problem illustrates. John Wolf (1981, p. 21) notes that from August 1968 until the execution of Dan Mitrione in August 1970, the police were unable to locate a single kidnap victim. The tactic appeared to work.

But although this tactic gained publicity, it also provoked a harsh police reaction. Torture increased, and police became more repressive. Ironically, the repression was greeted with public support. When forced to the brink, Uruguayan security forces turned to brutal repression, the one tactic they knew would work, and by 1972 it had become the legal norm.

In the final analysis, Tupamaro tactics failed. Ironically, the public supported a repressive government rather than the fight by the Tupamaros for national socialism, and the Tupamaro propensity toward violence was a chief reason for their loss of public support. Yet the tactics of the Tupamaros differ little from the tactics of most other terrorist groups. Even though the tactics ultimately failed, the organizational structure proved to be a model for others.

Organizational Characteristics

The Tupamaros were one of the most highly organized yet least structured terrorist groups in modern history. In some ways the Tupamaros seemed to anticipate the growth of networked organizations. By the same token, the Tupamaros maintained a hierarchy. Only groups like the Palestine Liberation Organization (PLO) and the Irish Republican

Army (IRA) rivaled the hierarchical organization of the Tupamaros. Yet although both the PLO and the IRA enjoy a tremendous amount of external support, the Tupamaros existed almost entirely inside the borders of Uruguay. Because they were virtually self-sufficient, the growth, operations, and organization of the Tupamaros were amazing. If they failed to achieve success in the long run, at least their organizational structure kept them in the field as long as possible. The Tupamaros were nominally guided by a National Convention, which had authority in all matters of policy and operations. In reality, the National Convention seldom met more than once per year and was disbanded in the 1970s. Christopher Hewitt (1984, p. 8) notes the National Convention did not meet at all after September 1970. John Wolf (1981, p. 31) believes an executive committee controlled all activities in Montevideo. Arturo Porzecanski (1973), probably the most noted authority on the Tupamaros, makes several references to this same executive committee. For all practical purposes, it seems to have controlled the Tupamaros (see Memorial Institute for the Prevention of Terrorism, n.d.).

The executive committee was responsible for two major operations. It ran the columns that supervised the terrorist operations, and it also administered a special Committee for Revolutionary Justice. The power of the executive committee derived from internal enforcement. The job of the committee was to terrorize the terrorists into obedience. If an operative refused to obey an order or tried to leave the organization, a delegation from the committee would usually deal with the matter. It was not uncommon to murder the family of the offending party, along with the errant member. The Tupamaros believed in strong internal discipline.

In day-to-day operations, however, the executive committee exercised very little authority. Robert Moss (1972, p. 222) states the Tupamaros lacked a unified command structure for routine functions. The reason can be found in the nature of the organization. Because secrecy dominated every facet of its operations, it could not afford open communications. Therefore, each subunit evolved into a highly autonomous operation. There was little the executive committee could do about this situation, and the command structure became highly decentralized. The Tupamaros existed as a confederacy.

Operational power in the Tupamaros was vested in the lower-echelon units. Columns were organized for both combatant (operational) and staff (logistical) functions. Wolf (1981, p. 35) writes that most of the full-time terrorists belonged to cells in the combatant columns. They lived a precarious day-to-day existence and were constantly in conflict with the authorities. According to Wolf, they were supported by larger noncombatant columns that served to keep the terrorists in the field.

The importance of the noncombatant columns cannot be overemphasized—the strength of the Tupamaros came from its logistical columns. Without the elaborate support network of sympathizers and part-time helpers, the Tupamaros could not have remained in the field. Other

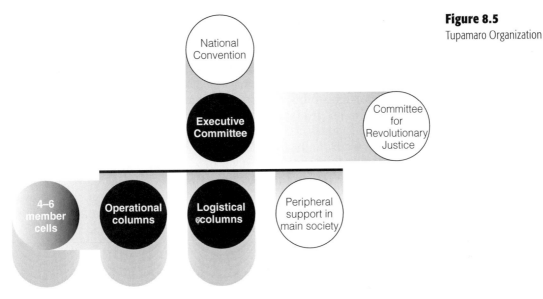

Figure 8.5
Tupamaro Organization

Source: Wolf, 1981.

groups that have copied their organizational model have not had the ability to launch a campaign because they lacked the same support.

Wolf's analysis of the support network includes peripheral support that was not directly linked to the Tupamaro organization. With Porzecanski, Wolf classifies supporters into two categories. One group operated in the open and provided intelligence and background information to the noncombatant sections. The other type of supporters worked on getting supplies to the operational sections. These sympathizers provided arms, ammunition, and legal aid. Both groups tried to generate popular support for the Tupamaros. When the government attacked the terrorists in 1972, its primary target was the support network. Police officials reasoned that if they destroyed the logistical network, they would destroy the Tupamaros.

In looking at the organizational chart of the Tupamaros in Figure 8.5, it is easy to envisage the entire operation. The executive committee was in charge, but it ran a highly decentralized operation. Its main power came from the internal rule enforcement provided by the Committee for Revolutionary Justice. Columns were the major units, but they tended to be tactical formations. The real operational power came from the cells, which joined for column-style operations on rare occasions. The combat striking power of the Tupamaros came from the four- to six-person groups in the cells. This organization epitomized Marighella's concept of the firing unit. Peter Waldmann (1986, p. 259) sums up the Tupamaros best by stating that they became the masters of urban terrorism. He believes that in terms of striking power, organization, and the ability to control a city, no group has ever surpassed the Tupamaros. They epitomized the terrorist role.

The influence of the Tupamaros spread far beyond Latin America. When violence erupted in western Europe and the Middle East in the 1960s and 1970s, terrorists cited Guevara and Marighella as their icons. The Tupamaros served as the model. As groups emerged in Africa, central Asia, and the United States in the 1980s and 1990s, they patterned themselves after groups who studied Guevara, Marighella, and the Tupamaros. Jihadist groups, with the exception of hierarchies like Jamaat Islamiyya in Indonesia, have a new structure, but their tactics have been deeply affected by Latin American influence. General James Mattis, U.S. Marine Corps, probably sums it up best. People have been fighting on this planet for five thousand years and more, and Alexander the Great would not be perplexed by the problems of counterterrorism. We will learn how to fight terrorism, Mattis concludes, if we study the past (cited in Ricks, 2006, p. 317).

Self-Check

- *Why should the Tupamaros be studied nearly forty years after their campaign?*
- *How might Tupamaro tactics reflect the actions of terror networks?*
- *Do the organizational characteristics of the Tupamaros apply to modern terrorist groups?*

SUMMARY

- Modern terrorism was influenced by theories from Latin America. The primary architects of modern terrorism were Carlos Marighella and Ernesto Guevara. The theoreticians behind the movements were Frantz Fanon and Regis Debray.
- Marighella developed a theory of urban terrorism. Guevara wrote a description of guerrilla war as used in the Cuban Revolution.
- The nationalistic revolutions of the post–World War II period incorporated the theories of urban terrorism and guerrilla warfare.
- Guerrillas use terrorist tactics selectively and do not engage in indiscriminate terrorism.
- Terrorists lack the structural capabilities of guerrillas, and their tactical operations are limited to terrorism. They cannot wage a guerrilla war.
- The Tupamaros of Uruguay embodied the concept of urban revolution. It is possible to gain an understanding of modern terrorism by studying the structure and tactical operations of the Tupamaros.

KEY TERMS

Frantz Fanon (p. 162)   Carlos Marighella (p. 164)
Mao Zedong (p. 164)   urban terrorism (p. 165)

Cuban Revolution (p. 166)   Raul Sendic (p. 171)
Ernesto "Che" Guevara (p. 167) coyuntura (p. 177)
Cuban guerrilla war (p. 168)

WRITING ASSIGNMENTS

1. Outline the concept of urban revolution. Use the concepts of Carlos Marighella. What are the strengths and weaknesses of the model? How does the concept of rural guerrilla war complement and contradict the urban model?

2. Do practitioners like Marighella and Guevara need theorists like Fanon and Debray? Do theories justify violence?

3. Using the information on terror networks presented in Chapter 3 and the conclusion at the end of this chapter, argue either that the historical study of terrorist organizations is important for understanding present forms of terrorism or that networks have transformed terrorism, rendering past experiences with terrorism irrelevant.

9

Background to the Middle East

AP Photo/Mohammed Zaatari

A young Lebanese girl holds an Israeli rocket launcher captured by Hezbollah in 2006. Divisions in the Middle East are rooted deeply in history, and prejudices are frequently socialized and accepted at an early age.

Learning Objectives

After reading this chapter you should be able to

- Define the Middle East as a historical, geographical, and cultural metaphor.
- Briefly sketch the origins of Islam.
- Describe the difference between Shiites and Sunnis.
- Explain the emergence of militant theology.

- Discuss the historical significance in the decline of the Ottoman Empire and the birth of Zionism.
- Summarize the impact of World War I on the Middle East.
- Describe the formation of Israel and the Arab-Israeli wars.
- Explain the emergence of terrorism after the 1967 Six Days' War.
- Briefly sketch the history of modern Iran.

We have reviewed in preceding chapters the origins of modern terrorism in terms of its spread from western European
ideology to Russia and then back to the West by the incorporation
of Russian revolutionary thought in the nationalistic struggle in
Ireland. Latin America also influenced the development of modern
terrorism. Before discussing current events, it is necessary to look
at another area, the historical development of conflict in the Middle
East. Although many people think Middle Eastern terrorism is a
recent phenomenon, the area has been the center of violence, misunderstandings, and cultural confrontations for centuries. Confrontations involve sectarian fighting about religion, clashes between
differing religions, the legacy of imperialism, and economics—
especially the economic issues surrounding gas and oil.

What Is the Middle East?

Bernard Lewis (1995, pp. 64–67) implies that the Middle East is not a
geographical region; it is a concept. It is based on a Western orientation to the world. Historically, *Middle East* was used by Captain Alfred
Thayer Mahan, the most important naval theorist in American history,
to describe a section of the world that encompasses part of North Africa and southwest Asia directly south of Turkey, including the Arabian
Peninsula, Iran, and Afghanistan. Geographically, *Middle East* is a term
of convenience with a European bias. If Europe and America are the
West, and China and Japan are the Far East, then there is an east "near"
Europe, one "far" away, and one in the "middle." Albert Hourani (1997),
in a comprehensive history, says the area is dominated by two major
concerns: the religion of Islam and the history of the Arab people. Yet
many people who live in the Middle East are not Arabs. Culturally, the
Middle East is an area dominated by a religion, Islam, but John Esposito
(1999, pp. 214–222) demonstrates that there are many differing cultures
inside Islam as well as myriad interpretations of the religion.

Bernard Lewis (1995, p. 65) also says the term *Middle East* is used
out of convenience. In a broader scope, many people are really speaking
about the sociogeographical relationship between Islam and Christianity. Yet distinctive social meanings attach to the term *Middle East*. It is
a region that witnessed the birth of three great monotheistic religions:
Judaism, Christianity, and Islam. The Middle East is an area dominated
by Islam, but most Muslims live outside the region. The social mores of
the Middle East—family and tribal loyalty, male dominance, honor, and

resentment of Western imperialism—extend across northern Africa and into central Asia. The traditional Middle East includes Arabs, but many other people live there.

The Middle East is a historical, social, and geographical concept. It seems to be dominated by questions about Palestine and Israel, but Lewis (2004, pp. 196–204) demonstrates that many other problems engulf the region. Lewis (1995, pp. 45–55) also points out that it is the historical tinderbox that ignited several centuries of conflict between Muslims and Christians. The area is the home of Islamic conquests and Arabic empires. It also witnessed the Crusades and Western and Mongol invasions, which were followed by Turkish then European domination. It gave birth to modern nations in the twentieth century, including Lebanon, Syria, Jordan, Yemen, the independent **Gulf States**, Iraq, Saudi Arabia, Iran, and Israel. It is the home of multiple ethnic groups, and violence in the region has influenced international terrorism. Three issues help illustrate the importance of the region: (1) the birth and spread of Islam, (2) historical confrontations between Christianity and Islam, and (3) the expansion of conflict beyond the traditional geographical realm of the Middle East.

Gulf States

Small Arab kingdoms bordering the Persian Gulf. They include Bahrain, Qatar, the United Arab Emirates, and Oman.

Introduction to Islam

Many aspects of Middle Eastern and, subsequently, international terrorism are ensconced in rhetorical religious sloganeering. If terrorism is to be understood in this context, it is necessary to become familiar with the basic aspects of Islam. For those readers of this book unfamiliar with the basics of Islam, this section is necessary; others may wish to skip it. It is not always possible to capture the theological richness of any major religion in several volumes, much less in a short section in a college text. This is not an exegetical exercise; rather, it is a simple overview to provide background in understanding terrorists who employ religious imagery.

The description here is taken primarily from Western scholars and Islamic sources in English. It is based on the work of Karen Armstrong (2000a, 2000b), Abdullah Saeed and Hassan Saeed (2004), Thomas W. Lippman (1995), Caesar Farah (2000), John Esposito (1999, 2002), Haneef Oliver (2002), Bernard Lewis (1966, 1995, 2004), Heinz Halm (1999), Malise Ruthven (2000), Moojan Momen (1985), Robin Wright (2000), Edward Said and C. Hitchens (1989), Charles Kurzman (2004), Rudolph Peters (1996), and Rueven Firestone (1999). See Expanding the Concept: Moving beyond an Introduction if you wish to read further.

The Centrality of Mohammed's Revelation

Mohammed was born about 570 C.E. on the Western calendar in the Arabian city of Mecca. He was orphaned at an early age and taken in by his uncle, Abu Talib. He was extremely spiritual, by most accounts,

EXPANDING THE CONCEPT

Moving beyond an Introduction

Most Americans know about Islam from skewed media images. However, several good books introduce English-speaking audiences to the religion. If you would like to read more, here is a suggested path:

Start with Karen Armstrong's (2000a) *Islam: A Short History*. It is thorough yet easy to read. Armstrong outlines the major figures and theological issues that have developed over the past 1,400 years.

If you are interested in theology, Thomas W. Lippman's *Understanding Islam* is a good place to begin. His review of most of the major theological developments in Islam is written crisply and with a news reporter's passion for the facts. Caesar Farah (2000) presents a more detailed view in *Islam*, and Malise Ruthven offers an extremely comprehensive view with *Islam in the World*. Start with Armstrong, then read Lippman. If you want more detail, Farah and Malaise will take you deeper into the ideas.

For works on Shiites, Heinz Halm's *Shi'a Islam* is an easy place to start. Halm will take you through the birth and growth of Shiaism to the modern period. One of the definitive English-language works is Moojan Momen's *An Introduction to Shi'a Islam*. It is detailed, comprehensive, and informative.

If you would like to read about the misunderstandings between Western Jews and Christians and the Islamic world, two authors have several books that will help you grasp the ideas. Bernard Lewis and John Esposito are two Princeton scholars with differing views. They are internationally recognized as leading scholars in Islamic and Middle Eastern studies. Any of their works will deepen your understanding.

Ali

(circa 599–661) Also known as Ali ibn Abi Talib, the son of Mohammed's uncle Abu Talib and married to Mohammed's oldest daughter Fatima. Ali was Mohammed's male heir because he had no surviving sons. The followers of Ali are known as Shiites. Most Shiites believe that Mohammed gave a sermon while perched on a saddle, naming Ali the heir to Islam. Differing types of Shiites accept authority from diverse lines of Ali's heirs. Sunni Muslims believe Ali is the fourth and last Rightly Guided caliph. Both Sunnis and Shiites believe Ali tried to return Islam to the purity of Mohammed's leadership in Medina.

and exposed to three great monotheistic religions, Judaism, Christianity, and Zoroastrianism. As he grew older, Mohammed became a trader under the tutelage and protection of his uncle. He also became close to his cousin **Ali**, who looked upon Mohammed as an older brother. While on a caravan he met an older widow, Khadijah. They were married and had a daughter, Fatima. Khadijah was impressed with Mohammed's character and by his spiritual nature. She encouraged him to continue a religious quest, but Mohammed was confused. He had been exposed to several religions, yet he did not know which aspect of spirituality was correct. That changed when he was meditating at age forty.

Mohammed had a vision of the angel Gabriel (Jabril), who told him that God had chosen Mohammed to be a prophet to the Arabs. (Jews, Christians, and Muslims have a similar theology of angels, and *Allah* is not a name. It is Arabic for "the God." Muslims believe that Jews, Christians, and Zoroastrians worship the same Deity.) Mohammed was overwhelmed by the voice of Gabriel, and he begged for silence. Gabriel did not agree. He told Mohammed that Moses had been sent to tell the Jews of the one true God, and Jesus had been sent to the world with the same message. Mohammed, the angelic voice said, had been chosen as the final Prophet to complete the message. The first vision stopped after forty days, and Mohammed came to accept that he had been chosen. Visions would continue periodically until 632, the year of his death.

Mohammed's role as a prophet, as *the* Prophet, is crucial in Islam. He stands in a long line of Jewish prophets—the visionaries later adopted by Christians—and Jesus of Nazareth. Muslims believe that Mohammed was given the direct revelation of God through Gabriel. In Muslim theology God is vast, all encompassing, and without form. The pronoun *he* is used, but God is gender neutral. The little that can be known about God comes through revelations from the four major Prophets—Abraham, Moses, Jesus, and Mohammed—and the law that God has given them. The Hebrew and Christian Bibles contain those revelations, but humans corrupted the message when writing the stories, according to Islamic theology. One of the greatest mistakes, according to Muslims, was the deification of Jesus. All the Prophets are human, and they will be judged by God according to their deeds with an overwhelming, loving mercy that comes from God's benevolence. God has given divine law through the Prophets. Mohammed was chosen to correct the errors of the past.

Creating the Muslim Community at Medina

Mohammed won early converts in Mecca, including his cousin Ali, his wife Khadijah, and three influential friends: **Abu Bakr**, **Umar**, and **Uthman**. Many of the wealthy merchants of Mecca were not impressed. Messages of God's love were acceptable, but Mohammed's emphasis of social egalitarianism called on them to share wealth. They resented that and asked Abu Talib to remove familial protection from the young Prophet, a request Abu Talib refused. After Abu Talib's death, Mohammed's life was in jeopardy. At the same time representatives from warring Jewish and polytheistic tribes in Yathrib, later Medina, asked Mohammed to serve as their leader and make peace. Mohammed agreed, provided that they would acknowledge the one God and the legitimacy of Mohammed's calling. They agreed, with the Jews reserving the right to judge Mohammed's call as a prophet. Legend says he left for Medina in 622 with 72 families. Most Western historians believe that the families left in waves and that Mohammed escaped to Medina, even as Meccans were plotting his death.

Muslims believe Mohammed created the perfect Islamic community at Medina, combining a just government with religion. Mohammed stressed the importance of community over tribal relations and the governance of God's law in every aspect of life. In addition, there were not enough resources to live in Mecca, so Mohammed's followers chose a traditional Bedouin path for survival: raiding passing caravans. In 624

Abu Bakr

(circa 573–634) Also known as Abu Bakr as Saddiq, the first caliph selected by the Islamic community (*umma*) after Mohammed's death in 632. Sunnis believe Abu Bakr is the rightful heir to Mohammed's leadership, and they regard him as the first of the *Rishidun*, or Rightly Guided caliphs. He led military expeditions expanding Muslim influence to the north of Mecca.

Umar

(circa 580–644) Also known as Umar ibn al Khattab, the second Rightly Guided caliph, according to Sunnis. Under his leadership the Arab empire expanded into Persia, the southern part of the Byzantine empire, and Egypt. His army conquered Jerusalem in 637.

Uthman

(circa 580–656) Also known as Uthman ibn Affan, the third Rightly Guided caliph, according to Sunnis. He conquered most of the remaining parts of North Africa, Iran, Cyprus, and the Caucasia region. He was assassinated by his own soldiers for alleged nepotism.

this led to a confrontation with an army from Medina at **Badr**. It was a small battle, but politically important. Because of their victory at Badr Muslims increasingly came to believe that God was on their side and that their cause would be championed in heaven. Mohammed eventually conquered Mecca, and the new religion spread along trade routes. Suddenly, in 632, Mohammed died, leaving the community of believers to chart the path for the new religion.

The Shiite-Sunni Split

The Muslims who followed Mohammed agreed on many aspects of the new faith. God's revelation to Mohammed was critical. The poetic utterances of Gabriel were eventually codified in a single book, the Quran. The things Mohammed had said and done were recorded, and his actions became the basis for interpreting the Quran. All Muslims came to believe that it was necessary to confess the existence of one God and Mohammed as God's Prophet. They were also expected to pray as a community, to give to the poor, to fast during holy times, and to make a pilgrimage to Mecca when able. Problems came, however, in the question of leadership. According to Arabic tradition, Mohammed's male heir should lead the community, but Mohammed claimed to have revealed a new law that said the importance of the community would take precedence over tribal rules of inheritance. Questions over leadership spawned a debate and eventually a civil war. The questions still affect the practice of Islam today.

The question of leadership focused on the community. One group of people believed the community should select its own leaders, but another group believed that Mohammed had designated Ali, his cousin and son-in-law, as the Muslim leader. The proponents of community selection carried the day, but Ali's followers came to believe that God had given a special inspiration to Mohammed's family. The community selected a political and religious leader, a caliph, but Ali's followers encouraged him to exercise the leadership authority they believed God had provided. When Ali's sons, Hasan and Hussein, were born, his followers believed they also carried special gifts based on their relationship with their grandfather Mohammed.

The Muslim community eventually split over this question. Mohammed's friend Abu Bakr became the first caliph in 632. After his death in 634, Umar became caliph. The Arabs expanded under his leadership, handing defeats to the Romans, or Byzantines, and the Persians. Umar was assassinated in 644 by a Persian captive, and another of Mohammed's friends, Uthman, was selected as caliph. The Arabs continued to expand, and they soon held a vast empire. All was not well, however. As Uthman consolidated wealth, groups of Arab soldiers came to feel he favored his own family over the community. They broke into his house in 656 and assassinated him. The followers of Ali came forward, and proposed that he become caliph. Ali believed that Uthman's family and Muslims in general were forgetting the straight path that had been

Badr
The site of a battle between the Muslims of Medina and the merchants of Mecca in 624. Mohammed was unsure whether he should resist the attacking Meccans, but decided God would allow Muslims to defend their community. After victory, Mohammed said that Badr was the Lesser Jihad. Greater Jihad, he said, was seeking internal spiritual purity.

revealed to Mohammed. He led an army against Uthman's family but sought a negotiated peace between both factions of Muslims. His hopes were in vain, and he was assassinated. The family of Uthman assumed control of the Islamic movement and ruled the first Arab empire.

Umayyads

The first Arab and Muslim dynasty ruling from Damascus from 661 to 750. The Umayyads were Uthman's family.

The followers of Ali were not satisfied. They felt that the **Umayyads**, Uthman's family, had abandoned the principles of Islam in favor of worldly goods. This split came to dominate the Muslim community. The Umayyads believed they represented Islam, even as they fought other Muslims to maintain control of the new Arab empire. Some of the followers of Ali invited **Hussein**, Ali's oldest living son, to meet with them in what is present-day Iraq. They wanted him to lead a purified Islamic movement, returning to the simple principles of his grandfather, Mohammed. The Umayyad governor was alarmed and sent an army to intercept Hussein. He was killed with a small band of followers at Karbala in 680. His martyrdom cemented the schism between the Umayyad dynasty and the followers of Ali.

Hussein

(626–680) Also known as Hussein ibn Ali, Mohammed's grandson and Ali's second son. He was martyred at Karbala in 680. Twelver Shiites believe that Hussein is the Third Imam, after Imam Ali and Imam Hasan, Ali's oldest son.

Mainstream Muslims following the caliph were conventionally called Sunnis, and the followers of Ali became known as Shiites. In actuality, though, several differing types of Shiites developed in the formative years of Islam. Zaidi Shiites recognize a line of succession differing from Hussein. Many Zaidi Shiites live in Yemen today. Ismalis believe there were seven Imams who followed Mohammed. They sponsored a cult known as the Assassins in the Middle Ages, but they live quite peacefully on the Indian subcontinent today (see Lewis, 2003a). Ithna Ashari, or Twelver, Shiites compose the majority of Shiite Muslims. Ithna Ashari Shiites dominate Iran, southern Iraq, and southern Lebanon.

Initially, there were few theological differences between Sunnis, who compose an estimated 85 to 90 percent of all Muslims today, and Shiites. The main difference focused on the line of succession from Mohammed. Over the years, however, differences did emerge. Ithna Ashari Shiites believe that the Twelfth Imam went into hiding in 934. Some of them believe he divinely transcended life with a promise to return. Another group of Shiites believe that he died but was resurrected, and a final group believes that God hid the Twelfth Imam, but left part of the imam's spirit on earth. Sunnis claim that all three beliefs are more reminiscent of Christianity than Islam. The split between Sunnis and Shiites remains today.

The Golden Age of Arabs

Abbasids

The second Arab and Muslim dynasty ruling from Baghdad from 750 to 1258. The Abbasids lost influence and power to Turks after 950, and their empire collapsed to Mongol conquest.

Mohammed's followers spread Islam and Arabic culture through the Middle East in the years after his death. Two dynasties, the Umayyads (661–750) and the **Abbasids** (750–1258), ruled the area in the years following Mohammed. Hourani (1997, pp. 25–37) points out that these caliphs theologically divided the world into the Realm of Islam and the Realm of War. The purpose of Islam was to subject the world to God's will. Indeed, *Islam* means "submission to the will of God," and a *Muslim* is "one who submits."

About 1000 C.E. the Turks began to take the domains of the Abbasids. Struggles continued for the next hundred years, until a Mongol advance from east Asia brought the Abbasid dynasty to an end. The Mongols were eventually stopped by an Egyptian army of slaves, giving rise to a new group of Turks known as Ottomans. The Ottomans were aggressive, conquering most of the Middle East and large parts of Europe. The Ottomans fought the Iranians on one border and central Europeans on the other border for many years.

European relations with Islamic empires were not characterized by harmony. The West began its first violent encounters by launching the Crusades, attempts to conquer the Middle East lasting from 1095 to about 1250. These affairs were bloody and instigated centuries of hatred and distrust between Muslims and Christians. European struggles with the Ottoman Empire reinforced years of military tensions between the two civilizations. Modern tensions in the area can be traced to the decline of Ottoman influence and the collapse of Iranian power in the eighteenth century. When these Islamic powers receded, Western Christian powers were quick to fill the void.

Bernard Lewis (1995) points to the Age of Discovery as the origin of modern confrontation between the West and Islam. Americans might think of 1492 as the beginning of European discovery through Christopher Columbus, but Lewis says it is also the year that the final Islamic stronghold in Spain was destroyed. In addition, although Ottoman Turks conquered Constantinople in 1453, renaming it Istanbul, 1492 represented a reversal of fortune for expanding Islamic armies. Western Christian military forces gradually gained the upper hand in world affairs through their superior navies and military technology. When the Turks were driven back from the gates of Vienna, nearly 200 years later, it symbolized the ascendancy and domination of the West.

Agrarian Response to Political Crisis

Karen Armstrong (2000b, pp. 32–42) argues that Islam went through a series of crises before and after 1492, and she describes both a theological and political response to events. Armstrong believes that when agrarian empires falter, religious zealots arise to call the faithful back to the true meaning of religion. The pattern goes like this: As agrarian empires expand, winning victories in the name of their deity, all is going well. The chosen people prosper under the protection of a divine force. At some point, however, the empire eventually suffers a strategic military reverse. Because the empire grew under the favor of a deity, the only logical conclusion is that the deity is no longer with the people. In other words, they are no longer chosen. Inevitably, prophets call the people back to religious purity, to the golden age of the faith. Prophets obscure the past with an idealistic remembrance of the Golden Age, and they separate the pure from the impure. This happened several times in the history of Islam, including the invasion of Mongol and Crusader armies in the eleventh and twelfth centuries, the stagnation of Arab thought and technological development after 1200, and the collapse of the Ottoman caliphate in 1924. Each instance brought a theologically driven political reform movement.

Self-Check

- *Why is it necessary to understand orthodox Islam?*
- *What is the difference between Sunnis and Shiites?*
- *Explain a theory of the rise and fall of agrarian empires.*

Militant Philosophy

Abdul Wahhab
(1703–1792) Also known as Mohammed ibn Abdul Wahhab, a religious reformer who wanted to purge Islam of anything beyond the traditions accepted by Mohammed and the four Rightly Guided caliphs. He conducted campaigns against Sufis, Shiites, and Muslims who made pilgrimages or who invoked the names of saints.

As religions develop, various interpretations follow, and this is especially true in times of crisis. As Armstrong suggests, reformers emerged in Islam, calling believers to an idealized past when crisis erupted. Many people argue that this gave rise to militancy, but others argue that militants misused the theology of the reformers (see Oliver, 2002; Esposito, 2002; Saeed and Saeed, 2004). Taqi al Din ibn Taymiyya introduced new ideas about militancy and the faith after Arab setbacks by Mongols and Crusaders. Mohammed ibn **Abdul Wahhab** "rediscovered" ibn Taymiyya when preaching puritanical reform of Islam 500 years later. **Sayyid Qutb**, who lacked theological training, militarized the ideas of ibn Taymiyya and Wahhab in the twentieth century. Although apologists defend these men as peaceful thinkers seeking a pure Islam, critics maintain that their theological writings gave rise to militancy.

Ibn Taymiyyah

Sayyid Qutb
(1906–1966) An Egyptian educator who called for the overthrow of governments and the imposition of purified Islamic law based on the principles of previous puritanical reformers. Qutb formed a militant wing of the Muslim Brotherhood.

Western Crusaders began waging war against the Muslims in the eleventh century, and Mongol invaders struck the Arab lands a hundred years later. Hundreds of thousands of Muslims were killed in each invasion. Taqi al Din **ibn Taymiyyah** (circa 1269–1328), an Islamic scholar, was appalled by the slaughter and sought to find an answer in his faith. He believed that Muslims had fallen away from the truth and must therefore internally purify themselves. He called for jihad (struggle or effort), the destruction of heretics and invaders, calling it the sixth pillar of Islam.

Ibn Taymiyyah
(circa 1269–1328) Also known as Taqi al Din ibn Taymiyya, a Muslim religious reformer in the time of the Crusades and a massive Mongol invasion.

Ibn Taymiyyah fled Baghdad to escape invading Mongols. He believed that the Crusaders and Mongols defeated Islamic armies because Muslims had fallen away from the true practice of Islam. Emphasizing *tawhid*, or the oneness of God, ibn Taymiyyah attacked anything that threatened to come between humanity and God. He forbade prayers at gravesites, belief in saints, and other practices that had worked their way into Islam. He was especially harsh on the mystical Sufis, who believed that deep prayer revealed the will of God beyond the prophecy of Mohammed and the Quran. Individual Sufis pledged allegiance to various masters and followed their masters even when actions violated Islamic law. According to ibn Taymiyyah, any belief that went beyond Mohammed's revelation was to be subjected to a purifying jihad. He preached that holy war should be waged against all people who threatened the faith. His targets included Muslims and non-Muslims.

Ibn Taymiyyah's shift is important. Islam is frequently described as a monotheistic religion based on five tenets, or pillars: (1) a confession of faith in God and acceptance of Mohammed as God's last and greatest Prophet, (2) ritual prayers with the community, (3) giving alms, (4) fasting, especially during holy periods, and (5) making a pilgrimage to Mohammed's birthplace, Mecca (Farah, 2000, pp. 132–148). Jihad has a place in this system, and different Islamic scholars (*ulema*) interpret jihad in various ways. There are many meanings, but most Muslims defined jihad as defending a community and waging an internal struggle against one's own tendency toward evil (Firestone, 1999, pp. 5, 65–91; Peters, 1996, pp. 1–8, 115–119).

Ibn Taymiyyah expanded the meaning of jihad by advocating attacks on nonbelievers and impure Muslims; however, he preached toleration for Muslims who accepted one of the more rigid versions of Sunni Islam. He claimed that this was another pillar of Islam (Hourani, 1997, pp. 179–181; Esposito, 2002, pp. 45–46; see Gerges, 2006, p. 209).

Abdul Wahhab

John Esposito (1999, pp. 6–10) says that reform movements are common throughout the history of Islam. Two recent movements became important to the jihadists. In the late eighteenth century a purification movement started by Mohammed ibn Abdul Wahhab (1703–1792), who was influenced by ibn Taymiyyah, took root in Arabia. Wahhab preached a puritanical strain of Islam that sought to rid the religion of practices added after the first few decades following Mohammed's death. This doctrine deeply influenced the Saud family as they fought to gain control of Arabia, and it dominates the theology of Saudi Arabia and the Gulf States today. Militant application of Wahhab's puritanical principles spread to India and other parts of Asia. Strict Muslims who follow the practices of Wahhab argue that they are trying to rid the religion of superstition and return it to the state envisioned by Mohammed and his first followers (Oliver, 2002, pp. 10–11; see Another Perspective: A Critique of Western Interpretations and Another Perspective: Wahhab as a Mainstream Reformer). Militants, however, force their puritanical views on those who disagree with them (Farah, 2000, p. 230).

Sayyid Qutb

Sayyid Qutb (1906–1966) was an Egyptian teacher and journalist who was initially employed by the Ministry of Education. He traveled to the United States and lived as an exchange professor in Greeley, Colorado,

ANOTHER PERSPECTIVE

A Critique of Western Interpretations

The strict Hanbali rite of Sunni Islam emphasizes the importance of the elders (*salafiyya* or *salafi*). Most of them revere Taqi al Din ibn Taymiyya and Mohammed ibn Abdul Wahhab, and they become incensed when the two Islamic scholars are linked to violence. Haneef James Oliver reflects this position in *The "Wahhabi" Myth* (2002). He points out the following:

- There is no such thing as a Wahhabi, or follower of Wahhab. Orthodox Muslims in Saudi Arabia and other areas emphasize the oneness of God and the importance of Mohammed and the Rightly Guided caliphs, the salafiyya. To call them Wahhabis suggests that there is more than one correct interpretation of Islam, Oliver says.

- Mohammed ibn Abdul Wahhab was not a radical Muslim. His call for reform was based on the Quran.

- Osama bin Laden, Ayman al Zawahiri, and other members of al Qaeda do not follow the teachings of Wahhab, the Quran, or Islam. They are mystics who believe their personal experiences and theologies are superior to Mohammed. Oliver believes, as did Wahhab, that mystical Sufis corrupted Islam by emphasizing their own encounters with the holy and that al Qaeda follows this tradition. Mohammed provided the last revelation. There are no more Prophets despite Sufism and mystics in other religions.

- When terrorists are called Salafis, Wahhabis, or Salafi-Wahhabis, it completely miscasts and misinterprets Islam. Terrorists follow the teachings of Sayyid Qutb, who was neither an Islamic scholar nor a good Muslim.

Muslim Brotherhood

An organization founded by Hassan al Banna designed to recapture the spirit and religious purity during the period of Mohammed and the four Rightly Guided caliphs. The Brotherhood seeks to create a single Muslim nation through education and religious reform. A militant wing founded by Sayyid Qutb sought the same objective through violence. Hamas has rejected the multinational approach in favor of creating a Muslim Palestine, and it considers itself to be the Palestinian wing of the Muslim Brotherhood.

from 1948 to 1950. Qutb's experience in America soured his opinion of Western civilization. He returned to Egypt and became an active member of the **Muslim Brotherhood**, an organization that seeks to create a single Muslim nation through education and religious reform. Qutb was arrested in 1954 after the Brotherhood tried to overthrow the Egyptian government, but he was released in 1964 because of health problems. He published his most famous work, *Milestones*, in 1965. The book outlines the theology and ideology of jihadist revolution, and its militant tone led to Qutb's second arrest and subsequent hanging in 1966.

Qutb's books and articles popularized many militant ideas, and they continue to influence jihadists today. He believed that the Islamic world descended into darkness (*jahaliyya*) shortly after the death of Mohammed (AD 632). The so-called Islamic governments of the Arab empires were really corrupt nonreligious regimes. Pure Islam had been lost, but a few people, such as ibn Taymiyyah, Mohammed ibn Abdul Wahhab, and Mawlana Mawdudi (1903–1979), kept the faith alive. Qutb rejected the West and called on Muslims to overthrow their corrupt governments. He argued that rulers should impose Islamic law on their subjects, and when pure Islamic states were created, they should confront the world (Esposito, 2002, pp. 56–64).

Wahhab as a Mainstream Reformer

Many American security experts use the Taymiyya-Wahhab-Qutb theological link to explain militant jihadist religion. Natana DeLong-Bas throws this assumption aside. In a study of Wahhab's original works, she concludes that he was a mainstream reformer who was trying to bring Islam back to its roots. She conducts a detailed examination of Wahhab's extensive writings and historical accounts of his life, combining these with an in-depth analysis of Wahhab's interpretation of the Quran, Mohammed's life and actions, and Islamic law. DeLong-Bas believes that Wahhab favored academic argument and logic over the use of force, and he subtly divorced himself from military conquests in the name of Islam. Wahhab opposed any action that detracted from faith in and prayer to the oneness and total unity (tawhid) of God. By the eighteenth century, many Muslims were praying at the tombs of the departed asking for their intercession, they wore charms, and some of them accepted older superstitions. These activities defied the sovereignty of God, Wahhab believed, and he challenged Islamic scholars (ulema) to justify them. He sought to restore the rights of women as established by the Prophet, and he wanted Muslims to guide their lives by practical interpretations of the Quran. This upset the established rulers and provoked strong reactions against Wahhab, DeLong-Bas says. Current militants like bin Laden and Zawahiri do not understand Wahhab's theological writings, and his interpretation of religion has little to do with jihadists who murder in God's name.

Source: DeLong, 2004.

In *Milestones* Qutb (1965, pp. 112–134) argued that Muslims were in a cosmic battle with the forces of darkness. Whereas Mohammed mandated tolerance of those who would not embrace Islam, Qutb called for the destruction of all enemies. The forces of darkness could not be tolerated, he wrote, and although God was ultimately responsible for the destruction of darkness, Muslims were called to fight it. Qutb's writings were banned in many Islamic countries, and they infuriated the Egyptian government under Gamal Nasser. Qutb was arrested and sent to prison after he returned from the United States. The *Al Qaeda Manual* (White, 2004a) cites Qutb as a source of inspiration.

Jihadists utilize ibn Taymiyya, Wahhab, and Qutb to justify violence (see Esposito, 2002, pp. 40–64). Esposito adds **Hassan al Banna**, founder of the Muslim Brotherhood, and **Mawlana Mawdudi** of central Asia to the list. Two other factors play into the rise of extremism: the birth of modern Israel and the collapse of Western imperialism. Both of these factors interact with the jihadist movement at points, but they have their own distinctions. In addition, the collapse of imperialism has influenced diverse forms of terrorism, from the 1979 **Iranian Revolution** to ethnic fighting in Africa and to Maoist rebellions in Nepal. Modern Middle Eastern terrorism extends far beyond the traditional concept of the Middle East and it involves far more than jihadist philosophy.

Hassan al Banna

(1906–1949) The founder of the Muslim Brotherhood. He was murdered by agents of the Egyptian government.

Mawlana Mawdudi

(1903–1979) A Pakistani reformer who saw jihad as both a spiritual struggle and the basis for political activism against European colonialism. Qutb was deeply influenced by Mawdudi's writings, but Mawdudi sought to reform Islamic countries without revolution much as Hassan al Banna did.

Iranian Revolution
The 1979 religious revolution that toppled Mohammed Pahlavi, the shah of Iran, and transformed Iran into an Islamic republic ruled by Shiite religious scholars.

Self-Check

- *Explain the relationship among the philosophies of Taymiyya, Wahhab, and Qutb.*

- *Does Qutb's theology represent orthodox Islam?*

- *How might Wahhab's and Qutb's ideas reflect the theory of agrarian empires suggested in the previous section?*

Modern Israel

Jihadist theology has come to dominate religious terrorism, but nationalism and secularism predated the late-twentieth-century movement. Ethnic violence can be traced to the founding of the modern state of Israel. The creation of Israel was the result of three events in the nineteenth century that involved the persecution of Jews in eastern Europe, the founding of the Zionist movement and its desire for a Jewish state, and the collapse of the Ottoman Empire. After the assassination of Czar Alexander II (1818–1881), Russian authorities blamed Jewish socialists for the rise of anarchism in Europe. They began a merciless purge of Jewish communities (Armstrong, 2000a, p. 147). At the same time a strong Zionist movement began in eastern Europe, demanding a homeland for displaced Jews. Russian and eastern European Jews joined the Zionist movement (Nasr, 1997, pp. 5–6). As a result a number of Jewish settlers began flocking to the Ottoman land of Palestine in the late nineteenth and early twentieth centuries. Weakened by a collapsing empire, Turkish forces were unable to stop the influx of Jews. These Zionist settlers began to carve out the nucleus of the land that would become modern Israel in 1948.

A Synopsis of Traditional Middle Eastern Issues

To understand terrorism in the Middle East, it is necessary to appreciate certain recent aspects of the region's history. To best understand the Middle East, keep the following assumptions in mind:

- The current structure of Middle Eastern geography and political rule is a direct result of nineteenth-century European imperial influence in the region and the outcomes of World War I.
- Many of the Arab countries in the Middle East place more emphasis on the power of the family than on contemporary notions of government. However, Israel rules itself as a parliamentary democracy.
- The modern state of Israel is not the biblical Kingdom of David mentioned in the Hebrew and Christian Bibles or the Islamic Quran. It is a secular power dominated by people of European descent.
- Arabs, and Palestinians in particular, do not hold a monopoly on terrorism.
- The religious differences in the region have developed over centuries, and fanaticism in any religion can spawn violence. Fanatical Jews,

Christians, and Muslims in the Middle East practice terrorism in the name of religion.

- Although the Middle East has been volatile since 1948, the year Israel was recognized as a nation-state, modern terrorism grew after 1967. It increased after 1973 and became a standard method of military operations in the following two decades.

- In 1993, however, the Palestine Liberation Organization (PLO) renounced terrorism, but instead of decreasing tension, that has created tremendous tension. On the Arab side, some groups have denounced the PLO's actions whereas others have embraced it. The same reaction has occurred in Israel, where one set of political parties endorses peace plans and another prepares for war. Middle Eastern peace is a very fragile process, and terrorism is a wild card. It can upset delicate negotiations at any time, even after a peace treaty has been signed and implemented (for an example, see Hoffman, 1995).

- All of these issues are complicated by a shortage of water and vast differences in social structure. The area contains some of the world's richest and some of the world's poorest people. Most of them are far from water sources.

One can best begin to understand the Middle East by focusing on the world of the late 1800s. During that time period, three critical events took place that helped to shape the modern Middle East.

First, the **Ottoman Empire**, the Turk-based government that ruled much of the Middle East, was falling apart in the nineteenth century. The Ottoman Turks encountered domestic challenges across their empire as various nationalistic, tribal, and familial groups revolted, and they faced foreign threats, too. The Iranian empire had collapsed earlier, but Great Britain, France, Germany, and Russia intervened in the area with military force. Each European country was willing to promise potential rebels many things if they revolted against the Turks. Turkey was reluctantly drawn into World War I, and the victorious Allies partitioned the empire after victory in 1918. A group of military officers took control of Turkey, banned religious government, and in 1924 brought an end to the caliphate (Fromkin, 2001, pp. 406–426).

The second critical event came from a political movement called Zionism. From 1896 to 1906, European Jews, separated from their ancient homeland for nearly 2,000 years, wanted to create their own nation. Some of them favored Palestine, whereas others wanted to move to South America or Africa. In 1906 those who backed Palestine won the argument, and European Jews increasingly moved to the area (Armstrong, 2000a, pp. 146–151). The sultan of the Ottoman Turks allowed them to settle, but refused to grant them permission to form their own government. Palestinian Arabs, the people who lived in Palestine, were wary of the Jewish settlers and tensions rose (Nasr, 1997, pp. 5–8).

Finally, European armies engulfed the Middle East from 1914 to 1918, as they fought World War I. European governments continued to

Ottoman Empire
A Turkish empire that lasted for 600 years, until 1924. The empire spanned southeastern Europe, North Africa, and southwest Asia, and it reached its zenith in the fourteenth and fifteenth centuries.

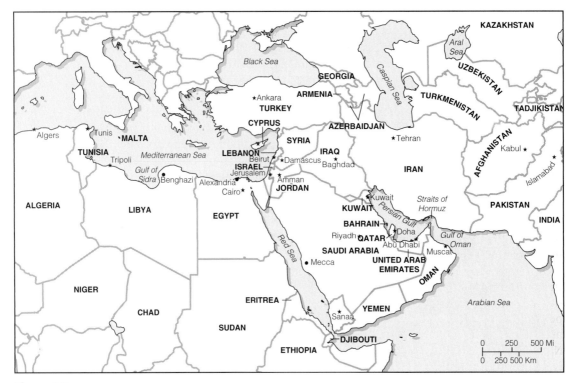

Figure 9.1
The Middle East

make contradictory promises as they sought to gain spheres of influence in the region. When the war ended, the victorious nations felt they had won the area from the Turks. They divided the Middle East, not with respect to the area's political realities, but to share the spoils of victory. This created long-term political problems. Historian David Fromkin calls this "the peace to end all peace," satirizing the Western depiction of World War I as the "war to end all wars" (Fromkin, 2002, pp. 15–20).

Three Sources of Violence in Mahan's Middle East

The situation at the end of World War I set the stage for developments over the next century, and it is the basis for terrorism in the traditional Middle East, defined by the U.S. Navy's Captain Mahan as Israel, Lebanon, Jordan, Egypt, Syria, Iraq, and the Arabian Peninsula. As events unfolded, three factors became prominent in Middle Eastern violence: (1) questions about the political control of Israel and Palestine, (2) questions of who would rule the Arab world, and (3) questions concerning the relations between the two main branches of Islam: Sunnis and Shiites. Stated another way, these problems are the following:

1. The Palestinian question (control of Palestine)

2. Intra-Arab rivalries and struggles

3. The future of revolutionary Islam

These problems are all separate, but they are also interrelated. The sources of terrorism in the Middle East are symbiotic. That is, they are independent arenas of violence with a dynamic force of their own, but they are also related to and dependent on each other (Figure 9.1).

All forms of Middle Eastern terrorism share certain traits. Primarily, many Arab groups express dissatisfaction over the existence of Israel. They are not necessarily pro-Palestinian, but they find the notion of a European-created, non-Arab state in their lands offensive. Most Middle Eastern terrorist groups are anti-imperialist. The intensity of their passion wavers according to the type of group, but terrorism has largely been dominated by anti-Western feelings. Another symbiotic factor is the pan-Arabic or pan-Islamic orientation of terrorist groups. Although they fight for local control, most wish to revive a united Arab realm of Islam. Finally, Middle Eastern terrorism is united by kinship bonds. In terrorism, as in Middle Eastern politics in general, familial links are often more important than national identification.

When the Israelis practice terrorism, they usually claim their activities are conventional military actions. At times, however, the Israelis have used the same tactics the PLO used in the 1960s and 1970s. It is perhaps more accurate to argue that all Middle Eastern violence, Arabic and non-Arabic, is locked into symbiosis; it is interdependent (see Nasr, 1997; Said and Hutchinson, 1990). We will approach this problem with an examination of the world of the Middle East as it emerged from World War I.

The Early Zionist Movement in Palestine

The Zionist movement took place at the same time the Ottoman Empire was breaking up. This encouraged several Arab groups to espouse nationalism for lands formerly dominated by the Turks. The Palestinians believed themselves to be part of Syria, and because the Turks had objected to Jewish settlement, the Palestinians were willing to consider Jewish immigration as an expression of Syrian nationalism. The Zionists held no such belief: the Jews had no intention of becoming part of Syria. Nasr (1997, pp. 6–7) argues that the Palestinian Arabs represented a cohesive mixture of Muslims and Christians and that they were leery of Jewish settlements. Regardless, Palestinians sold land to the Zionists, who linked their holdings with the ultimate purpose of creating a Jewish state.

Nasr (1997, pp. 9–16) points out that sporadic violence accompanied these new settlements. Tensions became apparent in ethnic confrontation and conflicts between individuals. Violence was seldom organized, however, and it did not reflect the forms of terrorism that would engulf the region within two decades. That situation changed in World War I.

In the years preceding the war, Zionism caused confusion in Palestine. Even though most of the Jewish immigrants were European, the Arabs thought of them as Semitic people, and both groups identified with Palestine. Furthermore, the Zionists originally stated they had no desire to displace the Palestinians; they wanted to coexist with them. As Jewish settlers bought land, however, they purchased large parcels next to each other. They established governing councils for their farmland and refused to sell land back to Arabs. They were acting in defiance of the sultan's refusal to allow Jewish self-government (see Hourani, 1997, pp. 323–324).

World War I and Contradictory Promises

Jewish immigration into Palestine played into the political issues of World War I. Because the Turks were allied with the Germans, the British encouraged the Arabs to revolt against the Turks. If the Arabs would fight for the British, the British promised to move the caliphate from Istanbul to Mecca and to name an Arab as caliph. The military commander in Cairo, who promised to restore the caliphate, thought he was promising the Islamic equivalent of a pope and that secular, individual Arab states would continue to exist. He did not understand the nature of the caliphate. On October 24, 1915, the British made an unclear promise to the Arabs. In return for a general Arab revolt against the Turks, the British agreed to support the creation of a united, independent Arab state at the close of the war. The British believed this to be sound foreign policy. They believed the nebulous understanding was not a promise of support to the Arabs. However, the Arabs felt they had received a promise for the ancient Arab realm of Islam. Although the British had gained an ally at little expense, the circumstances were ripe for resentments (Fromkin, 2001, p. 179).

The British made other promises. Partially in response to the Zionist movement and partially to keep the goodwill of American Jews, the British promised the Zionists a Jewish homeland in Palestine. The **Balfour Declaration** of November 1917 promised to create the state of Israel. It was backed by Protestant Christians who understood neither the nature of the caliphate nor the importance of Jerusalem (al Quds to Muslims) in Islam. Supporters of the Balfour Declaration were unaware that their promise directly contradicted the British commander's promise in Cairo, the promise to reestablish an Arab-dominated caliphate. All Arab Muslims would expect the caliphate to include the three most important cities in Sunni Islam: Mecca, Medina, and Jerusalem. The Balfour Declaration threatened to transfer Jerusalem to the new state of Israel (Fromkin, 2001, pp. 274–300).

The British also made promises to their allies. Sir **Mark Sykes**, a British foreign service officer, negotiated a treaty with the French to extend spheres of British and French influence in the states of the old Ottoman empire. On the other side of the region, in ancient Persia (modern Iran), the British approached the Russians with another deal. Iran would be divided into three parts, a northern area controlled by Russia, a southern zone under British rule, and a neutral area in between. When the war ended in 1918, the entire Middle East was controlled by the

Balfour Declaration

A policy statement signed by the British government in November 1917 that promised a homeland for Jews in the geographical area of biblical Israel. Sir Arthur Balfour was the British foreign secretary.

Mark Sykes

(1879–1919) A British diplomat who signed a secret agreement with Francois Georges-Picot in May 1916. The Sykes-Picot Agreement divided the Middle East into spheres of French, British, and Russian influence.

British, French, and Russians, but it was a powder keg (Fromkin, 2001, pp. 189–196, 291–293).

Explicable in a time when national survival was threatened, these contradictory promises were nothing more than an extension of prewar British imperial policies. They did not alleviate the tensions between the Palestinian Arabs and the newly arrived Palestinian Jews. At the end of the war, the British created a series of Arab countries dominated by strong, traditional family groups. Far from representing a united Arab realm of Islam, the British division was challenged internally by rival families and externally by other Arab states. Each family and each of the Arab leaders wished to unite Islam under their own banner. Major states eventually emerged from this scenario: Syria, Iraq, Saudi Arabia, Jordan, and the Gulf States. Some of the new nations dreamed of a pan-Islamic region, but none was willing to let another run it. Other ethnic groups, like the Kurds, wanted autonomy. Christian Assyrians and Jewish settlers in Palestine also wanted independence (Hourani, 1997, pp. 315–332; Fromkin, 2001, pp. 558–561).

The Arabs also could not counter the continuing British influence, and neither a pan-Arabic realm nor a Jewish national state could develop under the watchful eyes of the British. In 1922 Great Britain received permission from the League of Nations to create the **Mandate of Palestine**. The mandate gave Britain control of Palestine and placed the British in the center of Middle Eastern affairs. But it came with a cost. It left neither Arab nor Jew satisfied. The Arabs believed they had received a false promise, and the Jews avidly demanded their right to a homeland (Fromkin, 2001, pp. 562–565).

The Birth of Israel

While the British established the Protectorate, in Palestine feelings of nationalism and anger increased. Both Jews and Arabs resented the British, but neither side was willing to submit to the other if the British could be expelled. Sporadic violence began in the 1920s and spilled into open revolt before World War II (1939–1945).

An Arab revolt in Palestine began in 1936 and lasted until 1939. It was primarily aimed at the British, but the brewing hatred and distrust between the Arab and Jewish communities also came to the surface. Both Jews and Arabs fought the British, but they fought each other at the same time. Animosity was overshadowed by the events of the early 1940s but resurfaced after the war. Both Jews and Arabs firmly believed the only possible solution to the problems in Palestine was to expel the British and eliminate the political participation of the other (Nasr, 1997, pp. 17–25).

In late 1945 and into 1946, thousands of Jews displaced by the Nazi holocaust flocked to Palestine. Palestinian Arabs, sensing danger from this massive influx of Jews, began to arm themselves. They had little assistance. The British Empire was collapsing, and other Arabs were too concerned with their own political objectives to care about the Palestinians. Officially, the British had banned Jewish immigration, but there was

Mandate of Palestine
The British Mandate of Palestine was in effect from 1920 to 1948. Created by the League of Nations, the mandate gave the United Kingdom the right to extend its influence in an area roughly equivalent to modern Jordan, Israel, and the Palestinian Authority.

little that could be done about the influx of immigrants. Jews continued to arrive, demanding an independent state (Lewis, 2004, pp. 181–187).

In 1947 the situation was beyond British control. Exhausted by World War II, the British sought a UN solution to their quandary in Palestine. The United Nations suggested that one part of Palestine be given to the Arabs and another part be given to the Jews. The Zionists were elated; the Arabs were not. Caught in the middle, the British came to favor the UN solution, and they had reason to support it. The Jews were in revolt.

Modern terrorism resurfaced in Palestine just before the UN partition. A Jewish terrorist organization called the Irgun Zvai Leumi launched a series of attacks against British soldiers and Arab Palestinians. The purpose of the attacks was twofold. The Irgun believed individual bombings and murders of British soldiers would make the occupation of Palestine too costly. Second, the Irgun was concerned about the presence of Arabs in newly claimed Jewish areas. Threats, beatings, and bombings were used to frighten the Arabs away.

In a four-part series on terrorism, the History Channel (2000) pointed to one of the threads running through Jewish terrorism. Leaders of the Irgun studied the tactics of the Irish Republican Army's Michael Collins. They incorporated Collins's methods in the Jewish campaign. Within twenty years, Palestinian Arabs would make the same discovery.

On May 15, 1948, the United Nations recognized the partition of Palestine and the modern nation-state of Israel. The Arabs attacked the new Jewish state immediately, and the Irgun's terrorism fell by the wayside. Both Arabs and Jews shifted to conventional warfare and would fight that way until 1967.

Arab Power Struggles and Arab-Israeli Wars

Modern Middle Eastern terrorism is the result of continuing conflicts in the twentieth century. This section reviews the formation of some of the most important Arab states in North Africa and southwest Asia. Instead of considering each story separately, the narrative blends Israel's development with the symbiotic nature of the conflict. This approach explains the relationship between intra-Arab rivalries and terrorism.

Although control of Palestine is always mentioned when dealing with contemporary Middle Eastern violence, from as far back as after World War I the situation was not conducive to peace. Britain and France divided the ancient realm of Islam, known as dar al-Islam, and left the area ripe for confusion and bitterness. Aside from the Palestinian issue, other Arabs felt slighted by various peace settlements, and their dissatisfaction continued through the end of World War II. The French and British created states that did not reflect the realistic divisions in the Middle East.

North Africa was completely dominated by Britain and France. Libya was divided into British and French sections, and it did not become independent until 1951. In 1969 Colonel Muammar Gadhafi seized power in a military coup, claiming Libya as an anti-Western socialist state. Egypt achieved its independence before World War II but did not fully break with Britain until Gamal Nasser took power in 1954. Gadhafi sought to follow Nasser's footsteps but broke with Egypt after Nasser's death in 1970 (Halliday, 2005, pp. 167–175).

Syria was under French rule from 1922 to 1946. After several military coups and a failed attempt to form a united republic with Egypt, a group of pan-Arabic socialists, the Baath Party, seized power in 1963. They were purged by an internal Baath revolution in 1966, and Baathist president Hafez Assad came to power in 1970 and ruled until his death in 2000. Aside from internal problems (especially problems involving a minority group of Alawites who practiced Muslim, Christian, and pagan rituals), Assad believed that Lebanon and Palestine were rightly part of Greater Syria (Dawisha, 2003, pp. 160–213).

Lebanon has become one of the most violent regions in the area. Ruled by France until 1943, the government of Lebanon managed a delicate balance of people with many different national and religious loyalties. In 1948 when Palestinians displaced by Israel began flocking to the country, the delicate balance was destroyed. Lebanon has suffered internal conflict ever since. Violence includes civil wars in 1958 and 1975–1976, continued fighting to 1978, an Israeli invasion in 1978, another Israeli invasion in 1982, Iranian revolutionary intervention from the 1982 Israeli invasion, a fragile peace in 1990, and the growth of a terrorist militia from 1983 to 1996. Several large militias still roam the countryside, despite their agreement to disarm by the terms of the 1990 peace plan. Israel began abandoning Lebanon in the spring and summer of 2000. Militant Lebanese forces moved into the former occupied zones, seeking vengeance on the **South Lebanese Army**, whose members supported Israel (Friedman, 2000, pp. 126–137).

The Persian Gulf region has another history. In an effort to secure the land route to India, the British established several states from the Mediterranean to the Persian Gulf in the nineteenth and early twentieth centuries. One branch of the Hashemite family received Jordan as a reward for assisting the British; another branch received Iraq. Jordan became a constitutional monarchy ruled by King Hussein from 1952 to 1999 and his son, King Abdullah, from 1999 to the present. Iraq's path was more turbulent. A 1958 coup eliminated the Iraqi Hashemites from power, and another coup in 1968 brought **Baathist** rule. Saddam Hussein, a Baathist, came to power in 1979 (Dawisha, 2003, pp. 169–171, 276–277).

Saudi Arabia and the Persian Gulf States fared somewhat better because of their immense wealth and independence from Europe. In 1902 the Saud family began expanding its control of Arabia, which includes Mecca, the most sacred shrine in Islam, and it unified the kingdom in 1932. The Gulf States remained independent from the Saud family. The social situation changed in 1938 when oil was discovered on the Arabian peninsula. When operations intensified, explorers found that the entire region was rich with oil. Poorer states, such as Iraq and Jordan, look at the Persian Gulf with envy, believing the whole area should ben-

South Lebanese Army
A Christian militia closely allied with and supported by Israel. It operated with Israeli support from 1982 to 2000.

Baathist
A member of the pan-national Arab Baath Party. Baathists were secular socialists seeking to unite Arabs in a single socialist state.

efit all of dar al-Islam, but not all has been peaceful in the Persian Gulf or Saudi Arabia.

From 1947 to 1967, the Middle East was dominated by a series of short conventional wars. Arab states failed to achieve unity, often seeming as willing to oppose each other as they were to oppose Israel. Rhetorically, all the Arab states maintained an anti-Israeli stance, but Jordan and Saudi Arabia began to pull closer to the West. They were enthusiastically led by the shah of Iran (B. Rubin, 2003).

In the meantime, the Israeli armed forces grew. Composed of highly mobile combined combat units, the Israeli Defense Forces became capable of launching swift, deadly strikes at the Arabs. In 1967 the Israelis demonstrated their superiority over all their Arab neighbors. Although the combined Arab armies were equipped with excellent Soviet arms and outnumbered the Israeli forces, in six days Israel soundly defeated its opponents and doubled its territory (Armstrong, 2000b, p. 171; Dawisha, 2003, 250–258).

Six Days' War

A war between Israel and its Arab neighbors fought in June 1967. Israel launched the preemptive war in the face of an Arab military buildup, and it overwhelmed all opposition. At the end of the war Israel occupied the Sinai Peninsula, the Golan Heights, and the West Bank of the Jordan River. It also occupied the city of Jerusalem (al Quds to Muslims).

After the 1967 **Six Days' War**, the PLO began a series of terrorist attacks against civilian Israeli positions. It was a turnaround from the old tactics of the Irgun and its violent offshoot, the Stern Gang. These attacks embittered most Israelis and served to define Israeli relations with Arab neighbors. The PLO soon split between moderates and radicals, but terrorism against Israel increased. Israel struck back against the PLO, wherever they were located (Nasr, 1997, pp. 40–47).

In the meantime, the Arab states also split into several camps. One group, represented by King Hussein of Jordan, was anxious to find a way to coexist with Israel. A few nations, like Egypt, simply wanted to avenge the embarrassment of the Six Days' War. Egypt would negotiate with Israel, but as an equal, not as a defeated nation. Other Arab views were more militant. Represented by the Baath Party, groups of Arab socialists called for both Arab unity and the destruction of Israel. They formed the Rejectionist Front, a coalition that included several terrorist groups rejecting peace with Israel. Finally, a group of wealthy oil states hoped for stability in the region. They publicly supported the struggle against Israel, while privately working for peace. Peace would ensure sound economic relations with their customers in the West.

Despite the myriad positions, the embarrassment of the Six Days' War proved to be the strongest catalyst to action. The Egyptians and Israelis kept sniping at one another along the Suez Canal. Gamal Nasser, Egypt's president, vowed to drive the Israelis back and asked for Soviet help to do it. Breaking relations with the United States, Nasser moved closer to the Soviet camp. When he died in September 1970, Anwar Sadat, his successor, questioned the policy. By 1972 he had thrown the Soviets out, claiming they were not willing to support another war with Israel. Coordinating activities with Syria, Sadat launched his own war on October 6, 1973 (Esposito, 1999, pp. 72–73, 93–96).

Yom Kippur War

A war between Israel and its Arab neighbors fought in October 1973. Also known as the Ramadan War, hostilities began with a surprise attack on Israel. After initial setbacks, Israel counterattacked and regained its positions.

The **Yom Kippur War**, sadly named after a Hebrew festival celebrating God's atonement for all sin and reconciliation with humanity, psychologically reversed the defeat of the Six Days' War for many of Israel's Arab neighbors. Catching the Israelis by surprise, in 1973 the Egyptians drove Israeli forces back into the Sinai, while the Syrians drove on to the Golan Heights. The Syrians almost captured Jerusalem before the Israeli Defense Forces managed to stabilize the front. Israel counterattacked, driving their enemies back, but the Egyptians celebrated their initial victory. Peace came three weeks later, and the Egyptians felt they had restored the honor.

Satisfied with this sense of victory, Sadat took a series of bold initiatives. Responding to an overture from the United States, Sadat renewed relations with Washington and stopped the minor skirmishes with Israeli troops by 1975. He visited Jerusalem in 1977 and publicly talked of peace (Esposito, 1999, pp. 96–98).

Menachim Begin became prime minister of Israel in September 1977. Begin was committed to maintaining control of the occupied territories, including Jerusalem, that Israel had won in the Six Days' War. Begin's position precluded peace with the Arab states because the Arabs demanded the return of the occupied territories. Despite the obvious differences, Anwar Sadat maintained a dialogue with Washington. Under the mediation of U.S. president Jimmy Carter, Sadat agreed to a separate peace with Israel, provided Israel would withdraw from the Sinai Peninsula. Begin agreed, and on May 26, 1979, Egypt and Israel signed the **Camp David Peace Accord** under Carter's watchful eyes. The decision cost Sadat his life. He was assassinated by Muslim fundamentalists in 1981 for agreeing to peace.

Camp David Peace Accord

A peace treaty between Egypt and Israel brokered by the United States in 1979.

The Rise of Terrorism

The Arabs rejecting peace with Israel fell into two camps. The radicals rejected any peace or recognition of Israel. The more moderate group was concerned about the fate of the Palestinians. Egypt's peace with Israel did not account for the Palestinian refugees in Israel or the occupied territories. At the same time, much of the West failed to pay attention to legitimate claims of the Palestinians because radical Palestinians were involved in dozens of terrorist attacks.

In the symbiotic world of Middle Eastern terrorism, Palestine was frequently used as a cover-up for the intra-Arab struggle for power. In 1978 Israel launched a minor invasion of Lebanon followed by a full-scale attack in 1982. During this same time, Middle Eastern governments were consolidating internal power and looking at potential regional rivals. The Iranian government fell to revolutionary Shiites, and the American embassy and its inhabitants were seized by Iran's revolutionary government. As the United States eventually achieved the return of its embassy hostages, Saddam Hussein's Iraq and revolutionary Iran went to war. Terrorism increased as a horrible sideshow, and thousands died each month on conventional battlefields (Wright, 2000, pp. 15–19).

In the melee of the 1980s, Middle Eastern terrorism fell into several broad categories including (1) suicide bombings and other attacks on Israeli and Western positions in Lebanon; (2) various militias fighting other militias in Lebanon; (3) state-sponsored terrorism from Libya, Syria, and Iran; (4) freelance terrorism to high-profile groups; (5) terrorism in support of Arab Palestinians; (6) attacks in Europe against Western targets; and (7) Israeli assassinations of alleged terrorists. Terrorists mounted dozens of operations for supporting governments, and several nations used terrorists as commandos. Airplanes were hijacked; airports were attacked; the United States responded with naval action, once accidentally shooting down an Iranian civilian airplane and killing hundreds; and Europe became a low-intensity battleground (Pluchinsky, 1982, 1986).

Despite the appearance of terrorism, conventional war continued to dominate the Middle East, and Arabs struggled against Arabs. As the **Iran-Iraq War** neared its end, Saddam Hussein turned his attention to Kuwait. Feeling the British had unfairly removed Kuwait from Iraq before World War I, Saddam Hussein invaded the small country to gain control of its oil production. The result was disastrous for Iraq. Leading a coalition of Western forces and the Persian Gulf States, the United States struck with massive force. Saddam Hussein's army suffered greatly, and terrorism reemerged as a weapon to strike an overwhelming military power. As Iraq retreated in the Persian Gulf, terrorists began plotting new methods for striking the United States.

Iran-Iraq War
A war fought after Iraq invaded Iran over a border dispute in 1980. Many experts predicted an Iraqi victory, but the Iranians stopped the Iraqi Army. The war produced an eight-year stalemate and more than a million casualties. The countries signed an armistice in 1988.

Self-Check

- *Is Israel the manifestation of the biblical Kingdom of David or a modern political movement?*
- *How did misunderstandings between Arabs and Jews develop?*
- *Why did terrorism become a part of these misunderstandings?*

▼ Iran

Americans found it convenient in the 1980s to speak of Iranian terrorism. After all, the Iranians had violated international law in the early stages of their revolution by taking the American embassy in Tehran. They were alleged to have staged several bombings in Lebanon as well as attacks on other American interests in the Middle East. They had planted mines in the Persian Gulf and were responsible for the deaths of U.S. troops. Finally, intelligence sources reported that the Iranians were allied with other terrorist states and supported a shadowy group known as Islamic Jihad—which turned out to be a cover name for an operational group of Hezbollah. The media attributed this rise in terrorism to the rise of Islamic fundamentalism in Iran.

In some ways this popular conception is correct, but in other ways it is completely wrong. The 1979 revolution in Iran represented the flames from friction that started centuries earlier. Far from being a rebirth of fundamentalism, it was more indicative of a religious split in Islam.

Uniquely Persian

Iranians are not Arab; they are Persian and have strong ethnonational ties to the ancient Persian Empire. They have struggled with Arabs for centuries, and these struggles are indicative of Iran's place in Islam. After the martyrdom of Hussein ibn Ali, Mohammed's grandson, at Karbala, Shiite Islam moved east. It came to dominate Iran, further separating Persians from many Arab Sunnis. When conquering Arab and Mongol armies rode through Persia over the next centuries, the Persians maintained their historical cultural identity. It came into full flourish when Iran reestablished its own agrarian empire under Shiite domination. Iranians resisted Turks and later European imperialists. Bernard Lewis (2004, pp. 43–45) says Iran never adapted the habits of nations that conquered them; they remained uniquely Persian.

Reaction to European imperialism cannot be overemphasized when considering the politics of modern Iran. There is a healthy Iranian distrust of the West. Karen Armstrong (2000a) shows the religious side of the struggle. During the nineteenth century, Iranians developed a hierarchy of Shiite Islamic scholars, including local prayer leaders, masters of Islam, ayatollahs, and grand ayatollahs. Armstrong says the leading scholars formed a theological advisory board to the government called the **majilis council**. In the early twentieth century, the majilis resisted British exploitation by taking political leadership. The scholars' activities helped bring about a constitution in 1906 and they virtually shut the country down in a general strike against British policies a few years later.

majilis council
The Islamic name given to a religious council that councils a government or a leader. Some Islamic countries refer to their legislative body as a majilis.

British Influence and Control

British imperialism came to Iran in the 1800s. After 1850, the British began to view Iran as the northern gate to India. They were also very concerned about German imperialism and possible Russian expansion. For their part, the Russians saw a potential opportunity to gain a warm-water port and further their empire. They moved into northern Iran and prepared to move south. The British countered by occupying southern Iran. Both countries used the occupation for their own economic and military interests (Nima, 1983, pp. 3–27; see also Esposito, 1999, pp. 41–52).

Oil production had a tremendous impact on the way the British used Iran. The British established the Anglo-Persian Oil Company in 1909 and started taking oil profits out of Iran. Although direct economic imperialism has ended in Iran, Iranians still regard Western oil companies as an extension of the old British arrangement. They believe the shah stayed in power by allowing Western corporations to exploit Iranian oil.

To some extent, this attitude reflects the history of Iran. The British became very concerned about Iran in the 1920s after the communist revolution in Russia, believing Iran might be the next country the communists would target. No longer in direct control of the south, the British searched for a leader to stem the potential Soviet threat, a leader whose Iranian nationalism would make him a Russian enemy. They did not believe such a man would be difficult to find because working-class Iranians hated the Russians as much as they hated the British. The British found their hero in **Reza Shah Pahlavi**. In 1925, with British support, he became shah of Iran (Wright, 2000, pp. 44–46).

Robin Wright says that Reza Shah was under no illusions about his dependency on British power. For Iran to gain full independence, he needed to develop an economic base that would support the country and consolidate his strength among the ethnic populations in Iran. Dilip Hiro (1987, pp. 22–30) says Reza Shah chose two methods for doing so. First, he encouraged Western investment, primarily British and American, in the oil and banking industries. Second, he courted various power groups inside Iran, including the Shiite fundamentalists. At first, these policies were successful, but they created long-term problems.

Hiro points out that Reza Shah had to modernize Iran to create the economic base that would free his country from the West. He introduced massive educational and industrial reforms and embarked on a full-scale program of Westernization. This brought him into conflict with the Shiite holy leaders, who had a strong influence over the Iranian lower classes. Modernization threatened the traditional Shiite hold on the educational system and the Shiite power base. The Shiites, however, did not bring about the fall of Reza Shah; World War II did.

Reza Shah's long-term failure was a result of his foreign policy. In the 1930s Reza Shah had befriended Hitler, and he saw German relations as a way to balance British influence. He guessed that Iran would profit from having a powerful British rival as an ally, but his plan backfired. When World War II erupted, the British and Russians believed Reza Shah's friendship with the Nazis could result in German troops in Iran and Iranian oil in Germany. In 1941 the British overran southern Iran, while the Russians reentered the north (Wright, 2000, pp. 45–46).

Prelude to the 1979 Revolution

Reza Shah was finished. He fled the country, leaving his son, **Mohammed Reza Pahlavi**, nominally in charge of the country. Mohammed Pahlavi became the modern shah of Iran, but his ascent was traumatic. An Allied puppet in the beginning, the shah had to fight for the same goals his father had failed to achieve. When he was on the verge of achieving power in the early 1950s, he found himself displaced by democratic and leftist forces. Like his father, the shah fled the country (Kurzman, 2004, pp. 103–124).

In August 1953 Pahlavi returned to the office that had been denied him during Iran's brief fling with democracy. The Iranians had attempted to create a constitutional assembly, but the British believed they were moving too far to the left and would be swept into a communist

Reza Shah Pahlavi

(1878–1944) Shah of Iran from 1925 to 1941. He was forced from power by a British and Soviet invasion.

Mohammed Reza Pahlavi

(1919–1980) Shah of Iran from 1941 to 1979. The shah led a rigorous program of modernization that turned Iran into a regional power. He left the throne and accepted exile as a result of the 1979 Iranian Revolution.

revolution. Playing on their fear of communism, the British convinced the American CIA that the only hope for stability in Iran was to empower the shah, Mohammed Pahlavi. The CIA conducted propaganda operations, but the new government was so ineffective that it would have fallen without help from the United States. In the popular Iranian version of the story—the story that most Iranians believe today—the CIA launched a well-orchestrated coup against the government (B. Rubin, 2003). America looked on the shah as a friend, not realizing Iranians viewed America's actions as part of a long tradition of imperialism.

In an extensive account with primary sources, Dilip Hiro (1987, pp. 30–100) provides details of the shah's attempt to build his base and his eventual failure. Once back in power in 1953 the shah formulated a plan to stay in power. Like his father, he believed that only modernization would lead to Iranian autonomy. Yet he also feared his own people. He created a secret military police force, **SAVAK**, to locate and destroy his enemies. SAVAK was aggressive.

The shah used a fairly effective strategy to employ SAVAK. Rather than taking on all his enemies at once, he became selective. He allied with one group to attack another group. SAVAK's enthusiasm for the torture and murder of political opponents complemented the policy. After 1953 the shah found it convenient to ally with the Shiite holy men, who welcomed the shah's support and turned a blind eye to SAVAK's activities. Charles Kurzman (2004, p. 126) points out that SAVAK's fist, effective at first, would eventually fail.

According to Hiro, by 1960 the shah's tenuous relationship with the fundamentalist clergy began to waver. The shah no longer needed their support, and the Western reforms of Iranian society were popular with the middle class, the members of which profited from modernization. The Shiite clergy, however, felt the increasing power of the state as Shiite influences and traditions were questioned or banned. From their seminary in the holy city of Qom, the clergy began to organize against the shah, but it was too late. The shah no longer needed the fundamentalists.

As the clergy organized demonstrations among theology students in Qom and marches of the faithful in Tehran, the shah unleashed his forces. SAVAK infiltrated Shiite opposition groups in Tehran, and the army attacked Qom. There were thousands of arrests, and demonstrators were ruthlessly beaten or, in some cases, shot in the streets. By 1963 many potential opponents were murdered, and the shah had many others in custody. One of his prisoners was the *hojatalislam* (master of Islam) **Ruhollah Khomeini**. In a gesture of mercy, the shah ordered Khomeini deported to Iraq instead of executing him. That proved to be a mistake.

The Revolution

Khomeini's rise to power was a key to the revolution. He was intolerant, not only of the shah's American infatuation, but of other Shiites who refused to accept his narrow interpretation of Islam. The shah and

SAVAK
Mohammed Pahlavi's secret police empowered after the 1953 downfall of the democratic government.

Ruhollah Khomeini
(1900–1989) The Shiite grand ayatollah who was the leading figure in the 1979 Iranian Revolution. Khomeini toppled the shah's government and consolidated power by destroying or silencing his enemies, including other Shiite Islamic scholars. Iran transformed into a theocracy under his influence.

his father had been very successful in limiting the power of the clergy because of the popularity of Western-style reforms. The Shiite scholars wisely sidestepped the reforms and attacked the shah where he was most vulnerable, the apparent link to imperialism through America. Khomeini had spoken several times about the shah's love affair with America, and this raised the ire of common Iranians, to whom America seemed no different from their former Russian and British colonial masters (Esposito, 1999, pp. 60–66).

Khomeini's influence increased after he was arrested and deported in 1963. He was promoted to the rank of ayatollah and ran a campaign against the shah from Iraq. Under his leadership, the mosque came to be perceived as the only opposition to the shah and the hated SAVAK. Khomeini headed a network of 180,000 Islamic revolutionaries in addition to 90,000 mullahs (low-ranking prayer leaders), 5,000 hojatalislams (middle-ranking scholars), and 50 ayatollahs (recognized scholars with authoritative writings). The Shiite scholars were able to paint the shah in satanic terms owing to his relations with the United States; they called for a holy revolution and the restoration of Islam. Khomeini led the way while in Iraqi exile (Wright, 2000, pp. 46–48; Kurzman, 2004, pp. 44–45).

Revolutionaries gained momentum after the election of Jimmy Carter as president of the United States in 1976. Carter pressured the shah to end SAVAK's human rights abuses. Fearful of a loss of American aid, the shah ordered SAVAK to ease off the opposition, increasing the ability of revolutionaries to operate inside Iran. There were many different groups. Secular socialists sought to topple the shah and remove Iran from the cold war. Communists wanted to shift allegiance to the Soviet Union. Many democrats wanted to create an Iranian democracy, and Shiite scholars sought to reintroduce religious values within a secular government. Khomeini, who viewed Carter as a manifestation of satanic power, felt no gratitude toward the United States. He wanted to create an Iranian theocracy with the majilis in charge of spiritual and temporal life. Increasing revolutionary activities from Iraq, Khomeini moved against the shah and other Iranian groups (Rasler, 1996) (Figure 9.2).

The shah pressured Saddam Hussein, then president of Iraq, to remove Khomeini, who was forced to flee Iraq in fear for his life. He received asylum in Paris where, ironically, he was better able to control the revolution because Paris had a modern telephone system from which he could directly dial Tehran.

In 1977 Khomeini's revolutionary headquarters in Paris maintained an open telephone line to Tehran. Khomeini sent hundreds of revolutionary sermons to a multiple audiotape machine in Tehran, and his words were duplicated and delivered throughout the Iranian countryside. Khomeini's power increased dramatically (Wright, 2000, pp. 46–49).

Khomeini returned to Tehran in 1978. There was little the shah could do. Although he had unleashed SAVAK and ordered his troops to fire on street demonstrators, the public had risen against him. Sev-

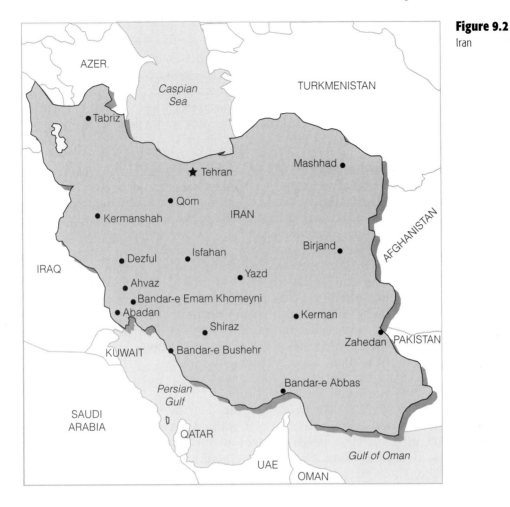

Figure 9.2
Iran

eral groups were vying for power, but Khomeini seemed to be on top. In February 1979, the shah fled Iran. Khomeini, riding victoriously through the streets of Tehran, was still faced with problems. It was necessary to eliminate all opposition if the Islamic revolution was to succeed. The starting point was to attack all things Western. In his first victory addresses, Khomeini pulled no punches. He said it was time to launch a holy war against the West and the traitors to Islam.

The Iranian Revolution of 1979 caused another form of terrorism to spread from the Middle East. Khomeini, filled with hatred for Saddam Hussein after being driven from Iraq, was content to wage a conventional war with his neighbor. However, such direct tactics would not work against a superpower. The United States and the Soviet Union, if they dared to intervene, would be subjected to a lower-level form of warfare. Because the superpowers would win any war fought out in the open, the Ayatollah Khomeini chose to fight in the shadows (Esposito, 1999, pp. 17–20).

In 1982 Israel invaded Lebanon, moving through the Shiite areas of the south. Revolutionaries left Iran and traveled through Syria, brokering deals with the Syrians to assist them in resisting the Israelis. The Iranian Revolutionary Guard arrived in the Bekaa Valley and established the nucleus of a new type of revolutionary force, Hezbollah. It subsequently became a multifaceted organization with elements representing terrorism, social services, Lebanese politics, and a military wing of Iranian foreign policy (Esposito, 1999, 154–157).

The Call to Karbala

Khomeini used a mixture of repressive tactics and political strategies to consolidate his power in Iran, and he is best understood within the Shiite tradition of Islam. Although many Western observers believe the fanaticism of the revolution was due to a resurgence of fundamentalism, in reality it gained its intensity from the repressed lower classes of Iran emerging to practice their traditional religion.

As imperialism made its way into nineteenth century Iran, public plays of Hussein ibn Ali's martyrdom at Karbala gained popularity. The emotional displays of Hussein's death at the hands of the Umayyads and his heroic acceptance of martyrdom became a Shiite equivalent of a Christian passion play. Such plays reinforced the distinction of the Shiites from all other religions, the uniquely Persian character of Iran, and the nobility of sacrifice for the sake of God (Armstrong, 2000b, pp. 299–319; see Rasler, 1996; Kurzman, 2001).

The Ayatollah Khomeini was guided by the message of Karbala, and he removed Islamic scholars and political leaders who disagreed with his message. He believed the Iranian Revolution was the first step in purifying the world. Israel must be eliminated and returned to Islamic rule. The West had become the handmaiden of the Jews, but the West was and remains the source of imperialism. Its influence is satanic and must be destroyed. Holy warriors are called to battle. After Khomeini's death in 1989, several competing schools of thought emerged in Iran. Although opposed by some Islamic scholars and almost all political moderates, a Khomeini-influenced majilis council came to dominate Iranian politics. It is guided by a belief that suggests the martyrdom of Karbala should be experienced every day. Many Islamic scholars reject this notion, and a number of political analysts believe that most Iranians, although proudly and uniquely Persian, do not wish to usher in a new age of martyrdom (Kurzman, 2001).

Self-Check

- *What social and political factors separate Iran from the Arab-dominated Middle East?*
- *How did British imperial policy help to shape modern Iran?*
- *How did reactions to Western policies influence the 1979 Iranian Revolution?*

SUMMARY

- The Middle East is a cultural concept. It can refer to a geographical area, but the boundaries are not distinct. *Middle East* means different things to different people.

- Islam is one of the world's great monotheistic religions. Believers contend that God is revealed through prophets and that Mohammed was the last and greatest Prophet. God's holy law is revealed in the Quran, and Islamic law can be interpreted by the sayings and actions of Mohammed.

- Islam has many different branches. The two main branches, Shiites and Sunnis, initially split over leadership of the Muslim community.

- Militant interpretations of Islam developed as the Islamic world faced military, political, and economic crises.

- When the Ottoman Empire collapsed, it led to the dissolution of the caliphate. British and French forces divided the Middle East into spheres of influence after World War I. European actions led to the creation of modern Israel within the British sphere.

- The Arabs and Israelis engaged in a series of conventional wars from 1948 to 1973, and the Israelis demonstrated their military superiority in each one. After the devastating defeat of June 1967, some Palestinians turned to terrorism as a method for confronting Israeli military superiority.

- Modern Iran formed within the context of European imperialism. The British were instrumental in placing Iranian leaders on the throne, and the United States took their place after World War II. Iran disavowed the United States after the 1979 Iranian Revolution.

KEY TERMS

Gulf States (p. 186)
Ali (p. 187)
Abu Bakr (p. 188)
Umar (p. 188)
Uthman (p. 188)
Badr (p. 189)
Umayyads (p. 190)
Hussein (p. 190)
Abbasids (p. 190)
Abdul Wahhab (p. 192)
Sayyid Qutb (p. 192)
Ibn Taymiyyah (p. 192)
Muslim Brotherhood (p. 194)
Hassan al Banna (p. 195)
Mawlana Mawdudi (p. 195)
Iranian Revolution (p. 196)

Ottoman Empire (p. 197)
Balfour Declaration (p. 200)
Mark Sykes (p. 200)
Mandate of Palestine (p. 201)
South Lebanese Army (p. 203)
Baathist (p. 203)
Six Days' War (p. 204)
Yom Kippur War (p. 204)
Camp David Peace Accord
   (p. 205)
Iran-Iraq War (p. 206)
majilis council (p. 207)
Reza Shah Pahlavi (p. 208)
Mohammed Reza Pahlavi (p. 208)
SAVAK (p. 209)
Ruhollah Khomeini (p. 209)

WRITING ASSIGNMENTS

1. Imagine that you are a talk show host on a listener call-in station. A person calls and says, "Islam is a religion full of suicide bombers and terrorists. It's time to stop being politically correct and deal with these terrorists." How would you respond?

2. Iran has a strained relationship with the West, especially the United States. Explain how this relationship developed, focusing on the transformation from being close allies to becoming openly hostile. Given their history, how might Iran and the United States engage each other in a series of dialogues to end the hostile environment?

3. Explain the reforms of ibn Taymiyya, Abdul Wahhab, and Qutb within the context of Karen Armstrong's view of agricultural empires and crisis.

PART

III

© Veer/Getty Images

TERRORISM TODAY

The Question of Israel and Palestine

AP Photo/Nasser Ishtayeh

A woman weeps at the ruins of her niece's bulldozed house. Her niece was a suicide bomber, and Israel routinely destroys the homes of such militants. Both terrorism and counterterrorist policies are devastating and controversial in the Middle East.

Learning Objectives

After reading this chapter, you should be able to

- Describe the rise of Fatah and the Palestine Liberation Organization (PLO).
- Identify the major Palestinian groups that emerged after the Yom Kippur War.
- Summarize the history of the Abu Nidal Organization.
- Discuss the origins of the Palestinian Islamic Jihad, its structure, and its operations.

- Explain the confusion surrounding the term *Islamic Jihad*.
- Outline the impact of the first Intifada and the birth of Hamas.
- Describe the current operational capabilities of Hamas.
- Define shifts that may cause Hamas to target the United States.
- Summarize the tactics of the al Aqsa Martyrs Brigades.

CHAPTER 10   The Question of Israel and Palestine   **217**

■ List and describe the activities of Jewish terrorist and extremist organizations.

■ Summarize controversial Israeli counter-terrorist policies.

During the summer of 2006, Iran began to support Hezbollah more aggressively than in the recent past, attempting to assert authority in foreign policy. Hezbollah, seeking a greater role in Lebanese politics, used Iran's increased support to make demands on the newly installed, fragile democratic government in Beirut. Syrian forces had recently been expelled from Lebanon, and many Lebanese did not want Hezbollah in their place. Hezbollah's Shiite militia maintained a strong hold on southern Lebanon, and it was more powerful than the Lebanese Army. Hezbollah refused to disband the militia and continued to move against its traditional enemy, Israel. Enraged, the Israeli prime minister ordered a conventional military invasion of Lebanon to destroy Hezbollah. This was a mistake. The touted military superiority of the Israeli Defense Forces (IDF) was shattered when determined Hezbollah militiamen stopped the Israeli offensive. The Israelis believed the Lebanese would assist with the destruction of Hezbollah, but the Lebanese instead rallied against the Israeli invaders. A year after the war, an Israeli review board chastised both the military and the prime minister for mismanagement of the conflict. The enemies of Israel had improved.

▼PLO from the Six Days' War to the Al Aqsa Intifada

In 1968 Cuba hosted revolutionary groups in a training session outside Havana (History Channel, 2000). Several leftist and nationalistic groups and individuals from around the world attended the event, including **Yasser Arafat** (1929–2004), leader of the Palestine Liberation Organization (PLO). Arafat stated that revolution united all revolutionaries from the past to the present. He embraced other terrorists in the Cuban training camps and promised to join them in international revolution. It seemed to some that Arafat's organization could be part of an international conspiracy.

In reality, however, the PLO was a secular organization attempting to establish a government for displaced Palestinians. Some PLO members lived in Israel, some in Palestinian areas controlled by Israel, and some simply moved to other countries, including a good number to Jordan. In 1957 Arafat gathered groups of disgruntled Palestinians in Jordan, form-

Yasser Arafat
(1929–2004) The name assumed by Mohammed al Husseini. Born in Cairo, he was a founding member of Fatah and the PLO. He merged the PLO and Fatah in 1964 and ran a terrorist campaign against Israel. After renouncing terrorism and recognizing Israel's right to exist, Arafat was president of the Palestinian National Authority from 1993 to 2004.

ing the PLO in 1964. His purpose was to create a political organization to help form a multinational alliance against Israel. He hoped Arab governments would jointly launch a war against the European-created state.

Fatah and the Six Days' War

In 1959 Arafat formed Fatah, a guerrilla organization, to wage a campaign against the Israelis. He advocated the use of small-unit tactics and terrorist actions, patterned after the Irgun Zvai Leumi. Fatah's attacks were annoyances to Israel, but they did not represent a serious threat. Israel was more concerned about the large armies of its Arab neighbors. Frustrated, Arafat merged Fatah into the PLO in 1964. See Expanding the Concept: Important Terms, Dates, Concepts, and People in the Middle East.

Arafat's frustrations multiplied after the Six Days' War in June 1967. After the Arab armies' sound defeat, Arafat's Fatah moved to center stage. An engineer educated in Cairo, the self-made leader of the PLO proposed terrorizing unfortified civilian targets (Wallach and Wallach, 1992). Using a group of Fatah warriors known as **fedayeen**, Arafat and **Kahlil Wazir** (also known as Abu Jihad, killed by Israeli intelligence in April 1988) began to attack Israel. The initial media coverage of Fatah's attacks caused the PLO's status to rise throughout the Arab world, and Arafat's fortunes rose along with it. All the conventional Arab armies were in disarray. Only the PLO had the courage and will to strike, despite being outnumbered, outgunned, and without a country. They had only the fedayeen (Dawisha, 2003, pp. 256–257).

Arafat conducted Fatah operations from Jordan, despite protests from **King Hussein**. Fatah had only a few hundred fedayeen, but their numbers slowly increased, allowing Arafat to launch more raids against Israel. With the Arabs in complete military disarray, Fatah's reputation rose. Rival groups tried to outdo Arafat, but it was Fatah's attacks that drew Israel's attention, making Arafat a hero in Palestinian eyes and moving Fatah into the leading role (Nasr, 1997, pp. 44–45).

Fatah after Karamah

The hit-and-run strikes from Palestinian bases in Jordan drew protests from Israel. They demanded that King Hussein put a stop to Fatah's operations. King Hussein sympathized with Israel, and he grew increasingly concerned by the growing militancy of Fatah. Still, he was afraid to act, fearing a rebellion among his own people if he moved against Fatah. Many Jordanians were of Palestinian origin, and they identified with the PLO. Israel, angered by a lack of action, decided to take matters into its own hands. On March 21, 1968, they sent a combined tank and mechanized infantry unit into Jordan to raid the Palestinians. They backed the attack with helicopters and artillery.

The target of the Israeli action was fedayeen in the village of Karamah, a tiny refugee center. They had no intention of holding the town or maintaining operations in Jordan. Their plan was to conduct a fairly

---

fedayeen

Warriors who sacrifice themselves. The term was used differently in Arab history; the modern term is used to describe the secular warriors of Fatah.

Kahlil Wazir

(1935–1988) A founder of Fatah and military leader for the PLO. His nom de guerre was Abu Jihad. He played a leading role in Black September and died in an Israeli-targeted assassination.

King Hussein

(1935–1999) King of Jordan. King Hussein drove the PLO from Jordan in September 1970. After his death his son Abdullah assumed the throne.

Important Terms, Dates, Concepts, and People in the Middle East

Arab-Israeli Wars: A generic term for several wars

1948 to 1949: Israel's War of Independence

1956 Suez Crisis: Britain, France, and Israel attack Egypt to keep the Suez Canal open; Israel takes the Gaza Strip

1967 Six Days' War: Pits Israel against its Arab neighbors; Israel takes Jerusalem, the West Bank, and other areas

1973 Yom Kippur War: Egypt and Syria strike Israel to regain occupied territories; Egypt is initially successful, but its major army is surrounded in a counterattack (Muslims frequently call it the Ramadan War)

Arafat, Yasser: Leader of the Palestine Liberation Organization (PLO), later the Palestine National Authority (PNA), and later the Palestine National Council (PNC); widely recognized secular leader of the Palestinian movement

Baalbek: Lebanese city in the Bekaa Valley; original headquarters of Hezbollah

Camp David Peace Accords: 1978 peace agreement between Egypt and Israel

Dome of the Rock: The place where Muslims believe Abraham (Ibrahim) had a vision of God

Eretz Israel: The land of Israel under King David; many Jewish fundamentalists feel God has called them to retake this land and expel the Arabs

Fedayeen: Warriors who sacrifice

Gaza Strip: Palestinian strip of land along the Mediterranean

Golan Heights: Region in Syria overlooking Israel

Gush Emunim: Literally, "Bloc of the Faithful"; Jewish group formed in 1974 that believes God literally promised Jews the Kingdom of David

Habash, George: Christian founder of the Popular Front for the Liberation of Palestine

Hawatmeh, Naiaf: One of the founders of the Popular Front for the Liberation of Palestine; later led the Democratic Front for the Liberation of Palestine

Interim Agreement: Follow-up to 1993 Oslo Accords in 1995 to allow elections in Palestinian territory

Intifada: 1987–1993 uprising in Palestinian areas; al Aqsa Intifada began in 2000

Jabril, Ahmed: Leader of the Popular Front for the Liberation of Palestine; later leader of the Popular Front for the Liberation of Palestine, General Command

(continued)

Important Terms, Dates, Concepts, and People in the Middle East (continued)

Jewish settlements: Legal and illegal settlements in Palestinians lands; in 2004 Israeli prime minister Ariel Sharon proposed withdrawing from the Jewish settlements

Knesset: The Israeli parliament

Labor Party: The liberal Israeli political party

Likud Party: The conservative Israeli political party

Mossad: The Israeli intelligence service

Mujahideen: Holy warriors

Muslim Brotherhood: An Islamic revivalist organization founded by Hassan al Banna in Cairo in 1928

Occupied territories: Palestinian territories under the post–World War I British division of Palestine that were occupied by Israel after the 1967 Six Days' War

Palestinian diaspora: The displacement in 1948 of Palestinians living in Israel

Palestine National Authority (PNA): Semiautonomous body established after the Oslo Accords

Palestine National Council (PNC): Representative body from the occupied territories, the Gaza Strip, and the Palestinian diaspora

Peace process: Generic term used to describe efforts to create a lasting peace between Palestine and Israel as well as general peace in the area

Rabin, Yitzak: Israeli Labor Party leader, politician, and prime minister; assassinated in 1995 by a Jewish extremist for brokering a peace plan

Rejectionist Front: A group of individuals, political parties, and states that reject Israel's right to exist

Road Map for Peace: The term used by president George W. Bush while trying to bring peace to the Middle East starting in 2002

Sharon, Ariel: Israeli military officer, defense minister, and prime minister; maintained a hard line against Palestinians

South Lebanon Army: The security force established by Israel to control south Lebanon after the withdrawal of the Israeli Defense Force in 1985

Sykes-Picot Agreement: A 1916 agreement between Britain and France for control of the Middle East

Tanzim: Fatah's militia

Temple Mount: The site of the ancient Jewish Temple, a former Christian church, and the al Aqsa mosque

Wailing Wall: The remaining western wall of the ancient Jewish Temple in Jerusalem

(continued)

Important Terms, Dates, Concepts, and People in the Middle East (continued)

West Bank: The West Bank of the Jordan River, formerly controlled by Jordan; seized by Israel in the 1967 war

Wye Accords: 1998 Israeli-Palestinian agreement to abide by previous commitments

Zion: The hill on which Jerusalem stands

Zionist: In contemporary usage, a Jew wishing to reestablish the Jewish homeland; Arabs and many Muslims frequently use the term to refer to all Jews

---

heavy hit-and-run operation of their own. As Israeli forces crossed Jordan's border, King Hussein ordered Jordanian tanks to counterattack. A tank battle ensued as the leading Israeli forces were hitting Karamah (Kometer, 2004, pp. 38–42).

Fedayeen grabbed their assault rifles and fought back. It seemed that they were going to be overrun when the Israelis pulled back. The Israelis had no intention of provoking a war with Jordan, and their tanks disengaged with the Jordanian counterattack. Infantry units in Karamah also pulled back, having lost their tank support. It was a small engagement, but the Israelis were retreating. Arafat became an overnight hero to the Arabs. That the Israelis had chosen to retreat and not been driven off was immaterial. The legend of the battle told of Fatah's fedayeen standing at Karamah and defeating the IDF. No other Arab forces had done so. Always one to strive for media attention, Arafat welcomed the role of the heroic commander of the fedayeen. Millions of donated dollars flowed into his coffers, making the PLO the most powerful Palestinian group—and corrupting the PLO leadership. Ironically, the Israeli raid on Karamah did not eliminate fedayeen but instead gave the PLO an aura of power. It would not be the last time an Israeli attack would backfire (Nasr, 1997, pp. 46–47; Dawisha, 2003, pp. 256–259).

The PLO Expelled

King Hussein of Jordan viewed the increasing strength of the PLO in his land with growing concern. He had entered the Six Days' War against Israel with some reluctance and preferred to take a moderate stance in the pan-Arabic struggle. Closely identified with British culture and friendly with the West, Jordan did not endorse the radicalism of Syria and other militant Arab states. King Hussein was especially wary of Syrian and Iraqi expansionist dreams and was more concerned with the protection of Jordan than with a united Arab realm (see Shlaim, 2001, pp. 298–299).

As the PLO grew, it drew closer to militant Arab states, giving them a potential base in Jordan. Concerned with the growing influence of foreign nationals in his own land, King Hussein ordered the PLO to stop attacking Israel. He was trying not to protect Israel but to stop the spread of rival influences in Jordan.

But the PLO was at an all-time high and not about to quit. Radical elements in Iraq and Syria encouraged Arafat to defy Hussein's order. Members of the Baath Party, the pan-Arabic socialist movement with branches in Syria and Iraq, saw the PLO as a tool that could be used against the Israelis. More importantly, they came to view the organization as a weapon to help the cause of revolution and socialism among all the Arabs. Arafat defied Hussein's order and stepped up operations against Israel.

Arafat continued training in Jordanian PLO camps and invited revolutionaries throughout the Middle East to participate. His exiled Palestinian government took no orders from its Jordanian host. Raids against Israel were conducted by a variety of PLO and foreign terrorist groups, and Arafat's reputation as a revolutionary hero spread beyond the Middle East. This became too much for King Hussein. After Palestinian terrorists hijacked three airplanes and destroyed them in Jordan, the king decided to act. In September 1970, Hussein attacked the PLO.

Arafat and the PLO were taken completely by surprise. The PLO terrorist offensive against Israel had worked because the terrorists operated in base camps that, although subject to Israeli attack, were relatively immune from annihilation. This was not the case when King Hussein's Jordanian army struck; the PLO had nowhere to run. As Jordanian regulars bombarded PLO camps and launched an all-out assault, Arafat had no alternative. Too weak to stand and fight, he fled to southern Lebanon. It was his only option.

Black September and Munich

Arafat blamed the Israelis for King Hussein's actions, and he wanted to strike back. He could not control terrorists in the many PLO splinter groups, so he created a new group after King Hussein's September attack. He called the group Black September. Using German leftist allies, Black September began planning a strike against the Israelis. It came, with German terrorist help, in Munich at the 1972 Olympic Games. Black September struck the Olympic Village and took most of the Israeli Olympic team hostage, killing those who tried to escape. German police moved in, and the world watched a drawn-out siege.

Black September terrorists negotiated transportation to Libya, but while moving to the aircraft designated to fly them from Germany, the German police launched a rescue operation. Plans immediately went awry. Reacting quickly, terrorists machine-gunned their hostages before the German police could take control. The Israelis and a German police officer were killed. It was a terrorist victory, and European leftists and nationalists saw it as partially their triumph (Shalev, 2006).

The 1982 Invasion of Lebanon

In southern Lebanon the mainstream PLO under Arafat became a fairly autonomous and potent force. Farther to the north, nationalistic Lebanese Christian and Islamic militias opposed each other, as well as the Palestinians and foreign interests. Syria backed its own militia in the hope of increasing its influence in Lebanon, and Iran joined the fighting after the Revolution of 1979, establishing a new terrorist organization called Islamic Jihad. Endemic civil war raged in Lebanon as dozens of terrorists slipped across the border to attack Israel (see Nasr, 1997, pp. 125–135).

By 1982 the Israelis had had enough. On June 6, a massive three-pronged IDF force invaded Lebanon in **Operation Peace for Galilee**. The PLO and other militias moved forward to take a stand, but they were no match for the coordinated efforts of IDF tanks, aircraft, and infantry. The Israelis rolled through Lebanon. Soon they were knocking on the doors of Beirut, and Lebanon's civil war seemed to be over (see Creed, 2002).

But Syria had other plans. Unable to tolerate Israel's presence in the area, the Syrians rallied all local militias, except the Christians, to their side and turned their own aircraft and tanks on the Israeli invaders. Israel found itself in a new war, and Arafat found himself out of options. Surrounded and bombarded by the Israelis in Beirut, even as the Syrian-backed forces fought the IDF, Arafat knew the Syrians had no love for him. If the Israelis won, Arafat would be doomed. If the Syrians won, they intended to install their own surrogates in place of the PLO. In August 1982 he left Beirut for Tripoli with 14,000 fedayeen. More than 10,000 guerrillas stayed, but they joined the Syrians.

Although the PLO left Lebanon in defeat, the Israelis had little to cheer. They formed an alliance with the northern Christian militias and tried to find a way out of the murderous mess their invasion had created. For their part, the Christian militias went on a rampage. They massacred Palestinians in two Lebanese villages, **Sabra and Shatila**. When international television viewers saw pictures of a dead Palestinian toddler in a bloody diaper lying on top of a pile of bodies, people began to wonder what type of Christians the Israeli allies professed to be. Israel was in a morass, and the violence continued (see Shahid, 2002).

With the PLO's retreat from Lebanon, Israel's fight with the group shifted to occupied Palestinian areas in Israel. Once again, Israel's military action resulted in more terrorism. As the fedayeen retreated, new terrorists came to take their place. The fighting in Lebanon continued with a new group, Hezbollah, which used an umbrella-style network (Chapter 11). Now we pause in the story of the PLO and step back to examine some of the groups that splintered from it before the war in Lebanon.

Operation Peace for Galilee
The code name for the Israeli invasion of Lebanon in 1982. It resulted in the expulsion of the PLO from Lebanon and the influx of Iranian revolutionaries who helped form Hezbollah. Israel occupied southern Lebanon for eighteen years, eventually leaving. Hezbollah claimed victory.

Sabra and Shatila
Two villages where Palestinian refugees were massacred in Lebanon in September 1982. Surrounded by IDF units who had guaranteed safety for the refugees, hundreds of Palestinians were massacred by Lebanese militiamen while the Israelis stood by. The IDF units claimed they had no idea of what was taking place. Critics dismiss this claim.

Self-Check

- *Explain the emergence of Fatah from the Six Days' War.*
- *How did Karameh and the Jordanian offensive change Fatah?*
- *What impact did the 1982 invasion of Lebanon have on Palestinians?*

▼ Factionalism in Palestinian Terrorism

The October 1973 Yom Kippur, or Ramadan, War caused a shift in the structure of Middle Eastern terrorism. The war eventually resulted in peace between Israel and Egypt, a peace that cost the life of the Egyptian leader who negotiated it, Anwar Sadat, and brought a domestic campaign of terrorism to Egypt. The end of the Yom Kippur War brought a sustained cease-fire between Jordan and Israel, and it returned Yasser Arafat to the forefront of Palestinian terrorism.

This brought another type of war, a war of internal battles for supremacy in the Palestinian movement. Karamah gave Fatah prestige, and Arafat tried to take advantage of his resulting popularity. Although he tried to exert control over the entire military campaign, Arafat was unsuccessful. New Palestinian groups formed and split from Fatah.

Divergent Terrorist Organizations

Sabri al Banna

(1937–2002) The real name of Abu Nidal. Al Banna was a founding member of Fatah, but split with Arafat in 1974. He founded militias in southern Lebanon, and he attacked Western and Israeli targets in Europe during the 1980s. In the 1990s he became a mercenary. He was murdered in Iraq, probably by the Iraqi government.

From 1967 to 1973 the PLO was characterized by internal splintering. Arafat found he could not retain control of the military wing, and several groups split from it. These groups included the Democratic Front for the Liberation of Palestine, the Popular Front for the Liberation of Palestine, and the Popular Front for the Liberation of Palestine, General Command. Another notable defector was **Sabri al Banna**, who would form an international terrorist group that operated in the 1980s. Kameel Nasr (1997, p. 46) concludes that all of these groups were at their best when they fought each other. Expanding the Concept: Divergent Groups lists many of these groups.

Arafat, trying to hold a diverse coalition of groups together, hinted that he would recognize the state of Israel if the world would recognize a Palestinian state (Halliday, 2005, p. 121). His words infuriated many Arab nationalists and socialists, and they were condemned by violent religious fanatics. By the early 1980s groups opposing Arafat gravitated to the Rejectionist Front, a coalition of groups rejecting Israel's right to exist. One of those groups was the Abu Nidal Organization, one of the deadliest groups in the Middle East (Gordon, 1999).

The Abu Nidal Organization

Black June

The rebel organization created by Abu Nidal in 1976. He changed the name to the Fatah Revolutionary Council after a rapprochement with Syria in 1981. Most analysts refer to this group simply as the Abu Nidal Organization.

Sabri al Banna (whose code name was Abu Nidal) and Yasser Arafat were once comrades in arms in the struggle for Palestine, but as others broke from Arafat, so too did Abu Nidal's rebel organization, called **Black June**. In the end, Abu Nidal and his organization became a mer-

Divergent Groups

Al Aqsa Martyrs Brigades: The al Aqsa Martyrs Brigades are based in West Bank refugee camps. Formed after the beginning of the al Aqsa Intifada, the Brigades appear to be Fatah's answer to the jihadists. Some members are motivated by Hezbollah, suggesting to some analysts that the Brigades have Shiite elements. Other analysts think that the Brigades are Fatah's attempt to take the Intifada's leadership away from Hamas and the PIJ. The Brigades are organized along military lines and became one of the first secular groups in the Middle East to use suicide bombers. Many experts believe that Arafat either directly controlled the Brigades or that they operated with his approval. A command council is responsible for leadership, and terrorist operations are divided into six geographical areas. If Yasser Arafat controlled the Brigades, members directly violated his orders on several occasions. The division commanders control the rank-and-file members, not the command council.

Black September: Named after the September 1970 Jordanian offensive against Palestinian refugees in western Jordan, Black September was the infamous group that attacked the Israeli athletic team at the 1972 Munich Olympics. Israel spent years hunting down and killing the members of Black September. The 1972 attack also prompted the Germans to create a new elite counterterrorist group, Federal Border Guard Group 9 (GSG-9), headed by Ulrich Wegener.

Democratic Front for the Liberation of Palestine (DFLP): A Christian, Naiaf Hawatmeh, created the DFLP in 1969 when he broke away from the Popular Front for the Liberation of Palestine. This Marxist-Leninist group seeks a socialist Palestine and was closely associated with the former Soviet Union. In 2000 the group joined Arafat in Washington, D.C., to negotiate with Israeli prime minister Ehud Barak. As a reward, the U.S. Department of State took the DFLP off its list of terrorist groups. The DFLP currently limits its attacks to the IDF.

Fatah: Fatah began as the military wing of the former PLO and was Yasser Arafat's strongest military muscle. Formed in the early stages of the PLO, Fatah was part of an underground organization formed in 1959. It emerged in the open in 1965 after making terrorist attacks against Israel in 1964. Fatah rose to prominence after the 1967 Six Days' War because it became the only means of attacking Israel. Fatah fought the Jordanians for ten days in September 1970 and regrouped in Lebanon. It joined in the Lebanese Civil War (1975–1990) and was eventually expelled to Tunisia. In the first Intifada (1987–1993), Fatah Hawks, political militants in the PLO, organized street demonstrations and disturbances, but emerging religious groups threatened Fatah's leadership among the militant Palestinian groups. Fatah went to the bargaining table in Oslo in 1993 and joined the

(continued)

Divergent Groups (continued)

peace process. It currently holds the majority of seats in the Palestinian government. Although it is now a political party, many analysts associate it with the al Aqsa Martyrs Brigades. The Tanzim Brigade and Force 17 (see p. 237) come from the ranks of Fatah, and it has traditionally championed Palestinian nationalism over ideology or religion.

Force 17: Officially known as Presidential Security, Force 17 is an arm of Fatah. It operated as Yasser Arafat's security unit.

Hamas: In December 1987, a few days after the first Intifada began, the Islamic Resistance Movement (Harakat al Muqawama al Islamiyya, or Hamas) formed. It was composed of the Palestinian wing of the Muslim Brotherhood. The Brothers advocated an international Islamic movement, and most of them did not support violence. Hamas differs from the Brothers' position in that it has localized the Islamic struggle and accepts violence as a norm. Hamas is organized as a large political union, and its primary mission is to oppose the PLO; today it represents an alternative to the Palestine National Council. Its military wing is called the Izz el Din al Qassam Brigades, named for a martyr in the 1935 Arab Revolt against the British in Palestine. In 2004 Israel assassinated Hamas's spiritual leader, Sheik Ahmed Yassin. As soon as Hamas appointed a new leader, the Israelis killed him, too. Hamas is a large organization, but its terrorist wing is rather small. Frequently allied with the PIJ, Hamas competes with other Fatah organizations.

Hezbollah: Hezbollah is the Iranian-backed Party of God operating from southern Lebanon. The local branch of the group forms alliances of convenience with other organizations participating in the al Aqsa Intifada. The international branch is believed to run the most effective terrorist network in the world. (See Chapter 11.)

Palestinian Islamic Jihad (PIJ): A small group emerging from the Muslim Brotherhood in Egypt in 1979, forming in the Gaza Strip in 1981. Whereas the Brothers spoke of an international Islamic awakening, the PIJ felt the struggle could be nationalized and had to become violent. PIJ leaders were enamored with the 1979 Iranian Revolution, and even though they were Sunnis, they sought contact with Iran's revolutionary Shiites. The PIJ operates out of the Gaza Strip and forms alliances of convenience with other organizations. It has grown closer to Hamas since the al Aqsa Intifada. The PIJ seeks to destroy Israel and establish an Islamic state in Palestine. The group has strong links to the United States, allegedly in Florida, and it is one of the groups that has mastered suicide bombing.

Palestine Liberation Front (PLF): Three different groups call themselves the Palestine Liberation Front: The Abu Abbas faction based in Iran follows the old-style leadership used by Arafat, the Abdal Fatah Ghanem faction received support from Libya, and the Talat Yaqub faction sought favor with

(continued)

Divergent Groups (continued)

Syria. The name used by all three groups comes from Ahmed Jabril, a former Syrian Army captain, who formed the first PLF in 1961. After the Six Days' War in June 1967, the PLF merged with two small radical groups to form the Popular Front for the Liberation of Palestine, but Jabril broke away and formed the Popular Front for the Liberation of Palestine, General Command (see p. 228). The PFLP-GC split in 1977 after Syria backed Lebanese Christians in the Lebanese Civil War (1975–1990), and the anti-Syrians formed a new group, reviving the PLF name.

The PLF had yet another internal war in 1984, and Abu Abbas, a militant leader who rebelled against Syria, returned one faction to Arafat, expelling all Syrian influence. Abdal Fatah Ghanem broke from Abbas and sided with Syria. His group remained active in Lebanon. Talat Yaqub tried to remain neutral. After Abdal Fatah Ghanem died of a heart attack, his faction gravitated toward Libyan support. All three factions of the PLF seek to destroy Israel. The PLF's most notorious action was the hijacking of an Italian luxury liner, the *Achille Lauro*, in 1985. American forces captured the hijackers, but Abu Abbas was released. He went to the Gaza Strip and eventually to Iraq. He was captured during the U.S. invasion of Iraq in 2003 and died in captivity.

Popular Democratic Front for the Liberation of Palestine (PDFLP): The PDFLP is the military wing of the DFLP.

Popular Front for the Liberation of Palestine (PFLP): The PFLP is a Marxist-Leninist Arab nationalistic group that emerged after the June 1967 Six Days' War. Egypt initially supported the PFLP but withdrew finances in 1968 when PFLP leaders criticized the Egyptian president. Operating in Lebanon under the command of Wadi Hadad, the PFLP began attacking Israeli airliners in 1968. In 1970 the group staged four hijackings in a six-day period; three of the planes were destroyed in the Jordanian desert in front of international media. Because the PFLP was closely linked to Arafat's Fatah, the Jordanians drove Arafat from their territory in September 1970. In 1975 it allied with Carlos the Jackal, a Latin American terrorist, and the Red Army Faction, a left-wing terrorist group from Germany, to attack an oil ministers' conference in Vienna. Although the PFLP has been successful at times, it has been riddled with factionalism. The first splits came in 1968 and 1969 when Ahmed Jabril and George Habash broke from the PFLP. Wadi Hadad left the organization in 1976 when the Palestine National Council disavowed the use of terrorism outside the vicinity of Israel and the territories it occupied. He formed the Popular Front for the Liberation of Palestine, General Command, but died in 1978. Habash returned to the PFLP in 1976 and directed the campaign against Israel. He eventually reconciled with Fatah and handed leadership over to Abu Ali Mustafa in 2000. Mustafa was assassinated by the Israelis in August 2001. Ahmed

(continued)

Divergent Groups (continued)

Sadat, his successor, retaliated by killing an Israeli official. The PFLP has grown in stature since the al Aqsa Intifada.

Popular Front for the Liberation of Palestine, General Command (PFLP-GC): The PFLP formed in 1967 when George Habash agreed to ally with Ahmed Jabril's PLF. Habash, a Christian, assumed leadership of the group, but he soon clashed with the Syrian-oriented Jabril. Syria continued to court Jabril, and he broke from Habash in 1968 to form the PFLP-GC. The PFLP-GC advocates armed struggle with Israel, and it became one of the most technically sophisticated organizations in the area. It originally operated from southern Lebanon with support from Syria. By the late 1980s, the PFLP-GC had followed the lead of the Abu Nidal Organization and rented its services to various governments. Some analysts believe the group was behind various international airline bombings. The PFLP-GC has been eclipsed by suicide bombers since 2000, but Jabril is increasingly emphasizing religion. This places the PFLP-GC closer to jihadist groups, but it still remains one of the most technically sophisticated terrorist organizations in the area. Jabril has always favored military action over sensationalized terrorist events.

Tanzim Brigade: Claiming not to be directly involved in terrorism, the Tanzim Brigade is the militia wing of Fatah.

---

cenary group, not only abandoning Arafat but also completely forsaking the Palestinian cause.

Patrick Seale (1992), a veteran Middle Eastern correspondent who has extensive contacts among Palestinian leaders, provides the most comprehensive and objective account of Abu Nidal to date in *Abu Nidal: A Gun for Hire.* According to Seale, Abu Nidal joined Fatah in the hope of regaining a homeland for the Palestinians, but he soon became disillusioned with Fatah, especially with Yasser Arafat. When Arafat began the gradual shift away from terrorism in the early 1970s, Abu Nidal began to take action. In 1973 after authorizing the murder of several leading Palestinian moderates, he left for Baghdad.

The Iraqis welcomed Abu Nidal with open arms and helped him build the infrastructure to support his own terrorist organization. At first, Abu Nidal's purpose was to purge Fatah of moderates, but the Lebanese Civil War (1975–1985) quickly drew his attention. He entered the war with his own agenda, also representing the interests of his Iraqi benefactors.

Seale states Abu Nidal's relations with the Iraqis started going bad after the rise of Saddam Hussein in 1979. Abu Nidal began courting his former enemy, **Hafez Assad** of Syria, and moved his operations to Damascus in 1983. The Syrians, using their newfound terrorist allies to

Hafez Assad
(1930–2000) President of Syria from 1970 to 2000. He brutally suppressed a rebellion of the Muslim Brotherhood in 1982. His son Bashir Assad assumed the presidency after his death.

augment their air force's intelligence service, hoped to employ Abu Nidal in Lebanon. They soon found, however, that Abu Nidal was not easy to control. Once ensconced in Damascus, Abu Nidal's terrorists set up a command-and-control structure that defied Syrian intervention. He provided some services to his Syrian patrons (for example, he waged an assassination war against Jordan), but the Syrians gradually tired of Abu Nidal's insubordination. By 1987 he had worn out his welcome (Wege, 1991).

Seale says **Muammar Gadhafi** was happy to bring Abu Nidal to Libya. Gadhafi offered financial help and gave Abu Nidal space for recruiting and training terrorists. Most of the group continued to operate from secret bases in Libya through the 1990s, but Abu Nidal himself was murdered in Iraq in 2002. Although he claimed to represent the Palestinian cause, Abu Nidal worked as a freelance assassin. Many of his hit teams have targeted other Arabs, including high-ranking officials of the PLO.

The birth of the Abu Nidal group may have mirrored standard Middle Eastern terrorism, but the group's exploits drew more attention than did those of its rival terrorist organizations. Abu Nidal was particularly ruthless. Making no distinction between targets and the people in and around targets, Abu Nidal's terrorists became noted for the harsh brutality of their murderous attacks. His organization's international exploits gained attention: the world was a battleground for Abu Nidal.

Abu Nidal changed the face of Middle Eastern terrorism. First, he increased activities in Europe, resulting in spectacular attacks in Rome and Vienna on December 27, 1985. Second, he created a large terrorist group, defying the trend to split, by maintaining a ruthless internal enforcement mechanism. Third, he threw himself into the **Lebanese Civil War** (1975–1990), maintaining militias in southern Lebanon. After the 1982 Israeli invasion of Lebanon, Abu Nidal established training centers and support camps in Lebanon. Finally, terrorism became the reason for existence. Abu Nidal dropped his ideological bent and started working as a mercenary for foreign governments.

The Rise of Palestinian Islamic Jihad

Another secular group arising after the Yom Kippur War was the Palestinian Islamic Jihad (PIJ). Discussions of the group are sometimes confusing because several small groups in various countries operate under the name of *Islamic Jihad* (see Expanding the Concept: Islamic Jihads). Confusion increases because founders of the PIJ structured the organization in secret. American intelligence sources believe that Hezbollah's umbrella included Palestinian Islamic Jihad from 1982 until sometime around 1988. But Hezbollah officials deny this and claim no relation with the PIJ (Harik, 2004, pp. 16–27, 164–175).

The PIJ emerged from Egypt. Its founders—**Fathi Shekaki**, **Abdul Aziz**, and **Bashir Musa**—were influenced by militant **Salafism** and disillusioned with the Muslim Brotherhood. Whereas the Brothers spoke of

Muammar Gadhafi

(1942–) The leader of Libya. Gadhafi took power in 1969 in a socialist revolution. He developed a unique theory of Arab socialism. His intelligence forces were responsible for planting a bomb on a Pan American flight over Lockerbie, Scotland, in 1988, killing 270 people. The attack was in response to an American bombing raid in Libya in 1986.

Lebanese Civil War

(1975–1990) A brutal factional war between several different religious militias for control of Lebanon. Several nations intervened, and Syria exerted control in the waning years of the war. Supporting Hezbollah, Syria retained control of Lebanon until 2005.

Fathi Shekaki

(1951–1995) The general secretary and founder of the PIJ. From Gaza, Shekaki was a Palestinian physician. He was killed in a targeted assassination.

Abdul Aziz

(1950–) A founding member and spiritual leader of the PIJ. He is also known as Sheik Odeh and has several aliases.

Bashir Musa

(1955–) A founding member of the PIJ. The U.S. government considers Musa to be a member of a terrorist

EXPANDING THE CONCEPT

Islamic Jihads

Several groups operate under the name *Islamic Jihad*, maintaining offices in Damascus, Beirut, Khartoum, and Tehran. They also raise funds in the United States.

Group	Location
Islamic Jihad	Lebanon, 1982–1988
Islamic Jihad Organization	Jordan
Islamic Jihad	Jordan
Islamic Jihad—the Temple	Israel
Pro-Iranian Islamic Jihad Organization, the al Aqsa Battalions	Israel
Islamic Jihad Squad	Egypt and Sudan
Islamic Jihad, Shekaki Faction	Syria, Lebanon, and Israel

organization. He currently teaches Islamic studies in the United Kingdom.

Salafism
A reform movement in Islam that started in North Africa in the nineteenth century. Its purpose is to purify Islam by returning to the Islam of Mohammed and his companions.

Gaza Strip
The westernmost area of Palestine territories.

occupied territories
Any number of territories controlled by Israel. The areas may become the independent nation of Palestine, if the Palestinians are able to create their own nation.

education and peaceful change, the founders of the PIJ wanted to create an Islamic state using military action. They moved the PIJ into the **Gaza Strip** in the late 1970s and eventually went to southern Lebanon. When they returned to the **occupied territories**, they believed they could become the vanguard of a local Islamic revolution (Institute for Counter-Terrorism, 1996), and they began to create a new terrorist organization.

To understand this geographical and religious journey, it is necessary to look at the PIJ's first leader. Fathi Shekaki fell under the influence of the Muslim Brotherhood in Egypt, but as Sayyid Qutb had, he longed to take direct action against corrupt Muslim governments and the infidels who influenced them. He felt the Brothers were too patient, waiting for the Islamic world to awaken and create a pan-Islamic society. This was too idealistic for the practical Shekaki. Revolutions, he believed, started in localized geographical areas. In other words, ideas spread violently after a revolution had taken place, not gradually as an entire people became enlightened through education. As Shekaki championed Islamicist theories in 1978, much of the world's attention was focused on Iran. In the wake of the Iranian Revolution, the Ayatollah Khomeini created an Islamic government and talked of spreading the revolution. Nothing could have been closer to Shekaki's heart (Donovan, 2002).

Shekaki supported the Iranian Revolution, hailing it as a model for bringing Islamic law to the community of believers throughout the Islamic world. He left Egypt with Abdul Aziz and Bashir Musa to settle in the Gaza Strip in 1981. In the shadow of the occupied territories, the PIJ grew, espousing revolution as a means of action. Shekaki wanted no social program or general political movement. He felt his small group should be devoted to one thing: military action. Bombings and other terrorist tactics would serve as the vanguard of the Islamic revolution in the same manner that Khomeini's revolution in Iran toppled the shah (Military.com, 2004). Shekaki and his cohort waited for a chance to strike.

His opportunity was not long in coming. In 1982 Israeli tanks rolled through the Shiite settlements of southern Lebanon, and as discussed in Chapter 9, Revolutionary Guards from Iran went to the area to fight the Israelis under the umbrella of Hezbollah. Shekaki and his newly formed PIJ also went to Lebanon. While there, he recruited terrorists and formed relations with local Shiites. These overtures brought the PIJ into contact with Iran and the spiritual leaders who had been trained in **Najaf**, Iraq, including Mohammed Hassan Fadlallah (Israeli Foreign Ministry, 1996). Shekaki soon discovered that he and his Iranian allies had a similar vision.

Shekaki was also impressed with two of Hezbollah's innovations: the umbrella-style organization and the suicide bomber. He copied both of them. Many researchers are not sure whether the PIJ became one of the groups operating under Hezbollah's umbrella or whether it remained completely autonomous in 1982, but it is known that the PIJ formed its own umbrella in 1983. Shekaki found that by letting his group split he became virtually invisible to his enemies. The United States had never seen anything like the PIJ (Taubman, 1984). It was a "nongroup." Both Hezbollah and the PIJ took the West totally by surprise; their structures gave terrorism a new kind of power (Wright, 1986, pp. 84–86).

The U.S. Department of State (1996, 2004a) sees the structure of the PIJ as a pillar of its strength. PIJ terrorists gained power through the group's hidden structure because it made them invisible. As Robin Wright (1986, p. 86) notes, the PIJ had no infrastructure or visible means of support. It was not concerned with claiming credit for operations, but it was concerned about killing. Shekaki's terrorists lived and died for one thing: to kill their enemies. Action, not slogans and ideas, caused revolution.

The group's invisibility was partially due to the growing number of groups claiming the name "Islamic Jihad." Shekaki's group had no concern about who called themselves Islamic Jihad as long as they killed PIJ enemies. Even a single action from a group would help confuse investigators. After all, it seemed impossible to fight an organization that was not an organization. There was no place to launch a counterstrike.

When the first **Intifada** broke out in 1987, the PIJ increased political action and joined the battle in the streets. Shekaki was captured and deported from Gaza in 1988, but he returned in short order. When the 1993 **Oslo Accords** promised some hope for an end to violence, Shekaki joined a new Rejectionist Front. Allying with various other groups, including the other Islamic Jihads, Shekaki called for a wave of violence. The PIJ struck Israeli targets, assassinated soldiers, and perfected the tactic they copied from Hezbollah, suicide bombing. This was too much for the Israelis. If they could not figure out how to strike a nebulous network of groups, they could strike its figurehead. Shekaki was assas-

Najaf
A city in Iraq one hundred miles south of Baghdad. It is a holy site for Shiites who believe that the Imam Ali, Mohammed's cousin and son-in-law, is buried there.

Intifada
The first spontaneous uprising against Israel that lasted from 1987 to 1993. It began with youths throwing rocks and creating civil disorder. Some of the violence became more organized. Many people sided with religious organizations, abandoning the secular PLO during the Intifada.

Oslo Accords
A 1993 agreement between Palestinians and Israel. It resulted in the Palestinian National Authority and limited self-rule.

sinated in Malta in 1995; most sources believe the Israelis were behind the attack.

Time magazine reporters interviewed Shekaki nine months before his death (*Time*, 1995). There would be no peace, he said, until Israel was destroyed. He also reiterated his willingness to use human missiles—the suicide bombers. He stated that Palestinian Islamic Jihad, unlike Hamas, was willing to accept a liberated Palestine even without a united Arab realm. The U.S. Department of State (1996) took such statements at face value and feared an expanded suicide-bombing campaign in 1995.

Ramadan Abdullah Sallah

(1958–) The leader of the PIJ after Shekaki's assassination. He is wanted by the FBI and believed to be in Syria.

Shekaki's successor, **Ramadan Abdullah Sallah**, maintained the Shekaki philosophy. Raised in Gaza and educated in the United Kingdom, Sallah continued the campaign against Israel. He formed a loose alliance with Hamas and conducted joint PIJ-Hamas operations. True to its original design, the PIJ remained small, consisting of no more than a few dozen members (Donovan, 2002).

The September 2000 al Aqsa Intifada sent the PIJ into a frenzy of activity as the group launched a suicide-bombing campaign. Divisions among the various factions narrowed, and the PIJ sought deeper ties to Hezbollah and Hamas. Yet the PIJ could not match the number of bombings from other terrorist groups during the early stages of the al Aqsa Intifada, so it tried to create more spectacular bombings. These actions included deadly strikes on civilian targets designed to kill and maim ordinary Israeli citizens. It also endorsed the use of women and children as suicide bombers.

The U.S. Department of Justice (2003) believes that, despite its indistinct infrastructure, the PIJ has an organized network of financial supporters around the world, including in the United States. The U.S. government claims it has uncovered a PIJ financial and administrative network at a Florida university, and it has charged several alleged members. Steven Emerson (2002, pp. 112–124) claims that the PIJ distributes literature and raises funds throughout the United States. The U.S. Department of State (2004a) still believes that some funds come through Iran and possibly Syria.

Self-Check

- *Why did the Palestinian militant movement split into factions?*
- *How did the Abu Nidal Organization emerge from this split?*
- *Why did the Palestinian Islamic Jihad establish its own operations?*

Arab nationalism

The idea that the Arabs could create a European-style nation based on a common language and culture. The idea faded after the 1967 Six Days' War.

Hamas and the Rise of Religious Organizations

Arab nationalism grew through the early part of the twentieth century and flourished until the June 1967 Six Days' War. Groups spawned from Fatah and independent organizations like the PIJ began their activities by embracing some form of nationalism. Before he degenerated into mercenary activities, Abu Nidal favored **Arab socialism** as a form of nationalism. In the 1970s and 1980s Baathist nationalists in Syria and Iraq also believed in socialism. Adeed Dawisha (2003, pp. 253–280) points out that nationalism ultimately failed. It did not unite the Arabs nor did it raise their standard of living. As nationalism waned, religious fervor took its place. The PIJ began using religious imagery, and other groups were born from religious fervor.

An Overview of Hamas

The story of Hamas is tied to the late Sheik **Ahmed Yassin**. Born in 1938, Yassin grew up in Gaza under the influence of the Muslim Brotherhood. He believed that Islam was the only path that could restore Palestine, and he preached reform and social welfare. Many Palestinians in Gaza began to follow Yassin's powerful call. When he told followers to secretly gather weapons in 1984, they obeyed, but it cost him his freedom. The Israelis discovered Yassin's plans and jailed him. He was released in 1986 and decided that in the future his organization would have a military wing. The Palestinian Muslim Brothers would become the nucleus of Hamas (Institute for Counter-Terrorism, 2004).

Hamas was formed in December 1987 at the beginning of the first Intifada (Isseroff, 2004). Yassin was disappointed with the secular direction of the PLO and wanted to steer the resistance movement along a religious course. Several technically trained university graduates, engineers, teachers, and Islamic scholars joined the movement. They published the Hamas Charter in 1988, declaring that Palestine was God-given land, from the Jordan River to the Mediterranean. There could be no compromise with the Israelis, and Israel could not be allowed to exist. Unlike Arafat's PLO, Hamas would fight Israel with religious zeal. Unlike the PIJ, Hamas would be much more than a military organization. It would be a Muslim government, the forerunner of a Palestinian Muslim state (Levit, 2006, pp. 17–18, 30–32).

Hamas's organization reflects this original charter (Hamas, 1988), maintaining a political wing to oversee internal and foreign relations. Its largest unit, especially in Gaza, is its social wing. According to the third pillar of Islam, *Zakat*, Muslims are to give alms and share with the poor. Hamas runs charities, schools, hospitals, and other social service organizations in Gaza where unemployment is sometimes as high as 85 percent. These social services have made Hamas popular among the Palestinians. Hamas's military wing, the **Izz el Din al Qassam Brigades**, is named after a martyr from the time of the British occupation of Palestine.

Hamas's relationship with the PLO and the Palestinian National Authority (PNA) has been shaky (Westcott, 2000). The reason can be traced to its religious orientation. Although Yassin and his followers vowed never to use violence against fellow Palestinians, they have always opposed Arafat.

Arab socialism

A school of Arab nationalism contending that a single Arab nation should have a socialist economy.

Ahmed Yassin

(1937–2004) One of the founders and leaders of Hamas. Yassin originally started the Palestinian Wing of the Muslim Brotherhood, but merged it into Hamas during the Intifada. He was killed in an Israeli-targeted assassination.

Izz el Din al Qassam Brigades

The military wing of Hamas, named after the Arab revolutionary leader Sheik Izz el Din al Qassam (1882–1935), who led a revolt against British rule.

Struggles for Leadership

After the first Intifada, Hamas faced an internal power struggle. Yassin was jailed from 1989 to 1997, and during that time, the American-educated **Musa Abu Marzuq** took over Hamas. His strategy was much more violent than Yassin's had been. He also sought financial backing from Syria and Iran in an attempt to assert greater power in the organization. He assembled a new leadership core and based it in Jordan, leading others to call it the "outside" leadership, in contrast to the "inside" leadership group of Yassin, who believed the struggle should remain inside Palestine (Levitt, 2002, pp. 34–37).

Marzuq's leadership also caused a struggle with the PNA (Institute for Counter-Terrorism, 2004). In 1996 Marzuq authorized a campaign of suicide bombing inside Israel. The PIJ launched one at the same time, and both campaigns continued into 1997. They were especially savage, targeting civilians and public places. Bombs were designed to kill, cripple, and maim. Some bombs were even laced with rat poison to cause wounds to continue bleeding after treatment. Israel gave Arafat an ultimatum: crack down on Hamas or Israel would. The PNA arrested a number of Hamas's leaders, and Marzuq's offensive waned.

After Yassin was released from prison in 1997, he gradually reasserted control over Hamas, even though he remained under house arrest. He moved operations back to the Gaza Strip. Violence continued to 2000 but slowly decreased. Leaders of the al Qassam Brigades were incensed at the decrease, claiming that both the inside and outside leadership were placing too much attention on political solutions (see Levitt, 2002, pp. 33–51). In the meantime, Jordanian officials closed Hamas operations in Amman, Jordan, and the outsiders who could avoid arrest fled to Syria. By 2000 some observers believed a lasting peace might be at hand. They were disappointed (Karman, 2000; Wikas, 2002). The al Aqsa Intifada started in September.

The Al Aqsa Intifada

It is hard to overstate the effect of the **al Aqsa Intifada** on Hamas. Quarreling between the al Qassam leaders and the political wing came to a standstill. Moderates and hard-liners drew closer together. As the IDF swarmed into Palestinian areas, Arafat's makeshift government, the PNA, lost much of its power. Hamas, therefore, had the opportunity to assert its muscle. The distinction among the various Palestinian forces began to blur, and Hamas grew stronger by forming alliances with Hezbollah and the PIJ. It then joined the largest suicide-bombing campaign the Middle East had ever seen.

In the summer of 2003 Palestinian prime minister **Mahmud Abbas** brokered a limited cease-fire, asking Hamas, the PIJ, and related groups to end their campaigns. But the peace effort ended in August after a suicide bombing on a bus in Jerusalem. The Israelis responded by renewing a policy of selective assassination, that is, they identified leaders of Hamas and systematically murdered them (see Expanding the Concept:

Musa Abu Marzuq
(1951–) The "outside" leader of Hamas, who is thought to be in Damascus, Syria. He is believed to have controlled the Holy Land Foundation.

al Aqsa Intifada
An uprising sparked by Ariel Sharon's visit to the Temple Mount with a group of armed escorts in September 2000. The area is considered sacred to Jews, Christians, and Muslims. Muslims were incensed by the militant aspect of Sharon's visit. Unlike the 1987 Intifada, the al Aqsa Intifada has been characterized by suicide bombings.

Mahmud Abbas
(1935–) The president of the Palestinian National Authority since 1995; founding member of Fatah and an executive in the PLO.

EXPANDING THE CONCEPT

Israeli Selective Assassination

Israel has targeted Hamas leaders throughout the al Aqsa Intifada.

Person	Position	Israeli Action
Riyad Abu Zayd	Military commander	Ambush, February 2003
Ibrahim Maqadah	Military commander	Helicopter attack, May 2003
Abdullah Qawasmah	Suicide bomb commander	Ambush, June 2003
Ismail Shanab	Political leader	Bomb strike, August 2003
Sheik Ahmed Yassin	Head of Hamas	Helicopter attack, March 2004
Abdel Aziz Rantisi	Replaced Yassin	Helicopter attack, April 2004

Israeli Selective Assassination). Hamas passed another milestone in the campaign against Israel: it used a female suicide bomber in a joint operation with a newer group, the al Aqsa Martyrs Brigades (J. Stern, 2003a). Hamas had followed the lead of the Liberation Tigers of Tamil Eelam (LTTE), the Kurdistan Workers Party, and the Chechen rebels, who have also used female suicide bombers.

The Future

The future of Hamas may lie outside the Middle East. In March 2004 Yassin was leaving a mosque in Gaza when Israeli helicopters appeared and fired three missiles at him. He met the fate of other Hamas leaders before him and was killed instantly. Hamas announced his replacement, **Abdel Aziz Rantisi**, an old member of the inside faction. However, the Israelis assassinated Rantisi in the same manner shortly after he took office. A new leader was appointed, but Hamas kept his identity secret (Oliver, 2004; Keinon, 2004).

Some analysts believe the new leader is **Khalid Mashal**, an outsider operating from Damascus. If this is true, Hamas may develop an international orientation and present a threat to the United States (Lake, 2004). Reuven Paz (2004) senses a shift in Hamas thinking. In August 2004 U.S. and Iraqi forces battled the Shiite militia of **Muqtada al Sadr** in Najaf, Iraq. Paz points out that Hamas issued two very interesting communiqués in the wake of this battle. The first one condemned the United States for fighting around Najaf, the site of a Shiite holy shrine, and it called on all Iraqi people to band together to defeat America. The second statement was different, and Paz notes that it looked like a correction. The new release called on Iraqis to support the militia of Muqtada al Sadr.

Abdel Aziz Rantisi
(1947–2004) One of the founders of Hamas along with Ahmed Yassin. He took over Hamas after Israeli gunships assassinated Yassin. He, in turn, was assassinated by the Israelis a month after taking charge.

Khalid Mashal
(1956–) One of the "outside" leaders of Hamas, in Damascus, Syria. Mashal is described as a political leader by Hamas.

Muqtada al Sadr
(1974–) An Iraqi ayatollah. Al Sadr leads the Shiite militia known as the Mahdi Army.

Paz concludes that Hamas is shifting targets and focus. Hamas began as a strong Sunni organization, a Palestinian extension of the Muslim Brotherhood, influenced by militant Salafi puritanism. Much of its monetary support came from Saudi sympathizers, and Sheik Yassin and the inside group kept Hamas in the Salafi camp. Even though the outsiders operated in other countries, Hamas remained focused on Israel. The jihad was not international; it belonged to Hamas, the Islamic resistance movement in Palestine. The assassinations of Yassin and Rantisi, however, may have changed the equation.

Paz points to Hamas's two communiqués as evidence. The first was addressed to the Iraqi people. Logically, it expresses Sunni concern for U.S. intervention in the area and calls for unification. The second version, the corrected version according to Paz, asks for support of a junior Shiite scholar in defense of a Shiite holy site. Al Sadr is not a senior scholar; he is a young radical confronting the senior Shiite scholars of Iraq. He is also a disciple of the Ayatollah Khomeini. A Sunni Salafi militant would not be concerned with the defense of a holy mosque in Najaf or an Iranian-style Shiite scholar, Paz argues, but a member of Hezbollah would be.

Paz comes to an interesting conclusion. He believes that leadership has passed to Khalid Mashal or someone very close to him in the outsider Damascus group. Mashal and his followers are abandoning the "Palestine first" philosophy of Hamas and drawing closer to the revolutionary Shiite views of Hezbollah and Iran. Hamas condemned the Wahhabi-supported al Qaeda violence of the **Tawhid** and its allied group Ansar al Islam, groups headed by **Abu Musab al Zarqawi** until his death in 2006 (Dakroub, 2004). Paz believes that by voicing support for Iranian-style Shiites and not Shiites in general Hamas is falling into Hezbollah's orbit. If this is true, the organization will move closer to Syria and Iran, both on the U.S. State Department's list of nations supporting terrorism. Hamas may well end up becoming an enemy of the United States, targeting Americans and American interests.

Matthew Levitt (2002, pp. 204–227), an American governmental intelligence chief, says that Hamas routinely engages in anti-American rhetoric, but it has several disincentives for attacking the West in general and the United States in particular. It has refused to join al Qaeda and the international jihad because its focus is on Israel. Hamas does not want new enemies. In addition, Hamas has used the United States and other Western countries as a financial resource. Some officials believe Hamas raised quite a bit of money through charities, such as the **Holy Land Foundation**—a charge the foundation denies.

Despite these disincentives, Levitt notes that Hamas has an international reach. The Israelis claim to have arrested a member of Hamas who intended to target Canada. Hamas also recruited British citizens to engage in suicide bombings. Although these attacks were aimed at Israel, Hamas could target the West. Finally, the militant theology behind Hamas may encourage individual terrorists to take action. Levitt con-

tawhid

"Oneness." In Islamic theology *tawhid* refers to unity of God. Abu Musab al Zarqawi once led a terrorist organization known as Tawhid.

Abu Musab al Zarqawi

(1966–2006) The nom de guerre of Jordanian-born Ahmed Fadel al Kaleyah. He left Jordan after getting out of prison to join the Afghan jihad in 1989. Training in al Qaeda camps, he returned to Jordan and formed Tawhid. After another arrest and imprisonment, Zarqawi returned to Afghanistan in 2001 to fight for al Qaeda. He re-formed Tawhid, but called it al Qaeda in Iraq. He was killed after being targeted by American forces.

Holy Land Foundation

An Islamic charity based in the United States. Federal authorities closed the foundation in 2001, alleging that it sponsored terrorist activities.

cludes that if Hamas engages in international attacks, it will most likely attack Jewish or pro-Israeli targets. The greatest threat to American and Western targets comes from religiously inspired terrorists operating outside Hamas's leadership, and individual cells or single terrorists simply operating on their own.

Self-Check

- *Why did religion merge with the Palestinian movement?*
- *Explain the birth of Hamas.*
- *Is Hamas a united movement?*

The Al Aqsa Martyrs Brigades

Suicide bombing became the most important tactic of all the Palestinian terrorist groups at the beginning of the al Aqsa Intifada in September 2000. Hezbollah, Hamas, and the PIJ were in the forefront, giving leadership to local religious groups. Fatah also became involved, but it continued its secular orientation. Its two main forces were the politically oriented Force 17 and the Tanzim Brigade. Other Fatah splinter groups joined the intifada, and although they resisted Arafat's control, they also steered clear of religion. This became a problem because local jihadists and religious terrorists dominate the al Aqsa Intifada (Shahar, 2002). If Fatah wanted to play a leading role, it had to move from the secular to the religious realm.

BBC News (2003) reports that Fatah has shown a newfound religious streak that comes from the grass roots of Palestinian society. The al Aqsa Brigades were formed to put Fatah at the center of the new Intifada. The Brigades began as a secular group, but they increasingly used jihadist rhetoric. They were also the first secular Palestinian group to use suicide tactics. Hezbollah, Hamas, and the PIJ do not recognize Israel's right to exist. This is not so with the Brigades. They claim their purpose is limited: their goal is to stop Israeli incursions and attacks in Palestinian areas, and they intend to punish Israel for each attack. Whether this explanation is accepted or not, one thing is clear: the Brigades have become the most potent Palestinian force in the al Aqsa Intifada.

Effective Tactics

The Council on Foreign Relations (2004) believes the tactics of the al Aqsa Martyrs Brigades have made the group particularly deadly to the Israelis. At first, shadowy spokespeople said they would strike Israeli military targets only inside Palestinian territory. This practice was soon abandoned, however, and attacks moved into Israel proper. The Brigades' primary tactics have been drive-by shootings, sniper shootings, ambushes, and kidnap-murders. Yet, as with so many other terrorist groups, their most devastating tactic has been the use of suicide bombers.

Yael Shahar (2002) says the al Aqsa Martyrs Brigades suicide bombers were frightening for two reasons: they were secular, and they sought out targets crowded with civilians. They delivered human bombs filled with antipersonnel material designed to inflict the maximum amount of casualties. Their purpose was to kill and maim as many victims as possible in the most public way possible. Furthermore, as mentioned above, they used the first female suicide bomber in the Middle East on January 27, 2002, in conjunction with Hamas. They expanded their targets and their casualties increased; after initially allowing the PIJ and Hamas to play the leading role in the rebellion, the Brigades moved to the forefront of the rebellion.

Leadership in the Martyrs Brigades

Leadership of the Brigades is a controversial topic. They seem to be directly associated with their parent group, Fatah, but it is unclear how their operations are directed and from where. One school of thought maintains that Arafat led and paid for the Brigades. Israeli intelligence claims they have proof of Arafat's involvement. Shahar (2002) says that the IDF raided Arafat's headquarters in Ramallah in 2002 and captured PNA documents that show payments to various factions inside the Brigades, payments personally approved by Arafat. The Israelis say that Arafat may not have determined targeting and timing, but he paid the expenses and set the agenda.

Marwan Barghouti

(1969–) A leader of Fatah and alleged leader of the al Aqsa Martyrs Brigades. A Brigades statement in 2002 claimed Barghouti was their leader. He rose to prominence during the al Aqsa Intifada, but he is currently held in an Israeli prison.

Other investigations point to another conclusion. The Council on Foreign Relations (2004) believes Arafat may have run the Brigades but admits there may be another source of leadership. A BBC News (2003) investigation points to **Marwan Barghouti** (currently in Israeli custody) as the commander. A Palestinian spokesman, Hassan Abdel Rahman, says the documents Israel seized in 2002 are false and claims the Israelis planted them (Rothem, 2002). Arafat claimed he knew nothing about the Brigades.

PBS's *Frontline* (2002) conducted an interview with a Palestinian leader code-named Jihad Ja'Aire at the height of the first bombing campaign. Ja'Aire claimed that he and all the other Brigades commanders were under Arafat's control. Arafat provided the direction, Ja'Aire said, and all the members obeyed him. This does not condemn Arafat, Ja'Aire pointed out, because the group operates with a different philosophy. The al Aqsa Martyrs Brigades will accept a negotiated peace. If Israel had accepted the 1967 borders, that is, the borders before Israel added the West Bank and Gaza Strip after the Six Days' War, and stopped incursions into Palestinian areas, Arafat could have called off the attacks.

Whether Arafat had direct control of the Brigades remains a subject of debate, partly because of the way the Brigades are organized. Taking a cue from the international jihadist groups, the al Aqsa Martyrs Brigades have little centralized structure. Their administration has been pushed down to the lowest operational level so that they may function almost autonomously. Cells exist in several Palestinian communities, and leaders are empowered to take action on their own without approval from a hierarchy. In addition, Israel has targeted the Brigades' leadership for selective assassination, but the organization continues.

Beginning a Network

No matter where leadership authority lies, the managerial relations within the Brigades remain a paradox, even to the Palestinians. In June 2004 some of the leading figures in the Palestinian territories formed the **Fatah General Council** to investigate the al Aqsa Martyrs Brigades and Arafat's relation to them. This enraged some in the Brigades because they believed Arafat was manipulating the entire investigation. Claiming that Arafat had abandoned them, disgruntled members of the Brigades surrounded his house and threatened him. If Arafat controlled the Brigades, his hold may not have been very tight (Algazy, 2004).

Fatah General Council
The leadership group of Fatah.

The structure of the Brigades is testimony to Michael Scheuer's (2006) comments about the nature of modern terrorism, and it harks back to points made by Marc Sageman (2004). Although the leaders of the group are unknown, the Brigades have been effective without centralized leadership. Their strength comes from the ability of small cells to operate without a strong leader. The Brigades have been effective because they operate in a network (MIPT, n.d.).

Self-Check

- *What started the al Aqsa Intifada?*
- *What tactics did terrorists use in the al Aqsa Intifada?*
- *Do the al Aqsa Martyrs Brigades unite the Palestinians in a common effort?*

▼Violent Jewish Fundamentalism

Religious violence in the Middle East is not limited to militant Islam. Jewish groups have also been involved in terrorist violence, and some of them have direct links to the United States. Militant Judaism is based on the biblical notion that God has promised to restore the state of Israel. The theology is racist, eschatological, and linked to the conquest and possession of territory. No other groups are permitted to control sacred territory, according to militant Judaism, and the Messiah can appear only when the state of Israel has been restored. Such thinking has produced deadly results.

Kach

One militant group is called Kach ("Thus!"). It was created by **Rabbi Meir Kahane**, an American Jewish cleric who immigrated to Israel in 1971. Serving synagogues in New York City in the early 1960s, Kahane's descriptions of religion and the superiority of Jews began to grow more militant. In 1968 he created the Jewish Defense League, a group that

Rabbi Meir Kahane
(1932–1990) Founder of the Jewish Defense League and Kach. Kahane was assassinated in New York City in 1990.

was involved in several terrorist incidents in the United States. Moving to Israel in 1971, Kahane combined politics and biblical literalism to demand that all Arabs be expelled from territories occupied by Israel. He called for the militant creation of Greater Israel, the ancient Israel of King David. He was assassinated in 1990 in the United States.

Kahane Chai

Kahane's son, Benjamin, created a new group, Kahane Chai (Kahane Lives), shortly after Kahane's assassination. According to the U.S. Department of State (1999), both groups have been involved in harassing and threatening Palestinians, and they have threatened to attack Arabs and Israeli officials who seek peace. **Baruch Goldstein**, a member of Kach, killed nearly two dozen Muslims as they worshipped in the al Aqsa mosque in 1994. When Kach and Kahane Chai issued statements in support of Goldstein's terrorism, the Israeli government declared both groups to be terrorist organizations. President Clinton signed an executive order in 1995 prohibiting Americans from involvement in the groups. Kach and Kahane Chai are committed to stopping any peace proposal that recognizes the territorial rights of Palestinians.

Laurence Hanauer (1995) states that Kach and Kahane Chai have defined God's biblical promises in terms of territory. In the Hebrew Bible, God makes a covenant with Abraham and his descendants. (Muslims have the same story in the Qu'ran and believe they are also Abraham's children.) Hanauer argues that militant Judaism takes the focus away from a covenant with people and focuses it on conquering new lands. This creates a climate for increased terrorism.

Baruch Goldstein

(1956–1994) An American physician who immigrated to Israel. In February 1994 he entered a religious site in Hebron wearing his Israeli military uniform. He then began shooting Muslim worshippers, killing twenty-nine and wounding more than a hundred.

Gush Emunim

The leaders of these ethnocentric movements are sophisticated and socially connected. Whereas Kach and Kahane Chai alienate most Israelis because of their violent rhetoric, other movements with the same views have grown. Gush Emunim, a fundamentalist Israeli settlement in Palestinian territory, is one such movement (Hanauer, 1995). Gush Emunim has the same set of beliefs as the violent fundamentalists, but their rhetoric appears normative compared with the violent rhetoric of the other groups. This has generated political support for Gush Emunim inside Israel.

Hanauer sees several problems with Jewish militant extremism and the prospects for peace. First, the extremists denounce the existing social order because it is not racially pure. All social, economic, and political problems are blamed on the failure to ascend to the moral high ground of Jewish biblical literalism. Second, the extremists claim the exclusive right to determine the truth. Third, they advocate an ideal order, and Gush Emunim and Kach claim that the Messiah can come only once the existing order is purified. Fourth, the national identity of Israel and its political legitimacy can be determined only through religion. Finally, all current events are defined within a narrow set of beliefs that

ANOTHER PERSPECTIVE

David's Kingdom and Israeli Settlements

Many supporters of Israel and a good number of Israeli peace activists do not favor expansion into Palestinian areas. Moshe Amon (2004) writes that although Israel is a secular democracy, it is being influenced by religious extremists. Ultraorthodox rabbis, he maintains, seek to conquer the biblical Kingdom of David. Jewish extremists, with the support of the state, have moved into Palestinian areas to establish permanent settlements. Many militants believe that when David's kingdom is restored every person on earth will follow the teachings of the God of Israel. Amon says some of the militants fight Israeli soldiers, and some of their leaders call for the murder of non-Jews. Amon believes this behavior threatens not only Israel's moral character but its very survival.

encompass a limited worldview and identify only a few people as being chosen by God.

Hanauer believes such extremism may result in increased terrorist violence. Extremists do not answer to democratic ideals; they answer directly to their concept of God. The land of Israel is deified in their theology, so any attempt to achieve a land settlement is denounced. Jewish extremism leads to violence. Hanauer concludes that Baruch Goldstein, the terrorist who murdered the Muslim worshippers in 1994, was not a loner who simply snapped. He was the product of a Jewish extremism rooted in territorialism. Hanauer believes this structure will produce more religious terrorism.

Moshe Amon (2004) agrees with Hanauer and takes the argument further. He believes that Israel was founded on secular principles but that Jewish Orthodox extremists gained control over governmental policy (see Another Perspective: David's Kingdom and Israeli Settlements). This is suicidal, Amon argues, because the only chance of peace is negotiation with the Palestinians and the Arab nations. If Israeli extremists prevent the government from negotiating some type of settlement with their Arab neighbors, militant Arabs will win control of Arab foreign policy. A time will come when Israel cannot stand against them or when the entire area will be destroyed with weapons of mass destruction. To create the opportunity for a peaceful settlement, Amon believes, all religious extremism must come to an end.

Self-Check

- *Do all Jews and Israelis passively accept the existence of Muslims in Israel?*
- *What terrorist actions are taken by fundamentalist Jewish groups?*
- *Describe the religious basis of fundamentalist Jewish violence.*

Controversial Counterterrorist Policies

Mossad

The Israeli intelligence agency formed in 1951. It is responsible for gathering foreign intelligence. Shin Beth is responsible for internal security.

Many Israeli police and military units have established excellent reputations in counterterrorist operations. **Mossad**, the Israeli intelligence service, is known for its expertise. Shin Beth, the domestic Israeli security service, is one of the most effective secret police forces in the world. The IDF is an excellent fighting machine. The Israeli police know how to handle bombs, snipers, kidnappings, and everyday crime. The tactical operations of these units are second to none.

Tactical operations, however, differ from policies. Governments decide the broad philosophy and practice of a policy, and tactical operations take place within the guidelines of long-term political goals. Policy involves a strategic view of a problem and the means to settle it. Unlike Israel's excellent tactical record, its counterterrorist policies have stirred international controversy (see Another Perspective: Controversial Tactics).

Bulldozing

When Israel first faced suicide bombings, the government implemented a controversial policy called bulldozing whose purpose was to destroy the family homes of suicide bombers. If militant charities and governments were going to compensate families of martyrs, the Israelis reasoned, bulldozing homes would be more painful than the pleasure of economic reward. Soon, the homes of not only families but of suspected leaders in militant groups and others were targeted for bulldozing. In 2004 farms and other areas were bulldozed. The policy expanded to include clearing ground for military reasons and clearing space to build a security fence, that is, a wall separating Israel from Palestinian areas (*Palestine Monitor*, 2004; *New York Times*, International, 2004). Critics maintain that bulldozing takes place to further Israel's self-interests.

Invading Lebanon

Judith Harik (2004, pp. 117–124) describes another controversial policy: punishing Lebanon for the sins of Hezbollah. As discussed earlier in the chapter, Israel launched its first invasion of Lebanon to rid the south of the PLO. That ended after an eighteen-year occupation and the creation of a new enemy, Hezbollah.

Operation Grapes of Wrath

The code name for the April 1996 attack on Lebanon. The IDF attacked Lebanese targets for sixteen days in retaliation for Hezbollah's activities.

In 1996 Israel launched a limited offensive in Lebanon to disrupt Hezbollah operations. They destroyed bridges, power plants, and other infrastructure targets in **Operation Grapes of Wrath**. Dozens of innocent Lebanese were killed in the process. Israel hoped to drive a wedge between the Lebanese and Hezbollah. Like bulldozing, the theory behind the invasion was based on punishment. The Israelis wanted to hurt Lebanon to force the government to clamp down on Hezbollah. The policy was not only controversial, it backfired. Harik believes the attack brought the Lebanese closer to Hezbollah and strengthened Syr-

Controversial Tactics

Israel has engaged in tactics that have enraged the Palestinians and many others. Critics call these tactics Israeli terrorism. Defenders say that Israel has a right to protect itself. The United States almost always supports Israel, frequently using its veto power in the UN Security Council to keep the United Nations from condemning Israeli actions. Controversial tactics include

- Destroying the homes of suicide-bomber families
- Selective assassination of Palestinian leaders
- Killing innocents when striking militants
- Excessive use of force
- Commando raids in neighboring countries
- June 2006 invasion of Lebanon

ia's hand in Lebanese affairs. She thinks Israel's offense was an abysmal failure.

The Israelis responded with force again in July 2006. Israel was surprised when Hezbollah launched **Katyusha rockets** into Israel while sending ground forces across the border to ambush an Israeli patrol. Hezbollah killed three soldiers and kidnapped two others. Israel launched an immediate attack, losing five more soldiers and failing to free the two soldiers taken hostage. The rockets injured another ten people.

Most of the world expected an Israeli response, but few believed it would become a massive retaliation. Israel announced that it planned to destroy Hezbollah, and it launched air strikes and set up a naval blockade of Lebanon. The IDF followed with a ground invasion a few days later, but Hezbollah fought the Israeli soldiers to a standstill (al Jazeera, 2006). Israel defended its action, with support from the United States, by stating the massive strike was necessary because the Lebanese government was not able to confront and disarm Hezbollah's militia (*Daily Mail*, 2007). Critics maintained the operation was overkill. In a war that lasted nearly a month, hundreds of Lebanese civilians were killed, nearly a million Lebanese were displaced, and Lebanon's infrastructure was destroyed (Chomsky, 2006; Salem, 2006).

The Wall

In an effort to stop Palestinian attacks, the government of Ariel Sharon proposed an idea that dated back to Hadrian of the Roman Empire. The Israelis began constructing a massive wall. On the surface, this might seem to be an uncontroversial issue, but the path of the wall grabbed the attention of the world. The concrete and barbed-wire barrier snaked through Palestinian areas, often putting water and other resources in

Katyusha rockets
A type of mobile rocket. Developed by the Soviet army during World War II, the rockets were originally mounted on the beds of trucks. Katyuhsa rockets target a general area and are effective when used in barrages. The latest generation is much more accurate, and one may have been so precisely guided that it hit an Israeli ship during the 2006 war. The name means "Little Katie."

the hands of the Israelis. It also separated people from services, jobs, and their families. Much of the international community condemned the wall (I. Black, 2003).

Selective Assassination

The most controversial aspect of Israel's counterterrorist policy is selective assassination. Israel has maintained a consistent policy against terrorism. When it is struck, it hits back hard. Israeli commandos and IDF units have allegedly killed opposition leaders in the past, such as Abu Jihad of the PLO and Fathi Shekaki of the PIJ, but the policy expanded during the al Aqsa Intifada when Israel began the wholesale assassination of Hamas leadership.

Reuven Paz (2004) questions the effectiveness of this policy, suggesting that it might internationalize the conflict. Left-wing political leaders in Israel deplore the policy, calling such assassinations "gangster murders" (Kafala, 2001). Human rights groups have condemned the policy and challenged it in Israeli courts (BBC News, 2002). Nations all over the world have condemned Israel for these targeted assassinations as well.

Daniel Byman (2006) argues that Israel's selective assassinations are publicly transparent. Each proposed attack must go through several stages, excluding legal review. The public is aware of the moral dilemma and various tradeoffs. Rather than being secretive, the policy is open to debate. Byman states that the policy remains controversial, but the process is open. He intimates that it would be stronger if the judiciary were involved in the process. It is important to note that Israeli deaths from terrorism have dropped since it employed its controversial policy.

Charles Krauthammer (2004) reflects the feelings of those who support these controversial policies. Israel is under attack, he writes. Whereas the United Nations, for instance, condemned the security fence, Krauthammer maintains that its construction reduced suicide attacks. Many Israelis feel that harsh policies must be implemented to deter terrorism (Kafala, 2001). Furthermore, the United States has repeatedly taken the position that Israel cannot be condemned for harsh measures until the international community also denounces Palestinian terrorism.

Although supporters claim that Israel should be allowed to take the steps necessary for self-defense, the policies remain controversial. The important question to try to answer is Do harsh policies reduce terrorism or increase the cycle of violence? Thus far, the question remains unanswered, and violence continues from both sides of the fence.

Self-Check

- *Why might Israeli policies toward Lebanon be described as a failure?*
- *Is collective punishment for terrorist violence effective?*
- *Do retribution and intensive security measures stop terrorism?*

SUMMARY

- The PLO emerged in 1964 and took center stage after the June 1967 Six Days' War. Fatah was its main military wing, but groups kept splitting off. After the 1982 invasion of Lebanon, the PLO retreated to North Africa and the occupied territories. Still sponsoring terrorism, Fatah's activities were eclipsed by other groups.
- A number of groups emerged from Fatah, and they were active in the 1970s. The Abu Nidal Organization was one of the most effective groups splintering from the PLO. Other groups came from outside the PLO. The PIJ was one of the groups with the most staying power.
- The Abu Nidal Organization began as a member of the Rejectionist Front. It then worked for various countries, and finally became a mercenary group. Its leader, Sabri al Banna, was murdered in Iraq in August 2002.
- The PIJ emerged from Egypt in the 1970s. It evolved into a religious organization with the philosophy that religious law would be implemented after victory, but the more immediate objective was the destruction of Israel. By 1995 most of its founding leaders had been killed. New leaders purposely maintain a small group of operatives in a rigid hierarchy.
- Several groups use *Islamic Jihad* in their names. There are even factions in the PIJ.
- Hamas emerged from the first Intifada. It embraced the principles of religious law and expressed disgust for the secular policies and corruption of the PLO. It formed a large organization and mastered the art of suicide attacks. It opposes any peace with Israel, and its charter calls for the destruction of Israel. Hamas won control of the Palestinian government in 2006. Although the United States has refused to negotiate with Hamas, many people believe Hamas will target neither the United States nor other Western countries.
- The al Aqsa Martyrs Brigades formed from Fatah, embracing religion and suicide attacks. There are many questions about its leadership. Currently, it operates in a network of independent cells with no central command structure.
- Several militant Jewish groups have called for the elimination of non-Jewish people in traditional Jewish lands. They believe the biblical kingdom of Israel is a literal and geographical gift to them from God.
- Israel has responded to terrorism with controversial policies. These include bulldozing, invasions of Lebanon, constructing a wall to separate Palestinians from Israelis, and targeted assassinations.

KEY TERMS

Yasser Arafat (p. 217)
fedayeen (p. 218)
Kahlil Wazir (p. 218)

King Hussein (p. 218)
Operation Peace for Galilee
    (p. 223)

WRITING ASSIGNMENTS

1. Both Bruce Hoffman and David Rapoport argue that terrorism has developed in overlapping patterns since the end of World War II. Excluding Hezbollah (discussed in the next chapter), is there a particular pattern in the development of terrorism in Israel and Palestine? How does the movement from the secular PLO to the religious Hamas affect your argument? Does your answer change when considering violent Jewish groups?

2. Does leadership make a difference in the effectiveness of terrorist organizations? Most of the groups described in this chapter had strong leaders like Arafat, al Banna, Shekaki, and Yassin. How important was their presence? Why can the al Aqsa Martyrs Brigades operate without strong leaders?

3. Describe each controversial counterterrorist policy summarized in this chapter. Do they work? Is there a point where counterterrorism becomes terrorism?

International Umbrella Groups and Terror Networks

AP Photo/B. K. Bangash

The Egyptian Embassy in Islamabad, Pakistan, after a terrorist attack in 1995. Central Asia is a major source of emerging terror networks in the early twenty-first century.

Learning Objectives

After reading this chapter you should be able to

- Describe the birth and growth of Hezbollah after the 1982 Israeli invasion of Lebanon.

- Explain the current political and military aspects of Hezbollah.

- Summarize critical and sympathetic views of Hezbollah.

- Describe the terrorist networks created in North Africa.

- Explain Egyptian Islamic Jihad's influence on Zawahiri and subsequently on al Qaeda's organization.

- Outline the birth and growth of al Qaeda.

- Briefly explain the theological misnomers guiding the jihadist movement.

- Explain bin Laden's decision to target the far enemy.

- Define and describe the eclectic disassociation of fifth-generation jihadists.

247

- Explain why jihadists began to create their own media force multipliers.
- Relate the American experience in Iraq to international jihadist networks.

l Qaeda was not the first international jihadist group. The first such organization evolved from the Syrian and Iranian-backed Shiite group Hezbollah. Over the years, Hezbollah has evolved. Today, supporters claim it is a political organization with a military arm, but detractors believe it to be one of the deadliest international terrorist groups in the world. Before al Qaeda's September 11 attacks, Hezbollah was responsible for more American deaths than any other terrorist group. Jihadist groups in North Africa started organizing local networks in the 1990s, and one of them even created an international cell based in New York City. Al Qaeda formed a large international network after 1996, and small terrorist groups began to spread under the shield of al Qaeda's umbrella. They began to operate in a leaderless network after the American offensive in Afghanistan in 2001. Today these eclectic groups function without structure, and they form and re-form new local patterns constantly.

Hezbollah: Local and International

Hezbollah, a Shiite group, provided the model for jihad under an umbrella. It was spawned in Lebanon after the Iranian Revolution (1978–1979), which culminated in the overthrow of the secular shah of Iran. Hezbollah's purpose is to spread the Islamic law of Shiite Islam. Although it is most frequently associated with violence in Lebanon and Israel, Hezbollah has an international jihadist wing. It also created the organizational style that groups like the Egyptian Islamic Group, the Egyptian Islamic Jihad, the Armed Islamic Group in Algeria, and al Qaeda would use. Therefore, it is appropriate to consider Hezbollah apart from the localized groups of Palestine and Israel and their neighbors.

Hezbollah's international branch appears to have three major functions. In Europe and in the United States, Hezbollah raises money to support operations (*United States of America v. Mohamad Youseff Hammoud, et al.*, 2002). Iran uses Hezbollah as an extension of its own power. It protects Iranian interests in Lebanon, and projects an Iranian-influenced military presence in other parts of the Middle East. It also acts as a buffer between Iran and Israel (Byman, 2003). Finally, Hezbollah has established a strong presence in South America. It uses this base to raise funds through legitimate and illegitimate methods, conduct propaganda, and launch terrorist operations. Should the United States and Iran enter a war, South American members of Hezbollah plan to attack the United States (Gato and Windrem, 2007).

The Metamorphosis of Hezbollah

Hezbollah is a product of the 1979 Iranian Revolution and the struggle between Israel and its neighbors. Shiite scholars, known as **ayatollahs**, gained control of the revolution through the **Revolutionary Guards**, a group of young fanatic Shiites who evolved into a paramilitary arm of the revolution. There are many different types of Shiites, and the Shiites who dominate Iran and southern Iraq are **Ithna Asharis**, or Twelvers.

Whereas Sunnis, another Islamic sect, believe that Mohammed and the entire Muslim community are equal before God and that everybody will be judged equally at the end of time, Twelver Shiites believe that one of Mohammed's descendants must return before God judges humanity. They also believe that Mohammed's power flowed through his heirs. Twelver Shiites believe that Mohammed had twelve direct heirs, or **imams**, and that the last imam was taken directly into heaven. He will return as a prelude to final judgment, and until that time ayatollahs are given some of the characteristics of the Twelfth Imam. In 1979 the ayatollahs ruled Iran, and the Grand Ayatollah Khomeini commanded the Revolutionary Guards.

The Iranian Revolution made many Sunni Muslims nervous because the Revolutionary Guards vowed to create revolutionary Shiite governments throughout the Muslim world. An eight-year war with Iraq, however, seemed to block Khomeini's plans for revolution, and his Revolutionary Guards spent less time spreading ideals and more time keeping Iran's ayatollahs in power during the first year of the Iran-Iraq War (1980–1988). The situation changed in 1982 when Israel invaded Lebanon.

Judith Harik (2004, pp. 29–39) explains the complicated factors that moved Shiite revolutionaries from Iran to Lebanon, giving birth to Hezbollah. Secular Syrian Baathists wanted to establish power in Lebanon to regain control of the Golan Heights, an area taken by Israel in the 1967 Six Days' War (see Chapter 9). At the same time, Lebanon was locked in a multifaceted civil war that began in 1975 and would last fifteen years. Secular Palestinians in the Palestine Liberation Organization (PLO) moved into the Shiite areas of southern Lebanon after they were expelled from Jordan in 1970. The Syrians backed the southern Shiites in the civil war, and this pitted the Shiites and Syrians against the PLO. The PLO also used its bases in southern Lebanon to attack Israel. The Israelis, incensed, invaded Lebanon in 1982 to drive the PLO from the south.

The Israeli invasion of Lebanon created an unlikely alliance among Iran's Revolutionary Guards, secular Syrian Baathists, and southern Lebanese Shiites. Iran's foreign policy under the Ayatollah Khomeini's Revolutionary Guards was designed to spread religious revolutionary thought throughout the Muslim world. On the surface, the fervently religious Khomeini had little in common with the secular socialists in Syria, but the Syrians were supporting Shiites in southern Lebanon. When Israeli

ayatollahs
Ranking members of the Shiite scholars, or ulema. Ayatollahs have written a theological work. They rank under grand ayatollahs, who are recognized as master scholars.

Revolutionary Guards
The militarized quasi-police force of the revolutionary government during the Iranian Revolution.

Ithna Ashari
Literally, *twelvers*. Twelver Shiites believe that some of the power God gave to Mohammed passed to a line of twelve chosen descendants.

imam
In Shiite Islam, one of the twelve descendants of Mohammed. It is a title of respect for certain Shiite ulema.

Figure 11.1

Hezbollah Umbrella,
circa 1985

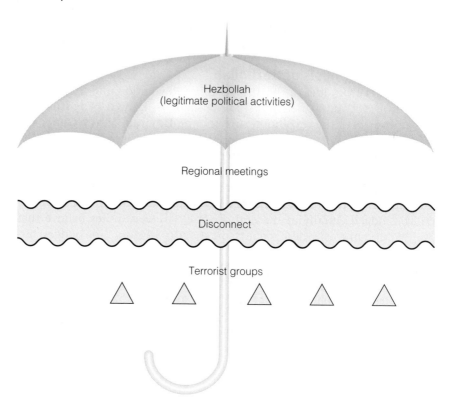

tanks rolled through southern Lebanon, they passed through Shiite villages, and the Revolutionary Guards begged the Ayatollah Khomeini for a chance to protect their fellow believers in Lebanon. Secular Syria and religious Iran now had a common enemy.

Harik points out that both nations needed a surrogate to fight the Israelis. If Iran openly intervened in the Lebanese Civil War (1975–1990), Israel or the United States might attack Iran. Syria also needed a proxy because its troops were no match for the Israeli Defense Forces (IDF) and, like Iran, it feared the United States. As Shiite militias resisted the Israeli invasion, one group began to form in the shadows of the civil war. It centered on a nonorganization, that is, a governing council to share ideas, plans, and money but designed to disappear and leave autonomous groups to carry out attacks under a variety of names. They called themselves Hezbollah, or the Party of God, and their shadowy nature was ideal for the plans of Syria and Iran (Figure 11.1).

Iranian officials made contact with the Syrians in 1982. Promising reduced oil prices to Syria, the Iranians asked for permission to move 1,000 Revolutionary Guards from Syrian territory across its borders and into the Bekaa Valley in eastern Lebanon (Figure 11.2). The Revolutionary Guards made links with the emerging Hezbollah and provided the Lebanese Shiite group with money, weapons, and training. Both Syria and Iran wanted to maintain their distance, and the religious leaders of

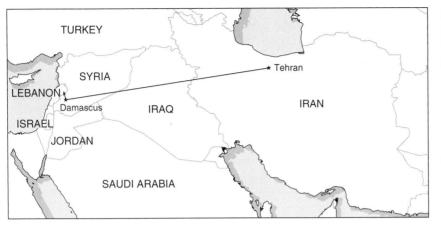

Figure 11.2
Movement of the Revolutionary Guards through Syria to Lebanon, 1982

Al Dawa
Literally, *the call*. A Shiite militia group in the Lebanese Civil War.

Islamic Amal
A Shiite militia in the Lebanese Civil War. Abbas Musawi entered into an alliance with Iranian revolutionaries in Lebanon and formed Islamic Amal to counter Nahbi Berri's Amal.

Sheik Mohammed Hassan Fadlallah
(1935–) A grand ayatollah and leader of Shiites in Lebanon. The spiritual leader of Hezbollah. He was the target of a 1985 U.S. assassination plot that killed seventy-five people.

Abbas Musawi
(1952–1992) A leader of Hezbollah killed with his family in an Israeli attack in 1992.

Hassan Nasrallah
(1960–) The secretary-general of Hezbollah. He took over leadership of Hezbollah after Musawi's death in 1992. Nasrallah is a lively speaker and charismatic leader.

Hezbollah wanted to deny any affiliation with military action. As a result, Hezbollah became a terrorist organization like no one had yet seen (see Hiro, 1987, pp. 113–181, 240–243; Taheri, 1987; Kurz, 1994; Wege, 1994; Ranstorp, 1994, 1996).

Hezbollah grew from a council of Shiite scholars who claimed to be part of a spiritual movement. In essence, this council became a large umbrella. Syrian and Iranian money and supplies poured into the movement, but Hezbollah denied any direct connection. Below the umbrella, several Shiite cells operated autonomously and received money, weapons, and ideas through hidden channels linked with the spiritual leaders. The leadership also formed alliances with two Lebanese Shiite groups, **Al Dawa** and **Islamic Amal**, while claiming to be a religious movement designed to support Lebanon's Shiite community (Gambill and Abdelnour, 2002).

During the first few years of its existence, Hezbollah acted more or less like a terrorist clearinghouse (Reuters, 1996). Following orders from Iran, Hezbollah met as an independent organization, always willing to deny its Iranian connections. According to Israeli intelligence (Israeli Foreign Ministry, 1996), Hezbollah developed under the leadership of three central figures: **Sheik Mohammed Hassan Fadlallah**, **Abbas Musawi**, and **Hassan Nasrallah**. Fadlallah, the target of an attempted U.S.-sponsored assassination, was a charismatic spiritual leader. Musawi provided the loose connections to Iran. Nasrallah was a practical militarist, leaving the Islamic Amal militia to organize Hezbollah into a regional force.

In phase one of the development of Hezbollah, from 1982 to 1985 (see Timeline 11.1: Phases of Hezbollah), the Hezbollah umbrella covered many terrorist groups, including a shadowy organization known as Islamic Jihad. According to Amir Taheri (1987), Hezbollah leaders met in the city of Baalbek in Lebanon's Bekaa Valley and issued vague "suggestions" to **Islamic Jihad**. They also provided financial and logistical support for terrorist operations but kept themselves out of the

TIMELINE 11.1	1982–1985, Organizing	Different groups carry out attacks under a variety of names.
Phases of Hezbollah	1985–1990, Kidnapping and bombing	A terrorist organization is created.
	1990–2000, Legitimacy	The group organizes social services, a political party, and a military wing.
	2000–2004, Coalition	Hezbollah forms temporary alliances with others in the September 2000 Palestinian uprising against Israel (the al Aqsa Intifada).
	July 2006	Israel launches offensive in Lebanon.
	August 2006	Israel withdraws, Hezbollah claims victory.
	September 2006	Iran begins to rebuild Lebanese infrastructure.

Islamic Jihad

Not to be confused with the PIJ or other groups of the same name, this Islamic Jihad was a small group under Hezbollah's umbrella. It was responsible for the 1983 U.S. Marine barracks bombing that killed more than 200 U.S. service personnel and a second attack that killed 58 French paratroopers. Hezbollah denies all connections with the attacks.

Amal

One of the largest militias in the Lebanese Civil War. Amal was a Shiite militia started by an Iranian Shiite scholar and eventually commanded by Nahbi Berri, a successful Lebanese leader who transformed the organization into a political party.

day-to-day affairs of the terrorist group. By keeping their distance, Hezbollah's leaders were able to claim they had no direct knowledge of Islamic Jihad, and more importantly, they kept Iran from being directly linked to Islamic Jihad's terrorist campaign against Israel and the West. The tactic was successful, and other groups formed under the umbrella.

After 1985 Hezbollah began to change. As part of an organization designed to spread the Shiite revolution, Hezbollah was not content to act only as an umbrella group to support terrorism (Enteshami, 1995; Reuters, 1996). Its leaders wanted to develop a revolutionary movement similar to the one that gripped Iran in 1978 and 1979. Lebanon was inundated with several militias fighting for control of the government, and Nasrallah saw an opportunity. By following the pattern of the **Amal** militia, he began changing the structure of Hezbollah. In 1985, he established regional centers, transforming them to operational bases between 1987 and 1989.

Hezbollah went on the warpath. After introducing suicide bombers in its initial phase, Hezbollah struck U.S. Marines and the French army in October 1983, forcing a withdrawal of a multinational peacekeeping force. The marine barracks bombing resulted in the deaths of 200 marines, and a second suicide bomber killed 50 French soldiers. In its second phase, Hezbollah's leadership launched a kidnapping campaign in Beirut. Westerners, especially Americans, were taken hostage, but Hezbollah always denied any affiliation with the group conducting the operation.

Tactics were extremely effective in the first two phases. Suicide actions and other bombings disrupted Lebanon. The U.S. embassy was targeted for a bomb attack, and Hezbollah managed to kill the top six CIA operatives in the Middle East. Two of Hezbollah's kidnappings were simply designed to murder the victims. Hezbollah kidnapped, tortured, and murdered the CIA station chief in Beirut, as well as a marine colonel working for the United Nations. Judith Harik (2004, p. 37) points out that no evidence directly linked Hezbollah to these actions, and the

Nasrallah's Management of Image

What is Hezbollah? Judith Harik (2004) says the answer to this question depends on the audience. For the four audiences below, Hassan Nasrallah has four different answers.

1. *Jihadists*: He uses militant language and speaks of holy war.

2. *Nationalists*: He avoids jihad analogies and calls on Sunnis, Shiites, Christians, and secularists to fight for Lebanon.

3. *Pan-Arabic*: He points to Israel as a colony of the West and denounces Europe's imperial past.

4. *International*: He cites UN resolutions and claims that Israel violates international law.

Harik concludes that this is not the pattern of an intolerant religious fanatic. Instead, this ability to compromise for various purposes demonstrates Nasrallah's political skills.

Source: Harik, 2004.

group denied links to terrorism, denouncing terrorism as a tactic. This strategy made the group extremely effective.

The third phase of Hezbollah's metamorphosis came in 1990. Taking over the organization after the death of Musawi, Nasrallah created a regional militia by 1990. In 1991 many of Lebanon's roving paramilitary groups signed a peace treaty, but Hezbollah retained its weapons and revolutionary philosophy and became the primary paramilitary force in southern Lebanon (U.S. Department of State, 1996; Reuters, 1996). It claimed to be a legitimate guerrilla force, resisting the Israeli occupation of the area. Hezbollah's militia, however, soon found itself in trouble. Squabbling broke out among various groups, and Hezbollah was forced to fight Syria and Islamic Amal. Diplomatic pressure increased for the release of hostages. Nasrallah took bold steps in response. He sought peace with the Syrians, and with Syrian approval, Western hostages were gradually released. Far from claiming responsibility for the hostages, both Hezbollah and Syria claimed credit for gaining their freedom. Hezbollah's militia began to operate in the open, and it stepped up its campaign against the Israelis in Lebanon. This made the organization popular among Lebanese citizens and gave the group the appearance of a guerrilla unit.

Nasrallah had one more trump card. With the blessing of fellow council members, Hezbollah joined the Lebanese political process. Hezbollah's fourth phase brought the organization from the shadows. Its militia, while operating as a guerrilla force, repeatedly struck the Israelis in Lebanon. The success of this action brought political payoffs, and by 1995 Hezbollah developed strong political bases of support in parts of Beirut, the Bekaa Valley, and its stronghold in southern Lebanon. It created a vast organization of social services, including schools, hospitals, and public works. This final change worked. In 1998 Hezbollah won a number of seats in Beirut while maintaining control of the south. When Palestinians rose against the Israelis in 2000, Hezbollah embraced their cause, and its transformation was complete (see Another Perspective:

Figure 11.3

Hezbollah, circa 2004

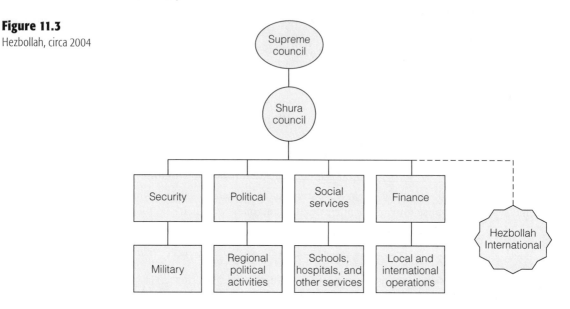

Nasrallah's Management of Image). It was a nationalistic group with a military wing, and its stated goals were to eliminate Israel and to establish an Islamic government in Lebanon.

Daniel Byman (2003) says Hezbollah managed to do something else in its last transition. It emerged as an international group. Watching the success of al Qaeda, Hezbollah spread its umbrella throughout the world. It established links in Asia, Africa, and the Triborder region of South America. It also created a presence in Europe and the United States. According to former deputy secretary of state Richard Armitage, Hezbollah is the A team among terrorist groups. Al Qaeda, Armitage says, is only the B team.

The Current State of Hezbollah

Magnus Ranstorp (1994) finds Hezbollah to be one of the strongest nonstate groups in the Middle East. Its leaders, who are called clerics in the Western press but *ulema*, or Islamic scholars, by Muslims, are associated with the Shiite seminary in Najaf, Iraq. It is organized in three directorates: a political wing, a social services wing, and a security wing (Figure 11.3). A separate international group, Hezbollah International, is managed by master terrorist **Imad Mugniyah** (J. Goldberg, 2002). A weak Lebanese government allows Hezbollah to maintain strongholds in southern Lebanon, the Bekaa Valley, and central pockets in Beirut. Each directorate is subservient to the Supreme Council, currently headed by Hassan Nasrallah.

Most of Hezbollah's activities deal with the politics of Lebanon and the vast social service network it maintains in the south. The security wing is based in Lebanon and is responsible for training guerrillas and terrorists. (Supporters of Hezbollah do not make a distinction between

Imad Mugniyah

(1962–) The leader of the international branch of Hezbollah. He has been implicated in many attacks, including the 1983 U.S. Marine and French paratrooper bombings. He is also believed to be behind bombings of the U.S. embassy in Beirut and two bombings in Argentina.

guerrilla and *terrorist*.) Guerrillas are assigned to militias that operate along Israel's northern border, especially in the **Shaba farm region**. These paramilitary fighters frequently conduct operations in the open, and they engage in conventional military confrontations with the IDF. Hezbollah can maintain all of these operations because it receives funding from Iran.

Terrorists also operate along the border with and sometimes in Israel, engaging in murder and kidnapping. Although Israel is their acknowledged enemy, Hezbollah terrorists have targeted Lebanese Christians and other Arabs not sympathetic to their cause. The primary terrorist tactic is bombing, and Hezbollah has mastered two forms: suicide bombing and radio-controlled bombs for ambushes. Gilles Kepel (2004, p. 34), a specialist in French and Middle Eastern terrorism, believes Hezbollah suicide bombings are directly related to the Shiite emphasis on martyrdom.

Hezbollah International is a shadowy group, and the Supreme Council denies its existence (J. Goldberg, 2002). The international section has cells in several different countries, including the United States, and maintains an extensive international finance ring partially based on smuggling, drugs, and other criminal activity. Imad Mugniyah keeps close ties with operatives in the Triborder region and Ciudad del Este and also runs a terrorist training camp off the coast of Venezuela. Mugniyah met with al Qaeda, possibly Osama bin Laden, in the mid-1990s and allegedly taught al Qaeda terrorists methods for attacking buildings.

A Sympathetic View of Hezbollah

Many voices in Lebanon and elsewhere claim that Hezbollah is a legitimate self-defense force. Hala Jaber (1997, pp. 38–39) summarizes this view in a journalistic examination of Hezbollah. Although Western analysts date the origin of Hezbollah to 1982, the organization claims it was formed in 1985. Members say they had nothing to do with the suicide bombings of U.S. Marines and the French army in 1983, and they deny they were behind the kidnappings of Westerners in Beirut from 1983 to 1990. Instead, they claim that Hezbollah grew from the Lebanese Civil War.

According to Jaber's research, supporters claim that Hezbollah had no intention of spreading the Iranian Revolution; they merely wanted to defend their community. Although they began to fight against the Israeli invaders in 1985, they also fought the Syrians and the Amal militia in 1988. Supporters claim they are a religious and political organization supporting a guerrilla army, and the purpose of the army is to defeat Israel.

According to Jaber (1997, pp. 207–212), Hezbollah members maintain that it is not a crime to resist the Israelis. In fact, many Hezbollah guerrillas simply refer to themselves as the "Islamic resistance." The military wing is a small part of the organization. The main focus is social service in the form of education, health services, and social security.

Shaba farm region

A small farming region in southwest Lebanon annexed by Israel in 1981. When Israel withdrew from southern Lebanon in 2000, it remained in the Shaba farm region, creating a dispute with Lebanon, Hezbollah, and Syria.

Jessica Stern (2003b, p. 47) says that Hezbollah knows it cannot confront the IDF in a conventional war so it uses guerrilla tactics, and Hezbollah guerrillas believe that fighting the Israelis is not an act of terrorism.

Research by the Council on Foreign Relations (2004) concludes that most Arabs find Hezbollah to be a source of inspiration. Although no Arab nation has ever beaten the Israelis or the West, Hezbollah has a track record of success. If one dates the origin of the group to 1982 and credits Hezbollah with the October 1983 suicide bombings, Arabs believe that Hezbollah forced the French and Americans to withdraw from Lebanon. In 1985 the IDF fled from Hezbollah in central Lebanon, and Israel abandoned the south in 1990. Far from being viewed as a terrorist organization, Hezbollah has achieved heroic status in the eyes of many Arabs.

Mohammed Fneish

(age unknown) A Hezbollah politician and minister of energy in the Lebanese prime minister's cabinet.

Gary Gambill and Ziad Abdelnour (2002) say that Hezbollah's entry into politics further legitimized its activities. **Mohammed Fneish**, a Hezbollah representative in the Lebanese parliament, told journalist Tim Cavanaugh (2004) that Hezbollah has the right to resist Israeli aggression after Israel invaded Lebanon. Even after the Israelis left, Fneish claims, the Israelis continued to strike targets in Lebanon and to occupy Palestinian lands. Fneish says Hezbollah is a political and social service organization, but it will resist Israel. He says there is no relation with Iraqi Shiites, but the Iraqi Arabs are inspired by Hezbollah's example.

Alasdair Soussi (2004) writes that most Hezbollah members share Fneish's feelings, pointing to Hezbollah's large-scale health care and education systems as evidence that their emphasis is primarily humanitarian. They also claim that the group's goal is to assist the 400,000 Palestinians living in Lebanon. Hezbollah supporters believe the organization is nothing more than a resistance movement against Israel and that its soldiers are the guerrillas and commandos stationed along the border. Supporters point to the condemnation by Hassan Fadlallah, Hezbollah's spiritual leader, of the September 11 attacks as un-Islamic, refusing to call the hijackers "martyrs" and maintaining they committed suicide while murdering innocent people (Council on Foreign Relations, 2004).

A Critical View of Hezbollah

Despite the above arguments, many people in the world consider Hezbollah to be a terrorist organization. The U.S. Department of State (2004b) summarizes this point of view in its 2004 revised report on terrorism: Hezbollah is a deadly international terrorist organization that has developed international links and uses international crime to finance operations. Its primary sponsor is Iran, and it receives secondary support from Syria, nations that are listed as state sponsors of terrorism. In addition to its murders of Israelis, Hezbollah has killed U.S. citizens and kidnapped and tortured Americans. The State Department sees Hezbollah as a group of international murderers.

The Council on Foreign Relations (2004) echoes the State Department's view. Hezbollah is a terrorist organization because of the suicide attacks it carried out against civilian and peacekeeping forces and because of its kidnapping rampage from 1983 to 1990. It was also involved in the **1985 hijacking of a TWA flight**, during which an American was murdered, and two bombings in **Argentina in 1992 and 1994**. It has been responsible for a campaign of suicide bombings, the murders of Lebanese Christians, international arms smuggling, and a host of international criminal activity, including crimes in the United States.

Critics also point to Hezbollah's uncompromising political stand, saying that it exists for only two reasons: to impose a Shiite government on Lebanon and to destroy the state of Israel. Hezbollah parliamentary representative Mohammed Fneish says that Hezbollah will not force Lebanon to become an Islamic republic like Iran, but his party will campaign for it. After Hezbollah is elected, it can take the necessary steps of consolidating power. As far as the elimination of Israel goes, Fneish says Israel was created illegally by Europeans and Americans who felt guilty about the Nazi death camps. They created Israel, he says, as a way of apologizing. Hezbollah does not recognize Israel's right to exist, and it must be eliminated (Cavanaugh, 2004).

Other researchers also condemn Hezbollah. Alasdair Soussi (2004) says Hezbollah exports its revolutionary ideals, claiming that contacts exist between Hezbollah and the Iraqi resistance movement. Muqtada al Sadr, the Shiite leader of the Mahdi Army in Iraq, is linked to Hezbollah's Hassan Nasrallah. Daniel Byman (2003), a professor in security studies at Georgetown University, says there is no question about the terrorist agenda of Hezbollah. It might have credibility in the Islamic world, but its record of bloodshed and hostility speaks for itself. It is not a question of whether the United States should stop Hezbollah, Byman writes, but of how.

Jessica Stern (2003b) points out that Hezbollah interacts with other terrorist groups around the world. Rather than standing alone as a terrorist group, it is part of a network of groups that range from jihadists to traffickers in narcotics. Jeffery Goldberg (2002) says that the director Imad Mugniyah of Hezbollah International is the primary culprit behind these links. Both Stern and Goldberg believe the network blends Hezbollah with al Qaeda. The existence of the international aspect of Hezbollah, according to such research, proves that the organization is part of an international jihadist struggle that uses crime and state support to wage a campaign of terrorism.

Jaber (1997, p. 1) characterizes the practical outcome of Hezbollah in the lives of everyday people in the opening scene of her book. In her scenario, a boy named Mohammed Ghandour and his younger sister watch a video showing a car laden with explosives driving into an Israeli convoy. When the car explodes, Mohammed exclaims, "There's my daddy." In her moving portrait of the Ghandour family, Jaber describes the differing views of the Israelis and the Lebanese.

Hezbollah is part of the jihadist network, but its origins and reasons for existing are found in the struggle over Palestine. It has reluctantly

1985 hijacking of a TWA flight
The hijacking of TWA Flight 847 by a group believed to have links to Hezbollah while it was en route from Athens to Rome. The plane went to Beirut and then to Algeria where terrorists tortured and murdered U.S. Navy diver Robert Dean Stethem, a passenger on the flight. The plane returned to Beirut, and passengers were dispersed throughout the city. Terrorists released hostages throughout the incident, and all hostages were freed from Beirut after Israel released more than 700 Shiite prisoners.

Argentina in 1992 and 1994
Two bombings in Buenos Aires. Terrorists struck the Israeli embassy in 1992, killing twenty-nine, and the Jewish Community Center in 1994 killing eighty-five. Imad Mugniyah is suspected to be behind the attacks.

formed alliances with many of the non-networked groups such as the Palestinian Islamic Jihad, Hamas, the Popular Front for the Liberation of Palestine, and the al Aqsa Martyrs Brigades. Since the start of the al Aqsa Intifada, a Palestinian uprising starting in September 2000, the distinction among many of the pro-Palestinian groups has blurred. Daniel Byman (2003) concludes that the international operations of Hezbollah could potentially be neutralized if the United States were to repair its relationship with Syria and Iran.

Hezbollah provided a model for the formation of an international umbrella of terrorist organizations. The international section remains a conglomeration of like-minded semiautonomous groups. The model inspired the formation of other networks, and none was as important as the groups related to al Qaeda. As Osama bin Laden and Ayman al Zawahiri modified the Hezbollah model within al Qaeda, a plethora of terrorist groups exploded from the Afghan jihad. The allied and semiautonomous groups add to the al Qaeda mystique, and the jihadist network strengthens al Qaeda's striking power.

Self-Check

- *Explain the four phases in the evolution of Hezbollah.*
- *What is the current state of Hezbollah?*
- *Summarize critical and sympathetic views toward Hezbollah.*

Umbrellas and Networks in North Africa

Inspired by Qutb and moving to a new organizational model, the decentralized networks moved into North Africa. Whereas Hezbollah started as an umbrella, moved to centralization, and sought political legitimacy, the path taken by groups in North Africa was different. Three groups moved from an original umbrella structure to further decentralization. These groups eventually provided a model for al Qaeda after it formed a new coalition in 1996. They represent the movement to terrorist networks (see Sageman, 2004; Scheuer, 2006).

The Armed Islamic Group

Algerian Civil War
(1991–2000) The war that ensued after the military assumed control of the government when an Islamist party won a democratic national election. More than 100,000 people were killed.

In 1991 an Islamic party won the national election in Algeria. This frightened the West, especially France and the United States, who were worried that narrow-minded Islamicist governments would spread through the region (see Kepel, 2002, pp. 159–176). When the Algerian military took control of the government and voided the elections, several Western nations breathed a sigh of relief. North Africa was too close to Europe for comfort; the West was not eager to see a government based on strict Islamic law so close to its southern door (Figure 11.4). Unfortunately, the military coup resulted in the deadly **Algerian Civil War**, during which more than 100,000 people died between 1991 and 2000.

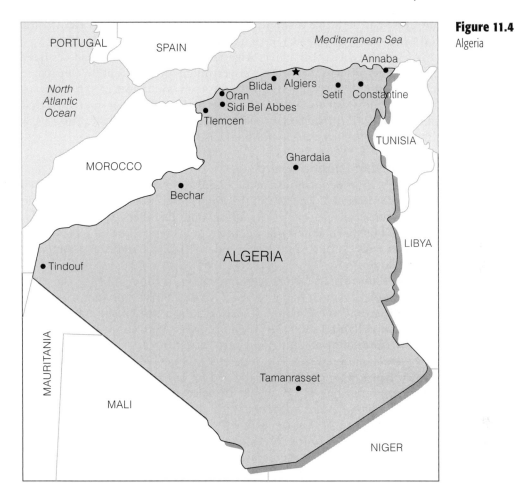

Figure 11.4
Algeria

The Algerian Armed Islamic Group (GIA) grew to resist the military (see Kepel 2002, p. 169; Esposito, 1999, p. 187). The GIA consisted of new Algerian recruits as well as several jihadists who had fought in the Soviet-Afghan War. By 1995 new jihadist groups were springing up in Algeria, and the war became a bloodbath. Violence and jihadist groups spread throughout North Africa. Egypt found itself in the midst of a war with three of them; Libyan leaders were threatened for criticizing jihadists; Tunisia started to move toward a more strict form of Islam; and Morocco, one of the West's closest allies in the region, spawned its own jihadist movements.

The GIA was particularly ruthless. Following the Qutb philosophy that no believer was really a Muslim unless he or she accepted Qutb's narrow theological path, the group specialized in the murder of civilians. GIA terrorists specialized in slitting throats; their victims, they said, wore an Algerian smile (see Esposito, 2002, pp. 103–104). One of the founding members of the GIA, Hassan Hattab, became so disgusted with civilian

Hassan Hattab

To come.

Salafi Group for Call and Combat (GSPC)

murders that he broke away in 1998 and formed the **Salafi Group for Call and Combat (GPSC)**. It remains active in Italy (Haahr, 2006).

Although GIA is still active, Algerian military and police forces have damaged its effectiveness. The government also sought to repatriate many of the jihadists jailed during the civil war. Most of the Algerian jihadists who want to fight have gravitated to the global network that characterizes terrorism today, or they have joined the GPSC. The GIA is so weak that it moved its operational base to Italy.

The Egyptian Islamic Group

Press reports tended to present the jihadist movements in North Africa as an expansion of al Qaeda, but this interpretation is incorrect. In some cases jihadist groups shared training and members with al Qaeda, but they had been emerging on their own before the Soviet-Afghan War. One such group was the Egyptian Islamic Group (al Gamaat al Islamiyya, or IG).

Three interrelated factors were prevalent in the rise of IG: the 1981 assassination of Anwar Sadat by religious extremists, the failure of Arab nationalism, and the decline of Arab socialism. When the nationalistic movement collapsed after the 1967 Six Days' War, dreams of an Arab socialist state followed suit. Religious extremism took the place of socialism and nationalism. The religious fanatics dismissed nationalism because Muslims should not be divided by European-style borders, and they feared that socialism would displace God. Sadat's assassination electrified the Egyptian militants.

According to the U.S. Department of State (2007), IG formed in the early 1970s. It came to the forefront after mujahideen returned from the Soviet-Afghan War, and it embraced a new style of organization. Instead of a centralized hierarchy, it operated in a loosely structured network spanning several Egyptian cities. It also established foreign wings, and IG was even active in the United States. It was connected with the **1993 World Trade Center bombing** and with plans for further attacks in New York City.

A prominent member of IG known to many Americans is **Sheik Omar Abdel Rahman**. He has been convicted of complicity in the World Trade Center bombing. Less known to many Americans are IG members in Egypt, even though they have caused more death and destruction. IG has been responsible for attacks on Egyptian security forces, Christians, and tourists. An attack on a group of tourists in Luxor drew international attention to the IG.

At the time it seemed an isolated event. On November 17, 1997, four Egyptian jihadists dressed in police uniforms approached a group of fifty-eight tourists visiting the Pyramids (Figure 11.5). Most of the tourists were Swiss. As the tourists disembarked from a bus, the jihadists attacked. They shot more than fifty tourists. In a gruesome act, they pulled out small knives and worked their way through the dead and wounded. Victims were mutilated and decapitated to increase the drama

1993 World Trade Center bombing

A car-bomb attack by a cell led by Ramzi Youseff. The cell had links to the Egyptian IG.

Sheik Omar Abdel Rahman

(1938–) A Sunni Islamic scholar linked to the Egyptian IG. He came to the United States in 1990 even though his name was on a State Department watch list. He was arrested and convicted of conspiracy after the 1993 World Trade Center bombing. He is gravely ill in an American federal prison.

Mustafa Hamza

(1957–) A leader of the Egyptian IG, believed to be involved in several terrorist incidents, who agreed to a cease-fire in 1997. He has been sentenced to death in absentia in Egypt.

of the attack. The jihadists were later killed by Egyptian security forces (Plet, 1999).

The IG declared a cease-fire in 1997, but this led to factionalism. **Mustafa Hamza**, one faction's leader, supported the cease-fire, but **Rafai Taha Masa**, another faction's, did not. Hamza's wing renewed the pledge for peace in 1999, but Taha Masa continued to advocate violence. He published a book denouncing the cease-fire in 2001 and disappeared shortly thereafter (U.S. Department of State, 2007). Stephen Ulph (2004) says that Taha Masa was arrested by the Syrians shortly after the September 11 attacks, and they handed him over to the Egyptians. He was pressured to renounce violence under pain of execution.

Figure 11.5

Luxor

Egyptian Islamic Jihad

Ayman al Zawahiri was the driving force behind another terrorist group in Egypt, the Egyptian Islamic Jihad (EIJ). Zawahiri and EIJ demonstrate both the power of an ideology to hold a group together and the evolutionary path of terrorist networks. Like IG, EIJ was bound loosely with autonomous cells taking action on their own. Unlike IG, EIJ specifically targeted the Egyptian government (Keats, 2002).

Zawahiri did not get along with either IG's leaders or its philosophy. He felt that targeting Christians and tourists would turn Egyptians against the jihadist movement. The government repressed the people; therefore, the government should be the sole target of the terrorist campaign (L. Wright, 2006, pp. 53–55). Zawahiri believed the government represented the **near enemy**. It was the so-called Muslim government that should be overthrown, as Sayyid Qutb had argued. Zawahiri believed local groups could defeat their own governments and then unite the entire Islamic community. When this was achieved, the united jihadists could focus on the **far enemy**: Israel, the United States, and the West (see Gerges, 2005).

After returning from the Afghan jihad, Zawahiri threw himself into the Egyptian Islamicist revolt. Using Egyptians trained in camps in Afghanistan, EIJ focused on governmental targets. Terrorists tried to assassinate Egypt's interior minister. After that failed, they pulled off a bombing attack on the Egyptian embassy in Islamabad, Pakistan. Although Zawahiri believed the true Muslims of Egypt would arise when EIJ began its religious revolt, the opposite happened. The government cracked down, and few people stepped forward to take up EIJ's version of jihad. Zawahiri left for Afghanistan, and several members of EIJ followed (BBC, n.d.).

In 1998 EIJ was absorbed into al Qaeda when Osama bin Laden announced that he was forming the **World Islamic Front against Jews and Crusaders**. The story of EIJ is taken over by al Qaeda at this point; however, the experience of EIJ dominated al Qaeda's new alliance as al Qaeda evolved into a sophisticated international network. Interestingly,

Rafai Taha Masa
(age unknown) A militant leader of the IG. He split with Hamza over the 1997 cease-fire and signed the 1998 declaration with bin Laden and Zawahiri.

near enemy
A jihadist term referring to forms of Muslim governments and Islamic law (sharia) that do not embrace the narrow-minded philosophy of Sayyid Qutb.

far enemy
A jihadist term referring to non-Islamic powers or countries outside dar al Islam. It is a general reference to Israel, the West, and the United States.

World Islamic Front against Jews and Crusaders

An organization created in 1998 by Osama bin Laden and Ayman al Zawahiri. It represents a variety of jihadist groups that issued a united front against Jews and the West. It is commonly called al Qaeda.

Zawahiri announced that IG joined the network in 2006. This might have been just propaganda by Zawahiri because the past animosity between EIJ and IG would seem to prohibit their joining forces. Regardless, bin Laden and Zawahiri brought a new style of organization to the world of international terrorism.

Self-Check

- *How could Hezbollah inspire the creation of umbrella groups in North Africa?*
- *Explain the evolution of jihadist groups in Algeria.*
- *How did the Egyptian experience reflect the umbrella philosophy?*

The Growth of International Jihadist Networks

In May 2004 the ABC news service reported that the terrorist organization al Qaeda, operated by Osama bin Laden, had 18,000 fighters poised throughout the world and the group was ready to strike Western interests (ABC News, 2004). The report's source was the United Kingdom's Institute for Strategic Studies, as originally reported by the Reuters news service. Various news agencies around the world ran their own versions of the Reuters story without doing their own research. If they had, they would have found that many people had passed through al Qaeda training camps, but the actual number of terrorists was much lower. The real problem was the secret nature of al Qaeda's structure. It seemed that al Qaeda was capable of running an organized international operation even though it had been surrounded and pounded by U.S. military forces in Afghanistan. Before 2001 al Qaeda maintained a command hierarchy. After 2001 its leaders ran virtual networks and inspired autonomous jihadists around the globe (see Scheuer, 2006). Intelligence agencies still do not have a full grasp of al Qaeda's operational capabilities. (See Another Perspective: Examining Terms: Fundamentalists, Islamicists, and Jihadists.)

The Birth of Al Qaeda

Taliban

The Islamicist group that governed Afghanistan from 1996 to 2001.

Mullah Omar

(1959–) The leader of the Taliban. After the collapse of the Taliban government in 2001, Omar went into hiding.

Al Qaeda was born in the last stages of the Soviet-Afghan War, and it grew until the U.S. offensive in Afghanistan in October 2001, when U.S. forces struck the al Qaeda and **Taliban** forces there. Led by **Mullah Omar**, the group was composed of Islamic students who wanted to bring order to Afghanistan through the forced imposition of Islamic law (Matinuddin, 1999, pp. 21–22, 41). As Peter Bergen (2001, pp. 195–235) says, al Qaeda transformed after 2001. It became what he calls al Qaeda 2.0, a group he believes to be a decentralized alliance of al Qaeda terrorists spread throughout the world. Yet al Qaeda is simply one manifestation of the jihadist movement, a movement with millions of supporters and sympathizers.

ANOTHER PERSPECTIVE

Examining Terms: Fundamentalists, Islamicists, and Jihadists

Popular media sources and some scholarly works frequently use two terms to describe terrorists who claim to be acting under the banner of Islam: *Islamic fundamentalist* and *Islamicist*.

Fundamentalist is usually a term that refers to a movement in twentieth-century Protestantism, but it has also come to refer to anyone who stresses strict and literal adherence to, in this case, religious principles. All Muslims have fundamental beliefs, but they differ on the interpretation of Islamic law.

Islamicist is a much better term because it differentiates between Muslims and violent extremists acting in the name of Islam. A person practicing Islam is a Muslim. Although Muslims combine religion with government as the prophet Mohammed did in Medina, they do not endorse violence to impose their views on others. Islamicists not only advocate violence but attack mainstream Muslims and those outside the religion. They seek to impose their version of Islamic law on others.

Lately, many terrorism specialists have been using the term *jihadist* to describe Islamicists. A jihadist is someone who

- Worships by waging holy war, or jihad
- Wants to force a strict code of Islamic law on all people
- Believes in killing non-Muslims
- Believes in killing Muslims who disagree with their strict interpretation of Islamic law
- Uses terrorism to wage jihad

Most Muslims believe jihad is an internal journey of purification or a willingness to carry arms in defense of the community. Militants have transformed jihad's meaning and claim they are called to wage an offensive holy war against non-Muslims and Muslims who disagree with them.

As al Qaeda transformed, its symbolic name came to mean more than its actual power (Windrem and Gubash, 2004). Several groups sympathetic to al Qaeda claimed to be part of a vast network, but sometimes they had no direct relationship with each other. Jihadist ideology held these groups together. In short, the jihadist ideology contends that Islam has become corrupt and needs to be purified. Although they blame heretical Islamic leaders, jihadists believe much of the corruption is due to the values and economic power of the West, especially the United States. They feel called to destroy this evil influence, but they are not necessarily affiliated with and certainly not controlled by al Qaeda. They are independents bound by common ideas.

Misappropriated Theology

Because jihadists make religious claims, many Muslims become upset when their faith is portrayed in terms of violent terrorism. Many Christians feel similarly, for instance, when the fighting in Ireland is described as a "religious war." They believe that even though militant thugs invoke either Protestantism or Catholicism, Irish violence is a violation of

Christian principles. Mainstream Muslims feel the same way. In fact, Magnus Ranstorp (1998) says the jihadists are doomed to failure within their own culture because their theology of violence does not convey the meaning of Islam.

Many Muslims agree with Ranstorp's conclusion. Feisal Rauf (2004, pp. 41–77) responds with a popular theological treatise explaining the strengths of Islam. Islam is a religion, Rauf says, that values peace and toleration. There are violent passages in the Quran, but there are violent passages in the writings of all major religions, including Judaism and Christianity. Islam teaches universal human love, submission to God's will, and a life of morality preparing for the final judgment of God. He calls Muslims to embrace the roots of their faith and the commonalities among Muslims, Jews, and Christians.

Former congressman Paul Findlay (2001), who is Christian, is enraged by attacks on stereotyped Muslims. Findlay recounts stories and actions of friends who have embraced the Islamic faith. He tells of personal travels to Islamic lands to demonstrate his belief in a simple fact: people are people everywhere. The religion of Islam, he concludes, does not foster militancy.

Others point to violent sects in Islam. Steven Emerson (2002, pp. 221–233) says Islam has always been associated with political expansion and that militancy is a product of the twentieth century. His research shows that many seemingly legitimate Islamic organizations support the jihadists and directly or indirectly fund radical Muslim terrorist groups. Missionaries from intolerant sects within Islam travel to the West by the hundreds, Emerson says, and millions of dollars from such sects build mosques in Europe and the United States.

madrassas
Islamic religious schools.

Confusion about mainstream Islam complicates attempts to understand jihadists. Misunderstandings increase when jihadists use religious rhetoric. For example, Catholic IRA terrorists do not publicize their operations in the name of God. Jihadists do. In addition, some **madrassas** (Islamic schools) in many areas of the world glamorize violence and inspire young people to join terrorist organizations (J. Stern, 2003b, pp. 258–259). Samuel Huntington (1996, p. 176) points out that Christians, Hindus, and Buddhists do not create international associations of nation-states that are based on religion. Muslims do. Such religious and cultural issues are factors that complicate attempts to understand the nature of jihadist networks.

Militant Muslims embrace the reforming doctrines of Wahhab, the Salafiyya, and the Muslim Brotherhood but depart from the path of Islam and endorse violence. They see jihad as a duty and means for imposing their strict form of Islam on others. Their goal is to unite the world in a pure Islamic state through the force of arms. Most Muslims reject these ideas, even though they distrust the policies of the United States and dislike America in general (Palmer and Palmer, 2004, pp. 9–34).

The Origins of Jihadist Networks

John Cooley (2002, pp. 64–104) believes the foundation of modern jihadist power grew from the cold war, and he blames the West for incubating the network. The idea of using militant reformers against the Soviet Union was born in France. The French intelligence community knew that Islamic militants hated the communists for several reasons and therefore suggested to intelligence counterparts in Washington and London that militant Islamic reformers might be used against communist countries. America, Great Britain, and France soon began to seek alliances with militant Islamic radicals. Using ties with oil-rich Muslim states, especially Saudi Arabia and Kuwait, the Western allies channeled support to both militant and nonviolent purification movements within Islam.

Western efforts to support Islamic reformers came to fruition in 1979. In December of that year the Soviet Union invaded Afghanistan to bolster a failing communist regime. According to Cooley, this was the chance the West had been waiting for. President Jimmy Carter's State Department encouraged Arab and other Islamic allies to send money and religious puritans to fight the Soviets in a guerrilla war. The puritans were called *mujahideen*, or "holy warriors." The United States formed an alliance with Pakistan, and the Pakistani **Interservice Intelligence Agency (ISI)** began to train and equip the mujahideen. When Ronald Reagan became president in 1980, American efforts against the Soviets increased.

Several researchers have looked at the relationship between the United States and the mujahideen during the Soviet-Afghan War (see, for example, Benjamin and Simon, 2002, pp. 98–102; Cooley, 2002, pp. 64–75; Gunaratna, 2002, p. 18; Kepel, 2002, pp. 136–150; Ruthven, 2000, p. 365). Their research points to several important conclusions. First, the United States helped Saudi Arabia develop a funding mechanism and underground arms network to supply the mujahideen. Second, the United States agreed to give most of the weapons and supplies to the ISI, which built mujahideen groups with little American participation. Third, Islamic charities flourished in the United States, and their donations supported the mujahideen. Finally, when the Soviets left Afghanistan in 1989, the United States rejoiced and abandoned war-torn Afghanistan.

The mujahideen were not united at the end of the Soviet-Afghan War. Up to thirty-one different groups fought the Soviets, with six major mujahideen guerrilla armies controlling most operations. The power that held the many groups together was a mutual hatred of the Soviets (Shay, 2002, pp. 108–109). When the Soviets finally retreated, the Afghan mujahideen believed the power of God had prevailed over Satan. The major leaders wanted to turn their efforts against the other enemies of God: apostate Islamic governments, Israel, and the West. Some mujahideen returned to their homes to spread holy war, but others had

Interservice Intelligence Agency (ISI)
The Pakistani domestic and foreign intelligence service created by the British in 1948. Supporters claim that it centralizes Pakistan's intelligence. Critics maintain that it operates like an independent state and supports terrorist groups.

grander schemes. Virtually ignored by the United States, the jihadist movement grew, and terrorism grew with it.

Jihad Continues in Afghanistan

As the Soviets began leaving Afghanistan in April 1988, the United States celebrated a vicarious victory. The Soviets were on the run and in full retreat from the battlefields of the cold war. The defeat was another blow to a crumbling empire, and by 1991 the Soviet Union had dissolved. The cold war was over, and it appeared that a new world of peace was at hand. As the world stepped back from the brink of nuclear annihilation, America's leaders and people paid very little attention to events in far-off Afghanistan (see Crile, 2003, pp. 470–484).

But the fighting was not over in Afghanistan. Shaul Shay (2002, pp. 76–81) writes that the mujahideen groups continued to fight for control of the country. Al Qaeda was one of many paramilitary organizations to join the fray, and the United States failed to recognize the problem on two levels. Cooley (2002, p. 122) and Napoleoni (2003, pp. 189–191) say that American oil companies sought alliances with some groups in hopes of building an oil pipeline from central Asia to the Indian Ocean. The oil would run through Afghanistan. Americans paid more attention to potential profits than the political problems brewing in Afghanistan. On another level, the United States simply ignored issues. As the Afghan groups continued to build and strengthen, Americans celebrated the ending of the cold war and the beginning of the **peace dividend**—the money the United States diverted from military spending.

Osama bin Laden was a large part of America's blissful ignorance. The report of the **9/11 Commission** (2004, pp. 53–54) notes that bin Laden's reputation began to grow as the mujahideen searched for a continuing jihad (see Another Perspective: The 9/11 Commission's Analysis of Counterterrorism). When international terrorist violence increased in Africa and Asia during the 1990s, bin Laden emerged as a symbol of Islamic discontent. Oil-rich Muslim countries were faced with a growing population of young men who had technical educations with no broad understanding of humanities, social sciences, and the larger world. They also faced unemployment due to the distribution of wealth. Bin Laden emerged as a spokesman for the discontented, and his own movement began to take form.

peace dividend

A term used during President William Clinton's administration (1992–2000) to describe reducing defense spending at the end of the cold war.

9/11 Commission

The bipartisan National Commission on Terrorist Attacks upon the United States created after September 11, 2001, to investigate the attacks.

The Rise of Osama bin Laden

Rohan Gunaratna (2002) documents the origins of al Qaeda and its actions from the end of the Soviet-Afghan War until the attacks of September 11, 2001. Yoseff Bodansky (1999) offers a biography of bin Laden that predates the September 11 attacks. The 9/11 Commission Report (2004, pp. 47–70) also documents the growth of al Qaeda. All three works point to the importance of the personality of Osama bin Laden.

Osama bin Laden was the son of Mohammed bin Laden, a wealthy construction executive who worked closely with the Saudi royal family.

The 9/11 Commission's Analysis of Counterterrorism

Chapter 3 of the 9/11 Commission Report summarizes some of the mistakes government agencies made as al Qaeda was growing.

1. The Department of Justice (DOJ) was geared to gather evidence, prosecute, and convict. It was not designed to look into additional intelligence after a verdict was rendered.

2. The FBI measured success by crime rates, arrests, and crime clearances. It did an outstanding job when investigating terrorist incidents, but the bureau did not emphasize the role of intelligence gathering and analysis.

   a. It did not place resources in intelligence gathering.

   b. The division established to analyze intelligence faltered.

   c. The bureau did not have an effective intelligence-gathering system.

3. A series of rulings by the attorney general and mandates from Congress limited the FBI's ability to collect domestic intelligence.

   a. DOJ officials were confused about the relationship between criminal investigations and intelligence operations.

   b. The Foreign Intelligence Surveillance Act of 1978 (FISA) was misinterpreted by DOJ, the FBI, and the FISA court. (The FISA court approves warrants for surveillance under FISA.)

   c. Misinterpretations of FISA prevented intelligence agencies from sharing relevant information with FBI criminal investigators.

4. The Immigration and Naturalization Service focused on the southwestern U.S. border and did not have enough personnel to deal with terrorism.

5. The Federal Aviation Administration (FAA) had layered defensive measures in place to gather intelligence, single out suspected terrorists, screen passengers, and provide in-flight procedures for emergencies at differing points in the security process.

   a. The FAA intelligence division was not adequately staffed.

   b. The no-fly lists did not contain the names of terrorists known to other governmental agencies.

   c. Airport security screening performed poorly.

   d. The FAA rejected a ban on small knives, fearing screeners could not find them and searches would create congestion at screening areas.

   e. Procedures for in-flight emergencies did not include plans to counter suicide hijackers.

   f. In defense of the FAA, the 9/11 Commission notes that hijackings had diminished for a decade, and they did not seem to be an immediate threat.

6. Intelligence agencies in general were not prepared to deal with terrorism.

   a. The intelligence community remained geared to fight the cold war.

   b. There was no overall director of intelligence.

   c. Intelligence operations were hampered by reduced resources.

   d. American universities did not produce scholars with in-depth knowledge of jihadist issues and appropriate foreign-language capabilities.

(continued)

The 9/11 Commission's Analysis of Counterterrorism (continued)

7. The Department of State had lost much of its ability to establish foreign policy.

   a. Foreign policy planning had been shifting to the National Security Council and the Department of Defense since 1960.

   b. Former secretary of state Warren Christopher tried to lump counterterrorism into drug and crime control but was prevented from doing so by Congress.

   c. The screening system for visas was full of holes.

8. The Department of Defense sought to deter terrorism by retaliating against acts of terrorism with limited air strikes. This policy was not effective against a loosely bound international terrorist organization.

9. Congress bears much of the responsibility for the state of affairs in government.

   a. There were too many committees overseeing intelligence.

   b. Like the intelligence community, Congress was structured for a cold war enemy.

   c. Congressional priorities were in areas other than terrorism.

   d. Congress was slow to react to terrorism and favored local domestic issues over those of national security.

   The 9/11 Commission (2004, pp. 340–344) points out that it was easy to develop this critique with hindsight. As the jihadist network developed, only a few people, such as Dale Watson of the FBI and Richard Clarke of the White House staff, were focused on counterterrorism. American institutions and, more importantly, the American people were not overly concerned with jihadist terrorism. As the jihadist network grew, Americans looked the other way.

Source: 9/11 Commission Report, 2004.

The elder bin Laden divorced Osama's mother, but he continued to provide for the family. Osama decided that he wanted to become a good Muslim at an early age. Because of his father's connections, bin Laden was raised in the Saudi royal court, and his tutor, Mohammed Qutb, was the brother of the Egyptian radical Sayyid Qutb. Bin Laden was influenced by Sayyid Qutb's thought. While attending university, bin Laden left the nonviolent Wahhabism of the Saudi royal family and turned to Qutb's philosophy (see H. Oliver, 2002, pp. 10–38). Eventually, bin Laden dropped out of college to join the Soviet-Afghan War. At first, he lent his support to the mujahideen, but later he formed his own guerrilla unit (L. Wright, 2006, pp. 60–83).

While in Afghanistan, bin Laden fell under the influence of **Abdullah Azzam**, a doctor of Islamic law. Azzam was a Palestinian scholar who was influenced by Qutb's writings. He came to believe that a purified form of Islam was the answer to questions of poverty and the loss of political power. He had been working for the Palestinians in the mid-1970s, but he became disillusioned with their nationalism and emphasis

Abdullah Azzam

(1941–1989) The Palestinian leader of Hizb ul Tahrir and spiritual mentor of bin Laden.

on politics over religion. Azzam believed Islam should be the guiding force for war, and he would not abandon religious principles for the sake of a political victory. He left the Palestinians for a Saudi university to teach Islamic law, later joining the Afghan jihad (L. Wright, 2006, pp. 99–106).

According to Azzam, the realm of Islam had been dominated by foreign powers for too long. It was time for all Muslims to rise up and strike Satan. He saw the Soviet-Afghan War as just the beginning of a holy war against all things foreign to Islam. At first, bin Laden found the theology of Azzam to his liking and the answer to his prayers for a path to holy war.

According to the 9/11 Commission Report (2004, p. 58), bin Laden and Azzam "established what they called a base or foundation (al Qaeda) as a potential general headquarters for future jihad" toward the end of the Soviet-Afghan War. Bin Laden was its leader, and the organization included an intelligence component, a military committee, a financial committee, a political committee, and a committee in charge of media affairs and propaganda.

Bodansky (1999) points out that the United States would hardly have considered funding such a group of rebels, but the Pakistani ISI intervened. The 9/11 Commission (2004, pp. 55–56) writes that the ISI was concerned with the growing threat of the Soviet Union, but it had its own agenda for national security. Pakistan offered to act as the surrogate for the United States and Saudi Arabia, as both nations poured money into the war against the Soviets. The ISI, however, did not tell either America or Saudi Arabia how the money was being spent, nor was the ISI truthful when anti-Soviet hostilities ended in Afghanistan. Various mujahideen groups struggled to gain power in Afghanistan, and the ISI backed its favorite allies. It also hoped to use groups like al Qaeda in Kashmir, a province in northern India that Pakistan claims. In essence, the ISI developed the structure that would support al Qaeda with U.S. and Saudi funds during the Soviet-Afghan War.

Training in Pakistan and Afghanistan under Azzam's spiritual mentoring, bin Laden financed mujahideen operations and taught the guerrillas how to build field fortifications. By 1986 he had left the training field for the battlefield. Enraged with the Soviets for their wholesale slaughter of Afghan villagers and use of poison gas, bin Laden joined the front ranks of the mujahideen. Allied with hundreds of radical militants throughout the world, Osama bin Laden became a battlefield hero. (When interviewed by John Miller for *ABC News* [1998], bin Laden would not discuss these exploits. He simply stated that all Muslims are required to fight in the jihad.) After taking part in the war, bin Laden returned to Pakistan and joined Azzam in a new venture: to register all the foreign jihadists in a single computer database.

Things did not go well for Azzam, however. When the Soviets prepared to withdraw from Afghanistan in 1988, the ISI created its own Afghan guerrilla force and used it to take control of major areas of the country. Azzam believed the United States was behind this action, and he broke with the ISI. According to a U.S. federal agent I interviewed who spent many months in Pakistan and Afghanistan apprehending and interrogating jihadists, Azzam called together five mujahideen leaders, including bin Laden and Ayman al Zawahiri, a leader of the EIJ, in an attempt to unite the jihadist movement. But the meeting ended in shambles, with each leader declaring the other four heretics. Bin Laden and Zawahiri left, disillusioned and angry with Azzam. At this point, Zawahiri began sketching out a grand model for al Qaeda, proposing a structure like the umbrella organization of the EIJ.

According to Gunaratna (2002, p. 25), Zawahiri became the brains behind a new operation. Using bin Laden's notoriety and charisma among the Afghan mujahideen, he transformed the organization. Zawahiri knew from experience that an umbrella-style organization was difficult to penetrate. In Egypt he had witnessed the effectiveness of EIJ, which had terrorized the country with a small centralized organization supplying logistical support and advice to a set of semiautonomous groups. Al Zawahiri persuaded bin Laden that this was the type of organization to take control of Afghanistan and spread the new Islamic empire.

With Zawahiri's ideas, Osama bin Laden took advantage of America's inattention and Azzam's waning power. He began to recruit into al Qaeda the mujahideen registered in his computer database, while al Zawahiri organized training camps and cells. He also expressed a willingness to work with the Shiite terrorist organization Hezbollah (Waxman, 1998a; J. Goldberg, 2002). Yael Shahar (1998) says bin Laden saw the Soviet collapse in Afghanistan as a sign of God's victory. Islamic law was to be imposed on the world, and bin Laden believed al Qaeda to be the organization that could do it.

The only problem was Azzam, who resisted bin Laden and Zawahiri's takeover. But in November 1989, Azzam was killed by a remote-controlled car bomb. Whether the assassination was by Egyptian radicals or perhaps bin Laden himself, the result was that bin Laden and Zawahiri became the undisputed leaders of al Qaeda. Following the philosophy of Sayyid Qutb, their enemies were the United States, the West, Israel, and Muslims who refused to accept jihadist theology.

Bin Laden's first cause was the Saudi government and its "corrupt" royal family. As bin Laden's mujahideen fighters, or "Afghans," as he called them, either went home to their native lands to wage jihad or stayed in Afghanistan to train and fight, bin Laden returned to Saudi Arabia, enjoying warm relations with the ISI. But the Saudi Arabian government, which does not tolerate diverse opinions and dissension, was not happy to see him return. When bin Laden brought several of his Afghans into his Arabian construction business, the Saudis watched carefully. While they looked on, bin Laden became independently wealthy and his agents began making real estate purchases in Sudan (see L. Wright, 2006, pp. 140–156).

The situation changed in 1990 when Iraq invaded Kuwait. The United States joined Saudi Arabia in a large international coalition opposing the invasion, and bin Laden was infuriated. As thousands of non-Muslim troops arrived in Saudi Arabia, radical Muslims were appalled to find Muslims fighting Muslims under U.S. leadership. The U.S.-led coalition called this military buildup **Desert Shield**, and it became **Desert Storm** in February 1991 when American, British, and other allied forces poured into Iraq and Kuwait. For bin Laden, however, it was a desert apostasy.

After Desert Storm the Saudi government allowed U.S. troops to be stationed in Saudi Arabia, the site of the cities of Mecca and Medina, two of the most holy shrines in Islam. Millions of Muslims believe that these sacred sites must be protected. Having foreigners so near was too much for bin Laden, who now thought of declaring his own war on the Saudi royal family and the United States. By April he was training and financing terrorist groups and calling for the overthrow of unsympathetic Muslim governments.

Declaring War on the United States

The PBS television show *Frontline* (2002) noted that bin Laden's protests against Desert Storm brought a Saudi crackdown on his operations, and he was forced to flee the country. Bin Laden found friends in Sudan's radical government formed under the influence of **Hasan al Turabi**. Turabi was the intellectual leader of the jihadist cause and connected to radical and mainstream Muslims throughout the world. He could provide respectability to jihadist philosophy, and bin Laden and Turabi formed a helpful alliance. Turabi served as the philosopher, and bin Laden provided organizational skills. Bin Laden brought five hundred Afghan veterans to Sudan and built a network of businesses and other enterprises. By the end of 1992 bin Laden employed Afghan-hardened mujahideen in Sudan. He also began to internationalize, creating multinational corporations, false charities, and front companies. Al Qaeda became stronger with each economic expansion (Bergen, 2001, pp. 76–91; for further discussion, see Reeve, 1999, pp. 45–134; Gunaratna, 2002, pp. 1–15; 9/11 Commission Report, 2004, pp. 63–70, 108–143; Randal, 2004, pp. 115–162, 201–221; Palmer and Palmer, 2004, pp. 100–105).

While bin Laden's fortunes increased in Sudan, Americans were on the move in Somalia. President George H. W. Bush sent U.S. forces to **Mogadishu** to end a humanitarian crisis there, and they were joined by other armies, including Muslim forces. The people of Somalia were threatened with mass starvation due to continual struggles among several rival warlords. President Bush hoped peacekeeping efforts could open the area for food distribution. When the Democrats came to power in 1992, President Clinton continued the effort. Most of the world saw the multinational peacekeeping force as a method for feeding the starving Somalis, but not bin Laden. He believed it was another U.S.-led assault on a Muslim nation.

Desert Shield

The name of the defensive phase of the international coalition, created by President George H. W. Bush after Iraq invaded Kuwait on August, 2, 1990, to stop further Iraqi attacks and to liberate Kuwait. It lasted until coalition forces could begin an offensive against Iraq in January 1991.

Desert Storm

The military code name for the January–February offensive in the 1991 Gulf War.

Hassan al Turabi

(1932–) A Sudanese intellectual and Islamic scholar. He served in the Sudanese government during the time bin Laden was in exile in Sudan.

Mogadishu

The capital of Somalia. U.S. troops moved into Mogadishu during Operation Restore Hope from December 9, 1992, until May 4, 1993, when the United Nations took over operations. American forces were involved in a major battle in October 1993 while serving under U.N. command.

In December 1992 a bomb exploded in a hotel in Yemen that had been housing American troops. According to *Frontline* (1999), U.S. intelligence linked the attack to bin Laden. It was the opening shot in bin Laden's war against the United States and an international campaign of terrorism. In the 1980s terrorism was frequently associated with a particular state. Bin Laden, however, transcended the state and operated on his own, with the wealth of his construction empire providing financial backing. Yael Shahar (1998) argues that bin Laden's entrepreneurial efforts gave him the freedom to finance and command the al Qaeda terrorist network. His connections with the Afghan mujahideen and his reputation as a warrior gave him legitimacy. Bin Laden did not need a government to support his operations. He had the money, personnel, material, and infrastructure necessary to maintain a campaign of terrorism. The 9/11 Commission Report (2004, pp. 185–186) disagrees with Shahar. The commission believes bin Laden was and remains funded by wealthy sympathizers. Financial operations in Sudan covered only day-to-day expenses, and many of the companies were not profitable. Regardless of its source, bin Laden had financing and did not need the support of a rogue nation. He needed only a place to hide.

According to *Frontline*, bin Laden went on the offensive in 1993. Using his contacts in Sudan, he began searching for weapons of mass destruction. His Afghans sought to purchase nuclear weapons from underground sources in the Russian Federation, and he began work on a chemical munitions plant in Sudan. Bodansky (1999) says he also sent terrorists to fight in other parts of the world, including Algeria, Egypt, Bosnia, Pakistan, Somalia, Kashmir, and Chechnya. U.S. intelligence sources believe bin Laden's Afghans also came to the United States.

Bin Laden was active in Somalia when U.S. troops joined the forces trying to get food to the area. In October 1993, a U.S. Army Black Hawk helicopter was downed while on patrol in Mogadishu. U.S. Army Rangers went to the rescue, and a two-day battle ensued in which eighteen Americans died. In an interview with John Miller of ABC News (1998), bin Laden claimed he trained and supported the troops that struck the Americans.

Bin Laden was also involved in assassination attempts. In 1993 his Afghans tried to murder Prince Abdullah (now King Abdullah) of Jordan. In 1995 U.S. intelligence sources believe he was behind the attempted assassination of Egyptian president Hosni Mubarak. According to *Frontline*, bin Laden called for a guerrilla campaign against Americans in Saudi Arabia in 1995.

Bin Laden was forced from the Sudan in 1996 by international pressure, and Zawahiri fled Egypt when security forces began cracking down on the jihadists. Both men went to Afghanistan, where many displaced jihadists joined them. Bin Laden consolidated power and absorbed the new jihadists in his ranks. And then he made a most unusual declaration. Seated in front of a camera with Zawahiri and al Qaeda's security director, Mohammed Atef, bin Laden declared war on the United States in 1996. He followed this by having his religious council issue two religious rulings, called fatwas, in 1998, even though few Muslims recognized the validity of the council's religious scholars and bin Laden has no theological credentials.

Magnus Ranstorp (1998) argues that these writings reveal much about the nature of al Qaeda and bin Laden. First, bin Laden represents a new phase in Middle Eastern terrorism. He is intent on spreading the realm of Islam with a transnational group. Second, he uses Islam to call for religious violence. Bin Laden is a self-trained religious fanatic ready to kill in the name of God. Finally, bin Laden wants to cause death. Whether with conventional weapons or weapons of mass destruction, bin Laden's purpose is to kill. In his fatwas of February 1998, he calls for the killing of any American anywhere in the world.

In August 1998 bin Laden's terrorists bombed the U.S. embassies in Nairobi, Kenya, and Dar es Salaam, Tanzania. The Nairobi bomb killed 213 people and injured 4,500; the Dar es Salaam explosion killed 12 and wounded 85. These attacks signaled a new phase in al Qaeda terrorism. The Nairobi and Dar es Salaam bombs demonstrated how al Qaeda had matured. For the first time, the group could operate a cell planted in a country hundreds of miles away from al Qaeda training camps. It used sophisticated bombs and demonstrated complicated planning. Then came the attack on the USS *Cole* in 2000, a failed millennium plot, and the attacks of September 11, 2001 (see L. Wright, 2006). After the United States and allied forces struck al Qaeda bases in Afghanistan in October 2001, the structured operations gave way to the loose network.

Self-Check

- *Explain the "umbrella effect" on the international jihadist movement.*
- *How did al Qaeda misappropriate Islam?*
- *Does the rise of bin Laden signal a declaration of war between Islam and the West?*

▼ Eclectic Disassociation: Fifth-Generation Jihadists

By 2007 al Qaeda was trying to reestablish some type of leadership structure in Pakistan along the Afghan border, but al Qaeda's strength came not from its ability to command but by its inspirational ability to motivate. Terrorism from the Middle East underwent a new transformation. The secular members of Fatah had been the first generation, and the mercenary Abu Nidal Organization, Hezbollah, Palestinian Islamic Jihad (PIJ), EIJ, IG, and Hamas became the first religious terrorist groups and the second-generation. Some of these organizations formed a new organizational structure, the umbrella group, which became the third generation. Al Qaeda, the fourth generation, transformed into an international umbrella and it formed a network with a command center

eclectic disassociations
A term used to describe international networks. There is no pattern for forming groups so they are called eclectic. The groups and the external alliances they form are temporary and disassociate from each other after operations.

Ramzi Youseff
(1967–) A jihadist of Palestinian, Kuwaiti, or Pakistani descent. He is known by many other names. Youseff was linked to Sheik Omar Abdel Rahman and was responsible for the 1993 World Trade Center bombing. Involved in other plots, including an attempt to bring down a number of American airliners over the Pacific Ocean (Operation Bojinka), Youseff was arrested in Pakistan in 1995 and convicted of terrorist-related crimes in 1996. He is serving a life sentence without chance of parole.

Khalid Sheik Mohammed
(1964–) The uncle of Ramzi Youseff and probably the mastermind behind the 9/11 attacks and several other major international and domestic terrorist incidents. These include the World Trade Center bombing (1993), Operation Bojinka (1996), a thwarted attack on the Los Angeles airport (2000), an attempt to bring down an American

in Afghanistan. The breakup of al Qaeda created a fifth generation of jihadist terrorist networks, the all-channel networks that operate without central leadership or permanent structures (see Arquilla and Ronfeldt, 2001; Arquilla, Ronfeldt, and Zanini, 1999). The new organizations were not organizations at all but **eclectic disassociations**.

Decentralized Operations

International jihadist operations actually began operating in networks before al Qaeda took an ideological leading role. In 1993 a group of jihadists tried to destroy the World Trade Center in New York City with a massive car bomb, and a year later a blind Egyptian cleric inspired a group to attempt several other attacks in New York City. In 1995 **Ramzi Youseff** planned to attack the United States by downing airliners over the Pacific during a thirty-one-hour period. These actions illustrate the evolving nature of jihadist ideology. It was not the result of a mastermind terrorist pulling strings from a secretive lair. It was a loose confederation of like-minded people who had limited interactions. Youseff was linked to **Khalid Sheikh Mohammed**, a bin Laden operative and master planner of the September 11 attacks, but he took no orders from bin Laden. In addition, Khalid Sheikh Mohammed admired bin Laden, but he did not officially join al Qaeda until 1999. Individual jihadist operators took actions influenced by al Qaeda's interpretation of jihad (Reeve, 1999, pp. 186–189).

Bin Laden's use of Zawahiri's umbrella or hub organization brought cohesion to jihadists with differing causes (Arquilla, Ronfeldt, and Zanini, 1999, p. 50; Gunaratna, 2002, pp. 75–84). Before the U.S. offensive in Afghanistan in October 2001, al Qaeda existed with a leadership group in Afghanistan and semiautonomous **sleeper cells**—or cells designed to "sleep," or to stay hidden, until the time they were called to action—placed in various countries throughout the world. After leadership in Afghanistan was neutralized, sleeper cells began operation on their own.

Jihadist groups struck many areas, including Bali (October 2002) and U.S. compounds in Riyadh (May 2003), Morocco (August 2003), and Madrid (March 2004). Jihadists have also specialized in beheading hostages in front of international audiences, and they have mastered roadside bombs, suicide attacks, and mass murders in Iraq. Many times these groups claim to be the local version of al Qaeda or they operate by their own name.

Michael Doran (2002) points out that even though the network provided motivations for the various jihadists, it would be a mistake to think the groups presented a united front. They were fueled by local issues and diverse goals. The different jihadist organizations say they all believe in the same thing, Doran says, but when local situations are examined, jihadist causes are varied. Bin Laden's strength came from trying to focus Islamic rage on the United States. In the words of Brian Jenkins (2004a), jihadists see a holy war against the United States as a method for uniting political Islam. It is one of the few issues holding the jihadists together. Doran agrees.

Irm Haleem (2004) says that U.S. operations in Afghanistan caused al Qaeda to completely decentralize. When their Afghan base was rendered inoperable, al Qaeda reformed from an umbrella or hub into a series of autonomous organizations driven by local concerns. John Arquilla and colleagues (1999, p. 50) call this a chain organization, and as such, al Qaeda serves as more of an inspiration than a hub.

Communication and Sympathy

The dispersion of the al Qaeda organization in Afghanistan also created new forms of terrorism. Bin Laden and Zawahiri, or cleverly disguised substitutes, began releasing audiotapes claiming that actions were imminent or claiming credit for attacks in other areas of the world. Jessica Stern (2003b) concludes that by decentralizing to a chain organization, supporting terrorist allies, and maintaining the ability to threaten the world, al Qaeda ideology was more dangerous than ever. This was ironic, given its quick rout from Afghanistan.

James Rubin (2003) points to another problem. On September 11, 2001, the United States had the sympathy and support of the world. When it launched its offensive in Afghanistan, it again had international allies and support. As U.S. law enforcement took action, it received support from police forces in Southeast Asia, the Middle East, Africa, and Europe. But Rubin points out that when President G. W. Bush shifted his attention from al Qaeda to Iraq, America lost the support it had enjoyed after September 11.

Other television and Internet support networks sprouted in the jihadist movement. In addition, the jihadists learned to use the media as a force multiplier. They accomplished this in three ways. First, they used the Internet as a communication and planning tool. They held virtual meetings and linked themselves through computer networks. Second, they created propaganda videos. Sometimes a leader like Zawahiri would make a statement, and at other times individual bombers gave their last words to the world through broadcasts. These tapes were released to Arab media outlets. Finally, the jihadists began posting their own productions on the Internet (Glasser and Coll, 2005).

Operation Iraqi Freedom and the Jihad

On March 19, 2003, President Bush ordered U.S. forces to attack Saddam Hussein, the longtime authoritarian president of Iraq. Officially dubbed **Operation Iraqi Freedom**, the invasion intended to preempt Hussein from launching a terrorist attack on the United States. Two suppositions by the Bush administration supported the invasion: that Iraq was holding weapons of mass destruction and that Hussein had established ties with al Qaeda. The Bush administration feared that Hussein would put weapons of mass destruction in the hands of bin Laden. No weapons of mass destruction were found.

airliner (2001), the murder of a *Wall Street Journal* reporter (2002), and the Bali nightclub bombing (2002). He was captured in March 2003 by Pakistani ISI agents.

sleeper cells
Terrorist cells that operate for long periods doing nothing to stand out from their social surroundings. They become active just before an operation.

Operation Iraqi Freedom
The code name for the 2003 U.S.-led invasion of Iraq. The military operation was code named Cobra II, a reference to George S. Patton's Third Army breakout in France in 1944.

Fawaz Gerges (2006, pp. 17, 266–267) says the invasion of Iraq rejuvenated the jihadist movement. Ironically, the loose confederation of international terrorist groups found a common cause on their home turf. As President Bush declared an end to major combat operations in Iraq, the real battle with the jihadists was just beginning. With their common enemy so close to home, various jihadist groups and individuals made their way to Iraq to attack the United States. Supporters of the Iraq policy believe that Iraq has presented the battleground for America to strike and defeat international terrorists (Wolfowitz, 2004). Critics claim that it has given jihadists the incentive to fight (Gordon and Trainor, 2006, pp. 497–501).

Robert Kagan (2004) argues that whether or not the decision to go to war in Iraq was correct, the long-range focus should be on building international political hegemony there. Kagan also points out that the jihadist network takes strength from two main factors: the dynamic nature of the network and its ability to create so much hatred for the United States that differences between jihadists disappear. When America cooperates with other nations, terrorist networks are disrupted. When jihadists are able to take sanctuary in countries that oppose the United States, it is another story. The United States needs international support, Kagan says, but other nations may not give it. This would be a tragedy, he says, because America is less dangerous than jihadists and other terrorists.

Another opinion regarding the U.S. role in Iraq suggests that the United States has alienated the Arab world and many millions of Muslims for launching the wrong war against the wrong target (M. Lynch, 2003; Albright, 2003). Former secretary of state Madeleine Albright champions this reasoning. Under President George W. Bush, America has taken many actions unilaterally or with minimal international support. Secretary Albright and others argue that the United States must act in conjunction with other nations, especially Islamic countries. This argument maintains that the United States needs to fight terrorism by allying with the international community and alienating terrorists from potential support.

Self-Check

- *How did the allied offensive in Afghanistan impact the jihadist movement?*
- *How do networks differ from hierarchies?*
- *Explain the characteristics of fifth-generation jihadists.*

SUMMARY

- Hezbollah grew when Revolutionary Guards joined Shiites in Lebanon after the 1982 Israeli invasion. Today it has established several different functions. It is a social and welfare organization in southern Lebanon, and it holds seats in the Lebanese parliament. Hezbollah operates a successful militia that engages in military operations and supports terrorism. The group also has an international wing.

- Sunni jihadist organizations embracing umbrella-style organizational structures grew in North Africa during the 1990s. The three major groups were the GIA, IG, and EIJ. They evolved into localized networks, but IG had an affiliated cell in New York City.

- Osama bin Laden returned to Afghanistan in 1996 and formed an alliance with Ayman al Zawahiri. In 1996 bin Laden "declared war" on the United States. In 1998, under Zawahiri's influence, several groups merged to form the international network known generically as al Qaeda.

- Al Qaeda's theology is based on a militarized version of Islam. It is inspired by Sayyid Qutb.

- Bin Laden and Zawahiri decided that internal revolutions had failed, and they turned to the far enemy. Al Qaeda became a loosely organized network of ideological cells, but it maintained a hierarchy in Afghanistan. After an American-led offensive in October 2001 the hierarchy was dispersed, and al Qaeda served to inspire activities around the globe. Most terrorism analysts believe that Zawahiri and possibly bin Laden are trying to reassemble the al Qaeda hierarchy in Pakistan.

- *Eclectic disassociation* is a term used to describe the fifth-generation jihadists inspired by al Qaeda. They are eclectic because many organizational styles change with each operation. Their patterns of operations are dissociated. They form an ad hoc terrorist group, join with local jihadists and criminals, attack, and disperse. The next group to form has little to do with the previous group.

- Jihadists have created their own media outlets to multiply force. Hezbollah uses al Manar television, and fifth-generation jihadists produce videos and propaganda on the Internet.

- After the successful U.S. ground offensive in Iraq ended, several different types of insurgent groups began fighting foreign armies and each other. Jihadists came to Iraq to fight Americans, but they constitute a small percentage of the number of people fighting.

KEY TERMS

ayatollahs (p. 249)
Revolutionary Guards (p. 249)
Ithna Ashari (p. 249)
imam (p. 249)
Al Dawa (p. 251)
Islamic Amal (p. 251)
Sheik Mohammed Hassan Fadlallah (p. 251)
Abbas Musawi (p. 251)
Hassan Nasrallah (p. 251)

Islamic Jihad (p. 251)
Amal (p. 252)
Imad Mugniyah (p. 254)
Shaba farm region (p. 255)
Mohammed Fneish (p. 256)
1985 hijacking of a TWA flight (p. 257)
Argentina in 1992 and 1994 (p. 257)
Algerian Civil War (p. 258)

Salafi Group for Call and Combat (GSPC) (p. 260)
1993 World Trade Center bombing (p. 260)
Sheik Omar Abdel Rahman (p. 260)
Mustafa Hamza (p. 260)
Rafai Taha Masa (p. 261)
near enemy (p. 261)
far enemy (p. 261)
World Islamic Front against Jews and Crusaders (p. 262)
Taliban (p. 262)
Mullah Omar (p. 262)
madrassas (p. 264)

Interservice Intelligence Agency (p. 265)
peace dividend (p. 266)
9/11 Commission (p. 266)
Abdullah Azzam (p. 268)
Desert Shield (p. 271)
Desert Storm (p. 271)
Hassan al Turabi (p. 271)
Mogadishu (p. 271)
eclectic disassociations (p. 274)
Ramzi Youseff (p. 274)
Khalid Sheik Mohammed (p. 274)
sleeper cells (p. 275)
Operation Iraqi Freedom (p. 275)

WRITING ASSIGNMENTS

1. Hezbollah's charter calls for establishing an Islamic republic in Lebanon. Does this mean that there can be no negotiation with Hezbollah leadership? If Hezbollah takes different positions with different audiences, are there opportunities to talk with Hezbollah's leaders? The United States claims that it does not negotiate with terrorists and it officially labels Hezbollah as a terrorist group. Is Hezbollah a terrorist group? If no, how might the United States and other nations communicate with Hezbollah? If yes, how might the United States and Hezbollah communicate? Do you think America has never negotiated with terrorists?

2. Imagine that you are in a political science class. The professor says that the CIA created and paid for al Qaeda. Challenge the professor's assumption. Use information from the program that assisted ISI and U.S. actions after the Soviet-Afghan War. Using the same information, explain why the professor is not completely incorrect.

3. Does the term *eclectic disassociation* help you understand the lack of structure in jihadist networks after the collapse of al Qaeda's hierarchy in October 2001? Why or why not?

Black Tigers parade in Sri Lanka. Old-style hierarchies, umbrella groups, and new terror networks have spread in areas of Africa and Asia.

AP Photo/Gemunu Amarasinghe

Learning Objectives

After you read this chapter you should be able to

- Define the three issues at the root of terrorism in Africa.

- Explain the relative importance of terrorism in light of Africa's other issues.

- Summarize political conditions in western and central Africa.

- Outline the issues surrounding terrorism in the Horn of Africa.

- Explain the multiple sources of conflict in Iraq and Afghanistan.

- Define the three sources of terrorism in central Asia.

- Summarize the political issues surrounding terrorism in Pakistan.

- Explain religious militancy in Bangladesh.
- Outline the history of terrorism in Sri Lanka.
- Describe the sources of terrorism in India.
- Summarize the state of terrorism in Southeast Asia.
- Discuss three recent Japanese experiences with terrorism.

Sub-Saharan Africa

Many years ago, J. Bowyer Bell (1975, pp. 10–18) used the term "endemic terrorism" to describe the state of terrorist violence in Africa. He defined this as a form of terrorism created by artificial divisions of tribes, families, and ethnic groups. When moving south of the Sahara, it is possible to see the extent of endemic terrorism, but problems in sub-Saharan Africa extend beyond terrorism. War, famine, and disease are more pressing. Both children and women are exploited, and totalitarian governments control some countries. Africa is the poorest region on earth.

In western and central Africa, terrorism represents a potential problem. The Horn of Africa has active groups, including a jihadist movement, but even there ethnic cleansing, revolts, slavery, and starvation outweigh the problems presented by terrorism. Africa is suffering from a colonial past, poverty, and a modern epidemic. Some policy makers believe that these issues must be addressed but they are separate from terrorism. Others argue that a comprehensive approach to Africa's massive social problems is a more effective method of controlling terrorism.

Sources of African Terrorism

It is difficult to single out terrorism because Africa is the source of conventional and guerrilla wars, several revolutions, and criminal violence. One of the primary reasons for this is Africa's position in the world. It is the most poverty-stricken region on earth, and the sub-Saharan portion of the continent has negative economic growth. In other words, the countries in the south produce less income year by year. Health conditions in Africa are also the worst on the planet, and the **AIDS pandemic** is creating havoc. There are hundreds of thousands of homeless orphans (Sachs et al., 2004). Tribal violence has led to genocide and countless deaths (see Berkeley, 2001). Child armies, slavery, and starvation are part of the social problems plaguing the region (Singer, 2001; Polack, 2004). Terrorism is one problem among many in Africa.

Thomas P. M. Barnett (2004, p. 351) points out that certain regions have specialized problems. The center of the continent is plagued by tribal strife, and the Horn—the eastern section bordered by the Red Sea and Indian Ocean—witnesses religious and ethnic conflicts. The southwestern coastal countries along the Atlantic Ocean are involved in struggles for resources. There was a recent deadly political racial struggle in South Africa, and there is political turmoil in Zimbabwe. Despite this, Barnett points out that there are large portions of Africa where people are getting along. The continent is not completely awash

AIDS pandemic
The number of people with HIV/AIDS (human immunodeficiency virus/acquired immunodeficiency syndrome). In 2005 Africa had 25.8 million HIV-positive adults and children. Africa has 11.5 percent of the world's population but 64 percent of its AIDS cases. From 1982 to 2005, AIDS claimed 27.5 million African lives (Cook, 2006).

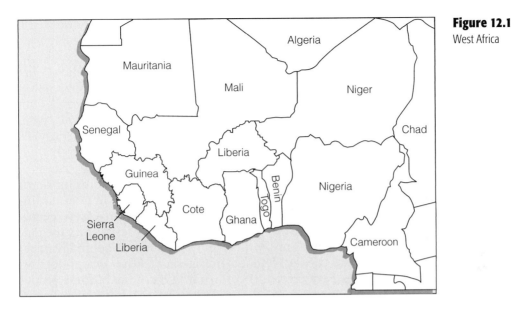

Figure 12.1
West Africa

in violence, and Barnett believes the long-term solution to most African violence, including terrorism, is to bring economic development and stabilization.

Oil Regions

In sub-Saharan Africa most of the oil resources are located in the west (Figure 12.1). These fields are attractive to the United States for several reasons. The oil is **sweet crude**; that is, it has a lower concentration of sulfur and it is easier and cheaper to refine into gasoline. The oil fields are closer to the U.S. East Coast than the Middle East, reducing transportation costs. Finally, Africa is increasing its oil production. It is estimated that by 2020 the United States will purchase one quarter of its oil imports from western Africa (Donnelly, 2005).

Although violence, crime, and warfare threaten oil production, terrorism has not been a major issue. It should be viewed as a potential problem. Princeton Lyman, the former U.S. ambassador to Nigeria, and Stephen Morrison, a specialist in AIDS policy for the Center for Strategic and International Studies (2004), are concerned about the potential for terrorism and America's approach to the areas outside the Horn of Africa and the Middle East. They are critical of America's naïve foreign policy approach to western and central Africa.

Lyman and Morrison argue that U.S. foreign policy has focused on jihadists and the areas where jihadists are most prevalent. Although this is important, they say, it misses the areas where jihadists have tremendous potential and other areas where they can move without scrutiny. This occurs in western and central Africa, areas where criminal networks are in league with corrupt leaders and governments and rebels struggle for power. These situations are exploited by jihadists, but the

sweet crude

A type of oil with less than 0.5 percent sulfur content. Nigeria sits on a large sweet crude field, giving the country potential wealth. The people who live above the oil, however, are poverty stricken, and oil production has been harmful to the environment.

United States has not sufficiently reacted to the situation because it is so closely focused on other areas. The United States does not have a holistic approach to Africa.

Stated more bluntly, Lyman and Morrison do not believe that countries like Nigeria and Liberia appear on the strategic foreign policy radar screen. Nigeria has a population of 133 million, with 67 million Muslims, making it the second largest Islamic country, behind Egypt, in Africa. Its economy is crucial to the United States, and America currently gets 7 percent of its oil imports from Nigeria. Yet America has not paid attention to violence in Nigeria or the rest of western Africa.

From 1999 to 2003 fighting in Nigeria between the Muslim north and the Christian south claimed 10,000 lives. The conflict did not involve established terrorist cells, but the conflict's source is so deeply rooted in the community that terrorism could easily result from the tensions. Lyman and Morrison say this is due to the factors behind regional conflict. There are tribal differences in Nigeria and the surrounding regions, and tribes have created their own armies. Many of these armies have children as recruits. Tribal rivalries intermingle with religious differences, which have become sharper since 1970. In the past, Christians and Muslims tolerated one another, and western African Islam, strongly influenced by local mystical, or Sufi, traditions, was especially tolerant. After 1970, however, Wahhabi missionaries came to the area, and they were extremely critical of the religious practices of western African Muslims. In Nigeria this resulted in an internal struggle among the country's Muslims about the purity of Islam. There is no evidence that terrorist cells have formed, but all of the predictive signs are there.

Lyman and Morrison argue that Liberia, another country in the region, presents a second example of misguided U.S. policy. The **Liberian Civil War**, from which Liberia is only now emerging, fostered criminal networks, corrupt leaders, and local military adventurers. The country's former leader, **Charles Taylor**, was known for corruption. In 2003 it looked like the United States was going to intervene in Liberia's problems, and leaders of all independent armies and militias stated that they would accept a U.S. enforced peace. Instead of intervening, President George W. Bush, under pressure from the military and his vice president, stated that all American efforts would be limited to humanitarian aid. Marines landed but departed in three months. Taylor eventually fell to the **Liberians United for Reconciliation and Democracy (LURD)**. Although not supporting Taylor, Lyman and Morrison believe such actions are shortsighted. When a state fails, they argue, it creates a haven for terrorist groups.

The International Crisis Group (ICG; 2006c) agrees with Lyman and Morrison's approach. In Nigeria an insurgent group emerged in January 2006 to eliminate governmental control of the oil industry. One of its primary tactics has been kidnapping foreign oil workers. Oil production has suffered. Failure to support democracies in other countries leads to further disruptions (see ICG, 2006e). The International Crisis

---

Liberian Civil War

Two episodes of conflict involving rebel armies and militias as well as neighboring countries. The First War, 1989–1996, ended when a rebel army brought Charles Taylor to Monrovia, the capital. The Second War, 1999–2003, toppled Charles Taylor from power. Both wars were characterized by village massacres and conscription of child soldiers.

Charles Taylor

(1948–) A warlord in the First War of the Liberian Civil War and president of Liberia from 1997 to 2003.

Liberians United for Reconciliation and Democracy (LURD)

A revolutionary movement founded in 1999 in western Africa. LURD was instrumental in driving Charles Taylor from power in 2003.

Group (2005b) sees western Africa as a region that is delicately balanced between moderate Islam and an undercurrent of jihadism. If the United States and West in general would approach the area's problems in a way to ensure economic stability, fair and democratic elections, and an end to corruption, a political crisis could be averted. The threat of terrorism can be eliminated with supportive foreign policies, and Africa has much to offer the West. Active diplomacy supporting democracy would prevent terrorism, they argue.

Lyman and Morrison (2004) apply the same logic outside western Africa. In the central region of Africa, tribal conflicts and lack of governmental control have created large lawless areas. Jihadists have exploited this. They have created criminal enterprises and links with criminal organizations to expand their financial structures. In addition to the human tragedies of ethnic cleansings, child exploitation, and slavery, failing states encourage the emergence of a jihadist solution.

Another potential problem in central and western Africa is the **Big Man**. An autocratic ruler—a Big Man—may ally with other countries at crucial times, but he does so only at the expense of the people. A Big Man might be a tempting ally, but he may present a short-term payoff. After a revolution topples the Big Man, such as the 1978–1979 revolution in Iran, the new government may be openly hostile to any country that supported the Big Man. Thomas P. M. Barnett (2004, p. 133) points out another problem. Big Men are often followed by Little Men. In other words, autocrats tend to put their children in power. A distasteful alliance can be carried into the next generation.

For example, Joel Barkan (2004) points out that Kenya is vital to the U.S. struggle against terrorism. It houses several U.S. governmental entities and allows the U.S. military to use its ports. The United States gained its foothold there by courting Kenyan Big Men, who tended to favor their own tribes. In addition, prosperity was based on tribal relations. In 2002 Kenya achieved a hard-won, fragile democracy that terrorism, if allowed to establish itself, could destroy. Barkan concludes that the best way for the United States to fight terrorism in the region is to help Kenya consolidate its democracy. A strong autocratic ruler may be the best ally in the world, but when the ruler falls—they all fall sometime—there is no guarantee the next government will maintain the old alliances. When Western governments support a Big Man, they frequently incur the wrath of common people.

Ted Dagne (2002) has another perspective on American foreign policy in sub-Saharan Africa. Reporting for the Congressional Research Service, Dagne says that the government is aware that Africa represents potential bases for terrorism. He argues that dozens of African governments have voiced their support for the war on terrorism. They have cooperated with investigations and intelligence-gathering efforts, provided bases and staging areas for military forces, and shared intelligence. Because they are aware that Africa might be a haven for terrorist groups, they monitor activities in their own countries. He says that the Bush

Big Man

An anthropological term to describe an important person in a tribe or clan. *Big Man* is sometimes used by political scientists to describe a dictator in a totalitarian government.

administration is pleased with the support it receives from sub-Saharan African governments.

By the same token, Dagne acknowledges concerns among African governments. Some of them feel they are not full partners with the United States. Others feel that although they have given support, the United States has refused to assist them economically. Other leaders express concerns that regions in their own lands might become targets for American military action. Some governments would prefer that international antiterrorist efforts be led by the United Nations, not the United States. The greatest fear is the Big Man. Many Africans believe that the United States will ally with governments that support antiterrorist efforts even if they have poor human rights records.

Rita Abrahamsen (2004) offers an alternative view by focusing on the post-9/11 African policy of the United Kingdom. She states that, unlike the United States, Britain has maintained a moral and humanitarian approach to Africa. Its primary foreign policy efforts have been aimed at expanding economic development and increasing human rights. She is worried that the new U.S. approach in the antiterrorist environment favors security. She admits this is a subtle policy shift but sees it taking shape in Africa. Abrahamsen believes that the long-term security policy would be better served by emphasizing development and human rights. In the long run such an approach is more successful than seeking short-term security objectives. She also believes that Britain's approach emphasizing economic development has been far more productive than America's preoccupation with security.

Over the past few decades France has maintained an African policy that sharply differs from either the United States or the United Kingdom (Gauthier-Villars, 2007). Faced with anticolonial revolts after World War II, France created a special military unit known as the **African Cell**. Its purpose was to extend French influence in the oil- and mineral-rich areas of Africa. It has been used to support Big Men, overthrow governments, and protect tribes loyal to France in times of war. The African Cell operates outside the normal channels of French government and is responsible to neither the legislature nor the courts. It reports directly to the president. Supporters view it as a means to deal with terrorism. Critics think its tactics border on terrorism. When **Nicolas Sarkozy** was elected president of France in 2007, he promised to review the activities of the African Cell.

Terrorism is a threat in western and central Africa. Although Thomas Barnett is correct in saying that the area is not awash in violence, it has been the scene of countless tragedies, mass murders, genocides, and epidemics. Terrorism is not the overriding issue. Hunger, disease, violence, and human rights abuses are. Abrahamsen is probably correct. If the developed nations would aggressively intervene for humanitarian purposes, it would do much to prevent state failures that provide an environment supporting terrorism. The same argument could be made for the Horn of Africa.

African Cell

A French military unit stationed in Africa and France. It retains between 10,000 and 15,000 troops in various African countries, about half its strength, and answers directly to the president of France.

Nicolas Sarkozy

(1955–) The president of France. During the election of 2007, Sarkozy promised to review the activities of the African Cell. Sarkozy is a conservative who seeks closer French ties with the United Kingdom and the United States.

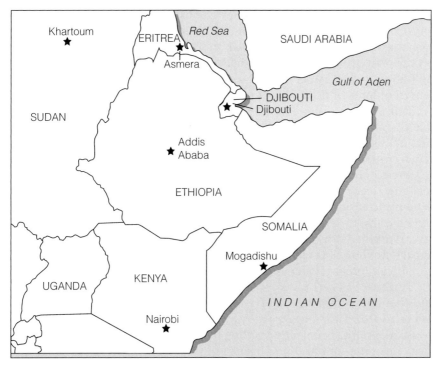

Figure 12.2
Horn of Africa

Horn of Africa
An eastern region of Africa, although some geographers include parts of southwest Asia in their definitions. It usually includes Djibouti, Eritrea, Ethiopia, Kenya, Somalia, and Sudan. Some definitions also include Yemen. The Darfur region is usually implied in the definition.

Terrorism in the Horn

Central and western Africa represent the potential for terrorism, but terrorists are currently active in the **Horn of Africa**, which as a result receives more interest from America (Figure 12.2). After 9/11 the United States worked with governments in the region to create the **Combined Joint Task Force, Horn of Africa (CJTF-HOA)**. Its purpose was similar to the domestic Joint Terrorism Task Forces (JTTFs) in the United States. The CJTF-HOA detects and disrupts terrorist activities before the terrorists can commit violence. Unlike a JTTF, CJTF-HOA relies heavily on military force and national security intelligence. It is not limited to law enforcement activities. Francis Miko (2004) states that although the CJTF-HOA has been effective, terrorism in the Horn will remain a problem because of porous borders, lax security, and political instability.

The United States has been active in the Horn, and its policies support governments in the area, even when friendly governments take repressive actions. Miko (2004) says America justifies its actions by the regional presence of al Qaeda and other jihadist groups. Kenya is the only sub-Saharan country with known al Qaeda cells, but there are many other known jihadist organizations in the Horn. Jihadist activities bleed across Kenya's borders into Somalia. The **Islamic Courts Union**, for example, represents a coalition of groups wanting to rule Somalia with Islamic law.

Debra West (2005) says the United States faces differing terrorist threats in the Horn of Africa, and each threat requires a different policy

Combined Joint Task Force, Horn of Africa (CJTF-HOA)
An American-led counter-terrorist unit combining military, intelligence, and law enforcement assets of several nations in the Horn.

Islamic Courts Union
A confederation of tribes and clans seeking to end violence and bring Islamic law to Somalia. It is opposed by several neighboring countries and internal warlords. Some people feel it is a jihadist organization, but others see it as a grouping of clans with several different interpretations of Islamic law.

response. The most obvious threat comes from the ability of terrorist groups to take immediate action. From bases in the Horn they attack American interests and stage operations. Another threat is the ability of terrorist groups, especially jihadists, to organize in the region. They are able to do this because of two other threats: (1) unstable political environments and (2) a population that supports terrorism against the United States and its allies. The CJTF-HOA is an answer for immediate threats, West believes. Diplomatic relations, foreign aid, and governmental assistance are required to deal with threats from the political environment.

West points to the success of the CJTF-HOA as a measure of tactical effectiveness. When the CJTF-HOA first began to operate in 2002 it sought three terrorist organizations and 25 supporters. By 2004 it had killed or captured 65 terrorists and had identified 550 probable supporters. Working with other military forces, the CJTF-HOA has successfully struck numerous targets. Yet, West concludes, the biggest challenge for American foreign policy is promoting political stability.

Andrew Feickert (2005) says that the CJTF-HOA has been so successful that some observers believe it should be used as a model for the war on terrorism. The struggle against terrorism cannot be measured in conventional military terms, according to this logic, but success comes when American military and intelligence units are able to work hand in hand with local military and police forces. The CJTF-HOA's close relationship with indigenous forces will build a long-term partnership with governments in the Horn. Security forces from local governments can operate in places where American troops cannot go. In a report for Congress, Feickert says that champions of this policy point to the number of terrorists that the CJTF-HOA approach has identified, captured, or killed, but he acknowledges that not everyone agrees with this assessment.

Two people who disagree are John Prendergast and Colin Thomas-Jensen (2007). They argue that the Horn represents the hottest war zone in the world, and it is a region of massive humanitarian crises and ethnic conflicts. Two clusters of conflicts lay at the heart of the matter. The first involves rebellions in Sudan, particularly Darfur. These conflicts have spilled into Uganda, Chad, and the Central African Republic. The second cluster of conflicts involves a dispute between Ethiopia and Eritrea over complicated fighting in Somalia. This includes a new secular faction trying to take power in Mogadishu, Islamic militias, anti-Islamic militias, private armies of united tribes, individual warlords, and terrorist groups. The problems are far beyond simply eradicating terrorism, but American policy has been shortsighted.

Prendergast and Thomas-Jensen believe that political stability will make the situation better and solve terrorism in the long run, but stability involves more than calling out the CJTF-HOA. In fact, by approaching the Horn as a military problem, the United States has actually made the situation worse. The United States has supported authoritarian governments that encourage repression. In addition, foreign policy favors covert military action over long-term diplomacy. This has been a disaster, the authors argue. Nearly 9 million people have been displaced, and the 16 million people who do not have access to aid could become a humanitarian crisis. People are murdered, entire populations are "cleansed," children are taken into slavery, and children are used as soldiers. Prendergast and Thomas-Jensen believe that a long-term policy to stabilize the region is the most effective counterterrorist policy, but they feel the United States has acted without an overall strategy.

The International Crisis Group (2005b, 2005d) summarizes the foreign policy problem from this perspective. The International Crisis Group maintains that the United States stereotypes as jihadists Muslims who want to live under Islamic law. The situation is much more complicated than that. For example, the Islamic Courts Union briefly took power in Somalia in mid-2006 (and lost power in December of the same year). Some analysts immediately feared that Somalia would follow the path of Afghanistan under the Taliban (see Nzwili, 2006). The International Crisis Group says a review of the Courts Union is in order before jumping to this conclusion. It is hardly a jihadist organization, although jihadists are certainly in it. The Courts Union is simply a tribal confederation of leaders who are tired of constant warfare and criminal activity in Somalia. The International Crisis Group warns that if the United States treats the Courts Union like a radical terrorist regime, it will transform into a jihadist organization.

The Horn and its problems engender hot debate because people suffer so greatly in the area and the region contains jihadist terrorists. The Bush administration has tended to militarize the problem of terrorism. People who agree with this approach are more inclined to favor the methods of the CJTF-HOA. Critics of militarization tend to agree with the position of the International Crisis Group. Although both positions have strengths and weaknesses, issues in the Horn reflect the problems of western and central Africa. Social and humanitarian issues present far greater problems than terrorism, yet the violent, unstable political environment makes the area ripe for it.

Self-Check

- *What types of social problems plague Africa?*
- *What are the primary criminal problems in sub-Saharan Africa?*
- *Describe the state of terrorism in the Horn of Africa.*

Unconventional War

In 2001 an American-led coalition struck Afghanistan in an attempt to destroy al Qaeda. Two years later another much smaller coalition, essentially an American and British force with nominal support from other countries, invaded Iraq to topple Saddam Hussein and prevent Iraq from

Figure 12.3

Iraq

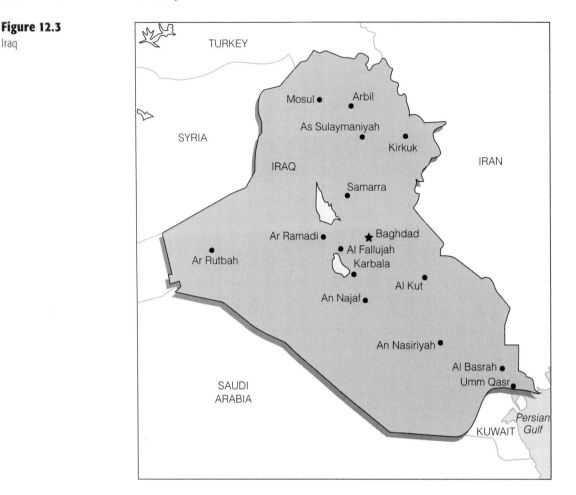

passing weapons of mass destruction to al Qaeda and other jihadists. Both campaigns resulted in unconventional wars. The official governmental stance was that both invasions were part of the Global War on Terrorism (GWOT). However, one was directly related to terrorism, and the other was not.

Iraq

In March 2003 U.S.-led forces launched an invasion of Iraq (Figure 12.3). There were several official objectives. First and foremost, the United States sought to enforce a mandate from the United Nations to end the production and possession of weapons of mass destruction in Iraq. The United States also wanted to end the reign of Saddam Hussein and implement a democratically elected government. Finally, the stated purpose was to end collusion between Saddam Hussein and al Qaeda. The U.S.-led offensive rolled through Iraq, and opposition dissolved. On May 1, 2003, President George W. Bush landed on an aircraft carrier and dramatically announced the end of major combat operations. Neither he nor most Americans understood that major combat operations were only beginning (for a variety of views, see Simon and Stevenson, 2004; Lopez and Coright, 2004; Diamond, 2004; Dobbins, 2005; Gordon and Trainor, 2006; Ricks, 2006).

After the major offensive, the campaign of violence against the United States and its allies was horrendous. Hostages were savagely beheaded, and suicide bombers killed indiscriminately. American soldiers were murdered while roaming through areas thought to be safe. Innocent Iraqis were killed as targets and in accidental strikes, or sometimes they were simply caught in the crossfire. On the other side, American military personnel abused Iraqi prisoners, and tremendous battles occurred around suspected insurgent strongholds, causing injuries and even death to innocent bystanders. Democratic elections took place in Iraq in January 2005, but the Iraq insurgency continued (Benjamin and Simon, 2003; Diamond, 2004).

President Bush and many other governmental officials referred to the insurgents as terrorists. Media outlets vacillated on what to call them; they were "terrorists," "fighters," "suicide bombers," "homicide bombers," "outlawed militiamen," or "followers" of various leaders. Both the administration and the media identified Tawhid and Ansar al Islam as two of the terrorist organizations fighting Americans and claimed that al Qaeda allies had come to Iraq. There seemed to be no clear enemy (Benjamin and Simon, 2003).

There are terrorist organizations in Iraq, and there are terrorists who kidnap and murder soldiers, diplomats, journalists, and businesspersons from several nations. Yet the insurgency in Iraq is not simply terrorism. The most helpful way to think about the insurgency is to look at different categories of groups opposing the occupation and the Iraqi government and to consider the differences in cultures (U.S. Army, 2003).

The United States and allied forces are not engaged in a battle against Iraqis in general or against one group of Iraqis in particular. There are three main insurgent groups. The first is composed of displaced Baathists who were part of Saddam Hussein's regime (Benjamin and Simon, 2003). Although some of these people have been incorporated in the new Iraqi government, others remain outside. Many Baathists believe they can reclaim power. At times they use terrorist tactics—car bombs and murder—but they see themselves engaged in a guerrilla campaign in the style of Frantz Fanon.

The second group of insurgents is composed of Iraqis who want the United States to leave their country. Sunni militants who do not belong to the Baathists generally fight along tribal lines. Militant Shiites want to make Iraq an Islamic republic like Iran. The most noted militant Shiite leader is Muqtada al Sadr with his Mahdi Army. Al Sadr is a product of the Najaf seminary, where many Hezbollah and Iranian Islamic scholars were trained. Al Sadr is not overly popular among the upper classes, but his name is revered among the poor. Many Shiites oppose his brand of

Islam and do not want to see an Islamic republic (Raman, 2004). Others think he is a renegade. The Iranians approve of al Sadr and sent him support. For the most part, al Sadr's followers avoid terrorist tactics, and he wants to build political legitimacy. This second group of insurgents also includes Iraqi criminals who do not care about the country's leadership and engage in crime to make a profit.

The third group of insurgents is composed of jihadists who have come to Iraq to fight the United States. There are two classes of jihadists. Some flock from surrounding areas to fight as guerrillas. If they use terrorism, it is highly selective and its purpose is to kill Americans and their supporters. The other group is composed of terrorists within an al Qaeda–style umbrella. Some, such as Abu Musab al Zarqawi, who was killed by American forces in 2006, were trained in al Qaeda camps (Thompson, 2003). Others have an ideological link to al Qaeda and affiliated groups, but they exist on their own. Terrorism is the primary tactic of the jihadists, and they are behind many of the murderous kidnappings and suicide bombings. America's confrontation with this third group of terrorists is a fight against terrorism (A. Cronin, 2003).

The three insurgent groups do not share a common vision for the future of Iraq and they are frequently at odds with each other (Paz, 2004). The Shiite organizations condemned Zarqawi's kidnap-murders, and al Sadr has intervened in other kidnappings to have hostages freed. Power struggles are occurring in Iraq among several different groups.

The cultural factors behind the violence in Iraq become extremely important. The boundaries of Iraq, and most parts of the Middle East, are the product of European boundary settlements at the end of World War I. The lines remain somewhat artificial today, and they frequently cross a more important boundary—the one delineating tribes. Families and extended-family groups are one of the most important aspects of Arab culture (Nydell, 2002, pp. 91–99).

Raphael Patai (2002, pp. 78–100) says that ideally Arabs see their ancestors as one of two great tribes in Arabia, one from the north and the other from the south. Although this idea is part of the Arab myth or sacred story, it is a practical part of the situation in Iraq today. Relations begin within the immediate family and reach out to extended families, clans, and tribes. These family ties are so crucial that when a U.S.-dominated coalition of non-Arab nations invaded an Arab country, tribal loyalties came to the forefront. An old Arab folk saying illustrates the overriding importance of family ties in Arab culture and the response to "the stranger": "I and my brothers against my cousins; I and my cousins against the stranger" (Patai, 2002, p. 22).

When such cultural aspects combine with the various ideologies motivating insurgent groups, it is possible to see that a major portion of the insurrection does not involve terrorism. At the same time, many of the actions against Americans and their allies do involve terrorism. Fighting takes place on multiple levels. The tactics that work against terrorists do not work against guerrillas or conventional militias. If the United States

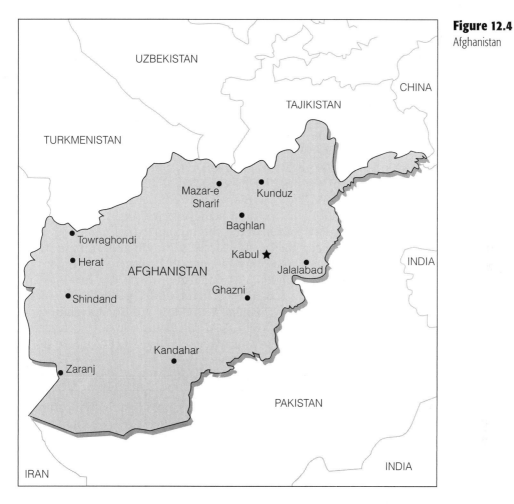

Figure 12.4
Afghanistan

is to end major combat operations in Iraq, it will need to implement a strategy that addresses the major issues that insurgents and terrorist groups use to justify violence. Not all of the enemies can be combined into a simple category, and the battle is not merely a war against terrorism. Failure to make such distinctions may lead to defeat (S. Hoffman, 2003; Wheeler, 2003).

Afghanistan

Operation Enduring Freedom began on October 7, 2001. Like the Iraq invasion, it was a counterterrorist operation using military force against an enemy country. Unlike the Iraq invasion, the campaign in Afghanistan had several different objectives. To begin, Afghanistan hosted the terrorist group responsible for 9/11. The United States demanded the arrest of al Qaeda members and leadership, but the government of Afghanistan refused. American-led forces entered Afghanistan with international support (Figure 12.4). Old allies and old enemies offered as-

Operation Enduring Freedom

The code name for the American-led coalition's military intervention in Afghanistan.

sistance and troops. It was truly a coalition of international proportion (United Kingdom, House of Commons, 2001). The American forces attacked with small, highly mobile combat teams that quickly took objectives and forced al Qaeda leadership into hiding (Shumway, 2005).

The Afghanistan invasion enjoyed international support because most of the world community felt that America was justifiably responding to the 9/11 attacks. **NATO** even took command of operations in eastern Afghanistan in 2006, assuming control of 12,000 American troops. Afghanistan was an allied effort. Civilians did suffer heavy casualties, causing them to turn against coalition forces at times. They also suffered from the variety and deadly capacity of new munitions (Benini and Moulton, 2004). The operation initially hinged on the belief that a small, highly mobile force could achieve objectives. Some members of the Defense Department believed the initial Afghan operation, with its mobility and speed, had been a success (Gordon and Trainor, 2006, p.53), despite bin Laden and others escaping. The other side argues that counterinsurgency campaigns take many troops who can relate to and support the civilian infrastructure (Conetta, 2001, pp. 25–27; Petraeus, 2006). Critics maintain that the invasion unduly punished Afghan civilians, destabilized the region, and failed to capture top al Qaeda terrorists, including Osama bin Laden and Ayman al Zawahiri (Conetta, 2001, pp. 12–25).

The purpose here is not to discuss counterinsurgency, but to place Afghanistan within the context of terrorism in central Asia. Three issues appear. First, in terms of a network, al Qaeda and jihadist sympathizers were able to reconstitute leadership in the eastern areas of Afghanistan and tribal regions of Pakistan (Schuster, 2006). Second, their ability to inspire or directly control the network destabilizes the area and gives the jihadists a long reach (see Scheuer, 2006). Finally, as in Iraq, Taliban and other jihadist forces use terrorist tactics against military forces in an unconventional role. Military forces can handle this, but they literally fight a counterterrorist campaign (Barnett, 2004, pp. 315–327).

NATO

The North Atlantic Treaty Organization, which is headquartered in Brussels, Belgium. Formed in 1949, it was a cold war alliance between the United States and Western Europe against the Soviet Union and Warsaw Pact. NATO has expanded into five eastern European countries since 1991, and it remains the primary military alliance between the United States and Europe.

Self-Check

- *Why did fighting in Iraq shift from conventional to unconventional warfare?*
- *Compare fighting in Iraq to fighting in Afghanistan.*
- *Why would General David Petraeus argue that troops must relate to local civilians when fighting an insurgency?*

▼ Asia

Aside from the areas discussed earlier in the text, Asia has witnessed further growth of terror networks in the early part of the twenty-first century. Even earlier, in central Asia five former communist states—

Figure 12.5
Central Asia, the "Stans,"
and Xinjiang

Turkmenistan, Uzbekistan, Tajikistan, Kyrgyzstan, and Kazakhstan—
moved from the Soviet orbit into self-government shortly after the fall of
the Soviet Union (Figure 12.5). Islamicists emerged in these states, and
some of them grew militant. Bangladesh has militant movements, and
Nepal is home to a Maoist rebellion. India and Pakistan squabble over
ownership of Jammu and Kashmir, and jihadists moved into the area.
Both countries also faced internal terrorist movements. Indonesia became the breeding ground for several jihadist organizations, and one of
them, Jamaat Islamiyya, spread to Thailand, Singapore, and Myanmar
(also known as Burma). The Philippines faced its own rebellions based
in nationalism and religion. Many of these networks are loosely tied to
jihadist networks, but local issues dominate agendas.

Central Asia

Ahmed Rashid (2002, pp. 46–56) describes the growth of terrorism in
central Asia, noting that as the Russian Federation formed after the 1991
breakup of the Soviet Union, the Russians wanted little to do with their
old possessions in central Asia. Turkmenistan, Uzbekistan, Tajikistan,
Kyrgyzstan, and Kazakhstan, all of which lie north of Pakistan and
Afghanistan, struggled for political existence as jihadist organizations
joined resurgent Islamic movements. The new governments ended up
as authoritarian regimes far removed from the common people. Rashid
believes this led to unrest across the region, and the climate became ripe
for religious radicals to gain influence.

Rashid argues that the situation after 1991 gave rise to three movements. The Hizb ul Tahrir (HT), a Palestinian organization, moved to cen-

Islam Karimov

(1938–) President of
Uzbekistan since 1991.
Karimov is known for
authoritarian leadership
and repression of political
dissent.

Fergana Valley

A rich farming region in
central Asia that lies inside
Uzbekistan, Kyrgyzstan,
and Tajikistan. It partially
borders China's Xinjiang
province.

Uighars

A Turkish ethnic group in
central Asia. Many Uighars
seek an autonomous state
within China's Xinjiang
province.

**Islamic Renaissance
Party (IRP)**

A Tajikistan religious political party. Banned in the
Tajik Civil War, it reemerged
as a political party in 1998.

tral Asia to preach conversion to Islam. The group saw this area as a fer-
tile ground for Islamic converts. A second group, the Islamic Movement
of Uzbekistan (IMU), proposed a violent jihad against **Islam Karimov**,
the dictator of Uzbekistan. Disillusioned HT followers gravitated toward
the IMU, and the IMU gained strength in the **Fergana Valley**, a rich
agricultural area shared by Tajikistan, Uzbekistan, and Kyrgyzstan and
that is important for any political group that wishes to have control
of central Asia. A third group of jihadists appeared from western China's ethnic Turkmen. The **Uighars** organized to revive an eighteenth-
century Islamic state in China's Xinjiang province. Using Kyrgyzstan
and Kazakhstan as a base, they operate in China.

HT is growing in central Asia and spreading to the Middle East, Turkey, and Europe (Rotar, 2004b). One of the most powerful groups in
central Asia, it is banned by most Muslim governments. Growing from
a Palestinian missionary organization in 1953, HT took root in central
Asia and began to spread after the fall of the Soviet Union. Its purpose
was evangelism, and it preached the peaceful formation of the caliphate,
although HT leadership believes the caliphate can be centered in central
Asia instead of Arab lands. In official literature and pronouncements,
HT denounces violence. Yet there appears to be a struggle inside the
group, and it may split over disagreements about peace versus violence
(Rotar, 2004a).

Madeleine Gruen (2004) explains the demographic expansion and
recruitment patterns of HT. It targets young males who feel abandoned
by society. Claiming that Islam is under attack, it calls potential recruits
to join in the struggle for the caliphate. HT groups have spread to the
Middle East, Europe, and the United States using aggressive personal
recruiting and an Internet campaign. In addition to young marginal-
ized men, HT targets local Islamic leaders and law enforcement officers.
Although evangelical and peaceful on the surface, it tolerates neither democracy nor other religions. Some researchers believe it may encourage
violence (see Novikov, 2004).

When HT appeared in Europe, it raised concerns. The Russian Federation, having witnessed HT's operations in central Asia, banned it. The
German government soon followed, and officials in the United Kingdom
fear that HT glorifies and encourages terrorism while claiming to be
peaceful (Strieff, 2006). Rohan Gunaratna (2004) points to the central
issue of HT. It may proclaim nonviolence, but members of several violent
terrorist groups were members of HT. In addition, some members of the
IMU, a self-described violent group, have been found with HT literature.

According to the Uzbek government, HT has been behind violence
and terrorism in Uzbekistan, Tajikistan, and Kyrgyzstan. Many analysts doubt this claim and blame much of the violence on another group,
the IMU. The origins of IMU can be traced to the Fergana Valley after
the collapse of the Soviet Union. According to Mark Burgess (2002), the
movement began when a group of young Muslims approached the communist mayor of Namangan, the second-largest city in Uzbekistan, and

demanded the right to build a mosque. The young men called themselves the **Islamic Renaissance Party (IRP)**. The mayor refused and the men seized Communist Party headquarters in Namangan. Two IRP leaders, **Tohir Yoldash** and **Jumaboi Khojaev**, tried to place Namangan under Islamic law and enforce a strict Islamic dress code. The Uzbek government reacted by moving against Yoldash and Khojaev, and the IRP ordered its members not to take violent action against the government. Feeling abandoned, Yoldash and Khojaev broke with the IRP. Khojaev assumed the nom de guerre **Juma Namangani** and formed the IMU, leading it against Uzbekistan.

Yoldash and Namangani wished to restore the caliphate in central Asia and believed they had the support to do so. They formed a new organization, but the Uzbek government moved against it. Members of the new organization were arrested, but Yoldash and Namangani fled to Tajikistan. When the **Tajik Civil War** began, Yoldash fled to Afghanistan and Namangani joined the Tajik Islamicists. Yoldash became an ambassador of sorts for the Central Asian Caliphate movement. Burgess says that he established contact with Pakistan's ISI and raised funds from Saudi Arabia. The funds fortified the conservative caliphate, or **Deobandi**, movement.

In the meantime, Namangani attained a reputation as a fierce warrior. A former Soviet paratrooper in the Soviet-Afghan War, he fought hard for the Islamist forces in the Tajik Civil War. When the war ended, the Islamists entered the Tajik government in a power-sharing arrangement. Burgess says that Namangani went to Afghanistan to join the Taliban government somewhat impressed with the Tajik settlement. He thought he could establish the same type of power-sharing relationship in Uzbekistan, and this would be a prelude to a religious government. After all, the Taliban had taken control of Afghanistan. Namangani believed Islamist movements in other countries would become successful, and they could unite into a single caliphate after victory. He joined Yoldash to form the IMU in Kabul in 1998 (see Weitz, 2004).

The IMU launched its campaign the next year with bombs in Tashkent, the capital of Uzbekistan, almost killing Islam Karimov, the leader of Uzbekistan. Karimov struck back and arrested its members. Namangani moved to Kyrgyzstan and made attacks there, catching the military by surprise. In 2000 Karimov's forces moved to the Fergana Valley in conjunction with Kyryzstan security forces, and both countries pressured Tajikistan to clamp down on Namangani. Mattais Ericksson (2006) says that Karimov demonized the entire religious movement, including the IMU, calling them Wahhabi extremists. This drew Russian sympathy as the IMU battled Uzbek police and military forces.

After it received between $2 million and $5 million for the safe return of the kidnapped Japanese geologists, the IMU seemed to notice for the first time that it could raise money through crime. Namangani began a twofold campaign. He continued terrorist activities to create the caliphate, and he increasingly turned to crime for money. This brought

Tohir Yoldash

(1967–) A founder of the Islamic Movement of Uzbekistan, now associated most closely with external relations, funding, and political leadership.

Jumaboi Khojaev

(1969–2001) The main founder and military leader of the Islamic Movement of Uzbekistan. Khojaev is better known by his nom de guerre, Juma Namangani. He was killed in a battle with U.S. forces in November 2001.

Juma Namangani

Nom de guerre of Jumaboi Khojaev.

Tajik Civil War

(1992–1997) The war fought between the government of Tajikistan and a confederation of opponents known as the United Tajik Opposition. The war resulted in democratic elections and power sharing between different political and religious groups. More than 100,000 people were killed during the war.

Deobandi

A conservative religious school of thought originating in India and influential in central Asia. Many observers equate its conservative positions with Saudi Arabian Wahhabism.

a closer alliance with the Taliban and narcotics traffickers in Afghanistan. He also developed ties with al Qaeda and possibly personal links with Osama bin Laden. Yoldash continued as an ambassador at large, raising funds and building relations with the ISI and religious conservatives throughout the Islamic world. Despite Uzbekistan's efforts, the IMU maintained a base of an estimated 300 fighters and joined the Taliban in a fight against the **Northern Alliance**. Things fell apart after al Qaeda attacked the United States on September 11 (Burgess, 2002; Weitz, 2004; Cornell, 2005).

When the U.S.-led coalition struck Afghanistan in October 2001, the IMU fought for the Taliban. American forces killed Namangani in heavy fighting a month later, and the IMU went underground. Its operations are diminished and have been limited to bombing and ambushes in Uzbekistan, Kyrgyzstan, and the Fergana Valley. Yoldash remains its primary spokesperson, probably from Pakistan. Karimov's government is quick to blame both IMU and HT for all political opposition (International Crisis Group, 2005c).

Svante Cornell (2005) has an interesting interpretation of IMU activities. Instead of seeing the IMU as a terrorist group, he points to a transformation that took place after the Japanese kidnappings of 1999. Cornell believes the IMU changed its focus from political terrorism to criminal networking. The IMU began raising funds through kidnapping, and then it turned to a larger cash opportunity, narcotics. Joining the Taliban, Cornell says, the IMU became narcotics traffickers. It may be doing so to raise funds for an international jihad—a concept abhorrent to mainstream Muslims—or it may simply enjoy the fruits of criminal profits. Cornell concludes that an aggressive counterterrorist policy in central Asia should include emphasis on criminal networks and drug trafficking. Despite rhetoric to the contrary, the jihadists are organized criminals.

China's Problems in Xinjiang

After September 11, China was eager to join America's "war on terror." Beijing claims that international jihadists, trained in Afghanistan and Pakistan, are attempting to overthrow Chinese rule in the Xinjiang (New Frontier) province and establish an Islamic state. In 2003 China asked for international assistance in clamping down on what the government claims to be its own "jihadist terrorists," Uighar nationalists who believe Xinjiang is their homeland. Although the Chinese communists link the Uighars to al Qaeda and the 9/11 attacks, the movement pre-dates al Qaeda by 245 years (Lufti, 2004).

The Uighars are ethnic Turkmen, mostly Sufi Muslims, and they have lived in and governed parts of the Xinjiang province for 200 years (Figure 12.6). Many of them are fighting to become independent of China. Chien-peng Chung (2002) says the ethnic Uighars are mostly Islamic mystics who are inspired by the collapse of the Soviet Union, not Osama bin Laden. As the former central Asian Soviet republics gained autonomy after 1991, the Uighars saw it as an opportunity to reassert their

Northern Alliance

A military-political organization formed in 1996 in northern Afghanistan to fight the Taliban. During the early part of Operation Enduring Freedom, the Northern Alliance fought closely with U.S. Special Forces. Osama bin Laden ordered suicide bombers to kill Ahmad Masood, then general of the Northern Alliance, just before the 9/11 attacks. It was composed mainly of Tajiks, Uzbeks, and Afghan (Hazara) Shiites.

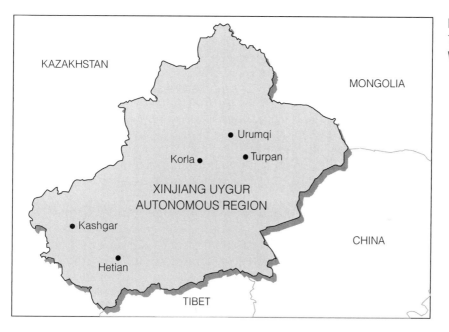

Figure 12.6
The Region the Uighars Wish to Be Autonomous

independence. Separatists launched a terrorist campaign in the Xinjiang province aimed at throwing the Chinese out. Despite their best efforts, Chung says, the Chinese have not been able to eradicate the rebellion.

China annexed the area in 1759, and the first uprising came in 1865, lasting twelve years. Chung says the revolt set the stage for Muslim independence from China, which the Uighars achieved two times, 1931–1934 and 1944–1949, calling their land East Turkestan (see Figure 12.5). The communist Chinese brutally repressed the Uighars and reasserted control in 1949. The Chinese have settled the area with ethnic Chinese, displacing the Uighars, in an effort to assimilate the area. In 1949 the area was 90 percent Uighar, but it may be less than 50 percent today. Displaced Uighars throughout the world support the separatists. Beijing has asked Washington to list militant Uighar organizations as terrorist groups, and the United States has been sympathetic to Chinese demands. Washington needs Beijing as an ally.

Although one of the militant groups fighting for independence trained in Afghanistan, the majority of militants are not jihadists. To be sure, some separatists are terrorists. Bombings and assassinations have cost almost 200 lives and 600 casualties. Ahmed Lufti (2004) says it is important to remember that China is experiencing a terrorist campaign. Aside from religious differences causing strife, China fights for Xinjiang because it has China's largest oil and gas reserves. The growing Chinese economy needs its resources, but the Uighars feel it is their country. Fighting continues. Groups based in Kyrgyzstan and Kazakhstan raid across the Chinese border, and internal groups run their own campaigns.

Chung says that, although this is terrorism, there are two problems with that classification. Most Uighar terrorism is not part of the jihadist movement. Uighars are not fighting an international jihad for a caliphate; they want independence. The greater problem, however, is that many of the separatists are not violent and they do not endorse terrorism. Chung says they only want independence. Through the process of labeling, the Chinese have deemed all expressions of Uighar separatism as terrorism based in the jihadist movement. The United States, disinclined to lose China's support against central Asian terrorism, is reluctant to criticize China when it justifies repression in the name of counterterrorism.

The Maoist Rebellion in Nepal

Brad Adams (2005), director of the Asia Division of Human Rights Watch, points to a sad situation in Nepal that involves terrorism in the forms of revolution and repression. Over the past ten years more than 12,000 people have died in a war between a Maoist revolutionary group and the Nepalese government. Both sides engage in horrid human abuses, Adams says. The government, in the person of the authoritarian **King Gyanendra**, unleashed the military after taking the throne in 2001. It conducts summary executions, torture, and abductions. The Communist Party of Nepal responds by conducting its own abductions and executions. The population is caught in the middle. If they side with the government, rebels label them as "class enemies" and they are liable to be murdered. If they give in to rebel demands for food and shelter, governmental forces punish them.

King Gyanendra
(1947–) The king of Nepal. After the attack and murder of several members of the royal family, Gyanendra became king of Nepal in 2001. Gyanendra took complete power in 2005 to fight the Maoist rebellion. In the spring of 2006 he was forced to return power to parliament.

Nepal's problems do not follow the path of other forms of terrorism in Asia. The Nepalese government gave out the impression that its people were happy, spiritually enlightened citizens. Adams says the reality was much different, and a small group of powerful elites ruled the country in conjunction with the king. Faced with a series of nationwide strikes, the monarchy allowed establishment of opposing political parties in 1990, but this led to a series of unstable governments. A civil war started in 1996 when Maoists launched attacks in different parts of the country. King Gyanendra, abandoning attempts to expand democratic government, took direct control of Nepal in February 2005, cutting Nepal off from the rest of the world. The result has been a bitter circle of revolution and repression.

The government and the Maoists signed a peace agreement in late 2006, with both sides promising to agree to a power-sharing arrangement and to write a new constitution. The International Crisis Group (2007b) believes the only way the process will work is if the Maoists control the extremists in their own ranks. Whereas the government has concluded that it cannot continue the war, the Maoists are divided. If all the parties agree to share power, the International Crisis Group believes, the militant factions of the Maoists will find it difficult to back away. If Maoist leaders cannot control their more radical members, however, then the violent cycle of terrorism and counterterrorism will continue.

Self-Check

- *What are the major causes of terrorism in central Asia?*
- *What issues separate the Uighars from the Chinese?*
- *How do both the government and the rebels support forms of terrorism in Nepal?*

Terrorism on the Indian Subcontinent

The Indian subcontinent includes Pakistan, Bangladesh, Sri Lanka, and India. Although the jihadist movement is one of the dominating features of terrorism in the region, each country has its own specific problems. Pakistan is caught amid tribal tensions, a strong jihadist movement, potential conflict with India, and the delicate internal problem of cooperating with the United States against jihadists. Bangladesh has witnessed growing religious extremism. India has problems in a disputed province with Pakistan, internal religious strife, and international religious terrorists. Sri Lanka has been home to an ethnic revolt for the last two decades.

Pakistan

Two international issues dominate Pakistan's relations with the United States and the problem of terrorism. Leon Hadar (2002) summarizes these as the nuclear and tactical dimensions of Pakistani decision making. To begin, Pakistan is the only Islamic country with nuclear capabilities, and it has shared technology with other nations. While the West lives in fear of a radical regime gaining control of atomic weapons, Pakistan already has them. Second, after 9/11 Pakistani president **Pervez Musharraf** became an ally of the United States. In a televised address to the Pakistani people he explained that this was a tactical decision. Pakistan could either accept America as an ally or confront it as an invader. The United States was coming after Islamic extremism, and one of the paths was through Pakistan (Figure 12.7).

Pakistan's efforts to curb terrorism are complicated by dissenting views. Some Pakistani leaders support terrorism, some want to establish the caliphate while rejecting terrorism, and some want to fight the jihadists. The Council on Foreign Relations (2005) summarizes the issues well. Musharraf has allowed Coalition forces fighting in Afghanistan to enter Pakistani airspace, allowed American personnel to operate within its borders, and had its military conduct counterterrorist operations, especially in the northwest where al Qaeda, Taliban, and other jihadist forces are housed. Musharraf does not have the support of his people for allowing these measures. He walks a fine line every time he takes actions against terrorism.

The International Crisis Group (2006e, 2006g, 2007a) points to another internal problem. Pakistan is not so much a modern country as

Pervez Musharraf

(1943–) The president of Pakistan. A career army officer, Musharraf took power in a 1999 military coup and declared himself president in 2001. After 9/11 he sought closer relations with the United States, while trying to mollify sources of domestic religious strife.

Figure 12.7

Pakistan: States and Tribal Areas

North-West Frontier Province (NWFP)

One of four Pakistani states, inhabited primarily by ethnic Pashtuns. Several areas of the NWFP are controlled by tribes, and jihadists operate in the area. Peshawar, NWFP's capital, served as a base for organizing several mujahideen groups in the Soviet-Afghan War.

Waziristan

Literally, the land of the Waziris, a tribal region between the North-West Frontier Province and Balochistan. Waziri tribes clashed with the Pakistan Army from 2004 to 2006, and they support several jihadist operations in Afghanistan and Pakistan. Al Qaeda and Taliban forces operate in Waziristan.

Balochistan

The largest of four states in Pakistan dominated by the Baloch tribe. Many Balochs are fighting a guerrilla war against the Pakistan Army in a dispute over profits from natural resources. The central government is creating a deepwater port and international trade center in Gwadar, Pakistan's principal seaport, and displacing many Balochs.

it is a modern series of tribal confederations. Pakistan formed in 1947 when British rule in India and the region ended. Divided into East and West, East Pakistan revolted in 1971 and formed the new country of Bangladesh. The Pakistan Army, probably the most respected and certainly the most powerful institution in the country, is the power behind the president's office. The jihadist movement is strong in the **North-West Frontier Province** and strongest in the province's tribal area **Waziristan**. Balochs are staging a revolt in **Balochistan**, and two major religious parties resent Musharraf's relationship with the United States. Bombings, kidnappings, and terrorist assaults from multiple groups are commonplace.

There is also tension between Pakistan and India all along their border, especially in the area of **Jammu and Kashmir**, where both countries claim sovereignty (Figure 12.8). Kashmir is a flashpoint because Pakistan and Muslim residents want the area under Islamic control, whereas India sees Kashmir as part of a secular multiethnic state. The ISI has supported

Figure 12.8

India, Pakistan, and Jammu and Kashmir

some of the Islamic groups operating in Kashmir, and Pakistan accuses India of attacks on Muslims. The Council on Foreign Relations (2006) says that Kashmir has its own homegrown Muslim terrorists, and international jihadists have also come to the area.

Bangladesh

The ports of Bangladesh have become centers for international crime, including drug trafficking and illegal weapons trade, and the country has a strong internal jihadist movement. Wilson John (2005) concludes that this makes Bangladesh an ideal place for militant religion to emerge. Radical religious parties have grown over the past decade, fueled by an increase in madrassas funded by Saudi Arabia and other Gulf States.

John believes the growth of militant fundamentalism threatens Bangladeshi political stability and promotes terrorism. The militant religious climate has spawned the birth of ul-Jihad ul-Islami (Islamic Jihad), a local group that John believes is the Southeast Asian wing of al Qaeda.

Jammu and Kashmir

A mountainous region in northern India claimed by India and Pakistan. It has been the site of heavy fighting during three wars between India and Pakistan in 1947–1948, 1971, and 1999. Kashmir is artificially divided by a line of control (LOC), with Pakistani forces to the north and India's to the south. India and Pakistan made strides toward peace after 2003, but many observers believe the ISI supports jihadist operations in the area.

> **EXPANDING THE CONCEPT**
>
> ## The Sri Lankan Conflict
>
> *The Issue.* In 1948 the British granted Sri Lanka independence. The island was inhabited by the dominant Sinhalese and the Tamils. Although the constitution granted Tamils representation in the government and civil service, by 1955 they felt they were being systematically excluded from Sri Lanka's economic life.
>
> *The Group.* As ethnic tensions increased, some Tamils turned to violence. The Liberation Tigers of Tamil Eelam (LTTE, or Tamil Tigers) formed in 1976 to fight for the Tamil minority.
>
> *The Campaign.* The Tigers began a campaign against the Sri Lankan Army, and they targeted India when the Indian prime minister tried to bring peace by deploying security forces. The LTTE is known for kidnapping young children and socializing them in LTTE camps. The Tigers also became masters of assassination and suicide bombings. The LTTE was the first modern secular group to use suicide bombers. Many members live in a virtual death cult, and the Black Tigers, the suicide wing of the LTTE, are known for carrying cyanide capsules around their necks when they attack.
>
> *The Cease-fire.* The LTTE agreed to a cease-fire in December 2001 and began peace negotiations in 2002. Although occasional outbreaks of violence have occurred, many experts believed the LTTE was suffering from a lack of resources.
>
> *Renewed Fighting.* Hostilities renewed in late 2006. After four years of relative peace, the Sinhalese refused to recognize a Tamil homeland. Both sides began sporadic fighting and terrorism returned to Sri Lanka.
>
> *Source*: Council on Foreign Relations, 2004; ICG, 2006f.

Of more concern, he says, is the creation of the Harkat ul-Jihad (Jihad Organization), a clone of ul-Jihad ul-Islami. In addition to terrorist violence, these groups threaten to bring a larger revolution to Bangladesh. He also fears the strong presence of HT because its infrastructure tends to intersect with local radical groups. If crime and corruption problems overwhelm Bangladesh's weak government, the religious militants have their standard answer. It is the same answer the Taliban offered Afghanistan (see ICG, 2006b).

Sri Lanka

The Liberation Tigers of Tamil Eelam (LTTE, or Tamil Tigers), have been fighting for an independent homeland for nearly 3 million **Tamils** in northern and eastern Sri Lanka (see Expanding the Concept: The Sri Lankan Conflict). The LTTE has waged a guerrilla campaign using terrorism as both a prelude to guerrilla warfare and a way to support uni-

Tamils
An ethnic minority in southern India and Sri Lanka. The Tamils in Sri Lanka are primarily Hindu, and the Sinhalese majority mostly Buddhist. Ethnicity, however, not religion, defines most of the conflict between the two groups.

1972	New constitution favors Buddhist Sinhalese.	The Sri Lankan Civil War
1983	Anti-Tamil riots; Tamils hunted and killed.	
1987	First LTTE suicide bombing.	
1991	Indian prime minister Rajiv Gandhi killed by a suicide bomber.	
1996	Suicide bomber kills ninety-one people at Colombo Central Bank.	
2002	Government and Tamil Tigers sign a cease-fire.	
2004	Cease-fire threatened when a tsunami kills thousands.	
2006	Fighting renews.	

Sources: Wall Street Journal Research Staff, January 2005; International Crisis Group, 2006f.

formed guerrillas in the field. They have killed thousands and assassinated prominent political figures, such as Indian prime minister **Rajiv Gandhi** and President **Ranasinghe Premadasa** of Sri Lanka. They also continue to attack moderate Tamils who oppose their cause. The basis of ethnic conflict is exacerbated by struggles between Hindus and Muslims. The struggle for Sri Lanka has been a long, dirty, and terrible war (Timeline 12.1: The Sri Lankan Civil War).

Manoj Joshi (1996) traces the struggle's origins to the autonomy India gained at the end of World War II. As India sought to bring internal peace among Hindus and Muslims, the island of Sri Lanka (formerly known as Ceylon) faced a similar problem. In addition to religious differences, the Tamil minority in Sri Lanka was concerned about maintaining its ethnic identity among the Sinhalese majority. Tamils along the southeastern coast of India supported the Sri Lankan Tamils in this quest (Figure 12.9). As the Sri Lankan government was formed, some Tamils found themselves in positions of authority. Although they accounted for only 17 percent of Sri Lanka's population, the Tamils were well represented in the bureaucracy. This changed in 1955.

Claiming that Tamils dominated the Sri Lankan government, the Sinhalese majority forced the government to adopt a Sinhalese-only policy. Tamils began to grumble, and some spoke of violence. A Tamil assassin killed the Sinhalese leader in 1959, setting the stage for further violence. Seeking sanctuary in the Tamil region of India, militant Tamils filtered across the short expanse of ocean from Sri Lanka to India to wage a low-level terrorist campaign through 1975. Spurred by their successes, they began larger operations.

The Tamil experience was similar to the situation in Ireland. Buoyed by religious differences and ethnic support, Tamil separatists could begin a guerrilla campaign by waging terrorist war. Their ethnic support base gave them the opportunity to do so. In 1975 **Velupillai Pirapaharan**, a young Tamil militant, took advantage of the situation and formed the LTTE. (*Eelam* means "homeland.") Pirabhakaran faced problems similar to those of other terrorists. He had to raise money, which he did through

Rajiv Gandhi
(1944–1991) Prime minister of India from 1984 until 1991, when he was assassinated by an LTTE suicide bomber.

Ranasinghe Premadasa
(1924–1993) President of Sri Lanka from 1989 until 1993, when he was killed by an LTTE suicide bomber.

Velupillai Pirapaharan
(1954–) Founder and current leader of the LTTE. Pirapaharan's terrorists have conducted more successful suicide bombings than any other terrorist group in the world.

Figure 12.9

Sinhalese and Tamil Areas in Sri Lanka; Tamil Areas in India

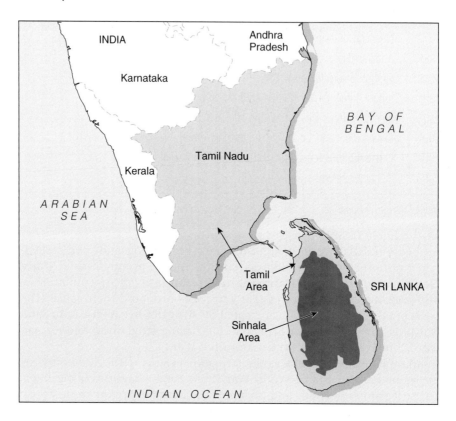

Colombo

The capital of Sri Lanka.

bank robberies and assassinations, and he needed to eliminate rival terrorists to claim leadership of the movement.

The LTTE eventually emerged as the leading revolutionary group and launched Sri Lanka into a full-blown terrorist campaign. The Tigers were not satisfied with this, however, wanting to build a guerrilla force and eventually a conventional army. The Sinhalese majority reacted violently in 1983, and Sinhalese protesters flocked to the streets of **Colombo**, Sri Lanka's capital, in a series of anti-Tamil riots. Many Tamils fled to India, and the LTTE returned to terrorism.

Reactions to the riots were a turning point for the LTTE. Unable to foment the revolution from above, the group established contacts with the Popular Front for the Liberation of Palestine. Since that time, the Tamil Tigers have mounted three on-again, off-again terrorist campaigns. At first, India responded by forming a joint peacekeeping force with Sri Lanka. India's primary purpose was to keep violence from spilling over into the mainland. India reevaluated its policy after several assassinations and violent encounters, and the government has vowed never to send troops to Sri Lanka again.

The LTTE has incorporated a variety of tactics since 1984. Their ability to operate is directly correlated to the amount of popular support they enjoy during any particular period. In 1988 and 1992 they sought to control geographic areas, and they moved using standard guerrilla tactics, forming uniformed units. They even created an ad hoc navy. In times of weakness, they relied on bank robberies, bombings, and murder. In the weakest times, they have employed suicide bombers. They used suicide attacks in 1995 on land and at sea.

Joshi estimates that before 1983 the LTTE had only forty followers. The anti-Tamil riots were a catalyst to growth, as links were formed in the Middle East. Terrorist training camps appeared in the Tamil region of India in 1984 and 1985, and the training cadre included foreign terrorists. India responded by signing a joint peace agreement with Sri Lanka and soon found itself under attack from a highly organized terrorist group of between 10,000 and 16,000.

When not attacking India, the Tamil Tigers launched operations in Sri Lanka. Although they had once struggled to be recognized as the leaders of the independence movement, the Tigers now ruthlessly wiped out their opponents and terrorized their own ethnic group into providing support. Yet security forces enjoyed several successes, and by 1987 the Tamil Tigers were in retreat.

According to Joshi, this was a very dangerous period for the group. In fact, it was almost wiped out. Driven into the jungle, the Tamil Tigers practiced terrorism from jungle hideaways. They increased contact with Tamil bases in India, using India for logistical support. Politically adept, the LTTE asked for a cease-fire in 1989, giving India a chance to withdraw from the joint security force. No sooner had the Indians left than the LTTE renewed its attack on the Sri Lankans.

In 1990 the LTTE expanded its operations by converting a fishing fleet into a makeshift navy. Suicide boats and other seaborne operations threatened shipping between Sri Lanka and India. By 1991 India was once again targeted by Tamil terrorists, and the Indian Navy was forced to respond to the growing threat. Not only did the LTTE fight small-scale sea battles with the Indians, but its terrorists also succeeded in assassinating Prime Minister Gandhi on May 21, 1991. When Indian authorities cracked down on Tamil bases, the Tamil Tigers increased their terrorist attacks against India.

From 1994 to 1995 the Tamil Tigers waged another bombing and assassination campaign, and they did what no other terrorist group has been able to do. Although their bases in India were limited, they had strongholds on Sri Lanka. Supported by guerrilla strongholds, Tamil Tigers appeared in uniforms in 1994 and fought pitched battles with the Sri Lankan security forces. Suicide bombings increased during the same time. Faced with open revolution, the Sri Lankan government signed a peace agreement in January 1995.

Joshi's research ended in the summer of 1995. The peace accord broke down, and the Sri Lankan Army went on the offensive. The LTTE suffered several setbacks, but the group made headlines in 1996 with suicide bombings in Colombo. In the spring of 1996, Sri Lankan security forces launched an all-out assault on Tamil strongholds on the northern portion of the island. Some commentators (de Silva, 1996; Berthelsen, 1996) believed this would be the end of the LTTE. They were wrong.

Rohan Gunaratna (1998) argues that the LTTE is in a unique position because it has such a large guerrilla base. The guerrillas are perfectly capable of fighting a protracted war against security forces, and if defeated, the LTTE can revert to terrorism. Indeed, this has been the LTTE's tactic. In the wake of new fighting, the LTTE has followed the path of suicide bombing. Although the guerrilla campaign subsided a bit in 1999, suicide bombings increased in 2000. The hard-core LTTE is a long way from any negotiated settlement. The hope of the Sri Lankan government is to attract moderate Tamils into a coalition government and deprive the Tamil Tigers of their ethnic and guerrilla support.

In December 2001 the LTTE agreed to a cease-fire with the government of Sri Lanka. Although the Tigers still threaten violence, their resources may be depleting. The Council on Foreign Relations (Zissis, 2006) believes that the international community's efforts to thwart terrorism after September 11 are responsible for this situation. Arms shipments have been virtually eliminated, and expatriate Tamil communities in Australia, Canada, and the United States are no longer allowed to gather and ship resources to Sri Lanka. The largest hit was economic. LTTE assets were frozen in the wake of September 11. The Council on Foreign Relations believes the LTTE may no longer be able to fight.

The Tamil Eelam website (http://www.eelamweb.com) suggests that negotiations may work. The Tamils believe that Sri Lanka is the home of two sovereign peoples: the Tamils and the Sinhalese. They argue that the island can be divided into two sovereign areas and that both groups can live together, albeit separately. They also claim they are operating their own governmental, economic, and educational systems. According to the website, the LTTE is not a terrorist organization; it is the army of the Tamil people. It may well be that the Sinhalese and Tamils are able to negotiate peace from the recent cease-fire, but most of the world would not agree with this assessment of the Tigers. A group that conscripts children and fosters suicide bombings is and will remain a terrorist group in the eyes of most people.

India

India has a variety of terrorist problems coming from political, religious, and ethnic strife (Timeline 12.2: A Sample of Terrorist Events in India). Carin Zissis (2007) maintains that great economic disparities have caused the growth of left-wing movements that demand a more equal distribution of resources. One of these movements has turned violent. The Naxalites emerged in a 1967 uprising in West Bengal. Composed of radical Maoists, the Naxalite rebellion was short-lived after Indian security forces targeted the group. The Naxalites broke into many smaller movements, and reemerged in 2004 when two violent Maoist groups united to form the Communist Party of India.

1948	Mahatma Gandhi assassinated by Hindu extremist.
1984	Prime Minister Indira Gandhi assassinated by Sikh bodyguards.
1985	Air India Flight 182 bombed, 329 killed.
1990	Muslim separatists launch campaign in Kashmir.
1991	Prime Minister Rajiv Gandhi assassinated by LTTE.
1995	Sikh bomb kills Beant Singh, the chief minister of Punjab.
2001	Jihadists attack legislative assembly in Srinagar.
2001	Jihadist suicide attack on Indian parliament building.
2003	Jihadists execute 24 Hindu civilians in Kashmir.
2003	Jihadist terrorist bombs kill 46 in Bombay.
2006	Seven explosions kill 185 on train in Mumbai.

Sources: BBC News, December 2001; Scaruffi, 2007.

Zissis says the Naxalites operate in a **red corridor** extending from Nepal through central India. Approximately 10,000 to 20,000 strong, the Naxalites attack Indian security forces and economic targets with small arms and homemade bombs. Like the LTTE in Sri Lanka, they often kidnap potential recruits and force them to join their ranks. The Naxalites were responsible for 740 deaths in 2006.

Politics and religion combine in Jammu and Kashmir, where three main groups and a host of smaller splinter organizations carry out a campaign of religious violence. Although Pakistan reduced its operations in India after coming to the brink of nuclear war in late 2002, the ISI has played a leading role in Kashmiri violence. ISI's efforts can be linked to the Soviet-Afghan War. Shaul Shay (2002, pp. 107–108) says the ISI took control of several mujahideen groups at the end of the Soviet-Afghan War. Using its influence within the groups, the ISI sponsored new intolerant religious schools and brought new recruits into Jammu and Kashmir. Violence escalated on both sides, and the death toll soared into the thousands. In Kashmir frustrated police and military officials, disobeying orders, have formed death squads and quasi-official militias to attack Muslims (J. Stern, 2003b, pp. 118–119).

Zissis (2007) identifies three ISI-inspired jihadist groups in Jammu and Kashmir. The Lashkar-e-Taiba (LeT), or Army of the Pure, receives funding from the ISI in exchange for two services: target Hindus in the Jammu and Kashmir region and send operatives into India to train native jihadists. On July 7, 2006, a series of bombs exploded on a crowded train near Mumbai, India. The attack set fire to the exits, trapping people inside the train cars and burning them to death, killing 185 people. The Lashkar-e-Qahar, a small group claiming to be an offshoot of the LeT, claimed responsibility for the attack. India has been quick to blame the ISI for all jihadist terrorism, but many experts believe the ISI backed away from supporting such organizations after 2003 (E. Kaplan, 2006).

red corridor

The area of Naxalite violence in India. The length of the corridor runs from Nepal through southern India, and the width extends from India's east coast to the central regions.

The Harakat-ul-Mujahideen (HuM), the Organization of Holy Warriors, is another group operating in Jammu and Kashmir. Sean Hill and Richard Ward (2002, pp. 903–905) believe the HuM formed from the merger of two mujahideen groups after the Soviet-Afghan War. Originally called the Harakat al Ansar, or Organization of Helpers, HuM changed its name after the U.S. Department of State designated the organization as a terrorist group. HuM targets beyond India. One of its senior members signed a 1998 letter from al Qaeda calling for terrorist attacks on Americans all over the globe.

Hill and Ward (2002, pp. 929–932) identify the third major group in Jammu and Kashmir, the Jaish-e-Mohammed (JeM), or Army of Mohammed. Headquartered in Pakistan, JeM has ambitions beyond Jammu and Kashmir. The group operates a string of radical madrassas that preach Islamic revolution. In other words, JeM produces jihadists. Its graduates are encouraged to carry the war to Kashmir but also to move into the Muslim areas of India. JeM states that it wants Jammu and Kashmir as well as several provinces in India.

Outside of Jammu and Kashmir, India faces other jihadist terrorist activities. B. Raman (2002) says India is concerned with growing terrorism by its own internal jihadists. Dennis Kux (2002) believes India's counterterrorist policy is complicated by the complexity of terrorist threats. Although the ISI activity seems to have decreased, there are several ethnic and communal tensions involving terrorism as well as internal jihadist threats.

India has a diverse population, including a religious group known as the Sikhs. *Sikh* is a Punjabi word meaning "disciple." Founded over 500 years ago, Sikhism emphasizes an inner journey to seek spiritual enlightenment followed by external behavior to live in peace with the world. The religion has enshrined ten great teachers, or gurus, and it embodies elements of Islam and Hinduism (Singh, 1999; Brar, 2003). After India was partitioned in 1947, some Sikhs sought independence in Punjab, a state where they represented the majority of the population. This gave birth to a small, violent independence movement in 1977.

India responded to the revolt by increasing central authority in Punjab. This move divided the Sikhs into a majority orthodox group that wanted to peacefully resolve the situation and a small radicalized group that wanted to fight India. Issues came to a head in 1984 when Indian military forces entered the Sikhs' most sacred site, the **Golden Temple**, and engaged in a bloody battle with armed militants. Thousands of people were killed (Singh, 1999, pp. 214–215). Small groups of Sikhs formed terror cells and they targeted Indian security forces, unsympathetic journalists, and the majority community of Sikhs who called for the restoration of peace (GlobalSecurity.org, n.d.). A few months after the Golden Temple raid, the Sikh bodyguards of the prime minister of India assassinated him.

Sikh extremists planned assassinations all over the world, including the United States. Several cells were active in North America. Extrem-

Golden Temple
The most sacred shrine of Sikhism. Its official name is the Temple of God.

ists compiled a hit list of moderate Sikhs in Canada, and radical members preached violence. One radical pleaded guilty in 2003 to making the bomb that brought down Air India Flight 182, an explosion that killed 329 people in 1985 (Commission of Inquiry, 2007). By 1988 more than a hundred people per month lost their lives. Fighting took place as militant Sikhs attacked police and nonmilitant Sikhs, while the police struck back. Violence continued in India through 1994 and then decreased. When one Sikh was asked to explain why the violence had tapered off, he responded succinctly. The militants are all dead (Juergensmeyer, 2000, pp. 86–101).

Self-Check

- *How do problems with Jammu and Kashmir spill into Pakistan and Bangladesh?*
- *How important are religious differences in Sri Lanka when compared to ethnic differences?*
- *What are the sources of terrorism in India?*

Southeast Asia and the Pacific Rim

Other areas of Asia have experienced varying forms of terrorism. Local religious militants operate in some countries, and other nations have been targeted by international jihadists. Sometimes local terrorists and jihadists combine operations. The North Korean Intelligence Service (NKIS) exports its own brand of terrorism. Japan has experienced nationalistic violence, radical international groups, and a religious group that launched an attack that could have resulted in thousands of deaths.

Thailand

Thailand is experiencing a rebellion in its southern provinces. Although the country is dominated by Buddhism, Islam is the primary religion of the three most southern states, states that border Islamic Malaysia. Zachary Abuza (2006) says that Muslims failed in a revolt about forty years ago because they were ideologically divided. Another revolt today is smaller yet more united. Abuza identifies the main groups involved in the fighting.

The Pattani United Liberation Organization (PULO) formed in India in 1968 to create a Muslim state through armed struggle. Its leadership is aging, but it maintains a propaganda campaign through the Internet. It held a reunification meeting in Damascus in 2005, hoping to support the insurgency in the south. PULO controls no insurgents, but some of its leaders have made public threats. It claims to be secular, but Abuza says it has Salafi undertones. New PULO, formed in 1995, is much more effective. Its leaders trained in Syria and Libya and have considerable bomb-making skills.

Figure 12.10

Indonesia

The Barisan Revolusi Nasional, Coordinate (BRN-C), is leading the insurgency and carries a jihadist agenda. One of three BRN groups involved in the insurgency, BRN-C is active in southern Thailand's mosques. Running a network of madrassas, the BRN-C has become the training ground for militants and fundamentalists. More than 2,500 madrassa graduates went for further training in the Middle East before returning to Thailand. BRN-C membership is estimated at 1,000, and it controls eighteen schools and a number of teachers. Thai security forces estimate that 70 percent of the southern villages have at least one cell.

Complementing the BRN-C is the Gerakan Mujahideen Islami Pattani (GMIP), with forty active cells. Afghan veterans reassembled the group in 1995, but it deteriorated into a criminal gang. Abuza says that it began to embrace the insurgency by 2003, and that GMIP has contacts with Jamaat Islamiyya in Indonesia and the Moro Islamic Liberation Front (MILF) in the Philippines. The GMIP staged raids on police and army outposts in 2002.

Ian Storey (2007) notes that the southern insurgency is becoming an international affair. Militant groups in Malaysia have embraced the Muslim rebellion in Thailand, even though the Malaysian government does not. Radicals in the Philippines and Indonesia see the revolt as part of the international jihad.

Indonesia

Jihad also grew in Southeast Asia. Zachary Abuza (2003b, pp. 121–187), in an analysis of terrorism in that region, says that jihadist groups began forming in Indonesia in the early 1990s. The International Crisis Group (2004, 2005a) says these movements had their origins after World War II when Indonesia gained its independence from the Netherlands. Islamic associations became part of the political process, but they were suppressed by the government and the army in the name of nationalism. Abuza notes that new leadership gained power in 1998, and Islamic groups blossomed, asserting their independence. In 1999 fighting broke out between Christians and Muslims in the eastern islands, and militant Islamic groups grew (Figure 12.10).

Figure 12.11
Philippine Islands

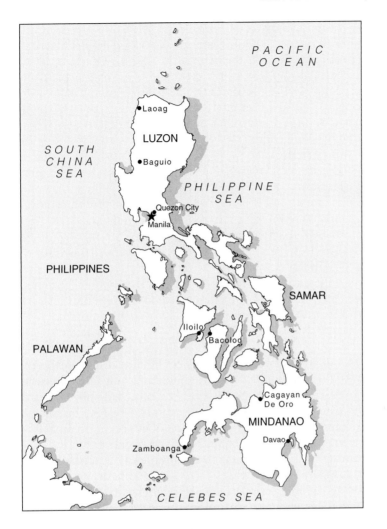

The political situation in Indonesia provided a climate for the growth of jihadist groups. According to Abuza, many of the members of jihadist movements had been trained in the mujahideen camps of Afghanistan. Lashkar Jihad formed to fight Christians in the east. A more sinister group, Jamaat Islamiyya, formed with the purpose of placing Indonesia under strict Islamic law. Both groups had contacts with al Qaeda (Gunaratna, 2002, pp. 174–203; Abuza, 2003b, pp. 138–142), although leaders of both groups claimed to be independent of Osama bin Laden (J. Stern, 2003b, pp. 75–76).

The Philippines

The Philippines also experienced jihadist violence. Historically, the relationship between the Christian islands in the north and a few Muslim islands in the south has been marked by strife (Figure 12.11). The U.S. Army fought Muslim rebels after the Spanish-American War (1898), and the Philippine government faced both Muslim and communist rebellions in the 1950s. Religious and ideological rebellions were repeated themes for the Philippines during the twentieth century.

Abuza (2003b, pp. 89–120) outlines the formation of three recent terrorist groups in the Philippines. The Moro National Liberation Front (MNLF) is a continuation of the old religious struggle. Having proposed negotiations with the Philippine government, the MNLF seeks an independent Islamic state. Breaking away from the MNLF is the more radical Moro Islamic Liberation Front (MILF). It has ties with jihadist movements and seeks to create an Islamic state under strict interpretations of Islamic law. A third group, Abu Sayyuf, claims to be part of the jihadist movement, but it is most closely associated with criminal activity and seems more interested in money than religion.

Ideology is also active in the Philippines (Hill and Ward, 2002, pp. 281–291). The New Peoples Army (NPA) operates throughout the Philippines. Originally established to fight both the government and its American allies, the NPA hopes to turn the Philippines into a communist state. The group has been responsible for several murders, including those of U.S. military personnel.

Radicals and Religion in Japan

On March 20, 1995, Tokyo was subjected to a technological terrorist attack by a radical religious sect. Members of Aum Shinrikyo (Supreme Truth) released a poisonous gas into the crowded subway system. The terrorists were not individuals seeking social release or some vaguely defined political revenge; they were members of an organized religious group trying to destroy the Japanese government.

According to the U.S. Department of State (1996), the poison gas attack in the Tokyo subway was the first large-scale use of chemical agents by terrorists. Diplomatic officials estimated that cult members hoped to destabilize the Japanese government and seize power in the confusion. Aum Shinrikyo terrorists struck five subway trains simultaneously, killing 12 and sending approximately 5,500 to hospitals for treatment. Subsequent investigations by Japanese police linked Aum Shinrikyo to a previous gas attack in 1994, which killed 7 and injured 500 (Muir, 1999).

The group's charismatic leader, Shoko Asahara, planned murders, conducted dress rehearsals before the subway attack, and developed a mechanism for funding, developing, and supporting a program of weapons of mass destruction (Brackett, 1996). All of this came not from a nation-state but from a cultlike terrorist group whose members included technicians and scientists.

The technology behind the attack was frightening. The terrorists used sarin, a deadly, odorless, colorless gas developed by Nazi researchers during World War II. They placed innocent-looking packets containing chemicals under their subway seats. Each terrorist punctured the lethal container just before 8:00 a.m.; upon exposure to air, sarin gas clouds began working their way through the subway cars with immediate results.

The Japanese Red Army, a unique group that intertwined leftist ideology with Japanese nationalism, forged relations with terrorist groups all over the world. Incongruously, it was a Japanese leftist group, but its most active cell would operate in Lebanon, fighting in the Palestinian cause. The Red Army's uniqueness came from its willingness to embrace many differing issues, ranging from left-wing political action to recapturing Japan's historical nation-of-warriors society. It can be classified as a left-wing group in the Western tradition (that is, in the Western economic tradition), but it exhibited some cultic characteristics as it engaged in ritualized behavior designed to subjugate members to a particular leader (Farrell, 1990).

The group splintered into many factions. One segment operated with the North Korean Intelligence Service, another joined Palestinians in the Middle East. The main group stayed in Japan to wage a criminal campaign. Part of the Japanese faction internalized violence, and other members sought connections with Asian communists. The Middle Eastern faction continued to identify itself as the Japanese Red Army, but it became consumed with the Palestinian cause. Some members in the Middle East eventually evolved into mercenaries, hiring themselves out to the highest bidder. The Japanese Red Army tried to take too many directions for it to remain viable in the twenty-first century.

Joseph Ferguson (2004) says that international jihadists are prepared to target Japan. Although it would be extremely difficult for jihadists to infiltrate the islands, Japanese have been targeted overseas (for example, the IMU kidnapping of four Japanese geologists and targeting of Japanese diplomats in Iraq). Japan quickly announced its support of the United States after 9/11, and that did not escape the notice of the jihadists. In October 2003 Japan received its first videotaped threat from Osama bin Laden, in which he threatened suicide attacks in all countries supporting the United States. The United Kingdom has experienced such attacks, and at least one has been thwarted in Australia. Japan has not been hit within its national boundaries, Ferguson concludes, but the war on terrorism is still young.

Self-Check

- *Is the rebellion in southern Thailand similar to jihadist movements in other parts of the world? Why or why not?*
- *What are the sources of terrorism in Indonesia and how do they relate to terrorism in Southeast Asia?*
- *What are the differences among the groups fighting in the Moro area of the Philippines?*
- *Describe the unique nature of terrorism in Japan.*

SUMMARY

- Poverty is an overriding issue in sub-Saharan Africa. The area also suffers from the AIDS pandemic and tribal violence. These issues are more pressing than terrorism.
- Terrorism is a potential problem in western and central Africa. Failed states combine with governmental corruption and organized crime to create a potential haven for terrorist groups. Jihadist groups are present in the Horn of Africa.
- Afghanistan and Iraq are plagued by tribal violence. Afghanistan has never had a strong central government. Strong authoritarian leaders in Iraq formed tribal alliances to maintain a central government, but after Saddam Hussein's fall, tribal violence is on the rise. In addition, Iraq has religious and ethnic splits. International jihadists operate in both Afghanistan and Iraq.
- Tribal areas in Pakistan harbor militants and international jihadists. This creates problems for all of central Asia. Religious militants spread throughout the region from Bangladesh to Kazakhstan. The ISI has supported jihadist groups in Jammu and Kashmir, further fanning the flames of religious violence.
- Sri Lanka is experiencing ethnic conflict. The LTTE emerged from the Tamil population in Sri Lanka. It became so strong that it was able to move from terrorism to guerrilla warfare. In 1995 the LTTE began a campaign of suicide bombing. Today, a fragile peace is threatened by ethnic divisions.
- India has several forms of internal terrorism. Maoists operate in the red corridor, and tensions run high in Jammu and Kashmir, which has jihadist groups. Other jihadists operate within India, and India blames the ISI for their actions. India has also experienced ethnic violence and religious terrorism apart from militant Islam.
- Southeast Asia has a variety of jihadist movements, but groups generally operate within nationalistic contexts. Thailand has a rebellion in its southern provinces, and Indonesia's groups can be tied to madrassas. The Philippines has three active groups, but one of them behaves more like a criminal gang.
- Japan experienced terrorism with two internal groups, a radical political group that splintered and a religious cult that attempted to kill thousands. Recently, al Qaeda threatened Japan because of its support for American policies.

KEY TERMS

AIDS pandemic (p. 280)
sweet crude (p. 281)
Liberian Civil War (p. 282)
Charles Taylor (p. 282)

Liberians United for Reconciliation and Democracy (p. 282)
Big Man (p. 283)
African Cell (p. 284)

Nicolas Sarkozy (p. 284)

Horn of Africa (p. 285)

Combined Joint Task Force, Horn of Africa (CJTF-HOA) (p. 285)

Islamic Courts Union (p. 285)

Operation Enduring Freedom (p. 291)

NATO (p. 292)

Islam Karimov (p. 294)

Fergana Valley (p. 294)

Uighars (p. 294)

Islamic Renaissance Party (p. 294)

Tohir Yoldash (p. 295)

Jumaboi Khojaev (p. 295)

Juma Namangani (p. 295)

Tajik Civil War (p. 295)

Deobandi (p. 295)

Northern Alliance (p. 296)

King Gyanendra (p. 298)

Pervez Musharraf (p. 299)

North-West Frontier Province (p. 300)

Waziristan (p. 300)

Balochistan (p. 300)

Jammu and Kashmir (p. 301)

Tamils (p. 302)

Rajiv Gandhi (p. 303)

Ranasinghe Premadasa (p. 303)

Velupillai Pirapaharan (p. 303)

Colombo (p. 304)

red corridor (p. 307)

Golden Temple (p. 308)

WRITING ASSIGNMENTS

1. Some analysts believe that African nations need to take a more active role in the war on terrorism. Yet many social scientists think social and economic problems dwarf terrorism. Which position is correct? Could policies be developed to address both issues effectively?

2. Compare Iraq and Afghanistan. Were either (or both) of the wars waged there by the United States justified? How might America's allies answer this question?

3. How does violence on the Indian subcontinent affect central Asia? Does this violence have the same type of impact on Southeast Asia?

13 Europe, Turkey, and Russia

AP Photo/Alexander Zemlianichenko

Women mourn in the ruins of the Beslan school in North Ossetia, where terrorists took hundreds of people hostage. The attack ended up killing over 300 people, including 186 children. Terrorism in the names of ethnicity, political radicalism, and religion haunts regions of the former Soviet Union, Turkey, and Europe.

Learning Objectives

After reading this chapter you should be able to

- Discuss the differences between ethnic and nationalist extremists in Europe.
- Describe the peace process in Ireland.
- Describe the history and renewal of violence in the Basque region of Spain.
- Explain the demise of leftist terrorist cells in western Europe.
- Describe the transformation of international jihadist groups in Europe.
- Summarize the terrorist issues facing Turkey.
- Outline the origins and current status of the PKK in Turkey.
- Cite examples of breakaway states in the Russian Federation.
- Explain the danger posed by Russia's breakaway states.
- Describe the political and security issues surrounding violence in Chechnya.

The term *terrorism* originated in Europe, and governments managed to apply it to revolutionary struggles in the nineteenth century. Terrorism returned to Europe around 1965 with the rise of leftist violence and the movement of Middle Eastern battlefields to Europe after 1972. This coincided with the rebirth of ethnic terrorism in the Basque region of Spain and nationalistic violence in Ireland. The process of terrorism changed in the 1990s and these changes extend into the twenty-first century. In the West, some ethnic violence remains, but the violent political left has virtually disappeared. International jihadist groups have been operating in western Europe for the past decade. Turkey, officially part of Asia but seeking closer ties with Europe, has witnessed ethnic tensions and jihadist violence. The Russian Federation faces problems in breakaway provinces and in the Transcaucasia region.

Terrorism in Western Europe

Despite the influence of religion on modern terrorism, other forms of terror continue to exist. National and ethnic struggles still dominate certain regions of Europe. For many years, analysts of terrorism examined nationalist terrorists within the same framework as older left-wing terrorist groups. Robert Trundle Jr. (1996) questions this approach, saying that because the structure of ethnic violence has changed, the old models are no longer applicable. At one time, this process may have worked, but it is currently obscuring the understanding of ethnic violence.

Ideological violence has also shifted. Ideological terrorism refers to small groups who terrorize for the purpose of imposing their political ideals on others. The term was first used to describe left-wing, anarchist, and communist revolutionaries. Small groups in Europe and South and North America fought to impose a new social order from about 1960 to 1985. They found economic and governmental systems to be oppressive, and they sought to replace them with an ideal form of socialism. Around 1980 resurgent right-wing groups began to grow in Europe and the United States. These groups wanted to turn back the clock and restore an ideal form of patriotism and strength. Around 1995 left- and right-wing groups started drawing closer together, but the majority of ideological violence has been based on single issues in the early years of twenty-first-century Europe. Such groups tend to operate in networks, swarming to achieve numerical advantages (see Arquilla, Ronfeldt, and Zanini, 1999). European ideological terrorism has waned in recent years.

Ethnic and nationalistic terrorism has lost some of its strength, too, but still continues in Spain and some areas of Ireland. Kurdish nationalism remains strong in Turkey. Daniel Byman (1998) of the RAND Corporation says ethnic terrorism differs from terrorism carried out in the name of ideology, religion, or economic gain. He acknowledges the growing influence of religion on terrorism, but he believes ethnic terrorism is a unique entity, even though the line between ethnic and religious violence is blurred. Ethnic terrorists are usually more nationalistic than their religious counterparts. He uses evidence from the Liberation Tigers of Tamil Eelam (LTTE), the Kurdistan Workers Party (PKK), the Provisional Irish Republican Army (PIRA), and the Basque Nation and Liberty (ETA) as evidence for his thesis.

Ethnic terrorists try to forge national identity. Their primary purpose is to mobilize a community, and they do so by appealing to the nationalistic background of a particular ethnic group. Byman says terrorist activity is used to make a statement about the group's identity. When the inevitable governmental persecution follows terrorist actions, it draws attention to the group and allows the terrorists to present themselves as victims. This process may increase public awareness of ethnic or nationalistic grievances and it may lead to new sources of support. Terrorism also polarizes other ethnic groups and forces them to either ally with the terrorists or oppose them.

Violence plays a special role in ethnic terrorism. Whereas political terrorists use violence in a symbolic manner and religious extremists use it to make a theological statement, violence is the raison d'être of ethnic terrorism. It keeps an idea alive. As long as a bomb goes off or a police officer is murdered, the identity and existence of ethnic differences cannot be denied. Violence sustains the conflict, even when political objectives are far out of reach. The fear created by violence serves ethnic interests. Violence also serves to undermine moderates who seek peaceful solutions.

In the past decade, jihadist networks have come to play a significant role in European terrorism. North African groups operate in Spain and Italy. Middle Eastern networks are active in Germany, Belgium, the Netherlands, France, and the United Kingdom. France also has ties with groups from Algeria (Kohlman, 2004).

Ireland and the Peace Process

In 1985 the United Kingdom and the Republic of Ireland signed a peace accord regarding the governance of Northern Ireland. Known as the Anglo-Irish Peace Accord, the agreement seeks to bring an end to terrorism by establishing a joint system of government for the troubled area. Seamus Dunn and Valerie Morgan (1995) believe many Protestant groups feel betrayed by this agreement. They surmise such groups may resort to violence if they feel they have no voice in the political system, and they believe that all groups must feel they have a vested interest in peace if the process is to work. It took militant Protestants and Catholics nearly ten years to lay down the weapons of terrorism, and sporadic outbursts of violence still occur.

J. Bowyer Bell (1998) describes the process of achieving peace in Ireland as a long ending to a lengthy process. The IRA declared a cease-fire in 1994 but broke it in 1996. Trying to bring life into the Anglo-Irish Peace Accord, British prime minister **Tony Blair** invited the most militant Irish nationalists to the peace table in 1998 and continued negotiations. This brought the ethnic Irish party Sinn Fein to the table, but more militant Irish Republicans broke ranks. This led to the birth of the Real Irish Republican Army, or the True Irish Republican Army, as well as several other Orange and Green terrorist organizations. These groups renewed a campaign of violence in 1998, hoping to destroy the Anglo-Irish peace initiatives.

Bell is not optimistic about the ability of any political entity—government or otherwise—to bring peace to the island nation by avoiding every avenue of conflict. Bell says there are too many agendas and too many people served by ethnic violence. Protestant violence may also increase because many Protestants believe the British government has abandoned them (Dunn and Morgan, 1995). The growth of Orange organizations like the **Red Hand Defenders** and **Orange Volunteers**, two new terrorist groups that have disavowed the peace accords, reinforce these conclusions.

More recent research (Monaghan, 2004; Hughes and Donnelly, 2004; Carmichael and Knox, 2004) suggests that although low-level violence may continue, the amount of terrorism is decreasing. For example, paramilitary shootings on both the Unionist and Republican sides have been reduced. Radical parties are using rhetoric inside the political process. Although still using the nationalistic and ethnic rhetoric of the past, they tend to operate peacefully. In addition, people who were jailed for terrorism and violent political activity have seemed to be more concerned with reintegrating into their families and communities after their incarceration than with carrying on the struggle.

By 2005 the road to peace seemed more secure. The Irish Republican Army has seemed less interested in Green issues than it has in organized crime. It has been associated with armed robbery, including a major bank robbery, and in late 2004 several IRA members allegedly murdered **Robert McCartney** in a Belfast bar fight. The murderers were particularly brutal, and IRA terrorists threatened to kill anybody who testified against them. When McCartney's sisters took the threats to the press, officials from the IRA offered to kill the offenders. The murder and the IRA's response to it resulted in the marginalization of the IRA and Sinn Fein. Several U.S. politicians shunned Sinn Fein's leadership during the 2005 Saint Patrick's Day celebrations in the United States, and Senator Ted Kennedy and President George W. Bush condemned the IRA (BBC News, 2005b). At long last, the people of Ireland seem to be tired of radical violence.

Tony Blair

(1953–) The Labour Party prime minister of the United Kingdom from 1994 to 2007.

Red Hand Defenders

A Unionist extremist group in Northern Ireland. The newest group to use the name formed in 1998.

Orange Volunteers

A Unionist paramilitary group in Northern Ireland. Volunteers for the House of Orange have joined Unionist causes in Northern Ireland since William of Orange saved the Protestant cause at the Battle of the Boyne in 1690.

Robert McCartney

(1971–2005) A Catholic supporter of Sinn Fein allegedly murdered by the IRA during a bar fight in Belfast. The murder had nothing to do with McCartney's politics, but it revealed the thuggish nature of the IRA.

Dennis McGinn (2006) points to attempts to control violence among paramilitary groups. The United Kingdom and Republic of Ireland created the **Independent Monitoring Commission (IMC)** to investigate claims of both terrorist and governmental abuses. The IMC believes the IRA has stopped recruiting terrorists and is trying to send members to Sinn Fein. It also believes that all paramilitary groups have stopped gathering information on security force members. Actions of the IMC have resulted in the arrests of Republican and Loyalist terrorists as well as members of the security forces who acted beyond the law (Henderson, 2006).

Independent Monitoring Commission (IMC)

A commission created in 2004 to investigate paramilitary actions and alleged governmental abuses during the Irish peace process.

Criminal elements and tactics in the IRA still remain. After Robert McCartney's murder, police interviewed seventy-two witnesses, but no one would provide evidence out of fear of retaliation. McCartney had been a sympathizer of Sinn Fein and supporter of republicanism. When Sinn Fein responded to McCartney's murder by saying that the **Police Service of Northern Ireland (PSNI)** was using the incident to undermine Republican politics, many Irish people, Republicans and Loyalists alike, were disgusted. Later, Gerry Adams, disavowed terrorist and president of Sinn Fein, urged his followers to cooperate with the police (BBC News, 2005a).

Police Service of Northern Ireland (PSNI)

The police force created in November 2001 to replace the Royal Ulster Constabulary.

The Basque Nation and Liberty

In March 2004 a series of bombs exploded in the central train station of Madrid, Spain, killing nearly 200 people. Although the plot was eventually tied to jihadists, the first response from Spain and the international media pointed to the group Euskadi ta Askatasuna (ETA, or Basque Nation and Liberty). The ETA has waged a campaign of violence since 1959 that has killed more than 800 people (see Expanding the Concept: The Basque Conflict). They have specialized in car bombings and assassinations, and they have targeted Spain's number-one industry, tourism. The ETA's goal is to establish an autonomous homeland in northern Spain and southern France (Foreign Policy Association, 2004; Council on Foreign Relations, 2002; Goodman, 2003).

The Basque region of France and Spain has long been a source for major nationalistic terrorism in Europe. Primarily located in Spain, the Basque region extends over the Pyrenees into France. Basque separatists believe they should be allowed to develop a homeland in Spain, and since the 1950s Basque separatism has been an important issue in Spanish politics. Many Americans are not aware of the Basque lands because they are unaware of the evolutionary nature of many European nations. The Basque region of Spain has always had its own language (R. Clark, 1979), and even though it had not existed as an independent kingdom since 1035, it had maintained its own culture. This changed when **Francisco Franco**, the fascist Spanish dictator (1939–1975), forcibly campaigned against Basque national identity. A resurgence of Basque nationalism during the 1950s reflected a centuries-old tradition of unique language and culture.

Francisco Franco

(1892–1975) Leader of the nationalistic forces during the Spanish Civil War and the fascist dictator of Spain from 1939–1975.

The Basque Conflict

The Issue. Basque separatists want a homeland completely independent of Spain. The nationalists control a semiautonomous Basque parliament, but they are divided in their desire for autonomy. A substantial minority of Basques want to remain united with Spain.

The Group. Although the Basque region has never been independent, it has its own language and culture. Francisco Franco, the Spanish dictator, tried to crush Basque culture and force the Basques to become Spanish.

The Campaign. The Basque Nation and Liberty (ETA) began a campaign against Spain in 1959. The group was responsible for assassinating Franco's probable successor and many other officials. They agreed to a cease-fire in 1998 but broke the treaty a year later. The Spanish government has given the Basques regional governing authority, and Basques use their own language and run their own schools. The majority of Spaniards believe the ETA to be the most important issue in Spain, and both Basques and Spaniards are tired of ETA violence. Spain also has a strong jihadist movement, but there is no connection between the jihadists and the ETA.

The Future. The ETA released a statement in October 2004 stating that it wished to achieve freedom through dialogue with France and Spain. In the past, radicals in the ETA have returned to violence after suggesting peace.

Sources: Goodman, 2003; Agence France Presse, 2004.

Edward Moxon-Browne (1987) examines the Basque separatist movement and its relation to terrorism. Moxon-Browne maintains that current problems are the result of a gradual loss of national identity that began in the nineteenth century when Madrid assumed greater control of the region, and accelerated in the early twentieth century because of industrialization. After the **Spanish Civil War** (1936–1939), Franco completely incorporated the Basque region into Spain, banning its language and expressions of national culture. Regaining them became the focus of the modern struggle.

Terrorism grew out of the nationalistic movement. The ETA formed as an offshoot of a nationalistic political party in 1959. Composed of young, frustrated nationalists who wanted regional autonomy, the ETA was not originally violent, but its members turned to violence when Franco tried to repress the movement. In 1966 the ETA voted to follow the example of the third world and engage in armed revolution. In 1968 the group started a terrorist campaign. A more militant group, the ETA-M, broke away from the ETA in 1974. ETA-M described itself as the military wing

Spanish Civil War

(1936–1939) A war that pitted pro-communist Republicans against pro-fascist Nationalists. The war ended with a Nationalist victory and a fascist dictatorship under Franco.

of the ETA and, according to Moxon-Browne, was responsible for the worst atrocities of the 1970s and 1980s.

Both the ETA and the ETA-M have waged a campaign under the name ETA. Violence reached its zenith between 1977 and 1980 and declined steadily throughout the 1980s. The ETA conducted a sporadic campaign during the 1990s, agreeing to a short cease-fire in 1998. In 1999 the ETA broke the cease-fire with a car bomb. In 2001 the ETA was responsible for murdering thirty foreign tourists, and it has tried to conduct major bombings, including an attempt to bring down one of Spain's largest buildings.

Robert Clark (1984) has studied the characteristics of Basque terrorists, and Moxon-Browne uses this as a basis to describe the characteristics of the ETA. Membership matches the composition of the local population, although most terrorists are males. The ETA is primarily a working-class movement, as are many nationalistic terrorist groups. Its members were not necessarily raised in a Basque family, but they were raised in Basque enclaves and feel a strong ethnic identity. The overwhelming majority feel they are fighting for all the members of their community.

One of the most interesting characteristics of the ETA is that its members did not view terrorism as a full-time activity. According to Moxon-Browne's research, they maintained some type of employment while serving in the ETA. In addition, most members engaged in terrorism for only about three years. After this, they returned to their full-time occupations.

Clark (1984) says the eventual goal of Basque terrorism is regional independence. In this sense, the ETA is very similar to the IRA. Another parallel is that the majority of Basques do not support the terrorist campaign, even though most support nationalism and some form of independence. Given these circumstances, one of the prime tasks of the Spanish government has been opening the political system to the Basques and allowing them to maintain their cultural heritage. This strategy has served to delegitimize terrorism.

In the late 1980s, the Spanish government began to further delegitimize the ETA by fostering democracy in the Basque region. Although this did not limit nationalistic desire, it gave nationalists a peaceful outlet for their views. They became participants in the control of their destiny. Steven Greer (1995) points to the national police force as evidence of the effects of democratization. It turned the tables on the ETA. By opening peaceful avenues, such as self-policing, both the Spanish and the Basques were able to denounce violence. The ETA found it harder to operate.

Francisco Llora, Joseph Mata, and Cynthia Irvin (1993) point to another change in the ETA. As Spanish authorities opened opportunities for democracy and national expression, the ETA transformed itself into a social movement. Only hard-core militants were left to preach violence, and faced with decreasing support in Spain, they began seeking sanctuary in France. The French government, however, began taking actions of its own; although the government traditionally has been sympathetic to Basque nationalism, French prosecutors reversed their position, charging more than seventy ETA members with terrorism in 1994 and convicting more than sixty members by 1995. The base of ETA support appears to be eroding.

Michel Wieviorka (1993) believes that Spain's attempt to open the political system will eventually deter the ETA. In the past, he says, the ETA has claimed to represent the Basque people. Now that the Basques have their own school system, governmental institutions, and local parliament, the ETA can no longer make that claim. In the end, Wieviorka says, the struggle was twofold: cultural and political. When the political system opened, the desire for ethnic cultural identity was not strong enough to support violence. Repressive policies created the tension, and when they were removed, the support for fighting eroded. If Wieviorka's thesis is correct, ETA actions will eventually be limited to sporadic violence, or the group may even disappear. At this time, however, the ETA still engages in terrorist violence.

Siamik Khatami (1997) summarizes the situation well, and his thesis reflects Byman's conclusions about the logic of ethnic terror. Khatami says that since the fall of the Soviet Union, the ETA and its political wing have become more entrenched in a working-class ideology. They believe the economic structure of the Basque region provides its ethnic identity. Khatami believes the ETA will not compromise on ethnic identity. This gives Spanish authorities a solid opportunity to open the doors of political participation to middle-class Basque moderates. Khatami believes this will become the best weapon against ETA violence.

The issues remain volatile. In the first decade of the twenty-first century, it first appeared that the ETA and Spain might negotiate a settlement. Moved by the events of 9/11, ethnic terrorism seemed to no longer have a place in a Europe that was seeking greater unification (Rabasa et al., 2006, pp. 115–117). When jihadist terrorists struck Madrid on March 11, 2004, it drew attention to the ETA. Although some reporters immediately blamed the ETA for the Madrid train explosions, the ETA was quick to deny it and denounce the bombing. Terrorism analysts in Spain pointed out that indiscriminate murder did not follow the ETA's tactical philosophy. Many people hoped it would lead to a political solution between the Spanish government and the Basque region. Unfortunately, even though violence has waned, sporadic ETA bombings began again in 2006.

The Demise of the Left in Europe

A group taking action under the name of the Red Brigades set several fires and conducted a bombing in Italy in 2004, but few analysts of terrorism were overly alarmed. The Red Brigades had not been very active since 1995, although they had carried out one or two minor events every year. Analysts were instead more concerned with single-issue terrorism.

Europe has experienced a pattern of declining left-wing revolutionary terrorism and its reemergence into single-issue violence. A brief overview explains the reason.

Researchers in the 1980s were noting the left's declining role in European terrorism. Raymond Corrado and Rebecca Evans (1988, pp. 373–444) examine western European terrorism and conclude that it has developed into a variety of forms with few common threads. Dormant after World War II, terrorism among indigenous native groups began to reemerge during the 1960s. Corrado and Evans believe this renewed growth was a response to western European modernization and industrialization. The ideological terrorists of the 1960s, on both the left and the right, were expressing their frustration with the social structures imposed by a modern industrial society.

Nationalistic violence remained, but ideological terrorism could not maintain a base of support. Corrado and Evans argue that the fundamental difference between ideological and nationalist terrorists can be found in their goals. Ideological terrorists in Europe reject the economic and social structure of industrial capitalism; they want a new order. Despite ideological division, both the left and the right fight for this goal. Nationalists, on the other hand, frequently embrace capitalism and fight for ethnic self-determination. They desire economic opportunity within the context of a strong national identity. Nationalism stays, ideology does not.

By 1988, Corrado and Evans conclude, the popularity of nationalistic and left-wing terrorism was changing. They suggest that the pluralism of Western democracies opened the door to peaceful participation in the political system and offered opportunities for change. Violence no longer seemed an attractive method for groups to express their grievances. As pluralistic governments worked to relieve frustration, the attractiveness of terrorism waned, and terrorists lost their support base. Corrado and Evans predicted that terrorist violence would fade away, reappearing in only a few sporadic incidents. Had the political structure of Europe remained constant since their writing, they would have been correct: left-wing terrorism was out of vogue, and nationalistic terrorism was on the decline.

Few analysts of terrorism—indeed, few scholars, politicians, soothsayers, or prophets—predicted three key events that changed the political landscape of Europe and the world. In 1989 the Berlin Wall came down, leading to the reunification of Germany. To the south, new nations emerging from the former Yugoslavia took up arms and resumed a centuries-old struggle. But the greatest change of all came in the East. The Soviet Union dissolved, along with the authoritarian rule of the Communist Party in the republics of the former Soviet Union and Eastern Europe. These three changes occurred at a time when Western Europeans were taking bold steps toward economic and political unity.

A State Department terrorism specialist, Dennis Pluchinsky (1982, pp. 40–78), saw potential changes a decade before they occurred. The left might decline, but he feared Europe would become a terrorist battle-ground. Pluchinsky also believed international and state-sponsored terrorism would grow in Europe, and a greater threat was posed by what he called supraindigenous terrorism. By this, Pluchinsky meant that local terrorist activities would extend beyond local boundaries. Each time a government checks one variety of terrorism, Pluchinsky argued, a new strain appears. Unfortunately, no analyst of terrorism was more correct. Middle Eastern religious terrorism spilled into Europe, and murderous ethnic cleansing, that is, killing or driving out ethnic or religious groups inhabiting an area, dominated the Balkan Peninsula.

As the structure of Europe and the world changed from 1989 to 1992, European terrorism also changed, just as Pluchinsky had predicted. Ideological terrorism swung from left to right, changing its structure as it moved. Nationalistic terrorism remained, but conflict rose in the form of ethnic violence. Ethnic violence grew into open warfare in the Balkans. New criminal organizations appeared, and old ones were revitalized. The threat of jihadist terrorism replaced threats from the left, and Europe experienced new strains of terrorism.

After growth unprecedented since 1968, left-wing terrorism began to decline by 1986. Whereas Corrado and Evans correctly saw the demise of the left as evidence of eroding political support for terrorism, other analysts believed it was a prelude to a new leftist campaign. Pointing to the unification of left-wing terrorist groups, these analysts feared conspiracy was at its zenith around 1985. They believed all the radical groups in Europe were forming to create a single superterrorist network. They warned that a new terrorist campaign would be worse than anything the West had experienced.

Stephen Segaller (1987, pp. 36–40) saw an additional pattern. Several European leftist groups formed a coalition. Direct Action in France, the Communist Combat Cells of Belgium, the Red Army Faction of Germany, the Red Brigades in Italy, and other groups were all uniting, but the reason for unification was exactly the opposite of what many analysts thought. The leftists were seeking unity out of *weakness*, not strength. The political assumptions Corrado and Evans made were correct. Left-wing extremism had run its course. The very societies the terrorists were trying to undermine had won the struggle. How had this happened?

Segaller had the answer, and it matched the Corrado-Evans thesis. Modern European terrorism emerged in the 1960s as an extreme reflection of left-wing activism. Fueled by the Vietnam War, European leftists were influenced by events in Latin America, as well as by revolutionary leaders such as Carlos Marighella. The **Red Army Faction (RAF)**—known as the Baader-Meinhof Gang in its early days—began a campaign in Germany, followed by copycat groups and more long-term terrorist organizations in other countries.

By 1970 most left-wing groups and the resurgent nationalistic groups modeled themselves after the Marighella model. Segaller said that al-

Red Army Faction (RAF)
A left-wing German terrorist group operating from the mid-1970s to 1998. While under the leadership of Ulrike Meinhof and Andreas Baader, the RAF was known as the Baader-Meinhof Gang.

though European terrorists longed for a Marighella-style revolution, they never achieved it because they were too weak. In 1985 they faced their weakness and tried to form a confederation to gain momentum.

The left-wing coalition was an effort to pool dwindling resources and support. Members of the Communist Combat Cells of Belgium went to Paris searching for the French terrorist group Direct Action. Shortly afterward, the leadership of Italy's Red Brigades also made overtures to Direct Action. West Germany's Red Army Faction (RAF) expressed an ideological union with these groups, and Direct Action responded by publishing several communiqués, claiming that a new left-wing unified terrorist movement had formed. In reality, the left-wing terrorist groups were sounding a retreat, possibly even a death knell.

Some authors like Claire Sterling (1986) and Benjamin Netanyahu (1986, 1997) have argued that this represented an organized international campaign of terrorism against the West. A closer scholarly analysis suggests this is not the case, however. Once again, Pluchinsky (1993) gave the reason. The left had played out. No longer supported by the Soviet Union, the groups simply could not stand alone. Western European leftists lacked the support and the appeal to remain operational. He pointed to Germany's RAF as an example.

On May 28, 1998, the RAF issued a communiqué stating that it was ceasing operations. Christoph Rojahn (1998) says the RAF mirrored the demise of the European leftists, but they were responsible for Germany's massive security apparatus. In addition, mainstream left-wing politicians had limited effect while the RAF was in the streets. The RAF ceased operations because it was a miserable failure. Although it had maintained a campaign of violence for decades, it was never able to link with a mainstream issue. The group could not attract the support of the radical left, with the exception of the following in its own narrow circle. Rojahn concludes that the 1998 declaration of peace was the group's recognition of its failure.

Southern Europe has experienced a similar decline in left-wing terrorism, and Xavier Raufer (1993) looks at Italy's Red Brigades as another example of the weaknesses in the left. When the Red Brigades approached Direct Action in 1985, they were already rapidly fading from their glory days of headline-grabbing murders. Raufer believed the Red Brigades would soon follow the unilateral peace declaration of the RAF.

There were nearly 300 left-wing groups in Italy appearing between 1967 and 1985, and most of them had a Marxist-Leninist orientation. The best-known group was the Red Brigades, which formed in Milan after **Renato Curcio** broke away from a left-wing working-class political organization. Leaders gathered more militant followers and announced plans for a terrorist campaign in 1970. **Margherita Cagol** joined Curcio and later became his wife. The future militants called their organization the Red Brigades, and Curcio's 1970 group of militants became known as the Historical Nucleus.

Renato Curcio

(1941–) The founder and leader of the Red Brigades in Italy.

Margherita Cagol

(1945–1975) Also known as Mara Cagol, the wife of Renato Curcio and a member of the Red Brigades. She was killed in a shoot-out with Italian police a few weeks after freeing her husband from prison.

The Red Brigades' violent communist ideology made no mystery of its strategy for revolution. Curcio and Cagol sought to make the cities unsafe for any governmental official or sympathizer. They believed a climate of violence would help bring about a revolution in Italy and eventually in all of Europe. Members of the Brigades saw themselves as the vanguard of a worldwide communist revolution. They believed sensational violence would be their key to the future. The group taking action in the early part of the twenty-first century, however, has little resemblance to the Red Brigades of the past.

The organization of the Red Brigades was unique in European terrorism. They came closer to matching the Marighella model than did any other group in Europe. They were bound in a loose confederation, with a central committee meeting periodically to devise a grand strategy. A key difference, however, was that whereas the Tupamaros operated only in Montevideo, the Red Brigades had a variety of urban centers. Each unit, therefore, became a fairly autonomous organization within its own area. The Red Brigades managed to establish independent headquarters in several major Italian cities (see Pisano, 1987).

Currently, left-wing terrorism in Europe is out of vogue. Only three groups remained active in the mid-1990s: Dev Sol in Turkey, GRAPO in Spain, and 17N in Greece (Pluchinsky, 1993). Raymond Corrado and Rebecca Evans were correct: the ideological basis for left-wing terrorism has been eliminated. Yet Pluchinsky's earlier prediction has also proved to be correct. Single-issue terrorism is in its infancy in Europe. It centers on globalization, the environment, genetic engineering, animal rights, and the power of multinational corporations. The bigger threat comes from international jihadists, who have targeted Germany, Belgium, the Netherlands, France, Spain, and the United Kingdom. Cultlike groups, such as Aum Shinrikyo, also threaten to become involved in the next wave of ideological terrorism. As Pluchinsky suggests, new strains replace the old.

Anonymous left-wing groups set off or attempted to detonate sporadic bombs in the first decade of the twenty-first century, but they failed to establish any pattern or mount a campaign. Albena Azmanova (2004), a sociologist at the University of Kent in the United Kingdom, may have the explanation. Mainstream left-wing political groups have failed to offer any type of positive agenda in the face of changing economic patterns. As globalization takes control of the international economy, Azmanova argues, the former split between labor and capitalism, the traditional strength of the left, no longer has an agenda. The only thing the left can offer is an antiglobalization stance. It has nothing positive to offer. If an analogy can be made with the decades before the new century, it is that violent left-wing extremists claimed the political agenda of the mainstream left. They wanted to impose reforms violently. The left and the right peacefully instituted reforms. Pluchinsky argues that the mainstream stole the extremist agenda. When mainstream political views are out of vogue, extreme interpretations of those views are insignificant.

Jihadist Operations in Western Europe

Western European terrorism has been increasingly characterized by jihadist activity. Evan Kohlman (2004) argues jihadist networks can be traced to the civil strife and **ethnic cleansing** in Bosnia in the early 1990s. By 1995, Kohlman argues, jihadists had a new network of cells in several European countries. He says they expanded activities through a network of charities and ended with operational terrorist cells. These cells were responsible for a number of attacks around the world, including several in Europe. Kohlman also believes the jihadist networks in North Africa are internationalized through their relations with Europe.

The European connection with North Africa gave a foundation to jihadists returning from Afghanistan, and they allied with new home-grown violent radicals who longed to wage war on an international front. Spain has seen an increase in foreign jihadists from Morocco, and it has paid the Moroccan government €40 million to develop antiterrorist safeguards. Although it has had a frosty relationship with the United States since withdrawing from Iraq in 2005, it has not ignored the North African threat. Italy's approach has been different. Having been targeted by jihadists over the past decade, the Italian government has approached international jihadist networks in cooperation with the United States and its European neighbors (Boustany, 2005).

Spain has reason to be concerned. On March 11, 2004, ten bombs placed in knapsacks on trains were detonated by cell phones during the morning rush hour. The bombs killed 191 people and injured more than 2,000. Spanish police went to work, forming their own network of differing Spanish bureaucracies, and found an eclectic jihadist terrorist organization poised to conduct further attacks. They made initial arrests and closed in on four suspects within three weeks. The suspects committed suicide by blowing themselves up rather than surrendering. Police action had prevented further attacks, but five suspects managed to escape.

Javier Jordan and Robert Wesley (2006) analyzed the group by looking at its origins, its members, and the operational characteristics of the network. Two al Qaeda groups in Madrid were broken up by Spanish authorities shortly after 9/11. These terrorists had connections with jihadists in North Africa. Jordan and Wesley believe these North African connections kept the jihadist movement alive in Spain, even though the original terrorists had been arrested and convicted. When Spain entered the American-led alliance in the Iraq War in 2003, Osama bin Laden promised to bomb Spain. Jordan and Wesley believe that this promise inspired the transplanted North African jihadists to take action. (See Timeline 13.1: The Madrid Train Bombings of March 11, 2004.)

The group contained long-term Spanish residents who were recruited to Islamic militancy. The culprits were reasonably well-to-do, most were

ethnic cleansing
A term to describe genocide in a geographical area. Ethnic cleansing occurs when one group decides to rid an area of another group.

March 11	Ten bombs explode on Spanish trains during early morning commute; police discover one bomb unexploded, an explosive agent wired to a cell phone.	
March 13	Five suspects arrested; one has a suspicious-looking cell phone.	
March 14	A video appears criticizing Spanish support for the coalition in Iraq.	
March 18	Five suspects arrested, later released.	
March 20 to March 23	More arrests of members of a cell linked to Moroccan immigrants.	
March 24	A Syrian suspect is arrested.	
March 26	Another Moroccan arrested.	
March 30	Police link the Moroccan Islamic Combat Group to the bombing.	
April 3	Four suspects commit suicide during a police raid.	
April 5 to April 16	Eight more suspects arrested with Moroccan connections but from other North African countries; police find fax saying that Spanish actions in Afghanistan and Iraq will cause blood to flow in Spanish streets.	

TIMELINE 13.1

The Madrid Train
Bombings of
March 11, 2004

Source: BBC News, 2004.

legal Spanish residents, and many of them were married with children. Although many immigrant Muslims are excluded from Europe's middle class by educational barriers, Jordan and Wesley believe exclusion did not play a major role in the Spanish jihadist network. They feel that propaganda and the creation of a radical religious culture were the primary reasons members of the Madrid network joined the jihad. They also believed missionary organizations like the **Tablighi Jamaat** played a role.

Jordan and Wesley point out that none of the members of the Madrid network attended training camps. Essentially, they were a group of amateurs who planned, prepared, and executed a devastating terror attack. The group financed the operation by selling drugs. The date of the attack was chosen to affect the outcome of the Spanish national elections. The Spanish prime minister supported the United States in Iraq, but his challenger vowed to bring Spanish troops home. The terrorists hoped the attack would encourage voters to support the challenger, but they were fully prepared for Spanish anger to turn against the jihadists. The challenger won the election, and the terrorists won their gambit.

Spain's withdrawal from the Iraq War has not stopped jihadist activities. Terror networks remain active throughout Spain and violent Salafi preaching and recruiting remains part of the agenda at many mosques. In late May 2007, fifteen jihadists were arrested in raids across Spain for recruiting Muslims for international jihad. They were mostly North Africans. Whether Spain is in Iraq or not, al Qaeda wants to return **al Andulus** to Islamic rule (Associated Press, 2007).

Europe has also experienced jihadist activity from networks in central Asia. On July 7, 2005, jihadists bombed three trains in the **London**

Tablighi Jamaat
An Islamic missionary society founded in Northwest India (Pakistan today) in the early twentieth century. Its original purpose was to teach Muslims how to behave piously. Critics maintain that it has become dominated by a militant philosophy.

al Andulus
The Arabic name for Muslim Spain, 711–1492.

London Underground
The subway system in London.

Londonistan

A slang term for areas of
London dominated by
Muslims. The areas were
known as a haven for
radical jihadists, but police
began to crack down on
militant activities after jihadist attacks in the United
Kingdom.

Underground and a fourth bomb blew up on a bus following the subway explosions. British security and intelligence services had been preparing for violent jihadist terrorism since 9/11. The primary focus had
been on overseas operations, but they initiated domestic investigations
in 2002. By 2005 the number of domestic inquiries had risen to 500.
Yet security services were surprised to find that their attackers were not
foreign-born Muslims from a militant community called **Londonistan**
by jihadists around the world. The July 7 attacks were carried out by
young British citizens in conjunction with al Qaeda (United Kingdom,
Intelligence and Security Committee, 2006).

Early in the morning of July 7, three suspects drove from Leeds to
London. They arrived at an Underground station and met a fourth suspect. The four young men exchanged items, and each left with a knap-
sack later determined to be full of explosives. When police searched the
car they found more explosives and a pistol. Some witnesses believed
that the four young men behaved strangely as they boarded a train for
King's Station in London, but others thought they behaved quite nor-
mally. When the suspects reached King's Station, they each took a knap-
sack and split up. Three men detonated their knapsacks on crowded
trains. A fourth tried calling the other three on their cell phones, and
then detonated his backpack on a bus. All four young men died in the
blasts (United Kingdom, House of Commons, 2006). Fourteen days
later five more suspects were arrested for apparently trying to copy the
crime.

Peter Bergen and Paul Cruickshank (2007) say the link between the
bombings is indicative of the networked structure of jihadist terrorism.
In the successful bombing, at least one of the suicide bombers attended
an al Qaeda training facility in Pakistan under the orders of a militant
leader affiliated with al Qaeda. The bombers made statements praising
religious violence, and Ayman al Zawahiri claimed credit for the attack. The unsuccessful bombers appeared to have connections to jihadist
groups in Kashmir. In August 2006 British police stopped would-be suicide bombers from bringing down as many as ten transatlantic flights.
Although British nationals were involved, they were linked to networks
in Afghanistan and Pakistan.

Europe's experience with jihadist networks does much to explain
the shift of terrorism. Although ethnic and political violence present
problems, jihadist terrorism may be Europe's greatest threat. It appears
from two different sources: international jihadists who come to target
the West and homegrown religious militants who embrace the extremist
violence. Esther Pan (2005a) believes that the major reason for homegrown religious extremism is Europe's inability to assimilate Muslim
youths. When looking at Spain, Jordan and Wesley (2006) think radical
missionaries are more to blame. No matter which position is correct, jihadist networks have come to Europe (Timeline 13.2: Jihadist Incidents
in Europe). It is important to remember that 9/11 bomber Mohammed
Atta started his al Qaeda cell in Hamburg, Germany.

December 1994	Air France flight hijacked in Algiers.	
July 1995	Train bombing, Paris.	
December 2000	French and German police prevent bombing, Strasbourg.	
September 2001	Police prevent Dutch cell from bombing U.S. embassy in Paris.	
November 2003	Synagogue bombings, Istanbul.	
November 2003	Secondary suicide bombings on bank and British consulate, Istanbul.	
March 2004	Madrid train bombings.	
November 2004	Theo Van Gogh, a filmmaker, murdered by jihadists in Amsterdam.	
July 2005	London mass transit bombings.	
July 2005	British police prevent copycat bombings.	
August 2006	British police prevent attacks on transatlantic flights.	
January 2007	British police stop a kidnapping and beheading, Birmingham.	

TIMELINE 13.2

Jihadist Incidents in Europe

Self-Check

- *What course has violent Irish Republican and Unionist extremism taken in recent years?*

- *Why do militant Basques reject Spanish rule?*

- *Why has the jihadist movement replaced western European concerns about left-wing violence?*

Turkey

Turkey is an enigma in its standing with Europe. The country is 99 percent Muslim and was the home of the last caliphate. Long ago it was the seat of the Eastern, or Byzantine, Roman Empire, but when its capital Constantinople fell to **Mahmet II** in 1453, it became the center of Islam. Ironically, Mustafa Kemal, better known as **Kemal Ataturk**, dissolved Islamic government in 1923 and established Turkey as a secular republic. Although most of the country is in Asia, Turkey was accepted as a partner in NATO, and it sought close trade ties with Europe and the United States after World War II. It was the first Muslim-majority country to recognize the state of Israel.

Esther Pan (2005b) says that Turkey looks to Europe for both cultural and economic reasons. Many Europeans and Americans encourage it, hoping that Turkey will join the **European Union (EU)**. Other Europeans have been reluctant to accept Turkey, citing demographic, cultural, and religious differences. They fear that if Turkey joins the EU, Europe will be flooded with poorly educated workers and radical jihadists will strengthen their foothold in Europe. They also worry about Turkey's human rights record.

Mahmet II
(1432–1481) Ottoman sultan and conqueror of Constantinople in 1453.

Kemal Ataturk
(1881–1938) Also known as Mustafa Kemal, a Turkish military and political leader. Ataturk dissolved the caliphate in 1923 and created the Republic of Turkey with a Western-style constitution.

European Union (EU)
An economic consortium of several European states formed in 1992. It was designed to remove trade barriers and to create a unified European economy.

For its part, Turkey has many people who like the idea of blending religion and government. Other Turks are not enamored with this idea. In May 2007 nearly 500,000 people demonstrated to protest the influence of Islam in Turkey's internal affairs. The Turkish Army has declared it will not accept a religious government (Associated Press, 2007). In the midst of this dilemma, Turkey has attempted to modernize its law enforcement agencies and military within the norms of Western democracies. It has opened its doors to Western police agencies, and the **Turkish National Police** has one of the most highly educated police command staffs in the world. Turkey has also experienced several different types of terrorist campaigns over the past three decades.

Turkish National Police
The national uniformed and plainclothes investigative service of Turkey, established in 1909.

Turkey's Struggle with Terrorism

Turkey has several problems with terrorism. Although the largest issue is with the Kurdistan Workers Party (see the next section), other groups operate in Turkey. In the mid-1980s a group known as Turkish Hezbollah appeared in eastern Turkey. It has no connection with the Hezbollah that is the Lebanese Shiite group. Formed from a Sunni Kurd–Turk Islamic base, Hezbollah sought to counter the activities of the Kurdistan Workers Party. Critics claim that it received some forms of clandestine support from the government in the 1990s, but Turkish security forces might disagree. Hezbollah expanded its targets in the 1990s to businesses and other establishments that it deemed to be un-Islamic. Following the path of other terrorist groups, Hezbollah began to kidnap and torture Muslim businesspersons who refused to support its activities. Hezbollah's goal is to establish an Islamic state by force of arms (BBC News, 2000).

Brian Williams and Fezya Altindag (2004) point out that Turkey developed an internal jihadist problem after 1994. They believe that Hezbollah is part of this problem, and they state that it is blowback from the government's attempt to create Hezbollah as a counterterrorist movement against the Kurdistan Workers Party. Yet the real problem started in 1994 when several thousand Turkish young people began to attend militant madrassas in Pakistan. They returned to Turkey with an Islamic agenda. Ataturk's secular Turkey was anathema to them.

Williams and Altindag believe that the Pakistani-trained young people eventually led to a jihadist movement in Turkey, including an al Qaeda splinter group, El Kaide Turka, or al Qaeda in Turkey. By 2001 a group of madrassa-trained young men placed themselves under the leadership of **Habib Akdas**, who had undertaken a task from Osama bin Laden. Bin Laden wanted to punish Turkey for its partnerships with the United States and Israel, and he believed Akdas was the man to lead the charge. With bin Laden's encouragement, Akdas sought to strike American and Israeli interests in Turkey. Al Qaeda in Turkey would eventually expand attacks to other Westerners.

Habib Akdas
(birth date unknown) Also known as Abu Anas al Turki, the founder of al Qaeda in Turkey. Akdas left Turkey to fight in Iraq after the American invasion. He was killed in a U.S. air strike in 2004.

Habib Akdas and his followers returned to Turkey after the American-led coalition attacked al Qaeda strongholds in Afghanistan in October 2001. Williams and Altindag say that coalition forces found training manuals translated into Turkish, and this prompted the United States to send a warning to Turkey's police and military forces. Akdas sat biding his time. Not wanting to rush his attacks, he planned for the next two years. Bin Laden wanted Akdas to attack an American air base in Turkey, but Akdas believed it was guarded too well. He searched for softer targets. The U.S. embassy in **Ankara** and U.S. consulate in Istanbul also proved to be too well fortified. Akdas decided to turn to British and Israeli targets. He launched suicide attacks against two synagogues in Istanbul on November 15, 2003. He struck the British consulate and a British bank with suicide bombers less than one week later.

The double bombings backfired. Infuriated by the attacks, Turkish citizens demanded the government take action because the majority of people killed in the al Qaeda bombings had been Muslims. The Turkish National Police unleashed their full power against al Qaeda in Turkey. Williams and Altindag say that dozens of al Qaeda operatives and supporters were arrested, and Akdas removed himself to Iraq to fight the Americans. The militants fanned across Turkey and began a low-level bombing campaign. Akdas is believed to have been killed in fighting around Fallujah in November 2004 (NewsMax.com, 2006). BBC News (2006) reported that Turkish police were able to arrest several important al Qaeda in Turkey leaders in December 2006, including Akdas's replacement.

The Kurdistan Workers Party and Its Alter Egos

Turkey is currently facing a wave of religious terrorism, but for the past three decades its major problem came from Kurds, an ethnic group inhabiting parts of southern Turkey, northern Iraq, and northern Iran (see Expanding the Concept: The Kurdish Conflict). The Kurdistan Workers Party (PKK) is a Marxist-Leninist terrorist organization composed of Turkish Kurds. Officially changing its name to Kurdistan Freedom and Democracy (KADEK) in 2002 (see Another Perspective: The PKK by Any Other Name), it operates in Turkey and Europe, targeting Europeans, Turks, rival Kurds, and supporters of the Turkish government. It represents the same ruthless brand of Maoism as the Peruvian guerrilla organization Shining Path, murdering entire villages whose residents fail to follow its dictates. The PKK/KADEK has developed chameleon-like characteristics, and although it is a revolutionary Marxist group, since 1990 it has employed the language of nationalism. Even more startling, since 1995, it has also used the verbiage of religion.

The PKK was founded in 1974 to fight for an independent Kurdistan (Criss, 1995). Unlike other Kurdish groups, the PKK wanted to establish a Marxist-Leninist state. Although the PKK targeted Turkey, the Kurds claim a highland region spanning southeast Turkey, northeast Iraq, and northwest Iran (see Figure 13.1 on page 336). Taking advantage of Kurdish nationalism, the PKK began operations in 1978, hoping to launch a guerrilla war.

The plans for revolution, however, proved too grandiose. There was sentiment for fighting the Iraqis, Iranians, and Turks, but not enough

Ankara
The capital of Turkey since the birth of the Republic of Turkey. Ataturk and the Young Officers moved the capital there from Istanbul in 1923.

EXPANDING THE CONCEPT

The Kurdish Conflict

The Issue. The Kurds are an ethnic group inhabiting northern Iraq, southern Turkey, and northern Iran. When other groups received national sovereignty at the end of the World War I, the Kurds remained divided among the three nations. The Treaty of Sevres (1920) created an independent Kurdistan, but it was never implemented. About 12 million Kurds live in Turkey.

The Group. The Kurdistan Workers Party (PKK) formed in 1978 as a Marxist-Leninist group. Its goal was to create an independent socialist Kurdistan.

The Campaign. After training in Syria, the PKK launched a guerrilla campaign in Turkey. By the early 1990s, the PKK turned to urban terrorism, targeting Turks throughout Europe and in Turkey. After its leader, Abdullah Ocalan, was captured in 1999, the PKK pledged to work for a peaceful solution; however, it maintained various militant organizations operating under a variety of names. The PKK maintains links with other revolutionary groups in Turkey and with some international terrorist groups.

The Future. Turkey is being considered for admission to the European Union. The EU, NATO, and the United States list the various entities of the PKK as terrorist organizations. In October 2003 the United States agreed to crack down on the PKK in northern Iraq, and a solution to the Kurdish question might result from negotiation among the United States, the Kurds, and the Turks.

Sources: Council on Foreign Relations, 2004; Dymond, 2004; U.S. Department of State, 2004b.

support for the communists. Most Kurds wanted autonomy, not communism. The PKK was not strong enough to wage a guerrilla war without some type of support, and its political orientation prevented them from allying with other Kurdish groups. The PKK had two choices: it could either wage a propaganda campaign or throw itself into terrorism. Its leadership chose the path of terrorism.

PKK leaders increased their efforts to build a terrorist organization by moving into Lebanon's Bekaa Valley in September 1980. While training there, they met some of the most accomplished terrorists in the world, and after the 1982 Israeli invasion of Lebanon, they quickly found allies in the Syrian camp. For the next two years, the group trained and purged its internal leadership. In the meantime, some PKK members cultivated sympathy among several villages in southern Turkey. By 1984 the PKK was ready for a campaign against Turkey.

Support turned out to be the key factor. Moving from base to base in Turkey, the PKK also received money and weapons from Syria. The

ANOTHER PERSPECTIVE

The PKK by Any Other Name

The PKK operates under a variety of names. According to the U.S. Department of State, these include

- Freedom and Democracy Congress of Kurdistan
- Kurdistan Peoples' Congress (KHK)
- Peoples' Congress of Kurdistan
- Liberation Units of Kurdistan (HRK)
- Kurdish Peoples' Liberation Army (ARGK)
- National Liberation Front of Kurdistan (ERNK)
- Kurdistan Freedom and Democracy Congress (KADEK)
- Kongra-Gel (KGK)

The PKK officially changed its name to KADEK in April 2002 and to Kongra-Gel in 2003.

Source: U.S. Department of State, 2004.

relatively weak group of 1978 emerged as a guerrilla force in 1984, and it ruthlessly used terrorism against the Turks and their allies. Civilians bore the brunt of PKK atrocities, and within a few years the PKK had murdered more than 10,000 people. The majority of these murders came as a result of village massacres (Criss, 1995). Turkey responded by isolating the PKK from their support bases and counterattacking PKK groups. Turkish security forces operated with a heavy hand.

The tactics had a negative effect on the Kurds. Although they were ready to fight for independence, they were not willing to condone massacres and terrorist attacks. The PKK responded in 1990 by redirecting offensive operations. Rather than focusing on the civilian population, the PKK began limiting its attacks to security forces and economic targets. Having expanded into western Europe a few years earlier, PKK leaders stated they would strike only "legitimate" Turkish targets. The PKK also modified its Marxist-Leninist rhetoric and began to speak of nationalism.

In a 1995 interview (Korn, 1995), PKK leader **Abdullah Ocalan** reiterated the new PKK position. When asked whether he was a Marxist, Ocalan stated that he believed in "scientific socialism." Ocalan said this would become a new path because the Muslim population and the Kurds in particular had suffered at the hands of Marxist-Leninists. He cast his statements in anti-imperialist format, stating that Kurdistan was only resisting imperialist powers.

In October 1995, Ocalan asked the United States to mediate between the PKK and Turkey, saying the PKK was willing to settle for a federation instead of complete autonomy. U.S. officials immediately rejected the terrorist's rhetoric, which was nothing new. The PKK had started speaking of federal status in 1990 (Criss, 1995). Irrespective of the form

Abdullah Ocalan

(1948–) The leader of the PKK. Ocalan was captured in 1999 and sentenced to death, but his sentence was commuted. He ordered the end of a suicide-bombing campaign while in Turkish custody and called for peace between Turkey and the Kurds in 2006.

Figure 13.1

Kurdish Region: Turkey, Iraq, and Iran

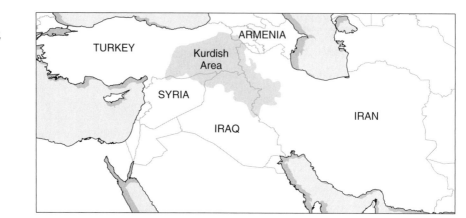

of government, Ocalan wanted semiautonomy. In the October 1995 letter to the United States, Ocalan asked for federal status "like the United States." Earlier that year, he had asked for the same thing, but "like the Russian Federation" (Korn, 1995). The most dramatic announcement came later. By December, the PKK was using the rhetoric of Islam, citing religious texts instead of Marxist-Leninist ideology. Ocalan appealed to Muslim Kurds, in the name of God, to revolt against the so-called secular Turkish government.

At first it might sound surprising to hear the Marxists of the PKK using religious language, but it is politically understandable. The PKK shifted its position to achieve the greatest amount of support. Ocalan had been moving in an anti-Western direction for many years. His terrorists attacked a NATO base in 1986, and they kidnapped nineteen Western tourists in 1993. As jihadist rhetoric grew against the West, Ocalan simply copied the verbiage. Additionally, there was something more. In June 1996 an Islamic religious government came to power in secular Turkey. Ocalan wanted to prove he was not an ogre who massacred civilians in their villages but simply a good Muslim.

Ocalan's shift to religion gave the PKK new life. Leftist movements in Turkey followed the path of their European counterparts: they went into hibernation. When Ocalan proclaimed a doctrine of Marxist Islam, the PKK managed to survive. A unilateral cease-fire on the part of the PKK in December 1995 placed Turkey in an awkward position. According to Nur Bilge Criss (1995), Ocalan's religious rhetoric played well not only among Kurds but also throughout the Middle East. Writing before the 1996 election, Criss predicted Turkey would move closer to the Islamic world to counter this threat. He also said the supreme irony is that Turkey may be drawn away from NATO to an alliance with Iraq or Iran in an effort to counterbalance the Kurds and the Syrians. His predictions turned out to be incorrect.

The PKK represents the pejorative nature of terrorism. When the terrorist label is applied to a group like the PKK, the whole movement is questioned. Kurds have long suffered at the hands of their neighbors.

The Iranians have slaughtered them, Saddam Hussein used rockets and poison gas to destroy entire Kurdish villages, and the Turks have repressed them. The PKK is a terrorist organization, but expressing Kurdish nationalism is not a terrorist act. Many thousands of Kurds were victimized by state terrorism long before the PKK unsheathed its sword.

Turkish authorities captured Abdullah Ocalan in Kenya in February 1999, and a security court sentenced him to death in June. Ocalan offered to chart a new course for the PKK a few weeks later. Because Turkey was lobbying to join the EU, it delayed and eventually reversed the death sentence. (Members of the EU may not invoke capital punishment.) It appeared as if there might be a window for peace.

The question of ethnic violence remains open, and the problem has increased since the U.S.-led invasion of Iraq. Turkey casts a wary eye on the Kurds, and many Kurdish guerrillas would actively fight Turkey and Iran for an autonomous homeland. Today, the PKK has thousands of supporters in Turkey and in Europe, but the United States agreed to crack down on the organization in northern Iraq in late 2003 (Dymond, 2004). This may create new possibilities for a negotiated peace between the Turks and the Kurds. By the same token, an autonomous Kurdish area in Iraq worries the Turks (Karon, 2003).

Self-Check

- *How is Turkey's struggle against terrorism similar and dissimilar from the issues in Europe?*
- *Cite the types of groups that practice terrorism in Turkey.*
- *How does the PKK differ from the jihadist movement?*

The Russian Federation

Since the collapse of the Soviet Union, the Russian Federation has been seeking its place among the world's powers. Weakened by the growth of its former eastern European holdings, Russia faces internal economic and political problems. Its leadership is becoming increasingly centralized and relations with the United States have grown sour. Two issues dealing with terrorism surface in the federation. The first deals with the problem of breakaway states. The second problem is nearly two centuries old, the status of Chechnya.

Breakaway States and Crime

After the collapse of the Soviet Union, Russia experienced widespread economic dislocation and a drop of close to 50 percent in gross domestic product (GDP). Stuart Goldman (2007), reporting for the Congressional Resource Service, says the economy was worse than the American economy during the **Great Depression**. Economic conditions have improved, but Russia still suffers from environmental troubles, a poor health system, and sharp declines in life expectancy. It also suffers from

Great Depression
The description of the international economy from the time of the U.S. stock market crash of 1929 until the beginning of World War II.

Figure 13.2

States in the Russian Federation That Have Declared Independence from Russia

organized crime and corruption. All of these factors serve to destabilize the country. One of the other problems that plague the country is the rise of de facto states. These are parts of the Russian Federation that simply refuse to accept Russian government and control from Moscow.

Dov Lynch (2004, pp. 22–39) explains the situation. The former Soviet Union broke into fifteen new nations in the early 1990s. Each nation had its own problems, and each one had to establish new relations with Moscow and the rest of the world's governments. The issue for the Russian Federation, however, was that five states declared their independence from Russia. Four are Nargorno-Karabakh in Azerbaijan, South Ossetia and Abkhazia in Georgia, and Transnistria in Moldova (Figure 13.2). The fifth, Chechnya, is the only one whose claim Russia has been successful in countering, but fighting continues to rage there.

Lynch says the inability to pull these states back into the country creates a haven for organized crime and terrorism. Because they lie outside the authority of Russia but remain unrecognized by the community of nations, they become failed states where arms trade, organized crime, and narcotics trafficking flourish. These regions are a hotbed for terrorism. Lynch concludes that if this situation is to be addressed, the international community must adopt methods for dealing with the regions so that some type of legal order can be introduced. The rebellion in Chechnya is another issue.

Chechnya

Unlike ideological terrorists, ethnic terrorist organizations tend to be long lasting. They can build logistical structures much more easily than ideological terrorists because they appeal to an ethnic group, and they can hide in a ready-made population (see Byman, 1998). Guerrillas and terrorists in the Russian-controlled province of Chechnya call on nationalism in a struggle for autonomy. Jihadist ideologues have not been able

Many jihadists have flocked to the Transcaucasia region, thinking it to be another Afghanistan. However, if the history of the area is examined, Chechnya can be explained as a revolt based in nationalism or ethnicity.

1830	Imperial Russia expands into the Caucasia region.
1859	Russia annexes Caucasia, including Dagestan and Chechnya.
1917–1923	Dagestan and Chechnya declare independence.
1923	The Communists conquer Caucasia, adding Dagestan and Checheno-Ingush to the USSR.
1944	Stalin purges the Caucasia area, fearing Chechens and others were influenced by Germany.
1991	The USSR falls; Chechens declare independence, but Russia rejects the claim.
1994–1996	Russia invades Chechnya; agrees to a cease-fire after severe casualties.
1997	Chechens launch bombing campaign in Russia; rebels enter Dagestan.
1999	Russia renews the war, takes Dagestan and launches devastating strikes on Chechnya.
2002	The Moscow theater takeover.
2004	The Beslan school takeover.

Sources: Walker, 2001; D. Lynch, 2004; Johnson and Brunner, 2004.

to create a large base of support for the cause, but Chechen nationalists have many followers because of their appeal to patriotism. This has not stopped either the Russians or international jihadists from claiming that Chechnya is a microcosm representing the West's struggle with al Qaeda. Although Russia has been able to assert more control in Chechnya than in its other breakaway states, it has experienced savage fighting in the region and terrorism in the Russian homeland as a result. In Daniel Byman's words, the tried-and-true methods of counterterrorism do not work against ethnic violence. Chechnya serves as an example (Timeline 13.3: Chechnya as a Nationalistic Revolt).

Groups in Asia have made their presence felt in the ethnic struggle between the Russian Federation and the would-be breakaway state of Chechnya. They seek legitimacy in the nationalistic struggle, but issues started long ago. Imperial Russia sought to impose Russian power in Chechnya in the early nineteenth century. Felix Corley (2004) says the current dispute can be traced directly to the communist era when Joseph Stalin (ruled 1922–1953) imposed Soviet power in the region. Since the fall of the Soviet Union, the Russians and Chechens have fought two conventional wars for control of the area. The first war lasted from 1991 to 1996. The current round of fighting began in 1999. Faced with overpowering Russian military force, some Chechens decided to strike inside Russia using the tools of terrorism. International jihadists came and sought to expand the war to the entire Caucasus region. They felt this could become the base for the new caliphate.

Figure 13.3

Chechnya and Dagestan

Despite the presence of international jihadists, the U.S. Department of State (2004c) says that Chechen rebels should not be lumped with other jihadist movements. According to the U.S. ambassador to Russia, Chechens are engaged in a legitimate war of independence and are not like other jihadist terrorists (Turks.US, 2004). Al Qaeda has tried to claim the Chechen-Russian conflict, the ambassador said, but Chechnya has been seeking independence for many years, and the struggle predates the jihadist movement by 200 years. Others believe jihadists influence the violent nature of the independence movement. Chechnya thrives on support from jihadist groups and imports jihadist tactics. Ayman al Zawahiri went to Chechnya to recruit and fight with new mujahideen groups after the Soviet-Afghan War. The Russians even jailed him, but released him through an oversight (Sud, 2004).

Stuart Goldman (2007) says the current wave of fighting began when international jihadists moved from Chechnya to Dagestan in 1999 in an attempt to broaden the conflict (Figure 13.3). An irregular militia, claiming to be members of the international jihadist struggle, occupied several villages in Dagestan. The group's leaders, two ruthless men known for hostagetaking and murder, proclaimed an Islamic republic and the beginning of a new caliphate. At the same time a series of explosions in a Moscow apartment complex killed more than 300 people. **Vladimir Putin**, the newly elected Russian prime minister, blamed the Chechens for both attacks and sent overwhelming military force into the breakaway state.

Paul Murphy (2004) believes there were three primary characters in the 1999 rebellion. The first was **Shamil Basayev**, a man who had gained fame by taking an entire hospital hostage in 1995 during the first Chechen war and whose 1999 actions in Dagestan started the second. Murphy describes Basayev as a Che Guevara–type figure who led by charisma and example. Basayev would increase his reputation by planning the takeover of a **Moscow theater** in 2002. An estimated 200 people—130 hostages and the remainder terrorists and security forces—

Vladimir Putin

(1952–) The president of the Russian Federation. He succeeded Boris Yeltsin in 1999.

Shamil Basayev

(1965–2006) A jihadist leader in Chechnya, Basayev engineered several operations resulting in mass civilian casualties.

Moscow theater

(Theatrical Center, Dubrovka, Moscow, 2002) The site of a Chechen attack where approximately 40 terrorists took 850 hostages. Russian forces stormed the theater on the third day of the siege, killing 39 terrorists and at least 129 hostages.

were killed. Two years later, on the opening day of the **Beslan school**, Basayev masterminded another takeover. Using children as hostages, his terrorists killed an estimated 300 to 400 people, mostly children. Basayev was killed in the summer of 2006 (see Expanding the Concept: Learning to Be Ruthless in Chechnya).

Murphy identifies two other jihadists. The second international jihadist leader, a mysterious leader known by the nom de guerre **ibn al Khattab**, was a Saudi. Basayev brought Khattab to Chechnya in 1995. Described as the "Black Wahhabi," he became known for ruthlessness. He was assassinated by Russian agents in 2002. The third leader, Salman Raduyev, took more hostages than any other terrorist. Before he went mad, Raduyev threatened to attack Russian nuclear facilities, Murphy says. Khattab and Basayev were responsible for the Dagestan invasion.

Although the Russian Army took **Grozny**, the capital of Chechnya, after heavy fighting in 2000, conflict continued. Murphy (2004) describes the pattern of both wars. At times the Chechens would stand and fight. This would give rise to conventional battles where the Russians were generally successful at a heavy cost. At other times the Chechens used the hit-and-run tactics of guerrilla warfare. These were more effective but brought reprisals from the Russians. The Russian Army used massed bombardments, summary execution, rape, and torture to counter guerrilla tactics. The Chechens responded in kind. Although this was a savage war, it was not entirely linked to the jihadist movement. Most Chechens fought for state autonomy.

Murphy points out that Basayev and Khattab approached the situation differently. They called for international jihadists to flock to Chechnya to begin an Islamic revolution. With this in mind, their tactics went far beyond guerrilla warfare. They introduced the tactics of terrorism and suicide bombings. Given the Russian tendency to ravage areas where they were attacked, the jihadists sought a new weapon, female suicide bombers called the **Black Widows**, who were women who had suffered at the hands of the Russians and who gained a reputation for effectiveness (Timeline 13.4: Chechen Suicide Attacks: The Black Widows).

In October 2002 about 50 Chechen rebels took over the Theatrical Center in Moscow during an evening performance. They took about 700 hostages. The group contained men and self-described Black Widows, and they demanded that Russian troops leave Chechnya. In the early morning on the third day of the siege, Russian special forces assaulted the theater, thinking hostages were being killed. The plan called for the introduction of sleeping gas, then the actual assault. It was a disaster. Aware that something was happening, the male terrorists engaged in a prolonged gun fight with the rescuers. The Black Widows, who may have been armed with explosives, were to set off their suicide explosives in an effort to kill as many hostages as possible. Fortunately, they hesitated while awaiting instructions from the men. Before Russian forces had restored order about 200 people were dead, many killed by the sleeping gas (CNN, 2002).

Beslan school

A Chechen terrorist attack on the first day of school in September 2004 in North Ossetia. The scene was chaotic and Russians forces were never able to establish a security perimeter. Although details remain unclear, the incident resulted in the murder of nearly 400 people, including more than 100 children.

ibn al Khattab

(1969–2002) Also known as Emir Khattab or the Black Wahhabi, an international Saudi jihadist who went to fight in Chechnya. He tried to move the Chechen revolt from a nationalistic platform to the philosophy of religious militancy. He was killed by the Russian secret service in 2002.

Grozny

The capital of Chechnya.

Black Widows

Chechen female suicide bombers. They are known as Islamic martyrs in the Chechen language.

Learning to Be Ruthless in Chechnya

Of the many suicide operations carried out by Chechens, two gained the most attention in the United States: the October 2002 attack on a Moscow theater and the September 2004 attack on a school in Beslan. Both attacks were suicide missions designed to produce massive casualties. A comparison of the two attacks demonstrates the way jihadists learned and corrected previous mistakes.

Moscow Dubrovka Theatrical Center: October 2002

What went as planned:

1. Terrorists took over a theater and isolated it.

2. Terrorists segregated hostages in small groups.

3. Terrorists planted enough bombs to kill most of the people in the theater.

4. Terrorists drew international attention to their cause.

What went wrong:

1. Terrorists formed partial bonds and relationships with some hostages.

2. Female terrorists took orders from males; therefore, when Russian special forces attacked, females waited for instructions to detonate bombs. But the males were busy fighting and could not give them.

3. Some hostages kept and used cell phones.

What the terrorists learned:

1. Ruthlessness, including random executions, keeps human bonds from forming.

2. Bombers should be readily prepared to detonate explosives at the first sign of an assault.

3. Cell phones must be destroyed.

The Beslan Middle School Number 1 Attack: September 2004

Jihadists learned lessons from the theater attack. To eliminate bonding and maintain control they did the following:

1. Publicly executed hostages at the beginning of the incident.

2. Destroyed cell phones.

3. Executed a terrorist who stated he never intended to attack a school.

4. Humiliated and intimidated the children taken hostage.

5. Played psychological games to keep parents in fear.

6. Denied food and water to hostages.

7. Bayoneted a young boy when he cried for a drink of water.

8. Gave selected females leading roles.

9. Placed bombs to detonate upon any counterattack without orders.

Sources: Ostovsky, Beliakov, and Franchetti, 2004; Spechard et al., 2004.

In the twenty-first century, the Chechen Black Widows have become a terrorist force in Russia. They get their name from the fact that many of them are widows of Chechen fighters.

June 2000	Suicide car bomb against Russian troops.
November 2001	A single attacker kills herself and a Russian officer with a hand grenade.
June 2002	A single bomber kills herself on a bus loaded with Russian pilots.
October 10–26, 2002	Forty-one rebels with female suicide bombers take hostages in a Moscow theater. One hundred twenty-nine people die when Russian forces attack.
May 12, 2003	Two females explode a truck at a Russian checkpoint.
May 14, 2003	Two females explode body bombs at religious service.
July 5, 2003	Two females attack a rock festival in Moscow.
July 10, 2003	A bomb carried by a single bomber accidentally explodes as the bomber is en route to a Moscow target.
July 27, 2003	A single bomber kills herself and a security guard when she's stopped for an inspection.
December 5, 2003	Three females kill 44 people on a commuter train. More than 150 are injured.
December 9, 2003	A single bomber attacks the National Hotel in Moscow.

Source: Saradzhyan, 2004.

In March 2003, Russia agreed to a new Chechen constitution, giving the region limited autonomy within the federation. Although Russia hoped this would help resolve the fighting, hopes were in vain. The Russian-appointed leader was assassinated in May 2004. Russia quickly introduced a new pro-constitution candidate who was elected in August of the same year. It appeared that an end to the fighting might be negotiated. Unfortunately, another Basayev-engineered disaster was on the horizon.

Jihadists staged the deadliest raid of all in September 2004 by crossing from Chechnya into Beslan, a village in North Ossetia. This time the terrorists herded the hostages into the school's gymnasium and wired it with explosives. Outside, the situation was a mess. Russian security forces responded, but so did parents. There were soldiers, police officers, and civilians running around with weapons. One of the Russians observing the situation told me that there was no chance to establish a perimeter. A bomb went off in the building and people started to flee. Gunfights broke out, parents ran to get their children, and children fled the building as terrorists shot them. There were at least 330 people killed, including 156 children (*Time Europe*, 2004).

By 2005 Moscow had been able to suppress large-scale military action, but it faced the prospect of prolonged fighting. The Russians managed to kill Basayev in 2006. Stuart Goldman (2007) is not optimistic about a quick settlement. Many foreign governments have criticized Russia's heavy hand. In addition, separatists conduct terrorist attacks inside Russia. Goldman estimates that Russia has lost more than 15,000 troops in Chechnya from 1999 to 2006. He says this is comparable to total Soviet losses in Afghanistan (1979–1989). He also writes, "Russian authorities deny there is a 'humanitarian catastrophe' in the North Caucasus and strongly reject foreign 'interference' in Chechnya. The bloodshed continues on both sides. Russian forces regularly conduct sweeps and 'cleansing operations' that reportedly result in civilian deaths, injuries, and abductions" (Goldman, 2007, p. 7). Chechnya will be a source of terrorism and state repression for the near future.

Self-Check

- *How are breakaway states related to terrorism?*
- *How do jihadists describe the two wars in Chechnya?*
- *How do Chechen nationalists view the conflict?*

SUMMARY

- Terrorism in Europe grew from renewed violence in the 1960s and 1970s. Ideology and nationalism drove the terrorist agenda. Nationalistic revolts were classified as ideological terrorism, but further research demonstrated that nationalists behaved differently than ideologues.
- Ireland may be coming to the end of a centuries-long struggle. Extremists seem to be moving to the mainstream, even though northern Unionists feel abandoned by the United Kingdom.
- Basque violence against Spain continues, but Spanish authorities are increasingly preoccupied by jihadist networks.
- When the United States began to take notice of European terrorism, it feared leftist violence. Many analysts pointed to a leftist conspiracy, but others noted that it was a conspiracy of the weak. European governments virtually stole the leftist agenda, leaving leftist terrorist groups irrelevant.
- Jihadist terrorism is Europe's greatest threat. Coming to Europe through the fighting in the Balkan Peninsula, jihadist networks established footholds in Europe. Countries have been targeted by international and homegrown violent religious extremists.
- Turkey has experienced terrorism for three decades. Domestic and international jihadists have attacked recently, but Turkey's largest problem has been the PKK.
- When the former Soviet Union broke apart in 1991, the old Soviet republics formed fifteen separate nations recognized by Moscow and the rest of the world. Five separatist states demanded their own rec-

ognition as independent nations, but neither the Russians nor other nations have recognized them.

- Chechnya sought independence after the collapse of the Soviet Union, but the Russians were able to respond. The majority of Chechens fight for nationalistic causes, but Russian and religious extremists have painted the struggle in terms of an international jihad. Terrorists complicated the issue by bringing violence to the Russian homeland.

KEY TERMS

Tony Blair (p. 319)
Red Hand Defenders (p. 319)
Orange Volunteers (p. 319)
Robert McCartney (p. 319)
Independent Monitoring Commission (p. 320)
Police Service of Northern Ireland (p. 320)
Francisco Franco (p. 320)
Spanish Civil War (p. 321)
Red Army Faction (p. 325)
Renato Curcio (p. 326)
Margherita Cagol (p. 326)
ethnic cleansing (p. 328)
Tablighi Jamaat (p. 329)
al Andulus (p. 329)
London Underground (p. 329)

Londonistan (p. 330)
Mahmet II (p. 331)
Kemal Ataturk (p. 331)
European Union (p. 331)
Turkish National Police (p. 332)
Habib Akdas (p. 332)
Ankara (p. 333)
Abdullah Ocalan (p. 335)
Great Depression (p. 337)
Vladimir Putin (p. 340)
Shamil Basayev (p. 340)
Moscow theater (p. 340)
Beslan school (p. 341)
ibn al Khattab (p. 341)
Grozny (p. 341)
Black Widows (p. 341)

WRITING ASSIGNMENTS

1. Modern European terrorism has changed since it reemerged around 1960–1965. Explain these transformations, including ethnic and ideological divisions. Focus on the ideological left, Ireland, and Spain.
2. Many analysts believe jihadist networks dominate modern European terrorism. Explain this perspective by tracing the movement of jihadist groups from the Balkan Peninsula to the remainder of Europe from the early 1990s to the present.
3. Is the unrest in Chechnya a result of international jihadist operations or local unrest? If local, explain the terrorist events at the Moscow theater and Beslan. If international, explain the nationalistic aspects of Chechnya.

14

The Structure and Study of Domestic Terrorism

The remains of a research lab at Michigan State University after an attack by the Animal Liberation Front. The United States has a wide array of violent domestic extremist groups.

Learning Objectives

After reading this chapter you should be able to

- Outline findings from the early studies of domestic terrorism.

- List the reasons law enforcement agencies have trouble understanding terrorism.

- Describe how the FBI's conceptual framework can be used in empirical studies.

- Explain the various aspects of the jihadist movement in the United States.

- Summarize the issues regarding the Puerto Rican nationalistic movement.

- Outline the history of right-wing extremism in the United States.

- Explain the demise of left-wing terrorism and the rise of single issues.

- Discuss antiabortion attacks.

Even given the deadly bombing in Oklahoma City in April 1995 and the attacks of September 11, 2001, America's recent experience with terrorism has been limited. Most attacks involve low-level strikes. Small ideological groups, violent activists, political extremists, and actions by foreign nationals have accounted for the bulk of domestic terror. September 11 suddenly thrust the United States into a jihadist conflict. Homegrown violent extremists, even homegrown jihadists, have joined the mixture. Right-wing extremists seem to be forming leaderless networks, and left-wing violence has given way to single issues. Antiabortion violence increased during the 1990s, but it appears to have leveled off in the next decade. Several noted scholars, law enforcement agencies, and bureaucratic organizations have tried to come to grips with all of these problems.

Early Studies of Domestic Terrorism

The United States has a long history of political violence, but until recently, few scholars characterized it as "terrorism." Three exceptions were H. H. A. Cooper, J. Bowyer Bell, and Ted Robert Gurr, all three of whom initiated work in this area before it was popular to speak of domestic terrorism. Bell is a leading authority on terrorism, and he completed one of the best-known scholarly works on the Irish Republican Army. Gurr is a political scientist and an expert on domestic political violence. Cooper directed the preparation of a report on terrorism by the National Advisory Commission on Criminal Justice Standards and Goals. Cooper and the National Advisory Commission provided the conceptual framework for domestic terrorism, and Bell and Gurr placed terrorist violence within the perspective of the American political experience.

Nixon's National Advisory Commission

Cooper and coauthors (1976) produced a presidential report on the political context of domestic terrorism. Combining the examination with work on civil disorders, Cooper and colleagues demonstrated the need to prepare law enforcement departments and other supporting agencies for emergencies. They presented a series of recommendations for emergency response. Although the report of the **Task Force on Disorders and Terrorism** is three decades old, the standards of performance it suggests remain valid, especially in the wake of 9/11.

The report focused on the police role in responding to terrorism. It outlined the differences between criminal investigations and counter-

Task Force on Disorders and Terrorism
The report issued by the National Advisory Commission Task Force on Disorders and Terrorism, the first presidential commission to investigate terrorism. Formed under the order of President Richard Nixon, the task force was headed by H. H. A. Cooper and was composed of some of the most noted terrorism analysts of the time.

terrorist operations, something American police agencies have finally started to master with the expansion of Joint Terrorism Task Forces (JTTFs) and specialized counterterrorist units. It talked about the need to collect, store, and analyze information. In the spring of 2007 the Department of Justice, Department of Homeland Security, the FBI, the United States attorney general, and the National Directorate for Intelligence hosted the first national conference on fusing criminal information and national defense intelligence. The Task Force on terrorism had suggested this course of action thirty years earlier.

Bell and Gurr: Examining the History of Domestic Terrorism

Cooper's team developed a pragmatic emergency-response planning model, whereas Gurr placed terrorism within its historical context. In an article written with J. Bowyer Bell (Bell and Gurr, 1979), Gurr argues that terrorism is a tactic used by the weak to intimidate the strong and, in turn, used by the strong to repress the weak. In this sense, America's history is filled with terrorist activities. Various political movements have used forms of terrorism to seek political gains. At the same time, industrial giants and those holding power have historically used terrorism to maintain control over workers and unions.

Bell and Gurr begin their review by looking at the late 1800s. Despite the American paranoia about radicals at that time, terrorism in the nineteenth century was primarily aimed at protecting the status quo and the economic environment. The actions of company security police and private corporations were often terroristic in nature, designed to keep workers from disrupting production. Labor radicals, however, also behaved violently; the labor movement of the late nineteenth century was replete with violence. Bell and Gurr call all these actions a form of terrorism.

Labor violence was not the only source of early U.S. terrorism. The frontier had its own special form of violence. As people moved west, the laws of the United States trailed far behind. Settlers developed their own brand of makeshift justice. At times, this type of justice spilled over into vigilante activities. Bell and Gurr believe that some vigilante actions equaled terrorism. In more recent times, the actions of the Ku Klux Klan are an example.

Although America has a long history of political violence, Bell and Gurr separate modern American terrorism from its historical precedents. In the 1960s, they argue, the character of domestic terrorism began to change, becoming rooted in radical politics, nationalism, and the international community's experience with terrorism. The use of terrorism to maintain social order was forgotten in the modern setting, and domestic terrorism was defined as a radical phenomenon.

Bell and Gurr believe the shift toward left-wing violence was derived from foreign models. Both political revolutionary groups and nationalistic groups in the United States took their ideas from terrorists in the Middle East and Asia. In this sense, both types of groups saw themselves as being involved in a broader struggle of international proportions.

Their logic had a catch, however. Bell and Gurr note that American terrorist groups did not have the same impact as their foreign counterparts. The American public rejected the violence of the revolutionary groups, and they never fully achieved popularity, even among their most sympathetic audiences. Revolutionary terrorists in the United States ended up as small bands of social misfits who had very little effect on the political system. As a result, the United States has been spared the excesses of revolutionary terrorism.

Bell and Gurr issue two caveats with their conclusion. First, even though the United States has avoided significant domestic terrorism, both criminals and political activists have used terrorist tactics on a local level, particularly the tactics of bombing and hostagetaking. Second, nationalist terrorists from Puerto Rico have been far more successful than revolutionaries at launching terrorist campaigns because they have an indigenous base of support. Although they have not had a major impact, Puerto Rican terrorists have enjoyed more success than revolutionary terrorists because of this support.

In a later work, Gurr (1988a) updates some of these ideas about domestic terrorism and outlines three types of terrorism: (1) vigilante terrorism, (2) insurgent terrorism, and (3) transnational terrorism.

Vigilante Terrorism. The growth of right-wing extremists is indicative of vigilante terrorism. The purpose of vigilantes is to defend the status quo or return to the status quo of an earlier period. Gurr points to the Ku Klux Klan, the Christian Identity movement, and other white supremacy organizations as examples of vigilante terrorism that rely on right-wing rhetorical traditions.

Insurgent Terrorism. Gurr describes insurgent terrorists in revolutionary terms. Black militants, white revolutionaries, and Puerto Rican nationalists fall into this category. Insurgent terrorism aims to change political policies through direct threats or action against the government. It is the political antithesis of vigilante terrorism because it attacks the status quo.

Transnational Terrorism. Transnational terrorism occurs when nonindigenous terrorists cross national borders. Gurr identifies several sources of transnational terror in the United States. Some foreign nationals have carried their fights onto U.S. soil, and some domestic groups have been inspired by foreign events. In other cases, foreign countries may have begun to target Americans at home. However, Gurr does not think the threat of transnational terrorism has been as great as popularly believed. Of course, he was writing before the bombing of the World Trade Center in 1993 and the jihadist movement inside the United States.

Self-Check

- *Characterize the nature of domestic terrorism from 1960 to 1985.*
- *In what ways do older research findings apply to terrorism today?*
- *What have more recent studies revealed?*

The Problem of Understanding Terrorism by Law Enforcement

Some American police agencies have gone to great lengths to prepare for terrorism; others have not. American law enforcement is a localized affair, and chiefs of police and sheriffs report to local boards. At the same time various state and federal agencies also exercise law enforcement power. This leads to confusion in preparing for terrorism.

For example, one senior Utah law enforcement officer, charged with coordinating security in preparation for the 2002 Winter Olympics in Salt Lake City, related the following story to me. After the initial security meeting, the director of France's security detail approached him to ask which agency was in charge. When the officer explained the federal, state, local, and tribal law enforcement systems in the United States, the French officer replied that he understood those divisions; he wanted to know which agency was in charge. The officer responded that each agency had its own leaders, and the leaders coordinated the response. The Frenchman shook his head, saying he would never understand American policing. Law enforcement is a local affair in the United States, complicated by layers of competing state and federal bureaucracies. Agencies approach terrorism with their own interpretations.

Terrorism Happens in Other Places

One of the reasons law enforcement has difficulty understanding terrorism is that it does not occur in most jurisdictions. American police officers do not spend a lot of time thinking about terrorism. They are faced with traffic accidents, gang problems, domestic disputes, and a host of tasks dealing with social order. Even in the wake of standoffs with domestic religious extremists, the Oklahoma City bombing, and al Qaeda's attacks, many U.S. law enforcement agencies remain focused on local issues. Most police managers do not think in the abstract and pride themselves on localized pragmatism. City councils and county commissioners look at local crime and the immediate concerns of their constituents. They rarely ask their police executives to apply critical thought in hypothetical exercises. Many people believe terrorism happens somewhere else (NBC/*The Wall Street Journal*, 2004). Terrorism is simply too exotic for most agencies until gun-toting students shoot their way through a local high school, a jihadist sleeper cell is caught running live-fire exercises, or a lone gunman goes on a killing spree in a state university.

Classifying Terrorism as Normal Crime

Another problem is that, although U.S. law enforcement officers routinely deal with terrorism, they call it something else. Even the FBI labels the majority of domestic terrorist activities with common crime designations in the Uniform Crime Report, an annual standard measure of criminal activity in the United States. In addition, the FBI's reports on domestic terrorism do not classify many terrorists' acts as "terrorism";

they are excluded from the terrorism report and classified as regular crimes in the FBI's annual Uniform Crime Report. Nonetheless, in the 1980s the FBI slowly learned practical methods for countering terrorism, and it became the only agency that could coordinate thousands of local U.S. police departments in counterterrorism. The irony of their efforts was that the FBI simply did not call much of their work counterterrorism. In addition, when terrorists are successful, as in Oklahoma City in 1995 or in New York City and Washington, D.C., in 2001, Congress is quick to point a finger at the FBI, forgetting about past successes (see FBI, 2002).

Closely related to this problem is that even after September 11 most domestic terrorism goes unnoticed. William Dyson (2004) tracks terrorist incidents in the United States and has identified nearly 300 that occurred between September 11, 2001, and December 2004. Most of these incidents were limited to threats or extensive property damage, and none of them involved massive numbers of deaths. These are probably the reasons most Americans fail to notice terrorist activity. Bombing serves as an excellent example. According to a *New York Times* News Service (1996) analysis, domestic bombings almost tripled between 1985 and 1994, from 1,103 to 3,163. Large explosions capture the world's attention, but the overwhelming number of bombings in the United States deal with individual criminal vendettas and single-issue terrorism.

Uneven Historical Development

Another reason for the lack of concern is that recent terrorism developed slowly in America. Terrorism grew with radical groups beginning about 1965, and although there were some sensational activities, terrorists did not routinely target the United States until 1982. Before then, most American terrorist movements died for lack of support. Since 1982, however, terrorists have produced an increasing number of victims in the United States. Even though the majority of incidents still involve low-level criminal activity, Americans have sadly learned that they cannot automatically dismiss terrorism as something that happens somewhere else.

Confusing Hate Crime and Terrorism

Daniel Levitas (2002, pp. 341–342) says that hate groups in America may launch the next major terrorist attack. Even if they choose not to do so, they bear watching, he says. Who are these hate groups? According to Levitas they include certain violent right-wing extremists, the Ku Klux Klan, paramilitary organizations (or militias), abortion clinic bombers, violent anti-immigrant groups, and others who are violent in the name of race or ethnicity. Many police officers would agree with this analysis, but it confuses the issue of domestic terrorism. Specifically, it brings up the problem of differentiating between hate groups and terrorist groups, and hate crime and terrorism.

The term **hate crime** is frequently used in conjunction with domestic terrorism. Hate crime is a relatively new term defined by federal law

hate crime
A crime motivated by race, ethnicity, or other category defined as a protected status by federal law.

and dozens of state statutes. It is a legal definition, not a manifestation of terrorism. Mark Hamm (1994, 1996) says that a hate crime is an illegal act designed to target a particular social group. With Hamm's definition in mind, it is possible to see that terrorists may use hate crimes just as they use other types of crime, but a hate crime is a specific violation of law.

The issue of hate crime complicates the understanding of domestic terrorism. The following scenario illustrates this. A group of teenage Jewish boys are walking down a street somewhere in a large American city. They spot two Arab immigrants and begin taunting them with racial and nationalistic slurs. If the jurisdiction has statutes that outlaw racial taunting, this may be a hate crime. It is not terrorism. As the Arabs try to walk away, several adult members of an anti-Semitic neo-Nazi group see the boys. They fold their arms in a neo-Nazi stance and stare at the Jewish teenagers, and their intent is to intimidate and threaten violence. This too can be a hate crime if the jurisdiction has outlawed nonverbal threats based on race, religion, sexual orientation, or ethnicity. Are the neo-Nazis terrorists?

The answer depends on who is responding. Some would say yes, others would classify them as a hate group, and still others would label the neo-Nazis extremists. Both incidents in this imaginary scenario involve hate, and both present a problem for the local police agency. If the Jewish teenagers belong to a gang dedicated to rid the neighborhood of Arab immigrants, it changes the situation completely. The neo-Nazis, by definition, probably belong to a group that wants to drive Jews away or to kill them. All of this involves hate, and it might involve terrorism.

Perhaps the best way to approach the definitional problem is to remember that terrorists commit crimes when they conduct operations. They are armed robbers, bombers, kidnappers, and murderers, but most armed robbers, kidnappers, and murderers are not terrorists. The same applies to hate crime. Hate crimes involve specific violations of criminal law. It may or may not be terrorism. Terrorists always commit crimes; criminals rarely commit terrorism.

Self-Check

- *What factors distort law enforcement's understandings of terrorism?*
- *Why is it difficult to recognize domestic terrorism?*
- *What is the difference between hate crime and terrorism?*

Classifying Terrorism in Criminal Justice

There is a great deal of tension between theoretical criminologists and practical analysts who look for an immediate solution to a specific problem. Classical criminologists look for an explanation of social phenomena, and they search for theories to explain crime or behavior in general. This crucial work produces theories that guide policies. From a tactical perspective, however, an immediate response to crime does not depend on general explanations. It is more important to understand the nature of the immediate problem and possible practical solutions. The same goes for terrorism: a label appropriate for theoretical criminology will not always lead to a response that solves an immediate problem. U.S. police officers routinely handle terrorism even though they call it by a variety of names. It would be helpful if law enforcement officers had a practical framework that explained their counterterrorist role.

Tactically, police and security forces should keep two issues in mind. First, a beat police officer is usually the first responder to domestic terrorism. Second, the investigation techniques used in large, sensationalized terrorist incidents are the same techniques a local agency would use to investigate a stink bomb placed in the locker room of a high school football team. From a practical perspective, counterterrorism depends on the fundamentals. Good investigative skills, such as the collection and preservation of evidence and good interviewing techniques, are important, and it is also important for law enforcement officers to understand the context of the crimes they investigate. Yet terrorism investigations also differ from routine crime scenes because terrorists behave differently. This calls for increased intelligence, long-term surveillance, and informant development. Therefore, it is important for officers to recognize terrorism when they investigate it.

The FBI Classification System

After handling left-wing domestic political violence, then focusing on racial and right-wing violence, the FBI developed a general classification system of domestic terrorism in the 1980s. John Harris (1987, pp. 5–13) summarized the FBI view by listing five types responsible for domestic terrorism in the 1980s: (1) white leftists, (2) Puerto Rican leftists, (3) black militants, (4) right-wing extremists, and (5) Jewish extremists. Like the FBI reports on domestic terrorism, Harris did not include criminal incidents involving terrorist tactics, and he limited his topic to the problem of political terrorism.

According to Harris, all domestic terrorist groups, with the exception of Puerto Rican nationalists, lacked an indigenous base, and they tended to have localized ideological bases. Types of groups were generally defined by location. For example, white supremacy groups tended to be rural, and revolutionary groups were generally urban. Because it tended to be geographically confined, American terrorism did not seem to affect all local police agencies in the same manner. In the 1990s the FBI began to issue a report called *Terrorism in the United States*. This provided a de facto definition of terrorism because it listed terrorist groups and related crimes. The FBI ceased publishing this report in 2002.

Today, the FBI approach is much more pragmatic. The FBI categorizes activities on the basis of origin. It is based on information gathering and sharing, but, as discussed earlier in the chapter, information sharing still remains difficult in police work. According to publicly released information (FBI, 2004), two categories cover the classification system: domestic terrorism (DT) and international terrorism (IT). DT involves violent political extremism, single-issue terrorism, and lone-wolf activities. IT is defined as threats that originate outside the United States. In 2002 the FBI's JTTF arrested six suspects near Buffalo, New York, for supporting jihadists. The JTTF called this DT because the activities originated in the United States. The attacks of September 11 are called IT because they originated outside U.S. borders (see FBI, 2002).

Although not included in the official categories of the Uniform Crime Report, this FBI system for defining terrorism provides a format for guiding investigations. For DT, political extremism involves violent left- and right-wing extremists. Single issues include violent activities associated with debates over abortion, **ecoterrorism**, **animal rights**, and **genetic engineering**. Lone wolves are included in the category when their actions are politically motivated. It is composed of three subsets: state-sponsored terrorism, clearly defined autonomous groups, and jihadists. The FBI focuses attention on the most active categories, so in the past five years emphasis has been placed on single-issue terrorists and jihadists.

The guidelines for reporting DT and IT are not part of the formal process of crime control. Rather, they serve as pragmatic guides for investigation. For example, when a JTTF or local FBI-police partnership conducts a counterterrorist investigation, state, local, tribal, and federal agencies use counterterrorist tactics: intelligence gathering, long-term surveillance, and informant development. These guidelines make little difference in official reports, and when prosecutors bring charges, suspects are generally accused of conspiracies or other normal crimes. However, the guidelines impact the practical manner for conducting the investigation (see G. Lee, 2004).

Using the Classification System

The classification system can also be used in practical criminological investigations. Using the FBI classification system, Brent Smith (1994; Smith and Roberts, 2005) places terrorist groups into three broad categories: (1) right-wing extremists, (2) left-wing and single-issue terrorists, and (3) international terrorists. Smith believes that right-wing groups form a category by themselves but that left-wing groups are different. Single-issue groups, criminal gangs, ecoterrorists, and old-style leftists fit neatly into the left-wing extremist category. International terrorists form the remaining group. Smith went on to do something that many terrorism analysts do not do. He conducted in-depth **empirical studies** within the classification system.

ecoterrorism
Terrorism against alleged environmental abusers.

animal rights
In this text, the single-issue focus of some extremists who attack in the name of animal rights.

genetic engineering
The manipulation of plant or animal genes to increase food output. Anti–genetic engineering activists frequently sabotage experimental crops and farm equipment.

empirical studies
A social science method that uses unbiased observations as a method to test ideas.

Self-Check

- *How do crime-classification systems confuse the meaning of terrorism?*
- *How does the FBI classify terrorism?*
- *Why can many different classification systems be used to study domestic terrorism?*

From Pipe Bombs and Dreams to Geospatial Analysis

Using data from official sources, Brent Smith and his colleagues approach terrorism through empirical research (Smith, 1994; Smith and Damphousse, 1998; Smith, Damphousse, Jackson, and Sellers, 2002; Damphousse and Smith, 2004; Smith and Roberts, 2005). They present some of the best factual summaries of recent terrorism in the United States in a criminological-based analysis of domestic terrorism. In his first work, Smith (1994) says the factor separating the average criminal from the average terrorist is *motivation* (see Another Perspective: Brent Smith's Approach to Domestic Terrorism). According to Smith, terrorists are criminals, but in addition they are motivated by ideology, religion, or a political cause. Smith also says that terrorists engage in another activity avoided by most criminals. They *plan* (Smith and Roberts, 2005).

Pipe Dreams

Smith's early research reveals several important findings. American terrorism grew, reaching its high level about 1985, just at the time the government was improving its counterterrorist tactics. Better governmental efficiency led to a series of arrests that decimated terrorist groups by the late 1980s. Right-wing groups tried to reemerge, but the left-wing groups did not. Left-wing terrorism remained a viable entity, however, because left-wing extremists were typically more loyal to their causes than were their right-wing counterparts. Puerto Rican nationalists and single-issue groups such as ecological terrorists accounted for much of the activity by left-wing groups. In fact, Smith believes ecological terrorists have a great potential for violence in the future.

Many analysts have tried to profile terrorists, but because terrorism is a fairly infrequent crime and most often handled as a normative violation of criminal law, Smith says it is difficult to conduct research on domestic terrorism because the database is so small. Smith takes two methodological steps that give a better picture of American terrorists: he lists the characteristics of domestic terrorists, and he compares left-wing and right-wing extremists. His findings indicate that American terrorists differ from their international counterparts. Native-born U.S. terrorists tend to be older than international terrorists, and foreign operatives

Brent Smith's Approach to Domestic Terrorism

Among the several classification systems for terrorism, Brent Smith has developed a simple and effective approach. He classifies terrorism as

1. Violent left-wing activities (including revolutionary nationalists and single-issue violence)

2. Violent right-wing activities

3. Foreign terrorism

Source: Smith, 1994.

working in the United States follow that trend. Many domestic terrorists are older than thirty, whereas international terrorists in the United States tend to be older than the young extremists in other parts of the world.

Although ideological groups differ in their beliefs, Smith notes that those on both the left and the right tend to fund themselves through armed robberies. Despite this similarity, the left and right actually differ quite a bit. Smith compares left- and right-wing terrorists in five categories: (1) ideology and beliefs about human nature, (2) economic views, (3) geographical bases of support, (4) tactics, and (5) selection of targets. Left-wing terrorists favor Marxism, target the economic status quo, base themselves in urban environments, and select symbolic targets of capitalism. Right-wing terrorists are vehemently anti-Marxist and very religious. In addition, they support the economic system without supporting the distribution of wealth, base themselves in rural areas, and focus attacks on symbols of governmental authority. Although their ideologies differ, both groups use similar terrorist tactics.

Smith offers several ideas for further examination. For example, he points out that left-wing terrorists were more active in the 1980s than right-wing terrorists. Official data show the truth of this, but it possibly is the case because of the way official data are reported. Many right-wing terrorist activities, such as assaults, arsons, bombings, and robberies, are reported as regular crimes. Would the levels of left-wing and right-wing activity be the same if the FBI counted all possible terrorist incidents as terrorist activities?

In another comparison, Smith notes that left-wing groups tend to follow the Marighella model of revolution, whereas right-wing groups stay in fortresses in rural areas. Again, the data demonstrate this is correct. But is this a difference in philosophy or geography? Right-wing groups frequently barricade themselves, but other activities, such as Louis Beam's "leaderless resistance" (discussed later in this chapter) are straight from Carlos Marighella. Perhaps the fortress mentality of right-wing groups is primarily due to geographical factors, particularly their favoring of rural locations.

In terms of the extremist right, Smith traces the resurgence of right-wing terrorism during the 1980s. He believes the right-wing groups began the decade on a high note but fell apart by 1984. Although they formed several organizations to try to rejuvenate the movement, Smith believes they failed.

Smith says left-wing terrorists have undergone no major transformation, remaining essentially the same from the 1960s to the present. Several protest groups began conglomerating around anti–Vietnam War movements after 1967, and by the end of the decade, some of them had become violent revolutionaries. After 1970, left-wing groups began acting in concert and frequently joined with Puerto Rican nationalists. When the Macheteros, a violent Puerto Rican nationalistic group, emerged in 1979, they soon found allies among violent leftists. Smith says left-wing groups tended to act in a coordinated fashion, and evidence indicated they were linked internally.

According to Smith, the May 19 Communist Organization (M19CO) was one of the more recent successful left-wing terrorist groups. Emerging from elements of the Students for a Democratic Society (SDS), Black Panther Party, and Student Non-Violent Coordinating Committee, the M19CO united several violent leftists under a common umbrella. The group formed in 1977, taking the "May 19" in its name from the birthdays of the North Vietnamese communist leader Ho Chi Minh and American Muslim leader Malcolm X. The M19CO was racially mixed, and approximately half of the members were women. A few months after its formation, members of the group launched a campaign to free "political" prisoners and attack capitalism.

The M19CO was most active from 1980 to 1984. The group conducted several robberies, planted bombs at military installations and private businesses, and murdered some of its victims. It attracted members of many other left-wing groups, and Smith found that it spawned temporary splinter groups under a variety of names. Its most infamous activity occurred in 1981, when M19CO members robbed an armored car, killing a guard and wounding another, and then murdered two New York police officers who were deployed at a roadblock.

In 1984, the group's luck began to run out. Several members were indicted for myriad crimes, and others were on the run. Some members were incarcerated on simple charges to give the government time to investigate more serious offenses. The JTTF, managed by the FBI, the New York City Police Department, and the New York State Police, proved successful against the M19CO. By 1989 all members of the M19CO were either in prison or in hiding.

Another left-wing group operating in the 1980s was the United Freedom Front (UFF). The UFF was composed mainly of anti–Vietnam War activists and protesters. Although not as active as the M19CO, the UFF became infamous for its ability to bomb American businesses. Members of the UFF and its clone group, the Armed Resistance Unit, were captured and jailed after the murder of a New Jersey state trooper. Despite some attempted activities through the late 1980s, left-wing terrorists virtually disappeared after 1990.

In Smith's analysis, ecological terrorists are following a trend similar to that of older left-wing groups. In the past several years, ecological terrorists have manifested their movement in two areas. First, some groups, such as the Evan Mecham Eco-Terrorist International Conspiracy (EMETIC), have focused on environmental and land-use issues, attacking developers and loggers. A second type of group, most famously the Animal Liberation Front, protests the use of animals in scientific experimentation. Both groups mirror the characteristics of left-wing terrorists, and members are fanatically dedicated to their causes. Smith believes such groups may lead domestic terrorist activities in the twenty-first century.

Smith also focuses on international terrorism in the United States, stating that since 1985, the country has experienced foreign terrorism as surrogate warfare. Although this is not fully discussed until the next section, let us examine here the interesting point about American policy that Smith raises. When terrorists attack the United States, law enforcement agencies frequently need the help of the military and intelligence communities. This creates the possibility that military forces will be used to fight political crimes. The internment of al Qaeda suspects in Cuba would seem to indicate that Smith's predictions were correct. In addition, in response to international terrorism, the U.S. Congress gave FBI agents the power to arrest terrorists on foreign soil even if the suspects are outside American jurisdiction.

Smith's early work concludes with a criminological analysis of domestic terrorism. He finds that laws regarding terrorism in the United States are exceptionally vague. International terrorists tend to plead guilty more frequently than right-wing and left-wing terrorists. Left-wing terrorists fare the best in court, whereas few right-wing cases are dismissed. Smith says there are insufficient data for determining whether sentences differ. Although the public may think that terrorists are not punished harshly enough, limited data indicate terrorists receive substantially longer sentences than traditional criminals. Finally, terrorism is a matter of attitude. Smith believes a person is not a terrorist until the government applies the label. And that label can have long-term effects.

American Terrorism Study

A study conducted with the cooperation of the FBI's Terrorist Research and Analytical Center, started in 1988, and sponsored by the U.S. House of Representatives Judiciary Subcommittee on Crime.

Leaderless Resistance and Geospatial Findings

Paxton Roberts, Kelley Damphousse, and Smith (Damphousse and Smith, 2004; Smith and Roberts, 2005) assembled a nationwide research team to examine data from the **American Terrorism Study**, and it reveals even more information about domestic terrorism. Relying on some of the best-known criminal justice scholars in the country, the team examined every recent case in which terrorists have been brought to trial and convicted. The team found common behavioral characteristics surrounding terrorist events. Arguing that most information about terrorism is not based in theory and observation, the social scientists sought to explain domestic terrorism through empirical research.

During the 1990s several domestic extremists advocated the use of **leaderless resistance**. Although this tactic seemed to be an American invention, it can be loosely related to the first phase of Marighella's revolutionary model, and it was incorporated in umbrella organizations like Hezbollah, Egyptian Islamic Jihad, and the Egyptian Islamic Group and by fifth-generation jihadists after the breakup of the al Qaeda hub in October 2001. The idea has been championed by members of the extremist right in America **Louis Beam** and **William Pierce**. The Earth Liberation Front, the Animal Liberation Front, and various anarchist groups have also gravitated to the idea. The purpose of leaderless resistance is to remain independent of other groups.

If violent extremist groups have changed tactics to leaderless resistance, data should exist to show that a switch in tactics and group structure has taken place. The press has written about the idea, and it has been championed by proponents on the extreme left and right, but Smith's purpose was to see whether researchers could find evidence that the shift had taken place. Louis Beam gave an infamous leaderless-resistance speech in 1992. If there was a shift in organizational structure, it could be argued that it came in 1992; groups before 1992 differed from groups after. Damphousse and Smith issued a report and suggested that a shift may well have taken place.

Damphousse and Smith (2004) argue that terrorism research has suffered from two shortcomings. There is a lack of theory and a lack of evidence to test theories. Tactics and organizational structures should be measurable. If groups have moved from hierarchies to engaging in **unstructured violence**, it should be measurable. The researchers use data from the American Terrorism Study to see if the shift has taken place. The most important measurement, they argue, would be a shift in group size. If groups are truly leaderless, groups should be smaller. Damphousse and Smith present three measurable ideas. If right-wing groups have adopted leaderless resistance, then federal criminal cases should indicate that the number of defendants per terrorist case has declined. Closely related to this idea is a second concept. If individuals are truly alone, then they should be committing more crimes because they rely only on themselves. They have no support network to coordinate activities. Finally, if criminals are more committed, then they should be less likely to cooperate with the government.

Damphousse and Smith limit their research to data gathered from prosecutions that matched the FBI approach to terrorism. They say this provides the greatest consistency of data from 1980 to 2002. It also provides objective public data. When suspects are charged in a federal criminal case, the indictment is part of a public record. The American Terrorism Study had more than 500 such records, and the pre-leaderless-resistance data could be compared to the leaderless-resistance period. Damphousse and Smith found 108 indicted suspects in nine terrorist

leaderless resistance
The concept that small unorganized, unmanaged groups or individuals can launch a revolution with disorganized violence.

Louis Beam
(1946–) Ku Klux Klan leader who popularized the idea of leaderless resistance in 1992.

William Pierce
(1933–2002) Leader of the National Alliance and author of *The Turner Diaries* and *Hunter.*

unstructured violence
Disorganized violence from unmanaged groups or individuals.

groups before 1992 and 73 suspects from sixteen groups after that date. They asked three questions: Did the number of defendants per case indicate a drop in group size? Were individuals arrested after 1992 charged with more crimes? And do post-1992 defendants plead innocent more often, demonstrating greater commitment to the cause?

The research results indicate that the size of domestic terrorist groups has been decreasing since 1992. Damphousse and Smith say this might show that leaderless resistance has affected terrorist activity, but they caution that it may also indicate that the federal government is prosecuting cases differently. They also tentatively say that terrorists are committing more crimes. They call for more data and further research in this area. Finally, they find less **plea bargaining** among suspects, but again they caution this may be due to either a change in federal plea bargaining tactics or lone wolves not making deals because they do not have fellow criminals they can testify against. It appears, although more research is needed, that leaderless resistance may be a pattern of modern right-wing terrorism.

Brent Smith has also used data from the American Terrorism Study to demonstrate patterns in terrorist behavior. Smith and Roberts (2005) examine the geography and timing of domestic terrorism. Smith and Roberts want to know the relationship between the place where terrorists prepare for an event and the place where they conduct an attack. They also search for the amount of time it takes to plan an attack. By looking at this data, they argue, it will help law enforcement identify the areas where terrorists prepare and the types of activities they conduct.

Smith and Roberts examine several geospatial variables. First, they look at the location of the residences of terrorists and compare that to the areas where they were recruited. They compare both of these areas to the places where terrorists trained and the areas where they prepared an attack. In terms of timing, Smith and Roberts look at the amount of time it takes to prepare for an attack and the activities taking place during preparation. For example, they consider the time it takes to steal weapons, gather explosives, make bombs, create false identification, enhance weapons, and establish laboratories or other bases. All of this data is compared to sixty-three actual or attempted domestic terrorist attacks.

Their findings are interesting. Attacks occurring within fifty-four miles of a suspect's residence account for 48 percent of domestic terrorist attacks. In other words, domestic terrorists tend to operate close to their home base. Even though international terrorists may travel great distances to arrive in the United States, once they settle they also operate near their bases. Most domestic terrorists also are recruited close to home. Cells operate for an average of 470 days before an incident. Smith and Roberts argue that this provides a key for counterterrorist investigations. When a group prepares an attack, they commit about four crimes three or four months before the actual attack. If law enforcement

plea bargaining
When a defendant pleads guilty to a charge of less severity than the original criminal indictment. For example, after being charged with breaking and entering, a suspect might plead guilty only to illegal entry, if the prosecutor agrees. The prosecutor gets a conviction, and the suspect, although guilty of the greater charge, receives a shorter sentence.

is aware of the types of crime terrorists commit and possible terrorist activities in their jurisdictions, they are in a better position to stop an attack before it occurs.

Self-Check

- *What is geospatial analysis?*
- *Define the transformation of domestic terrorism from group structures to leaderless resistance.*
- *What does geospatial analysis reveal about the characteristics of domestic terrorism?*

Jihadists in America

Jihadists appeared in the United States before the 9/11 attacks and they remain active today. There are two types of jihadist terrorist groups, and the interaction of the two may create a third style of organization. The first group is composed of international jihadists who have come to the United States to launch an attack or engage in criminal activities to support jihadist terrorism. The second style is the homegrown jihadist group. These are Americans who adopt the jihadist philosophy. Many law enforcement officials fear that a new style of jihadist group is appearing, a hybrid of foreign and homegrown terrorists. Such groups were involved in foiled attacks on Fort Dix, New Jersey, and JFK Airport, New York City, in the late spring of 2007.

International Jihadists

In the wake of September 11, jihadist terror dominated America's media and political institutions. It also generated controversy. The debate started in 1994 after Steven Emerson, an investigative journalist who spent several years covering the Middle East, produced a PBS program titled "Jihad in America" (Emerson, 1994). Emerson was already known for his analysis of Iraq (Emerson and Del Sesto, 1991), and his program touched off a heated debate between his supporters and his critics. Emerson (2002, 2006) stayed at the center of the controversy by creating a research group called the Investigative Project. Although the project infuriates his critics, this group has gathered more information about jihadists than most other organizations.

According to "Jihad in America," jihadist organizations took root in the United States during the Soviet-Afghan War. Undeterred by U.S. intelligence agencies, mujahideen traveled through the country to raise funds and establish charitable organizations. When the war ended in 1989, many mujahideen and their fund-raising mechanisms remained in the country, giving jihadists a base in the United States. Unfortunately, their wrath turned on the United States. For instance, Emerson linked the 1993 World Trade Center bombing to the domestic terrorist

ANOTHER PERSPECTIVE

Hamas in the United States

There is evidence beyond Steven Emerson's allegations of international terrorists operating in the United States. Consider these examples:

- In the summer of 2004 the Department of Justice charged several people with terrorist activities, including laundering money, threatening violence, possessing weapons, and a series of other related crimes. The indictment charges the suspects with being members of Hamas.

- In October 2003 law enforcement officers found small Cincinnati grocery stores raising millions of dollars for Hamas through price fraud.

- In September 2003 agents seized two men in the Virgin Islands after they left the mainland to launder money for Hamas.

- In Dearborn, Michigan, law enforcement officials charged two men with bank fraud. The alleged purpose was to raise money for Hamas.

Sources: United States of America v. Mousa Mohammed Abu Marzook, et al., 2003.

Tamim al-Adnani

One of the most vigorous fund-raisers for jihadist causes in the United States before the 1993 World Trade Center bombing.

networks before the government convicted some of their members. (See Another Perspective: Hamas in the United States.)

Former associate deputy FBI director Oliver B. "Buck" Revell, interviewed on Emerson's PBS program, stated that once the mujahideen and their associates came to the United States, they found a hospitable environment. They could raise money, film videos, run printing presses, and eventually attack the very country whose freedoms they enjoyed. For the first time in its history, the United States housed a terrorist infrastructure that stretched from the American heartland all the way through the Middle East to Southeast Asia. According to Revell, it is the most global network of terrorists the United States has ever faced.

Emerson credits Abdullah Azzam, one of the founders of al Qaeda, with the construction of the financial network. Azzam understood the vast amount of support available in the United States after helping to establish the Alkifah Refugee Center in New York City. According to Emerson, U.S. officials did not realize that the center was the front for another organization that called for jihad. But in fact, the Alkifah Refugee Center's Arabic letterhead called for holy war.

Azzam spread his jihadist network through thirty-eight states, with multiple bases in Pennsylvania, Michigan, California, Texas, and New England (see Expanding the Concept: The Charlotte Hezbollah Cell). Azzam returned to Pakistan in 1989, only to be killed by an assassin, but his work was completed by several supporters, including his cousin Fayiz Azzam.

Emerson names several prominent officials working in various radical groups in the domestic jihad. **Tamim al-Adnani** is the most vigorous recruiter and successful fund-raiser among all the leaders. Emerson

EXPANDING THE CONCEPT

The Charlotte Hezbollah Cell

A deputy sheriff moonlighting as a security guard in Charlotte, North Carolina, noticed a group of people buying cigarettes at a discount tobacco store. He noticed them because they were buying hundreds of cigarette cartons and loading them into vans. The deputy assumed it was a cigarette smuggling operation and called the Bureau of Alcohol, Tobacco, and Firearms (ATF). Buying cigarettes in one state and then selling them in another can be criminally profitable because of varying state tobacco laws and tax systems. When the ATF agents started investigating, they were surprised at what they found. The FBI, CIA, and many other agencies were also interested in the case.

Hezbollah was operating in Charlotte.

In this case the suspects purchased cigarettes in North Carolina and ran them to Michigan. North Carolina had a tax of five cents per pack on the cigarettes and a charge of fifty cents per carton. Michigan, however, taxed cigarettes at seventy-five cents per pack and $7.50 per carton. North Carolina did not require a tax stamp, but Michigan did. Smugglers transported the cigarettes from North Carolina to Michigan, stamped them with Michigan tax stamps, and then sold them at regular prices without paying taxes.

The U.S. attorney for western North Carolina, Robert Conrad, assumed the suspects were smuggling North Carolina cigarettes to Michigan and profiting by not paying tax. This turned out to be the base of the investigation, as the smugglers kept some of the money, but other illegal profits took a strange path. Conrad followed some money to Vancouver, Canada, and other profits went overseas. Conrad's office traced the money to Lebanon. Far from a simple cigarette scheme, the smuggling operation turned out to be an operation to support Hezbollah. The Charlotte Hezbollah cell, as it came to be known, was broken because investigators and prosecutors looked beyond the surface.

Source: United States v. Mohamad Hammoud, et al., 2002.

says al-Adnani has assisted in domestic terrorist incidents, including the 1993 World Trade Center bombing. Fayiz Azzam gives speeches calling for blood and holy war. **Elsayyid Nossair**, who was charged with the murder of militant rabbi Meir Kahane and convicted of lesser offenses, maintained a clearinghouse for terrorist literature before his arrest. Even in prison, Emerson says, Nossair helped plan the World Trade Center bombing.

Emerson says the most important terrorist operating in the United States was Sheik Omar Abdel Rahman. Before being charged with acts

Elsayyid Nossair
(1955–) An American jihadist associated with violence in New York City.

ANOTHER PERSPECTIVE

Some of Emerson's Conclusions

- Al Qaeda is recruiting in American prisons.

- Saudi contributors fund jihadists in America and elsewhere.

- Wahhabism, or the puritanical movement in Saudi Arabia associated with Mohammed ibn Abdul Wahhab, leads to attacks on non-Muslims and moderate Muslims.

- Radical Islamic schools promote violent actions against Jews.

- Many charities are fronts for jihadists.

- Hamas and al Qaeda may have established links.

Sources: Emerson and Levin, 2003; *Countdown with Keith Olberman*, May 5, 2004; Fesperman, 2004.

of terrorism in the United States, Rahman had been expelled from Egypt for conspiracy in the 1981 assassination of Egyptian president Anwar Sadat. He moved to New York City, where members of Rahman's group helped plan the assassination of Rabbi Kahane and recruit terrorists for a holy war against the United States. Emerson's PBS program caught Rahman in Detroit in 1991 calling for conquest of the infidel's land. Rahman has since been convicted for acts of terrorism, including complicity in the 1993 World Trade Center bombing. Emerson states that Sheik Abdul Wali Zindani, who has been involved in assassinations and bombings around the world, has taken Rahman's place.

Emerson also says well-known terrorist groups have established bases in the United States. He claims the Islamic Association for Palestine (IAP) is Hamas's chief propaganda arm in the United States. Under the name Aqsa Vision, the IAP produces many films, including military training videos. Based in Richardson, Texas, the IAP is one of several organizations with links to Hamas. Palestinian Islamic Jihad (PIJ) has a base in Tampa, Florida. Hezbollah also has a network in the country.

Emerson claims to have found more than thirty radical Middle Eastern groups in the United States, adding that the FBI has confirmed that terrorist groups have command centers in California, Nevada, Texas, Florida, Illinois, and New Jersey. Oliver Revell says the intention of these groups is to harm the United States and prevent it from being able to take international action.

Emerson (2002) followed the PBS broadcast with the book *American Jihad*, which documents his charges (see Another Perspective: Some of Emerson's Conclusions). Both efforts found a network of terrorist cells, false charities, and training camps in the United States. Emerson (2006) points to an international jihadist network in the United States that emerged after the 9/11 attacks, but he says there were many indications of activity long before September 2001. International jihadists operating in the United States followed the pattern of jihadists in

ANOTHER PERSPECTIVE

The Critics Attack Emerson

Steven Emerson has been the recipient of a storm of criticism. Some of his critics allege that he

- Attacks Muslims.
- Lumps all Islamic groups under one umbrella.
- Distorts information.
- Does not report facts.
- Is part of a pro-Israeli movement.
- Acts as an intelligence agent for Israel.

Sources: FAIR, February 2, 1999; Sugg, 1999; Hooper, 2000; Awad, 2003.

other areas of the world. They began with a structure, but shifted to the umbrella-style networks fashioned by groups like Hezbollah and Egyptian Islamic Jihad. Today they operate as a network, seeking inspiration from Qutb's philosophy and avoiding a centralized hierarchical structure.

Emerson (2006) says the network involves covert autonomous cells linked to the al Qaeda philosophy. They do not limit their activities to America. They are part of an international jihad. Although domestic cells exist, they feel a kindred spirit and seek contact with jihadist networks in other countries. The goal is to attack Americans anywhere in the world. Emerson links groups in Europe, central and Southeast Asia, and the Middle East with the domestic jihadist network. He is especially attuned to Pakistan, believing that the Pakistanis run madrassas and networks in the United States. He also argues there is a complex web of companies, charities, and other organizations that support jihadist networks.

Emerson's research stirs controversy in several communities (see Another Perspective: The Critics Attack Emerson). Some journalists ignore his conclusions. John Sugg (1999) wrote a scathing diatribe against Emerson, claiming that he is sloppy with facts and arrives at incorrect conclusions after major terrorist incidents. A journal on terrorism that features Emerson's work refuted Sugg's allegations in a press release. Sugg's publisher responded by saying that the journal's press release contained errors and misstated facts consistent with Emerson's inaccurate reporting (FAIR, 1999). In essence, Sugg believes that Emerson's conclusions about terrorism are painfully incorrect, but Emerson's Investigative Project can point to the arrest of alleged PIJ members in southern Florida as evidence of success.

Ibrahim Hooper (2000), a representative of a Muslim organization known as the **Council on American-Islamic Relations (CAIR)**, believes that Emerson is overly critical of Islam. Responding to an editorial

Council on American-Islamic Relations (CAIR)

An organization that maintains that it is a Muslim civil rights and advocacy group.

opinion Emerson expressed in the *Wall Street Journal,* Hooper said that Emerson is an attack dog of the American pro-Israeli lobby. He claimed that Emerson is "Islamophobic" and his purpose is to smear the image of Islam. *The Wall Street Journal* did not print Hooper's response.

Nihad Awad (2003), the head of CAIR, attacked Emerson's research in written testimony to the Senate Subcommittee on Terrorism, Technology, and Homeland Security. Awad says Emerson is a self-appointed terrorism expert who began making false charges in 1991; he agrees with Hooper's charge of Islamophobia. He criticizes "Jihad in America," saying that it places every Muslim institution in America under a general terrorist umbrella.

It is difficult to conduct inquiries when a specific ethnic or religious group risks being painted with a broad brush and given an incorrect label. Some people may call jihadists dangerous heretics, but they are *Muslim* heretics. Some of the institutions with which they associate also claim to be Islamic. This necessitates contacts between Islamic groups and researchers, journalists, and law enforcement personnel. It will always be a delicate situation at best. Many law enforcement authorities find Emerson's work valuable.

Homegrown Jihadists

In 2006, after British authorities uncovered a homegrown jihadist plot, FBI director Robert Mueller stated that the United States had to be vigilant against similar plots. International jihadists are a threat, Mueller said, but like the United Kingdom, the United States could be threatened by its own citizens. One of the incubators for homegrown jihadists is the American prison system. America's prisons are already awash with many variations of Islam, and Wahhabi missionaries covertly preach religious militancy in them. Aware of this danger, some institutions have established special units to gather information about religious militancy and to intercept violent missionaries (Moore, 2006).

Although prisons and jails are recruiting grounds, homegrown jihadists appear in different areas. In June 2006 JTTF officers arrested a group of jihadists in Miami and Atlanta who were not involved in any network, but authorities claimed they were plotting to blow up the Sears Tower in Chicago. The group did not even follow Islam. Its leader made up a religion combining Islam and other beliefs. According to media reports, the suspects were amateurs who had no real understanding of explosives, Islam, or the jihadist movement. Mueller said such groups might become the greatest domestic threat. They are self-recruited, self-motivated, and self-trained. Their only direct contact with the jihadists is the Internet (Josson, 2006). The jihadists who pulled off the March 11, 2004, Madrid attacks were amateurs, too.

Bodrero et al. (forthcoming) say homegrown terrorists are produced a number of ways. Some are born in the United States and prepare to wage the jihad even though they have little contact with jihadists. Others immigrate and find themselves alone. They gravitate to the jihad to find a purpose in life. Others, like **John Walker Lindh** and **Adam Gadahn**, leave the United States to join the jihad overseas. A third type threatens to become a hybrid form. Authorities fear that American citizens may join experienced international sleeper cells hiding in America.

The potential hybrid jihadist comes in several varieties. Bodrero et al. point to a case in Virginia where foreign-born and U.S. citizens recruited people from Washington, D.C., to train in Jammu and Kashmir. Another hybrid involves Black Muslims recruited away from their faith to a traditional form of Islam, and then they experience further conversion into militancy. Still another model comes from normative American Muslims radicalized in their mosques. Finally, some Muslims are radicalized while in foreign countries, and they return to the United States. Bodrero and his colleagues agree that prison recruiting creates a problem because it is much easier to radicalize people in jail. They cite a group of convicted armed robbers in Southern California who formed a jihadist cell in this manner, but they think prison recruiting is overemphasized. Most recruiting takes place outside prison.

Bodrero et al. say homegrown terrorism is not an American problem alone nor is it limited to radical Islam. It is a "bottom up event" where a person hears a radical message and decides to pursue the radical goal. It is difficult to develop effective law enforcement strategies to counter this process, especially if they are limited to reactive policing. Bodrero and his colleagues argue that law enforcement must be proactive, but sadly conclude that *proactive* has become one of the most overused buzzwords in American policing.

Although reacting to a crime will not work, practical steps—proactive measures—will work. Police need to be trained to recognize potential indicators of terrorist activity, they need to know what information they can collect and how to obtain it legally, and they need to participate in systems that share information. The British police have learned to do this. American law enforcement needs to learn it, too.

The need to understand homegrown jihadists appeared in 2007. In May 2007 a group in New Jersey planned to enter Fort Dix and murder American soldiers. They were indicted after police were informed of their videotaped training exercises (Hauser and O'Connor, 2007). A month later the New York City Police Department and the New York JTTF completed an eighteen-month investigation of an attack planned for JFK Airport (MSNBC, 2007). A year earlier, FBI director Mueller predicted that homegrown terrorism was an emerging problem. His predictions have come true.

John Walker Lindh
(1981–) An American captured while fighting for the Taliban in 2001 and sentenced to twenty years in prison.

Adam Gadahn
(1958–) The American spokesperson for al Qaeda. His nom de guerre is Azzam the American.

Self-Check

- *What different types of jihadists seem to operate in America?*
- *Is there a domestic American jihad?*
- *Why might Muslims be offended at the idea of a domestic jihad?*

Nationalistic Separatism: The Case of Puerto Rico

Ronald Fernandez (1987, 1996) offers two insightful views of Puerto Rico. In *Los Macheteros* he explores the reasons for terrorism conducted by Puerto Rican nationalists in the United States, and in *The Disenchanted Island* he explains the island's relationship with the United States from the Puerto Rican view. Puerto Rico was colonized by the Spanish shortly after the European discovery of America, and the Spanish ruled the island for nearly three centuries. This changed in 1898, when the United States captured Puerto Rico in the Spanish-American War.

At first, the Puerto Ricans welcomed the United States as liberators, believing they were going to be granted independence, but they were disappointed. Instead of freeing the island, the United States granted Puerto Rico commonwealth status. Its special relationship to the United States grew with the increasing military importance of the island. Currently, the population is divided by three opinions. Some desire Puerto Rican statehood. Others want to create an independent country, and some of these people favor a Marxist government. A third constituency wants to maintain commonwealth status. This leaves the United States with a paradox: No matter which group it satisfies, two other groups will be disappointed.

The Evolution of Revolutionary Groups

Violent revolutionaries in Puerto Rico appeared more than fifty years ago. Puerto Rican nationalists tried to assassinate President Harry Truman in 1950 and entered the chambers of the House of Representatives in 1954, shooting at members of Congress on the floor. Holes from the bullets remain in some desks in the House chambers today. Like their nationalist counterparts in Europe, revolutionary groups merged with left-wing organizations around 1970 through roughly 1980. Puerto Rican groups were able to continue operating despite the decline in left-wing terrorism (Smith, 1994).

A number of revolutionary organizations embraced the nationalistic terrorist campaign. The Armed Forces of National Liberation (FALN) began operating in the United States after 1945, and they were joined by other Puerto Rican terrorists in following decades. One of the most notorious groups was the Macheteros. Other groups included the Volunteers for the Puerto Rican Revolution (OVRP), the Armed Forces of Liberation (FARP), the Guerrilla Forces of Liberation (GEL), and the Pedro Albizu Campos Revolutionary Forces (PACRF). Before the decline of the left, Puerto Rican terrorists routinely joined left-wing operations.

The Future of Puerto Rican Terrorism

Smith (1994) notes that the Puerto Rican groups were the only domestic terrorists with strong international links during the 1980s. He believes Puerto Rican revolutionary support comes primarily from Cuba, and many members are in hiding there. Aside from carrying out the largest armored car robbery in the history of United States in 1983, Puerto Rican groups have conducted several bombings, assassinations, and even a rocket attack against FBI headquarters in San Juan. They have selectively murdered U.S. citizens, especially targeting U.S. military personnel stationed in Puerto Rico.

Since the fall of the Soviet Union, Puerto Rican terrorists have been less active, but their infrastructure remains intact. According to Fernandez (1987), terrorism has become one means of revolution. Smith believes the problem of Puerto Rican violence will not simply evaporate. Law enforcement officers must continue to respond to Puerto Rican terrorism, but at some point, American policy makers need to resolve the status of Puerto Rico to the satisfaction of its people. Currently, as Fernandez (1996) argues, Puerto Rico is economically dependent on the United States. In 1998 the House of Representatives asked for a binding vote to determine Puerto Rico's status, but the vote failed to alter the future. Only 3 percent of Puerto Rican voters wanted independence; 46 percent wanted statehood; and 50 percent said they did not want to accept statehood, commonwealth status, or independence, but they did not say what they did want (Rivera, n.d.). The future of Puerto Rico remains uncertain, although terrorist violence decreased in the first decade of the twenty-first century.

Self-Check

- *How did revolutionary ideas emerge and evolve in Puerto Rico?*
- *What major nationalistic groups have operated in recent years?*
- *What three possible political solutions divide opinion in Puerto Rico?*

Right-Wing Violence

On the morning of April 19, 1995, television and radio special-news reports indicated that some type of explosion had occurred in Oklahoma City in or near the federal building. These reports were quickly amended, and reports of the size and extent of damage increased with each moment. By noon it was apparent that the United States had suffered a devastating terrorist attack. As scenes of the injured and dead, including children, and smoldering wreckage dominated the nation's television screens, attention turned toward the Middle East. Conventional wisdom placed blame for the incident on some militant Islamic sect. Many Arab Americans were harassed, and some were openly attacked. The country was shocked when a young white man with a crew cut was arrested for the bombing. It was hard to believe that the United States had produced terrorists from its own heartland.

The Development of Right-Wing Violence

Although many people were surprised, even a cursory look at the history of right-wing extremism in the United States reveals that extremist ideology and violent political behavior is nothing new (J. White, 2001). The first incident of antifederal behavior came shortly after the American Revolutionary War (1775–1783). In 1791 the federal government levied an excise tax on the production of whiskey. Farmers in western Pennsylvania, a top whiskey-producing area in the country, were incensed. The unpopular tax provoked riots and created general disorder. In October 1794, President George Washington mobilized the National Guard of several states and sent the troops to Pennsylvania. The **Whiskey Rebellion** quickly ended, but not the resentment against the federal government (Phillips, 1999, pp. 332–334).

Antifederal attitudes were common in some circles in the early 1800s. The so-called **Know-Nothings** operated in the eastern United States before the Civil War (1861–1865). Organizing under such names as the Order of the Sons of America and the Sons of the Star Spangled Banner, these groups were anti-Catholic, anti-Irish, and anti-immigration. They felt Catholic immigrants were destroying American democracy. When confronted by authority, party members would claim to "know nothing," hence their name (McPherson, 1988, pp. 135–143).

Although the Civil War had many causes—slavery, farming versus industry, and sectionalism—one of the greatest was disagreement over the power of the federal government. Southerners questioned the legitimacy of the federal government, and they believed Congress was taking the powers reserved for the states. Most Southerners were not fighting to preserve slavery; they were fighting to keep the power of local governments. When the Confederacy was defeated in 1865, the issue did not die (McPherson, 1988, pp. 858–859; Foote, 1986a, pp. 35–40; 1986b, p. 1042).

Agrarian failures and depressions gave life to radical economic theories during the 1870s and 1880s. These rural movements were complemented by labor violence and the introduction of anarchism from the left. Businesses and local and state governments frequently repressed both left-wing and right-wing versions of extremism. After the turn of the century, though, mainstream Americans came to believe that the left posed a greater threat to democracy. This attitude increased after 1919, when a wave of left-wing terrorism swept the country. As a result, right-wing extremist organizations grew. They popularized extremist views and claimed judges, elected officials, and police officers in their ranks. Right-wing extremists also turned to an organization that had been created in the wake of the Civil War, the Ku Klux Klan (KKK).

The KKK had been the brainchild of Confederate cavalry genius General **Nathan Bedford Forrest** (Berlet and Lyons, 2000, pp. 58–62). Forrest had intended to create an anti-unionist organization that would preserve Southern culture and traditions. When the newly formed KKK began terrorizing freed slaves, Forrest tried to disband the organization.

Whiskey Rebellion
The uprising that took place in 1797 when a group of Pennsylvania farmers refused to pay a federal tax on corn used to make alcohol. The rebellion ended when President George Washington sent troops to stop the rebellion.

Know-Nothings
Different groups of American super-nationalists in the early nineteenth century who championed native-born whites over immigrants.

Nathan Bedford Forrest
(1821–1877) A famed and gifted Confederate cavalry commander who founded the Ku Klux Klan in Pulaski, Tennessee. Forrest tried to disband the KKK when he saw the violent path that it was taking.

Knight Riders
The first terrorists of the Ku Klux Klan. Donning hoods and riding at night, they sought to keep newly freed slaves from participating in government and society.

But it was too late, and the KKK began a campaign of hate. By the early twentieth century, the organization had nearly died, but it revived in the extremist atmosphere after World War I (1914–1918).

The KKK has operated in three distinct phases through history (Berlet and Lyons, 2000, pp. 58, 85–103, 265–286). Shortly after the Civil War, hooded **Knight Riders**, as they were called, terrorized African Americans to frighten them into political and social submission. This aspect of the Klan faded by the end of the century. The second phase of the Klan came in the 1920s as it sought political legitimacy. During this period, the KKK became popular, political, and respectable. But it collapsed in the wake of a criminal scandal. The modern KKK grew after World War II (1939–1945), becoming, up to the present day, fragmented, decentralized, and dominated by hate-filled rhetoric.

The development of the modern Klan parallels the growth of right-wing extremism from the 1930s to the present. Michael Barkun (1997) describes the growth of extremism from a religious view. Barkun says that a new religion, Christian Identity, grew from the extremist perspective. Starting with a concept called **Anglo-Israelism**, or British Israelism, American right-wing extremists saw white Americans as the representatives of the lost tribes of Israel. Wesley Swift preached this message in a radio ministry from California beginning in the late 1940s. Two of his disciples were **William Potter Gale** and **Richard Butler**. Gale went on to form several right-wing associations, including Posse Comitatus. Butler retired from an engineering career, moved to Idaho, and formed the **Aryan Nations**. Gale and Butler preached Swift's message of Christian Identity.

Christian Identity

Christian Identity is a strange blend of Jewish and Christian biblical passages and is based on the premise that God was white (J. White, 1997, 2001). Because Adam and Eve were created in the image of God, they were also white. Nonwhites, or "mud races," evolved from animals and eventually produced the Jews, who try to destroy God's white race and establish a kingdom of the devil. Jesus, who is the ultimate white man, came to help the white Israelites in their struggles, but the Jews crucified him. God intervened, promising that a militant resurrected Jesus would return to reclaim the world for white people. White Israelites eventually migrated to Europe, and each white tribe founded one of the countries in the northern and western parts of the continent. These became the Aryan Nations.

Christian Identity theology is based on a story of conflict and hate. According to this theology, Jews have gained control of the United States by conspiring to create the Federal Reserve System. The struggle between whites and Jews will continue until whites ultimately achieve victory with God's help. At that point, the purpose of creation will be fulfilled. Such theological perversions are necessary when converting a religion of love into a doctrine of hate.

Anglo-Israelism

The belief that the lost tribes of Israel settled in western Europe. God's ancient promises to the Hebrews become promises to the United Kingdom, according to this belief. Anglo-Israelism predated Christian Identity and is the basis for most Christian Identity beliefs.

William Potter Gale

(1917–1988) An American military leader who coordinated guerrilla activities in the Philippines during World War II. Gale became a radio preacher and leader of the Christian Identity movement after returning home.

Richard Butler

(1917–2004) A self-made millionaire and white supremacist. Butler founded the Aryan Nations in Hayden Lake, Idaho.

Aryan Nations

An American antigovernment, anti-Semitic, white supremacist group founded by Richard Butler. Until it was closed by a suit from the Southern Poverty Law Center, the group sponsored a Christian Identity Church called the Church of Jesus Christ, Christian.

Barkun points out that Christian Identity helped to provide the basis for violence among the extremists. Before the Christian Identity movement, American extremism was characterized by ethnocentrism and localized violence. Christian Identity gave a new twist to the extremist movement: it was used to demonize Jews. Christian Identity provided a theological base for stating that white people originated with God and Jews came from the devil. Such eschatological presumptions are deadly (see Stanton, 1991, p. 36).

Contemporary Right-Wing Behavior, Beliefs, and Tactics

The appearance of modern right-wing extremism came to fruition around 1984 and has remained active since that time. According to my research (J. White, 1997, 2000, 2002), several issues hold the movement together. First, the right wing tends to follow one of the forms of extremist religions. The name of God is universally invoked, even by leaders who disavow theism (a belief in God). Second, the movement is dominated by a belief in international conspiracy and other conspiracy theories. Followers feel sinister forces are conspiring to take away their economic status and swindle them out of the American dream. The primary conspiratorial force was communism, but after the fall of the Soviet Union, it became the United Nations. The extremist right believes a conspiracy of Jewish bankers works with the United Nations to create a New World Order, in which Jews control the international monetary system. Finally, right-wing extremists continue to embrace patriotism and guns. They want to arm themselves for a holy war (see Barkun, 1997; Berlet and Lyons, 2000, pp. 345–352).

In his popular historical work *Dreadnought: Britain, Germany and the Coming of the Great War*, Robert K. Massie (1991) points to the hysteria in Great Britain and Germany during the naval race before World War I. Both the British and the Germans demonized one another, and their national rivalries often gave way to irrational fears. In one of the more notable British reactions, the fear of German naval power gave rise to a particular genre of popular literature. These stories had a similar theme. Secret German agents would land in the United Kingdom and destroy the British Empire through some type of subversive plot. Whether poisoning the water supply, destroying the schools, or infiltrating the economic system, the fictional Germans never attacked directly. They were mysterious, secretive, and everywhere.

The actions of right-wing extremists fit Massie's description of the hysterical fears in Britain. Extremists believe alien forces are conspiring to destroy the United States. Bill Stanton (1991, pp. 78–82) says that in 1978 the KKK led the way into the modern era when it emerged in Georgia and North Carolina as a paramilitary organization. Within a decade, many members of the extremist right had followed suit. They were not only willing to accept conspiracy theories but also ready to fight the hordes that they believed would destroy the American way of life.

Brent Smith (1994) paints a realistic picture of right-wing extremism, arguing that terrorism from the right wing is fairly limited. Groups are rural and tend to emerge from farm-based compounds. For example, Posse Comitatus formed as a tax-protest group and engaged in violent resistance to local law enforcement. The most well-known case of Posse Comitatus resistance dealt with Gordon Kahl, who killed three law enforcement officers in North Dakota and Arkansas before being killed in a shoot-out. Another group, The Order, was a militant offshoot of the **white supremacy movement**. By 1987, however, The Order was defunct, and the right wing was fading.

Even while this was happening, most right-wing criminal activities were not labeled as terrorism, and even though the notorious cases of violent right-wing extremism faded from public awareness in 1987, the ideology that fueled them did not. So-called hate crimes increased, creating concern among criminal justice researchers (Hamm, 1994). Membership in extremist groups grew after their apparent collapse in 1987, and by 1994, the extremists were back in business. The late Richard Butler, former leader of the Aryan Nations, interacted with the leaders of several white supremacy movements and held an Aryan Congress each year to draw the white supremacists together.

Three issues rejuvenated the extremist right (K. Stern, 1996). First, the **Brady Bill** (named for President Reagan's press secretary, who was disabled in an assassination attempt on Reagan) caused many conservatives to fear federal gun-control legislation. The extremist right played on these fears, toning down issues like white supremacy and Christian Identity and claiming that the intrusive federal government was out to eliminate gun ownership. Extremists felt they had an issue that appealed to mainstream conservatives. By stressing the fear of gun control, right-wing extremists hoped to appear to be in the mainstream.

The second issue dealt with a botched U.S. Marshal's office attempt to arrest Randy Weaver on a bench warrant at Ruby Ridge in the mountains of Idaho. A white supremacist and adherent of Christian Identity, Weaver was charged with selling illegal firearms to undercover agents from the Bureau of Alcohol, Tobacco, and Firearms (ATF). Weaver was arrested and released on bail. When he refused to appear for the assigned court date, U.S. marshals tried to bring him in. Tragically, U.S. Marshal William Degan and Weaver's young son, Sammy, were killed in the ensuing shootout. The FBI responded by laying siege to Weaver's mountain cabin. In the following days, an FBI sniper shot and killed Weaver's pregnant wife before Weaver surrendered (Walter, 1995).

The **Ruby Ridge** incident had a strong symbolic impact on the extremist right. According to K. Stern (1996), Bo Gritz, a leading extremist figure, drew national attention to the siege when he came to negotiate surrender. Gritz is an articulate, charismatic individual who retired as a colonel from the U.S. Army Special Forces, and his voice and opinions carry far beyond the extremist right. He left Ruby Ridge saluting Skin-

white supremacy movement

A political philosophy claiming that white people are superior to all other ethnic groups.

Brady Bill

A law that limits gun ownership, named for President Ronald Reagan's press secretary after he was disabled in a 1981 assassination attempt.

Ruby Ridge

The location of a 1992 standoff between alleged survivalists and U.S. federal law enforcement officers in Idaho during which a U.S. marshal and survivalist Randy Weaver's wife and son were killed.

head demonstrators and calling for the formation of SPIKE groups (special resistance forces) to prevent further standoffs (Walter, 1995).

Closely related to Ruby Ridge, in the minds of the extremist right, was a third event: the federal siege of the **Branch Davidian** compound near Waco, Texas. In 1993 ATF agents attempted to serve a search warrant on the compound, but they were met with a hail of gunfire. Four agents were killed, and several were wounded. After a three-month siege, FBI agents moved in with tear gas. Unknown to the agents, the compound was laced with gasoline. When the FBI moved in, the Branch Davidians burned their fortress, killing eighty-two people, including several young children, inside the compound.

Stern says the **Waco siege** also became a symbol for the extremist right, even though it had very little to do with the right-wing movement. An ATF report (1995) said that in reality the Waco siege involved a group of people led by a dismissed Seventh Day Adventist, **Vernon Wayne Howell**, who changed his name to David Koresh. Taking advantage of the weak and distraught, Koresh established the Branch Davidian compound outside Waco. According to the ATF, Koresh gathered illegal weapons and engaged in a variety of unlawful activities. He ruled his flock in accordance with his messianic illusions, claiming that the end was near and he would save the world. In the end, he simply murdered his followers rather than admit his messianic failings, but he set the stage to be embraced by the extremist right. Although Koresh had nothing to do with right-wing extremists per se, he had the right formula: guns, a survivalist compound, and a belief in a warrior God.

If Stern is correct, the Brady Bill, Ruby Ridge, and Waco gave new life to the fading right-wing movement, and a shift in the religious orientation of the extremist right helped to rejuvenate their ranks. Although many American Protestants would agree that the United States was the new chosen land, perhaps even a new Israel, few could stomach the blasphemy and hatred of Christian Identity. In the 1990s, however, the religious message changed. Patriotism and anti-Semitism proved to be as strong as the Christian Identity message.

Today, the situation has shifted again. After being revitalized in the 1990s, the movement mutated after September 11, 2001. Violent members of the right-wing movement melted away from large organizations and began to congregate in small groups. Following the pattern of international terrorist groups, they organized chains or hubs, small groups operating autonomously. The days of large meetings seemed to fade as well. One Montana criminal-intelligence commander told me he believed that the current leaders of the movement do not know how to arrange large rallies. As a result, he said, the movement in the Pacific Northwest, for instance, looks more like a conglomeration of terrorist cells. But they remain violent and anticipate that white Christians will experience an anti-Jewish awakening.

More, smaller groups led to more individual violence (see Another Perspective: Criminal Behavior among Right-Wing Extremists). Addi-

Branch Davidians
Followers of Vernon Wayne Howell, also known as David Koresh. They lived in a compound outside Waco, Texas.

Waco siege
The 1993 standoff between members of the Branch Davidian cult and federal law enforcement officers. The standoff ended when FBI agents tried to bring the siege to an end. Eighty-two people were killed.

Vernon Wayne Howell
(or David Koresh, 1959–1993) The charismatic leader of the Branch Davidian cult.

ANOTHER PERSPECTIVE

Criminal Behavior among Right-Wing Extremists

Right-wing extremists fall into three categories:

Nonviolent offenders. Tend to be high school dropouts, engage in rhetoric or publication, disrupt public meetings, use "constitutional" driver's licenses and permits, use "common law" court documents. Common criminal behavior: fraud schemes.

Violent defenders. Stockpile survivalist materials and weapons, wait for the U.S. government to attack. Violent defenders call the government the Zionist Occupation Government (ZOG) or the Jewish Occupation Government (JOG) because they believe it is controlled by an international conspiracy of Jewish financial interests. Common criminal behavior: violent standoffs.

Violent attackers. Use standard terrorist tactics such as weapons violations, assaults, bombings, arsons, ambushes, and murders. Common criminal behavior: shooting sprees.

Sources: Pitcavage, 1999a, 1999b, 1999c, 2000.

tionally, these groups began to form linkages with single-issue groups, including anarchists and left-wingers. The trend is currently unclear. The groups may be fading as the left-wing did in the 1980s, or they may be repositioning themselves. Militias tended to turn to patriotism and more normative behavior after September 11. The path of the violent offshoot groups remains undetermined.

The wild card is the vacuum in leadership. Richard Butler, leader of the defunct Aryan Nations, died in September 2004. No one had been able to unite the extremist right like Butler. Leaders are jockeying for power, but no single leader with Butler's charisma and organizational skills has moved to the forefront. A number of potential leaders are due for release from prison, so a leader may emerge. In the meantime, small groups dominated by Christian Identity theology and Christian patriotism engage in localized violence.

Right-Wing Conspiracies, Militias, and the Call to Arms

Christianity has undergone some strange transformations in the violent circles of right-wing extremism, sometimes known as the hate movement (J. White, 1997, 2001). For example, some extremists adopted Norse mythology. Following Erich Luddendorff, a German general from World War I, extremists began preaching **Nordic Christianity** in northern Germany. This belief system migrated to the United States and took root in Michigan, Wisconsin, Montana, and Idaho in the 1990s. Using ancient Norse rites, they claimed to worship the Triune Christian Deity, but they added Odin (Wotan) and Thor. Odin, the supreme Norse god, called Nordic warriors to racial purification from Valhalla, or the Viking heaven. Thor, the god of thunder, sounded the call with a hammer that shook the heavens.

Nordic Christianity
A religion that incorporates the ancient Norse gods in a hierarchy under the Christian triune deity. It is similar to Odinism, but does not completely abandon Christianity.

Creatorism

The deistic religion of the Creativity Movement. It claims that white people must struggle to defeat Jews and nonwhite races.

Ben Klassen

(1918–1993) The founder of the Creativity Movement.

skinheads

Young people or groups who embrace racial hatred and white supremacy. Some groups claim not to be based on racism.

New World Order

A phrase used by President George H. W. Bush to describe the world after the fall of the Soviet Union. Conspiracy theorists use the phrase to describe what they believe to be Jewish attempts to gain control of the international monetary system and subsequently to take over the U.S. government.

free-wheeling fundamentalists

White supremacists or Christian patriots who either selectively use Bible passages or create their own religion to protect the patriot agenda.

survivalist

A person who adopts a form of right-wing extremism advocating militant rejection of society. Advocates withdrawal from society in

In another religious derivation, **Creatorism** rejects Judaism and Christianity altogether (see Creativity Movement, n.d.). Formerly called the World Church of the Creator, the movement changed its name to the Creativity Movement after being challenged by a Christian church with a similar name. Founded by **Ben Klassen** in 1973, Creatorists claim the Creator left humanity on its own, and each race must fend for itself. Embracing the urban **skinheads**, Creatorists call for a racial holy war, or RAHOWA. They produce racially oriented comic books designed to appeal to alienated white youth. They also publish *The White Man's Bible*, which emphasizes racial purity. Creatorists argue that an intervening, loving God is nothing more than an idle lie. White people have been left on their own by a deistic Creator, and they are expected to fight for their survival. Essentially, Creatorism is a deistic religion with more violent tendencies than Christian Identity.

If extremists were trying to achieve mainstream political acceptance through issues like gun control, taxation, and the **New World Order**, however, they could not merely appeal to Odin. The majority of right-wing extremists retreated to more conservative churches and relied on individual interpretations of scripture to justify antigovernment actions. This group can loosely be described as **free-wheeling fundamentalists**.

Unlike the hate religions, the free-wheeling fundamentalists do not believe the American government is part of a satanic conspiracy. They do believe, however, that the federal government and local governments are their enemies and that God will assist them in their confrontation with evil. Using antifederalist rhetoric, they boost their call to revolution with appeals to the Christian theology of lay preachers. They call on a personal God—a self-defined concept of divinity usually not recognizable in the Hebrew, Muslim, or Christian scriptures. By 1995 this movement became popular in the rural West and Midwest, and it has set the stage for right-wing extremism into this century (see O'Conner, 2004).

Free-wheeling fundamentalism affected the Christian patriot movement. Although many Christian patriots believe that the United States is God's promised land, many of them are not willing to demonize other races or religions. Many Christian patriots believe that the government no longer serves average Americans, and they believe bankers and businesspersons work together against farmers and other rural Americans. They believe in God, America, and freedom, but they do not accept the hate-filled tenets of Identity theology and reject Nordic Christianity as a collection of heretical myths. They feel that the government will not defend the country against foreign enemies and that it favors the United Nations over the United States. As **survivalist** ideology grew in the 1980s, the Free-Wheeling Fundamentalists turned to a new idea—the **militia movement**.

Paramilitary organizations, or unauthorized armed civilian militias that organize themselves in a military manner, thrive on conspiracy theories. They believe the U.S. government is leading the country into a single world government controlled by the United Nations and that the New World Order is a continuation of a conspiracy outlined in the **Protocols of Zion**, a document written after World War I, claiming that Jews are out to control the world (Stern, 1996). The militias play on conspiracy fears, fear of government, racism, antiabortion rhetoric, and anti-Semitism. In Stern's analysis, militia leaders and white supremacy leaders are one and the same. Stern links the militia movement to **Christian Identity** (see Maise and Burgess, n.d.).

ATF analysts believe militias tend to be issue oriented. Groups gather around taxes, abortion, gun control, or Christian Identity. Other research reflects the ATF findings (J. White, 1997, 2001). Militias are almost always religious, but few embrace Christian Identity, Nordic Christianity, or Creatorism. For justification, they rely on Free-Wheeling Fundamentalism and violent passages of Christian scripture quoted out of context. Most simply interlace their antitax, anti–gun control rhetoric with such biblical passages.

There is one more thing to say about the militia movement. Simply joining a militia group does not make a person a terrorist. Incidental observations have indicated that several people have joined the militias out of a sense of powerlessness. As a reporter from the *Toledo Blade* quipped to me, these are folks who never quite made it. The reporter says the militia makes them feel important, and he is probably correct. Many militia members are frustrated, feel overwhelmed, and are socially unable to cope with the rapid pace of change in the modern world. They may be extremists, but they are not terrorists.

Paramilitary groups operate on different levels. For example, the Arizona Vipers allegedly planned to blow up federal installations in 1996, and many of them eventually pleaded guilty to possessing illegal explosives. Interviews with several prominent members of other militias indicate, however, that they had never heard of the Arizona Vipers. The Freemen of Montana represent another variation. They allegedly terrorized a small town, Jordan, Montana, by flouting laws like they were an urban gang. When the federal government took action in 1996, creating another siege, militia members across the country expressed support but took steps to increase their ideological distance from the Freemen. Paramilitary groups come in a variety of shapes and sizes, and most of their action is rhetorical. The Arizona Vipers and the Freemen of Montana are exceptions. Rhetoric turns to violence when small, detached groups emerge from larger extremist groups.

A new trend emerged after the sieges of Ruby Ridge in 1992, Waco in 1993, and the Freemen standoff in 1996 in Jordan, Montana. Old left-wing extremists and new right-wing extremists began to search for common ground. One philosophy, the **Third Position**, tried to unite both extremes. Radicals (left wing) and reactionaries (right wing) found that they had some things in common. They hate the government, they have no use for large corporations, and they distrust the media. The Third Position serves to blur the line between left and right by uniting former

preparation for a coming internal war. Secluded in armed compounds, they hope to survive the coming collapse of society.

militia movement
A political movement started in the early 1980s, possibly spawned from survivalism. Militias maintain that the Second Amendment gives them the right to arm themselves and form paramilitary organizations apart from governmental control and military authority.

Protocols of Zion
A forged document written in czarist Russia allegedly explaining a Jewish plot to control the world. It was popularized in the United States by Henry Ford. It is frequently cited by the patriot and white supremacy movements. Jihadists also use it as evidence against Jews.

Christian Identity
An American extremist religion proclaiming white supremacy. Adherents believe that white Protestants of western European origin are the true descendants of the ancient Israelites. Believers contend that Jews were spawned by Satan and that nonwhites evolved from animals. According to this belief, white men and women are the only

people created in the image of God.

Third Position

A movement started after the Branch Davidian stand-off at Waco. It attempts to unite left-wing, right-wing, and single-issue extremists in a single movement.

enemies around common themes. This becomes more apparent when examining the newest form of domestic terrorism, ecological violence.

The small violent groups after September 11 began taking action without a centralized structure. In several areas two or three people began to operate without contacting other groups or conglomerating at large convocations. They planned bombings, chemical attacks, and spoke of a spontaneous revolution (CNN, 2004b; CBS News, 2004). These unrelated groups felt that any act of violence would help to create the mayhem necessary to topple the government (Damphousse and Smith, 2004). The organization style was new, but the ideology that drove the groups had been transplanted earlier from the hills of West Virginia. It was contained in the philosophy of William Pierce.

The Turner Diaries and *Hunter*: Blueprints for Revolution

National Alliance

The white supremacist organization founded by the late William Pierce and headquartered in Hillsboro, West Virginia.

William Pierce was a white supremacist with headquarters in rural West Virginia. He led an organization called the **National Alliance** and purchased Resistance Records, a recording label for skinhead hate music. Pierce held a doctoral degree and worked as a college professor. Until his death in 2003 he drew the attention of watchdog groups, scholars, and law enforcement officers (Pitcavage, 1999a). Pierce wrote two novels that summarized his thought and provided a blueprint for revolution.

Pierce's most noted novel, *The Turner Diaries*, was written under the pseudonym Andrew MacDonald (1985) and is a fictionalized account of an international white revolution. The work begins as a scholarly flashback from "New Baltimore" in the "year 100," and it purports to introduce the diary the protagonist, Earl Turner, kept during the "Great Revolution," a mythical race war set in the 1990s.

Robert Matthews

(1953–1984) The leader of The Order, killed in a shootout with the FBI.

For the most part, *The Turner Diaries* is a diatribe against minorities and Jews. It is well written and easy to read. The danger of the work is that from a technical standpoint, it is a how-to manual for low-level terrorism. Using a narrative, or storytelling, format, Pierce describes the proper methods for making bombs, constructing mortars, attacking targets, and launching other acts of terrorism. Anyone of average intelligence who reads *The Turner Diaries* will come away with an elementary idea of how to become a terrorist.

Bruder Schweigen

German for *silent brothers*, the name used by two violent right-wing extremist groups, Bruder Schweigen and Bruder Schweigen Strike Force II. The late Robert Miles, leader of the Mountain Church of Jesus in Michigan, penned an article about the struggle for white supremacy, "When All of the Brothers Struggle."

The second potential danger of *The Turner Diaries* is more subtle. The book could serve as a psychological inspiration for violence; that is, it could inspire copycat crimes. The frequent diatribes in and the philosophy behind the book justify murder and mayhem. Pierce presents the destruction of nonwhite races, minorities, and Jews as the only logical solution to social problems. Although Pierce himself was not religious, he used a general cosmic theology, presented in a "holy" work called The Book, to place Earl Turner on the side of an unknown deity.

Some extremists who read this book have taken action. **Robert Matthews**, for example, founded a terrorist group called the **Bruder Schweigen** (the Silent Brotherhood), or The Order, based on Turner's fictional terrorist group. When arrested, the Oklahoma City bomber Timothy McVeigh was carrying a worn copy of *The Turner Diaries*.

Written in 1989, *Hunter* is another novel by Pierce as Andrew Mac-Donald. Although not as popular as *The Turner Diaries*, *Hunter* tells the story of a lone wolf named Hunter who decides to launch a one-person revolution. He stalks the streets to kill African Americans, interracial couples, and Jews. The book is dedicated to a real-life killer, and like *The Turner Diaries*, it could inspire copycat crimes. In 1999 two right-wing extremists went on killing sprees in Chicago and Los Angeles in a style reminiscent of the violence in *Hunter*.

Extremist literature is full of hate, instructions, and suggestions. Pierce has introduced nothing new in the literature of intolerance. However, he has popularized terrorism in two well-written novels. Unfortunately, they could also serve as a blueprint for violence.

Self-Check

- *Why do modern right-wing groups reflect a long history of extremism?*
- *What is Christian Identity and how is it related to other right-wing movements?*
- *Describe various models for right-wing violent extremism.*

The Decline of the Left and the Rise of Single Issues

Left-wing terrorist groups dominated terrorism in the United States from about 1967 to 1985. Fueled by dissatisfaction with the Vietnam War, violent radicals broke away from student protest movements. Soon, various groups emerged, and they separated from the student movement to join ranks with nationalist terrorists. Their favorite tactic was bombing, but unlike right-wing groups, they tried to avoid causing casualties. Various groups made headlines, but their influence faded. By the late 1980s, several leftist groups formed coalitions such as the Armed Resistance Unit, but they were forced to do so out of weakness rather than strength (Wolf, 1981, pp. 40–43).

Several things contributed to the demise of left-wing terrorism in the United States. One of the major problems was that intellectual elites controlled the movement (Serafino, 2002). During a time of student activism, leftist elites developed followings and sympathy across a broad spectrum of collegiate and highly educated people. Kevin J. Riley and Bruce Hoffman (1995) note that this gave the left a broad constituency. Yet the movement lost its base when student activism began to disappear from American academic life. As the mood of the country shifted toward more conservative patterns of behavior, the left-wing terrorists had little sympathetic ideological support.

Riley and Hoffman surveyed several U.S. law enforcement agencies in the mid-1990s to determine their concern with domestic terrorism. Police departments were worried about terrorism, but left-wing groups were not at the top of their agenda. Only 25 percent of the urban agencies surveyed reported any left-wing activity; the responding departments reported much more activity from other types of groups. Riley and Hoffman say that the left-wing groups had engaged in symbolic violence. Some identified with Marxist-Leninist ideology, whereas others worked against specific political issues such as U.S. military involvement in Central and South America. The collapse of the Soviet Union did not help left-wing popularity. In 1995 police perceived right-wing and Puerto Rican groups to be the greatest threats. The greatest concentration of left-wing groups was on the West Coast, but they posed a comparatively weak threat.

Loretta Napoleoni (2003, xix–xxiii) finds that guilt was a factor as left-wing terror faded in Europe. People who may have been sympathetic to the ideology of left-wing terrorists could not tolerate their violent activities as terrorism increased. This may have been a factor in American terrorism as well. Furthermore, left-wing violence waned with the fall of the Soviet Union, and police tactics improved with time, putting many terrorist groups on the defensive (Peacetalk, 2003).

The decline of American left-wing terrorism may reflect a similar trend in Europe. Xavier Raufer (1993) says German leftists failed when the government stole their agenda. The conservatives of the Reagan era certainly did not take the left-wing agenda, but they did take the country's heart. American mainstream interests turned from the extremist left. Donatella della Porta (1995) points to this process in Italy. The Red Brigades were able to attract a broad sympathetic audience, but the government and authorities came to understand this and turned the tables, winning the support of the public. Unfortunately, as their power base waned, the Red Brigades increased violence in an effort to gain new recruits. American groups were too weak to do this, although they grabbed headlines.

Transformation to Single Issues

Left-wing terrorism did not disappear, however; it was transformed. Leftist movements became more specific, focusing not only on certain political behavior, but on particular causes. When the left faded, single-issue groups emerged to take their place. These new groups grew and began a campaign of individual harassment and property destruction.

Ecoterrorism, Animal Rights, and Genetic Engineering

According to the FBI (Jarboe, 2002), supporters of ecoterrorism and animal rights, and opponents of genetic engineering came together in the United Kingdom in 1992. The new group called itself the Earth Liberation Front (ELF). Composed of radicals from Earth First! the Animal Liberation Front (ALF), and other disaffected environmentalists, the group migrated from Europe to the United States. The alliance has been responsible for more than 600 criminal acts since 1996. Its tactics include sabotage, tree spiking, property damage, intimidation, and arson, resulting in tens of millions of dollars of damage. One ELF member recently called for violent action, but both ELF and ALF deny this.

Formation of ELF was augured when radical ecologists began to sabotage road-working and construction machinery in the late 1970s. As was the case with the right wing, a novel inspired the ecoterrorists. *The Monkey Wrench Gang*, a 1975 novel by Edward Abbey, told the story of a group of ecologists who were fed up with industrial development in the West. Abbey, however, is an environmental activist rather than a hate-filled ideologue like William Pierce. His novel is a fictional account that inspired others. In *The Monkey Wrench Gang*, the heroes drive through western states sabotaging bulldozers, burning billboards, and damaging the property of people they deem to be destroying the environment. (This is the same type of low-level terrorism German leftists used in the mid-1990s.) Such monkey wrenching has become a key tactic of ecoterrorists.

Bryan Denson and James Long (1999) conducted a detailed study of ecological violence for the *Portland Oregonian*. They found that a shadowy conglomeration of violent ecologists was not willing to watch developers move into undeveloped areas. ELF had no hierarchy and was not associated with any particular location. They used a terrorist tactic long associated with the past, however: ELF targeted its victims with arson.

Denson and Long found that damage from ecoterrorism reached into the millions of dollars. They conducted a ten-month review that considered only crimes that caused more than $50,000 damage. Cases that could not be linked to environmental groups were eliminated. They found one hundred cases with very few successful law enforcement investigations. ELF mastered firebombs and would not strike their targets when people were present. Their goal was to destroy property. Their firebombs grew increasingly sophisticated, and they placed bomb-making instructions on the Internet.

According to Denson and Long, most violence associated with ecoterrorism has taken place in the American West. From 1995 to 1999, damages totaled $28.8 million. Crimes included raids of farms, destruction of animal research laboratories at the University of California at Davis and Michigan State University, threats to individuals, sabotage of industrial equipment, and arson. ELF activities have increased each year since 1999 and have expanded throughout the country (Schabner, 2004). At least some members want to take their actions in a new direction. In September 2002 an ELF communiqué stated that it would "no longer hesitate to pick up the gun" (Center for Consumer Freedom, 2004).

In the past decade ecological and animal-rights extremists have united and are known by a variety of names with a myriad of extremist causes. For instance, ELF, Earth First! and a group satirically calling itself the Justice Department are interested in preserving the planet. The

ALF, Animal Rights Militia, Band of Mercy, and Paint Panthers champion animal rights. Like their right-wing counterparts, many of these groups merely engage in rhetoric or disruptive behavior. The violent groups, such as ELF and ALF, advocate and engage in economic damage. They want to economically harm land developers, ski lodges, farms, and research labs, forcing them out of business.

Ecoterrorists are uncompromising, illogical extremists just like their right-wing counterparts. A review of their ideological literature shows they use ecology as a surrogate religion; that is, they are attached to their ideology in the same way many religious people attach themselves to faith (J. White, 2000). Like all extremists, their positions are full of contradictions, but they brush these aside because they feel their cause is more important than being consistent.

Black Hebrew Israelism: An Apocalyptic Single Issue

In the public version of the FBI's **Project Megiddo**, a report about possible religious and cult terrorism at the turn of the millennium, FBI analysts say that **Black Hebrew Israelism** has the potential to become a violent group. Some critics have scoffed at this suggestion, saying the FBI overreacted to a set of beliefs. Others believe the FBI has identified a dangerous violent religious trend.

What is Black Hebrew Israelism? In a nutshell, it is Christian Identity with an African twist. According to Tory Thorpe (1996), Black Hebrew Israelites believe that the original Israelites were dark-skinned Africans. They migrated to Nigeria during the Jewish Diaspora and waited for God to fulfill promises to the Hebrews. The white slave traders interfered, however, and created a greater diaspora of black African Israelites.

The mythology of Black Hebrew Israelites and their beliefs dates back to the Civil War. In the latter part of the twentieth century, again like Christian Identity, the group developed an elaborate theology to explain the status of African Americans. For example, according to **Yehuda ben Yisrael**, a proponent of Black Hebrew Israelism, whites conspired to cancel the relationship between Africa and God. Another source explains that curly hair is evidence of the divine origins of black skin. The *African Heritage Study Bible* is used to prove that the Jews whom Moses led out of Egypt were black.

The First Amendment grants freedom of religion, so anyone is free to believe the tenets of Black Hebrew Israelism. In fact, the theology of Black Hebrew Israelism does not constitute a need for law enforcement investigation or even curiosity. However, some segments of Black Hebrew Israelism have a history of cultic violence, and some have demonized non-African races. Like the potential violence in Christian Identity, this merits law enforcement's attention, but a police agency inquiring about the religion is bound to create controversy. This is the reason some people criticized the FBI for examining the group in Project Megiddo.

The actions of Hulon Mitchell Jr. generated the most attention. According to court records (U.S. Court of Appeals, 1996), Mitchell and

---

Project Megiddo
A 1999 FBI research project designed to assess potential domestic terrorism, especially from groups espousing eschatological violence.

Black Hebrew Israelism
An African American version of Christian Identity. Followers maintain that God is black and the original Hebrews were black Africans. The idea is nearly 200 years old, and most followers are nonviolent. In extreme forms, whites and Jews are demonized. In one extreme version, Death Angels were dispatched to kill white people.

Yehuda ben Yisrael
A proponent of Black Hebrew Israelism, claims that whites conspired to keep African Americans from learning of their divine origin.

Linda Gaines moved to Miami, Florida, in 1979 and laid the foundation for a Black Hebrew Israelite group known as the **Nation of Yahweh**. Mitchell told followers that God and Jesus were black and he, Mitchell, had been chosen to lead blacks back to Israel. By 1980 he ordered followers to abandon their given names and assume Hebrew identities. Gaines became Judith Israel and Mitchell took the name **Yahweh ben Yahweh**. (Yahweh is an anglicized version of the Hebrew tetragrammaton YHWH, or the name of God.) Mitchell's new name could be translated as "God son of God."

By 1985 the Nation of Yahweh developed into a group of worshippers who focused their attention on Mitchell. He kept social order through violent discipline as members pledged their loyalty to him. Mitchell built the Temple of Love and stationed armed guards around its entrance. Gaines controlled the income of all temple members, and Mitchell ruled his followers with an iron hand. Mitchell began expanding his theology, teaching that whites were devils and his followers were to kill them in the name of God. He created an internal group called the Brotherhood, and one could obtain membership only by killing a white person.

When some members tried to leave the group, they were beaten and beheaded. Over the next few years, Mitchell dispatched **Death Angels** to kill whites in the Miami area. The Death Angels were ordered to bring victims' severed body parts back to Mitchell as proof that the murders had occurred. After a five-month trial, Mitchell, Gaines, and some of the other followers were convicted under federal organized-crime statutes.

Black Hebrew Israelism is indicative of the tension between believing and acting, and it presents a dilemma for those charged with security. The theology of Black Hebrew Israelism is not violent, and most of its adherents would never follow in Hulon Mitchell's footsteps. The problem for those charged with preventing violence, however, is that when a belief system degrades or demonizes another group, violence often follows. Any time extremist beliefs are fused with hatred, the larger community may be at risk.

Nation of Yahweh
A violent offshoot of Black Hebrew Israelism founded in Miami by Hulon Mitchell Jr., also known as Yahweh ben Yahweh. The group is best known for Mitchell's dispatching of Death Angels with instructions to kill whites.

Yahweh ben Yahweh
(1935–) The name Hulon Mitchell Jr. used as leader of the Nation of Yahweh. It is Hebrew for "God the son of God."

Death Angels
Select members of the Brotherhood in the Nation of Yahweh. They were sent to murder white people in the Miami area.

Self-Check

- *Did violent left-wing extremists from the 1960s and 1970s disappear?*
- *What issues dominate violent left-wing extremism today?*
- *How are single-issue groups related to left-wing extremism?*

▼ Antiabortion Violence

For the past three decades the amount of violence against abortion clinics and personnel has risen. Violent antiabortionists began with bombing and arson attacks more than twenty years ago, and they have enhanced their tactics since then. Doctors and nurses have been assaulted when entering clinics. A gunman murdered Dr. David Gunn as he entered

Tactics in Violent Antiabortion Attacks

- Suspected anthrax sent through the mail
- Malicious destruction of property
- Threatening letters and phone calls to workers
- False bomb threats
- Individual harassment
- Bombing and arson
- Bombing with secondary devices (designed to kill the people who respond to the first bombing)
- Assaults
- Intentional murder on the premises
- Assassination-style murders

a clinic in Pensacola, Florida, in 1993. A year later the Reverend Paul Hill killed another doctor and his bodyguard when he entered the same clinic (Risen and Thomas, 1998). Hill was convicted of murder and executed in 2003. Dr. Barnett Slepian was killed at home in 1998 when a sniper shot him through a window. Eric Rudolph evaded federal authorities for years after bombings at the 1996 Olympics, a gay night club, and an abortion clinic in Birmingham, Alabama.

Abortion is a heated topic pitting pro-life and pro-choice advocates against one another. Most pro-life advocates abhor and denounce antiabortion violence because it is a contradiction of what they represent. Violent antiabortion advocates, however, justify their actions in the same manner as other political extremists. According to Risen and Thomas (1998), both murderers in Pensacola felt a specific holy duty to kill the doctors they confronted. Paul Hill, for example, shot his victims five times, laid his gun down, and walked away. Michael Griffin, Gunn's murderer, felt that God gave him instructions to give Gunn one final warning. When Gunn ignored him, Griffin waited for five hours and then shot him three times in the back as he left the clinic. To these people, accepting the status quo is more evil than using violence to change behavior. It is the standard justification for terrorism (see Another Perspective: Tactics in Violent Antiabortion Attacks).

Violence is not the only illegal action among those who break the law. The manual of the Army of God (n.d.) includes "99 Ways to Stop an Abortionist." It discusses low-level tactics such as gluing locks, shutting off water, and slashing tires. These are the tactics of radical ecologists in Germany (Horchem, 1986), but the manual does not credit a source or inspiration for the suggested tactics. The manual also describes methods for confronting workers and those seeking an abortion.

David Nice (1988) attempts to build a theory of violence by examining trends in abortion clinic bombings. Though done in 1988, Nice's research remains applicable today. He notes that the literature reveals several explanations for violent political behavior. One theory suggests that social controls break down under stress and urbanization. Another theory says that violence increases when people are not satisfied with political outcomes. Violence can also be reinforced by social and cultural values. Finally, violence can stem from a group's strength or weakness, its lack of faith in the political system, or its frustration with economic conditions.

Nice matches trends in abortion clinic bombings against these theories of violence. His examination of thirty bombings during a three-year period revealed some patterns. First, bombings tended to be regionalized. Along with two in Washington, D.C., the bombings occurred in eight states, only three of which had more than four bombings. Nice compares the social factors in the detonation areas with the theories about violent political behavior.

Nice concludes that abortion clinic bombings are related to several social factors. Most of the bombings occurred in areas of rapidly expanding population and declining social controls. This means bombings tended to occur in urban areas. The slowest-growing states in the United States did not experience bombings, whereas half of the fastest-growing states did.

Bombings also reflected a method of communicating frustration with political processes and outcomes. Bombing is a means of taking direct action. Nice notes that most bombings took place where the ratio of abortions to live deliveries is relatively high. Abortion bombers feel compelled to take action by social and political circumstances. They believe they are making a positive impact on the political situation. Nice also notes that bombings predictably occur more frequently in states that have a highly active militant antiabortion constituency.

States that experience bombings also exhibit a greater toleration for crimes against women. Clinic bombings are highest in areas where cultural and social violence against women is considered more acceptable. States that have passed laws against domestic violence experience fewer bombings than states with no such laws.

Bombings are also a sign of weakness. Although it seems paradoxical, areas having strong concentrations of antiabortion sentiment do not experience as much bombing. If an area experiences antiabortion activism, however, the bombing rate tends to be higher. In addition, Nice says that when the population of the area has high numbers of Roman Catholics, Baptists, or Mormons, the number of bombings declines. When potential bombers feel outnumbered, however, they may take action because they feel weak.

In summary, Nice found that abortion clinic bombings were positively correlated with every theory of violence, except the theory of economic deprivation. There was no relation between abortion clinic bombings and economic conditions. Nice concludes that antiabortion violence appears in areas of rapid population growth where the abortion rate is high. As social controls decrease and the desire to substitute political controls increases, bombings develop into a form of political action.

Some of Nice's findings seem applicable to antiabortion violence that has occurred since his study. According to Risen and Thomas (1998), the murderers who killed doctors who performed abortions felt the killings were necessary to make a political statement. Killing was a means of communication. Paul Hill was so excited by Gunn's murder that he successfully publicized it by appearing on *The Phil Donahue Show* and confronting Gunn's son. Activists were also prominent in the area where the shootings took place. All these factors created an atmosphere in which the killers sought to make a stronger statement than merely persuading women entering the clinic to not have an abortion.

Other issues have changed since Nice's study. Deana Rohlinger (2002) argues that current media coverage of abortion issues differs from the 1980s and early 1990s. She states that organizations favoring a woman's right to an abortion understood two critical aspects of media coverage in the previous decades. They knew how certain news organizations framed the debate and how they would cover a story. They also understood the power of news coverage and were able to attract media coverage for their point of view. Organizations against abortion did not know how to either attract media coverage or utilize it as a propaganda tool. If Rohlinger is correct, it would be wise to follow Brent Smith's path of empirical analysis. Nice's theory of bombing and frustration could be tested against the ability of the antiabortion movement to affect outcomes by media publicity.

Carol Mason (2004) argues that frustration may be building on the pro-choice side. She believes that the antiabortion movement has not only effectively conveyed a message but glorified apocalyptic violence. Antiabortion terrorists become heroes in the antiabortion movement, even though their actions are publicly denounced. She uses the case of **Eric Rudolph** to illustrate her point. Wanted for a string of antiabortion violence, Rudolph was finally captured after years of being a fugitive. Rudolph was allowed to play the role of right-wing folk hero, Mason says, after he was taken into custody. She believes such glorification may lead to a backlash.

There is no easy solution to the abortion debate, as proponents of each side believe they are morally correct. The side favoring the right to choose feels it is defending constitutional rights, and those against abortion often believe they are following God's will. The abortion debate represents a political issue in which the positions have been defined by extreme political positions, and this frustrates other people who believe a moral solution lies between the extremes. The atmosphere surrounding the abortion debate is similar to extremist positions surrounding terrorist conflicts in other parts of the world.

Eric Rudolph

(1966–) A right-wing extremist known for bombing the Atlanta Olympics, a gay night club, and an abortion clinic. Rudolph hid from authorities and became a survivalist hero. He was arrested in 2003 and received five life sentences in 2005.

Self-Check

- *Do early studies of antiabortion violence reveal patterns that are applicable today?*
- *Describe the forms of antiabortion violence.*
- *Is antiabortion violence terrorism?*

SUMMARY

- Cooper, Bell, and Gurr provided the first summaries of domestic terrorism by focusing on differing forms of social violence; the nature of terrorism began to change by the time of Cooper's report.
- Conceptualizing domestic terrorism is challenging because many law enforcement agencies do not deal well with the problem; terrorism is reported in different ways, and there are different classification systems for defining terrorism and terrorists. Smith points to several research difficulties, and Emerson's research shows the difficulty of isolating jihadist terrorism.
- The FBI system for classifying domestic terrorism is similar to Smith's. It focuses on international terrorists in America, left- and right-wing terrorism, lone-wolf violence, and single-issue terrorism. Smith finds declining levels of ideological terrorism and increasing threats from single-issue terrorists. Groups may be moving toward the network structure of international terrorists.
- Emerson's research supports the existence of a network of jihadist terrorist organizations in the United States. Critics believe that he has categorized too many Muslims as terrorists. Regardless, Emerson's research group, the Investigative Project, has assembled an array of reports, many of which point to a jihadist network inside America's borders. Homegrown jihadists are appearing in America and they are inspired by the international network.
- Puerto Rican nationalistic groups seek independence from the United States. However, many Puerto Ricans want to either keep commonwealth status or seek statehood.
- Right-wing extremism can be traced to the Whiskey Rebellion of 1794. It continued through the next two centuries. Contemporary right-wing extremism is based on Christian patriotism or similar movements, white supremacy, and types of survivalism. Frequently, an individual extremist belongs to more than one phase of the movement.
- Left-wing terrorism dwindled much in the way it did in Europe. Single-issue violent extremists dominate the left-wing movement today. Radical ecologists and animal-rights activists primarily engage in property destruction in the name of their causes. Their goal is economic disruption. There are alliances among the groups today.

- Black Hebrew Israelism is an African American version of Christian Identity. It claims that black Africans were the original Israelites. One violent group, the Nation of Yahweh, demonized whites and called for their destruction.
- Antiabortion violence began with bombing and arson but moved into assault and murder. The same factors that spawned bombing seem to surround selective assault and murder.

KEY TERMS

Task Force on Disorders and
    Terrorism (p. 347)
hate crime (p. 351)
ecoterrorism (p. 354)
animal rights (p. 354)
genetic engineering (p. 354)
empirical studies (p. 354)
American Terrorism Study
    (p. 358)
leaderless resistance (p. 359)
Louis Beam (p. 359)
William Pierce (p. 359)
unstructured violence (p. 359)
plea bargaining (p. 360)
Tamim al-Adnani (p. 362)
Elsayyid Nossair (p. 363)
Council on American-Islamic
    Relations (p. 365)
John Walker Lindh (p. 367)
Adam Gadahn (p. 367)
Whiskey Rebellion (p. 370)
Know-Nothings (p. 370)
Nathan Bedford Forrest (p. 370)
Knight Riders (p. 370)
Anglo-Israelism (p. 371)
William Potter Gale (p. 371)
Richard Butler (p. 371)
Aryan Nations (p. 371)
white supremacy movement
    (p. 373)

Brady Bill (p. 373)
Ruby Ridge (p. 373)
Branch Davidians (p. 374)
Waco siege (p. 374)
Vernon Wayne Howell (p. 374)
Nordic Christianity (p. 375)
Creatorism (p. 376)
Ben Klassen (p. 376)
skinheads (p. 376)
New World Order (p. 376)
free-wheeling fundamentalists
    (p. 376)
survivalist (p. 376)
militia movement (p. 377)
Protocols of Zion (p. 377)
Christian Identity (p. 377)
Third Position (p. 378)
National Alliance (p. 378)
Robert Matthews (p. 378)
Bruder Schweigen (p. 378)
Project Megiddo (p. 382)
Black Hebrew Israelism (p. 382)
Yehuda ben Yisrael (p. 382)
Nation of Yahweh (p. 383)
Yahweh ben Yahweh (p. 383)
Death Angels (p. 383)
Eric Rudolph (p. 386)

WRITING ASSIGNMENTS

1. Governmental projects and noted scholars have provided frameworks for understanding terrorism since 1967, yet local American law enforcement does not seem to understand terrorism. Why? Is it important

for state, local, and tribal agencies to understand and recognize terrorism? Is terrorism only a problem for federal law enforcement?

2. How do right-wing organizational structures reflect the international trend toward networks instead of organizations? Are there similarities between right-wing religious interpretations such as Christian Identity and violent interpretations of Islam? Do these similarities play a role in the movement to network or are there other organizational factors at work? Will single-issue groups follow this pattern?

3. Many people against abortion believe it is murder. If this is true, how do they justify antiabortion bombings or assassinations? Are these actions murder, too?

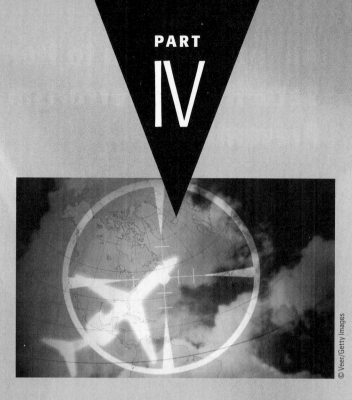

© Veer/Getty Images

HOMELAND SECURITY

15

An Introduction to Homeland Security and Terrorism Prevention

AP Photo/Kathy Willens

Officers from the New York Police Department search for potential terrorists in Grand Central Station. While a variety of agencies are responsible for preventing terrorism, state, local, and tribal law enforcement agencies play a leading role in homeland security.

Learning Objectives

After reading this chapter you should be able to

- Define *homeland security* and explain why confusion surrounds the term.
- List the agencies responsible for homeland security and describe their functions.
- Explain the issues involved in rethinking conflict.

- Summarize Clausewitz's and Sun Tzu's concept of war.
- Explain the difference between the attack on Pearl Harbor and the attacks of September 11.
- Outline the influence of a changing mode of conflict on military thought.
- Describe the intelligence process.

- Differentiate between criminal and national security intelligence.
- List some of the organizations responsible for processing intelligence.
- List and discuss some of the major issues in homeland security.

In the years since September 11, 2001, Americans routinely speak of *homeland security*, and the federal government has created a new cabinet-level department, the Department of Homeland Security, responsible for it. But the country is not quite sure what it means by homeland security. On one hand, it seems to mean something less than a military action because the Department of Homeland Security is separate from the Department of Defense, and more than half of the agencies that make up the department have arrest power. On the other hand, Department of Homeland Security leadership is full of retired military personnel, and it controls the U.S. Coast Guard, an organization that assumes a military role in wartime. The department's role remains confused. America is slowly coming to grips with the meaning of *homeland security* as government and industry fashion new relationships, but the nation has a long way to go. This is partially due to the changing nature of modern conflict and the role that terrorism plays in it.

Defining Homeland Security

In the autumn of 2004 the Department of Defense held a conference on special operations that combined the military's counterterrorism efforts with American law enforcement's. Three leading officials from the Bush administration spoke about homeland security, outlining the national strategy. One of the speakers cited the three major elements of the administration's policy. Another official said there were five major elements to President Bush's plans, and the last speaker, an advisor from the White House, said there were four elements to the national strategy. A frustrated Army officer asked the last speaker if the United States had three, four, or five elements to its counterterrorist policy. The speaker answered that he did not know, but it was not important.

A few years later in Destin, Florida, several federal agencies sponsored a training session that combined federal law enforcement, military, and intelligence agencies with state, local, and tribal law enforcement. Michael Chertoff (2007), secretary of the **Department of Homeland**

Department of Homeland Security (DHS)
A federal agency created in 2003 by Congress from the Office of Homeland Security after the attacks of September 11, 2001.

Security (DHS), spoke of the necessity to operate as a multifaceted team of differing organizations to stop terrorism before it occurs. A retired general in charge of assessing counterterrorist intelligence spoke of fighting international terrorist networks with our own network (Burgess, 2007). Another speaker outlined the changing face of conflict and explained how counterterrorist policy had become a complex network comprising educational, private sector, law enforcement, intelligence, and societal elements (J. White, 2007). Former ABC news analyst John Miller (2007), an FBI deputy director, closed the conference by outlining national policy and the roles of differing levels of government. In terms of policy, there had been a lot of changes in three years.

Searching for Defined Roles

There is a reason for policy transition. It was one thing to transform bureaucracy by reorganization and congressional authorization of a new cabinet position in 2003. It was quite another to define the roles and functions of agencies that would provide homeland security. Agencies have made progress over the last few years, especially in the area of information sharing and cooperation. There is still much to do, but some people believe the situation is better (Reese, 2007).

The reason for the initial confusion about policy is that America had no common definition of homeland security. Issues surrounding homeland security were confused because the country was dealing with a new concept, a new meaning of conflict, and a change in the procedures used to defend the United States. In the past, military forces protected the homeland, projecting power beyond U.S. borders, but the world changed with the end of the cold war in 1991. Another reason for confusion lies in the fact that the new Department of Homeland Security (DHS) was responsible for protecting the borders and the country's interior. Coupled with this state of affairs were bureaucratic efforts to redefine relations among agencies. The situation was further complicated when state and local governments became involved. Finally, a host of private businesses, nonprofit organizations, and health care systems were involved in security efforts. It was not easy to find a common definition for homeland security.

Confusion remains. For example, there are debates about the constitutionality of some aspects of governmental functions and laws that followed the 9/11 attacks (Raab, 2006). There are tremendous differences of opinion about the use of the military in the war on terrorism, and this is highlighted in passionate debates about the effectiveness of the Iraq War. Foreign policy relationships and the use of intelligence also are debated within the homeland security discussion (Pillar, 2006). Many federal, state, local, and tribal police agencies still search for their mission (J. White, 2007).

Despite the initial confusion, the first steps toward role definition have been taken, and agencies are beginning to understand their roles. Roles are divided into three functions: preventing terrorism, responding to attacks, and providing technical support to local agencies (Chertoff, 2007). Agencies are coming to grips with the concept of homeland security because, in its most rudimentary form, the term means *keeping the country safe*. The concept formed in the wake of a jihadist attack, but it has expanded beyond September 11. Basically, homeland security protects lives, property, and infrastructure. It is designed to secure the United States.

Critics maintain that confusion remains and that the country is not prepared to thwart an attack. Stephen Flynn (2002, 2004a, and 2004b) points to weaknesses in port security. Robert Poole (2006) told Congress that aviation security remains inadequate even after the disasters of 9/11. The greatest criticism is aimed at the borders. Although illegal immigration is a hotbed of political debate, the southern border is not secure by any measure. Many counterterrorist experts believe it will become one of the main infiltration routes for jihadists. The northern border, which does not receive the same amount of attention, is also difficult to secure (Clarke, 2007).

Security Missions

It might be more appropriate to move beyond the confusion about homeland security and look at the missions of various organizations and their common understanding of the concept. Essentially, *mission* and *understanding* mean the same thing, but there are many different understandings of homeland security because many agencies have differing missions. For example, the Department of Energy (DOE) is responsible for protecting nuclear materials, power grids, and gas lines. DOE's understanding of homeland security is related to its mission. Customs and Border Protection in the DHS, on the other hand, uses its agents to secure U.S. borders and points of entry, with customs agents collecting revenue. It has a law enforcement mission and defines homeland security within this context. The elements of security expand or contract depending on an organization's mission.

There is confusion, to be sure, but it centers on policy, not mission. The policy guiding homeland security in the United States has not been fully developed, and agency leaders are not quite sure how all the missions of various agencies fit together. Several groups inside and outside government are adjusting to new roles. The intelligence community was criticized after the attacks, and the 9/11 Commission and its supporters were successful in implementing reform in the intelligence community. Critics, however, are not impressed with the commission's version of reform. They maintain that the 9/11 Commission was established to investigate the attacks and that it had neither the expertise nor the capability to reform intelligence gathering (Posner, 2004). This leaves the roles of various intelligence groups in transition. The law enforcement and military communities are trying to find policies to define their roles. The functions of domestic and international laws have not been fully established. Various levels of government and private industry are trying to figure out where they interact. All of these maneuvers take time.

Homeland security also involves civil defense, that is, citizens engaged in homeland security. Civil defense did not develop overnight; rather, it emerged slowly from civilian functions during World War II. After 1960 civil defense structures were intended to help government protect citizens in areas such as emergency communications through private and public broadcasting, direct assistance during emergencies, evacuation routes, and fallout shelters. During the cold war various organizations involved in **civil defense** gradually learned specific missions. The idea of "civil defense" will take on a new meaning in the coming years because the nature of conflict has changed. Homeland security is much more than the sum of agencies charged with protecting the United States. A major portion of security is a civic responsibility.

civil defense

Citizens engaged in homeland security.

Self-Check

- *Why do law enforcement and domestic security agencies search for defined roles?*
- *Why do they compete with one another?*
- *How does an agency's mission provide a role definition?*

Agencies Charged with Preventing and Interdicting Terrorism

Congress approved the creation of the Department of Homeland Security by uniting twenty-two agencies in 2002, but many other governmental organizations also focus on homeland security. These organizations exist in all levels of government: federal, state, local, and tribal. Two types of private-sector organizations participate in homeland security: businesses providing critical infrastructure and businesses centered on security technology and service. The health care system and energy sector are also part of the infrastructure in homeland security.

The Department of Homeland Security

The DHS was created from the Office of Homeland Security in 2003 as a direct result of the 9/11 attacks. It has several different missions (see U.S. Department of Homeland Security, http://www.dhs.gov/xabout/structure/). One group of internal organizations responds to natural and human disasters, and this function is complemented by a group of agencies charged with health and policy. Closely related to this are organizations charged with monitoring science and technology, including the detection of nuclear activities. Other parts of the department are tasked with managing both DHS affairs and some functions external to it. DHS also coordinates response with thousands of state, local, and tribal organizations. There are several internal agencies that have security functions directly related to terrorism prevention.

The U.S. Coast Guard was formerly under the Department of Transportation, except in time of war when it is subsumed by the U.S. Navy. It was the first agency to be assigned to the DHS. The Coast Guard has many duties, including the protection of coastal and inland waterways, environmental protection, the interdiction of contraband, and maritime law enforcement. For counterterrorism its primary mission is to intercept terrorists and weapons from the high seas. Coast Guard personnel also serve wherever U.S. military personnel are deployed under the command of the armed forces.

Other departments inside DHS have counterterrorist responsibilities. Many DHS agencies are involved in intelligence; its Office of Intelligence and Analysis coordinates intelligence with other agencies. The Transportation Security Administration is responsible for airport security. The U.S. Customs and Border Protection contains customs agents and the Border Patrol. Their work is augmented by an investigative agency, Immigration and Customs Enforcement (ICE), which is DHS's largest investigative arm. The Secret Service also serves in DHS. In addition to providing presidential security, the Secret Service retains its former role in countering financial crime. It is also involved in investigating identity theft, banking practices, and cyberattacks (Figure 15.1).

Many DHS employees are employed in law enforcement tasks and have arrest powers. In the new Homeland Security structure, these special agents and federal police officers are trained in the Federal Law Enforcement Training Center (FLETC) in Glencoe, Georgia. FLETC instructors also teach basic and advanced classes on terrorism. Before 2003 FLETC was responsible for training all federal law enforcement officers except special agents from the FBI and DEA. These agencies have their own training academies at the Marine Corps base in Quantico, Virginia.

The Department of Justice

The Department of Justice (DOJ) maintains several functions in the realm of counterterrorism. The most noted agency is the FBI (FBI, n.d.). Before 9/11 the FBI was designated as the lead agency for handling cases of terrorism in the United States. After 9/11 Director Robert Mueller maintained that preventing terrorism would be the bureau's chief mission. The FBI enhanced its Counterterrorism Division and increased the number of intelligence analysts assigned to it under Mueller's direction. As discussed at other points in this text, the FBI also coordinates state and local law enforcement efforts in Joint Terrorism Task Forces (JTTFs). The bureau also maintains Field Intelligence offices in its local agencies (see "Building Intelligence Systems" later in this chapter).

The DOJ is involved in other areas (U.S. DOJ, 2006). U.S. Attorneys investigate and prosecute terrorism cases and coordinate intelligence sharing (see "Building Intelligence Systems"). The U.S. Marshals Service (2005) provides protection to federal officials under threat from terrorism. The Bureau of Alcohol, Tobacco, and Firearms (ATF) has

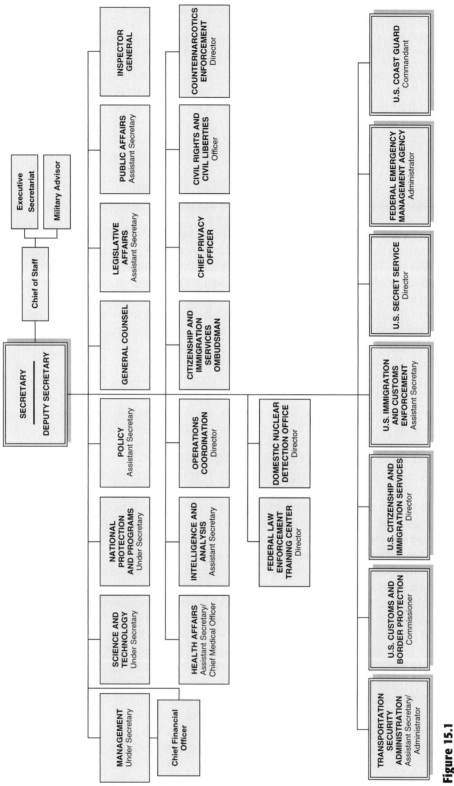

Figure 15.1
DHS Organizational Chart

played a leading role for years in counterterrorism. Bombs are one of the most frequent weapons used in terrorism, and the ATF has some of the best explosives experts in the world. It is also charged with federal firearms enforcement. Although the FBI is the lead agency in domestic terrorism, ATF's role in explosives and firearms enforcement is crucial. Many FBI investigations would be less productive without ATF help (ATF, 2007). The Bureau of Justice Assistance (BJA) has trained more than 100,000 state, local, and tribal officers since 9/11 in the BJA State and Local Anti-Terrorism Training (SLATT) program (Nedelkoff, 2002). SLATT trainers have also been used with various federal law enforcement agencies and the armed forces.

The Department of Defense

Obviously, in time of war, the military organizations in the Department of Defense (DOD) play the leading role. The DOD has also assumed counterterrorist functions. It does this in two ways. First, DOD operates the U.S. Northern Command to ensure homeland security. Because the Constitution forbids military forces from enforcing civil law except in times of declared martial law, the Northern Command limits its activities to military functions. It participates in information gathering and sharing, but it is excluded from civil affairs. In times of emergency, however, military forces can provide much-needed assistance to local units of government. This is the second function of DOD. When civilian authorities request and the president approves it, military forces may be used to support civilians in counterterrorism (U.S. DOD, 2005).

The Intelligence Community

The federal intelligence community underwent massive changes after 9/11 and after the invasion of Iraq and the failure to find WMD. The Office of the Director of National Intelligence (ODNI) began operations in April 2005. The purpose of the ODNI is to unite America's national security intelligence under one umbrella. The idea dates back to 1955 when several intelligence experts suggested that the deputy director of the CIA should run day-to-day intelligence operations for the agency and the director assume the responsibility of coordinating all national intelligence. The 9/11 Commission report suggested sweeping intelligence reforms, including the creation of a single intelligence director. The ODNI resulted from those recommendations (U.S. Office of the Director of National Intelligence, 2007).

The ODNI is a new concept in intelligence gathering. It coordinates information from national security and military intelligence. These agencies include the CIA, the National Security Agency, the Defense Intelligence Agency, the National Geo-Space Intelligence Agency, and the National Reconnaissance Office. It also includes intelligence operations from the Department of State. Based on the recommendations of the 9/11 Commission, the ODNI has incorporated federal law enforcement intelligence under its umbrella, too. Law enforcement agencies that re-

Figure 15.2

Office of the Director of
National Intelligence

THE NATIONAL SECURITY
INTELLIGENCE COMMUNITY

Director of National Intelligence

Armed Forces Intelligence	National Security Agency
Central Intelligence Agency	National Reconnaissance Office
Defense Intelligence Agency	National Geospatial Intelligence Agency
Department of Energy	Federal Bureau of Investigation
Department of Home and Security	Drug Enforcement Administration
Department of State	Department of the Treasury

port to the director of National Intelligence include the FBI's National Security Branch, the Department of Energy's Office of Intelligence and Counterintelligence, the Department of Homeland Security's Office of Intelligence and Analysis, the Department of the Treasury's Office of Intelligence and Analysis, and the Drug Enforcement Administration's Office of National Security Intelligence (Figure 15.2).

State, Local, and Tribal Law Enforcement

The federal government also envisions three intelligence roles for local governments. David Carter (2005) explains the first two. State, local, and tribal law enforcement agencies need to collect tactical intelligence for the prevention of terrorism and other crimes. They must also use intelligence for planning and the deployment of resources. Chief Gary Vest (2007) explains the third role. Information sharing is at the heart of local intelligence systems. Vest says that agencies are sharing information at an unprecedented level, but they need to enhance the process by creating systems governed by policies. Vest believes that agencies need to form associations with governing boards that have the power to enforce rules and regulations. This will regulate intelligence within the law, prevent leaks, and provide routine methods to share information.

Carter (2004, pp. 2–6) says the role of intelligence and information sharing among state, local, and tribal law enforcement agencies enhances counterterrorism efforts. Large federal systems operate on a global basis, and officers in local communities know their jurisdictions better than anyone. Community partnerships enhance the amount and quality of information they can accumulate. The federal government does not have the resources or the community contacts to develop these links. The National Criminal Intelligence Sharing Plan comes to the same conclusion. The ability of state, local, and tribal agencies to share information is at the heart of preventing terrorist strikes within the borders of the United States (Daniels, 2003). When it comes to terrorism, state, local, and tribal agencies are crucial to homeland security.

Self-Check

- *What federal departments and agencies are charged with homeland security?*
- *Why does the intelligence community interface with law enforcement?*
- *What roles do state, local, and tribal law enforcement agencies have in homeland security?*

Rethinking Conflict

The rules of conflict have been changing since World War II, and homeland security takes place within a changing tactical environment. David Rapoport (1988) believes the world has witnessed four primary waves of terrorism that overlapped and changed with the currents of history. Bruce Hoffman (2006, pp. 43–60) refers to the changes as phases and believes the world has experienced anticolonial, ideological, and religious terrorism. Brian Jenkins (2006) speaks of the types of wars America will face on a spectrum of conflict ranging from small, short counterterrorist operations to major military conflicts. Wesley Clark (2001) speaks of the need to confront social disorder in dysfunctional states, and Michael Gordon and Bernard Trainor (2006) believe the rise of the Iraqi insurgency is due to the American failure to understand and follow the changing tactical nature of conflict, especially the need for nation-building operations. Thomas Ricks (2006) supports their conclusions.

Networks and Law Enforcement

Homeland security takes place within a new set of rules (see Barnett, 2004). Although nations can pose a security threat, the current major threat for the United States comes from terrorist networks. Yet homeland security is more than counterterrorism. It involves responding to disasters, managing health crises, maintaining order at special events, and protecting federal officials, including the president. This text focuses on terrorism, and the discussion of homeland security will be limited to the prevention of terrorist attacks.

Most terrorism experts have argued for nearly fifty years that counterterrorism was primarily an affair for law enforcement, not the military (see Cooper, 1978; Wilkinson, 1974; Wardlaw, 1982; Jenkins, 1983; Sageman, 2004; Scheuer, 2006). Law enforcement still has a major role in stopping international networks that wage modern conflict, but the times have made it necessary to discuss the nature of modern conflict, warfare, and warfare's relation to terrorism.

The primary job of law enforcement in preventing terrorism is to stop criminal activity within networks. Arquilla and Ronfeldt (2001) believe that five factors must be in place for networks to operate. These factors identify nodes where the network can be disrupted: technology, social support, narrative, organizational structure, and tactical doctrine. Networks may be able to operate without all five factors, but they are not as effective. Technology, a traditional force multiplier for terrorist groups, is crucial. It allows a small group to operate on more sophisticated levels. Social support is also crucial. Groups must effectively maintain internal and external social relations. This builds trust and identity. Narrative is myth; it provides a story, the raison d'etre. The story must be accepted by the group, but outsiders must also embrace the narrative if the group is to operate in society. Organizations have abandoned the old hierarchy that defined terrorist groups in the post–World War II era. Groups range from simple chains to hubs to all-channel networks. There is no leadership structure. Finally, the tactical doctrine involves a *swarm*. Whether a demonstration in Seattle or a wave of suicide attacks, the group assembles, conducts operations, and disperses.

It is important to note that networks have changed the tactical structure of conflict, but the principles of conflict remain the same. Targeting has shifted from military forces to societal structures. Civilians, symbols, and physical and technological infrastructures become the targets of attack in a war beyond traditional definitions. The manner and style of fighting have changed—for example, guerrilla movements and terrorism enhanced by technological weapons—but the principles of war that applied to Julius Caesar, Frederick the Great, and George Patton are applicable today (for example, see Keegan, 1993, pp. 386–392). Whether a small eclectic terrorist cell or an armored division, combatants must structure units for operations and effectively communicate with one another. They must move matériel, seize and maintain the initiative, mass at the enemy's weak point, and psychologically convince the enemy that there is no point in fighting (Jenkins, 2006, pp. 111–143). Military ventures led by fighters from Scipio Africanus to David Petraeus require shock action and exploitation to achieve victory. The rule set has changed, not the nature of war.

In the new rule set, one social network opposes another. Although networks share information, agencies do not change their roles. Police departments should not become military or secret intelligence organizations. Law enforcement has three primary responsibilities, duties that existed long before 9/11. These responsibilities include (1) maintaining public safety, (2) collecting criminal intelligence, and (3) sharing information in a legal manner. None of these activities requires extraconstitutional authority, and they do not imply that police tactics should be militarized. Most importantly, there is no need for special paramilitary law enforcement units beyond those needed for high-risk response. In fact, closer relations with local communities enhance the national defense role of policing, whereas militarization, which inevitably builds barriers between the police and the public, actually detracts from law enforcement's ability to protect a community and serve the nation (Murray, 2005; see also Carter, 2004).

Blurring War and Peace

Just below the surface of jurisprudence, the practice of terrorism has blurred the distinction between war and peace. As described in Chapter 1, President Bush and his administration are fond of speaking of the *war on terrorism*. The Democratic Party might criticize the way the Republicans manage the war, but Democrats also refer to a war on terrorism. Although Republicans tend to see the issue as a military problem and Democrats frequently speak of terrorism as a criminal act, the public rhetoric of both sides focuses on bringing the enemy to justice. As Daniel Pipes (2003, pp. 242–257) says, it is one thing to define your enemies as "evil doers" and quite another to actually identify them. Can you "declare war" on "evil doers" and "bring them to justice?" he asks. Philosophers of war answered the question many years ago.

Before the time of growing terrorism, Americans thought they knew the meaning of conflict. War was an extension of politics fought within the legal framework of the Constitution. Quite simply, the Constitution states that only Congress has the power to declare war, and Congress decides whether America is in a state of war or peace. However, the anticolonial struggles after World War II; the Vietnam War; and the battles in Somalia, Serbia, Afghanistan, and Iraq confused the issue. American troops fought limited wars in peacetime.

The situation grew more complex as violence spread at home and abroad. Civil agencies faced standoffs with militant groups; a U.S. citizen bombed the federal building in Oklahoma City; two teenagers went on a shooting spree at their high school in Colorado; the World Trade Center towers were destroyed and the Pentagon attacked on September 11; a student went on a killing rampage at Virginia Tech; and jihadists allegedly plotted an attack on Fort Dix and JFK International Airport. Clearly, the law enforcement and public service workers involved were not soldiers, but they were being called to restore order during military-style attacks. The FBI was empowered to seize suspects beyond territorial limits, and military forces joined them in the hunt. When suspects were identified, prosecutors issued arrest warrants, and when suspects were caught, they went to trial in U.S. courts. Terrorism is changing the nature of conflict. Law enforcement agencies, courts, and corrections joined in the battle, even though they are not constitutionally associated with military power.

Networks and Classical Theories of Conflict

The American concept of conflict has been deeply influenced by the Prussian general and military philosopher **Carl von Clausewitz** (1780–1831), who cut his teeth on war during the nationalistic wars against Napoleon (1795–1815). Joining the Prussian Army as a twelve-year-old drummer boy to fight against France, he came to believe that the French Revolution created a new type of war, and he began to study war as a philosophical problem (1984 [1831]; for critiques see Liddell Hart, 1967; Craig, 1968; Howard, 1988; Hanson, 2000).

The strength of the French, Clausewitz reasoned, came from their ability to place the nation in arms, that is, to rally the people to the belief that all citizens of a nation are potential soldiers or supporters of the military. To defeat the French, Germany must become a nation in arms, unite under a democracy, and employ its own citizen soldiers. The proof of victory would come when Germany's political will could be imposed on France. Clausewitz joined a group of reformers and tried to modernize the Prussian Army. The Prussians were destroyed, however, in 1806 after the Battle of Jena-Auerstädt, and Clausewitz was carried off to Paris in captivity. He began writing, formulating a philosophy of national war.

Clausewitz's notions (see Another Perspective: Clausewitz and War in the Western Tradition) were derived from his study of history, especially the Thirty Years' War (1618–1648) and the campaigns of Frederick the Great (1740–1786). They were also influenced by his experiences after joining the Russian Army in 1812 to fight Napoleon and the German War of Liberation (1813–1814). Clausewitz's ideas come to us from a book published by his wife Maria the year after he died. *On War* is a philosophical treatise on the nature of total, nationalistic wars. It has also been one of the most influential works on military force in the twentieth century. Clausewitz's understanding of the nation in arms clearly renders the meaning of war, but it may not help Americans who desire to bring terrorists to justice.

Victor Hanson (2000) criticizes Clausewitz's idea of a single decisive conflict and the Western way of battle, claiming the West is consumed with the way war was fought in ancient Greece. According to this line of thought, the purpose of military action is to seek a decisive engagement, and Clausewitz's philosophical treatise emphasizes this point. Terrorism, however, is designed to produce the opposite effect, seeking to avoid direct confrontation with force. In addition, since the emergence of professional, modern warfare in the West after the Peace of Westphalia (1648), the purpose of war has been to impose political will on the defeated party. American law enforcement does not seek a decisive battle with enemy forces, and its purpose can never be the imposi-

Carl von Clausewitz

(1780–1831) A Prussian field marshal and philosopher of war. His book *On War* helped to shape military doctrine in the twentieth century.

On War

One of the most influential philosophical works on the practice of warfare. Written by Carl von Clausewitz, it remains standard reading for military officers in the Americas, Europe, and Asia.

ANOTHER PERSPECTIVE

Clausewitz and War in the Western Tradition

Clausewitz made several points about war, including the following:

- A nation is either at war or at peace.
- The purpose of diplomacy is to impose your will on your enemy.
- When diplomacy has failed, war may result.
- War must unite the will and resources of the nation.
- War is to be waged with maximum violence to destroy the enemy's will to fight.
- Battle results from a mutual decision to fight.
- All resources should be aimed at the main point (*Schwerpunkt*) of the battle to decisively defeat the enemy.
- War plans should be aimed at the total defeat of the enemy.

tion of political will. The goals of terrorism are to create panic and cause social systems to break. These goals mean that criminal justice and other civilian agencies will be involved in combating terrorism. America is neither at war nor at peace, and another paradigm may be more helpful.

Nearly 2,000 years ago a Chinese philosopher, **Sun Tzu**, produced a treatise on the paradoxes of war (Giles, 2000). Rather than conceiving of times when a political realm is either at war or at peace, Sun Tzu saw war and peace as two sides of the same coin. War and politics were psychological forces held together by the belief in power. In Sun Tzu's philosophical structure, the highest form of military leadership comes in breaking the enemy's resistance without fighting. Leaders must be able to control their anger and project power. When military leadership is strong, the state will be strong and have less need to act. If the state appears to be weak, it is vulnerable despite its strength (see Another Perspective: Sun Tzu and the Logic of Terrorism).

Terrorism is based on Sun Tzu's relation of strength to weakness. In modern military parlance this is called **asymmetry**. Asymmetry simply means competing forces are out of balance; that is, a weak force fights a much stronger power. A good analogy is to think of a single angry hornet attacking a hiker in the woods. The hornet can sting the hiker and, if it is lucky, cause the hiker to panic or maybe induce a fatal allergic reaction. If the hiker stays calm, however, a single swat ends the attack. The odds are in the hiker's favor. Terrorists are much like the hornet with two exceptions: They tend to be true-believing fanatics who sacrifice lives, not an angry insect acting in defense of self or territory, and they are willing to attack, violating social conventions and societal norms. Hornets attack the same way following their natural instincts, but terrorists fight outside the rules.

Sun Tzu

A Chinese philosopher of war who made little distinction between war and peace. Subtle expressions of power that defeat the enemy are better than war or fighting. Many counterterrorism analysts believe that Sun Tzu's ancient approach to conflict is applicable for fighting modern terrorism.

asymmetry

A term used in guerrilla warfare and terrorism to describe how a small, weak force fights a stronger power. Asymmetrical wars are fought between sides that are grossly unequal. The less powerful side does not fight the more powerful side under the conventional rules of war because it cannot win by using these tactics. The weaker side uses unconventional methods of fighting.

ANOTHER PERSPECTIVE

Sun Tzu and the Logic of Terrorism

Compare the selected paraphrases of Sun Tzu with those of Clausewitz. Which statements are more applicable to conventional battles with front lines and uniformed soldiers? Which statements are more applicable to guerrilla warfare and terrorism?

- If you know yourself and your enemy, you will be successful. If you know yourself and do not know your enemy, you will fail many times. If you know neither yourself nor your enemy, you will never succeed.

- The worst way to take a town is to lay siege. The best way is to make the inhabitants believe they are beaten.

- A military leader who projects strength can settle a dispute without losing a soldier.

- The best leader subdues the enemy's troops without fighting.

- Reduce the enemy by creating problems, making trouble, and making them rush to any given point.

The reason terrorists fight outside the norms of society is revealed by the imbalance of power. The major powers hold all the cards in international trade, legal authority, and military power. It does no good to strike them in the open, but they are vulnerable when attacked outside the norms of standard international relations. The lesson is as old as terrorism: If you can't kill their soldiers, kill their civilians. The purpose of terrorism is to give the impression that powerful economic, military, and political forces cannot protect ordinary people going about their daily routine. Terrorists do not seek an open battle but want to show that the norms of civil society cannot protect the population of the superior force. Enemy forces prepared for combat are too strong, but police stations, off-duty military personnel, and schoolchildren make tempting targets.

Obviously, military forces must cope with this change, but criminal justice agencies become involved in homeland security precisely because terrorists fight outside the rules. They commit virtually every type of crime imaginable when preparing an attack. If they wore uniforms, struck military targets, and fought within recognized international conventions, they would not be terrorists (Crenshaw, 1983, pp. 14–32).

Of course, they will never do this because terrorists lack the military strength and political appeal to engage in such activities. This means they will be arrested, tried, and incarcerated. Because terrorists attack the homeland, all aspects of the criminal justice system will be involved in homeland security. It is a new role, but the world is fighting by Sun Tzu's rules. Yet principles remain constant, only the tactics change. Despite criticism of Clausewitz, all the agencies involved in homeland security should seek decisive engagement with the enemy. But instead of a frontline engagement involving an enemy army, it involves a long-term confrontation with a network conducted within the bounds of legality.

Pearl Harbor and 9/11: Two Different Worlds

December 7, 1941, is known as "a date which will live in infamy"; September 11, 2001, is certainly a day that is burned into the hearts of Americans. Both events held surprises. For example, both Pearl Harbor and the suicide strikes revealed that America was vulnerable to attack. Both events occurred with no formal declaration of war, and both involved civilian casualties. Pearl Harbor and September 11 also shook the soul of the United States.

Despite these similarities, September 11 differs significantly from Pearl Harbor. The purpose of the Japanese surprise attack was to destroy U.S. military capabilities in the Pacific. Japanese governmental and military officials knew the United States would go to war as soon as the surviving Zeros returned to their carriers. Their purpose was to temporarily destroy America's capacity to wage war, achieve political objectives with military might, and negotiate a truce from a position of strength. By contrast, the September 11 attacks were designed for drama. They were a tragedy performed on a subnational, not international, level, to create an aura of fear by murdering thousands of people. There could be no negotiation because it is not permissible to negotiate with the devil. If the hijackers killed the enemies of evil, then God won. If they died in the process, God would replace them with future martyrs. Failure was out of the question, and victory was assured by God's promise (Lichtblau, 2001; Juergensmeyer, 2000, pp. 143–155).

The goal of the 9/11 terrorists was not one of conventional military strategy. Their purpose was to create so much fear that Western institutions would change their behavior. There was no grand offensive to follow the attacks and no notion of a rational, negotiated peace. The terrorists who targeted the United States wanted the West to believe that mass murder can happen at any time. In the words of Thomas Barnett (2004, pp. 18–34), the terrorists of September 11 were playing by a new set of rules. They were attacking globalization whereas America was defending state power.

If Barnett is correct, the September 11 attacks and the subsequent world of international terrorism have ushered in a new style of conflict. Jihadists are not attacking state power; they are attacking the idea of Western, particularly American, culture. Their war is with a global system that they fear and hate, and they resist being included in an economic arrangement they resent. This logic is applicable not only to jihadists. When the ideology of domestic terrorists is examined, similar types of concerns emerge. Modern terrorism is aimed at the infrastructure of everyday life and the symbols that define that structure (see Homer-Dixon, 2002; Stevenson, 2003).

> ## Self-Check
> - *How does World War II differ from the "war on terrorism"?*
> - *Why is it necessary to counter networks with networks?*
> - *How does terrorism apply to Clausewitz? To Sun Tzu?*

Redefining Conflict: A New Approach to the Military

It is not enough to suggest that terrorism has affected criminal justice or that it is primarily a law enforcement problem. There will be times when counterterrorism and homeland security will involve military forces and the intelligence agencies charged with national defense. One of the people who recognized this was retired Vice Admiral **Arthur Cebrowski**. A former carrier pilot, Cebrowski was president of the Naval War College and a champion of military innovation. He focused on the concept of **network-centric warfare** and advocated the use of small, combined military forces outfitted with the latest technology. He believed that the U.S. Navy needed not only traditional ships but also light vessels able to operate in coastal waters and rivers to handle guerrilla warfare and problems with terrorism (see Cebrowski and Gratska, 1998; Cebrowski and Barnett, 2003; Cebrowski, 2004). Cebrowski passed away in November 2005, but his ideas remain and influence American military thought. He understood that terror networks transcend the boundary between war and peace.

The whole nature of military action has been changing since World War II. Clausewitz himself probably would have thought beyond his initial notions. He wrote during an age when states fielded armies and those armies faced each other. He quite naturally focused on state-to-state war, but Clausewitz pointed to two other factors. Sometimes wars are fought on frontiers against irregular armies. Clausewitz was familiar with this because of Prussia's partition of Poland with Russia and Austria. In addition, Clausewitz's most famous maxim was that *war is an extension of politics*. In other words, the only reason a nation fights is to win a political victory. It may be necessary to think beyond open-field battles, but Clausewitz would have been the first to shift military efforts if it meant victory.

Operating Deeply in Society

Arthur Cebrowski (2004) said that U.S. armed forces need to develop the ability to operate "deeply" in society, that is, to fully understand, accept, and defend America with a complete comprehension of American culture and combine that with the willingness to completely understand any enemy society. He believed that America needs to create a new defense culture that permeates all levels of society and that breaks down barriers between organizations. Military forces must be able to fight and

---

Arthur Cebrowski
(1942–2005) A U.S. naval officer and president of the Naval War College who championed the idea of "network-centric warfare." His ideas are instrumental in understanding methods to counter terror networks.

network-centric warfare
A concept championed by Arthur Cebrowski stating that an enemy's crucial strength is in its social, political, and communications networks, not in geography or national capitals. Network-centric warfare seeks to destroy or disable such networks.

defeat irregular forces, they must be able to find targets, and they must develop ways to avoid strategic surprise. This type of strategy involves social immersion, and military forces need to harness the power of higher education. The United States needs forces that thoroughly understand American culture and the cultures of our enemies and friends.

Martin van Creveld (1991, pp. 142–156) presents the same idea in a different way. War has changed, Creveld argues, and it no longer reflects the rationality of Clausewitz's state-to-state clashes. Most importantly, many communities outside the West feel their very existence is threatened. A war for existence changes the nature of conflict because the strategic rules of war and the rational extension of policy are thrown out the window. When a community fights to survive, fighting *is* the policy. In these situations outbursts of violence are statements of existence as well as celebrations of being. In such circumstances, there can be no study of political purpose. Violence is the purpose. It demonstrates life.

Creveld uses the French-Algerian War (1954–1962) as an example. It was not war in the classical sense. There were no front lines, the Algerians did not field an army, and their attacks on the French and other Westerners violated established codes of conflict and criminal law. The French responded with a Clausewitzian cost-benefit analysis. They looked at the cost of keeping Algeria and weighed it against the benefits. When they sent paratroopers and police officers to fight, they did so as a continuation of this policy. Their goal was to impose their political will on the Algerians.

The Algerian nationalists of the National Liberation Front (FLN) approached the situation differently. They never conducted an analysis; they fought for the community's survival. As the war dragged on, survival became more important. In other words, violence justified violence. War brought more and more recruits to the ranks of the FLN. Creveld notes that the ability of the Algerians to accept punishment was almost limitless. Estimates of Algerian casualties range up to 1 million. The French, in contrast, lost twenty-two thousand soldiers and three thousand civilians over eight years, less than they lost in traffic accidents over the same period. Fighting France became the FLN's policy. As long as they fought, they were succeeding. Creveld said this is why the French lost: Algerians were fighting for their lives, the French for a calculation.

Creveld's theory reflects part of Barnett's thesis. Barnett (2004, p. 11) implies that military forces must change for future battles. In the future, they will develop policelike capabilities. The reason for this is clear. The nature of conflict has changed. If we combine these two ideas, it is logical to conclude that a force fighting to impose political will operates differently from a force fighting for existence. If military forces approach homeland security as a continuation of national policy, they will bring the wrong weapons to the wrong war. They will also fail to utilize their ultimate striking power: American citizens.

A New Map for the Pentagon

Thomas Barnett (2004) takes the concept much further in *The Pentagon's New Map*. War as we know it has ended, he writes. The purpose of power is to create a new set of international rules in which all nations are included in economic development, prosperity, and peace. This, Barnett says, is a future worth creating. When nations are excluded, he argues, violent terrorists have no incentive to play within the rules. The purpose of preparing to fight is to create an environment where violence is nonrewarding. It is to extend opportunity and improve the human condition. This extends the meaning of war far beyond the realm of military force and gives new roles to a variety of governmental and private agencies.

The recent growth of terrorism has changed all aspects of military affairs, and the nation must be prepared to enter a new type of war. Barnett (2004, pp. 6–7) says the Pentagon prepared to fight state-to-state battles during the 1990s. They tried to stop enemy movement, waited for the chance to concentrate forces in a single effort, and secured bases and supply lines. Military forces must still be prepared to fight these battles, but their mission has been extended. Terrorists do not fight in field engagements; therefore, military forces must transform their structures to take the fight to terrorists. New capabilities must be developed to prevent violence, keep infrastructures operating, include the whole political spectrum, and defend the social structure. Although not contained in Clausewitz's work, these transformations certainly reflect his thesis.

Self-Check

- *Define operating "deeply" in society.*
- *How does this idea of operating deeply in society change the meaning of conflict?*
- *Why do the law enforcement, military, and intelligence communities have complementary roles in homeland security?*

▼ Building Intelligence Systems

Redirecting military and police forces is an essential part of developing a system to protect the nation. The most important aspect of security, however, is the information that guides security forces. If policies and strategy are important to the overall effort, information is crucial for day-to-day operations. For example, Thomas Barnett's (2004) idea of creating an inclusive geopolitical economic policy in which everybody wins is a long-term strategy for reducing international violence. Somewhere between the current state of affairs and the outcome of such a policy is the everyday world of homeland security. This world is driven by intelligence, and security forces can be no more effective than their ability to gain information and process it into a meaningful guide.

The Intelligence Process

Information gathering is akin to academic research. Before beginning, a researcher needs basic knowledge of a field and an understanding of subdisciplines. Much of this background information has no direct bearing on the actual question a researcher is trying to answer, but without background preparation, the researcher cannot address the question. Command of basic information allows the researcher to move toward applying results. Applied information, the specificity the researcher seeks, is divided into both in-depth knowledge about a specific topic and the latest information from the discipline. In the sciences and social sciences, this process leads a researcher from general concepts to applied ideas, from abstract principles to glimpses of reality.

Although academic in nature, this process is directly applicable to gathering intelligence. Police intelligence systems can be modeled after academic research. Basic intelligence involves general information about a subject and its subdisciplines. Applied intelligence involves gathering basic information about a target and real-time information about current activities.

The practical application of this process comes through organizing structures aimed at collecting, analyzing, and forwarding information. Someone in every American law enforcement agency should be assigned to collect and forward terrorist intelligence. In small agencies this may mean assigning a person who represents several police and sheriff's departments, and in moderate-size agencies the function could be performed in the detective bureau or the planning unit. Large metropolitan and state police agencies need full-time intelligence units. At the state and regional levels, efforts must be made to assemble, categorize, and analyze information and place it within national and international contexts.

National Security and Criminal Intelligence

As mentioned earlier, in network-to-network conflict, bureaucracies should not change their role. For example, if the CIA were to operate as if gathering evidence for a criminal prosecution, it would not be able to function. The same applies to all levels of law enforcement. Police agencies cannot gather information illegally. If they do so, they defeat the society they are trying to protect. Each organization in a network has its own function, and the key to success in a network is sharing information.

This leads to the need for two different types of intelligence. **National security intelligence** is gathered to defend the nation. It is not used in criminal prosecutions and is not subject to legal scrutiny. **Criminal intelligence** is gathered by law enforcement and prosecuting attorneys. It cannot be gathered, analyzed, or stored without reason to believe that a crime is about to take place or has taken place (J. White, 2004b, pp. 73–74).

Richard Best (2001) argues that national security differs from law enforcement. In police work, officers react to information provided voluntarily. Police actions are governed by the rules of evidence, and the

national security intelligence

A system of agencies and networks that gather information about threats to the country. Any threat or potential threat is examined under the auspices of national defense intelligence. Unlike criminal intelligence, people and agencies gathering defense information do not need to suspect any criminal activity. The FBI is empowered to gather defense intelligence.

criminal intelligence

Information gathered on the reasonable suspicion that a criminal activity is occurring or about to occur. It is collected by law enforcement agencies in the course of their preventive and investigative functions. It is shared on information networks such as the Regional Information Sharing System (RISS). Unlike national defense intelligence, criminal intelligence applies only in criminal law. Agencies must suspect some violation of criminal law before they can collect intelligence.

ultimate purpose is to protect the rights of citizens, including those who have been arrested. National security intelligence, on the other hand, is used to anticipate threats. It uses aggressive methods to collect information, including, at times, operations in violation of the law. National security intelligence is ultimately designed to protect targets, not individuals' rights.

Best quotes Stansfield Turner, a former director of the CIA, to summarize the differences between law enforcement and national security. Give the FBI a task, Turner once said, and it will try to complete the mission within the constraints of the law. Give the CIA the same mission, and it tries to complete the task without concern for legality. Law enforcement's prime concern is public service. The American police will lose public trust if they rely on covert illegal operations. Using Best's insight, law enforcement should plan and develop two channels for information.

One channel should be aimed at law enforcement intelligence, that is, the types of information police agencies collect. As Best (2001) describes it, this information is based on criminal activity and the protection of individual rights. It is governed by the rules of evidence. Yet police agencies will inevitably come upon defense information, especially when monitoring community indicators.

Much of this intelligence will not be used in criminal investigation. At this point, state and local police agencies should be prepared to pass such information along to defense sources. These two paths for information, one for criminal investigation and one for national security, can serve as the basis for dealing with intelligence collected by state and local police agencies (see Another Perspective: David Carter's Recommendations for Law Enforcement Intelligence).

A Checkered Past

COINTELPRO

An infamous FBI counterintelligence program started in 1956. Agents involved in COINTELPRO violated constitutional limitations on domestic intelligence gathering, and the program came under congressional criticism in the early 1970s. The FBI's abuse of power eventually resulted in restrictions on the FBI.

The CIA had tested drugs and biological agents on unknowing citizens, and the FBI's counterintelligence program, **COINTELPRO**, had exceeded the authority of law enforcement. The government, responding to such abuses, began to limit the power of intelligence operations, unintentionally hampering their effectiveness. Law enforcement and national defense intelligence came under difficult times during the administration of President Jimmy Carter (1976–1980). Carter was not seeking to dismantle intelligence operations; he wanted to protect Americans from their government. The president tried to correct the abuse of power and end the scandal of using covert operations against American citizens.

President Carter's reaction was understandable, but critics believe he went too far, and no other administration has been able to reconstitute effective intelligence organizations. A *Time* magazine article (Calabresi and Ratnesar, 2002) states the issue succinctly: America needs to learn to spy again. National security intelligence is crucial, but law enforcement has a role, the *Time* authors argue. They also censure bureaucratic structures for failing to share information, and they condemn the sys-

David Carter's Recommendations for Law Enforcement Intelligence

David Carter suggests refocusing law enforcement efforts. Police activity, he argues, should be led by intelligence. In order to accomplish this, police agencies should take an "R-cubed" approach: reassess, refocus, and reallocate.

1. Reassess the following:

   a. Calls for service

   b. Specialized units

   c. Need for new specializations

   d. Community resources

   e. Potential threats

   f. Current intelligence

   g. Political mandates from the community

2. Refocus

   a. Establish new priorities based on reassessment.

   b. Weigh priorities in terms of criticality.

   c. Actually implement changes.

3. Reallocate: Commit the resources needed to implement changes.

Law enforcement intelligence differs from intelligence gathered for national security. Law enforcement agencies must base their activities on a reasonable suspicion to believe that some criminal activity is taking place.

Source: Carter, 2004.

tem for relying too heavily on machine and electronic information. We need information from people, the *Time* authors state emphatically. Another weak point is the inability to analyze information. Intelligence is fragmented and ineffective. Their opinion has been reflected in other studies (Best, 2001; Betts, 2002; D. Wise, 2002). See Another Perspective: Types of Intelligence.

Unlike national defense or security intelligence gathering, police agencies are required to demonstrate a reasonable suspicion of criminal activity before they may collect information. As long as agencies reasonably suspect that the law is being broken, law enforcement departments may gather and store criminal intelligence. The USA Patriot Act increases the ability of law enforcement and intelligence agencies to share information, but David Carter (2004), one of the foremost academic experts on law enforcement intelligence in the country, solemnly warns that the abuses of the past must not be repeated if police agencies want to develop effective intelligence systems (see also Dreyfuss, 2002). If police agencies improve their intelligence-gathering operations, they

Types of Intelligence

There are different types of intelligence gathering systems. The differences are crucial when dealing with civil rights (see Chapter 16), but each intelligence system has its own practical methods for assembling information.

Criminal intelligence is gathered by law enforcement agencies investigating illegal activity. State, local, and federal police agencies are not allowed to gather, store, and maintain record systems on general activities. Their information must be based on a reasonable suspicion that some sort of criminal activity is taking place. Certain FBI operations may gather noncriminal intelligence if agents are assigned to national security. They do not use this evidence in criminal prosecutions.

National defense or security intelligence is gathered by several organizations in the Department of Defense, National Security Agency, Department of Energy, Department of Homeland Security, FBI, and CIA. Defense or security intelligence is usually based on one or more of the following sources:

- HUMINT: Human intelligence from spies, informers, defectors, and other people
- IMINT: Imagery intelligence from satellites and aircraft
- SIGINT: Signal intelligence from communications
- MASINT: Measures and signatures intelligence from sensing devices

Defense or security intelligence can be gathered whether the targets are involved in a crime or not.

will do so under more stringent rules than those required for national security.

The New Jersey Intelligence System

Gathering information within the bounds of criminal intelligence need not bar the path to efficiency. It is possible to build criminal-intelligence systems within the letter and spirit of legal regulations, and several agencies have an excellent track record in doing so. The New Jersey State Police (NJSP), for example, has an extensive intelligence-gathering apparatus (New Jersey State Police, 2002). The NJSP Intelligence Service Section is made up of three main divisions. The Intelligence Bureau is the largest division, composed of six units. The Analytical Unit is responsible for reviewing data from organized-crime families and street gangs. It synthesizes information to produce a broad picture of the entire state, and it also conducts threat assessments for major public events. The Casino Intelligence Unit collects information on gambling affiliations of traditional and nontraditional crimes. It also serves as the government's liaison for regulatory agencies and conducts background investigations on contractors working in the casino industry. The Electronic Surveillance Unit conducts court-authorized monitoring and assists federal agencies in national security investigations. Critical information is shared through the Liaison Computerized Services Unit, including the sharing of information with agencies outside New Jersey. The Services

Unit also codifies and organizes intelligence reports. Finally, the Street Gang Unit collects information and works with local gang task forces. The NJSP system is a model for gathering, organizing, analyzing, and sharing criminal information.

Two other divisions complete the picture of the NJSP system. The Central Security Division is responsible for New Jersey's counterterrorist mission. Its primary purpose is the prevention of terrorist activities through intelligence operations. In other words, it is a proactive organization designed to prevent terrorism through interdiction. According to its official public statement, the Central Security Division is primarily concerned with maintaining civil peace, protecting dignitaries, and monitoring known hate groups.

The Solid Waste Division, which gathers information about hazardous materials and keeps an eye on organized crime, and the Casino Bureau round out the organization of the NJSP Intelligence Service Section. The key to its organization and its preventive capabilities is the collection, analysis, and sharing of information. Recently, NJSP linked its intelligence service with federal law enforcement, giving it the potential for greater effectiveness.

The California Intelligence System

California also introduced a new concept in statewide intelligence systems, the California Anti-Terrorism Information Center (CATIC). Formed after September 11, this statewide intelligence system was designed to combat terrorism. The center linked federal, state, and local information services in one system and divided operational zones into five administrative areas. The design called for trained intelligence analysts to operate within civil rights guidelines and to use information in a secure communications system (California Department of Justice, 2002). Information was analyzed daily.

CATIC was unique in state and local law enforcement. It combined both machine intelligence, that is, the type of information that can be gathered by computers and other automated devices, with information coming from a variety of police agencies. The information was correlated and organized by analysts looking for trends. Future projections were made by looking at past indicators. Rather than simply operating as an information-gathering unit, CATIC was a synthesizing process. It combined public information with data on criminal trends and possible terrorist activities. Processed intelligence produced threat assessments for each area and projected trends outside the jurisdiction.

CATIC developed as a prototypical intelligence fusion center, but it hit a snag. According to records obtained by critics of the system, CATIC collected and maintained records on several individuals and groups that had nothing to do with terrorism. In fact, if critics are correct, it gathered and stored information on political dissidents who engaged in no criminal activity (B. Hoffman, 2003). This is an illegal activity. Despite the initial hopes, CATIC closed its doors.

California created new systems under the tight control of regional law enforcement agencies and in partnership with four regional JTTFs. The State Terrorism Threat Assessment Center now coordinates the activities of regional threat-assessment centers. Modeled after fusion center plans, the system works with only criminal intelligence. The regional centers are staffed with local law enforcement and infrastructure protection personnel, and they work with the local FBI field offices (California Highway Patrol, 2007). The new regional systems have the potential to be as effective as CATIC. The key to their success will be in strict monitoring of the type of information gathered and stored by the analysts.

The NYPD Intelligence System

The New York City Police Department (NYPD) has taken the offensive spirit a step further. Police Commissioner Raymond Kelly created two new units, one for counterterrorism and one for intelligence. Retired Marine Corps general Frank Libutti heads the counterterrorism section, and a former high-ranking CIA official, David Cohen, was selected to head the intelligence section. Kelly stated that he wanted the NYPD to do a better job of intelligence analysis and to work more closely with the federal government. The International Association of Chiefs of Police (IACP) said the plan was appropriate for New York City (K. Johnson, 2002).

Law enforcement agencies present their intelligence systems in a positive light, but there are some critics. The FBI and CIA have been resoundingly criticized for failing to gather information before the September 11 attacks and ineffectively analyzing the information they did have (Dillon, 2001; Nordland, Yousafzi, and Dehghanpisheh, 2002). The Bush administration and police agencies expressed disapproval of the FBI's information-sharing policies (Fields, 2002). Civil liberties groups fear growing power in agencies associated with homeland security, and others express concern over expanding executive authority (Herman, 2001; CNN, 2006; Keefer, 2006).

U.S. Attorneys and JTTFs

The DOJ has created two intelligence systems, one in federal prosecutors' offices and the other in law enforcement. According to the DOJ (U.S. DOJ, 2007), "There are 93 United States Attorneys stationed throughout the United States, Puerto Rico, the Virgin Islands, Guam, and the Northern Mariana Islands. United States Attorneys are appointed by, and serve at the discretion of, the President of the United States, with advice and consent of the United States Senate. One United States Attorney is assigned to each of the judicial districts, with the exception of Guam and the Northern Mariana Islands where a single United States Attorney serves in both districts. Each United States Attorney is the chief federal law enforcement officer of the United States within his or her particular jurisdiction."

Each U.S. Attorney's office has an Anti-Terrorist Assistance Coordinator (ATAC). The purpose of the ATAC is to coordinate the collection of criminal intelligence and to share intelligence among federal, state, local, and tribal law enforcement agencies. ATACs hold security clearances, so they can view secret national security intelligence. Although they do not use this information in criminal prosecutions, they are authorized to pass the information to agencies charged with national security.

The various JTTFs operate in a similar manner. Each JTTF is made up of officers from all levels of American law enforcement and from a variety of different types of agencies. This gives each JTTF a wide range of authority because different police officers have various types of law enforcement authority and power. Every JTTF agent also receives a national security intelligence clearance. Like the ATAC, JTTF agents may not use national security intelligence in criminal prosecutions, but they are allowed to collect and use it for national defense. They may also work with various intelligence agencies. In addition, each regional FBI office has a field intelligence coordinator who works with ATACs and JTTFs (Cumming and Masse, 2004).

Plans, Networks, and Fusion Centers

Shortly after 9/11, the IACP joined with the DOJ to create the **National Criminal Intelligence Sharing Plan (NCISP)**. The plan established norms for collecting, analyzing, and storing criminal intelligence within legal guidelines. It also suggested how information could be shared among agencies. Its primary function was to set minimum standards for criminal intelligence so that every American police agency knew the legal guidelines for using criminal information. It also sought to create standards for using technology and giving police officers access to information (U.S. Bureau of Justice Assistance, 2005).

David Carter (2004, pp. 123–143) points to a number of criminal-intelligence networks in operation after 9/11. The **Regional Information Sharing System (RISS)** was created in 1973. RISS has six centers, each serving a selected group of states, that share criminal information with investigators working on a variety of criminal activities, including terrorism. RISS expanded operations in April 2003 by creating the Anti-Terrorism Information Exchange (ATIX). Complementing these systems is the FBI's Law Enforcement Online (LEO), which provides FBI intelligence to state, local, and tribal agencies. The Law Enforcement Intelligence Unit (LEIU) was created by a variety of police agencies in 1956. Today, it serves as a venue to share secure information on organized crime and terrorism.

Carter notes that the Department of Homeland Security has also created an intelligence system. The Homeland Security Information Network (HSIN) is set up to connect all jurisdictions with real-time communication. It includes state homeland security officials, the National Guard, emergency operations centers, and local emergency service providers. HSIN provides encrypted communications on a secure network. Designed to combine the criminal information of RISS with critical infrastructure protection, HSIN is designed to unite all the different

National Criminal Intelligence Sharing Plan (NCISP)

A plan to share criminal intelligence among the nation's law enforcement agencies. It suggests minimum standards for establishing and managing intelligence operations within police agencies.

Regional Informational Sharing System (RISS)

A law enforcement network that allows law enforcement agencies to share information about criminal investigations.

ANOTHER PERSPECTIVE

Homeland Security Information Network

The Homeland Security Information Network (HSIN) is a computer-based counterterrorism communications system connecting all 50 states, five territories, Washington, D.C., and 50 major urban areas.

The HSIN allows all states and major urban areas to collect and disseminate information between federal, state, and local agencies involved in combating terrorism. It also

- helps provide situational awareness
- facilitates information sharing and collaboration with homeland security partners throughout the federal, state and local levels
- provides advanced analytic capabilities
- enables real time sharing of threat information

This communications capability delivers to states and major urban areas real-time interactive connectivity with the National Operations Center. This collaborative communications environment was developed by state and local authorities.

Source: U.S. Department of Homeland Security, 2006.

organizations involved in homeland security (see Another Perspective: Homeland Security Information Network). Critics maintain that the system is underused and that it duplicates the functions of proven systems like RISS (Jordan, 2005).

Despite the systems and networks that were developed to share information, many agencies still were not part of the information-sharing process. Fusion centers came about to correct this. Endorsed by the NCISP, fusion centers were designed to place all intelligence in a single center, combining multiple agencies in a single unit to analyze all types of threats. As a result a typical fusion center may have analysts and agents from several federal law enforcement and intelligence agencies, military personnel, and local police officers and criminal analysts. It merges information, earning the name *fusion*, into a single process of data analysis. Criminal information is channeled to investigations and national security intelligence is passed on to the appropriate agency. Once passed on, national security intelligence is not available for criminal analysis or storage in law enforcement files (U.S. DOJ, Office of Justice Programs, 2006).

Self-Check

- *How does raw information become intelligence?*
- *What is the difference between national security and criminal intelligence?*
- *How can existing systems be used to create or to expand future intelligence networks?*

Issues in Homeland Security

There are many organizational and bureaucratic problems inherent to organizations. These issues are discussed in the next chapter. Other aspects of homeland security are directly related to homeland security. These issues include understanding the role of law enforcement, the value of symbolic targets, threat analysis, planning, and the ability to create a culture of information sharing.

Law Enforcement's Special Role

If military forces are to transform themselves in a fashion suggested by Thomas Barnett (2004), law enforcement must seek and find new roles. More than half of the DHS agencies have police power, and state and local governments look to law enforcement for preventing attacks and responding to the unthinkable. Interestingly, federal, state, and local officers have taken the leading role in identifying and disrupting terrorism in the United States. Whether terrorists are homegrown or imported from foreign lands, police agencies are responsible for breaking some of America's most formidable terrorist cells. Law enforcement has a key function in homeland security (see Carter, 2004).

American law enforcement has a long tradition of reactive patrol; that is, responding to crimes and calls for assistance. With the advent of radio-dispatched motorized patrol, response time became the measure of police effectiveness. It was assumed that the sooner police arrived at the scene of a crime, the more likely they were to make an arrest. Like fire departments responding to smoke, police effectiveness was determined by its ability to respond quickly to crime.

The problem of terrorism brings the need for preemptive, offensive policing to a new level. If law enforcement simply responds, it will have little impact on the prevention of terrorism. Defensive reaction alone leaves the initiative with terrorist organizations. However, no government can afford to fortify all the potential targets in a jurisdiction. Even if all targets could be defended, the goal of asymmetrical warfare is not to destroy targets, but to show that security forces are not in charge. Terrorists are free to strike the least-defended symbolic target. Defensive thinking, like reactive patrol, cannot win a fight in the shadows.

If state and local agencies shift to offensive thinking and action, two results will inevitably develop. First, police contact with potential terrorists will increase, but as Sherry Colb (2001) points out, the vast majority of any ethnic or social group is made up of people who abhor terrorism. This increases the possibility of negative stereotyping and the abuse of power. Second, proactive measures demand increased intelligence gathering, and much of the information will have no relation to criminal activity. If not properly monitored, such intelligence may be misused.

Another issue appears in the private sector. Kayyem and Howitt (2002) find that offensive action begins in the local community. The weakness in local systems occurs, however, because state and local police departments frequently do not think beyond their jurisdictions, and they do not routinely take advantage of potential partnerships inside their bailiwicks. Kayyem and Howitt believe partnerships are the key to community planning. One of the greatest potential allies is private security. Unfortunately, many law enforcement agencies frown on private security and fail to create joint ventures with the private sector.

On the positive side of the debate, counterterrorism is not a mystical operation. It uses many of the skills already employed in preventive patrol, criminal investigation, and surveillance. With a few tweaks, police intelligence operations and drug enforcement units can add counterterrorism to their agendas, and patrol and investigative units can be trained to look for terrorist activities in the course of their normal duties. If properly managed, these activities need not present a threat to civil liberties.

The Role of Symbols and Structures

symbolic targets

Terrorist targets that may have limited military or security value but represent the power of the state under attack. Terrorists seek symbolic targets to strike fear into society and to give a sense of power to the terrorist group. The power of the symbol also multiplies the effect of the attack.

Asymmetrical war is waged against **symbolic targets**, and homeland security is designed to secure symbols. Just because a target has symbolic significance does not mean it lacks physical reality. The bombing of the Murrah Federal Building in Oklahoma City in 1995, for example, had symbolic value, and the casualties were horrific. Attacks against symbols disrupt support structures and can have a high human toll. Defensive measures are put in place to protect both the physical safety of people and property as well as the symbolic meaning of a target (see Juergensmeyer, 2000, pp. 155–163; Critical Incident Analysis Group, 2001, pp. 9–16).

Grenville Byford (2002) points out that symbolic attack may simply be designed to inflict massive casualties; that is, killing people has a symbolic value. Killing civilians serves a political purpose for terrorists. American citizens contribute economically to the well-being of the country, and because they participate in a democracy, they ultimately control military policy. Targeting them, Byford argues, may have practical as well as symbolic value. Rather than engaging in political rhetoric about morality, Byford concludes, it is more productive to understand that Americans represent symbolic targets of military value. His conclusion reflects the alleged saying of nineteenth-century Prussian prime minister Otto von Bismarck: "Righteous indignation is no substitute for a good course of action." There is little to be gained by ranting about evildoers, but much can be accomplished by developing strategies to protect targets.

Strategies for protection should be grounded in the understanding of the problem. Ian Lesser (1999, pp. 85–144) outlines three forms of terrorism: symbolic, pragmatic, and systematic. Symbolic terrorism is a dramatic attack to show vulnerability; pragmatic terrorism involves a practical attempt to destroy political power; and systematic terrorism is waged over a period of time to change social conditions. Lesser also points to several examples in which symbolic factors enter into attacks.

Community Threat Analysis

Examine the following considerations for defensive planning, or community threat analysis. What other items might be added?

- Find networks in and among communities. Look at transportation, power grids and fuel storage, water supplies, industrial logistics and storage, and the flow of people.

- Think like a terrorist. Which targets are vulnerable? Which targets would cause the most disruption? Which buildings are vulnerable? Where is private security ineffective?

- Obtain architectural plans for all major buildings. Protect air intakes, power supplies, and possible points for evacuation.

- Have detailed emergency information for each school.

- Practice tactical operations in each school building after hours.

- Prioritize. Assign a criticality rating to each target, assessing its importance, and rank targets according to comparative ratings.

- Coordinate with health services.

- Discuss triage and quarantine methods. Plan for biological, chemical, and radiological contamination.

- Look at emergency plans for other communities and use the appropriate methods.

- Prepare added security for special events.

- Designate an emergency command post and roles for personnel from other agencies. Practice commanding mock attacks.

- Study past emergencies and determine what law enforcement learned from its shortcomings.

Source: Management Analytics and others, 1995.

In other words, terrorists use symbolic attacks or attacks on symbols to achieve pragmatic or systematic results.

The University of Virginia's Critical Incident Analysis Group (CIAG) brought law enforcement officials, business leaders, governmental administrators, and academics together to discuss America's vulnerability to symbolic attack (CIAG, 2001). Symbols can have literal and abstract meanings, such as a capitol that serves literally and abstractly as the seat of governmental power. The key to security is to offer protection without destroying abstract meanings. For example, the words of one CIAG participant summed up the problem: We want to protect the Capitol building, he said, without making Washington, D.C., look like an armed camp (see Another Perspective: Community Threat Analysis).

All societies create symbols, and American democracy is no different. In a time of asymmetrical war, American symbols demand protection. The key to security, the CIAG concludes, is to enhance protection while maintaining openness. The irony is that every added security measure increases the feeling of insecurity. The CIAG report cites metal detectors at county courthouses as an example. Simply going through the detector before entering a building gives a person the feeling that all things might fall apart. The key is to make symbolic targets as secure as possible while giving the illusion that very few security precautions have been taken.

Planning for Homeland Security

Everyone knows that planning should take place before a problem emerges. Effective police planning incorporates a description of a goal and methods for achieving it (Hudzik and Cordner, 1983). Planning should be based on the assets available to an agency and a projection of resources needed to meet the goal. A good plan will show how different entities interrelate and may reveal unexpected consequences. Planning brings resources together in a complex environment to manage multiple consequences.

The complexities of terrorism can seem overwhelming, so planning is essential. It enhances the gathering, organizing, and analyzing of information (Bodrero, 2002). Police agencies have long been aware of the need to make reactionary plans. Emergency planning, for example, is a tool for dealing with weather disasters and industrial accidents. After riots in Dade County, Florida, in 1980, local agencies developed field-force-deployment plans similar to mutual aid pacts among firefighters. The tragedies of Oklahoma City and September 11 brought several plans to fruition. Successful efforts in planning can be transferred into offensive strategies.

The IACP (2001) believes planning can be guided by looking for threats inside local communities. Police agencies should constantly monitor communities to determine whether a terrorist threat is imminent. Indicators such as an increase in violent rhetoric, the appearance of extremist groups, and increases in certain types of crimes may demonstrate that a terrorist threat is on the horizon. Planning is based on the status of potential violence, and law enforcement can develop certain responses based on the threat. Prepared responses, the IACP contends, are proactive (see Another Perspective: Information for Planning).

Creating a Culture of Information Sharing

The National Strategy for Homeland Security (Office of Homeland Security, 2002, p. 56; U.S. Department of Homeland Security, 2004b, pp. 3–34) calls for increased information sharing among law enforcement agencies by building a cooperative environment that enables sharing of essential information. It will be a "system of systems that can provide the right information to the right people at all times." This is an excellent idea in principle.

D. Douglas Bodrero (2002) believes many of these systems are already in place. The six-part RISS information network, whose policies are controlled by its members, is ideal for sharing intelligence. It has secure intranet, bulletin board, and conference capabilities. The High Intensity

ANOTHER PERSPECTIVE

Information for Planning

Areas in the jurisdiction that make potential targets for terrorists:

- List available resources.
- Project potential attacks.
- Identify critical infrastructures.

Factors influencing plans, including

- Emergency command structures
- Coordination among agencies
- Mass casualties
- Victim and family support
- Preservation of evidence
- Crime scene management
- Media relations
- Costs
- Training and preincident exercises

Source: International Association of Chiefs of Police, 2001.

Drug Trafficking Areas (HIDTAs) system and the El Paso Intelligence Center (EPIC) are also sources for information sharing. International Association of Law Enforcement Intelligence Analysts (IALEIA) routinely shares information with member agencies. These established systems are now complemented by HSIN and a host of fusion centers (U.S. DOJ, Office of Justice Programs, 2006). Critics say these networks are underused. In the past Robert Taylor (1987) found two primary weaknesses in U.S. systems: intelligence is not properly analyzed, and agencies do not coordinate information. Today, critics say the same thing. They feel that information sharing is recommended on the highest levels, but it does not take place (Nilson and Burke, 2002).

Despite criticism, information sharing is growing into a law enforcement norm. The NCISP has been accepted by all levels of police administration. The systems created after 9/11, older systems such as RISS, fusion centers, and individual agency operations point to a new idea in law enforcement, **intelligence-led policing**. This concept is a continuation of community policing, where police officers anticipate and solve community problems with citizens before an increase in crime and social disorder. Community policing is based on information gathered from police-citizen partnerships, and intelligence-led policing systematically combines such information with other intelligence data from multiple sources. The purpose of intelligence-led policing is to redeploy resources

intelligence-led policing
A type of law enforcement in which resources are deployed based on information gathered and analyzed from criminal intelligence.

in areas where they are most needed based on the analysis of criminal information (Duekmedjian, 2006).

David Carter (2004, pp. 39–54) sees intelligence-led policing as the logical outcome of the intelligence process. When police agencies began to adopt community policing strategies, officers developed skills in problem solving, building community partnerships, and gathering and analyzing the information needed to deal with crime and social problems in a local community. Citing the NCISP, Carter says that these skills have created a reliable and continuous flow of information between the community and the police. It is a gateway to the prevention of terrorism. Intelligence-led policing is an extension of this process. It not only prevents terrorism but it becomes **total criminal intelligence (TCI)** and it serves to prevent and address all problems in a community.

total criminal intelligence (TCI)

All criminal intelligence gathered and analyzed for intelligence-led policing. Rather than focusing on one type of issue, such as terrorism, agencies focus on gathering information about all potential crimes and social problems.

Intelligence-led policing is part of a process to guide the deployment of law enforcement resources. Carter says that information from citizens defines the parameters of community problems. Law enforcement agencies need to provide information so that citizens can distinguish between normal and suspicious behavior. They are to organize community meetings and work with the community to gather information. In addition, they must also communicate with the community, working with citizens and advising them of police policy for problems. In this model, the police are to serve as an extension of community needs while advising citizens of the issues the police see as social problems. All data is scientifically analyzed to guide the distribution of law enforcement resources.

Intelligence-led policing, especially within the framework of counterterrorism, is not without its critics. Critics are afraid that information sharing will lead to massive databases on people who are not subject to criminal investigations. They also fear privacy violations as citizens share information, and they are afraid that anyone who casually encounters a known terrorist suspect will be labeled as a terrorist supporter. Critics say intelligence-led policing may work in conjunction with national security intelligence gathering, and there will be no oversight of the collection, analysis, and storage of information. They also fear misguided profiling. For example, when a Muslim family moves into a non-Muslim neighborhood, citizens who see the practice of Islam as a suspicious behavior could discriminate against the family (Abramson and Godoy, 2006).

Intelligence and the 9/11 Commission Report

The 9/11 Commission Report (2004, pp. 399–428) suggested several reforms for restructuring government in the wake of the September 11 attacks (see Another Perspective: 9/11 Commission Recommendations), and the recommendations became law in December 2004. The recommendations focused on defense, intelligence, information sharing, homeland security, and law enforcement. The most sweeping recommendation came with the creation of a national intelligence director. The commission argued that the government was structured to fight the

9/11 Commission Recommendations

The 9/11 Commission suggested the following reforms:

1. Create a National Counterterrorism Center.

2. Create a director of national intelligence to oversee intelligence gathering and all the agencies involved in national defense intelligence.

3. Refocus the CIA. Reporting to the director of national intelligence, the CIA director should

    a. Build the analysis capability of the CIA

    b. Increase information gathered from people

    c. Develop extensive language capabilities

    d. Recruit from diverse groups in order to have agents who can blend with a variety of cultures

    e. Establish routine communications with other agencies

4. Paramilitary operations should move to Special Operations in the Defense Department.

    a. Covert operations should move to the Defense Department.

    b. Northern Command should assume responsibility for military threats against the United States.

5. Make the intelligence budget public.

6. Demand that agencies share information.

7. Streamline and strengthen congressional oversight of intelligence and homeland security.

8. Accelerate the appointment of national security administrators during presidential transitions.

9. Introduce new structures in the FBI.

    a. Create career paths for agents and others assigned to intelligence and national security.

    b. Create a culture of cross-fertilization between criminal justice and national defense.

    c. Restructure the budget to emphasize (1) intelligence, (2) counterterrorism and counterintelligence, (3) law enforcement, and (4) criminal justice services.

10. The Department of Homeland Security should

    a. Assess threats

    b. Develop and test emergency plans

    c. Protect the critical infrastructure

    d. Create a system for response to threats and attacks

Source: 9/11 Commission Report, 2004.

cold war, not to counter terrorism. The commissioners felt that reorganization of the intelligence community and elevation of a director to presidential cabinet level would help safeguard America.

Members of the 9/11 Commission held meetings with citizens, lobbied Congress, appeared on television, and joined with the families of victims of the September 11 attacks to demand reform. Their campaign was emotional, and anyone who criticized the reforms they proposed seemed almost un-American. Yet criticism came.

Judge Richard A. Posner (2004) argues that the 9/11 Commission Report presents two competing parts. The first, he writes, is an excellent step-by-step analysis of the events that led up to the attacks on September 11 and an explanation of actions after the terrorists struck. The second part of the report is a series of recommendations. Posner says that he paused when he encountered the recommendations because the policies and directions the commission suggested were not altogether consistent with the analysis of the first part of the report.

Posner suggests that the FBI's record of combating terrorism was poor, and restructuring may not improve its capabilities. Combining fifteen different intelligence agencies designed to do everything from launching spy satellites to gathering criminal information is illogical, he says. The agencies exist for different reasons and are responsible for different tasks. The national intelligence director who is supposed to manage the new conglomerated menagerie of agencies will spend most of his or her time dealing with arguments among the intelligence community, the DOJ, and the secretary of defense. Posner writes that in the aftermath of September 11, governmental agencies have an incentive to work together, but restructuring bureaucracy will not automatically make the United States safer.

Congress mandated the 9/11 Commission's recommendations in an emotional atmosphere in December 2004. However, questions for the future remain, questions that deal with the nature of intelligence, democracy, and individual rights. The defense and intelligence establishments have the legal right and mission to collect information to protect the country. The central question for criminal justice focuses on the role of law enforcement. The 9/11 Commission recommends changes in the FBI, but the vast majority of law enforcement activities take place far from the federal criminal justice system. Other nations have models for collecting information while protecting individual rights, but the commission did not consider these models, assuming that an analysis of American activities was sufficient. Balancing security with freedom is a delicate matter, and the new intelligence infrastructure has not dealt with all the issues.

Self-Check

- *How do diverse, independent law enforcement agencies assist with homeland security?*

- *Why is planning an important process in protecting both infrastructures and symbols?*

- *Why do the recommendations of the 9/11 Commission fall short of creating a culture of information sharing?*

SUMMARY

- Americans define homeland security in several different ways. Its meaning is institutionally unclear. The best way to define it is to look at the mission of the particular agency dealing with homeland security.

- After 9/11 several federal agencies were tasked with homeland security. The Departments of Homeland Security, Justice, and Defense have major roles in preventing terrorism. The intelligence community contributes to counterterrorism, and there is a major role for state, local, and tribal law enforcement to play.

- Clausewitz viewed war as a rational political process between states. Sun Tzu viewed war as a psychological process at many different levels. The difference between the ideas of Clausewitz and Sun Tzu can be illustrated by comparing Pearl Harbor with September 11. The former was a military attack rationally designed to obtain a political objective. The latter was a psychological attack designed to create an aura of fear.

- The nature of conflict is changing because entire cultures fear for their existence. When threatened in this manner, they do not respond rationally.

- The intelligence process is very close to basic and applied academic research. It involves the legal recognition, collection, analysis, and distribution of information. Intelligence is analyzed information.

- Law enforcement has a leading role in homeland security because of its presence in communities and its ability to gather information. Several sectors of federal law enforcement and DHS have responsibilities in this arena, too.

- It is important to understand the legal differences between criminal intelligence and national security intelligence when using that information. National security intelligence is not meant to be used in criminal prosecutions.

- Model systems for information gathering can be found in the New Jersey State Police and the New York Police Department. There are several excellent federal networks such as RISS and HSIN. The HIDTA system and EPIC assist even though they were designed for drug interdiction. Fusion centers offer quite a bit of promise because they bring information to a central point for analysis.

- Planning for homeland security and the prevention of terrorism should anticipate community needs, solve issues before they become problems, and provide a response to crises with adequate resources. The crux of counterterrorism involves information sharing among all levels of government. Psychological attacks are aimed at structures and symbols of power. The reform recommendations of the 9/11 Commission became law in December 2004. The new law changes the structure of intelligence gathering and establishes a director of national intelligence.

KEY TERMS

Department of Homeland Security
    (p. 393)
civil defense (p. 396)
Carl von Clausewitz (p. 404)
On War (p. 404)
Sun Tzu (p. 405)
asymmetry (p. 405)
Arthur Cebrowski (p. 408)
network-centric warfare (p. 408)
national security intelligence
    (p. 411)

criminal intelligence (p. 411)
COINTELPRO (p. 412)
National Criminal Intelligence
    Sharing Plan (p. 417)
Regional Informational Sharing
    System (p. 417)
symbolic targets (p. 420)
intelligence-led policing (p. 423)
total criminal intelligence (p. 424)

WRITING ASSIGNMENTS

1. Is it difficult to define homeland security? Why do so many agencies have different roles in the process? Because the Department of Homeland Security was created, should other agencies be excluded from the task of homeland security? Does the need to prevent terrorism require more than a single agency?

2. Describe the intelligence process. What happens when information is not analyzed and shared? What different types of organizations share criminal intelligence? Is there a difference between sharing criminal and national security intelligence?

3. How has conflict changed from the state-to-state wars of the early twentieth century to counterterrorist operations today? Cite Cebrowski, Creveld, and Barnett in your answer.

Law Enforcement Bureaucracy and Homeland Security

16

AP Photo/Eric Gay

The U.S. Border Patrol on the Texas border. There are thousands of law enforcement agencies charged with preventing terrorism. Coordinating their activities is a monstrous task, and it is made more challenging when intelligence organizations are added to the mix.

Learning Objectives

After reading this chapter you should be able to

■ Outline law enforcement's bureaucracy challenge.

■ Explain the ways homeland security represents Weberian bureaucracy.

■ Summarize bureaucratic issues within criminal and national security intelligence agencies.

■ Explain issues involved in border protection.

■ Discuss the ways the immigration debate impacts homeland security.

■ Define and describe infrastructure protection.

■ Describe the need for partnerships in homeland security.

- Summarize the critical bureaucratic issues in law enforcement partnerships.
- Outline Flynn's recommendations for effective homeland security.

- Explain how the JTTF arrangement might become a model for law enforcement partnerships.

In the realm of terrorism and homeland security, the primary role of law enforcement is prevention. To fulfill their role, every agency involved in homeland security must deal with organization. The creation of the Department of Homeland Security (DHS) involved one of the most massive reorganizations of government in American history. It combined several agencies ranging from the Secret Service to the Coast Guard. DHS is responsible for protecting almost every facet of American life, but it must coordinate its activities with other federal agencies. It has its own intelligence analysts and capabilities—so do other federal bureaucracies. DHS also coordinates activities with thousands of other organizations on state, local, and tribal levels as well as in the private sector. Every law enforcement agency, from part-time one-person police departments to the FBI, has some role in homeland security. All of the roles and relationships must be negotiated among competing bureaucracies.

The Bureaucracy Challenge

The federal government undertook massive reforms and reorganizations from 2002 to 2005 in the wake of 9/11. Some officials and terrorism specialists applaud these actions (see Jenkins, 2006). Others say it has not gone far enough (see Flynn, 2004a, 2004b). Still others say that homeland security cannot be tackled until Congress reforms its oversight function and places homeland security under a single committee. Currently, a variety of Senate and House committees are responsible for different aspects of homeland security. Critics believe that the organizational problems involving federal, state, local, and tribal law enforcement cannot be handled until the nation's lawmakers restructure their own lawmaking **bureaucracy** (Meese, Robb, and Abshire, 2005). There are literally thousands of law enforcement organizations in the United States, and they need to form partnerships with each of tens of thousands of business and community organizations if law enforcement is to have a role in homeland security.

bureaucracy

Governmental, private-sector, and nonprofit organizations. It assumes that people organize in a hierarchy to create an organization that will solve problems.

The federal government cannot assume that the reforms will carry over into state and local governments. The states may cooperate with the federal government, but they are not mandated to do so. The states and their local governments have entrenched bureaucracies with their own managerial structures and agendas. These organizations will not suddenly change methods of operation simply because centralized executive authority has mandated new policies for homeland defense. In a nutshell, this is the epitome of the bureaucracy challenge, yet it does not imply that state and local governments will automatically reject chances to participate. Change can happen, and may even be welcome, if federal agencies enter into cooperative relationships with their local counterparts (Liptak, 2002; for classic studies see Downs, 1967; Warwick, 1975).

Some advocates believe federal reform has begun. A 1995 attempt to reduce paperwork in federal government is one example. An earlier effort came in the **1978 Civil Service Reform Act**, which gave special executives managerial authority and placed them in performance-based positions. The most recent overhaul of the federal bureaucracy came with the **Government Management Reform Act of 1994**.

1978 Civil Service Reform Act
A federal law designed to prevent political interference with the decisions and actions of governmental organizations.

Yet managing homeland security will still require attention to the issues raised in this chapter. Large organizations are difficult to manage, and problems increase rapidly when organizational effectiveness requires cooperation on several levels. Homeland security calls for new alliances among federal agencies and cooperative relations among local, state, and federal levels of government. All of the issues interact with law enforcement agencies.

Government Management Reform Act of 1994
A federal law designed to prevent political interference in the management of federal governmental organizations and to increase the efficiency of management.

If the Department of Homeland Security (DHS) can create effective partnerships with intelligence and law enforcement agencies on the federal level, it could focus attention on these issues. However, in addition to thwarting an attack, homeland security has a duty much larger than merely gathering and analyzing information: responding to an event. That is a subject beyond the scope of this book. Response involves massive coordination among agencies. Fortunately, all levels of government have extensive experience in this realm. The difficulty is *preventing* terrorism, and prevention requires bureaucratic change. Powerful bureaucrats and bureaucratic procedures do not change easily.

The Weberian Ideal

If you have studied public administration, you have most likely encountered the classic works on bureaucracy. **Max Weber** (1864–1920), one of the founding masters of sociology, coined the term *bureaucracy* to describe professional, rational organizations. For Weber, every aspect of organizational structure was to be aimed at rationally achieving a goal. In other words, people organize for a purpose and their organization should accomplish that purpose.

Max Weber
(1864–1920) One of the major figures of modern sociological methods, he studied the organization of human endeavors. Weber believed that social organizations could be organized for rational purposes designed to accomplish objectives.

For example, if your purpose is to keep dirt from washing over an embankment, you gather people who know how to channel dirt. You then select managers who know how to get people to accomplish the task. People who assist in managing are selected because they know how to manage people who can do the job. Managers impersonally direct the organization to build walls, dig trenches, and change drainage patterns. The managers use only people who can accomplish assigned tasks. They do not favor friends, relatives, or tradition. They avoid people who attract others through charisma. When the task is finished, dirt no longer washes over the embankment. The process is rational: there is a problem, people organize to solve it, they work together, and the problem is solved. Weber believed that impersonal, professional human groups (bureaucracies) converge to solve the problems of society. Weber argued that bureaucracy should be designed to accomplish specific purposes.

In Weber's ideal, labor is to be divided into specific functional areas, or bureaus, and all the bureaus of the organization are to assemble logically to produce the whole. The bureaus work together and produce a logical outcome. Management in the organization is rationally oriented and devoid of friendship, family, or political influences. Modern bureaucratic management ideally comes from leaders who excel at leadership. There is no place for inherited leadership or popular, elected managers in Weber's bureaucracy. Every aspect of the organization centers on rational efficiency (Weber, 1947).

More than a century has passed since Weber first outlined the field that would become known as bureaucratic organizational theory. To be sure, hundreds of other scholars have filled volumes of books with organizational theories. These works range from highly theoretical psychological treatises to practical business administration guides. The sheer number of these tracts indicates that running an organization is a complicated affair, and the larger and more complex the organization becomes, the more difficult it is to manage.

Bureaucracy and Preventing Terrorism

There are two views concerning expanded homeland security bureaucracy. Supporters of one position maintain that consolidating power is efficient. They argue that a large bureaucracy with a clear mission will empower the security forces to perform their mission. The decision to create DHS was based on this ideal (Office of Homeland Security, 2002). Proponents of the second position suggest that decentralizing power personalizes services and helps develop links to communities. They believe localized, informal offices are more adept at recognizing and handling problems. Support for this position can be found among those who seek to trim the homeland defense concept and those who favor limiting the involvement of state and local governments in a larger organization (see Another Perspective: Taking Aim at Bureaucracy). Although both ideas appear to be new in the wake of September 11, they are actually part of a long-time, ongoing debate.

Taking Aim at Bureaucracy

Critics level harsh attacks against public bureaucracies, making the following points:

- Bureaucracies work toward stagnation. Innovation, creativity, and individuality are discouraged.

- Career bureaucrats are rewarded with organizational power. Therefore, they look for activities that provide organizational power instead of solutions to problems.

- Public bureaucracies do not face competition.

- Within a bureaucracy, it is better to make a safe decision than the correct decision.

- Bureaucratic organizations protect themselves when threatened with outside problems.

- Bureaucrats postpone decisions under the guise of gathering information.

- Policies and procedures are more important than outcomes in bureaucracies.

- Centralized bureaucracy increases paperwork.

- As bureaucracies grow, simple problems result in complex solutions.

Whether or not you agree with these criticisms, consider this question: Is there an alternative to classic bureaucracy when organizing state and local police for homeland defense?

Intelligence and Bureaucracy

The role of law enforcement and intelligence in homeland security is not exempted from the issues surrounding bureaucracy. Whether federal, state, or local, bureaucratic police work is a political process occurring in the context of official, routine procedures. Intelligence agencies, whether involved with the military or not, face the same problems. Both intelligence-gathering and law enforcement organizations operate within the American political system. They reflect governmental power, and their actions have political ramifications. Internally, conflicts arise from personal rivalries, territorial fights, and power struggles. They are as much a part of these services as they are in any organization (Gaines and Cordner, 1999, pp. 179–180; see also Walker, 1992).

Homeland security involves the use of intelligence and law enforcement. The Bush administration argues that counterterrorism is mainly a military problem. In the United States, however, the lead agency for counterterrorism is the FBI (Best, 2001). The FBI has several charges in this realm. First, under Director Robert Mueller its charge is to prevent terrorism. Second, it is to coordinate intelligence-gathering and intelligence-sharing activities with the Border Patrol, Secret Service, and CIA. Third, it is to operate as a partner of state and local law enforcement. Finally, because the FBI is in the Department of Justice, it is to coordinate its activities with DHS and the Department of Defense (DOD). Under the intelligence reform law of 2004, all intelligence coordination

ANOTHER PERSPECTIVE

DHS and Intelligence

The Department of Homeland Security has a large intelligence section, but its effectiveness is open to question. Several factors plague DHS intelligence:

1. It is relatively powerless in the intelligence community.

2. DHS does not maintain terrorist watch lists.

3. The CIA has the leading role at the National Counterterrorism Center (NCTC), formerly the Terrorist Threat Integration Center.

4. The CIA and FBI compile the president's daily intelligence briefing.

5. DHS intelligence has been slow to develop its mission.

Source: Rood, 2004.

National Counterterror-ism Center (NCTC)

An organization designed to filter information from the intelligence process, synthesize counterter-rorist information, and share it with appropriate organizations.

must take place in the **National Counterterrorism Center (NCTC)** (U.S. Congress, 2004).

This face of homeland security involves a new role for the CIA. When it was originally established at the end of World War II, the CIA was supposed to be the agency that would coordinate all U.S. intelligence data, but the head of the agency, as director of central intelligence, never received the political authority to consolidate the information-gathering power. In addition, the CIA was to operate apart from U.S. criminal law and was not officially allowed to collect data on Americans inside the United States (Best, 2001). Today, the situation is somewhat modified. Chastised by public outcries and the 9/11 Commission, and with formal orders from the president, the CIA is to cooperate fully with the FBI on counterterrorism intelligence (Office of Homeland Security, 2002; Baginski, 2004). The FBI and CIA are to work jointly on intelligence gathering and sharing inside and outside America's borders.

The DHS was created from the Office of Homeland Security in 2003 and charged with counterterrorism. DHS includes law enforcement agencies, such as the Secret Service, the Border Patrol, the new Immi-gration and Customs Enforcement, the U.S. Customs Service, and other agencies. It has its own military force, the U.S. Coast Guard, which has limited law enforcement power. DHS is responsible for port security and transportation systems. It manages security in airports and the massive Transportation Security Administration. It has its own intelligence sec-tion (see Another Perspective: DHS and Intelligence), and it covers every special event in the United States, from political conventions to football games. It is clearly the largest organization involved in homeland secu-rity (DHS, 2004b).

The Department of Defense has a limited but critical role in home-land security. Currently, the main military role in counterterrorism is to project American power overseas. DOD's military forces take the fight to terrorists in other lands, rather than letting terrorists become a problem within America's borders (Barnett, 2004, pp. 299–303). It also augments civilian defense and provides special operations capabilities. In some cases military intelligence can also be used in counter-narcotics operations. Military forces can be used to protect the borders, and the president or Congress can request that the limitations of *posse comitatus* be temporarily suspended under the Fourth Amendment when dictated by emergency and necessity.

This is an impressive array of American power. In theory, led by the FBI and the CIA, multiple agencies will work together to gain information, analyze it together, and share the results with every bureaucracy concerned with homeland security. *Cooperation* and *sharing* are the two buzzwords of the day. This is a charge not only to federal bureaucracies but to the FBI and CIA, which are to create a cooperative, sharing atmosphere with thousands of state and local law enforcement agencies. And cooperation does not stop there. DHS calls on the entire system of homeland security bureaucracies to form relations with local communities and private industry. On paper this is a massive force designed to stop terrorism and protect the United States of America.

The federal bureaucracy is massive, which presents a problem for agency cooperation. Yet the bigger challenge is in coordinating the thousands of state, local, and tribal law enforcement agencies in the United States. They form a network of potential sources of information, and their ability to function and cooperate is crucial to the homeland security mission. If terrorism can be envisioned as netwar, state, local, and tribal police agencies are a vital element of America's counterterrorist network (J. White, 2007).

Administrators at DHS, DOJ, the FBI, and the Office of the Director of National Intelligence have recognized the importance of state, local, and tribal law enforcement agencies and the value they bring to homeland security. One of the priorities of the federal government is creating a system where information can flow among the various levels of government, from and through America's police agencies. This is the major bureaucratic challenge facing law enforcement (Johnson, 2007).

State, Local, and Tribal Law Enforcement Bureaucracies

As discussed in the previous chapter, American policing is localized. With more than 800,000 state, local, and tribal law enforcement officers in the United States, agencies must cooperate to transform organizations. Any plan for changing so many bureaucracies must allow each agency to have the flexibility to change according to local demands. There are issues to overcome and partnerships with external agencies to be created, but it is not an impossible task. America's law enforcement agencies have overcome these problems to build systems in the past, and they can do the same thing in homeland security (see Bodrero, 2002).

The first issue to overcome is building a consensus among police agencies on the task to be accomplished. **Task orientation** will focus

posse comitatus
A clause in the second article of the Constitution that forbids the government to use military force to enforce law. (Do not confuse this with the right-wing extremist group Posse Comitatus.)

task orientation
As used in this text, the ability to stay focused on the primary mission of an organization.

threat analysis

The process of examining a community to determine the areas that might be subject to attack and the criticality of those areas to the functions of the community.

the actions of individual departments as they meet the homeland security needs within their communities. The task is to provide security. This is accomplished by **threat analysis**, information gathering, and information sharing. Individual tasks will vary. As Richard Marquise (2006, pp. 27–29) says, law enforcement tasks differ in Oklahoma City and New York City, but the mission remains the same. For law enforcement, the primary job is to prevent terrorism. Agencies need emergency service plans and comprehensive preparedness to respond to disasters, but their mission is to stop the attack. When police officers become first responders, counterterrorism has failed.

If multiple agencies are to focus on the task of preventing terrorism, then executives must buy into the concept. Chiefs, sheriffs, and directors set the administrative tone for their agencies. When groups of executives are oriented toward prevention, middle managers—captains and lieutenants—implement policies and sergeants, as first line supervisors, ensure the work takes place. Preventing terrorism becomes one of many emergency functions that state, local, and tribal law enforcement agencies handle. Homeland security transforms into routine police work (J. White, 2007).

Smith and Roberts (2005) demonstrate that terrorists engage in criminal activities before a planned attack. This gives local agencies an opportunity to prevent attacks. To accomplish this, officers need to become aware of the types of activities that take place before an attack. These are known as **pre-incident indicators**. The indicators for terrorism are known, but they are too sensitive to list in a college textbook. It is enough to be aware that they exist, that officers can learn to recognize them, and that terrorists can be stopped when law enforcement either makes arrests or gathers relevant information.

pre-incident indicators

The criminal and social actions of individuals and groups before a terrorist attack.

If terrorism prevention is to be successful on the local level, agencies must participate in systems. Once again, American police agencies have a history of doing this. The Law Enforcement Information Network (LEIN) links agencies to a host of bureaucracies to provide valuable information on everything from vehicle registrations to warrants. The National Crime Information Center (NCIC) maintains information on a nationwide basis. The systems discussed in the intelligence section of the preceding chapter, such as Regional Information Sharing System (RISS), El Paso Intelligence Center (EPIC), and the numerous High Intensity Drug Trafficking Areas (HIDTAs), attest to the willingness of state, local, and tribal agencies to cooperate in regional and national networks.

Bureaucratic changes present challenges, but they also provide opportunities. Two recent national innovations demonstrate this, and both processes are crucial to homeland security. As discussed in the previous chapter, community policing changed the face of American law enforcement (Chermak and Weiss, 2006; Duekmedjian, 2006). It began as an idea and spread with support from the federal government, research from university criminal justice departments, creation of community associations and partnerships and regional organizations, and participation of law enforcement executives who oriented themselves to the task of increasing police effectiveness. Homeland security presents the same opportunity, and community police networks are ideal for the functions it requires.

The second recent innovation is the National Criminal Intelligence Sharing Plan (NCISP). The concept of information gathering, analysis, and sharing began with the Global Advisory Committee to the U.S. attorney general. It moved to a **working group** of executives from all levels of law enforcement. As the working group developed ideas for carrying the concept out, groups like the International Association of Chiefs of Police (IACP) reviewed and amended the recommendations. Like community policing, it was a national team effort of many different law enforcement agencies. When the NCISP was unveiled and endorsed by the IACP, a multitude of police agencies, law enforcement associations, intelligence organizations, and associated bureaucracies endorsed and adopted it.

The many different organizations that compose state, local, and tribal law enforcement agencies face a daunting task in transforming bureaucracy, but preventing terrorism requires the transformation. The cooperative efforts of community policing and the NCISP indicate that local law enforcement bureaucracies can meet a challenge and even participate with multiple federal agencies. Such transformation can happen again as agencies develop homeland security missions. In fact, homeland security is an extension of what state, local, and tribal agencies are already doing (see Carter, 2004).

working group
A term used in the federal government for a group of subject matter experts who gather to suggest solutions to common problems.

Self-Check

- *What is the Weberian ideal and how does it relate to modern bureaucracy?*
- *Why is terrorism prevention a bureaucratic problem?*
- *How might bureaucracies cooperate to prevent terrorism?*

Border Protection

Aside from the myriad of functions related to law enforcement and intelligence, the federal government has another major goal: to protect America's borders. The responsibility falls on the DHS and a grouping of agencies contained within it. The main agencies responsible for border protection include Customs and Border Protection, Immigration and Customs Enforcement (ICE), and the Coast Guard. The Transportation Security Administration (TSA) has supporting responsibilities at international airports inside the United States, and agents from the agencies protecting the border are trained at the Federal Law Enforcement Training Center (FLETC). Many of the agencies coordinate their efforts with local units of government, and many DHS personnel are armed and carry arrest power.

American borders are vulnerable in several areas. Long stretches of unprotected areas along the northern and southern borders are open to infiltration, and more than 300 seaports must be secured. The DHS has agencies responsible for securing entry into the United States at airports, and it is responsible for protecting air travel once the entry points are protected. Border agents are responsible for staffing entry points along the northern and southern borders. This activity is augmented by efforts by the Coast Guard as it patrols the ocean shores and Great Lakes. Finally, another DHS agency has the task of accounting for noncitizens within U.S. borders (DHS, 2005).

Policy Disputes

The scope of activities is daunting, even for an agency as large as DHS, and the variety of functions multiply the problems. In some cases, such as keeping track of noncitizens, DHS cooperates with the FBI and CIA. DHS has increased the number of people who patrol the border, and it has tried to shift agents to the least secure areas. DHS also uses technology, such as biometric measuring—that is, identification systems based on body characteristics such as fingerprints, facial patterns, or DNA—to maintain records on aliens (DHS, 2005).

These functions have not come without problems. Critics say that DHS activities, broad as they may be, are not altogether effective (Flynn, 2004a, 2004b). A union representing DHS employees surveyed 500 border patrol agents and 500 immigration inspectors from the Border Protection and U.S. Customs divisions. The union president stated that old bureaucratic procedures leave borders unprotected, and members of the union agreed. Only 16 percent were satisfied with DHS's efforts. The majority of respondents complained of low morale. DHS administrators countered that only rank and file personnel completed the survey (Z. Alonso, 2004).

Some DHS policies have not been popular with other countries. For example, DHS implemented a policy of fingerprinting and photographing visitors from some other countries; some of America's closest allies were exempted from the process. This policy met with a storm of criticism from nation after nation. Brazil even retaliated, requiring photographs and fingerprints of U.S. visitors to its land. DHS has also tried more advanced methods of biometric measuring, hoping to create a database of body types. Some have complained that the process was ahead of its time (CNN, 2004a).

Local governments have been asked to assist with border protection, but some of them have balked at the idea. Many local governments feel they need the trust and cooperation of foreigners living in their areas. If aliens distrust the actions of local governments, governmental functions could be hampered. The education system would be disrupted, aliens would not seek health care, and law enforcement officials would neither get information nor be able to serve people in the jurisdiction (National Immigration Forum, 2004).

The 9/11 Commission Report (2004, pp. 400–407) addressed the issue of border security and suggested sweeping reforms. The commission said that more than 500 million people cross U.S. borders each year, and 330 million of them are foreigners. Bureaucratic reform is essential if these crossings are to be monitored because the system before September 11 was unable to provide security or monitor foreigners coming into the United States. A single agency with a single format, the commission recommended, should screen crossings. In addition, an investigative agency should be established to monitor all aliens in the United States. The commission also recommended gathering intelligence on the way terrorists travel and combining intelligence and law enforcement activities to hamper their mobility. The commission suggested using a standardized method for obtaining identification and passports with biometric measures. In essence, the commission recommended standardizing the bureaucratic response for monitoring the entry of foreign nationals.

The Immigration Debate

One of the controversial issues surrounding border protection involves immigration. Many elected officials argue that the United States cannot be secure unless its borders are secure. A few people want to eliminate immigration, but more want to stop only illegal immigration and install tighter controls on immigration from countries that may harbor hostility toward the United States. Other people believe the immigration debate is overemphasized. They say the United States is a country based on immigration and that immigrants do not represent a terrorist threat.

Conservative political candidate and pundit Patrick Buchanan (2002, pp. 97–109, 235) summarizes one view. By allowing the unregulated flow of immigrants from the southern border, Buchanan argues, the United States opens the door to terrorist infiltration. The situation is made worse by allowing emigrants from hostile Muslim countries to enter the United States. They can operate as independent terrorists or as agents for a rogue regime. Buchanan takes the argument a step further. By allowing the unregulated influx of Hispanics from the south, the United States risks not only terrorism but the destruction of American culture. Some critics dismiss Buchanan as a right-wing ideologue, but scholars such as Samuel Huntington (2004) make the same argument.

Most of the people concerned with border security make the distinction between legal and illegal immigration, and their primary concern reflects a desire for the rule of law. Kerry Diminyatz (2003) puts forward this idea in a research paper written while training at the U.S. Army War College. The southern border is not secure, and DHS plans for securing the border have not been adequate. This is a security threat, not only in terms of terrorism but from a variety of other criminal activities. Diminyatz argues that it is possible to secure the border but it will take major reforms. The major issues involve economic, social, and political inequities and corruption on both sides of the border.

Diminyatz says the failure to protect the southern border presents four major national security threats: (1) terrorism and weapons of mass destruction (WMD), (2) drug trafficking, (3) human smuggling, and (4) infectious disease. The most significant threat of unregulated immigration comes in the form of terrorism and organized crime. Although this has been a problem for decades, no presidential administration has effectively approached the dilemma. Diminyatz argues that all agencies charged with border security need to be brought into a single organization. The multiple numbers of bureaucracies responsible for border security are inefficient and the structure fails to focus all efforts. To correct the situation, U.S. military forces should be deployed along the border until civilian law enforcement can be consolidated and physical and technological barriers can be established to prevent illegal border crossings.

The federal government seeks to form partnerships with local communities so that state, local, and tribal law enforcement officers can act as an extension of agencies charged with border security (Seghetti, Vina, and Ester, 2005). But these law enforcement officials might not welcome the idea of joining a federal partnership to secure the borders. Sometimes local law enforcement agencies refuse because they want to maintain informational relationships with the illegal community (National Immigration Forum, 2004). They need information from both legal and illegal immigrants to protect the community and investigate crime. Successful policing requires information, and crimes cannot be investigated without it.

Other methods of enhancing border security have nothing to do with a reorganization of bureaucracy. Congress has considered a number of methods (Garcia, Lee, and Tatelman, 2005). One tool could be the introduction of national identification cards. Another is a law regulating asylum for those from countries openly hostile to the United States. Some members of Congress have suggested creating special laws or legal reviews for legal immigrants who pose a security threat. Others have advocated holding illegal aliens and not deporting them. These positions represent controversies within the controversy. The problem of border security might be best addressed by enhancing an agency's legal authority to deal with the issue. Civil libertarians are wary of such approaches, believing it will result in the abuse of governmental power.

Janice Kephart (2005), a former legal counsel to the 9/11 Commission, believes the holes in border security come from lax enforcement of existing law. She says a study of the activities of ninety-four foreign-born terrorists who operated in the United States from 1990 to 2004 shows the inadequacy of enforcement. Two thirds of the terrorists engaged in criminal activities before or in conjunction with their terrorist attacks. Note that this reinforces findings from Brent Smith and Paxton Roberts (2005). Terrorists enter the United States with temporary visas and then fail to follow the provisions of entry. They make false statements on applications and lie on other official documents while in the country. They make sham marriages or utilize other loopholes to stay in the country. Kephart believes border protection starts with rigorous law enforcement and background checks.

Sebastian Mallaby (2007), writing an opinion column for the *Washington Post*, vehemently argues that the focus on illegal immigration is not important to homeland security. Undocumented workers commit less crime than natives, and there is no indication that they convert to jihadist ideology. Immigrants come to the United States because they want to live here, Mallaby says. Homeland security has little to do with immigration reform. Mallaby says security efforts should focus on two types of targets, those most likely to be hit and those that will cause the greatest loss of life. Immigration is not a factor.

The debate about immigration reveals the problems inherent to law enforcement bureaucracy. To start, the nature of the problem is under dispute. Some arguments claim that illegal immigration is not a problem, whereas the opposite side maintains that legal, let alone illegal, immigration is destroying civilization. There is confusion about the relationship between local law enforcement and federal agencies. This is complicated by the number of federal agencies that have a role in border security and immigration. Finally, there are concerns with the efficiency of immigration laws. Some people argue that they are not being enforced, some want tougher laws, and still others believe border security is not an issue in preventing terrorism. It is difficult to formulate policy in the face of so many contradictory positions.

Self-Check

- *How do political disputes affect border security?*
- *Why are state, local, and tribal agencies hesitant to enforce border security?*
- *Summarize the different positions on the immigration debate.*

Infrastructure Protection

Another area concerning DHS is infrastructure protection. Information, energy, communication, transportation, and economic systems are vulnerable to terrorist attack. Their vulnerability requires all levels of government to develop new capabilities to provide protection. The DHS (Office of Homeland Security, 2002, pp. xi–xii) states that law enforcement agencies will need to develop cooperative links with public and private bureaucracies, including private security organizations, educational institutions, and health care systems. Fortunately, state and local police agencies are not starting in a vacuum. The International Association of Chiefs of Police (IACP, 2001) issued guidelines to provide cooperation among all levels of government and private industry and identify threats to the infrastructure to defend against them.

Private versus Governmental Partnerships

Just because some units of government and private industry realize that the infrastructure needs to be protected does not mean that bureaucracies will jump to action. Critics feel too little is being done. Jeanne Cummings (2002) points to two primary weaknesses. As much as a year after September 11, the federal government had failed to provide funding to state and local governments. State emergency planners complain they received little federal direction and no federal money. Cummings says the problem is even worse in the private security industry. After a survey of security at America's largest shopping mall, in Minnesota, Cummings concludes that federal law enforcement does little to assist private security. Keeping Americans safe, Cummings says, depends on state and local efforts outside Washington.

Richard Clarke, a former special advisor to the president with an impressive bipartisan service record, testified before the Senate Subcommittee on the Judiciary on February 13, 2002 (Clarke, 2002). He outlined many of the threats facing the nation's infrastructure, painting a grim picture. Most computer systems are vulnerable to viruses, Clarke believes, because computer users will not pay for proper protection. The government has opened more communication channels with users and vendors, but more protection is needed. Clarke says the nation's power system and the technological organizations that support it are vulnerable to disruptions. The Internet and other computer networks that support these systems are also vulnerable to attack. Pointing to the railroad industry as an example, Clarke shows how many low-tech organizations have imported high-tech support systems. Shut down electrical grids and computers, Clarke maintains, and you'll shut down transportation and communication (see Another Perspective: Infrastructure Protection).

As Clarke stated in his testimony, the FBI should not have been the lead agency for infrastructure protection; the role is more suited to technological specialists. (On November 25, 2002, following Clarke's recommendation, the Bush administration ordered the National Infrastructure Protection Center to move to the DHS.) Extending Clarke's logic, it can also be argued that state and local law enforcement should not play the leading role in infrastructure protection. The key is to develop relationships so state, local, and tribal police agencies can support security functions.

The problem is that private industry uses information for competition and profit. When governmental agencies share information, they do so in the public domain for the public good. Corporations like Wal-Mart, General Motors, and Apple have excellent information-gathering and security systems, and they often share information with governments for the public good. It is quite another matter to hand corporations analyzed criminal and national security intelligence. Partnerships with private industry may involve a one-way flow of information to law enforcement with the understanding that it will be used to benefit the public.

Infrastructure Protection

President Clinton issued a directive declaring law enforcement to be part of the nation's critical infrastructure. Shortly after taking office, the Bush administration published a report based on the directive. Among its points are the following:

- Each law enforcement agency is responsible for the protection of its own infrastructure. The U.S. government mandates federal agencies to develop plans and encourages local agencies to do so.

- Local plans should be flexible, based on the recommended model but applicable to individual needs.

- Because police agencies use information systems, each department is asked to review its infrastructure and assess vulnerabilities. Factors recommended for the threat assessment include evaluating critical missions and capabilities, critical assets, critical interdependent relations, types of threats, and vulnerability to attack.

- Planning for protection should be based on a prioritized listing of critical services and vulnerabilities.

Source: Vatis, 1999.

The Need for Private Partnerships

All levels of law enforcement are faced with the need for technical specialists and access to privately owned portions of the infrastructure. Protection of the infrastructure does not result with acquisition of technical expertise equivalent to that of industrial specialists; it comes when specialists in crime fighting and protection establish critical links with the public and private organizations maintaining America's infrastructure. Linkages should be developed in two crucial areas. First, the police should be linked to the security forces already associated with infrastructure functions. The American Society of Industrial Security (Azano, 2003) has made great strides in this area, but more needs to be accomplished. Second, state and local law enforcement agencies must establish formal and informal networks with the organizations in their jurisdictions, and these networks should expand to a cooperative federal system.

Michael Vatis (1999) points to another area: cybersecurity. Police agencies need to protect their own information infrastructures (see Another Perspective: Recommendations for Cybersecurity). Following the trend of most American organizations, police agencies integrate electronic management and records systems in everyday routines. If these systems are disrupted, police agencies could lose their ability to function. Surveying major agencies throughout the country, Vatis argues that infrastructure defense begins at home. He worries that law enforcement agencies are not only unprepared to defend community infrastructures but unable to protect their own support systems.

Recommendations for Cybersecurity

The Institute for Security Technology Studies at Dartmouth College recommends following the "best practices" of security in the computer industry. Best practices include the following:

- Update software.
- Enforce rigid password security.
- Disable unnecessary services.
- Scan for viruses and use virus protection.
- Utilize intrusion detection systems.
- Maintain firewalls.

Source: Vatis, 2001, p. 19.

Self-Check

- *Why is the infrastructure under both public and private control?*
- *What problems are caused by private-public partnerships?*
- *Why must the government work with private agencies to protect infrastructure?*

Governmental Partnerships

One of the most important aspects of DHS operations is communicating with local communities, law enforcement agencies, and private industries as they relate to intelligence-gathering activities and infrastructure protection. DHS (2004) says that local efforts are essential to successful security plans. The International Association of Chiefs of Police (2001) believes that local law enforcement agencies will become the hinge on which all local efforts pivot. It will be the job of local law enforcement, the IACP says, to coordinate activities from a host of agencies throughout local jurisdictions all through the United States.

The Federal Mission

As envisioned by federal bureaucracy, homeland security entails co-ordinating efforts from several local organizations, including private industry, public service, health care systems, and law enforcement. Emergency-response planning falls in two broad categories: prevention and reaction (Cilluffo, Cardash, and Lederman, 2001). State and local agencies assume expanded roles in this concept because they are the obvious choice for prevention, and they will be among the first to respond to a domestic attack. If local agencies assume such a role, law enforcement officers will be forced to rethink the ways they do business.

As discussed in Chapter 15, national security intelligence is a function of the federal government. As local agencies become involved in homeland security, they will need to think beyond criminal intelligence. Two new functions become apparent. They must become involved in assessing terrorist threats in their jurisdictions. They must also learn to recognize possible items that may add to national defense intelligence and develop routines to forward such information. This creates a legal problem because law enforcement agencies need to have a reasonable suspicion that criminal activity is taking place before they can collect information (see Carter, 2004; O'Conner, 2004).

Expanding Local Roles

If engaged in homeland security, state and local police agencies will need to expand the role of traditional law enforcement. On the most rudimentary level, officers could be assigned to security tasks and trained to look for information beyond the violation of criminal law. On a more sophisticated level, police intelligence units could be established to gather and pass on intelligence information. The most effective initial practice would be to train patrol officers, investigators, and narcotics officers to look for indicators of terrorism during their daily activities. This would be an effective method of enhancing intelligence, but critics fear governmental infringement on civil liberties (see Chapter 17; Cole and Dempsey, 2002, pp. 186–187).

Assuming that local law enforcement agencies will collect information only within the context of criminal investigations, bureaucratic problems remain. The process of gathering defense intelligence is not readily apparent in American policing. Most law enforcement officers did not enter police ranks thinking that they were joining an army or aspiring to be part of DHS. Their motivation generally focuses on crime elimination, not national defense. In addition, local police policies and employment incentives reinforce their original notions. Officers are encouraged to maintain a local view, and police managers reinforce pragmatic actions while discouraging abstract thinking. Police work is extremely political, and law enforcement officers think locally. To paraphrase the late Speaker of the House Tip O'Neill, all law enforcement politics is local. The goal is not to alienate constituencies, but to develop strong community ties to help keep information flowing. Information about suspects, crimes, and criminal activity translates into power and successful individual performance with police agencies, and it solves crimes (Manning, 1976, p. 35).

Thinking Internationally

State and local officers are not rewarded for thinking in terms of international issues or national security. Chiefs of police and sheriffs do not usually praise abstract reasoning. In an early critique of collegiate criminal justice programs, Lawrence Sherman (1978) claims that higher education has done little to help this situation. Criminal justice programs do

ANOTHER PERSPECTIVE

New Approaches to Mission

If state and local law enforcement officers were to begin looking for signs of terrorism, they would need to frame basic questions about potential adversaries. For example, in addition to criminal briefings before patrol or investigative tours, officers would need to think of questions such as the following:

- What is the modus operandi of our enemy?
- How does the enemy's organization function?
- What types of tactics will the enemy use?
- What types of weapons will the enemy use?
- How can information be gathered while protecting the source?
- What activities in the community might indicate that terrorists may be operating in a jurisdiction?
- How can information be shared securely with other agencies?

not produce abstract, critical thinkers for law enforcement, Sherman believes; they impart skills. According to a recent survey by *Police: The Law Enforcement Magazine*, graduates steeped in academic preparation are not as welcome in law enforcement agencies as recruits with military experience (July 2002). Discipline and the willingness to obey orders are more important than individual thinking and creativity (see Another Perspective: New Approaches to Mission).

Modern terrorism is an abstract, nebulous concept, which fluctuates according to historical and political circumstances. To combat terrorism, security forces require groups of people with abstract reasoning skills, knowledge of international politics and history, and specialized expertise in particular regions (Betts, 2002). If the police are to participate as full partners in this process, they must bring skilled specialists to the table. The ethos behind policing, however, rejects this logic. American law enforcement relishes pragmatic information with immediate applicability on the beat.

Localized attitudes bring contempt from intelligence agencies. Unlike analysts in defense intelligence, state and local police officers frequently exhibit no concern for in-depth background information, the kind of information needed to understand intelligence. As a result, intelligence bureaucracies frequently question police competence. Intelligence analysts know information is not usually valuable until it is categorized and placed within social and political contexts. If police agencies are unable to engage in this type of examination, intelligence organizations are hesitant to form partnerships with them. These factors present enormous problems as the DHS tries to create a network of information.

Self-Check

- *Why must governmental agencies form homeland security partnerships with each other?*
- *Why is it necessary to think about international problems at all levels of law enforcement?*
- *Why might people fear the expansion of state, local, and tribal roles?*

Bureaucratic Problems

Unlike the ideal rational organizations described by Weber, public service organizations have foibles that emerge in the everyday social construction of reality. Personalities are important, varying levels of competency limit or expand effectiveness, and organizations tend to act in their own interests. If all the organizations involved in homeland security agree to pool their efforts, several bureaucratic hurdles need to be cleared (see Swanson, Territo, and Taylor, 2001, pp. 643–644; Best, 2001; Bodrero, 2002; Mitchell and Hulse, 2002).

Federal Rivalries

The standard administrative logic is that federal bureaucracies work together. In reality, this is not always true. Sometimes federal agencies act more like rivals than partners. The 9/11 Commission criticized agencies for not working together. Anyone who has worked in or with the federal government can relate stories of interagency rivalries. Former FBI director Louis Freeh (2005, p. 192) says talking about CIA-FBI rivalries might sell books, but it is not true. Former CIA director George Tenet (2007, p. 193) admits that the CIA and FBI had a history of contentious relations, but he and FBI directors Freeh and Robert Mueller worked hard to overcome it.

For example, as American troops were preparing to enter Iraq in 2003, there was a tremendous dispute between the CIA and the military about the validity of intelligence coming out of Iraq (Gordon and Trainor, 2006, pp. 198–199). Another example is that, despite claims to the contrary, individual CIA agents probably refused to share information with the Joint Terrorism Task Force (JTTF) in New York City before 9/11 (L. Wright, 2006, p. 353). Perhaps the best example can be found in the FBI's decision to locate its counterterrorism efforts in its Washington field office. Former FBI executive Richard Marquise (2006, p. 26) says that Washington was the best place to locate counterterrorist headquarters because it positioned the FBI for inevitable turf battles with the CIA and Department of State.

Unfortunately, federal agencies mistrust one another at times, and their failure to cooperate in some circumstances influences local police relationships. Many federal law enforcement agencies openly resent the

FBI, and this attitude is frequently reciprocated. In addition, the creation of new bureaucracies such as the Transportation Security Administration exacerbates rivalries. Some rivalry is natural because people tend to look at problems from the perspective of the agency where they are employed. In the real world of bureaucracy, organizations on every level frequently act out of self-interest rather than concern with an overall mission (Valburn, 2002).

FBI versus Locals

In October 2001, FBI Director Robert Mueller attended the IACP meeting in Toronto, Ontario. According to police chiefs who attended the meeting, it was not a pleasant experience for him. State and local law enforcement executives criticized Mueller for failing to share information. Mueller vowed the FBI would never allow this failure to happen again. American law enforcement would witness a new FBI. Despite the intentions of the most forceful bureaucratic leaders, however, orders are not always carried out as planned. There have been success stories with information sharing, but there have also been tales of woe. Many American police executives are not convinced that the FBI is in full partnership with them in efforts to stop terrorism (L. Levitt, 2002).

The purpose here is not to condemn the FBI, but to acknowledge a bureaucratic issue. Many state and local police executives do not trust the FBI, and the attitude extends down through the ranks of law enforcement agencies. If police in America are to become part of homeland defense, the relationship between the FBI and state and local law enforcement must improve (Riordan and Zegart, 2002).

Local Control and Revenue Sources

Some people feel cooperation between state and local law enforcement will result in the de facto concentration of police power. This attitude was alive and well at the turn of the twentieth century when state police agencies were forming. Many local governments believed that state police forces had too much power, and many states limited these agencies to patrolling state highways. Civil libertarians believe that consolidated police power will erode civil rights. Local governmental officials worry that their agendas will be lost in federalization. The bureaucratic arguments extend beyond these interest groups (Hitt and Cloud, 2002).

There is also frustration among local governments with the monetary costs of their homeland security responsibilities. Some local governments want homeland security money to be distributed evenly. Larger jurisdictions, like New York City, argue that money should be distributed according to the likelihood of attack. Even then, New York City officials complain, federal money does not cover the cost of security (Mintz, 2005). Other people worry that homeland security grants are given to local units of government for bizarre uses. For example, the state of Kentucky received $36,000 in federal money to keep terrorists from infiltrating bingo halls (Hudson, 2006).

Legal Bureaucracy

Another factor inhibiting police cooperation is the legal bureaucracy of criminal justice. For example, many criminal justice scholars believe that the justice system is actually not a system at all but a multifaceted bureaucracy with intersecting—or not—layers. Drawing on earlier research, they refer to the justice system quite humorously as the "wedding cake model." Rather than a smooth flow among police, courts, and corrections, they see a cake in which a large bottom layer represents misdemeanors, a smaller middle layer represents serious crimes, and the smallest tier at the top represents a few celebrated cases. Each layer has differing procedures for dealing with different types of crimes, and police departments, court systems, and correctional agencies work apart from one another in each layer (see Walker, 1985; Cole and Smith, 2004, p. 8).

Each entity in the criminal justice system is independent, although it interacts with the other parts. There is no overall leader, and law enforcement, courts, and correctional agencies refuse to accept single management. From a constitutional perspective, the courts are hardly designed to fit into a criminal justice system. Although police and correctional institutions represent the executive branch of government, the courts autonomously belong to the judicial branch (del Carmen, 1991, pp. 275–277). Efforts to increase the efficiency of homeland defense will not change these relationships.

Self-Check

- *Describe rivalries among law enforcement agencies.*
- *What might be done to overcome those rivalries?*
- *Why does inflexibility hamper an organization's ability to operate?*

Bureaucratic Solutions

Successful organizations, whether car manufacturers or universities, overcome problems. Bureaucracies contain inherent problems, but they too can work for solutions. Law enforcement, homeland security, and intelligence agencies produce a unique product, but all formal organizations have the same internal and external troubles. Law enforcement bureaucracies will interact to solve problems. The lead panel at the first National Fusion Center Conference focused on this issue (Johnson, 2007). Panel participants from local agencies, the National Guard, the FBI, DHS, and the intelligence community addressed the problem directly. To combat terrorism, every bureaucratic obstacle that hinders the flow of information and action must be directly addressed (Figure 16.1).

Coordination of the activities of many different types of agencies is essential. Panel members stated that agencies had to develop new methods of coordinating and communicating ideas. This involved coordination committees and communication among leaders. Every person involved

Figure 16.1

The Bureaucracy of
Information Sharing

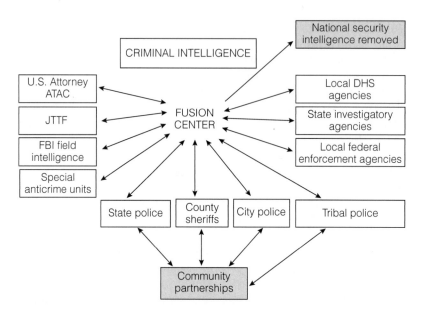

actionable intelligence

Information that law en-
forcement agencies, military
units, or other security
forces can use to stop an
attack or operation.

intelligence product

Any outcome or output of
analyzed information that
can be used by law enforcement agencies, military
units, or security forces to
take an immediate action.

in the intelligence effort needs to understand his or her role in the process. As law enforcement officers collect and forward information, analysts at local fusion centers turn the information into **actionable intelligence**. This intelligence is forwarded to the National Counterterrorism Center (NCTC) where it is analyzed with information from all other sources in the network. This newly created actionable intelligence is returned to the fusion centers as an **intelligence product**. It can be delivered to patrol officers, deputies, agents, and troopers.

Bureaucracies have problems, but they also offer a process. When law enforcement agencies and the other organizations for preventing terrorism stay focused on the goal, the process can produce results. It is possible to gather and analyze information, assess threats, and mobilize resources to prevent an attack.

Border Security: Critique and Reform

There are problems with border security, to be sure. Stephen Flynn, a senior fellow in national security studies at the Council on Foreign Relations (2002, 2004a, 2004b), believes the goals of homeland security are crucial and that America's bureaucracies and leadership are squandering the opportunity to really defend the United States. Flynn says America has made two crucial mistakes. First, homeland security has been separated from national security. Second, the infrastructure is vulnerable to attack. Despite all the rhetoric and departmental rearrangements for homeland security, the reality is that the United States has not organized its resources for defense.

Flynn vehemently argues that homeland security should be part of a national strategy to defend the United States. America needs to be able to strike a blow as well as to take one. Although both political parties speak of the war on terrorism, terrorism is not something that can be destroyed only by fighting in other areas of the world. There is no central front, Flynn argues, and America cannot always project its power to fight elsewhere. The United States has marshaled resources to fight overseas while neglecting to protect the home front.

To illustrate the point, Flynn points to the use of WMD. According to the CIA, the most likely scenario for smuggling WMD into the United States is by sea. It is difficult to inspect all of the cargo containers arriving in seaports; therefore, the oceans represent an opportunity for terrorists. Flynn points out that the Bush administration has done very little to protect the nation's 361 seaports. There has been a lot of rhetoric but insufficient action. He finds it hard to believe that in 2004 the United States spent more money every three days to fight the war in Iraq than it has in three years to protect seaports.

The nation's critical infrastructure remains open to attack, Flynn says. In the 2005 national budget, the DOD was allotted $7.6 billion to enhance the fortifications of its bases. In the same budget, the infrastructure for the *entire* nation received only $2.6 billion. Dirty bombs and chemical threats can be developed from hazardous material, yet over the past three years funds for secure disposal of such material have been drastically reduced. Police and firefighter numbers have been cut even though they are crucial for security.

Flynn also sees a problem in strategic thinking in DHS and other agencies. For example, the scientific and medical communities are essential elements of homeland security. Nearly 50 percent of the scientific and medical personnel employed by the federal government will retire before 2010. Currently, they are not being replaced quickly enough. The colleges and universities that would produce them are underfunded. In addition, the federal government has virtually ignored private industry, claiming that it is responsible for protecting its own infrastructure. However, Flynn finds that private industry is not doing this.

Even meeting the need for enhanced border security will not protect America against terrorist attack. Security is a dynamic process that combines intelligence, military, and law enforcement power. It requires international coordination and cooperation to counter the attacks planned overseas. Flynn says America needs an integrated system for defense.

Flynn believes that jihadists are fully aware of vulnerabilities in the infrastructure. They will not simply let the United States bring the fight to them; they intend to strike, and the safest and most effective way to hit America is to strike the infrastructure (see Another Perspective: Infrastructure Problems in the DOE). Jihadists understand the economic effect of their actions. For example, Flynn says that if terrorists managed to shut down the closed-container operations of America's shipping industry for just three weeks, the whole world could be thrown into an economic recession.

Flynn urges policy makers to reinvent homeland security. Defense at home is as important as the ability to wage military action overseas.

ANOTHER PERSPECTIVE

Infrastructure Problems in the DOE

60 Minutes reporter Ed Bradley examined the Department of Energy and its nuclear facilities. It has many problems, including the following concerns:

• Stolen keys to secure facilities that were not replaced for three years.

• Guards were sleeping on duty.

• Facilities were penetrated during mock terrorist attacks.

Bradley's report concluded that America's nuclear facilities are protected on paper but that DOE has not implemented real security measures.

Source: Bradley, August 29, 2004.

DHS and other federal bureaucracies should think of security from a broad perspective. There are many benefits for doing so. Flynn argues that developing an integrated system against terrorism would reduce the drug trade, contraband smuggling, and theft. These are residual benefits for a strategic program, he believes.

Despite the system's shortcomings, Flynn believes bureaucracies can overcome the problems. We will never have enough security to prevent every attack, he says, but we should follow the path of the aviation industry. Private and public aviation officials have worked together to lower the possibility of airplane accidents and reduce devastation when they do occur. Although the air industry experiences horrific disasters at times, people continue to fly. Flynn believes this is because of the faith people have in the air transportation system. They know that failures, although inevitable, are an aberration. They continue to use the system because they believe in its overall safety. Flynn says homeland security should have the same goal. In a system of civil defense, people have a civic responsibility to maintain the system. When bureaucracies recover from failure after an attack, people will believe life is getting back to normal and they will continue to function. This is the goal of bureaucracy, Flynn says. Americans must be able to absorb a major attack and continue to function. That, Flynn argues, should be the model for homeland security agencies.

If police departments follow Flynn's suggestions, they will see security as a "work in progress." Flynn says that if policies become a routine process, attention is focused on how work is accomplished rather than the results. Law enforcement agencies should look for weaknesses in the system, probe them, and make changes based on the results. Every agency needs to forge and sustain a variety of nontraditional partnerships with the community, different levels of government, private industry, and the nonprofit sectors. Flynn says our federalist system lends itself to these partnerships because many decision-making efforts are reserved for state governments.

Even though Flynn is critical of America's bureaucratic weaknesses, he is optimistic about the future. He believes that bureaucratic leaders, including police executives and managers, will grow to see the problems of terrorism from a more realistic perspective. This will cause them to improve homeland security *before an attack*. Although not every attack can be prevented, most terrorism can be deterred through cooperative partnerships. It demands new skills for law enforcement officers, a culture of information sharing, and new bureaucratic relationships, but interdiction of terrorism is an attainable goal.

Preparing for Successful Law Enforcement Processes

Imagine the following scene: On a snowy afternoon a road-patrol deputy stops a car on a Nebraska highway. Everything looks routine and the driver, a foreign national, is exceedingly polite. The deputy notices that the car is registered in South Carolina and that the driver has an operator's permit issued in Colorado. The deputy asks questions about the driver's country of origin, his South Carolina or Colorado residence, and his reason for driving through Nebraska. The answers are smooth, too smooth. Had they been rehearsed? When the deputy rephrases the questions, the driver repeats the same answers without variation and seems to be confused by the deputy's questions.

In the course of the interview, the deputy finds that the car is rented, and the driver's name is spelled one way on his license and another way on the rental agreement. Further questioning reveals immigration papers with a third spelling. At this point, the deputy begins to ask more in-depth questions. The deputy knows spelling names in multiple ways and creating false identification are methods mastered by many international terrorists.

The deputy returns to her vehicle and calls the local fusion center. The analyst puts the deputy in contact with the **Terrorism Screening Center (TSC)** in West Virginia. The TSC tells the deputy to gather as much information as possible but not to make an arrest. The deputy follows instructions and forwards the information. She does not know it, but the driver she has stopped is a suspect in an ongoing JTTF investigation in Florida, and the information she has provided will become valuable in the prevention of a terrorist attack and the arrest of the perpetrators *before* the event can take place.

The foregoing example is only imaginary, but recently a Midwestern police officer stopped a vehicle on an interstate highway for speeding. The car contained two men and a number of other items, objects the officer failed to see. The patrol officer failed to notice weapons and explosives in the car, including two loaded automatic weapons behind the driver and a semiautomatic pistol by the driver's hand. He also missed racist literature advocating violence and other extremist propaganda lying open in the car. He failed to see a clue when he first approached the car that would have given warning, a Ku Klux Klan symbol on the back window. Failing to do a proper warrant check, he did not know that one of the men was

Terrorism Screening Center (TSC)

A multiagency operation in West Virginia that evaluates information gathered from a variety of governmental sources.

a fugitive. He gave the driver a speeding ticket never knowing that his life had been in danger or that one of the men in the car was a member of a terrorist group planning a massive attack in Texas. The exact details of the stop are known because the other man in the suspect's car was an undercover police officer working the case (Keathley, 2002).

New Approaches to the Law Enforcement Mission

The JTTF system might well serve as an example for the first step in law enforcement cooperation. Critics like Cole and Dempsey (2002) believe that gathering security information in the course of criminal investigations is both legal and effective. The JTTF offers a sensible alternative by creating a system that separates criminal and national security intelligence. These units also combine local, state, and various federal police officers, as well as corrections officials and prosecutors, in regional units designed to combat terrorism. Local and state officers are given federal authority, and the presence of such officers gives federal agents the ability to act in local jurisdictions. The JTTFs have been effective in many cases (Watson, 2002).

An alternative for state and local agencies is to combine training in terrorism awareness with specialized training for selected officers. Rather than bringing an entire department into intelligence-gathering operations, select units could engage in counterterrorist activities. Intelligence specialists like David Carter (2004) see the value in this. Rather than bringing police officers into the intelligence process as full partners, police officers could be trained to look for indicators of terrorism in the course of normal operations and to pass the information along. Trained police officers may expand their efforts by creating public and private partnerships through community policing efforts.

On the surface JTTFs seem tailored to the needs of state and local law enforcement, but in some cases they meet opposition. Local governments have refused to allow their police forces to assist in counterterrorist activities, and some jurisdictions refuse to share criminal intelligence with federal law enforcement. Civil libertarians sometimes see the formation of a JTTF as too great of a consolidation of governmental power. In addition, although academics and governmental officials are fond of using the phrase "criminal justice system," the courts are not part of the system because they do not belong to the executive branch. State and federal courts may well limit the role of local agencies in homeland security, especially in intelligence-gathering activities.

On the other hand, police are in a perfect position to engage in intelligence-gathering activities and expand their role in national defense. Other Western democracies, such as France and Germany, have done this quite successfully. The Canadians and British accomplished the same thing but kept more of a public service model than the French or the Germans. The JTTF model may be a start, but law enforcement efforts need to go further. Partnerships with all types of formal and informal organizations and cooperation among all levels of law enforcement in an environment that rewards information sharing is the ultimate answer to preventing terrorism.

Self-Check

- *How can bureaucratic principles assist in the development of efficient organizations?*
- *What can be done to get agencies to work together?*
- *Where are the borders vulnerable?*
- *Why does the immigration debate spill into discussions of homeland security?*

Responding to Disasters

No security system can completely stop terrorism, and law enforcement agencies will be called to respond when an attack happens. The process for response and recovery involves planning. Fire departments, regional disaster teams, the health community, and other agencies have **emergency-response plans**. Law enforcement agencies have roles under these plans. Their primary responsibilities are to respond and restore order, assist emergency and rescue operations, and support health and human services. They also are charged with investigative and prosecutorial actions. With the exception of the last two functions, the procedures are similar when responding to natural disasters, civil disorders, or massive infrastructure failures. All of these functions involve reaction.

Response functions are critical and they save lives, but emergency-response planning differs from preventing terrorism. When law enforcement agencies respond to disasters, it does not matter whether the cause was an industrial accident, act of nature, or terrorist attack. Multiple agencies, including police departments, respond to emergencies. Plans and actions designed to stop terrorism involve different skills. Gathering information, analyzing it, and sharing findings are part of an intelligence process. Law enforcement's primary role is to prevent terrorism and crime, and its secondary purpose is to react to it to save lives. Reaction to a crisis, although one of the critical missions of police and homeland security agencies, is an emergency function. It has little to do with the cause of the disaster. For example, when a traffic officer responds to a car crash, it is reaction. Preventing automobile accidents is a different function. The same principle applies to preventing terrorism.

emergency-response plans
Preparations from any agency to deal with natural, accidental, or human-made disasters. They involve controlling the incident through an organized response-and-command system and assigning various organizations to supervise the restoration of social order.

Self-Check

- *How does prevention differ from emergency-response planning?*
- *Why do law enforcement roles differ in prevention and response?*
- *Has law enforcement failed when it engages in a responsive role?*

SUMMARY

- The problem of law enforcement bureaucracy with respect to homeland security and the prevention of terrorism is the sheer number of organizations in multiple layers of government. Max Weber's ideal bureaucracy rationally organizes people under goal-oriented leaders. Workers and managers are selected only according to their abilities.
- Most American governmental organizations, the military, and some private industry base their structures on the Weberian ideal of bureaucracy.
- Many bureaucracies are involved in homeland security, and their most important functions center on law enforcement and activities related to intelligence.
- DHS has assumed many roles in homeland security. It coordinates activities with the DOD, FBI, and CIA. It must also work with state, local, and tribal agencies.
- Border protection involves ports of entry—seaports, border checkpoints, and ocean shores—and vast expanses of land on the northern and southern borders.
- Infrastructure protection refers to security provided for the underpinnings of social life, such as roadways, computer networks, bridges, electrical grids, and pipelines.
- If state, local, and tribal law enforcement agencies are to take part in homeland security, the mission needs to be reconceived. Making the needed changes seems to make sense, but several factors work against change.
- Flynn maintains that the focus on homeland security is misplaced. People and products coming into the country need to be checked and monitored. America needs to become resilient to recover from terrorist strikes.
- The JTTF system may serve as a starting point for cooperation among police agencies. In the final analysis law enforcement agencies will need to create and sustain a variety of new partnerships in the public, private, and nonprofit sectors.

KEY TERMS

bureaucracy (p. 430)
1978 Civil Service Reform Act
   (p. 431)
Government Management Reform
   Act of 1994 (p. 431)
Max Weber (p. 431)
National Counterterrorism Center
   (p. 434)
posse comitatus (p. 435)
task orientation (p. 435)

threat analysis (p. 436)
pre-incident indicators (p. 436)
working group (p. 437)
actionable intelligence (p. 450)
intelligence product (p. 450)
Terrorism Screening Center
   (p. 453)
emergency-response plans
   (p. 455)

WRITING ASSIGNMENTS

1. What is the bureaucracy challenge? How does it apply to homeland security and law enforcement? What actions might overcome it?
2. Many agencies have different missions, yet these missions are all part of homeland security. Cite examples of the ways coalitions of agencies have worked together to solve problems in the past. Can this be done today? If so, how might agencies work together to prevent terrorism?
3. There are problems with competing bureaucracies in state, local, and tribal law enforcement and the way they interact with federal organizations. Identify some of the problems and possible solutions.

17

Homeland Security and Civil Liberties

Photo by Chip Somodevilla/Getty Images

FBI director Robert Mueller at a news conference about civil liberties. Perhaps the greatest challenge in homeland security is gathering enough information to prevent terrorism while preserving the individual liberties guaranteed by the U.S. Constitution.

Learning Objectives

After reading this chapter you should be able to

- Explain the dangers of restricting freedom in the name of security.
- Differentiate between civil liberties and human rights.
- Describe the relationship between the idea of defense in depth and civil liberties.

- Summarize the USA Patriot Act of 2001 and the renewal in 2006.
- List the constitutional issues that affect homeland security.
- Cite arguments to support and oppose increasing executive power to combat terrorism.

- Describe court responses to attempts to counter terrorism with increased governmental executive-branch power.
- Describe the role of law enforcement agencies in a social network opposed to terrorism.

- Discuss the dangers of militarizing police work.

September 11 changed the way America views terrorism. The wars in Afghanistan and Iraq claimed the lives of thousands, and massive counterterrorist measures were taken at home. The USA Patriot Act of 2001, which made significant changes in the structure of federal law enforcement, was passed within weeks of the September attacks. The act was renewed in 2006, after both the Senate and the House introduced several provisions curbing governmental authority. In 2004 the 9/11 Commission issued a report calling for the complete overhaul of the U.S. intelligence system, and in response a law was passed in December 2004. All of these activities generated tremendous controversy, and the debates took place as America waged foreign wars against an enemy who projected no central front. As America's internal debates continued, terrorist events around the world became deadlier.

Security and Liberty

There are always trade-offs when considering security. This applies to social structures and to physical aspects of security. It is possible to use force to create a social structure where people can have limited fear of crime and illegal violence. The underside is that people in such a society must often fear the powers of the civil government. Crime can be reduced through aggressive apprehension and punishment of criminals, but when the government goes beyond legal norms, people no longer fear only criminals; they fear the government that is supposed to protect their rights (Giroux, 2002).

This is both an ancient and modern principle. When the Athenians were threatened with invasion, they were often willing to suspend the rules of democracy in favor of protection. They shifted the structure of open democracy to grant more authoritarian power to leaders in times of crisis, and the power lasted until the threat abated (Finley, 1983, pp. 24–25). The Romans would follow a similar course in their republic, creating a dictatorship in times of war (Mackay, 2004, pp. 27–28). During the American Civil War, Abraham Lincoln imprisoned opponents without informing them of charges, suspending the right to habeas corpus (Goodwin, 2005, pp. 354–355). In times of emergencies some societies have been willing to sacrifice personal liberty in the name of security.

The question of the suspension of liberty lies at the root of arguments concerning homeland security. Proponents at one end of the spectrum argue that the open nature of democratic societies makes the social structure open to attack. They argue that some limitation on civil liberties is necessary to preserve the greater good. On the other end of the spectrum, people argue that limiting civil liberties is far more dangerous than the more limited threats posed by terrorism. Like Donald Black (2004), they argue that when governments suppress freedom in the name of counterterrorism, their actions are more violent than the terrorists they are trying to stop. There are many differing positions between these two extremes, and the debate complicates any approach to homeland security (Wise and Nadar, 2002).

Because the dispute is unsolvable, a metaphor might be helpful. More than a century ago tremendous debates raged in the navies of Japan, Europe, and the United States about the construction of battleships. The problem focused on three critical aspects of battleships: speed, armor, and firepower. Any time engineers increased one of the three, they had to decrease two of the others. For example, one set of nations decided to develop fast battle cruisers before World War I. This meant they had to reduce the number and caliber of big guns on the ships as well as the armor plating. Guns and armor added weight and slowed the cruisers. The battleship debate was a zero-sum game.

The debate about homeland security involves similar factors. Decreasing civil liberties limits individual freedom and increases governmental power. It may increase protection from terrorism, but it increases citizen vulnerability to the abuse of governmental power. Just as it was impossible to build a battleship that had the heaviest guns, the thickest amount of armored protection, and the fastest speed in any navy, so it is impossible to construct a counterterrorist system that ensures complete protection, allows for maximum civil liberty, and protects unrestricted freedom of movement. Issues need to be balanced, and the debate centers on the area that should be emphasized.

Human Rights and Civil Liberties

civil liberties

Individual rights granted to citizens under the U.S. Constitution.

Bill of Rights

The first ten amendments to the U.S. Constitution.

Civil liberties refer to the individual freedoms people have under a system of law. The Constitution is the law of the land in the United States. It establishes procedures for government and provides for civil liberties. The first ten amendments, known as the **Bill of Rights**, further limit the power of government. Americans enjoy particular freedoms under the Constitution, and the government cannot take these freedoms away. This is civil liberty.

Yet most people believe that all humans enjoy basic rights. They should not be enslaved, exploited, or subjected to arbitrary abuse such as genocide or unwarranted punishment. These issues are known as human rights, and they have been articulated by many governments and the United Nations (1948). **Human rights** focus on the legal right to exist in a society where people are free from arbitrary coercion. People have the right to be free, choose their religion, and have a fair trial (see Expanding the Concept: UN Declaration of Human Rights).

Human rights intersect terrorism and homeland security in two controversial areas. First, terrorist attacks on innocent civilians violate the human right of people to exist apart from political violence against innocent people. Second, governments must respect the human rights of their opponents. Ideally, they are not allowed to act outside the bounds of human decency and law when countering terrorists. Both positions create political and legal firestorms. Terrorists justify murders by stating that civilians are never innocent because they act within the governmental system (Pew Foundation, 2005). Governments frequently justify inhumane actions against terrorists by stating they have sacrificed the right to humane treatment because they use terrorism (Porteous, 2006).

Debates about terrorism, governmental authority, and homeland security almost always touch on these issues. Those who favor strong security at any cost tend to overlook human rights abuses and de-emphasize civil liberties. Those who favor civil liberties tend to de-emphasize security while emphasizing human rights. Many different positions between these extremes argue that the rule of law serves to mediate both positions.

human rights
The basic entitlements and protections that should be given to every person.

Defense in Depth

Changes in how war is fought affect the structure of civil society. For example, jihadist communities feel that their very existence is threatened. To paraphrase their most important philosopher, Sayyid Qutb (1965), jihadists are on a cliff and about to topple over its edge. They are threatened by Muslims who do not accept the jihadist philosophy and by the non-Muslim West. As a result, jihadists believe they can use any method for disrupting their enemies' societies. Stated another way, the target of terrorism is social order. Terrorists fight against the way a group of people live. Therefore, combating terrorism is not simply a matter of taking a battle to an enemy. It involves the preservation and protection of social order.

The logic of conflict becomes clear when the method of fighting and the targets of combat are placed together. Terrorism attacks *civil* society and *civilian* targets. Defending against terrorism implies that military force must extend beyond the military. In other words, to defend against terrorism, a nation or culture must use *civil defense*. The idea of **defense in depth** is that all levels of society must become involved in homeland security. Defense in depth is designed to protect a community fighting for its way of life (see Cebrowski and Barnett, 2003; Barnett, 2004).

Homeland security makes sense within this logic, but it raises a host of issues. This logic assumes that the community wants to fight for its

defense in depth
Using social networks in national defense. It is based on Arthur Cebrowski's idea of operating at all levels of society.

UN Declaration of Human Rights

In 1948 the United Nations adopted the Universal Declaration of Human Rights. The provisions include the following:

1. All human beings are born free and equal in dignity and rights. They are endowed with reason and conscience and should act towards one another in a spirit of brotherhood.

2. Everyone is entitled to all the rights and freedoms in the Declaration; and no distinction shall be made on the basis of the racial, religious, political, jurisdictional or international status of the country or territory to which a person belongs.

3. Everyone has the right to life, liberty and security of person.

4. No one shall be held in slavery or servitude; slavery and the slave trade shall be prohibited in all their forms.

5. No one shall be subjected to torture or to cruel, inhuman or degrading treatment or punishment.

6. Everyone has the right to recognition everywhere as a person before the law.

7. All are equal before the law and are entitled without any discrimination to equal protection of the law.

8. Everyone has the right to a legal remedy if human rights are violated.

9. No one shall be subjected to arbitrary arrest, detention or exile.

10. Everyone is entitled in full equality to a fair and public trial.

11. Every defendant has the right to be presumed innocent until proved guilty according to law in a public trial.

12. No one shall be subjected to arbitrary interference with his privacy, family, home or correspondence. Everyone has the right to the protection of the law against such interference or attacks.

13. Everyone has the right to freedom of movement, and the right to leave any country, including his own, and to return to his country.

14. Everyone has the right to seek political asylum from persecution.

15. No one shall be arbitrarily deprived of his nationality nor denied the right to change his nationality.

16. Men and women of full age have the right to marry and to found a family. Marriage shall be entered into only with the free will and consent of the spouses.

17. Everyone has the right to own property and no one shall be arbitrarily deprived of his property.

(continued)

UN Declaration of Human Rights (continued)

18. Everyone has the right to freedom of thought, conscience and religion.

19. Everyone has the right to freedom of opinion and expression.

20. Everyone has the right to freedom of peaceful assembly and association.

21. Everyone has the right to take part in the government of his country, directly or through freely chosen representatives. The will of the people shall be the basis of the authority of government.

Source: United Nations, http://www.un.org/Overview/rights.html.

---

existence, which implies that all members of the community are committed to a similar goal. Approaching conflict in this manner may solve logical issues, but it asks a society to engage in great sacrifice to achieve its objectives. As Martin van Creveld (1991, pp. 142–156) says, at some point violence serves to justify violence. This style of thought also asks members of a social group to be sufficiently ruthless with enemies to defeat them and to have the political will for rigid self-examination. In short, defense in depth may require citizens to alter the way they live and sacrifice the comforts of everyday life. For example, Americans have learned to tolerate increased security at airports and public schools.

The ideas of democracy and individual freedom have been developed in the West for the past thousand years. The United States, founded on these principles, struggles with the issues of democracy and civil rights. At the country's birth, property-holding males governed, women were noncitizens, and slavery was acceptable. The rights of citizenship have spread slowly for nearly 250 years, and the reality of individual freedom occurs in the tension between ideal freedom and state power. Defense in depth alters the balance by emphasizing state power. Laws, military behavior, police power, information gathering, and other aspects of civil existence are altered when an entire society engages in a conflict.

When homeland security is being discussed, the topic of individual rights usually becomes part of the discussion. To engage in a struggle against terrorism, Americans must examine themselves and honestly select a course of action they will accept. It cannot be imposed by legislative action, military force, or police power. It cannot be defined by self-appointed civil rights guardians. Attorneys and courts are fond of claiming this area for their exclusive jurisdiction, but the issue extends far beyond judicial logic. If Americans want to secure the homeland, they need to engage in a thorough self-examination and decide what they are willing to sacrifice and how they will maintain the most cherished aspects of social freedom (Cole and Dempsey, 2002, pp. 11–12).

This is not an abstract academic exercise. Many jihadists are engaged in a cosmic struggle, what they believe is a life-and-death struggle between good and evil. They believe they must not lose the battle for God and feel bound by no rules in the course of this holy war (Ruthven, 2000, p. 398). Killing their enemies—Muslims who disagree with the jihadist philosophy and non-Muslims—is a sacramental act. Death is the ultimate expression of their religion, and killing is horrific and spectacular. If the jihadists obtain weapons of mass destruction, they will use them. Americans will be better prepared to secure the homeland if they have engaged in a nationwide discussion of defense in depth and its impact on civil liberties before an attack. If the discussion takes place after a population center has been destroyed, emotions and reaction will guide the response. In that case, homeland security could become a threat to the American way of life.

Self-Check

- *Explain the difference between civil rights and human rights.*
- *Is it possible to increase security and preserve civil rights?*
- *How is defense in depth related to civil rights?*

▼ Civil Liberties and Federal Power

Federal counterterrorist laws were toughened after the 1995 Oklahoma City bombing. President William Clinton supported legislation to increase the government's power to limit civil liberties in the face of terrorism. Many civil libertarians criticized Clinton and Congress for these actions. President George W. Bush supported similar legislation in 2001 and again in 2005. After heated debate the president and Congress reached a compromise in 2006, and the pattern was clear: the United States has increased restrictions on civil liberties after each major terrorist attack.

USA Patriot Act
A law passed in October 2001 that expands law enforcement's power to investigate and deter terrorism. Opponents claim that it adversely affects civil liberties; proponents claim that it introduces reasonable measures to protect the country against terrorists. The act was amended and renewed in 2006.

The USA Patriot Act of 2001

The Bush administration sponsored legislation in the weeks following September 11 that contained increased responsibilities for criminal justice and other agencies. The **USA Patriot Act** has ten sections, or titles, outlining new powers for governmental operations (for a summary, see Doyle, 2002, and Expanding the Concept: An Overview of the USA Patriot Act). Title I is designed to enhance domestic security. It creates funding for counterterrorist activities, expands technical support for the FBI, expands electronic intelligence-gathering research, and defines presidential authority in response to terrorism. This section of the law also forbids discrimination against Arab and Muslim Americans.

Some of the most controversial aspects of the Patriot Act appear in Title II, which aims to improve the government's ability to gather elec-

An Overview of the USA Patriot Act

Critics of the USA Patriot Act say it infringes on civil liberties. Supporters believe it provides critical law enforcement tools. Here is an overview of the sections affecting law enforcement.

Title I, Designed to Enhance Domestic Security   Creates a counterterrorism fund, increases technical support for the FBI, allows law enforcement to request military assistance in certain emergencies, expands the National Electronic Task Force, and forbids discrimination against Muslims and Arabs.

Title II, Designed to Improve Surveillance   Grants authority to federal law enforcement agencies to intercept communication about terrorism, allows searches of computers, allows intelligence agencies to share information with criminal justice agencies, explains procedures for warrants, creates new definitions of intelligence, allows for roving wiretaps, and provides for expanding intelligence gathering. The USA Patriot Act has a sunset clause: If not renewed by Congress, it will automatically expire.

Title III, Designed to Stop Terrorism Finances   Grants expanded powers to law enforcement agencies to seize financial records, provides access to financial records, forces transactions to be disclosed, and expands investigative power in money laundering.

Title IV, Designed to Protect U.S. Borders   Outlines measures to protect the borders, tightens immigration procedures, allows foreigners to be photographed and fingerprinted, and gives benefits to victims of terrorism.

Title V, Enhances Investigative Powers   Provides a reward program, calls for sharing of investigative findings among law enforcement agencies, extends Secret Service jurisdiction, and forces educational institutions to release records of foreign students.

Title VI, Designed to Compensate the Families of Public Safety Officers Killed during a Terrorist Attack

Title VII, Designed to Expand the Information Sharing Network   Provides for the expansion of law enforcement's nationwide information exchange, the Regional Information Sharing System (RISS).

Title VIII, Strengthens Criminal Laws   Defines terrorist attacks, defines domestic terrorism, provides the basis for charging terrorists overseas, criminalizes support for terrorism, criminalizes cyberterrorism, allows investigation of terrorism as racketeering, and expands bioterrorism laws.

Title X, Contains Miscellaneous Addenda

tronic evidence. In other words, it allows police officials expanded authority to monitor communications. It also allows intelligence and federal law enforcement agencies to share noncriminal information with each other. In addition, it forces private corporations to share records and data with federal law enforcement departments during investigations and allows the FBI to seize material when it believes national security is jeopardized. Title II also contains a sunset clause, automatically ending the provisions of the Patriot Act unless it is renewed before a certain time limit, and enacts congressional oversight of the act.

Other sections of the law affect law enforcement and the criminal justice system in a variety of ways. Title III empowers federal law enforcement to interact with banking regulators and provides arrest power outside U.S. borders for U.S. agents investigating terrorist financing and money laundering. Title IV increases border patrols and monitoring of foreigners within the United States and mandates detention of suspected terrorists. Title VII focuses on police information sharing, specifically targeting a nationwide police investigative network known as the Regional Information Sharing System (RISS). Before the Patriot Act, RISS was used only in criminal investigations.

Supporters of the Patriot Act believe it will increase federal law enforcement's ability to respond to terrorism and will create an intelligence conduit to improve communication among local, state, and federal police agencies (U.S. Department of Justice, n.d.). They believe counterterrorism will be strengthened by combining law enforcement and national defense intelligence. Opponents of the law argue that it goes too far in threatening civil liberties and expanding police powers (Cole and Dempsey, 2002, pp. 186–187). Critics are especially concerned about sharing noncriminal intelligence during criminal investigations. The most pressing concern centers on the increased power of the government to monitor the activities of its own citizens.

The Debate about Governmental Power

The most controversial facets of counterterrorism are symbolized by the USA Patriot Act, and the most sensitive aspect of the law deals with intelligence gathering and sharing. Many diverse groups across the spectrum of American politics, from constitutional conservatives to civil libertarian activists, worry that the law will encroach on civil freedoms. The American government was founded on the idea of civil liberties. This means citizens are free from having their government infringe unreasonably on the freedoms guaranteed in the Constitution and the Bill of Rights. Stated simply, increasing the ability of the government to collect information increases executive-branch power. Therefore, opponents of increased governmental power focus their criticism on the government's intelligence activities, or information gathering. Supporters of increased intelligence activities say a nation cannot fight terrorism without gathering intelligence (for general comments on intelligence in U.S. law enforcement, see Carter, 2004).

When criminal justice and national security agencies gather information about organizations and people, they do so as an extension of the executive branch of government. Any effort to expand executive power will affect the other branches of government. The U.S. Constitution separates the powers of the three branches of government: executive, legislative, and judicial. This is known as the **separation of powers**, and these powers are also separated in the criminal justice system. Elected bodies of lawmakers (the legislative branch) pass laws, courts (the judicial branch) rule on them, and law enforcement and correctional agencies (executive branch) enforce them. This separation of powers acts as a check and balance to the amount of power wielded by each branch of government (Perl, 1998; Best, 2001; Cole and Dempsey, 2002, pp. 15–16; Carter, 2004, pp. 8–17).

A quick overview of constitutional issues illustrates points where homeland security policies and the Constitution intersect. The main body of the Constitution separates powers and prescribes duties for each branch of government. Powers not explicitly given to the federal government go to the states, and the *posse comitatus* clause forbids the use of military power to enforce civilian law. The Bill of Rights also comes into play by protecting free speech and the right to assemble (First Amendment), preventing the government from performing illegal search and seizure (Fourth Amendment), and preventing self-incrimination (Fifth Amendment). The Sixth Amendment helps to protect these rights by ensuring that suspects have access to an attorney. The **Fourteenth Amendment**, the most important amendment for law enforcement after the Bill of Rights, was added to the Constitution following the Civil War and ensures that suspects cannot lose their rights except by the due process of law. The interpretations of the Constitution and its amendments have protected American liberties for more than two centuries.

The Constitution guides the United States in war and peace, and it allows certain actions in times of emergency—actions that would be prohibited if there were no emergency. This makes terrorism a constitutionally murky subject, a cloudy area obscuring the boundary separating war and peace, because many people disagree about the nature of terrorism. Many legal scholars argue that terrorism is not a continuing emergency (Cole and Dempsey, 2002, pp. 189–201). For example, America's enemies of September 11 used terrorists trained in military-style camps to attack civilian targets and military forces engaged in peacetime activities. Logically, national security agencies, such as military forces and the CIA, try to prevent attacks whether they are engaged in a war or not. Criminal justice agencies do not take actions for war; they protect individual rights, and local, state, and federal courts are not charged with national defense (see del Carmen, 1991, pp. 73–176). Controversy arises when criminal systems and the defense establishment begin to blend their activities.

National Public Radio broadcast a special report focusing on constitutional issues in December 2001, and matters quickly lined up along

separation of powers
The distribution of power among the executive, legislative, and judicial branches of government. When powers are separated, they are assumed to be balanced. No one branch can take control of the government.

Fourteenth Amendment
A person cannot be deprived of freedom or property by the government unless the government follows all the procedures demanded for legal prosecution.

party lines. Attorney general John Ashcroft called for the right to deport suspected terrorists after secret hearings, and defense secretary Donald Rumsfeld gave orders to detain accused al Qaeda terrorists without trial. Two of the detainees were U.S. citizens. Critics argued that such actions endangered the rights of Americans (Seelye, 2002).

Senate Judiciary Committee chair Patrick Leahy (D-Vermont) said the executive orders coming from the Bush administration were disconcerting. According to Senator Leahy, President Bush's counterterrorist proposals threatened the system of checks and balances, giving the executive branch of government too much power. Attorney general Ashcroft disagreed with Senator Leahy's conclusions, arguing that the proposed guidelines were solely to protect the country from terrorists. This constitutional theme runs through discussions of homeland security. One group is skeptical of increased executive power, and the other sees it as logically necessary to protect the country.

Several other issues come to the forefront with regard to civil liberties. Civil rights attorney Nancy Chang (2001) criticizes the Patriot Act on the basis of democracy. She points out that the act was rushed through the House and Senate, with no public hearings and no time for public debate. There were no conference or committee reports. No time was allowed for security needs to be examined; the legislation came quickly in the emotional tide of September 11. The most important aspect, she finds, is the increased ability of the government to look into the affairs of its own citizens. By allowing the government to blur the distinction between defense intelligence and criminal evidence, the Patriot Act tramples on reasonable expectations of privacy.

Others argue that the Patriot Act is an unreasonable attack on electronic communication (Electronic Frontier Foundation, 2001b). According to this line of thought, the government overreacted to September 11. Technological societies are open to attack by subnational groups or even deranged individuals, and protection requires thoughtful, reflective analysis and reaction. Instead, Congress rushed legislation, amending fifteen different statutes. The law gives federal law enforcement agencies the right to monitor Internet searches and to keep tabs on individual queries. The government is allowed to conduct roving wiretaps without probable cause in the hope of obtaining information. For many, the provision in Title II forcing Internet service providers to give information on their users to federal law enforcement agencies is not acceptable.

Not everyone believes the Patriot Act represents an attack on individual rights. For example, two senators with strong civil liberties records think criticism of the act is premature (Straub, 2002). Senator Dianne Feinstein (D-California) believes we cannot rush to judgment. Time will show how the act is used in the real world. It may be necessary to revisit the law, but first we need to see how it is implemented. Senator Charles Schumer (D-New York) believes the law is balanced. It limits personal freedom while reasonably enhancing security. Both senators think it is necessary to balance civil liberties and social protection.

Championed by the Bush administration, the Patriot Act is a lightning rod in the debate pitting national security against civil liberties. Technological societies are vulnerable to technological attack—whether from individuals engaged in a killing spree, criminal gangs, or terrorist conspiracies—regardless of ideology. The more sophisticated the attackers, the greater the chances for multiple deaths. September 11 exacerbated the issue, but America was vulnerable before the hijackings and remains vulnerable today. Supporters claim that the Patriot Act and other governmental actions are necessary for security. Critics believe that loss of civil liberties in the name of security is unreasonable. This debate continues, and the courts have yet to rule on the issues.

Debate and the 2006 Law

The 2001 Patriot Act was scheduled for renewal in 2005. Although the House of Representatives voted to renew the law in December, in the Senate some believed the 2001 law passed too quickly. They argued that many of the provisions expanded governmental authority too far, and they were leery about making some of the intelligence-gathering practices permanent. Although many of the Republicans wanted to pass the extension of the Patriot Act before the 2006 elections, the Democratic Senate leaders urged caution. Some in the president's own party had reservations about some of the Patriot Act's provisions (Holland, 2005).

How the Patriot Act had been used in prior years caused the reservations. The Bush administration contended that law enforcement agencies employed the provisions carefully, using them only to stop terrorist attacks. In testimony before Congress, officials from the Justice Department assured the nation that no agency overstepped its bounds. Critics did not agree. They accused the government of selectively releasing information and hiding unfavorable reports. They also said that agencies were classifying public documents in an effort to hide governmental activities. They were especially critical of "sneak and peek" provisions that allowed the government to search for information without informing the person who was being investigated (Regan, 2004).

Several lawmakers, both Republican and Democratic, were concerned about provisions for gathering secret information and the original Patriot Act stipulations about the denial of legal representation in terrorism investigations. In the spring of 2006 the White House and Congress reached a compromise on some of the controversial articles of the Patriot Act and new provisions were approved. Under the renewed act, when the government seeks information, the request can be challenged in court. When information is requested in a terrorist investigation, suspects and others involved may talk about it. Suspects may also seek counsel from an attorney. The renewal also requires retailers to maintain information on sales of over-the-counter drugs that could be used to produce methamphetamines.

Some of the less controversial articles were renewed. The government has the right to intercept communications. Criminal intelligence can be given to agencies charged with national security, and the security community can openly communicate with the law enforcement community. The renewed law also extends the time suspects can be kept under surveillance and allows the government to seize electronic or other evidence with a warrant. The law also requires Internet and e-mail providers to hand over records. Finally, the renewed law allows federal law enforcement agencies to collect national security intelligence if that is their "significant purpose." Before the Patriot Act, national security could be the only purpose (Associated Press, 2006).

Self-Check

- *Why is it necessary to limit governmental power, even when the nation is threatened by terrorism?*
- *Describe the most controversial aspects of the 2001 Patriot Act.*
- *How were those issues addressed in 2006?*

Terrorism and the Constitution

One of the major stumbling blocks between civil rights advocates and the government during the Bush administration was the role of the president. When they came to power in 2000, both President Bush and Vice President Richard Cheney believed the power of the presidency had been watered down in past presidencies and that Congress and "activist judges" had taken too much authority from the president's office. They sought to increase presidential power (Mayer, 2006). This resulted in a series of confrontations about power, confrontations that spilled over into counterterrorist operations.

Constitutional Concerns

David Cole and James Dempsey (2002) sent out a warning after the 1996 counterterrorist law took effect in the wake of the 1995 Oklahoma City bombing. They reiterated their warning after passage of the 2001 USA Patriot Act. Stated simply, they fear that federal law enforcement power is growing too strong in a wave of national hysteria. Their thesis is that counterterrorist legislation empowers law enforcement agencies to enforce political law. By contrast, terrorists must violate criminal laws to practice terrorism. Therefore, Cole and Dempsey argue, it is best to keep the police out of politics and focused on criminal violations. If terrorists are prosecuted under criminal law, the Constitution will be preserved.

Cole and Dempsey point to four cases that illustrate their fears. In the late 1960s and early 1970s, the FBI trampled the rights of suspects and citizens through COINTELPRO, its counterintelligence program. Second, from 1981 to 1990, the FBI overreacted against U.S. citizens who expressed sympathy for revolutionaries in El Salvador. The FBI even designated friends of activists "guilty by association." Third, in the 1990s Muslims and Palestinians were targeted by investigations despite there being no reasonable suspicions they were involved in a crime. Finally, during the 1990s, political investigations of radical environmentalists and others expanded.

Citing a group of law professors that petitioned Congress to limit political investigations, Cole and Dempsey argue that law enforcement should gather intelligence only when there is reason to suspect criminal activity. They worry that the 1996 counterterrorist legislation and the 2001 Patriot Act and its 2006 renewal give the police power to regulate political activity. The real danger is not using reasonable efforts to fight terrorism, they say. There are certain instances when the intelligence community should share information with the criminal community. For example, when Osama bin Laden was charged in the bombings of Dar es Salaam and Nairobi, it would have been appropriate for the FBI and CIA to share information. Cole and Dempsey worry that Congress has given these and other agencies too much power to share intelligence without judicial review. The proper role of the courts, they argue, is to oversee the use of police power.

Their argument illustrates the passions involved in counterterrorism. The Cole-Dempsey thesis is endorsed by a host of jurists, civil rights organizations, legal scholars, and die-hard conservatives who support many of the Bush administration's other efforts. There is even support for their position inside law enforcement, especially within the FBI.

The Cole-Dempsey argument is directly applicable to two critical arguments made during the Bush administration, and both positions are applicable to the idea of increasing executive power as the primary method for countering terrorism. President Bush and Vice President Cheney maintain that the president has the power to designate certain terrorists as **enemy combatants** and subject them to trial by special military courts. They also contend that the president has the authority to allow national security intelligence agencies to intercept telephone calls that originate in the United States but are directed to suspected terrorists in foreign countries (Savage, 2006). Critics maintain that this is abuse of power (Leahy, 2006).

The issues about executive power form the crux of the debate about civil rights and security, and it is no different than the examples cited earlier from ancient Greece and Rome and the American Civil War. Some societies give presidents, prime ministers, and other leaders increased power when a nation is threatened. Because leaders sometimes abuse those powers, civil libertarians are almost always suspicious of additional authority. It is the primary issue involved in discussions about the Constitution, the role of executive authority, and the subsequent actions of law enforcement agencies.

enemy combatant
A legal term used to describe nonstate paramilitary captives from Afghanistan. The term was later applied to all jihadist terrorists by the Bush administration.

Increased Executive Powers

Several Constitutional scholars have examined the issue of increasing executive powers to combat terrorism. Lewis Katz (2001) believed in limited government before September 11, but he rethought his position in the wake of the attacks. He finds an analogy in drug enforcement. America launched its "war on drugs" and soon discovered it could not thwart drug traffickers under constitutional rules of evidence. As a result, police power has been growing since 1971, Katz argues, and citizen protection under the Fourth Amendment has been decreasing.

reasonableness

The actions an average person would take when confronted with certain circumstances. This is a Fourth Amendment doctrine.

Leery of government, Katz says the real test of the Fourth Amendment is **reasonableness**. In normal times, police officers can be held to a higher standard of behavior than in times of emergency. September 11 constituted an emergency. It was not unreasonable to interview Middle Eastern immigrants, Katz concludes, nor was it unreasonable to increase electronic surveillance powers. Although a long-time opponent of a national identification system, Katz now says such a system would not be unconstitutional, provided citizens were not ordered to produce identification without reasonable suspicion. Actions taken to prevent another September 11, he argues, do not violate the Fourth Amendment when they are reasonable.

Katz does believe some governmental actions are unreasonable. Eavesdropping on attorney-client conversations, for example, violates the Sixth Amendment, a suspect's right to counsel. Military tribunals deny the presumption of innocence. He argues that we cannot sacrifice the very liberties we are fighting to preserve. Katz's argument indicates that the balance of powers is a dynamic entity vacillating according to circumstances. In other words, there is no blanket policy of reasonableness, and care must be taken to balance security with civil liberties.

Sherry Colb (2001) of Rutgers University School of Law also applies a doctrine of reasonableness. Examining the issue of racial profiling, Colb concedes that police in America are facing a new enemy. Racial profiling has not helped the police control drugs, she argues, and it violates the due process clause of the Fourteenth Amendment. Yet the scope of September 11 calls into question previous assumptions about profiling, or targeting specific groups of people on the basis of race, ethnicity, religion, or other social factors. As police agencies assemble profiles of terrorists, one of the characteristics may be ethnicity.

Colb believes any profiling system, including one having ethnicity as a factor, will yield many more investigative inquiries than apprehensions. The reason is that there are only a small number of terrorists in any group, regardless of their profile. The population of people matching the profile is greater than the population of terrorists in the profile group. By the same token, a number of terrorists may fall within a particular ethnic group, and the urgency of September 11 may require action. If a terrorist profile develops and it includes race as one of the characteristics, Colb suggests that some opponents of ethnic profiling may find they endorse it in the case of counterterrorism.

The Bush administration moved quickly in the wake of September 11 (Van Natta, 2002). Wanting to do everything possible to catch terrorists, the Department of Justice scrapped the restrictions it placed on agents in earlier times. Issuing new guidelines, it freed the FBI from the requirement to rely on reasonable suspicion before launching an inquiry. Unless the courts rule otherwise or legislative bodies intervene, agents are free to search for indicators of illegal activity in open-source information, including the Internet. They can monitor chat rooms or engage in data mining. Agents can go undercover in political or religious organizations to search for threats to security. No longer required to seek central-office approval, local FBI offices would be empowered to launch inquiries based on their own information and initiative.

New guidelines, executive orders, and military tribunals have created strange twists in the criminal justice system. Reporter Katherine Seelye (2002) examines the summer of 2002 when two foreign-born terrorist suspects were arrested on the basis of probable cause and were sent to trial. At the same time, two U.S. citizens, Yaser Esam Hamdi and Jose Padilla, were held by military force without representation. Hamdi was fighting for al Qaeda when captured in Afghanistan in November 2001, and Padilla was arrested on May 8, 2002, for his alleged involvement in a plot to detonate a dirty bomb in the United States. Hamdi and Padilla, both of whom would have been criminally charged before September 11, were detained much like prisoners of war, whereas two alleged terrorists arrested on U.S. soil were afforded the rights of criminal suspects. Hamdi was released in September 2004.

Ruth Wedgwood (2002), a former federal prosecutor who now teaches law, offers an explanation of the irony of Americans being detained militarily and foreigners being held under civilian arrest. She says al Qaeda attacked civilian targets, gaining an advantage in the U.S. criminal justice system. Al Qaeda, Wedgwood says, has learned it is best to recruit U.S. citizens for operations because citizens are not subject to arbitrary arrest. Pointing to Jose Padilla, Wedgwood states that his arrest represents a conundrum between reconciling public safety and the law. The issues surface in the difference between intelligence operations and law enforcement administration. In short, she says, going to trial means exposing intelligence sources for the sake of a criminal conviction.

Wedgwood presents the logic of the two situations. Common sense dictates that the detention of terrorists does not follow the pattern of criminal arrests. Terrorists are detained because no writ, no law, and no court order will stop them from attacking. They must be physically restrained, Wedgwood says. The purpose of detention, she argues, is not to engage in excessive punishment but to keep terrorists from returning to society. She admits that the situation presents a public dilemma for a nation under the rule of law.

Wedgwood argues that indefinite detention by executive order is not the most suitable alternative. Terrorists could be given a military hearing to determine whether they continue to represent a threat. A panel of judges might rule on the danger of releasing suspected terrorists from custody. The Constitution is not a suicide pact, she says, citing a famous court decision. Common sense demands a reasonable solution to the apparent dichotomy between freedom and security.

E. V. Konotorovich (2002) is not as concerned about executive orders as Wedgwood. The stakes are so high, he argues, that the United States must make all reasonable efforts to stop the next attack. Torture is out of the question in this country, but drugs are a viable alternative. Police are allowed to do body-cavity searches for contraband in prison, Konotorovich argues, and the September 11 attacks make abhorrence for such searches pale in the face of massive terrorism. Drugs should not be used for prosecution, he says, but they are acceptable for gaining information. The threat is real, and legal arguments against obtaining information are illusory. Americans captured by al Qaeda have been quickly executed. Konotorovich believes Americans must take decisive actions against such terrorists.

Limiting Executive Powers

Susan Herman (2001) of Brooklyn Law School vehemently urges a different approach to counterterrorism, believing the Patriot Act to be a law that throws the balance of powers out of kilter. She asserts that Congress has relinquished its power to the president and failed to provide any room for judicial review. Congress, Herman argues, has chosen to fight terrorism by providing funding to the Bush administration, relinquishing its powers to check the executive branch. Proposals coming from the administration complement congressional actions by increasing the executive power to take actions without judicial review. For Herman, the beginning of the "war on terrorism" translates to a "war on the balance of powers." Herman's argument is based in constitutional law. She compares the USA Patriot Act with two previous sweeping pieces of legislation: the 1968 Crime Control and Safe Streets Act and the 1978 Foreign Intelligence Surveillance Act (FISA). Both laws provide guidelines for domestic surveillance.

Title III of the safe-streets act mandates judicial review of police surveillance. Under Title III, criminal evidence cannot be gathered without prior approval from a federal court, and although a judge reviews a request for surveillance in secrecy, the police must prove that wiretaps or other means of electronic eavesdropping will lead to establishing probable cause for a crime. FISA surveillance differs from Title III warrants. Under FISA, various forms of eavesdropping can be used to gather intelligence. A special judicial review is required before surveillance can be initiated, and any evidence gathered during the investigation cannot be used in a criminal prosecution.

The constitutional concern Herman voices partially focuses on judicial review. The courts have not been as vigilant in protecting individual rights during intelligence cases as they are in criminal trials. For example, she cites the record of FISA requests. Between 1978 and 2001 federal law enforcement officers applied for 4,275 FISA warrants. They were all granted.

In fairness to the judicial reviewers, you should remember that evidence gleaned from these warrants is not used in criminal prosecutions, but this is not the issue bothering Herman. She compares FISA warrants to the type of surveillance proposed under the Patriot Act and concludes that the Patriot Act allows the government to watch its own citizens with similar rules.

There is no guarantee that such surveillance will exclude evidence used in criminal prosecutions. The other part of Herman's argument focuses on the relationship between executive and legislative branches, and she feels the Patriot Act concentrates too much power in the executive branch. The act gives the attorney general power to detain and deport aliens with less judicial review than was required before September 11, and the attorney general is required only to have reason to believe the action is necessary. Courts, she states, would require a much higher standard of proof. The Patriot Act also gives the attorney general and the secretary of state the power to designate certain associations as terrorist groups, and they may take actions against people and organizations associated with these groups. Herman believes Congress has failed to aggressively seek a role in counterterrorism under the Patriot Act. By increasing executive powers, the Constitution is threatened. Her primary fear, she concludes, is that increased executive powers will be used to mask an attack on civil liberties.

The American Civil Liberties Union (ACLU) (2002) voices other concerns with civil liberties. Citing increased executive powers to detain immigrants, the ACLU charges the attorney general with trying to gut the role of immigration courts. The ACLU expresses two concerns. First, after September 11 the attorney general ordered the detention of several hundred immigrants. He refused to openly charge most of the detainees and refused to make the list known for several months. In addition, Attorney General Ashcroft sought to have the rules for detaining and deporting immigrants streamlined. He wanted to make the process more efficient by decreasing the amount of judicial review involved in immigration and naturalization cases. These issues alarmed the ACLU.

Tightening immigration laws, the ACLU argues, is a smoke screen for increasing executive powers at the expense of individual rights. The ACLU believes the attorney general will rely on political issues rather than the rules of evidence when deciding which cases to prosecute. With immigration courts streamlined, there will be no judicial body to oversee executive decisions. The ACLU also believes President Bush will appoint judges sympathetic to Attorney General Ashcroft's views. This process undermines civil liberties, the ACLU says, at the expense of the Constitution.

To demonstrate the point, the ACLU points to the post–September 11 case of Ali Maqtari. Married to a member of the armed forces, Maqtari was driving his wife to Fort Campbell, Kentucky, when police stopped him for questioning and detained him without probable cause to believe he had committed a crime. He was held for eight weeks without formal charges, according to the ACLU. After Maqtari was granted a hearing, a court ruled that the government's position was unjustified and he was released. Without effective judicial review, the ACLU says, Maqtari may not have been released. Coming to grips with terrorism should not involve scrapping personal freedoms protected by the Constitution.

Executive Power and the Courts

While the struggle between Congress and the president continued and legal scholars argued positions about executive authority, the courts began to review some of the issues involved in counterterrorism. One of the first issues involved the detention of enemy combatants in Guantánamo Bay, Cuba. The government contended it could try the defendants in special military tribunals, apart from normal criminal prosecutions and military law. Judges were not swayed by this argument.

Both civilian and military courts, using similar language, handed down decisions blocking the government's desire to establish special military courts that violate the civil rights established in the American legal system (Bravin, 2007). In the Hamdi case, previously discussed, courts ruled that defendants were entitled to contest the basis of their arrests. The government cannot hold a person without a hearing to ensure that an arrest is justified by probable cause.

There are several other cases where courts limited executive power. The Supreme Court ruled that the detainees in Guantánamo could contest the charges against them, much in the same manner as the Hamdi case. In 2006 the courts ordered the government to transfer Jose Padilla, the American originally accused of conspiring to use a dirty bomb, from the military to the civilian criminal court system where he was convicted of criminal conspiracy in 2007. Later in 2006 the Supreme Court declared that the military tribunal system established for enemy combatants was illegal. In 2007 a military court in Guantánamo dismissed cases against two defendants at Guantánamo Bay on the basis of the earlier Supreme Court decision (Bravin, 2007).

Although the Bush administration won some of its early battles to gain more power, the courts have been increasingly limiting executive power (see Expanding the Concept: Court Reversals). One of the primary reasons is that the president acted without specific congressional authority. The courts have historically supported special laws when Congress has given permission, but they are skeptical when no law is in place. According to an analysis in the *Wall Street Journal* (Bravin, 2007), the Bush administration did not seek such authorization after 9/11 because it feared that Congress would not grant it.

Interestingly, these court reversals of executive authority cannot be blamed on liberal courts or "activist judges." Few people would claim that the military tribunals established at Guantánamo were filled with overzealous civil libertarians. The last Supreme Court reversals came

Court Reversals

Despite the attempts to increase executive authority in counterterrorism, several court decisions have reversed policies from the White House. These include the following:

June 2004—Two decisions that allow enemy combatants the right to contest their arrests.

April 2006—A decision that prevents the prosecution of U.S. citizens arrested in the United States from being tried outside the criminal court system.

June 2006—The military tribunal system established at Guantánamo is declared illegal because it did not have congressional approval.

June 2007—A military tribunal dismisses charges against two enemy combatants based on the June 2006 Supreme Court decision.

Source: Bravin, 2007.

from a bench dominated by conservative appointees and a chief justice selected by President Bush. Despite all of the political debate about increasing executive power, the courts seem to be demonstrating that any effort to fight terrorism will be done within the rule of law.

Self-Check

- *Why are constitutional scholars concerned with intelligence gathering and the prevention of terrorism?*
- *Explain the benefits of expanding or limiting executive power.*
- *What effect do courts have on the power of the executive branch to confront terrorism?*

Civil Liberties and Police Work

The FBI, with an eye on the court system and a director's promise to fight terrorism within the law, conducted an internal audit to make sure that its actions were legal. The audit found that the FBI might have violated its own rules or federal laws in national security investigations more than 1,000 times since 2002. The vast majority of violations dealt with storing information from e-mails and Internet service providers that agents were not authorized to collect. This indicated a weakness in bureau procedures, and it unveiled something the FBI feared. Its agents did not understand their authority in national security investigations

(Solomon, 2007). Critics may point to overreaction, but it should be noted that the FBI performed this audit on its own.

As part of the executive branch of government, law enforcement agencies stand at the forefront of counterterrorism. Whether civil liberties are protected or whether they are abused most frequently depends on the way police officers handle their responsibilities. This applies to federal agencies such as the FBI, the Bureau of Alcohol, Tobacco, and Firearms (ATF), and the Secret Service, but it is also applicable to state, local, and tribal law enforcement departments.

Controversies in Law Enforcement

Effective counterterrorist policy is based on intelligence. The 9/11 Commission Report (2004, pp. 339–348) criticizes federal agencies for failing to recognize and share intelligence. The Patriot Act, before the commission's findings, was designed to facilitate intelligence gathering and to ensure intelligence sharing. Although this remains controversial on the federal level, sharing is logical because the federal government is constitutionally responsible for national defense. The government can make the argument that *any* federal agency can assist in this process. The problem comes when the federal government requests assistance from state and local governments. When the federal government asks state agencies to collect and forward national defense intelligence, many people take notice.

Any attempt to use state and local law enforcement in intelligence-gathering operations will have constitutional implications. The police may be used in homeland security, but there are strong and logical positions against this and equally powerful arguments supporting it. Regardless, even when the executive branch proposes a course of action, police operations will be influenced by court decisions. Local law enforcement's role in homeland defense cannot be developed in a constitutional vacuum.

The criminal justice system collects *criminal* intelligence, not information regarding national security. It collects information when it has reasonable suspicion to believe people are involved in crimes. Although some people may argue about the type of criminal intelligence the police gather, no one questions their right to gather information about criminal activity (see Commission on Accreditation for Law Enforcement Agencies, 1990; Walker, 1992; Radelet and Carter, 2000; Carter, 2004, pp. 8–17).

The dilemma emerges because terrorism moves the police into a new intelligence realm. Criminals engage in crime for economic gain or psychological gratification. Terrorists are political actors using crime to strike their enemies. This causes terrorists to encounter the police, but not from the standpoint of traditional criminals. To gather counterterrorist intelligence, the police are forced to collect political information. If state and local law enforcement agencies are included in national defense, they will collect information having no relation to criminal investigations. No matter which position you might support, this is a dilemma for American democracy. The police are not designed to collect political information (Schmitt, 2002).

Although lacking a defined role, the police in the United States have traditionally been associated with crime control. They respond to crime, prevent crime, and engage in social-maintenance tasks, such as traffic control, inside local communities. Although not a formal role, responding to and preventing crime has become the de facto purpose of American law enforcement. Local communities and states have empowered agencies to keep records to assist them in anticrime efforts, but many federal, state, and local laws, as well as civil rights groups, have imposed limits on the type of information the police may gather and retain. Any move to include the police in an intelligence-gathering system alters the expectations local communities have about law enforcement. Communities may decide to empower their police agencies to collect intelligence, but this means changing the focus of police work (see Manning, 1976).

Terrorism, both domestic and international, poses a variety of problems; Richard Best (2001) summarizes well the dilemma over the role for criminal justice. On the one hand, state and local law enforcement agencies are in a unique position to collect and analyze information from their communities. Corrections officials can perform the same role by both incarcerating terrorists and gaining information through jailhouse intelligence. Law enforcement and correctional agencies can become the eyes and ears of domestic intelligence. On the other hand, when the criminal justice system has participated in national defense in the past, abuses have occurred. The primary question is Does criminal justice have a role in homeland security? Secondary questions are Do criminal justice agencies want to assume this role? Does the public they serve want them to assume it? There are no easy answers to these questions.

National Security and Crime

Among the controversies surrounding the USA Patriot Act is the role for criminal justice, especially law enforcement. The debate comes to a head when the role of intelligence is discussed. There are two general schools of thought about the role of the police in intelligence gathering. One position can be summarized as "eyes and ears." Advocates of this position believe that state and local law enforcement should be used as extensions of, or the eyes and ears of, America's intelligence agencies. They believe the police should collect information and forward it to the appropriate intelligence unit. Extreme proponents of this position would use special police units to collect information beyond potential evidence used in criminal investigations. The purpose of such units would be to monitor the activities of political groups that might engage in violence.

Another way of thinking can be called traditional crime response and prevention. Supporters of this perspective fear that police intelligence-gathering activities will interfere with the traditional police missions of fighting crime and providing a social service. They believe that other agencies should gather intelligence. Some other people have a parallel view, fearing expanded police powers.

After September 11, the difference between these two positions became more than an academic debate. Local, state, and federal police agencies began to share information at an unprecedented level. State and local agencies expanded training activities in terrorism, and Attorney General Ashcroft ordered the FBI to create more Joint Terrorism Task Forces (JTTFs). The attorney general also used his prosecutors, the U.S. Attorneys who represent the government in the federal court system, to create Anti-Terrorism Task Forces (ATTFs) in all the nation's U.S. Attorneys' offices. The name changed to Anti-Terrorist Assistance Coordinators (ATACs) in 2003. All the federal efforts were based on the assumption that local, state, and federal agencies would work together. The attorney general also called for a seamless interface between law enforcement and defense intelligence. The intelligence role in law enforcement is what frightens civil libertarians.

Intelligence, Networks, and Roles

All levels of law enforcement form nodes in a network opposed to terrorism. Although police agencies have a multitude of other functions, their primary roles in preventing terrorism involve information gathering and sharing, protecting citizens and property, and investigating criminal conspiracies (J. White, 2007). Collecting, analyzing, and storing criminal intelligence requires a criminal predicate. Under the Fourth Amendment, law enforcement personnel cannot collect intelligence without the standard of reasonable suspicion. As stated in federal guidelines (28 CFR Part 23), the police must have evidence that a crime is taking or about to take place or that a person is engaged or about to engage in criminal activity, before information can be gathered, analyzed, and stored. Information involved in national security may not meet this test. Law enforcement is not to assume the national security mission. In other words, police officers should continue their assigned role in law enforcement and legally share information (Carter, 2004, pp. 5–18; J. White, 2004b, pp. 73–74). See Expanding the Concept: The War on Drugs as an Intelligence Model.

Networks encourage the flow of information. Carter (2004, pp. 192–193) argues that when information is not shared it loses its value. It is not enough to maintain community partnerships; agencies need to act in conjunction. Total criminal intelligence (TCI) involves sharing; indeed, TCI does not work unless agencies share criminal intelligence. Sharing information neither poses a threat to civil liberties nor reduces the effectiveness of partnerships. Shared information enhances crime prevention and decreases fear inside a community. It allows the intelligence function to operate effectively, when it is accomplished within legal guidelines.

The civil liberties danger appears when agencies inside a network either act illegally or forget their role. The growth of terrorism has thrown

The War on Drugs as an Intelligence Model

The war on drugs has produced a national system of police intelligence gathering and dissemination. Combined federal, state, and local law enforcement agencies operate in conjunction to gather intelligence and conduct operations.

Proponents hail this process as a model of sharing resources and intelligence. They point to cooperation among agencies and investigative information-sharing systems as the answer to the intelligence problem (National Drug Intelligence Center, 2002). At the national level, drug intelligence reports are synthesized and disseminated to state and local agencies. On the surface, these multijurisdictional efforts seem to be an effective tool in countering drug traffickers.

Opponents have a different view. Many police administrators believe the systems are not effective, and they refuse to participate in them (Herman, 2001). Other people outside law enforcement look at the intelligence network and claim it to be both a failure and an assault on the Fourth Amendment. Proponents of this position state that the war on drugs is ineffective, and the real loser in the process is civil liberty. Critics feel that trying to collect drug intelligence merely leads to labeling certain people or groups without making a dent in drug traffic.

law enforcement into an arena traditionally reserved for national security, but police officers are neither intelligence agents nor soldiers. Confronting a terror network requires resources for a long-term struggle and a solidified national will. It does not and should not require extraconstitutional law enforcement actions. Stated more succinctly, the ideological Salafi jihadist network does not threaten American civil liberties, but an improper police response may (see Jenkins, 2006, pp. 169–177). Law enforcement's role in national defense is to continue efforts at community partnerships.

In testimony before the House Subcommittee on Homeland Security (C-Span, 2007), Brian Jenkins, Frank Cilluffo, and Salam al Marayati offered an interesting assessment of the role of community partnerships in preventing terrorism. Rather than militarizing the problem, they presented terrorism, especially the jihadist movement, as a social idea. It appeals to young people, especially confused and potentially violent young men. There are times when force must be used, but Jenkins, Cilluffo, and al Marayati equated terrorism to other social problems such as child abuse, illegal drug use, gangs, drunk driving, and family fights. Law enforcement agencies became involved in education, intervention, information gathering, and enforcement in each of these areas. As Jenkins said, they play their role without violating civil rights.

War has not changed, tactics have. Terrorism represents a tactical change in conflict. Police work has not changed, nor has the police function. Deeper community relationships will enhance law enforcement's role in national security by preventing crime, reducing fear, solving problems, and increasing the flow of information. Returning to traditional crime fighting roles or militarizing the police will reduce police effectiveness. Police operating deeply in the community in the service role help to provide for the common defense (J. White, 2007).

Militarization and Police Work

There are roles for law enforcement in homeland security, but there are questions about the necessity of developing these functions along military lines. Some policy makers have responded by increasing the military posturing of the police. In other words, some police agencies have developed units that appear more suited for military functions than police work. On the other hand, some administrators and critics stress the civilian aspect of law enforcement, and they lament the paramilitary approach to controlling social problems. The debate between these two approaches will become more intense as the police role in homeland defense is institutionalized over time.

militarization

Responding to social problems with military solutions. In law enforcement militarization is usually characterized by martial law.

Before discussing the issue, it is necessary to define **militarization**. Military forces are necessary for national defense, and they are organized along principles of rigid role structures, hierarchies, and discipline. A military posture prescribes unquestioning obedience to orders and aggressive action in the face of an enemy. In Clausewitz's sense, military forces are either at war or at peace, and when engaged in war, their efforts are targeted toward an enemy. Any bureaucracy can be militarized when it adopts military postures and attitudes, and the police are no exception. If the United States is engaged in a war against terrorism, some policy makers will inevitably want the police to look more and more like a military force, especially because the Constitution prevents the American armed forces from enforcing domestic law. In this context militarization refers to a process in which individual police units or entire agencies begin to approach specific problems with military values and attitudes. They adopt paramilitary dress, behave with military discipline, and, most importantly, prepare to make war with an enemy.

In 1967 the International Association of Chiefs of Police (IACP) discussed the problem of confronting violent demonstrators (International Association of Chiefs of Police, 1967, pp. 307–327). The late 1960s was a time of social change and violent confrontation, and state and local police frequently found themselves facing hostile crowds. In response, the police often imported military maneuvers to control violent demonstrations, and the tactics were successful. The IACP, however, was not quick to jump on a military bandwagon. Its training manual instructs police officers to use minimal force to solve potential problems. The appearance of paramilitary force should be a last resort and developed only when a situation had deteriorated. The IACP, America's largest association of state and local police executives, has traditionally favored the civil role of policing over a militaristic approach.

Terrorism may bring a change in attitudes. For example, because many forms of terrorism require resources beyond the capacity of local police agencies, law enforcement has been forced to turn to the military for assistance. State and local law enforcement agencies have few international resources compared with the defense and intelligence communities. Finally, terrorism demands a team approach. Law enforcement officers exercise quite a bit of individual discretion when operating on calls or initiating activities, and they generally work alone or in small groups of two and three. Terrorism, like special events, changes the equation, bringing hundreds of officers together in a single function. The temptation may be to militarize the police response to terrorism.

Two trends may be seen in this area. The first comes from violent demonstrations. The Metro-Dade Police Department in Florida developed an effective method, called the field-force technique, for responding to urban riots after a particularly bad riot in 1980. By 1995 hundreds of U.S. police agencies were using the technique, and it now seems firmly established. The technique calls for responding to a growing disorderly crowd, a crowd that can become a precursor to a riot, with a massive show of organized police force. Officers assemble in an area away from the violent gathering; isolate the area, providing a route for the crowd to disperse; and then overwhelm it with military riot tactics. A field-force exercise looks as though a small army has moved into an area using nonlethal violence (see Christopher, 1999, pp. 398–407; Kraska and Kappeler, 1999, pp. 435–449).

A second source of militarization comes from police tactical units. These special operations units are called out to deal with barricaded gunmen, hostage situations, and some forms of terrorism. They are also frequently used on high-risk drug raids. Tactical units use military weapons, small-unit tactics, and recognized military small-unit command structures (see Cappel, 1979; Jacobs, 1983; Mattoon, 1987). In the past few years many of the units have abandoned the blue or brown tactical uniforms of police agencies for military camouflage, making it virtually impossible to distinguish them from military combat units.

Peter Kraska (1996) takes exception to these trends in militarization. He argues that police in America have gradually assumed a more military posture since violent standoffs with domestic extremists, and he fears terrorism will lead to a further excuse to militarize. This will adversely affect democracy, Kraska argues, because it will lead police to picture their jurisdictions as war zones and their mission as military victory. If the problem of terrorism is militarized, other social problems will see the same fate. Kraska's point is well taken. As Michael Howard (2002) states, calling our struggle with terrorism a "war" creates a variety of conceptual problems. In addition, Americans have become used to military metaphors for other social problems such as "wars" on drugs or poverty.

Most terrorism analysts believe terrorism is best left to the police whenever possible (see Wardlaw, 1982, pp. 87–102). The difficulty is that the growing devastation of single events sometimes takes the problem beyond local police control. In addition (U.S. Department of Defense, 2001; Perl, 2001), military forces are often targeted, and they must develop forces to protect themselves. Some of the same principles guiding military force protection will eventually spill into American policing. In the future, state and local police may face subtle social pressure to militarize the terrorist problem and respond to it with paramilitary force.

Self-Check

- *Why must civil libertarians be concerned with law enforcement power?*
- *Why should agencies in social networks maintain traditional roles?*
- *What might happen if law enforcement agencies move beyond their traditional role and act as an instrument of military force?*

SUMMARY

- Increased intelligence activities, homeland security measures, and using governmental power in preventing terrorism must be balanced with the protection of liberty. *Civil rights* refers to protection from governmental power. The basic freedoms and protection that should be granted to all people are known as human rights.
- Changes in the nature of conflict bring about a need to operate deeply in the social structure. This concept can be called *defense in depth*. Because it encompasses civil society, it is not possible to talk about such a concept with regard to homeland security without discussing civil rights.
- The USA Patriot Act, first enacted in 2001, enhanced the gathering and sharing of intelligence. It increased executive authority. Several aspects of the Patriot Act were modified in 2006. Supporters of the Patriot Act believe that it gives the government tools necessary for combating terrorism. Critics maintain that the Patriot Act threatens civil liberties.
- The Patriot Act affects the doctrine of the separation of powers, *posse comitatus*, the Bill of Rights, and the Fourteenth Amendment.
- An increase in executive-branch powers makes criminal justice more effective, but it threatens civil liberties. There are arguments for both increasing and reducing the power of the executive branch of government in preventing terrorism. Recent court decisions have emphasized the importance of balanced power among the branches of government and maintenance of civil rights.
- Criminal justice agencies protect individual civil rights. The key for successful performance is to continue preventing terrorism by

completing law enforcement functions and building community partnerships.

- Law enforcement remains a civilian entity. There is a danger when police work becomes militarized.

KEY TERMS

civil liberties (p. 460)

Bill of Rights (p. 460)

human rights (p. 461)

defense in depth (p. 461)

USA Patriot Act (p. 464)

separation of powers (p. 467)

Fourteenth Amendment (p. 467)

enemy combatant (p. 471)

reasonableness (p. 472)

militarization (p. 482)

WRITING ASSIGNMENTS

1. When societies are threatened they may look for strong leadership. Is this a new phenomenon? What tensions exist between governmental power and civil liberties? Use a metaphor to describe the zero-sum game of balancing governmental power, security, and individual rights.

2. How do the Patriot Act of 2001 and its renewal in 2006 increase executive authority? Describe some of the changes made in the 2006 compromise between Congress and the White House. What are the arguments for increasing executive power? Compare them to the arguments against such power. How have the courts reacted to the argument?

3. Should law enforcement be militarized to prevent terrorism?

Glossary

Abbas, Mahmud (1935–) The president of the Palestinian National Authority since 1995; founding member of Fatah and an executive in the PLO.

Abbasids The second Arab and Muslim dynasty ruling from Baghdad from 750 to 1258. The Abbasids lost influence and power to Turks after 950, and their empire collapsed to Mongol conquest.

Abu Bakr (circa 573–634) Also known as Abu Bakr as Saddiq, the first caliph selected by the Islamic community (*umma*) after Mohammed's death in 632. Sunnis believe Abu Bakr is the rightful heir to Mohammed's leadership, and they regard him as the first of the *Rishidun*, or Rightly Guided caliphs. He led military expeditions expanding Muslim influence to the north of Mecca.

Abu Marzuq, Musa (1951–) The "outside" leader of Hamas, who is thought to be in Damascus, Syria. He is believed to have controlled the Holy Land Foundation.

academic consensus definition A complex definition based on the work of Alex Schmid. It combines common elements of the definitions used by the leading scholars in the field of terrorism.

actionable intelligence Information that law enforcement agencies, military units, or other security forces can use to stop an attack or operation.

active cadre A military term that describes the people actually carrying out terrorist activity in an organizational hierarchy. The active cadre refers to the small terrorist group at the second level of a pyramid, under the command level.

Adnani, Tamim al- One of the most vigorous fund-raisers for jihadist causes in the United States before the 1993 World Trade Center bombing.

African Cell A French military unit stationed in Africa and France. It retains between 10,000 and 15,000 troops in various African countries, about half its strength, and answers directly to the president of France.

AIDS pandemic The number of people with HIV/AIDS (human immunodeficiency virus/acquired immunodeficiency syndrome). In 2005 Africa had 25.8 million HIV-positive adults and children. Africa has 11.5 percent of the world's population but 64 percent of its AIDS cases. From 1982 to 2005, AIDS claimed 27.5 million African lives (Cook, 2006).

Akdas, Habib (birth date unknown) Also known as Abu Anas al Turki, the founder of al Qaeda in Turkey. Akdas left Turkey to fight in Iraq after the American invasion. He was killed in a U.S. air strike in 2004.

al Andulus The Arabic name for Muslim Spain, 711–1492.

al Aqsa Intifada An uprising sparked by Ariel Sharon's visit to the Temple Mount with a group of armed escorts in September 2000. The area is considered sacred to Jews, Christians, and Muslims. Muslims were incensed by the militant aspect of Sharon's visit. Unlike the 1987 Intifada, the al Aqsa Intifada has been characterized by suicide bombings.

Al Dawa Literally, *the call*. A Shiite militia group in the Lebanese Civil War.

Algerian Civil War (1991–2000) The war that ensued after the military assumed control of the government when an Islamist party won a democratic national election. More than 100,000 people were killed.

Ali (circa 599–661) Also known as Ali ibn Abi Talib, the son of Mohammed's uncle Abu Talib and married to Mohammed's oldest daughter Fatima. Ali was Mohammed's male heir because he had no surviving sons. The followers of Ali are known as Shiites. Most Shiites believe that Mohammed gave a sermon while perched on a saddle, naming Ali the heir to Islam. Differing types of Shiites accept authority from diverse lines of Ali's heirs. Sunni Muslims believe Ali is the fourth and last Rightly Guided caliph. Both Sunnis and Shiites believe Ali tried to return Islam to the purity of Mohammed's leadership in Medina.

altruistic suicide The willingness of individuals to sacrifice their lives to benefit their primary reference group such as a family, military unit, ethnic group, or country. It may involve going on suicide missions in combat, self-sacrifice without killing others, or self-sacrifice and killing others.

Amal One of the largest militias in the Lebanese Civil War. Amal was a Shiite militia started by an Iranian Shiite scholar and eventually commanded by Nahbi Berri, a successful Lebanese leader who transformed the organization into a political party.

American Terrorism Study A study conducted with the cooperation of the FBI's Terrorist Research and Analytical Center, started in 1988, and sponsored by the U.S. House of Representatives Judiciary Subcommittee on Crime.

anarchists Those in the nineteenth-century who advocated the creation of cooperative societies without centralized governments. There were many forms of anarchy. In the popular understanding of the late nineteenth and early twentieth century, anarchists were seen as violent socialist revolutionaries. Antiglobalists calling themselves anarchists have little resemblance to their earlier counterparts.

Anglo-Irish Peace Accord An agreement signed in 1985 that was the beginning of a long-term attempt to stop terrorist violence in Northern Ireland by devising a system of political autonomy and protecting the rights of all citizens. Extremist Republicans rejected the accord because it did not unite Northern Ireland and the south. Unionists rejected it because it compromised with moderate Republicans.

Anglo-Israelism The belief that the lost tribes of Israel settled in western Europe. God's ancient promises to the Hebrews become promises to the United Kingdom, according to this belief. Anglo-Israelism predated Christian Identity and is the basis for most Christian Identity beliefs.

animal rights In this text, the single-issue focus of some extremists who attack in the name of animal rights.

Ankara The capital of Turkey since the birth of the Republic of Turkey. Ataturk and the Young Officers moved the capital there from Istanbul in 1923.

Arab nationalism The idea that the Arabs could create a European-style nation based on a common language and culture. The idea faded after the 1967 Six Days' War.

Arab socialism A school of Arab nationalism contending that a single Arab nation should have a socialist economy.

Arafat, Yasser (1929–2004) The name assumed by Mohammed al Husseini. Born in Cairo, he was a founding member of Fatah and the PLO. He merged the PLO and Fatah in 1964 and ran a terrorist campaign against Israel. After renouncing terrorism and recognizing Israel's right to exist, Arafat was president of the Palestinian National Authority from 1993 to 2004.

Argentina in 1992 and 1994 Two bombings in Buenos Aires. Terrorists struck the Israeli embassy in 1992, killing twenty-nine, and the Jewish Community Center in 1994 killing eighty-five. Imad Mugniyah is suspected to be behind the attacks.

Aryan Nations An American antigovernment, anti-Semitic, white supremacist group founded by Richard Butler. Until it was closed by a suit from the Southern Poverty Law Center, the group sponsored a Christian Identity Church called the Church of Jesus Christ, Christian.

Assad, Hafez (1930–2000) President of Syria from 1970 to 2000. He brutally suppressed a rebellion of the Muslim Brotherhood in 1982. His son Bashir Assad assumed the presidency after his death.

asymmetry A term used in guerrilla warfare and terrorism to describe how a small, weak force fights a stronger power. Asymmetrical wars are fought between sides that are grossly unequal. The less powerful side does not fight the more powerful side under the conventional rules of war because it cannot win by using these tactics.

The weaker side uses unconventional methods of fighting.

Ataturk, Kemal (1881–1938) Also known as Mustafa Kemal, a Turkish military and political leader. Ataturk dissolved the caliphate in 1923 and created the Republic of Turkey with a Western-style constitution.

ayatollahs Ranking members of the Shiite scholars, or ulema. Ayatollahs have written a theological work. They rank under grand ayatollahs, who are recognized as master scholars.

Aziz, Abdul (1950–) A founding member and spiritual leader of the PIJ. He is also known as Sheik Odeh and has several aliases.

Azzam, Abdullah (1941–1989) The Palestinian leader of Hizb ul Tahrir and spiritual mentor of bin Laden.

Baathist A member of the pan-national Arab Baath Party. Baathists were secular socialists seeking to unite Arabs in a single socialist state.

bacterial weapons Enhanced forms of bacteria that may be countered by antibiotics.

Badr The site of a battle between the Muslims of Medina and the merchants of Mecca in 624. Mohammed was unsure whether he should resist the attacking Meccans, but decided God would allow Muslims to defend their community. After victory, Mohammed said that Badr was the Lesser Jihad. Greater Jihad, he said, was seeking internal spiritual purity.

Balfour Declaration A policy statement signed by the British government in November 1917 that promised a homeland for Jews in the geographical area of biblical Israel. Sir Arthur Balfour was the British foreign secretary.

Balochistan The largest of four states in Pakistan dominated by the Baloch tribe. Many Balochs are fighting a guerrilla war against the Pakistan Army in a dispute over profits from natural resources. The central government is creating a deepwater port and international trade center in Gwadar, Pakistan's principal seaport, and displacing many Balochs.

Banna, Hassan al (1906–1949) The founder of the Muslim Brotherhood. He was murdered by agents of the Egyptian government.

Banna, Sabri al (1937–2002) The real name of Abu Nidal, Banna was a founding member of Fa-

tah, but split with Arafat in 1974. He founded militias in southern Lebanon, and he attacked Western and Israeli targets in Europe during the 1980s. In the 1990s he became a mercenary. He was murdered in Iraq, probably by the Iraqi government.

Barghouti, Marwan (1969–) A leader of Fatah and alleged leader of the al Aqsa Martyrs Brigades. A Brigades statement in 2002 claimed Barghouti was their leader. He rose to prominence during the al Aqsa Intifada, but he is currently held in an Israeli prison.

Basayev, Shamil (1965–2006) A jihadist leader in Chechnya, Basayev engineered several operations resulting in mass civilian casualties.

Beam, Louis (1946–) Ku Klux Klan leader who popularized the idea of leaderless resistance in 1992.

Belfast Agreement Also known as the Good Friday Agreement, an agreement signed in April 1998 that revamped criminal justice services, established shared government in Northern Ireland, called for the early release of prisoners involved in paramilitary organizations, and created a Commission on Human Rights and Equity. Its provisions led to the decommissioning of paramilitary organizations.

ben Yahweh, Yahweh (1935–) The name Hulon Mitchell Jr. used as leader of the Nation of Yahweh. It is Hebrew for "God the son of God."

ben Yisrael, Yehuda A proponent of Black Hebrew Israelism, claims that whites conspired to keep African Americans from learning of their divine origin.

Beslan school A Chechen terrorist attack on the first day of school in September 2004 in North Ossetia. The scene was chaotic and Russian forces were never able to establish a security perimeter. Although details remain unclear, the incident resulted in the murder of nearly 400 people, including more than 100 children.

Big Man An anthropological term to describe an important person in a tribe or clan. *Big Man* is sometimes used by political scientists to describe a dictator in a totalitarian government.

Bill of Rights The first ten amendments to the U.S. Constitution.

Black Hebrew Israelism An African American version of Christian Identity. Followers maintain that God is black and the original Hebrews were black Africans. The idea is nearly 200 years old, and most followers are nonviolent. In extreme forms, whites and Jews are demonized. In one extreme version, Death Angels were dispatched to kill white people.

Black June The rebel organization created by Abu Nidal in 1976. He changed the name to the Fatah Revolutionary Council after a rapprochement with Syria in 1981. Most analysts refer to this group simply as the Abu Nidal Organization.

Black Widows Chechen female suicide bombers. They are known as Islamic martyrs in the Chechen language.

Blair, Tony (1953–) The Labour Party prime minister of the United Kingdom from 1994 to 2007.

Bolsheviks Russian revolutionaries led by Lenin. The Bolsheviks overthrew the revolutionary government of Russia in October 1917, and Lenin established communist control in the newly formed Soviet Union.

bourgeois The middle class. *Bourgeoisie* (plural) in Marxist terminology refers to trades people, merchants, artisans and other nonpeasants excluded from the upper classes in medieval Europe. Marx called the European democracies after the French Revolution bourgeois governments, and he advocated a democracy dominated by workers.

Brady Bill A law that limits gun ownership, named for President Ronald Reagan's press secretary after he was disabled in a 1981 assassination attempt.

Branch Davidians Followers of Vernon Wayne Howell, also known as David Koresh. They lived in a compound outside Waco, Texas.

Bruder Schweigen German for *silent brothers*, the name used by two violent right-wing extremist groups, Bruder Schweigen and Bruder Schweigen Strike Force II. The late Robert Miles, leader of the Mountain Church of Jesus in Michigan, penned an article about the struggle for white supremacy, "When All of the Brothers Struggle."

bureaucracy Governmental, private-sector, and nonprofit organizations. It assumes that people organize in a hierarchy to create an organization that will solve problems.

Butler, Richard (1917–2004) A self-made millionaire and white supremacist. Butler founded the Aryan Nations in Hayden Lake, Idaho.

Cagol, Margherita (1945–1975) Also known as Mara Cagol, the wife of Renato Curcio and a member of the Red Brigades. She was killed in a shootout with Italian police a few weeks after freeing her husband from prison.

Camp David Peace Accord A peace treaty between Egypt and Israel brokered by the United States in 1979.

Capone discovery A term used by James Adams to explain the Irish Republican Army's entry into organized crime.

Cebrowski, Arthur (1942–2005) A U.S. naval officer and president of the Naval War College who championed the idea of "network-centric warfare." His ideas are instrumental in understanding methods to counter terror networks.

cell The basic unit of a traditional terrorist organization. Groups of cells form columns. Members in cells seldom know one another. In more recent terrorist structures, *cell* describes a tactical group dispatched by the network for selected operations.

chain organizations Temporary associations of diverse groups. Groups in a chain come together for a particular operation and disband after it is over.

Christian Identity An American extremist religion proclaiming white supremacy. Adherents believe that white Protestants of western European origin are the true descendants of the ancient Israelites. Believers contend that Jews were spawned by Satan and that nonwhites evolved from animals. According to this belief, white men and women are the only people created in the image of God.

civil defense Citizens engaged in homeland security.

civil liberties Individual rights granted to citizens under the U.S. Constitution.

Clausewitz, Carl von (1780–1831) A Prussian field marshal and philosopher of war. His book *On War* helped to shape military doctrine in the twentieth century.

COINTELPRO An infamous FBI counterintelligence program started in 1956. Agents involved in

COINTELPRO violated constitutional limitations on domestic intelligence gathering, and the program came under congressional criticism in the early 1970s. The FBI's abuse of power eventually resulted in restrictions on the FBI.

Colombo The capital of Sri Lanka.

column Groups of cells in a terrorist or guerrilla organization.

Combined Joint Task Force, Horn of Africa (CJTF-HOA) An American-led counterterrorist unit combining military, intelligence, and law enforcement assets of several nations in the Horn.

Committee of Public Safety Assembled by Maximilien Robespierre (1758–1794) to conduct the war against invading monarchal powers, and it evolved into the executive body of France. The Committee of Public Safety initiated the Reign of Terror.

communists Socialists who believe in a strong centralized economy controlled by a strong central government. Their ideas were summarized in *The Communist Manifesto*, written by Karl Marx and Friedrich Engels in 1848.

Council on American-Islamic Relations (CAIR) An organization that maintains that it is a Muslim civil rights and advocacy group.

coyuntura As used by Raul Sendic, the historical point where a series of ideas come together and force change.

Creatorism The deistic religion of the Creativity Movement. It claims that white people must struggle to defeat Jews and nonwhite races.

criminal intelligence Information gathered on the reasonable suspicion that a criminal activity is occurring or about to occur. It is collected by law enforcement agencies in the course of their preventive and investigative functions. It is shared on information networks such as the Regional Information Sharing System (RISS). Unlike national defense intelligence, criminal intelligence applies only in criminal law. Agencies must suspect some violation of criminal law before they can collect intelligence.

critical media consciousness The public's understanding of the media and the way stories are presented. A critically conscious audience would not simply accept a story presented in a news frame. It would look for the motives for telling the story, how the story affected social constructs and actions, and hidden details that would cause the story to be told another way.

Cuban guerrilla war A three-step process as described by Che Guevara: (1) revolutionaries join the indigenous population to form guerrilla *foco*, as Guevara called them, (2) small forces form columns and control rural areas, and (3) columns unite for a conventional offensive to overthrow government.

Cuban Revolution The guerrilla revolution led by Fidel Castro. Castro initially failed in 1956 and left for Mexico after a brief prison sentence. He returned with a small group of guerrillas and built a large guerrilla army. He overthrew the Cuban government in 1959, embracing communism shortly after taking power.

Curcio, Renato (1941–) The founder and leader of the Red Brigades in Italy.

Death Angels Select members of the Brotherhood in the Nation of Yahweh. They were sent to murder white people in the Miami area.

defense in depth Using social networks in national defense. It is based on Arthur Cebrowski's idea of operating at all levels of society.

Deobandi A conservative religious school of thought originating in India and influential in central Asia. Many observers equate its conservative positions with Saudi Arabian Wahhabism.

Department of Homeland Security (DHS) A federal agency created in 2003 by Congress from the Office of Homeland Security after the attacks of September 11, 2001.

Desert Shield The name of the defensive phase of the international coalition, created by President George H. W. Bush after Iraq invaded Kuwait on August, 2, 1990, to stop further Iraqi attacks and to liberate Kuwait. It lasted until coalition forces could begin an offensive against Iraq in January 1991.

Desert Storm The military code name for the January–February offensive in the 1991 Gulf War.

eclectic disassociations A term used to describe international networks. There is no pattern for forming groups so they are called eclectic. The groups and the external alliances they form are temporary and disassociate from each other after operations.

ecoterrorism Terrorism against alleged environmental abusers.

emergency-response plans Preparations from any agency to deal with natural, accidental, or human-made disasters. They involve controlling the incident through an organized response-and-command system and assigning various organizations to supervise the restoration of social order.

empirical studies A social science method that uses unbiased observations as a method to test ideas.

endemic terrorism Terrorism that exists inside a political entity. For example, European colonialists created the nation of Rwanda by combining the lands of two tribes that literally hate one another. The two tribes fight to eliminate one another. This is endemic to political violence in Rwanda.

enemy combatant A legal term used to describe nonstate paramilitary captives from Afghanistan. The term was later applied to all jihadist terrorists by the Bush administration.

Enlightenment An eighteenth-century intellectual movement following the Scientific Revolution. Also called the Age of Reason, the Enlightenment was characterized by rational thought and the belief that all activities could be explained.

eschatology (pronounced es-**ka**-taw-low-gee) A Greek word used to indicate the theological end of time. In Judaism and Christianity it refers to God bringing creation to an end. In some Shiite Islamic sects and among Christians who literalize biblical eschatological literature, believers contend that Jesus will return to lead a final battle against evil. Other major religions also have end-time theology.

Estates General An assembly in prerevolutionary France consisting of all but the lowest class. The Estates General had not been called since 1614, but Louis XVI assembled them in 1789 in response to demands from the Assembly of Notables who had been called to address the financial problems of France. Radical elements in the Estates General revolted, and the disruption led to the French Revolution.

ethnic cleansing A term to describe genocide in a geographical area. Ethnic cleansing occurs when one group decides to rid an area of another group.

European Union (EU) An economic consortium of several European states formed in 1992. It was designed to remove trade barriers and to create a unified European economy.

expropriation A term used by Carlos Marighella for armed robbery.

extrajuridical repression Violent repression outside the norms of criminal law. It can be used by governments, vigilantes, criminals, terrorists, or any group to enforce rules that violate criminal law. A death squad, for example, is a form of extrajuridical repression.

Fadlallah, Sheik Mohammed Hassan (1935–) A grand ayatollah and leader of Shiites in Lebanon. The spiritual leader of Hezbollah. He was the target of a 1985 U.S. assassination plot that killed seventy-five people.

failed state An area outside a government's control. Failed states operate under differing warlords, criminal groups, or competing governments.

Fanon, Frantz (1925–1961) A writer, psychiatrist, and revolutionary theorist. He was also one of the most influential philosophers in the awareness of colonialism. Fanon grew up in the French colony Martinique in the Caribbean, and he became acutely aware of racism and colonialism in experiences there. He joined the French Army in World War II, and won one of France's highest military decorations. After the war he studied psychiatry. Believing that mental illness was a result of imperialism, Fanon campaigned against racism and colonialism. He supported Algerian rebels in their struggle with France and advocated for violent revolution. He died of leukemia, but his ideas influenced anticolonial revolutionaries for decades.

far enemy A jihadist term referring to non-Islamic powers or countries outside dar al Islam. It is a general reference to Israel, the West, and the United States.

Fatah General Council The leadership group of Fatah.

fedayeen Warriors who sacrifice themselves. The term was used differently in Arab history; the modern term is used to describe the secular warriors of Fatah.

Fergana Valley A rich farming region in central Asia that lies inside Uzbekistan, Kyrgyzstan, and Tajikistan. It partially borders China's Xinjiang province.

Fneish, Mohammed (age unknown) A Hezbollah politician and minister of energy in the Lebanese prime minister's cabinet.

force multiplier A method of increasing striking power without increasing the number of combat troops in a military unit. Terrorists have four force multipliers: (1) technology to enhance weapons or attacks on technological facilities, (2) transnational support, (3) media coverage, and (4) religious fanaticism.

forensic accounting An investigative tool used to track money used in illegal activities. It can be used in any crime involving the exchange, storage, or conversion of fiscal resources.

Forrest, Nathan Bedford (1821–1877) A famed and gifted Confederate cavalry commander who founded the Ku Klux Klan in Pulaski, Tennessee. Forrest tried to disband the KKK when he saw the violent path that it was taking.

Fourteenth Amendment A person cannot be deprived of freedom or property by the government unless the government follows all the procedures demanded for legal prosecution.

Franco, Francisco (1892–1975) Leader of the nationalistic forces during the Spanish Civil War and the fascist dictator of Spain from 1939–1975.

Free State The name given to the newly formed Republic of Ireland after Irish independence in the Tan War.

Freedom of Information (FOI) Act A law ensuring access to governmental records.

free-wheeling fundamentalists White supremacists or Christian patriots who either selectively use Bible passages or create their own religion to protect the patriot agenda.

Gadahn, Adam (1958–) The American spokesperson for al Qaeda. His nom de guerre is Azzam the American.

Gadhafi, Muammar (1942–) The leader of Libya. Gadhafi took power in 1969 in a socialist revolution. He developed a unique theory of Arab socialism. His intelligence forces were responsible for planting a bomb on a Pan American flight over Lockerbie, Scotland, in 1988, killing 270 people. The attack was in response to an American bombing raid in Libya in 1986.

Gale, William Potter (1917–1988) An American military leader who coordinated guerrilla activities in the Philippines during World War II. Gale became a radio preacher and leader of the Christian Identity movement after returning home.

Gandhi, Rajiv (1944–1991) Prime minister of India from 1984 until 1991, when he was assassinated by an LTTE suicide bomber.

Gaza Strip The westernmost area of Palestine territories.

genetic engineering The manipulation of plant or animal genes to increase food output. Anti–genetic engineering activists frequently sabotage experimental crops and farm equipment.

globalization A common global economic network ideally uniting the world with production and international trade. Proponents believe it will create wealth. Critics believe it creates corporate wealth and increases distance between the rich and poor.

Golden Temple The most sacred shrine of Sikhism. Its official name is the Temple of God.

Goldstein, Baruch (1956–1994) An American physician who immigrated to Israel. In February 1994 he entered a religious site in Hebron wearing his Israeli military uniform. He then began shooting Muslim worshippers, killing twenty-nine and wounding more than a hundred.

Government Management Reform Act of 1994 A federal law designed to prevent political interference in the management of federal governmental organizations and to increase the efficiency of management.

Great Depression The description of the international economy from the time of the U.S. stock market crash of 1929 until the beginning of World War II.

Grozny The capital of Chechnya.

Guevara, Ernesto "Che" (1928–1967) Fidel Castro's assistant and guerrilla warfare theorist. Guevara advocated guerrilla revolutions throughout Latin America after success in the Cuban Revolution. He was killed in Bolivia in 1967 when trying to form a guerrilla army.

Gulf States Small Arab kingdoms bordering the Persian Gulf. They include Bahrain, Qatar, the United Arab Emirates, and Oman.

Gyanendra, King (1947–) The king of Nepal. After the attack and murder of several members of the royal family, Gyanendra became king of Nepal in 2001. Gyanendra took complete power in 2005 to fight the Maoist rebellion. In the spring of 2006 he was forced to return power to parliament.

Hamza, Mustafa (1957–) A leader of the Egyptian IG, believed to be involved in several terrorist incidents, who agreed to a cease-fire in 1997. He has been sentenced to death in absentia in Egypt.

Hapsburg The ruling family of Austria (1282–1918), the Austro-Hungarian Empire (1437–1918), and the Holy Roman Empire (1282–1806). Another branch of the family ruled in Spain (1516–1700). Reference here is to the Austrian royal family.

hate crime A crime motivated by race, ethnicity, or other category defined as a protected status by federal law.

hawala system A system of exchanging money based on trust relationships between money dealers. A chit, or promissory note, is exchanged between two hawaladars, and it is as valuable as cash or other traded commodities because the trust between the two parties guarantees its value.

Hohenzollern The ruling family of Brandenburg and Prussia that ruled a united Germany from 1871–1914.

Holy Land Foundation An Islamic charity based in the United States. Federal authorities closed the foundation in 2001, alleging that it sponsored terrorist activities.

home rule The dominant issue in Irish politics from the mid-1800s until independence. Advocates of home rule wanted to establish a parliament (*Dáil* in Gaelic) in Dublin that would be independent from the British parliament in Westminster. Some advocates of home rule were willing to swear allegiance to the United Kingdom. Others demanded complete autonomy.

Horn of Africa An eastern region of Africa, although some geographers include parts of southwest Asia in their definitions. It usually includes Djibouti, Eritrea, Ethiopia, Kenya, Somalia, and Sudan. Some definitions also include Yemen. The Darfur region is usually implied in the definition.

Howell, Vernon Wayne (or David Koresh, 1959–1993) The charismatic leader of the Branch Davidian cult.

human rights The basic entitlements and protections that should be given to every person.

Hussein (626–680) Also known as Hussein ibn Ali, Mohammed's grandson and Ali's second son. He was martyred at Karbala in 680. Twelver Shiites believe that Hussein is the Third Imam, after Imam Ali and Imam Hasan, Ali's oldest son.

Hussein, King (1935–1999) King of Jordan. King Hussein drove the PLO from Jordan in September 1970. After his death his son Abdullah assumed the throne.

ibn al Khattab (1969–2002) Also known as Emir Khattab or the Black Wahhabi, an international Saudi jihadist who went to fight in Chechnya. He tried to move the Chechen revolt from a nationalistic platform to the philosophy of religious militancy. He was killed by the Russian secret service in 2002.

Ibn Taymiyyah (circa 1269–1328) Also known as Taqi al Din ibn Taymiyya, a Muslim religious reformer in the time of the Crusades and a massive Mongol invasion.

imam In Shiite Islam, one of the twelve descendants of Mohammed. It is a title of respect for certain Shiite ulema.

Independent Monitoring Commission (IMC) A commission created in 2004 to investigate paramilitary actions and alleged governmental abuses during the Irish peace process.

intelligence product Any outcome or output of analyzed information that can be used by law enforcement agencies, military units, or security forces to take an immediate action.

intelligence-led policing A type of law enforcement in which resources are deployed based on information gathered and analyzed from criminal intelligence.

Interservice Intelligence Agency (ISI) The Pakistani domestic and foreign intelligence service created by the British in 1948. Supporters claim that it centralizes Pakistan's intelligence. Critics maintain that it operates like an independent state and supports terrorist groups.

Intifada The first spontaneous uprising against Israel that lasted from 1987 to 1993. It began with youths throwing rocks and creating civil disorder. Some of the violence became more organized. Many people sided with religious organizations, abandoning the secular PLO during the Intifada.

Iranian Revolution The 1979 religious revolution that toppled Mohammed Pahlavi, the shah of Iran, and transformed Iran into an Islamic republic ruled by Shiite religious scholars.

Iran-Iraq War A war fought after Iraq invaded Iran over a border dispute in 1980. Many experts predicted an Iraqi victory, but the Iranians stopped the Iraqi Army. The war produced an eight-year stalemate and more than a million casualties. The countries signed an armistice in 1988.

Islamic Amal A Shiite militia in the Lebanese Civil War. Abbas Musawi entered into an alliance with Iranian revolutionaries in Lebanon and formed Islamic Amal to counter Nahbi Berri's Amal.

Islamic Courts Union A confederation of tribes and clans seeking to end violence and bring Islamic law to Somalia. It is opposed by several neighboring countries and internal warlords. Some people feel it is a jihadist organization, but others see it as a grouping of clans with several different interpretations of Islamic law.

Islamic Jihad Not to be confused with the PIJ or other groups of the same name, this Islamic Jihad was a small group under Hezbollah's umbrella. It was responsible for the 1983 U.S. Marine barracks bombing that killed more than 200 U.S. service personnel and a second attack that killed 58 French paratroopers. Hezbollah denies all connections with the attacks.

Islamic Renaissance Party (IRP) A Tajikistan religious political party. Banned in the Tajik Civil War, it reemerged as a political party in 1998.

Ithna Ashari Literally, *twelvers*. Twelver Shiites believe that some of the power God gave to Mohammed passed to a line of twelve chosen descendants.

Izz el Din al Qassam Brigades The military wing of Hamas, named after the Arab revolutionary leader Sheik Izz el Din al Qassam (1882–1935), who led a revolt against British rule.

Jamaat, Tablighi An Islamic missionary society founded in Northwest India (Pakistan today) in the early twentieth century. Its original purpose was to teach Muslims how to behave piously. Critics maintain that it has become dominated by a militant philosophy.

Jammu and Kashmir A mountainous region in northern India claimed by India and Pakistan. It has been the site of heavy fighting during three wars between India and Pakistan in 1947–1948, 1971, and 1999. Kashmir is artificially divided by a line of control (LOC), with Pakistani forces to the north and India's to the south. India and Pakistan made strides toward peace after 2003, but many observers believe the ISI supports jihadist operations in the area.

Kahane, Rabbi Meir (1932–1990) Founder of the Jewish Defense League and Kach. Kahane was assassinated in New York City in 1990.

Karimov, Islam (1938–) President of Uzbekistan since 1991. Karimov is known for authoritarian leadership and repression of political dissent.

Katyusha rockets A type of mobile rocket. Developed by the Soviet army during World War II, the rockets were originally mounted on the beds of trucks. Katyuhsa rockets target a general area and are effective when used in barrages. The latest generation is much more accurate, and one may have been so precisely guided that it hit an Israeli ship during the 2006 war. The name means "Little Katie."

Khojaev, Jumaboi (1969–2001) The main founder and military leader of the Islamic Movement of Uzbekistan. Khojaev is better known by his nom de guerre, Juma Namangani. He was killed in a battle with U.S. forces in November 2001.

Khomeini, Ruhollah (1900–1989) The Shiite grand ayatollah who was the leading figure in the 1979 Iranian Revolution. Khomeini toppled the shah's government and consolidated power by destroying or silencing his enemies, including other Shiite Islamic scholars. Iran transformed into a theocracy under his influence.

Klassen, Ben (1918–1993) The founder of the Creativity Movement.

Knight Riders The first terrorists of the Ku Klux Klan. Donning hoods and riding at night, they sought to keep newly freed slaves from participating in government and society.

Know-Nothings Different groups of American super-nationalists in the early nineteenth century who championed native-born whites over immigrants.

leaderless resistance The concept that small unorganized, unmanaged groups or individuals can launch a revolution with disorganized violence.

Lebanese Civil War (1975–1990) A brutal factional war between several different religious militias for control of Lebanon. Several nations intervened, and Syria exerted control in the waning years of the war. Supporting Hezbollah, Syria retained control of Lebanon until 2005.

Lenin, Vladimir The Russian revolutionary who helped lead a revolution in February 1917 and who led a second revolution in October, bringing the communists to power. Lenin led the communists in a civil war and set up a dictatorship to enforce communist rule in Russia.

Liberian Civil War Two episodes of conflict involving rebel armies and militias as well as neighboring countries. The First War, 1989–1996, ended when a rebel army brought Charles Taylor to Monrovia, the capital. The Second War, 1999–2003, toppled Charles Taylor from power. Both wars were characterized by village massacres and conscription of child soldiers.

Liberians United for Reconciliation and Democracy (LURD) A revolutionary movement founded in 1999 in western Africa. LURD was instrumental in driving Charles Taylor from power in 2003.

Lindh, John Walker (1981–) An American captured while fighting for the Taliban in 2001 and sentenced to twenty years in prison.

London Underground The subway system in London.

Londonistan A slang term for areas of London dominated by Muslims. The areas were known as a haven for radical jihadists, but police began to crack down on militant activities after jihadist attacks in the United Kingdom.

madrassas Islamic religious schools.

Mahmet II (1432–1481) Ottoman sultan and conqueror of Constantinople in 1453.

majilis council The Islamic name given to a religious council that councils a government or a leader. Some Islamic countries refer to their legislative body as a majilis.

Mandate of Palestine The British Mandate of Palestine was in effect from 1920 to 1948. Created by the League of Nations, the mandate gave the United Kingdom the right to extend its influence in an area roughly equivalent to modern Jordan, Israel, and the Palestinian Authority.

Mao Zedong (1893–1976) Also known as Mao Tse Tung, the leader of the Chinese Communist Party. He seized power in a revolution in 1949 and ruled China until his death in 1976.

Marighella, Carlos (1911–1969) A Brazilian communist legislator and a revolutionary theorist. Marighella popularized urban terrorism as a method for ending repression and eliminating U.S. domination of Latin America. He was killed in a police ambush in São Paulo in 1969.

Masa, Rafai Taha (age unknown) A militant leader of the IG. He split with Hamza over the 1997 cease-fire and signed the 1998 declaration with bin Laden and Zawahiri.

Mashal, Khalid (1956–) One of the "outside" leaders of Hamas, in Damascus, Syria. Mashal is described as a political leader by Hamas.

Matthews, Robert (1953–1984) The leader of The Order, killed in a shoot-out with the FBI.

Mawdudi, Mawlana (1903–1979) A Pakistani reformer who saw jihad as both a spiritual struggle and the basis for political activism against European colonialism. Qutb was deeply influenced by Mawdudi's writings, but Mawdudi sought to reform Islamic countries without revolution much as Hassan al Banna did.

McCartney, Robert (1971–2005) A Catholic supporter of Sinn Fein allegedly murdered by the IRA during a bar fight in Belfast. The murder had nothing to do with McCartney's politics, but it revealed the thuggish nature of the IRA.

meaning The subjective interpretation people give to events or physical objects. Meanings are developed by individuals and groups, and different meanings can be attributed to the same event or physical object because the definitions are always influenced by interpretation. Social scientists in this tradition believe that meanings cause actions.

meaning framework The social construct providing definitional boundaries for a particular social meaning.

Mensheviks Russian socialists who allied with the Bolsheviks in the February 1917 Revolution to overthrow the czarist government.

militarization Responding to social problems with military solutions. In law enforcement militarization is usually characterized by martial law.

militia movement A political movement started in the early 1980s, possibly spawned from survivalism. Militias maintain that the Second Amendment gives them the right to arm themselves and form paramilitary organizations apart from governmental control and military authority.

Mogadishu The capital of Somalia. U.S. troops moved into Mogadishu during Operation Restore Hope from December 9, 1992, until May 4, 1993, when the United Nations took over operations. American forces were involved in a major battle in October 1993 while serving under U.N. command.

Mohammed, Khalid Sheik (1964–) The uncle of Ramzi Youseff and probably the mastermind behind the 9/11 attacks and several other major international and domestic terrorist incidents. These include the World Trade Center bombing (1993), Operation Bojinka (1996), a thwarted attack on the Los Angeles airport (2000), an attempt to bring down an American airliner (2001), the murder of a *Wall Street Journal* reporter (2002), and the Bali nightclub bombing (2002). He was captured in March 2003 by Pakistani ISI agents.

Moscow theater (Theatrical Center, Dubrovka, Moscow, 2002) The site of a Chechen attack where approximately 40 terrorists took 850 hostages. Russian forces stormed the theater on the third day of the siege, killing 39 terrorists and at least 129 hostages.

Mossad The Israeli intelligence agency formed in 1951. It is responsible for gathering foreign intelligence. Shin Beth is responsible for internal security.

Mugniyah, Imad (1962–) The leader of the international branch of Hezbollah. He has been implicated in many attacks, including the 1983 U.S. Marine and French paratrooper bombings. He is also believed to be behind bombings of the U.S. embassy in Beirut and two bombings in Argentina.

Musa, Bashir (1955–) A founding member of the PIJ. The U.S. government considers Musa to be a member of a terrorist organization. He currently teaches Islamic studies in the United Kingdom.

Musawi, Abbas (1952–1992) A leader of Hezbollah killed with his family in an Israeli attack in 1992.

Musharraf, Pervez (1943–) The president of Pakistan. A career army officer, Musharraf took power in a 1999 military coup and declared himself president in 2001. After 9/11 he sought closer relations with the United States, while trying to mollify sources of domestic religious strife.

Muslim Brotherhood An organization founded by Hassan al Banna designed to recapture the spirit and religious purity during the period of Mohammed and the four Rightly Guided caliphs. The Brotherhood seeks to create a single Muslim nation through education and religious reform. A militant wing founded by Sayyid Qutb sought the same objective through violence. Hamas has rejected the multinational approach in favor of creating a Muslim Palestine, and it considers itself to be the Palestinian wing of the Muslim Brotherhood.

Najaf A city in Iraq one hundred miles south of Baghdad. It is a holy site for Shiites who believe that the Imam Ali, Mohammed's cousin and son-in-law, is buried there.

Namangani, Juma Nom de guerre of Jumaboi Khojaev.

narco-terrorism A controversial term that links drugs to terrorism in one of two ways. Either drug profits are used to finance terrorism or drug gangs use terrorism to control production and distribution networks.

Nasrallah, Hassan (1960–) The secretary-general of Hezbollah. He took over leadership of Hezbollah after Musawi's death in 1992. Nasrallah is a lively speaker and charismatic leader.

Nation of Yahweh A violent offshoot of Black Hebrew Israelism founded in Miami by Hulon Mitchell Jr., also known as Yahweh ben Yahweh. The group is best known for Mitchell's dispatching of Death Angels with instructions to kill whites.

National Alliance The white supremacist organization founded by the late William Pierce and headquartered in Hillsboro, West Virginia.

National Convention Elected in 1792, it broke from the Estates General and called for a constitutional assembly. The Convention served as the major legislative body of France until it was replaced by the Directory in 1795.

National Counterterrorism Center (NCTC) An organization designed to filter information from the intelligence process, synthesize counterterrorist information, and share it with appropriate organizations.

National Criminal Intelligence Sharing Plan (NCISP) A plan to share criminal intelligence among the nation's law enforcement agencies. It suggests minimum standards for establishing and managing intelligence operations within police agencies.

national security intelligence A system of agencies and networks that gather information about threats to the country. Any threat or potential threat is examined under the auspices of national defense intelligence. Unlike criminal intelligence, people and agencies gathering defense information do not need to suspect any criminal activity. The FBI is empowered to gather defense intelligence.

NATO The North Atlantic Treaty Organization, which is headquartered in Brussels, Belgium. Formed in 1949, it was a cold war alliance between the United States and Western Europe against the Soviet Union and Warsaw Pact. NATO has expanded into five eastern European countries since 1991, and it remains the primary military alliance between the United States and Europe.

near enemy A jihadist term referring to forms of Muslim governments and Islamic law (sharia) that do not embrace the narrow-minded philosophy of Sayyid Qutb.

netwar One network fighting another network.

network-centric warfare A concept championed by Arthur Cebrowski stating that an enemy's crucial strength is in its social, political, and communications networks, not in geography or national capitals. Network-centric warfare seeks to destroy or disable such networks.

networks Organizations of groups, supplies, weapons, and any structure that supports an operation. Much like a traffic system or the World Wide Web, networks do not have central leadership, and they operate under a variety of rules.

new economy of terrorism A term used by Loretta Napoleoni to describe the evolution of terrorist financing from the beginning strategies of the cold war to the present. Economic support and antiterrorist policies interact to form the new economy.

New World Order A phrase used by President George H. W. Bush to describe the world after the fall of the Soviet Union. Conspiracy theorists use the phrase to describe what they believe to be Jewish attempts to gain control of the international monetary system and subsequently to take over the U.S. government.

news frames Visual, audible, or written packages used to present the news. Communication scholars do not agree on a single definition, but news frames generally refer to the presentation of the news story. They contain a method for beginning and ending the story, and they convey the importance of characters and actions as the story is told.

9/11 Commission The bipartisan National Commission on Terrorist Attacks upon the United States created after September 11, 2001, to investigate the attacks.

1985 hijacking of a TWA flight The hijacking of TWA Flight 847 by a group believed to have links to Hezbollah while it was en route from Athens to Rome. The plane went to Beirut and then to Algeria where terrorists tortured and murdered U.S. Navy diver Robert Dean Stethem, a passenger on the flight. The plane returned to Beirut, and passengers were dispersed throughout the city. Terrorists released hostages throughout the incident, and all hostages were freed from Beirut after Israel released more than 700 Shiite prisoners.

1993 World Trade Center bombing A car-bomb attack by a cell led by Ramzi Youseff. The cell had links to the Egyptian IG.

1978 Civil Service Reform Act A federal law designed to prevent political interference with the decisions and actions of governmental organizations.

nodes In counterterrorist or netwar discussions, the points in a system where critical components are stored or transferred. The importance of a node is determined by its relationship to the network.

Nordic Christianity A religion that incorporates the ancient Norse gods in a hierarchy under the Christian triune deity. It is similar to Odinism, but does not completely abandon Christianity.

Northern Alliance A military-political organization formed in 1996 in northern Afghanistan to fight the Taliban. During the early part of Operation Enduring Freedom, the Northern Alliance fought closely with U.S. Special Forces. Osama bin Laden ordered suicide bombers to kill Ahmad Masood, then general of the Northern Alliance, just before the 9/11 attacks. It was composed mainly of Tajiks, Uzbeks, and Afghan (Hazara) Shiites.

North-West Frontier Province (NWFP) One of four Pakistani states, inhabited primarily by ethnic Pashtuns. Several areas of the NWFP are controlled by tribes, and jihadists operate in the area. Peshawar, NWFP's capital, served as a base for organizing several mujahideen groups in the Soviet-Afghan War.

Nossair, Elsayyid (1955–) An American jihadist associated with violence in New York City.

Ocalan, Abdullah (1948–) The leader of the PKK. Ocalan was captured in 1999 and sentenced to death, but his sentence was commuted. He ordered the end of a suicide-bombing campaign while in Turkish custody and called for peace between Turkey and the Kurds in 2006.

occupied territories Any number of territories controlled by Israel. The areas may become the independent nation of Palestine, if the Palestinians are able to create their own nation.

Omar, Mullah (1959–) The leader of the Taliban. After the collapse of the Taliban government in 2001, Omar went into hiding.

On War One of the most influential philosophical works on the practice of warfare. Written by Carl von Clausewitz, it remains standard reading for military officers in the Americas, Europe, and Asia.

Operation Enduring Freedom The code name for the American-led coalition's military intervention in Afghanistan.

Operation Grapes of Wrath The code name for the April 1996 attack on Lebanon. The IDF attacked Lebanese targets for sixteen days in retaliation for Hezbollah's activities.

Operation Iraqi Freedom The code name for the 2003 U.S.-led invasion of Iraq. The military operation was code named Cobra II, a reference to George S. Patton's Third Army breakout in France in 1944.

Operation Peace for Galilee The code name for the Israeli invasion of Lebanon in 1982. It resulted in the expulsion of the PLO from Lebanon and the influx of Iranian revolutionaries who helped form Hezbollah. Israel occupied southern Lebanon for eighteen years, eventually leaving. Hezbollah claimed victory.

Orange Volunteers A Unionist paramilitary group in Northern Ireland. Volunteers for the House of Orange have joined Unionist causes in Northern Ireland since William of Orange saved the Protestant cause at the Battle of the Boyne in 1690.

Oslo Accords A 1993 agreement between Palestinians and Israel. It resulted in the Palestinian National Authority and limited self-rule.

Ottoman Empire A Turkish empire that lasted for 600 years, until 1924. The empire spanned southeastern Europe, North Africa, and southwest Asia, and it reached its zenith in the fourteenth and fifteenth centuries.

Pahlavi, Mohammed Reza (1919–1980) Shah of Iran from 1941 to 1979. The shah led a rigorous program of modernization that turned Iran into a regional power. He left the throne and accepted exile as a result of the 1979 Iranian Revolution.

Pahlavi, Reza Shah (1878–1944) Shah of Iran from 1925 to 1941. He was forced from power by a British and Soviet invasion.

peace dividend A term used during President William Clinton's administration (1992–2000) to describe reducing defense spending at the end of the cold war.

pejorative term A term that is loaded with negative and derogatory meanings.

philosophy of the bomb A phrase used by anarchists around 1848. It means that social order can be changed only through violent upheaval. Bombs were the first technological force multiplier.

Pierce, William (1933–2002) Leader of the National Alliance and author of *The Turner Diaries* and *Hunter*.

Pirapaharan, Velupillai (1954–) Founder and current leader of the LTTE. Pirapaharan's terrorists have conducted more successful suicide bombings than any other terrorist group in the world.

Plantation of Ulster The area of Northern Ireland selected by English monarchs for colonization in the seventeenth century. Irish peasants were displaced by Scottish and English settlers. The Irish were primarily Catholic and the settlers were mostly Protestant. The settlement was named Ulster because it encompassed the old Irish tribal area of Ulster.

plea bargaining When a defendant pleads guilty to a charge of less severity than the original criminal indictment. For example, after being charged with breaking and entering, a suspect might plead guilty only to illegal entry, if the prosecutor agrees. The prosecutor gets a conviction, and the suspect, although guilty of the greater charge, receives a shorter sentence.

Police Service of Northern Ireland (PSNI) The police force created in November 2001 to replace the Royal Ulster Constabulary.

posse comitatus A clause in the second article of the Constitution that forbids the government to use military force to enforce law. (Do not confuse this with the right-wing extremist group Posse Comitatus.)

postmodern Describing the belief that modernism has ended. Some events are inexplicable, and some organizations and actions are naturally and socially chaotic and defy explanation. A postmodern news frame leaves the consumer thinking there are many possible conclusions.

pre-incident indicators The criminal and social actions of individuals and groups before a terrorist attack.

Premadasa, Ranasinghe (1924–1993) President of Sri Lanka from 1989 until 1993, when he was killed by an LTTE suicide bomber.

Project Megiddo A 1999 FBI research project designed to assess potential domestic terrorism, especially from groups espousing eschatological violence.

proletariat A Marxist term to describe the working class.

Protocols of Zion A forged document written in czarist Russia allegedly explaining a Jewish plot to control the world. It was popularized in the United States by Henry Ford. It is frequently cited by the patriot and white supremacy movements. Jihadists also use it as evidence against Jews.

Provisionals The nickname for members of the Provisional Irish Republican Army. They are also known as Provos. The name applies to several different Republican paramilitary terrorist groups.

Putin, Vladimir (1952–) The president of the Russian Federation. He succeeded Boris Yeltsin in 1999.

pyramid An illustration of the way terrorists organize themselves into hierarchies. It is an analogy showing a large base of support culminating in a small group of terrorists at the top.

Qutb, Sayyid (1906–1966) An Egyptian educator who called for the overthrow of governments and the imposition of purified Islamic law based on the principles of previous puritanical reformers. Qutb formed a militant wing of the Muslim Brotherhood.

radical democrats Those who tried to bring democracy to all classes. They sought a more equitable distribution of wealth throughout all economic classes, believing that concentrated wealth and class inequities prevented societies from becoming truly democratic.

Rahman, Sheik Omar Abdel (1938–) A Sunni Islamic scholar linked to the Egyptian IG. He came to the United States in 1990 even though his name was on a State Department watch list. He was arrested and convicted of conspiracy after the 1993 World Trade Center bombing. He is gravely ill in an American federal prison.

Rantisi, Abdel Aziz (1947–2004) One of the founders of Hamas along with Ahmed Yassin. He took over Hamas after Israeli gunships assassinated Yassin. He, in turn, was assassinated by the Israelis a month after taking charge.

reasonableness The actions an average person would take when confronted with certain circumstances. This is a Fourth Amendment doctrine.

Red Army Faction (RAF) A left-wing German terrorist group operating from the mid-1970s to 1998. While under the leadership of Ulricke Meinhof and Andreas Baader, the RAF was known as the Baader-Meinhof Gang.

red corridor The area of Naxalite violence in India. The length of the corridor runs from Nepal through southern India, and the width extends from India's east coast to the central regions.

Red Hand Defenders A Unionist extremist group in Northern Ireland. The newest group to use the name formed in 1998.

reference group The primary group whose values with which individuals or other groups identify. It is an idealized group of peers that serve as a model for behavior.

Regional Informational Sharing System (RISS) A law enforcement network that allows law enforcement agencies to share information about criminal investigations.

Reign of Terror The name given to the repressive period in France 1794–1795. The revolutionary government accused thousands of French nobles and clergy of plotting to restore the monarchy. Executions began in Paris and spread through the countryside. Large mobs attacked and terrorized nobles in rural areas. Summary executions without trial were quite common.

reporting frame The simplest form of a news frame. It is a quick, fact-driven report that summarizes the latest information about a story. It does not need to contain a beginning or an end, and it assumes that the consumer understands the context of the facts.

repression Governmental actions that suppress freedom.

Revolutionary Guards The militarized quasi-police force of the revolutionary government during the Iranian Revolution.

Royal Irish Constabulary (RIC) The police force established by the United Kingdom in Ireland. It was modeled after the London Metropolitan Police, but it represented British interests. After the Free State formed, the RIC became the RUC, Royal Ulster Constabulary. In turn, the RUC gave way to the Police Service of Northern Ireland (PSNI) as part of Irish and British attempts to bring peace to Northern Ireland after 1995.

Ruby Ridge The location of a 1992 standoff between alleged survivalists and U.S. federal law enforcement officers in Idaho during which a U.S. marshal and survivalist Randy Weaver's wife and son were killed.

Rudolph, Eric (1966–) A right-wing extremist known for bombing the Atlanta Olympics, a gay night club, and an abortion clinic. Rudolph hid from authorities and became a survivalist hero. He was arrested in 2003 and received five life sentences in 2005.

Sabra and Shatila Two villages where Palestinian refugees were massacred in Lebanon in September 1982. Surrounded by IDF units who had guaranteed safety for the refugees, hundreds of Palestinians were massacred by Lebanese mili-

tiamen while the Israelis stood by. The IDF units claimed they had no idea of what was taking place. Critics dismiss this claim.

Sadr, Muqtada al (1974–) An Iraqi ayatollah. Sadr leads the Shiite militia known as the Mahdi Army.

Salafi Group for Call and Combat (GSPC) A jihadist group that emerged from the GIA. It is based in Italy.

Salafism A reform movement in Islam that started in North Africa in the nineteenth century. Its purpose is to purify Islam by returning to the Islam of Mohammed and his companions.

Sallah, Ramadan Abdullah (1958–) The leader of the PIJ after Shekaki's assassination. He is wanted by the FBI and believed to be in Syria.

Sarkozy, Nicolas (1955–) The president of France. During the election of 2007, Sarkozy promised to review the activities of the African Cell. Sarkozy is a conservative who seeks closer French ties with the United Kingdom and the United States.

SAVAK Mohammed Pahlavi's secret police empowered after the 1953 downfall of the democratic government.

Sendic, Raul (1926–1989) A Uruguayan revolutionary leader. Sendic founded the Movement of National Liberation (MLN), popularly known as the Tupamaros. Following governmental repression in 1973, he fled the country. Sendic died in Paris in 1989.

separation of powers The distribution of power among the executive, legislative, and judicial branches of government. When powers are separated, they are assumed to be balanced. No one branch can take control of the government.

Shaba farm region A small farming region in southwest Lebanon annexed by Israel in 1981. When Israel withdrew from southern Lebanon in 2000, it remained in the Shaba farm region, creating a dispute with Lebanon, Hezbollah, and Syria.

Shekaki, Fathi (1951–1995) The general secretary and founder of the PIJ. From Gaza, Shekaki was a Palestinian physician. He was killed in a targeted assassination.

shell state A political situation where a government nominally controls its own state but where large regions are either anarchic or under the control of others. A government is unable to enforce law or provide for other forms of social order in a shell state.

simple definition A definition of terrorism that involves three parts: (1) use of force, (2) against innocent people, (3) for political purposes.

Sinn Fein The political party of Republicans. Critics claim it represents terrorists. Republicans say it represents their political interests. Despite the debate, Sinn Fein historically has close connections with extremism and violence.

Six Days' War A war between Israel and its Arab neighbors fought in June 1967. Israel launched the preemptive war in the face of an Arab military buildup, and it overwhelmed all opposition. At the end of the war Israel occupied the Sinai Peninsula, the Golan Heights, and the West Bank of the Jordan River. It also occupied the city of Jerusalem (al Quds to Muslims).

six tactics of terrorism As defined by Brian Jenkins, (1) bombing, (2) hijacking, (3) arson, (4) assault, (5) kidnapping, and (6) hostagetaking.

skinheads Young people or groups who embrace racial hatred and white supremacy. Some groups claim not to be based on racism.

sleeper cells Terrorist cells that operate for long periods doing nothing to stand out from their social surroundings. They become active just before an operation.

social construct The way people view reality. Groups construct a framework around a concept, defining various aspects of their lives through the meanings they attribute to the construct.

social context The historical, political, and criminological circumstances at a given point in time. The social context affects the way terrorism is defined.

social geometry As used by Donald Black, the social space occupied by a structure and the direction it moves.

socialists Radical democrats who sought wealth equality in capitalist societies. Some socialists sought governmental guarantees of living standards. Others believed that the state should control industry and divide profits among all members of society. Others believed that people would form cooperative relationships on their own with no need of a government.

Society of United Irishmen An organization formed in Dublin with a second chapter in Belfast in 1791 that united both Protestants and Catholics. The purpose of the movement was to free Ireland from British rule. The society demanded Catholic emancipation (equal rights for Catholics and Protestants), the end of British rule, and a free Irish parliament.

South Lebanese Army A Christian militia closely allied with and supported by Israel. It operated with Israeli support from 1982 to 2000.

Spain in 1807 The Peninsula War (1808–1814), which began when Spanish and French forces divided Portugal in 1807. Napoleon, whose army entered Spain in 1807, attempted to use his forces to capture the Spanish throne in 1808. British forces under Sir Arthur Wellesley, later Duke of Wellington, joined Spanish forces loyal to the king of Spain and Spanish partisans to fight the French.

Spanish Civil War (1936–1939) A war that pitted pro-communist Republicans against pro-fascist Nationalists. The war ended with a Nationalist victory and a fascist dictatorship under Franco.

spectrum of conflict A system developed by the U.S. Army to define low-intensity conflict, mid-level wars, and wars of mass destruction. This text expands the definition to include many levels of social conflict far beneath traditional definitions of war.

Stalin, Joseph The dictator who succeeded Lenin. Stalin solidified communist control of Russia through a secret-police organization. He purged the government of all suspected opponents in the 1930s, killing thousands of people.

structural framework The idea that social constructs are based on systems that provide order. The systems are social structures that accomplish functions necessary to survive. Human activity occurs to accomplish the functions required to maintain the social structure of the system.

structure The manner in which a group is organized and its purpose. Social scientists from this tradition feel that a group's structure and purpose cause it to act. They also believe that groups are created for specific functions.

Sun Tzu A Chinese philosopher of war who made little distinction between war and peace. Subtle expressions of power that defeat the enemy are better than war or fighting. Many counterterrorism analysts believe that Sun Tzu's ancient approach to conflict is applicable for fighting modern terrorism.

Supreme Council The command center of several Republican terrorist organizations, including the Irish Republican Army, the Official Irish Republican Army, and the Provisional Irish Republican Army. The name was transposed from the Irish Republican Brotherhood.

survivalist A person who adopts a form of right-wing extremism advocating militant rejection of society. Advocates withdrawal from society in preparation for a coming internal war. Secluded in armed compounds, they hope to survive the coming collapse of society.

sweet crude A type of oil with less than 0.5 percent sulfur content. Nigeria sits on a large sweet crude field, giving the country potential wealth. The people who live above the oil, however, are poverty stricken, and oil production has been harmful to the environment.

Sykes, Mark (1879–1919) A British diplomat who signed a secret agreement with Francois Georges-Picot in May 1916. The Sykes-Picot Agreement divided the Middle East into spheres of French, British, and Russian influence.

symbolic targets Terrorist targets that may have limited military or security value but represent the power of the state under attack. Terrorists seek symbolic targets to strike fear into society and to give a sense of power to the terrorist group. The power of the symbol also multiplies the effect of the attack.

Tajik Civil War (1992–1997) The war fought between the government of Tajikistan and a confederation of opponents known as the United Tajik Opposition. The war resulted in democratic elections and power sharing between different political and religious groups. More than 100,000 people were killed during the war.

Taliban The Islamicist group that governed Afghanistan from 1996 to 2001.

Tamils An ethnic minority in southern India and Sri Lanka. The Tamils in Sri Lanka are primarily Hindu, and the Sinhalese majority mostly Buddhist. Ethnicity, however, not religion, defines most of the conflict between the two groups.

Task Force on Disorders and Terrorism The report issued by the National Advisory Commission Task Force on Disorders and Terrorism, the first presidential commission to investigate terrorism. Formed under the order of President Richard Nixon, the task force was headed by H. A. Cooper and was composed of some of the most noted terrorism analysts of the time.

task orientation As used in this text, the ability to stay focused on the primary mission of an organization.

tawhid "Oneness." In Islamic theology *tawhid* refers to unity of God. Abu Musab al Zarqawi once led a terrorist organization known as Tawhid.

Taylor, Charles (1948–) A warlord in the First War of the Liberian Civil War and president of Liberia from 1997 to 2003.

Terrorism Screening Center (TSC) A multiagency operation in West Virginia that evaluates information gathered from a variety of governmental sources.

theory of action A social science theory that assumes human beings take action based on the subjective meanings they attribute to social settings.

theory of suicide terrorism A theory developed by Robert Pape that states that a group of people occupied by a democratic power are likely to engage in suicide attacks when there are differences between the religions of the group and the democratic power and the occupied religious community supports altruistic suicide.

thermobaric bomb A two-stage bomb. The first stage spreads either a fuel cloud or finely ground powder through the air. The explosive material mixes with the oxygen present in the atmosphere. The second stage denotes the explosive material, which explodes in all directions in a series of shock waves. The cloud can penetrate a number of barriers. A person breathing the material explodes from the inside out when the material is ignited.

Third Position A movement started after the Branch Davidian standoff at Waco. It attempts to unite left-wing, right-wing, and single-issue extremists in a single movement.

Thirty Years' War A war beginning as a dispute between Protestants and Roman Catholics in

Prague and eventually pitting the north of Europe against the south. The war was savage and devastated the German states. France ended the war by leaving the Catholic alliance to fight against Austria. At the end of the war, Lutherans (and eventually Calvinists) and Roman Catholics agreed to tolerate each other's faith.

threat analysis The process of examining a community to determine the areas that might be subject to attack and the criticality of those areas to the functions of the community.

total criminal intelligence (TCI) All criminal intelligence gathered and analyzed for intelligence-led policing. Rather than focusing on one type of issue, such as terrorism, agencies focus on gathering information about all potential crimes and social problems.

Triborder region The area where Brazil, Paraguay, and Argentina join. The major city is Cuidad del Este.

Trotsky, Leon A Russian revolutionary who led foreign affairs in Stalin's government and later became the commander of the Red Army. He espoused terrorism as a means for spreading revolution. He was thrown out of the Communist Party for opposing Stalin and assassinated by communist agents in Mexico City in 1940.

Turabi, Hassan al (1932–) A Sudanese intellectual and Islamic scholar. He served in the Sudanese government during the time bin Laden was in exile in Sudan.

Turkish National Police The national uniformed and plainclothes investigative service of Turkey, established in 1909.

typology Classification of an issue by looking at different types. Because this text is designed for those studying criminal justice and related security functions, terrorism will be examined by looking at the different types of tactical behavior.

Uighars A Turkish ethnic group in central Asia. Many Uighars seek an autonomous state within China's Xinjiang province.

Umar (circa 580–644) Also known as Umar ibn al Khattab, the second Rightly Guided caliph, according to Sunnis. Under his leadership the Arab empire expanded into Persia, the southern part of the Byzantine empire, and Egypt. His army conquered Jerusalem in 637.

Umayyads The first Arab and Muslim dynasty ruling from Damascus from 661 to 750. The Umayyads were Uthman's family.

umbrella A group that shelters, supports, and inspires smaller terrorist groups. The RAND Corporation refers to this as a hub.

unstructured violence Disorganized violence from unmanaged groups or individuals.

urban terrorism A four-stage process described by Carlos Marighella: (1) unorganized violence accompanied by passive disruption, (2) governmental repression to stop violence, (3) massive uprising in response to repression, and (4) toppling of government.

USA Patriot Act A law passed in October 2001 that expands law enforcement's power to investigate and deter terrorism. Opponents claim that it adversely affects civil liberties; proponents claim that it introduces reasonable measures to protect the country against terrorists. The act was amended and renewed in 2006.

Uthman (circa 580–656) Also known as Uthman ibn Affan, the third Rightly Guided caliph, according to Sunnis. He conquered most of the remaining parts of North Africa, Iran, Cyprus, and the Caucasia region. He was assassinated by his own soldiers for alleged nepotism.

violent eschatology When a group believes it must wage war to purify the earth before the return of a deity.

viral weapons Enhanced forms of viruses. The virus is "hardened" so that it can live for long periods and enhanced for deadlier effects.

virtual organizations Associations that develop through communication, financial, and ideological links. Like a network, a virtual organization has no central leadership.

Waco siege The 1993 standoff between members of the Branch Davidian cult and federal law enforcement officers. The standoff ended when FBI agents tried to bring the siege to an end. Eighty-two people were killed.

Wahhab, Abdul (1703–1792) Also known as Mohammed ibn Abdul Wahhab, a religious reformer who wanted to purge Islam of anything beyond the traditions accepted by Mohammed and the four Rightly Guided caliphs. He conducted campaigns against Sufis, Shiites, and Muslims who made pilgrimages or who invoked the names of saints.

Wazir, Kahlil (1935–1988) A founder of Fatah and military leader for the PLO. His nom de guerre was Abu Jihad. He played a leading role in Black September and died in an Israeli-targeted assassination.

Waziristan Literally, the land of the Waziris, a tribal region between the North-West Frontier Province and Balochistan. Waziri tribes clashed with the Pakistan Army from 2004 to 2006, and they support several jihadist operations in Afghanistan and Pakistan. Al Qaeda and Taliban forces operate in Waziristan.

Weber, Max (1864–1920) One of the major figures of modern sociological methods, he studied the organization of human endeavors. Weber believed that social organizations could be organized for rational purposes designed to accomplish objectives.

Whiskey Rebellion The uprising that took place in 1797 when a group of Pennsylvania farmers refused to pay a federal tax on corn used to make alcohol. The rebellion ended when President George Washington sent troops to stop the rebellion.

white supremacy movement A political philosophy claiming that white people are superior to all other ethnic groups.

Workers Councils (or Soviets) The lowest-level legislative body in the Soviet Union following the October Revolution. *Soviet* is the Russian word for "council."

working group A term used in the federal government for a group of subject matter experts who gather to suggest solutions to common problems.

World Islamic Front against Jews and Crusaders An organization created in 1998 by Osama bin Laden and Ayman al Zawahiri. It represents a variety of jihadist groups that issued a united front against Jews and the West. It is commonly called al Qaeda.

Yassin, Ahmed (1937–2004) One of the founders and leaders of Hamas. Yassin originally started the Palestinian Wing of the Muslim Brotherhood, but merged it into Hamas during the Intifada. He was killed in an Israeli-targeted assassination.

Yoldash, Tohir (1967–) A founder of the Islamic Movement of Uzbekistan, now associated most closely with external relations, funding, and political leadership.

Yom Kippur War A war between Israel and its Arab neighbors fought in October 1973. Also known as the Ramadan War, hostilities began with a surprise attack on Israel. After initial setbacks, Israel counterattacked and regained its positions.

Youseff, Ramzi (1967–) A jihadist of Palestinian, Kuwaiti, or Pakistani descent. He is known by many other names. Youseff was linked to Sheik Omar Abdel Rahman and was responsible for the 1993 World Trade Center bombing. Involved in other plots, including an attempt to bring down a number of American airliners over the Pacific Ocean (Operation Bojinka), Youseff was arrested in Pakistan in 1995 and convicted of terrorist-related crimes in 1996. He is serving a life sentence without chance of parole.

Zarqawi, Abu Musab al (1966–2006) The nom de guerre of Jordanian-born Ahmed Fadel al Kaleyah. He left Jordan after getting out of prison to join the Afghan jihad in 1989. Training in al Qaeda camps, he returned to Jordan and formed Tawhid. After another arrest and imprisonment, Zarqawi returned to Afghanistan in 2001 to fight for al Qaeda. He re-formed Tawhid, but called it al Qaeda in Iraq. He was killed after being targeted by American forces.

Abbey, E. (1975). *The Monkey Wrench Gang*. Salt Lake City: Roaming the West.

ABC News. (1998). "John Miller Interview with Osama bin Laden." http://abcnews.co.com/sections/world/DailyNews/terror 1st person 980612.html.

———. (2004). "Al Qaeda Has 18,000 Militants for Raid—Think Tank." May 25. http://abcnews.go.com/sections/world/Investigation/Insider_DTR_040525.html.

Aboul-Enein, Y. H. (2004). "Ayman al-Zawahiri: The Ideologue of Modern Islamic Militancy." United States Air Force, Air University: Maxwell Air Force Base, AL. http://www.au.af.mil/awcgate/cpc-pubs/ward2.pdf.

Abrahamsen, R. (2004). "A Breeding Ground for Terrorists? Africa and Britain's War on Terrorism." *Review of African Political Economy* 31 (102): 677–684.

Abramson, L., and M. Godoy. (2006). "The Patriot Act: Key Controversies." National Public Radio. http://www.npr.org/news/specials/patriotact/patriot actprovisions.html.

Abuza, Z. (2003a). "Funding Terrorism in Southeast Asia: The Financial Network of al Qaeda and Jemaah Islamiya." *Contemporary Southeast Asia* 25, no. 2 (August): 169–200.

———. (2003b). *Militant Islam in Southeast Asia: Crucible of Terror*. Boulder, CO: Lynne Rienner.

———. (2006a). "JI Moneyman and Top Recruiter: A Profile of Noordin Mohammed Top." *Terrorism Focus* 3 (29) (July 25). http://jamestown.org/terrorism/news/article.php?issue_id=3811.

———. (2006b). "A Breakdown of Southern Thailand's Insurgent Groups." The Jamestown Foundation. *Terrorism Monitor* 4 (17). http://www.jamestown.org/terrorism/news/article.php?articleid=2370121.

Adams, B. (2005). "Nepal at the Precipice." *Foreign Affairs* 84 (5): 112–134.

Adams, D. (2003). "Narcoterrorism Needs Attention." *St. Petersburg Times*. March 10. http://www.sptimes.com/2003/03/10/columns/Narcoterrorism_need.shtml.

Adams, J. (1986). *The Financing of Terror*. New York: Simon & Schuster.

Agence France Presse. (2004). "Basque ETA Separatists Call for Unconditional Dialogue." http://www.elkarri.org/en/pdf/Agence_France_Pres_28_10_04.PDF.

Al Jazeera. (2006). "Timeline: Lebanon Conflict." English edition. August 17. http://english.aljazeera.net/English/archive/archive?ArchiveId=24660.

Albright, M. (2003). "Bridges, Bombs, or Bluster." *Foreign Affairs* 82 (September/ October): 2–19.

Alcohol, Tobacco, and Firearms (ATF), U.S. Department of the Treasury. (1995). *Violent White Supremacist Groups.* Washington, DC: ATF.

Algazy, J. (2004). "Amnesty: IDF Killed 100 Children Last Year." http://www .fromoccupiedpalestine.org/.

Alonso, R. (2001). "The Modernization in Irish Republican Thinking toward the Utility of Violence." *Studies in Conflict and Terrorism* 24 (2): 131–144.

Alonso, Z. (2004). "Border Guards Divided on Security Adequacy." *Los Angeles Times*, reported in *The Grand Rapids Press*, August 29, A5.

Althaus, S. L. (2002). "American News Consumption during Times of National Crisis." *Political Science and Politics* (September): 517–521. http://www .apsanet.org/imgtest/AmericanNewsConsumption-Althaus.pdf.

Altheide, D. L. (2006). "Terrorism and the Politics of Fear." *Cultural Studies ⇔ Critical Methodologies* 6 (4): 415–439. http://csc.sagepub.com.ezproxy.gvsu .edu:2048/cgi/reprint/6/4/415.

American Civil Liberties Union. (2002). "ACLU Decries Ashcroft Scheme to Gut Immigration Courts." March 20. http://www.aclu.org/ACLUPressRelease.

Amon, M. (2004). "Can Israel Survive the West Bank Settlements?" *Terrorism and Political Violence* 16 (Spring): 48–65.

Anderson, B. C. (2005). *South Park Conservatives: The Revolt Against Liberal Media Bias.* Washington, DC: Regnery.

Animal Liberation Front. (2000). Homepage. http://www.nocompromise.org/ alf/alf.html.

Appleby, R. S. (2000). *The Ambivalence of the Sacred.* New York: Rowman & Littlefield.

Armstrong, K. (2000a). *Islam: A Short History.* New York: The Modern Library.

———. (2000b). *The Battle for God.* New York: Random House.

Army of God. (n.d.). "The Army of God Manual." http://www.armyofgod.com/ AOGhistory.html.

Arquilla, J., and D. Ronfeldt. (1996). *The Advent of Netwar.* Santa Monica, CA: RAND.

———. (2001). *Networks and Netwars: The Future of Terror, Crime, and Militancy.* Santa Monica, CA: RAND.

Arquilla, J., D. Ronfeldt, and M. Zanini. (1999). "Networks, Netwar, and Information-Age Terrorism." In Ian O. Lesser et al. (eds.), *Countering the New Terrorism.* Santa Monica, CA: RAND.

Asprey, R. B. (2002). *War in the Shadows: The Guerrilla in History.* Lincoln, NE: iUniverse.

Associated Press. (2006). "Provisions in the USA Patriot Act." May 7. http://sf gate.com/cgi-bin/article.cgi?f=/n/a/2006/03/07/national/w134940S84.DTL.

———. (2007a). "Thousands Protest in Turkey Against an Islamic-Based Government." May 20. *The International Herald Tribune*. http://www.iht.com/articles/2007/05/20/africa/ankara.php.

———. (2007b). "Spain Arrests 15 on Terror Recruitment Charges." MSNBC, May 28. http://www.msnbc.msn.com/id/18903462/.

ATF. *See* Alcohol, Tobacco, and Firearms.

Awad, N. (2003). "Written Testimony of Nihad Awad Before the Senate Subcommittee on Terrorism, Technology, and Homeland Security." September 10. http://www.anti-cair-net.org/awadTestimony2003.html.

Azam, J. P. (2005). "Suicide Bombing as an Inter-Generational Investment." *Political Choice* 122:177–198.

Azano, H. J. (2003). "Can Security Help with Civil Defense?" *Security Management* (February). http://www.securitymagement.com/.

Azmanova, A. (2004). "The Mobilisation of the European Left in the Early Twenty-First Century." *European Journal of Sociology/Archives Europeénnes de Sociologie* 45 (2): 273–306.

Badey, T. J. (2003). "Defining International Terrorism: A Pragmatic Approach." In T. J. Badey (ed.), *Annual Editions—Violence and Terrorism 2003/2004*. New York: McGraw-Hill.

Baginski, M. (2004). "Statement of Maureen A. Baginski before the House of Representatives Select Committee on Homeland Security." August 22. http://www.gov/congress/congress04baginsky081704.htm.

Bakier, A. H. (2006a). "Jihadis Provide Internet Training for Female Suicide Bombers." *Terrorism Focus* 3 (40). http://www.jamestown.org/terrorism/news/article.php?issue_id=3890.

———. (2006b). "Lesson from al Qaeda's Attack on the Khobar Compound." *Terrorism Monitor*. http://jamestown.org/terrorism/news/article.php?issue_id=3830.

Bakunin, M. (1866). "Revolution, Terrorism, Banditry." Repr. 1987, pp. 65–68.

Ballard, J. D. (2003). *Nuclear Waste Transportation*. Reno: State of Nevada. http://www.state.nv.us/nucwaste/news2003/pdf/nas_ballard.pdf.

Barber, B. R. (1996). *Jihad vs. McWorld: How Globalism and Tribalism Are Reshaping the World*. New York: Ballantine Books.

Barkan, J. D. (2004). "Kenya After Moi." *Foreign Affairs* 83 (1): 87–100.

Barkun, M. (1997a). *Religion and the Racist Right: The Origins of the Christian Identity Movement*. Chapel Hill: University of North Carolina Press.

———. (1997b). "Leaderless Resistance and Phineas Priests: Strategies of Uncoordinated Violence on the Far Right." Paper presented at the American Society of Criminology, San Diego.

Barnett, T. P. M. (2004). *The Pentagon's New Map: War and Peace in the Twenty-first Century*. New York: Putnam's.

Baron, D. P. (2004). "Persistent Media Bias." http://www.wallis.rochester.edu/conferenceII/mediabias.pdf.

Basile, M. (2004). "Going to the Source: Why al Qaeda's Financial Network Is Likely to Withstand the Current War on Terrorist Financing." *Studies in Conflict and Terrorism* 27 (3): 169–185.

Bassiouni, M. C. (1981). "Terrorism and the Media." *Journal of Criminal Law and Criminology* 72:1–55.

BBC News. (2000). "Turkish Hezbollah: No State Links." January 23. http://news.bbc.co.uk/1/hi/world/europe/615785.stm.

———. (2001). "Time Line India Targeted Attacks." December 13. http://news.bbc.co.uk/2/hi/south_asia/1708861.stm.

———. (2002). "Challenge to Israel's Assassination Policy." January 24. http://news.bbc.co.uk/1/hi/world/middle_east/1780051.stm.

———. (2003). "Profile: Al Aqsa Martyrs' Brigades." BBC New World Edition. July 1. http://news.bbc.co.uk/z/hi/middle_east/1760492.stm.

———. (2004). "Timeline: Madrid Investigation." April 28. http://news.bbc.co.uk/1/hi/world/europe/3597885.stm.

———. (2005a). "Arrest after Stabbing Victim Dies." January 30. http://news.bbc.co.uk/1/hi/northern_ireland/4221599.stm.

———. (2005b). "Murder Witnesses Facing Threats." March 9. http://news.bbc.co.uk/1/hi/northern_ireland/4332747.stm.

———. (2005c). "IRA Weapons Report Handed Over." http://news.bbc.co.uk/1/hi/northern_ireland/4281104.stm.

———. (2006). "Turkey Seizes al Qaeda Members." December 9. http://news.bbc.co.uk/2/hi/europe/6164789.stm.

Bell, J. B. (1974). *The Secret Army: A History of the IRA, 1916–1970.* Cambridge, MA: MIT Press.

———. (1975). *Transnational Terror.* Washington, DC: American Enterprise Institute.

———. (1976). "Strategy, Tactics, and Terror: An Irish Perspective." In Yonah Alexander (ed.), *International Terrorism.* New York: Praeger.

———. (1998). "Ireland: The Long End Game." *Studies in Conflict and Terrorism* 21:5–28.

Bell, J. B., and T. R. Gurr. (1979). "Terrorism and Revolution in America." In H. D. Graham and T. R. Gurr (eds.), *Violence in America.* Newbury Park, CA: Sage.

Benini, A. A., and L. H. Moulton. (2004). "Civilian Victims in an Asymmetrical Conflict: Operation Enduring Freedom, Afghanistan." *Journal of Peace Research* 41 (4): 403–422.

Benjamin, D., and S. Simon. (2002). *The Age of Sacred Terror.* New York: Random House.

———. (2003). "The Real Worry: In Iraq We Have Created a New Field of Jihad." *Time*, September 1 (vol. 162), p. 35.

Bergen, P., and P. Cruickshank. (2007). "Al Qaeda-on-Thames: UK Plotters Connected." *Washington Post*, April 30. PostGlobal.com. http://newsweek.washingtonpost.com/postglobal/needtoknow/2007/04/al_qaedaonthames_plotters_well.html.

Bergen, P. L. (2001). *Holy War, Inc.: Inside the Secret World of Osama bin Laden.* New York: Free Press.

Berger, C. R., J. T. Johnson, and E. J. Lee. (2003). "Antidotes for Anthrax Anecdotes: The Role of Rationality and Base-Rate Data in Assuaging Apprehension." *Communication Research* 30:199–223. http://crx.sagepub.com/cgi/content/abstract/30/2/198.

Berkeley, B. (2001). *The Graves Are Not Yet Full: Race, Tribe, and Power in the Heart of Africa*. New York: Basic Books.

Berlet, C., and M. N. Lyons. (2000). *Right-Wing Populism in America: Too Close for Comfort*. New York: Guildford.

Berthelsen, J. (1996). "Room with No View." *Far Eastern Economic Review*, May 9, p. 159.

Best, R. A., Jr. (2001). *Intelligence and Law Enforcement: Countering Transnational Threats to the U.S.* Congressional Reference Service. CRS Report for Congress. December 3. http://www.fas.org/irp/crs/RL30252.pdf.

Betts, R. K. (2002). "Fixing Intelligence." *Foreign Affairs* 81:43–59.

Bew, P. (1999). "Moderate Nationalism and the Irish Revolution, 1916–1923." *The Historical Journal* 42 (3): 729–749.

Black, D. (2004). "The Geometry of Terrorism." *Sociological Theory* 22 (1): 14–25.

Black, I. (2003). "EU Hits Out at Israeli Fence." *The Guardian*. November 18. http://www.guardian.co.uk/israel/Story/0,2763,1087396,00.html.

Blank, S. (2003). "Testimony—Committee on International Relations, Subcommittee on the Middle East and Central Asia, U.S. House of Representatives." *Congressional Quarterly*, December 29. "Terrorism in Asia and the Pacific." http://homeland.cq.cm/hs/display.do?dockey=/usr/local/cqonline/docs/html.

Blomberg, S. B., G. D. Hess, and A. Weerapana (2004). "An Economic Model of Terrorism." *Conflict Management and Peace Science* 21:17–28.

Bodansky, Y. (1999). *Bin Laden: The Man Who Declared War on America*. Rocklin, CA: Forum.

Bodrero, D. D. (2002). "Law Enforcement's New Challenge to Investigate, Interdict, and Prevent Terrorism." *The Police Chief* (February): 41–48.

Bodrero, D. D., et al. (forthcoming). "Homegrown Terrorism." *FBI Law Enforcement Bulletin.*

Borum, R. (2004). *Psychology of Terrorism*. University of South Florida.

Boustany, N. (2005). "Spain Keeps a Vigilant Eye on al Qaeda Threat." *Washington Post*, April 20. http://www.washingtonpost.com/wp-dyn/articles/A2944-2005Apr19.html.

Bowers, S. R., and K. R. Keys. (1998). "Technology and Terrorism: The New Threat for the Millennium." *Conflict Studies* (May).

Bozell, L. B. (2005). *Weapons of Mass Distortion: The Coming Meltdown of the Liberal Media*. New York: Three Rivers Press.

Brachman, J. M., and W. F. McCants. (2006). "CTC Report: Stealing Al-Qaida's Playbook." West Point, NY: United States Military Academy. http://www.ctc.usma.edu.

Brackett, D. W. (1996). *Holy Terror: Armageddon in Tokyo*. New York: Weatherhill.

Bradley, E. (2004). *60 Minutes*. CBS.

Bradshaw, B. (1978). "Sword, Word, and Strategy in the Reformation in Ireland." *The Historical Journal* 21 (3): 475–502.

Brar, S. S. (2003). "The Sikhism Homepage." http://www.sikhs.org/.

Bravin, J. (2007). "Terror War Legal Edifice Teeters." *The Wall Street Journal*, June 13, A4.

Bruce, S. (2001). "Terrorism and Politics: The Case of Northern Ireland's Loyalist Paramilitaries." *Studies in Conflict and Terrorism* 13 (2): 27–48.

Buchanan, P. J. (2002). *The Death of the West: How Dying Populations and Immigrant Invasions Imperil Our Country and Civilization*. New York: Thomas Dunn.

Bunker, R. J. (1998). "Information Operations and the Conduct of Land Warfare." *Military Review*, September–November, pp. 4–17. http://www.iwar.org.uk/war/resources/milrev/bunker/pdf.

Burgess, C. A. (2007). "Opening Remarks." First National Fusion Center Conference, Destin, FL. Unpublished.

Burgess, M. (2002). "In the Spotlight: The Islamic Movement of Uzbekistan (IMU)." Center for Defense Information. http://www.cdi.org/terrorism/imu.cfm.

Burke, J. (2004). "Al Qaeda Launches Online Terrorist Manual." *Guardian Unlimited*. http://www.guardian.co.uk/alqaida/story/0,12469,1125879,00.html.

Burton, A. (1976). *Urban Terrorism*. New York: Free Press.

Butler, P. (2002). "Terrorism and Utilitarianism: Lessons from, and for, Criminal Law." *Journal of Criminal Law and Criminology* 93:1–22.

Butler, R. E. (1976). "Terrorism in Latin America." In Yonah Alexander (ed.), *International Terrorism*. New York: Praeger.

Byford, G. (2002). "The Wrong War." *Foreign Affairs* 81 (July/August): 34–43.

Byman, D. (1998). "The Logic of Ethnic Terrorism." *Studies in Conflict and Terrorism* 21:149–169.

———. (2003). "Should Hezbollah be Next?" *Foreign Affairs* 82 (6): 54–66.

———. (2006). "Do Targeted Killings Work?" *Foreign Affairs* 85 (2): 95–111.

Cahill, T. (2003). *How the Irish Saved Civilization: The Untold Story of Ireland's Heroic Role from the Fall of Rome to the Rise of Medieval Europe*. New York: Bantam/Doubleday.

Calabresi, M., and R. Ratnesar. (2002). "Can We Stop the Next Attack?" *Time*, March 11, pp. 24–37.

Calhoun, C. (1989). "Classical Social Theory and the French Revolution of 1848." *Sociological Theory* 7(2): 210–225.

California Department of Justice, Office of the Attorney General. (2002). Anti-Terrorist Information Center. http://caag.state.ca.us/antiterrorism/index.htm.

California Highway Patrol. (2007). "State Terrorism Threat Assessment Center." http://www.chp.ca.gov/offices/sttac.html.

Cappel, R. P. (1979). *S.W.A.T. Team Manual*. Boulder, CO: Paladin Press.

Carmichael, P., and C. Knox. (2004). "Devolution, Governance, and the Peace Process." *Studies in Conflict and Terrorism* 16 (Autumn): 593–621.

Carter, D. L. (2004). *Law Enforcement Intelligence: A Guide for State, Local, and Tribal Agencies*. U.S. Department of Justice. http://www.cops.usdoj.gov/default.asp?Item=1404.

———. (2005). "The Law Enforcement Intelligence Function: State, Local, and Tribal Agencies." *The FBI Law Enforcement Bulletin* (June). http://findarticles .com/p/articles/mi_m2194/is_6_74/ai_n15966184.

Cassara, J. A. (2006). *Hide and Seek: Intelligence, Law Enforcement, and the Stalled War on Terrorist Finance*. Dulles, VA: Potomac Books.

Casteel, Steven W. (2003). "Narco-Terrorism: International Drug Trafficking and Terrorism—A Dangerous Mix." Testimony, Committee on the Judiciary, U.S. Senate. May 20. http://www.judiciary.senate.gov/testimony .cfm?id=764&wit_id=2111.

Cavanaugh, T. (2004). "Meet Hizbollah." *Reasononline*, March 11. http://reason .com/interview/hizbollah.shtml.

CBS News. (2004). "Chicago Bomb Plot Stopped." August 5. http://www .cbsnews.com/stories/2004/08/05/terror/main634270.shtml.

Cebrowski, A. K. (2004). "Netwar." Unpublished speech at the Assistant Secretary of Defense Conference on Special Operations. September. Alexandria, VA.

Cebrowski, A. K., and T. P. M. Barnett. (2003). "The American Way of War." *Proceedings US Naval Institute*, January: 42–43.

Cebrowski, A. K., and J. J. Gratska. (1998). "Network-Centric Warfare: Its Origins and Future." *Proceedings of the U.S. Naval Institute*, January, pp. 28–35.

Center for Consumer Freedom. (2004). "Non-Violent Protests with Guns?" September 4. http://www.consumerfreedom.com/news_detail.cfm/headline/ 1561.

Center for Strategic and International Studies. (2004). *Cybercrime, Cyberterrorism, and Cyberwarfare*. Forward and Recommendations. http://www.csis.org/ pubs/cyberfor.html.

Chang, N. (2001). "The USA Patriot Act: What's So Patriotic about Trampling on the Bill of Rights?" Center for Constitutional Rights. http://www.ccr-ny.org/ whatsnew/usa_patriot_act.asp.

Chermak, S., and A. Weiss. (2006). "Community Policing in the News Media." *Police Quarterly* 9 (2): 135–160.

Chertoff, M. (2007). "Keynote Address." First National Fusion Center Conference, Destin, FL. February. Unpublished.

Chomsky, N. (2002). "Who Are the Global Terrorists?" http://secondpress.ca/ articles/151-may25-chomsky.pdf.

———. (2006). "On the U.S. Israeli Invasion of Lebanon." Znet, August 23. http://www.zmag.org/content/showarticle.cfm?ItemID=10811.

Chouvy, P. A. (2004). "Narco-Terrorism in Afghanistan." *Terrorism Monitor: In-Depth Analysis of the War on Terror* 2 (6) (March 25).

Christopher, W. (1999). "Report of the Independent Commission on the Los Angeles Police Department." In Larry K. Gaines and Gary W. Cordner (eds.), *Policing Perspectives: An Anthology*. Los Angeles: Roxbury.

Chung, C.-P. (2002). "China's 'War on Terror.'" *Foreign Affairs* 81 (4): 8–12.

Cilliers, J. (2003). "Terrorism and Africa." *African Security Review* 12 (4): 91–103. http://www.iss.org.za/pubs/ASR/12No4/Cilliers.pdf.

Cilluffo, F. J., S. L. Cardash, and G. N. Lederman. (2001). *Combating Chemical, Biological, Radiological, and Nuclear Terrorism: A Comprehensive Strategy: A Report of the CSIS Homeland Defense Project*. Washington, DC: Center for Strategic and International Studies.

Clark, C. (2006). *Iron Kingdom: The Rise and Downfall of Prussia, 1600–1947*. London: Oxford University Press.

Clark, J. K. (1988). "Guevara." Global Security. http://www.globalsecurity.org/military/library/report/1988/CJK.htm.

Clark, K. (1998). *Petersburg: Crucible of Cultural Revolution*. Cambridge, MA: Harvard University Press.

Clark, R. (1984). *The Basque Insurgents*. Madison: University of Wisconsin Press.

———. (1979). *The Basques*. Reno: University of Nevada Press.

Clark, W. K. (2001). *Waging Modern War*. New York: Public Affairs.

Clarke, R. (2002). Testimony on Cyberspace Security. U.S. Senate Subcommittee on the Judiciary. Washington, DC: U.S. Senate, recorded from C-Span, February 13.

Clarke, R. A. (2007). "A Back Door for Terrorists." *The New York Times*. June 1. Opinion, Editorial.

Clausewitz, C. (1831). *On War*. M. Howard and P. Paret (trans.). Repr., Princeton, NJ: Princeton University Press, 1984.

Clayton, M. (2005). "Is Black-Market Baby Formula Financing Terror?" *The Christian Science Monitor*, June 29. http://www.csmonitor.com/2005/0629/p01s01-usju.html.

Cloward, R., and L. Ohlin. (1960). *Delinquency and Opportunity*. New York: Free Press.

Clutterbuck, L. (2004). "The Progenitors of Terrorism: Russian Revolutionaries or Extreme Irish Republicans?" *Terrorism and Political Violence* 16 (Spring): 154–181.

Clutterbuck, R. C. (1975). *Living with Terrorism*. London: Faber & Faber.

CNN. (2002). "Russian Troops Storm Moscow Theater." October 26. http://archives.cnn.com/2002/WORLD/europe/10/25/moscow.siege/index.html.

———. (2004a) "Most Will Miss Biometric Passport Deadline." January 29. http://www.cnn.com/2004/US/01/28/biometric.passports/.

———. (2004b). "Cyanide, Arsenal Stirs Domestic Terror Fear." January 30. http://www.cnn.com/2004/US/Southwest/01/30/cynaide.probe.ap/index.html.

———. (2006). "House Approves Patriot Act." CNN.com. http://www.cnn.com/2006/POLITICS/03/07/patriot.act/.

Cochrane, P. (2004). "Is Al-Hurra Doomed?" Worldpress.org. http://www.worldpress.org/Mideast/1872.cfm.

Cohen, A. (2003). "Testimony—Committee on International Relations, Subcommittee on the Middle East and Central Asia, U.S. House of Representatives." *Congressional Quarterly*, October 29. "Terrorism in Asia and the Pacific." http://homeland.cq.cm/hs/display.do?dockey=/usr/local/cqonline/docs/html.

Colb, S. F. (2001). "The New Face of Racial Profiling: How Terrorism Affects the Debate." *Find Law's Legal Commentary*, October 10. http://writ.news.findlaw.com/200111010.html.

Cole, D. (2003). *Enemy Aliens: Double Standards and Constitutional Freedoms in the War on Terrorism*. New York: The New Press.

Cole, D., and J. X. Dempsey. (2002). *Terrorism and the Constitution: Sacrificing Civil Liberties in the Name of National Security*. New York: Free Press.

Cole, G. F., and C. E. Smith. (2004). *The American System of Justice*. Belmont, CA: Wadsworth.

Collin, B. (2004). "The Future of CyberTerrorism: Where the Physical and Virtual Worlds Converge." http://afgen.com/terrorism1.html.

Commission of Inquiry. (2007). "Terrorism, Intelligence, and Law Enforcement: Canada's Response to Sikh Terrorism." Commission of Inquiry into the Investigation of the Bombing of Air India Flight 182. http://www.majorcomm.ca/documents/dossier2_ENG.pdf.

Commission on Accreditation for Law Enforcement Agencies. (1990). *Accreditation Program Overview*. Fairfax, VA: CALEA.

Conetta, C. (2001). "Strange Victory: A Critical Appraisal of Operation Enduring Freedom and the Afghan War." Cambridge, MA: Project on Defense Alternatives. http://www.comw.org/pda/0201strangevic.pdf.

Cook, N. (2006). "AIDS in Africa." CRS Reports for Congress. http://fas.org/sgp/crs/row/IB10050.pdf.

Cooley, J. (2002). *Unholy Wars: Afghanistan, America, and International Terrorism*. London: Pluto Press.

Coolidge, S., and J. Prendergast. (2003). "Police Shut Down Crime Ring." *The Cincinnati Enquirer*, October 3. http://www.enquirer.com/editions/2003/10/03/loc_crimering03.html.

Cooper, H. H. A., et al. (1976). *Task Force Report on Disorders and Terrorism*. Washington, DC: National Advisory Committee on Criminal Justice Standards and Goals.

Cooper, H. H. A. (1977a). "Terrorism and the Media." In Yonah Alexander and Seymour Finger (eds.), *Terrorism: Interdisciplinary Perspectives*. New York: John Jay.

———. (1977b). "What Is a Terrorist? A Psychological Perspective." *Legal Medical Quarterly* 1:8–18.

———. (1978). "Terrorism: The Problem of the Problem Definition." *Chitty's Law Journal* 26:105–108.

———. (2001). "Terrorism: The Problem of Definition Revisited." *American Behavioral Scientist*. February (44): 881–893.

Corley, F. (2004). "Ruslan Gelayev: Feared Chechen Rebel-Turned-Bandit." *Independent News*, March 4. http://news.independent.co.uk/people/obituaries/story.jsp?story=497568.

Corman, S. R., and J. S. Schiefelbein. (2006). "Communication and Media Strategy in the Jihadi War of Ideas." Phoenix: Arizona State University. http://www.asu.edu/clas/communication/about/csc/publications/jihad_comm_media.pdf.

Cornell, S. E. (2005). "Narcotics, Radicalism and Armed Conflict in Central Asia: The Islamic Movement of Uzbekistan." *Terrorism and Political Violence* 17 (4): 577–597.

Corrado, R., and R. Evans. (1988). "Ethnic and Ideological Terrorism in Western Europe." In M. Stohl (ed.), *The Politics of Terrorism*. New York: Dekker.

Costigan, G. (1980). *A History of Modern Ireland*. Indianapolis, IN: Bobbs-Merrill.

Cottle, S. (2006). "Mediatizing the Global War on Terror," In A. P. Kavoori and T. Fraley (eds.), *Media, Terrorism, and Theory: A Reader*. Lanham, MD: Rowman & Littlefield.

Council on Foreign Relations. (2002). "Basque Fatherland and Liberty (ETA)." http://cfrterrorism.org/groups/eta.html.

———. (2004). "Al-Asqa Martyrs Brigades." http://cfrterrorism.org/groups/alasqa.html.

———. (2005b). "Terrorism Havens: Pakistan." http://www.cfr.org/publication/9514/#3.

———. (2006). "Kashmir Militant Extremists." http://www.cfr.org/publication/9135/.

Countdown with Keith Olberman. (2004). "Interview with Steven Emerson." MSNBC.

Craig, G. A. (1968). *The Politics of the Prussian Army, 1640–1945*. New York: Oxford University Press.

Creativity Movement. (n.d.). "The Creativity Movement." http://www.creativitymovement.net/ (accessed 2007).

Creed, R. D., Jr. (2002). "Eighteen Years in Lebanon and Two Intifadas: The Israeli Defense Force and the U.S. Army Operational Environment." Fort Leavenworth, KS: U.S. Army Command and General Staff College.

Crenshaw, M. (ed.). (1983). *Terrorism, Legitimacy, and Power*. Middletown, CT: Wesleyan University Press.

Creveld, M. van. (1991). *The Transformation of War*. Cambridge, MA: Harvard University Press.

Crile, C. (2003). *Charlie Wilson's War*. New York: Grove Press.

Criss, N. B. (1995). "The Nature of PKK Terrorism in Turkey." *Studies in Conflict and Terrorism* 18:17–38.

Critical Incident Analysis Group. (2001). *Threats to Symbols of American Democracy*. Charlottesville: University of Virginia.

Cronin, A. K. (2003). "Al Qaeda after the Iraq Conflict." Congressional Reference Service. CRS Report for Congress, Order Code RS21529, May 23.

Cronin, S. (1984). *Irish Nationalism: A History of its Roots and Ideology*. Dublin: University Press of Ireland.

C-Span. (2007). House Subcommittee on Homeland Security. "Testimony: Brian Jenkins, Frank Cilluffo, and Salam al Marayati." June 14.

Cumming, A., and T. Masse. (2004). "FBI Intelligence Reform Since September 11, 2001: Issues for Congress." Congressional Reference Service. http://www.house.gov/etheridge/CRSREPRT.doc.pdf.

Cummings, J. (2002). "States Mend Homeland Security Blanket." *Wall Street Journal*, August 13, p. A4.

Curtis, E. (2000). *A History of Ireland from the Earliest Times to 1922*. London: Routledge. (Orig. pub. 1936.)

Dagne, T. (2002). "Africa and the War on Terrorism." CRS Report for Congress. http://fpc.state.gov/documents/organization/7959.pdf.

Daily Mail. (2007). "Olmert: No Option but to Strike Hezbollah Immediately." *Daily Mail Online*, May 10. http://www.dailymail.co.uk/pages/live/articles/news/worldnews.html?in_article_id=453922&in_page_id=1811.

Dakroub, H. (2004). "Beheading Condemned by Hamas and Hizbollah." *Independent News*. http://news.independent.co.uk/world/middle_east/story.jsp?story=521094.

Daly, J. C. K. (2006a). "Saudi Oil Facilities: Al Qaeda's Next Target?" *Terrorism Monitor*. http://jamestown.org/terrorism/news/article.php?articleid=2369910.

———. (2006b). "The Baloch Insurgency and Its Threat to Pakistan's Energy Sector." *Terrorism Focus*. http://jamestown.org/terrorism/news/article.php?issue_id=3660.

Damphousse, K. R., and B. L. Smith. (2004). "Terrorism and Empirical Testing: Using Indictment Data to Assess Changes in Terrorism Conduct." In M. De-Flem, *Terrorism and Counter-terrorism: Criminological Perspectives*. Amsterdam: Elsevier.

Daniels, D. A. (2003). "Breaking Barriers: Sharing Information in a Changing World." Law Enforcement Information Sharing Symposium, Office of Justice Programs, U.S. Department of Justice, Arlington, VA. http://www.ojp.usdoj.gov/aag/speeches/deainfosharing.htm.

Danitz, T., and W. P. Strobel. (1999). "The Internet's Impact on Activism: The Case of Burma." *Studies in Conflict and Terrorism* 22: 257–269.

Darby, J. (1995). "Conflict in Northern Ireland: A Background Essay." In S. Dunn (ed.), *Facets of Conflict in Northern Ireland*. Basingstoke, UK: MacMillan.

Dawisha, A. (2003). *Arab Nationalism in the Twentieth Century: From Triumph to Despair*. Princeton, NJ: Princeton University Press.

Dawkins, R. (1998). *Unweaving the Rainbow: Science, Delusion, and the Appetite for Wonder*. Boston: Houghton Mifflin Company.

de Silva, M. (1996). "Sunshine over Jaffna." *Far Eastern Economic Review*, May 5, p. 159.

Debray, J. R. (1967). *Revolution in the Revolution?* Westport, CT: Greenwood.

del Carmen, R. (1991). *Civil Liberties in American Policing: A Text for Law Enforcement Personnel*. Englewood Cliffs, NJ: Prentice-Hall.

Della Porta, Donatella. (1995). "Left-Wing Terrorism in Italy." In M. Crenshaw (ed.), *Terrorism in Context*. State College: Pennsylvania State University.

Denson, B., and J. Long. (1999). "Ecoterrorism Sweeps the American West," *Portland Oregonian*, September 26; "Ideologues Drive the Violence," September 27; "Terrorist Acts Provoke Change in Research, Business, Society," September 28; "Can Sabotage Have a Place in a Democratic Community?" September 29. http://www.oregonlive.com/cgi-bin/printer/printer.cgi.

DHS. *See* U.S. Department of Homeland Security.

Diamond, L. (2004). "What Went Wrong in Iraq." *Foreign Affairs* 83 (September/October): 34–56.

Dillon, S. (2001). "A Forum Recalls Unheeded Warning." *New York Times*, October 4, p. A16.

Diminyatz, K. L. (2003). "Providing for the Common Defense: Securing the Southwest Border." United States Army War College. Project Paper. http://stinet.dtic.mil/cgi-bin/GetTRDoc?AD=ADA414219&Location=U2&doc=GetTRDoc.pdf.

Discovery Times Channel. (2005). *Media Jihad*.

Dixon, P. (2004). "Peace within the Realms of the Possible? David Trimble, Unionist Ideology, and Theatrical Politics." *Terrorism and Political Violence* 16 (Autumn): 462–482.

Dobbins, J. (2005). "Iraq: Winning the Unwinnable War." *Foreign Affairs* 84 (January/February): 16–25.

Dobson, C., and R. Payne. (1982). *The Terrorists.* New York: Facts on File.

Donnelly, J. (2005). "Oil in Africa: A Special Report by the Boston Globe." *The Boston Globe.* http://www.boston.com/news/specials/oil_in_africa/.

Donovan, M. (2002). "Palestinian Islamic Jihad." Center for Defense Information. http://www.cdi.org/terrorism/pij.cfm.

Doran, M. S. (2002). "Somebody Else's Civil War." *Foreign Affairs* 81 (January/February).

Downs, A. C. (1967). *Inside Bureaucracy.* Boston: Little, Brown.

Doyle, C. (2002). "The USA Patriot Act: A Sketch." Congressional Reference Service. CRS Report for Congress. http://www.fas.org/irp/crs/RS21203.pdf.

Drakos, K., and A. M. Kutan. (2003). "Regional Effects of Terrorism on Tourism in Three Mediterranean Countries." *Journal of Conflict Resolution* 45 (5): 621–641.

Dreyfuss, R. (2002). "The Cops Are Watching You." March 23. http://www.ccmep.org/hotnews2/cops_are_watching052302.htm.

Duekmedjian, J. E. (2006). "From Community to Intelligence: Executive Realignment of the RCMP Mission." *Canadian Journal of Criminology and Criminal Justice* 48 (4): 523–542.

Dunn, S., and V. Morgan. (1995). "Protestant Alienation in Northern Ireland." *Studies in Conflict and Terrorism* 18:175–185.

Durham, F. D. (1998). "News Frames as Social Narratives: TWA Flight 800." *Journal of Communication* 48 (4): 100–117.

Duyvesteyn, I. (2004). "How New is the New Terrorism?" *Studies in Conflict and Terrorism* 27 (2): 439–454.

Dymond, J. (2004). "U.S. and Turkey to Hit PKK." BBC News, October 2. http://news.bbc.uk/2/hi/europe/3158686.stm.

Dyson, W. E. (2001). *Investigating Terrorism: An Investigator's Handbook.* Cincinnati, OH: Anderson.

———. (2004). *Terrorism: An Investigator's Handbook* (2nd ed.). Cincinnati, OH: Anderson.

Economist. (2003). "Al Qaeda Operations are Rather Cheap." October 4, p. 45.

Ehlen, P. (2001). *Frantz Fanon: A Spiritual Biography.* New York: Crossroad 8th Avenue.

Ehrenfeld, R. (2003). *Funding Evil: How Terrorism Is Financed and How to Stop It.* Chicago: Bonus Books.

Elbe, P. (2000). "The Orange Order in the Wake of Drumcree: Parity of Esteem, Protest, and Propaganda in Northern Ireland, 1995–98." *Archive: A Journal of Undergraduate History.* http://www.sit.wisc.edu/~uwho/Archive/Archive%20 4%20orange%20order.pdf.

———. (2001). "EFF Analysis of the Provisions of the USA Patriot Act." http://www.eff.org/Privacy/Surveillance/Terrorism_militias/20011031_efft _usa_Patriot_analysis.html.

Ellingsen, T. (2005). "Toward a Revival of Religion and Religious Clashes?" *Terrorism and Political Violence* 17 (3): 305–332.

Emerson, S. A. (1994). *Jihad in America.* Public Broadcasting System.

———. (2002). *American Jihad: The Terrorist Living Among Us.* New York: Free Press.

———. (2006). *Jihad Incorporated: A Guide to Militant Islam in the U.S.* Amherst, NY: Prometheus.

Emerson, S. A., and Cristina Del Sesto. (1991). *Terrorist: The Inside Story of the Highest Ranking Iraqi Terrorist Ever to Defect to the West.* New York: Villard.

Emerson, S. A. and J. Levin. (2003). "Terrorism Financing: Origin, Organization, and Prevention: Saudi Arabia, Terrorist Financing and the War on Terror." Testimony, United States Senate, Committee on Governmental Affairs. July 31.

Enteshami, A. (1995). *After Khomeini: The Iranian Second Republic.* London: Routledge.

Epstein, B. (2001). "Anarchism and the Anti-Globalism Movement." *Monthly Review* 53 (4): 1–14.

Eriksson, M. (2006). "Islamic Extremism in Uzbekistan: Is It a Threat?" Stanford University. *Stanford's Student Journal of Russian, East European, and Eurasian Studies* (Spring). http://zhe.stanford.edu/spring06/extremism.pdf.

Esposito, J. (1999). *The Islamic Threat: Myth or Reality.* New York: Oxford University Press.

Esposito, J. L. (2002). *Unholy War: Terror in the Name of Islam.* New York: Oxford University Press.

FAIR. (1999). "Extra!'s Report on Steven Emerson: Setting the Record Straight." Fairness & Accuracy in Reporting, February 2. http://www.fair.org/press -releases/emerson.html.

Fanon, F. (1980). *A Dying Colonialism.* London: Writers and Readers. (Orig. pub. 1965.)

———. (1982). *The Wretched of the Earth.* New York: Grove.

Farah, C. (2000). *Islam.* Hauppage, NY: Baron's.

Farrell, W. R. (1990). *Blood and Rage: The Story of the Japanese Red Army.* Lexington, MA: Lexington Books.

FBI. (1999). *Terrorism in the United States: Special Report—Thirty Years of Terrorism.* Washington, DC: FBI.

———. (2000). "U.S. Embassy Bombings Summary." http://www.fbi.gov/majcase/eastafrica/summary.htm.

———. (2002). *Terrorism 2000/2001.* http://www.fbi.gov/publications/terror/terror2000_2001.htm (accessed 2006).

———. (2004). "Counterterrorism Website." October 12. http://www.fbi.gov/terrorinfo/terrorism.htm.

———. (2005). "Crime in the United States 2005." http://www.fbi.gov/ucr/05cius/ (accessed 2006).

———. (n.d.). "Counterterrorism." http://www.fbi.gov/terrorinfo/counterrorism/waronterrorhome.htm (accessed 2007).

Feickert, A. (2005). "U.S. Military Operations in the Global War on Terrorism: Afghanistan, Africa, the Philippines, and Colombia." CRS Reports for Congress. http://www.law.umaryland.edu/marshall/crsreports/crsdocuments/RL3275802042005.pdf.

Ferguson, J. (2004). "Al Qaeda's Threat to Japan: Tokyo's Wake Up Call to the War on Terrorism." The Jamestown Foundation. *Terrorism Monitor* 2 no. 2 (January 30). http://www.jamestown.org/terrorism/news/article.php?articleid=23504.

Fernandez, R. (1987). *Los Macheteros: The Wells Fargo Robbery and the Violent Struggle for Puerto Rican Independence.* Upper Saddle River, NJ: Prentice Hall.

———. (1996). *The Disenchanted Island: Puerto Rico and the United States in the Twentieth Century.* Westport, CT: Greenwood.

Ferrero, M. (2002). "Radicalization as a Reaction to Failure: An Economic Model of Islamic Extremism." The Economic Consequences of Global Terrorism. Berlin, June.

Fesperman, D. (2004). "Link between Hamas, al-Qaida feared." *The Baltimore Sun.* http://www.baltimoresun.com/news/local/bal-te.md.hamas25aug25,1,934840.story?coll=bal-local-headlines.

Fields, G. (2002). "U.S. Probe of Intelligence Lapses to Go beyond CIA and FBI." *Wall Street Journal*, May 3, p. A4.

Findlay, P. (2001). *Silent No More: Confronting America's False Images of Islam.* Beltsville, MD: Amana.

Finley, M. I. (1983). *The Politics of the Ancient World.* Cambridge, United Kingdom: Cambridge University Press.

Firestone, R. (1999). *Jihad: The Origins of Holy War in Islam.* New York: Oxford University Press.

Fitzpatrick, S. (2001). *The Russian Revolution.* New York: Oxford University Press.

Flemming, P. A., M. Stohl, and A. P. Schmid. (1988). "The Theoretical Utility of Typologies of Terrorism: Lessons and Opportunities." In M. Stohl (ed.), *The Politics of Terrorism.* New York: Dekker.

Flynn, S. (2002). "America the Vulnerable." *Foreign Affairs* 81:60–74.

———. (2004a). *America the Vulnerable.* New York: Harper Collins.

———. (2004b). "The Neglected Home Front." *Foreign Affairs*. 83 (September/ October): 20–33.

Foote, S. (1986a). *The Civil War: A Narrative. Volume I: Fort Sumter to Perryville*. New York: Vintage Books.

———. (1986b). *The Civil War: A Narrative. Volume III: Red River to Appomattox*. New York: Vintage Books.

Foreign Policy Association. (2004). "Great Decisions Guides: Terrorism—The Basque ETA." http://www.fpa.org/newsletter_info2478/newsletter_info _sub_list.htm?section=The%BasqueETA.

Foster, R. F. (2000). "Ascendancy and Union." In R. F. Foster, *The Oxford Illustrated History of Ireland*. New York: Oxford University Press.

———. (1989). *Modern Ireland, 1600–1972*. London: Penguin.

———. (2001). *The Oxford History of Ireland*. New York: Oxford University Press.

Fraley, F., and E. L. Roushanzamir. (2006). "Critical Media Theory, Democratic Communication, and Global Conflict." In A. P. Kavoori and T. Fraley (eds.), *Media, Terrorism, and Theory: A Reader*. Lanham, MD: Rowman & Littlefield.

Fraser, J., and I. Fulton. (1984). *Terrorism Counteraction. FC 100-37*. Fort Leavenworth, KS: U.S. Army Command and General Staff College.

Freeh, L. J. (2005). *My FBI: Bringing Down the Mafia, Investigating Bill Clinton, and Fighting the War on Terror*. New York: St. Martin's Press.

Friedman, T. L. (2000). *From Beirut to Jerusalem*. New York: Harper Collins.

———. (2004). "War of Ideas, Part 2." *The New York Times*, January 11, sec. 4, p. 15.

Fromkin, D. (2001). *A Peace to End All Peace: The Fall of the Ottoman Empire and the Creation of the Modern Middle East*. New York: Owl Books, Henry Holt.

Frontline. (1999). "Hunting bin Laden." PBS. http://www.pbs.org/wgbh/pages/ frontline/shows/binladen/.

———. (2002). "Interview: Jihad Ja'Aire, Al Asqa Martyrs Brigade Leader." PBS. http://www.fromoccupiedpalestine.org/node.php?id=745.

Gaines, L. K., and G W. Cordner. (1999). *Policing Perspectives: An Anthology*. Los Angeles: Roxbury.

Gambetta, D. (2005). *Making Sense of Suicide Missions*. Oxford, UK: Oxford University Press.

Gambill, G. C., and Z. K. Abdelnour. (2002). "Hezbollah: Between Tehran and Damascus. http://www.meib.org/articles/0202_l1.htm.

Garcia, M. J., M. M. Lee, and T. Tatelman. (2005). "Immigration: Analysis of the Major Provisions of the REAL ID Act of 2005." Congressional Research Service. http://www.mipt.org/pdf/CRS_RL32754.pdf.

Garrison, A. H. (2004). "Defining Terrorism: Philosophy of the Bomb, Propaganda by Deed, and Change Through Fear and Violence." *Criminal Justice Studies* 17 (3): 259–279.

Gato, P., and R. Windrem. (2007). "Hezbollah Builds a Western Base." NBC News, MSNBC. http://www.msnbc.msn.com/id/17874369.

Gause, F. G., III. (2005). "Can Democracy Stop Terrorism?" *Foreign Affairs* 84 (5): 62–76.

Gauthier-Villars, D. (2007). "Colonial-Era Ties to Africa Face a Reckoning in France." *The Wall Street Journal*, May 16, A1.

Gerges, F. A. (2005). *The Far Enemy: Why Jihad Went Global*. New York: Cambridge University Press.

———. (2006). *Journey of the Jihadist: Inside Muslim Militancy*. Orlando, FL: Harcourt.

Gilboa, E. (2005). "Global Television News and Foreign Policy: Debating the CNN Effect." *International Studies Perspectives* 6 (3): 325–341.

Giles, L. (2000). Sun Tzu, *The Art of War*. The Internet Classics Archive. http://classics.mit.edu/Tzu/artwar.html.

Gilio, M. E. (1972). *The Tupamaros*. London: Secker & Warburg.

Giroux, H. A. (2002). "Democracy and the Politics of Terrorism: Community, Fear, and the Suppression of Dissent." *Cultural Studies Critical Methodologies* 2 (3): 334–342.

Glasser, S. B., and S. Coll. (2005). "The Web as a Weapon." *Washington Post*, August 1. http://www.washingtonpost.com/wp-dyn/content/article/2005/08/08/AR2005080801018.html.

Global Security.org. (n.d.). "Sikhs in Punjab." GlobalSecurity.org. http://www.globalsecurity.org/military/world/war/punjab.htm (accessed May 2007).

Global Witness. (2003). *For a Few Dollars More: How al Qaeda Moved into the Diamond Trade*. London: Global Witness.

Goffman, E. (1959). *The Presentation of Self in Everyday Life*. Garden City, NY: Doubleday.

Goldberg, B. (2003). *Bias: A CBS Insider Exposes How the Media Distort the News*. New York: Perennial Editions (Harper Collins).

Goldberg, J. (2002). "In the Party of God: Hezbollah Sets up Operations in South America and the United States." *The New Yorker*, October 28.

Goldman, S. D. (2007). "Russian Political, Economic, and Security Issues and U.S. Interests." CRS Reports for Congress. http://www.fas.org/sgp/crs/row/RL33407.pdf.

Goodman, A. (2003). "Basque Question: Spain's Pressing Problem." CNN. http://www.cnn.com/SPECIALS/201/basque/stories/overview.html.

Goodwin, D. K. (2005). *Team of Rivals: The Political Genius of Abraham Lincoln*. New York: Simon & Schuster.

Gordon, M. R., and B. E. Trainor. (2006). *Cobra II: The Inside Story of the Invasion and Occupation of Iraq*. New York: Pantheon Books.

Gordon, N. (1999). "Terrorism in the Arab-Israeli Conflict." South Bend, IN: University of Notre Dame, Joan B. Kroc Institute for International Peace Studies, Occasional Paper.

Graber, D. (2003). "Styles of Image Management During Crises: Justifying Press Censorship." *Discourse and Society* 14 (5): 539–557. http://das.sagepub.com.ezproxy.gvsu.edu:2048/cgi/content/abstract/14/5/539.

Greer, S. (1995). "De-centralised Policing in Spain: The Case of the Autonomous Basque Police." *Policing and Society* 5: 15–36.

Grob-Fitzgibbon, B. (2004). "From the Dagger to the Bomb: Karl Heinzen and the Evolution of Political Terror." *Terrorism and Political Violence* 16 (Spring): 97–115.

Groseclose, T., and J. Milyo. (2005). "A Measure of Media Bias." *Quarterly Journal of Economics* 4 (November): 1191–1239. http://www.polisci.ucla .edu/faculty/groseclose/MediaBias.8.htm.

Grossman, M. (1999). "Cyberterrorism." *Computer Law Tip of the Week.* http:// www.mgrossmanlaw.com/articles/1999/cyberterrorism.htm.

Gruen, M. (2004). "Demographics and Methods of Recruitment." In Z. Baran, *The Challenge of Hizb ut Tahrir: Deciphering and Combating Islamist Ideology.* The Nixon Center. http://www.nixoncenter.org/Program%20Briefs/ PB%202004/confrephiztahrir.pdf.

Guevara, E. (1968). *Reminiscences of the Cuban Revolutionary War.* New York: Monthly Review Press.

Gunaratna, R. (1998). "International and Regional Implications of the Sri Lankan Tamil Insurgency." Institute for Counter-Terrorism. http://_www .ict.org.il/.

———. (2000). "Suicide Terrorism: A Global Threat." *Jane's Intelligence Review.* http://www.janes.com/security/international_security/news/usscole/ jir001020_1_n.s.html.

———. (2002). *Inside al Qaeda: Global Network of Terror.* New York: Columbia University Press.

———. (2004). "Links with Islamist Groups: Ideology and Operations." In Z. Baran, *The Challenge of Hizb ut Tahrir: Deciphering and Combating Islamist Ideology.* The Nixon Center. http://www.nixoncenter.org/Program%20Briefs/ PB%202004/confrephiztahrir.pdf.

Gurr, T. R. (1988a). "Some Characteristics of Political Terrorism in the 1960s." In M. Stohl (ed.), *The Politics of Terrorism.* New York: Dekker.

———. (1988b). "Political Terrorism in the United States: Historical Antecedents and Contemporary Trends." In M. Stohl (ed.), *The Politics of Terrorism.* New York: Dekker.

Haahr, K. (2006). "Authorities Break Up GSPC Cells in Italy." *Terrorism Focus* 3 no. 30, (August 1). http://www.jamestown.org/terrorism/news/article .php?articleid=2370090.

Hacker, F. J. (1976). *Crusaders, Criminals, and Crazies.* New York: Norton.

Hadar, L. (2002). "Pakistan in America's War on Terrorism: Ally or Unreliable Client?" The Cato Institute. http://www.cato.org/pubs/pas/pa436.pdf.

Haleem, I. (2004). "Micro Target, Macro Impact: The Resolution of the Kashmir Conflict as a Key to Shrinking al-Qaeda's International Terrorist Network." *Journal of Terrorism and Political Violence* 16 (Spring): 18–47.

Halliday, F. (2005). *The Middle East in International Relations: Power, Politics and Ideology.* New York: Oxford University Press.

Halm, H. (1999). *Shi'a Islam: From Religion to Revolution.* Princeton, NJ: Marcus Wiener.

Hamas. (1988). "Hamas Character." Translated and copied by MidEastWeb. http://www.mideastweb.org/hamas.htm.

Hambling, D. (Mar. 21, 2004). "Experts Fear Terrorists are Seeking Fuel-Air Bombs." *New Scientist.* http://www.newscientist.com/news/news.jsp?id=ns99994785.

Hamilton, I. (1971). "From Liberalism to Extremism." *Conflict Studies* 17:5–17.

Hamm, M. (ed.). (1994). *Hate Crime: International Perspectives on Causes and Control.* Cincinnati, OH: Anderson.

———. (1996). *American Skinheads: The Criminology and Control of Hate Crime.* New York: Praeger.

Hanauer, L. S. (1995). "The Path to Redemption: Fundamentalist Judaism, Territory, and Jewish Settler Violence in the West Bank." *Studies in Conflict and Terrorism* 18:245–270.

Hanson, V. D. (2000). *The Western Way of War: Infantry Battle in Classical Greece.* Berkeley, CA: University of California Press.

Harik, J. P. (2004). *Hezbollah: The Changing Face of Terrorism.* London: I. B. Taurus.

Harris, E. (1995). *Guarding the Secrets: Palestinian Terrorism and a Father's Murder of His Too American Daughter.* New York: Scribner.

Harris, J. W. (1987). "Domestic Terrorism in the 1980s." *FBI Law Enforcement Bulletin* 56:5–13.

Harris, M. (1991). *Our Kind: Who We Are, Where We Came From, and Where We Are Going.* New York: Harper Collins.

Harris, W. (1998). *Burglary for the Patrol Officer.* Longview, TX: Rough Edge Publications.

Hastings, M. (1970). *Barricades in Belfast.* New York: Taplinger.

Hauser, C., and A. O'Connor. (2007). "Arrested in Plot to Attack Fort Dix." *The New York Times,* May 8. http://www.nytimes.com/2007/05/08/us/08cnd-dix.html?ex=1336276800&en=85a2795016f8037f&ei=5088&partner=rssnyt&emc=rss.

Henderson, D. (2006). "Former Detectives Arrested in McCord Probe." *The Independent,* August 9. http://news.independent.co.uk/uk/ulster/article1217930.ece.

Hereen, M. W., and S. A. Brown. (2002). *Christ in Celtic Christianity: Britain and Ireland from the Fifth to the Tenth Century.* Rochester, NY: Boydell Press.

Herman, E. S. (1983). *The Real Terror Network.* Boston: South End Press.

———. (1999). *The Myth of the Liberal Media: An Edward Herman Reader.* New York: Peter Lang.

Herman, S. (2001). "The USA Patriot Act and the U.S. Department of Justice: Losing Our Balances." *Jurist,* December 3. http://jurist.law.pitt.edu/forum/forumnew40.htm.

Hewitt, C. (1984). *The Effectiveness of Anti-Terrorist Policies.* Lanham, MD: University Press of America.

Higgins, A. (2006). "Hezbollah Fund-Raiser's Mission: Money for Bullets and Loans." *Wall Street Journal,* December 26.

Hill, F. (2003). "Testimony—Committee on International Relations, Subcommittee on the Middle East and Central Asia, U.S. House of Representatives." *Congressional Quarterly.* "Terrorism in Asia and the Pacific." October 29. http://homeland.cq.cm/hs/display.do?dockey=/usr/local/cqonline/docs/html.

Hill, S., and R. Ward. (2002). *Extremist Groups.* Huntsville, TX: Sam Houston State University.

Hinnen, T. M. (2004). "The Cyber-Front in the War on Terrorism: Curbing Terrorist Use of the Internet." *The Columbia Science and Technology Law Review.* www.stlr.org/html/volume5/hinnen.pdf.

Hinton, H. L. (1999). *Combating Terrorism: Observations on Biological Terrorism and Public Health Initiatives.* Washington, DC: General Accounting Office.

Hiro, D. (1987). *Iran Under the Ayatollahs.* London: Routledge & Kegan Paul.

History Channel. (2000). "100 Years of Terror." Four Part Series. New York: A&E Television Networks.

Hitt, G., and D. S. Cloud. (2002). "Bush's Homeland Security Overhaul Faces Obstacles." *Wall Street Journal,* June 10, p. A4.

Hobijn, B. (2002). "How Much Will Homeland Security Cost?" Federal Reserve Bank of New York. http://www.securitymanagement.com/library/Bart_Homeland0203.pdf.

Hocking, J. (2004). *Terror Laws: ASIO, Counter-Terrorism, and the Threat to Democracy.* Sydney: University of South Wales Press.

Hoffman, B. (1995). "Holy Terror: The Implications of Terrorism Motivated by a Religious Imperative." *Studies in Conflict and Terrorism* 18:271–284.

———. (1998). "Old Madness, New Methods." Santa Monica, CA: RAND. http://www.rand.org/publications/randreview/issues/rr.winter98.9/methods.html.

———. (2006). *Inside Terrorism, Revised and Expanded.* New York: Columbia University Press.

Hoffman, S. (2003). "The High and the Mighty: Bush's National-Security Strategy and the New American Hubris." *The American Prospect* 13 (January 13): 28–32.

Holland, J. J. (2005). "House Approves Extension of Patriot Act." Associated Press, December 14. http://news.yahoo.com/s/ap/20051214/ap_on_go_co/patriot_act.

Homer-Dixon, T. (2002). "The Rise of Complex Terrorism." *Foreign Affairs* 81 (January/February): 52–62.

Hooper, I. (2000). "WSJ Rejects Muslim Reply to Steven Emerson." Council on American-Islamic Relations, November 15. http://www.musalman.com/islamnews/amj-wsjrejectsmuslimreply.html.

Horchem, H. J. (1986). "Terrorism in West Germany." *Conflict Studies* 186.

Hourani, A. (1997). *A History of the Arab Peoples.* Cambridge, MA: Belknap Press.

Howard, M. (1988). *Clausewitz.* New York: Oxford University Press.

———. (2002). What's in a Name? How to Fight Terrorism. *Foreign Affairs* 81 (January/February): 43–59.

Howard, R. D. (2004). "Understanding Al Qaeda's Application of the New Terrorism." In R. Howard and R. Sawyer (eds.), *Terrorism and Counterterrorism: Understanding the New Security Environment*. New York: McGraw-Hill.

Hudson, A. (2006). "Antiterror Grant to Probe Bingo Halls Criticized." *Washington Times*, April 12. http://washingtontimes.com/national/20060411 -115930-6028r.htm.

Hudzik, J., and G. Cordner. (1983). *Planning in Criminal Justice Organizations and Systems*. New York: Macmillan.

Huffman, I. (2003) "Lockyer's Spying Reforms Not Enough, Activists Say." *Oakland Tribune Online*, April 12. http://findarticles.com/p/articles/mi_qn4176/ is_20030803/ai_nl4555774.

Hughes, J., and C. Donnelly. (2004). "Attitudes to Community Relations in Northern Ireland: Signs of Optimism in the Post Cease Fire Period?" *Terrorism and Political Violence* 16:567–592.

Huntington, S. P. (1993). "The Clash of Civilizations." *Foreign Affairs* 72:22–49.

———. (1996). *The Clash of Civilizations and the Remaking of World Order*. New York: Simon & Schuster.

———. (2004). "The Hispanic Challenge." *Foreign Policy*, March/April.

IACP. *See* International Association of Chiefs of Police.

Ihsanoglu, E. (2005). "Speech of H. E. Professor Ekmeledin Ihsanoglu." The International Conference on Combating Terrorism. Riyadh, Saudi Arabia. http://www.oic-oci.org/press/english/2005/feb%202005/SG-terrrorism.htm. Accessed 2006.

Imperial Knights of the Ku Klux Klan of America. http://www.k-k-k.com/items .html (accessed January 2007).

Institute for Counter-Terrorism. (2001). *Countering Suicide Terrorism*. Herzliya, Israel: Institute for Counter-Terrorism.

———. (2004). "Hamas." ICT. http://www.ict.org.il/inter_ter/orgdet.cfm? orgid=13.

International Association of Chiefs of Police. (2001). *Terrorism Response*. Alexandria, VA: IACP.

International Crisis Group. (2004). "Indonesia Backgrounder: Jihad in Central Sulawesi." February 3. http://www.crisisgroup.org/library/documents/asia/ indonesia/074_jihad_in_central_sulawesi_mod.pdf.

———. (2005a). "Recycling Militants in Indonesia: Dural Islam and the Australian Embassy Bombing." February 22. http://www.crisisgroup.org/library/ documents/asia/indonesia/074_jihad_in_central_sulawesi_mod.pdf.

———. (2005b). "Islamist Terrorism in the Sahel: Fact or Fiction?" March 31. http://www.crisisgroup.org/library/documents/africa/west_africa/092_islam ist_terrorism_in_the_sahel___fact_or_fiction.pdf.

———. (2005c). "Uzbekistan: The Andijon Uprising." May 25. http://www.cri sisgroup.org/library/documents/asia/central_asia/b038_uzbekistan___the _andijon_uprising_edited.pdf.

———. (2005d). "Somalia's Islamists." December 12. http://www.crisisgroup .org/library/documents/africa/horn_of_africa/100_somalia_s_islamists.pdf.

———. (2006a). "Fuelling the Niger Delta Crisis." http://www.crisisgroup.org/home/index.cfm?id=4394&l=1.

———. (2006b). "Pakistan: The Worsening Conflict in Balochistan." http://www.crisisgroup.org/home/index.cfm?id=4373&l=1.

———. (Aug. 3, 2006c). "The Swamps of Insurgency Nigeria's Delta Unrest." International Crisis Group. http://www.crisisgroup.org/library/documents/africa/west_africa/115_the_swamps_of_insurgency_nigeria_s_delta_unrest.pdf.

———. (2006d). "Bangladesh Today." October 23. http://www.crisisgroup.org/library/documents/asia/south_asia/121_bangladesh_today.pdf.

———. (2006e). "Cote d'Ivoire: Stepping Up the Pressure." September 7. http://www.crisisgroup.org/home/index.cfm?id=4365&l=1.

———. (2006f). "Sri Lanka: The Failure of the Peace Process." November 28. http://www.crisisgroup.org/library/documents/asia/south_asia/sri_lanka/124_sri_lanka___the_failure_of_the_peace_process.pdf.

———. (2006g). "Pakistan's Tribal Areas: Appeasing the Militants." December 11. http://www.crisisgroup.org/library/documents/asia/south_asia/125_pakistans_tribal_areas___appeasing_the_militants.pdf.

———. (2007a). "Discord in Pakistan's Northern Areas." April 2. http://www.crisisgroup.org/home/index.cfm?id=4748&l=1.

———. (2007b). "Nepal's Maoists: Purists or Pragmatists?" May 18. http://www.crisisgroup.org/home/index.cfm?id=4842&l=1.

Isikoff, M., and M. Hosenball. (2004). "Paying for Terror." *Newsweek* Web Exclusive, March 12. http://www.msnbc.msn.com/id/4963025/.

Israel, J. I. (2001). *Radical Enlightenment: Philosophy and the Making of Modernity.* New York: Oxford University Press.

Israeli Foreign Ministry. (1996). "Hizbullah." April 11. http://www.israel-mfa.gov.il.

Isseroff, A. (2004). "A History of the Hamas Movement." MidEastWeb. http://www.mideastweb.org/hamashistory.htm.

Jaber, H. (1997). *Hezbollah: Born with a Vengeance.* New York: Columbia University Press.

Jackson, G. (1972). *Peoples' Prison.* London: Faber & Faber. (Published in the United States in 1974 as *Surviving the Long Night.* New York: Vanguard.)

Jacobs, J. (1983). *S. W. A. T. Tactics.* Boulder, CO: Paladin Press.

Jarboe, J. (2002). Testimony before the U.S. House of Representatives, House Resource Committee, Subcommittee on Forests and Forest Health. Reproduced from "FBI Testifies to House Ecoterror Hearing." February 12. http://www.furcommission.com/news/newsF04f.htm.

Jenkins, B. (1987). "Will Terrorists Go Nuclear?" In Walter Laqueur and Yonah Alexander (eds.), *The Terrorism Reader.* New York: Meridian.

Jenkins, B. M. (1983.) *New Modes of Conflict.* Santa Monica, CA: RAND.

———. (1984). *The Who, What, When, Where, How, and Why of Terrorism.* Paper presented at the Detroit Police Department Conference on "Urban Terrorism: Planning or Chaos?" November, Detroit.

————. (2004a). "The Operational Code of the Jihadists." Briefing prepared for the Army Science Board: RAND. April 1. Unpublished.

————. (2004b). "Where I Draw the Line." *The Christian Science Monitor*. http://www.csmonitor.com/specials/terrorism/lite/expert.html.

————. (2006). *Unconquerable Nation: Knowing Our Enemy Strengthening Ourselves*. Santa Monica, CA: RAND.

Jensen, R. B. (2004). "Daggers, Rifles, and Dynamite: Anarchist Terrorism in Nineteenth Century Europe." *Terrorism and Political Violence* Spring (16): 116–153.

John, W. (2005). "The Roots of Extremism in Bangladesh." The Jamestown Foundation. *Terrorism Monitor* 3, no. 1 (January 13). http://www.jamestown.org/publications_details.php?volume_id=411&issue_id=3196&article_id=2369092.

Johnson, B. R. (2007). Panel chair for "Information Sharing Between State, Local, and Tribal Agencies and the Federal Government—Discussion of the Common Framework." First National Fusion Center Conference, Destin, FL. March.

Johnson, D., and B. Brunner. (2004). "Timeline of Key Events in Chechnya, 1830–2004." http://www.infoplease.com/spot/chechnyatime1.html.

Johnson, K. (2002). "NYPD Adds CIA, Military Experts." *USA Today*, January 29. http://www.usatoday.

Jordan, J., and R. Wesley. (2006). "The Madrid Attacks: Results of Investigations Two Years Later." The Jamestown Foundation. May 9. http://jamestown.org/terrorism/news/article.php?articleid=2369921.

Jordan, L. J. (2005). "Homeland Security Information Network Criticized." *Washington Post*, May 10. http://www.washingtonpost.com/wp-dyn/content/article/2005/05/09/AR2005050901076.html.

Joshi, M. (1996). "On the Razor's Edge: The Liberation Tigers of Tamil Eelam." *Studies in Conflict and Terrorism*, 19:19–42.

Josson, P. (2006). "New Profile of the Home-Grown Terrorist Emerges." *Christian Science Monitor*, June 26.

Juergensmeyer, M. (1988). "The Logic of Religious Violence." In David C. Rapoport (ed.), *Inside Terrorist Organizations*. New York: Columbia University Press.

————. (2000). *Terror in the Mind of God: The Global Rise of Religious Violence*. Berkley, CA: University of California Press.

Kafala, T. (2001). "Israel's Assassination Policy." BBC News, August 1. http://news.bbc.co.uk/1/hi/world/middle_east/1258187.stm.

Kagan, R. (2004). "America's Crisis of Legitimacy." *Foreign Affairs* 83 (March/April): 65–87.

Kahan, D. M. (1997). "Social Influence, Social Meaning, and Deterrence." *Virginia Law Review* 83 (2): 349–395. http://www.jstor.org/view/00426601/ap030646/03a00020/0.

Kaplan, D. E. (2003). "The Saudi Connection: How Billions in Oil Money Spawned a Global Terror Network." *U.S. News and World Report*, December 15. http://www.usnews/issue/031215/usnews/15terror.htm.

———. (2005). "Paying for Terror." *U.S. News and World Report*, December 5 http://www.usnews.com/usnews/news/articles/051205/5terror.htm.

Kaplan, E. H., A. Mintz, S. Mishal, and C. Samban. (2005). "What Happened to Suicide Bombings in Israel? Insights from a Terror Stock Model." *Studies in Conflict and Terrorism* 28:225–235.

Karim, K. H. (2001). *Islamic Peril: Media and Global Violence.* Ottawa: Black Rose Books.

Karman, E. (2000). "Hamas' Terrorism Strategy: Operational Limitations and Political Constraints." *Middle East Review of International Affairs* (4): March. http://meria.idc.ac.il/journal/2000/issue1/jv4n1a7.html.

Karon, T. (2003). "Why Turks and Kurds Prize Kirkuk." *Time*, May 10. http://www.time.com/time/world/article/0,8599,425230,00.html.

Katz, L. R. (2001). "Anti-Terrorism Laws: Too Much of a Good Thing." *Jurist*, November 24. http://jurist.law.pitt.edu/forum/forumnew39.htm.

Kayyem, J., and A. M. Howitt (eds.). (2002). *Beyond the Beltway: Focusing on Hometown Security.* Cambridge, MA: Harvard University.

Keathley, J. (2002). "Conducting Undercover Terrorism Investigations." Tallahassee: IRR. Unpublished.

Keats, A. (2002). "In the Spotlight: Al Jihad (Egyptian Islamic Jihad)." Center for Defense Information. http://www.cdi.org/terrorism/aljihad.cfm.

Keefer, W. J. (2006). "The Patriot Act Reauthorized." *The Jurist.* http://jurist.law.pitt.edu/forumy/2006/03/patriot-act-reauthorized.php.

Keegan, J. (1993). *A History of Warfare.* New York: Vintage Books.

Keegan, J., and A. Wheatcroft. (1976). *Who's Who in Military History.* New York: William Morrow.

Keinon, H. (2004). "Israel Preparing for Wave of Terror." *Jerusalem Post*, May 21.

Keller, D. (2006). "September 11, Social Theory, and Democratic Politics." In A. P. Kavoori and T. Fraley (eds.), *Media, Terrorism, and Theory: A Reader.* Lanham, MD: Rowman & Littlefield.

Kellner, D. (2002). "September 11, the Media, and War Fever Television." *New Media* 3 (May): 143–151.

Kepel, G. (2002). *Jihad: The Trail of Political Islam.* Cambridge, MA: Belknap Press.

———. (2004). *The War for Muslim Minds: Islam and the West.* Cambridge, MA: Belknap Press.

Kephart, J. L. (2005). "Immigration and Terrorism: Moving Beyond the 9-11 Staff Report on Terrorist Travel." Center for Immigration Studies. Center Paper 24. http://www.cis.org/articles/2005/kephart.pdf.

Ketcham, C. C., and H. J. McGeorge. (1986). "Terrorist Violence: Its Mechanics and Countermeasures." In N. C. Livingstone and T. E. Arnold (eds.), *Fighting Back.* Lexington, MA: Heath.

Khashan, H. (2003). "Collective Palestinian Frustration and Suicide Bombings." *Third World Quarterly* 24 (6):1049–1067.

Khatami, S. (1997). "Between Class and Nation: Ideology and Radical Basque Ethnonationalism." *Studies in Conflict and Terrorism* 20:395–417.

Kohlman, E. F. (2004). *Jihad in Europe: The Afghan-Bosnian Network*. New York: Berg.

Kohlmann, E. (2005). "Spreading Terrorist Dogma." MSNBC. http://www .msnbc.msn.com/id/13848605.

Kometer, M. W. (2004). "The New Terrorism: The Nature of the War on Terrorism." Air War College, Maxwell Air Force Base, AL. http://www .maxwell.af.mil/au/aul/aupress/SAAS_Theses/SAASS_Out/Kometer/Kome ter.pdf.

Konotorovich, E. V. (2002). "Make Them Talk." *Wall Street Journal*, June 18, p. A12.

Korn, D. A. (1995). *Interview with Abdullah Ocalan*. http://kurdstruggle.org/ index.shtml.

Kransoboka, N. (2002). "Real Journalism Goes Underground: The Internet Underground." *The International Journal for Communications Studies* 64 (5): 479–499.

Kraska, P. B. (1996). "Enjoying Militarism: Political/Personal Dilemmas in Studying U.S. Police Paramilitary Units." *Justice Quarterly* 13:405–429.

Kraska, P. B., and V. Kappeler. (1999). "Militarizing American Police: The Rise and Normalization of Paramilitary Units." In Larry K. Gaines and Gary W. Cordner (eds.), *Policing Perspectives: An Anthology*. Los Angeles: Roxbury.

Krasna, J. S. (1997). "Narcotics and the National Security Producer States." *Texas Law Review*. http://www.lib.unb.ca/Texts/JCS/s96/articles/krasna.html.

Krauthammer, C. (2004). "U. N. Will Go to Any Length to Condemn Israel." *Jewish World Review*, July 16. http://www.io.com/~freeman/updates/950 .htm.

Kurz, A. (1994). "Palestinian Terrorism—The Violent Aspect of a Political Struggle." In Y. Alexander (ed.), *Middle Eastern Terrorism: Current Threats and Future Prospects*. New York: Hall.

Kurzman, C. (2001). "Critics Within: Islamic Scholars' Protest Against the Islamic State of Iran." *International Journal of Politics, Culture and Society* 15 (2): 341–359.

———. (2004). *The Unthinkable Revolution in Iran*. Cambridge, MA: Harvard University Press.

Kushner, H. W., and B. Jacobson. (1998). "Financing Terrorist Activities Through Coupon Fraud and Counterfeiting." *Counterterrorism and Security International* 5 (Summer): 10–12.

Kuusisto, A.-K. (2001). "Territoriality, Symbolism, and the Challenge." *Peace Review* 13 (1): 59–66.

Kux, D. (2002). "India's Fine Balance." *Foreign Affairs* 81 (3): 93–106.

Labeviere, R. (2000). *Dollars for Terror: The United States and Islam*. New York: Algora.

Laffan, M. (1999). *Resurrection of Ireland: The Sinn Fein Party, 1916–1923*. Port Chester, NY: Cambridge University Press.

Lake, E. (2004). "Hamas Agents May Be Lurking in U.S.: Fears Rantisi's Vow to Attack May Awaken Operatives Here." *The New York Sun*, April 29.

Langguth, A. J. (1978). *Hidden Terrors*. New York: Pantheon.

Laqueur, W. (1987). *The Age of Terrorism*. Boston: Little, Brown.

———. (1999). *The New Terrorism: Fanaticism and the Arms of Mass Destruction*. New York: Oxford University Press.

Laqueur, W., and Y. Alexander. (1987). *The Terrorism Reader*. Boston: Little Brown.

Latora, V., and M. Marchioni. (2004). "How the Science of Complex Networks Can Help Developing Strategies Against Terrorism." *Chaos, Solutions, and Fractals* 20:69–75.

Lau, S. (2003). "An Analysis of Terrorist Groups' Potential Use of Electronic Steganography." SANS Institute. http://www.sans.org/reading_room/white papers/steganography554.php.

Leahy, P. (2006). "Statement of Senator Patrick Leahy." Senate Committee of the Judiciary, United States Senate. http://judiciary.senate.gov/member _statement.cfm?id=2048&wit_id=3984.

Lee, A. M. (1983). *Terrorism in Northern Ireland*. New York: General Hall.

Lee, G. D. (2004). *Conspiracy Investigations: Terrorism, Drugs and Gangs*. Upper Saddle River, NJ: Prentice Hall.

Lesser, I. O. (1999). "Changing Terrorism in a Changing World." In I. O. Lesser, B. Hoffman, J. Arquilla, D. Ronfeldt, M. Zanni, and B. M. Jenkins, *Countering the New Terrorism*. Santa Monica, CA: RAND.

Levin, D. (2003). "Structure of News Coverage of a Peace Process." *Press/Politics* 8 (4): 27–53.

Levin, M. (2003). "John Stuart Mill: A Liberal Looks at Utopian Socialism in the Years of Revolution 1848–49." *Utopian Studies* 14 (2): 68–82.

Levit, L. (2006). *Hamas: Politics, Charity, and Terrorism in the Service of Jihad*. New Haven, CT: Yale University Press.

Levitas, D. (2002). *The Terrorist Next Door: The Militia Movement and the Radical Right*. New York: St. Martin's Press.

Levitt, L. (2002). "A Fed-Friendly NYPD? Not Yet." *News Day*, January 28. http://newsday.com/news/columnists/nynyplaz22256708jan28.

Levitt, M. A. (2002). "The Political Economy of Middle East Terrorism." *Middle East Review of International Affairs* 6 (4). http://meria.idc.ac.il/journal/2002/issue4/jv6n4a3.html.

Lewis, B. (1966). *The Arabs in History*. London: Hutchinson University Press.

———. (1993). *Islam and the West*. New York: Oxford University Press.

———. (1995). *Cultures in Conflict: Christians, Muslims, and Jews in the Age of Discovery*. New York: Oxford University Press.

———. (2002). *What Went Wrong? The Clash between Islam and Modernity in the Middle East*. New York: Oxford University Press.

———. (2003a). *The Crisis in Islam: Holy War and Unholy Terror*. New York: Random House.

———. (2003b). *What Went Wrong?: The Clash Between Islam and Modernity in the Middle East*. New York: Perennial.

————. (2003c). *The Assassins: A Radical Sect in Islam*. New York: Basic Books.

————. (2004). *From Babel to Dragomans: Interpreting the Middle East*. New York: Oxford University Press.

Lichtblau, E. (2001). "Impassioned Letter Left Behind by Hijackers Urges Them to Stay the Course in Return for Paradise." *Los Angeles Times*, September 29. http://www.latimes.com/news/nation world/nation/la-092901letter.story.

Liddell Hart, B. H. (1967). *Strategy*. New York: Praeger.

Liff, S., and A. S. Laegren. (2003). "Cybercafes: Debating the Meeting and Significance of Internet Access in a Café Environment." *New Media & Society* 5 (3): 307–312.

Lippman, T. W. (1995). *Understanding Islam: An Introduction to the Muslim World*. New York: Meridian.

Liptak, A. (2002). "Changing the Standard." *New York Times*, May 31. http://nytimes.com/2002/05/31/ national/31ASSE.html.

Livingstone, N. C., and T. E. Arnold (eds.). (1986). *Fighting Back*. Lexington, MA: Heath.

Llora, F., J. M. Mata, and C. L. Irvin. (1993). "ETA: From Secret Army to Social Movement: The Post-Franco Schism of the Basque Nationalist Movement." *Terrorism and Political Violence* 5:106–134.

Lopez, G. A., and D. Coright. (2004). "Containing Iraq: Sanctions Worked." *Foreign Affairs* 83 (July/August): 90–103.

Luft, G., and A. Korin. (2004). "Terrorism Goes to Sea." *Foreign Affairs* 83 (November/December): 61–71.

Lufti, A. (2004). "Uyghur Separatism and China's Crisis of Creditability in the War on Terror." The Jamestown Foundation. *China Brief* 4, no. 3 (February 4). http://www.jamestown.org/publications_details.php?volume_id=395&issue_id=2905&article_id=23510.

Lyman, P. N., and J. S. Morrison. (2004). "The Terrorist Threat in Africa." *Foreign Affairs* 83 (1): 75–86.

Lynch, D. (2004). *Engaging Eurasia's Separatist States: Unresolved Conflicts and De Facto States*. Washington, DC: United States Institute of Peace.

Lynch, M. (2003). "Taking the Arabs Seriously." *Foreign Affairs* 82 (September/October).

MacDonald, A. [William Pierce]. (1985). *The Turner Diaries*. Arlington, VA: National Vanguard.

————. (1989). *Hunter: A Novel*. Hillsboro, WV: National Alliance.

MacDonald, R. (1972). "Electoral Politics and Uruguayan Political Decay." *International Economic Affairs* 26:24–45.

Mackay, C. S. (2004). *Ancient Rome: A Military and Political History*. New York: Cambridge University Press.

Maier, T. (2003). "Counterfeit Goods Pose Real Threat." *Insight on the News*, November 10, p. 21.

Maise, M., and H. Burgess. (n.d.). "Extremist/Spoilers." BeyondIntractability.org. http://www.intractableconflict.org/m/extremists.jsp (accessed 2005).

Makarenko, T. (2002). "Terrorism and Transnational Organized Crime: The Emerging News." In Paul Smith (ed.), *Transnational Violence and Seams of Lawlessness in the Asia-Pacific: Linkages to Global Terrorism.* Hawaii: Asia Pacific Centre for Security Studies.

Mallaby, S. (2007). "The Low Risk of Immigrants." *Washington Post,* May 28. http://www.cfr.org/publication/13462/low_risk_from_immigrants.html.

Management Analytics and others. (1995). "Sun Tzu: The Art of War." http://www.all.net.books/tzu/html.

Manning, P. K. (1976). *Police Work: The Social Organization of Policing.* Cambridge, MA: MIT Press.

March, A. (2005) "Guerrilla War, a Method." Che Guevara Studies Center and Ocean Press. http://www.marxists.org/archive/guevara/1963/misc/guerrilla-war-method.htm.

Marighella, C. (1969). *The Minimanual of the Urban Guerrilla.* Unpublished copy of the U.S. Army Military Intelligence School. [(2002). http://www.marxists.org/archive/marighella-carlos/1969/06/minimanual-urban-guerrilla/.]

———. (1971). *For the Liberation of Brazil.* Translated by John Butt and Rosemary Sheed. Harmondsworth, UK: Pelican.

Marquise, R. A. (2006). *Scotbom: Evidence and the Lockerbie Investigation.* New York: Algora.

Martindale, D. (1965). *Functionalism in the Social Sciences: The Strength and Limits of Functionalism in Anthropology, Economics, Political Science, and Sociology.* Philadelphia: American Society of Political Science.

Marx, K., and F. Engels. (1848). *The Communist Manifesto.* http://www.marxists.org/archive/marx/works/1848/communist-manifesto/index.htm.

Mason, C. (2004). "Who's Afraid of Virginia Dare? Confronting AntiAbortion Terrorism after 9-11." *Journal of Constitutional Law* (April): 796–817. http://64.233.179.104/scholar?hl=en&lr=&q=cache:wXS6hyrjQHUJ:www.law.upenn.edu/conlaw/issues/vol6/num4/mason.pdf+%22eric+rudolph%22+abortion.

Massie, R. K. (1991). *Dreadnought: Britain, Germany and the Coming of the Great War.* New York: Random House.

Matinuddin, K. (1999). *The Taliban Phenomenon.* New York: Cambridge University Press.

Mattoon, S. (1987). *S. W. A. T. Training and Deployment.* Boulder, CO: Paladin Press.

Mayer, J. (2006). "The Hidden Power." *The New Yorker,* July 3.

Mazur, Allan. (1982). "Bomb Threats and the Mass Media: Evidence for a Theory of Suggestion." *American Sociological Review* 47:407–410.

McElrath, K. (2000). *Unsafe Haven.* London: Pluto Press.

McGinn, D. (2006). "IRA Has Changed Drastically." *The Independent,* October 4. http://news.independent.co.uk/uk/ulster/article1794267.ece.

McPherson, J. M. (1988). *Battle Cry of Freedom: The Civil War Era.* New York: Ballantine.

Meese, E., C. Robb, and D. Abshire. (2005). "Reform Congress, Improve Homeland Security." The Heritage Foundation. http://www.heritage.org/Press/Commentary/ed010505b.cfm.

Melton, J. V. H. (2001). *The Rise of the Public in Enlightenment Europe*. Cambridge: Cambridge University Press.

Memorial Institute for the Prevention of Terrorism. (n.d.). "Group Profile: Tupamaros." MIPT. http://www.tkb.org/Group.jsp?groupID=235 (accessed 2007).

Mid East Forum. (2004). "Perceptions of the United States in the Middle East." C-Span 2, February 14.

Miko, F. T. (2004). "Removing Terrorist Sanctuaries: The 9/11 Commission Recommendations and U.S. Policy." CRS Reports for Congress. http://www.fas.org/irp/crs/RL32518.pdf.

Military.com. (2004). "Palestinian Islamic Jihad." Military.com. http://www.military.com/Resources/ResourceFileView?file=PIJ-Organization.htm.

Miller, A. (1982). *Terrorism, the Media, and the Law*. New York: Transnational.

Miller, J. (2007). "Plenary Session." First National Fusion Center Conference, Destin, FL. Unpublished.

Miller, J., S. Engelberg, and W. Broad. (2001). *Germs: Biological Weapons and America's Secret War*. New York: Simon & Schuster.

Miller, L. (2006). "The Terrorist Mind: II. Typologies, Psychopathologies, and Practical Guidelines for Investigation." *International Journal of Offender Therapy and Comparative Criminology* 50 (3): 255–268. http://ijo.sagepub.com/cgi/content/abstract/50/3/255?rss=1.

Miniter, R. (2005). *Disinformation: 22 Media Myths that Undermine the War on Terror*. Washington, DC: Regnery.

Mintz, J. (2005). "Security Spending Initiates Disputes." *Washington Post*, March 13. http://www.washingtonpost.com/wp-dyn/articles/A47964-2005Apr12.html.

MIPT. *See* Memorial Institute for the Prevention of Terrorism.

Mitchell, A., and C. Hulse. (2002). "Accountability Concern Is Raised over Security Department." *New York Times*, June 27. http://www.nytimes.com/2002/06/27/national/27RIDG.html.

Momen, M. (1985). *An Introduction to Shi'a Islam*. New Haven, CT: Yale University Press.

Monaghan, R. (2004). "An Imperfect Peace: Paramilitary Punishments in Northern Ireland." *Terrorism and Political Violence* 16:439–461.

Moore, R. F. (2006). "Deep Inside City Jails, Top Cops Keep a Watchful Eye Out for Terror." *New York Daily News*, August 13. http://www.nydailynews.com/front/story/443116p-373179c.html.

Moss, R. (1972). *Urban Guerrillas*. London: Temple Smith.

Moxon-Browne, E. (1987). "Spain and the ETA." *Conflict Studies* 201.

MSNBC. (2007). "DOJ Statement on JFK Airport Plot Arrests." MSNBC, June 2. http://www.msnbc.msn.com/id/19002569/.

Muir, A. M. (1999). "Terrorism and Weapons of Mass Destruction: The Case of Aum Shinrikyo." *Studies in Conflict and Terrorism* 22:79–91.

Mullendore, K., and J. R. White. (1996). "Legislating Terrorism: Justice Issues and the Public Forum." Paper presented at the Academy of Criminal Justice Sciences Annual Meeting, March, Las Vegas, NV.

Munck, R. (1992). "The Making of the Troubles in Northern Ireland." *Journal of Contemporary History* 27 (2): 211–229.

Murphy, P. (2004). *The Wolves of Islam: Russia and the Faces of Chechen Terrorism.* Washington, DC: Brassey's.

Murray, J. (2005). "Policing Terrorism: A Threat to Community Policing or Just a Shift in Priorities?" *Police Practice and Research* 6 (4): 347–361.

Nacos, B. L. (2000). "Accomplice or Witness? The Media's Role in Terrorism." *Current History* April, pp. 174–178.

Nance, M. W. (2003). *The Terrorist Recognition Handbook.* Guilford, CT: Lyons Press.

Napoleoni, L. (2003). *Modern Jihad: Tracing the Dollars Behind the Terror Networks.* London: Pluto.

Nasr, K. B. (1997). *Arab and Israeli Terrorism.* Jefferson, NC: McFarland.

National Commission on Terrorist Attacks Upon the United States. (2004). *The 9/11 Commission Report: Final Report of the National Commission on Terrorist Attacks Upon the United States.* New York: Norton. http://www.9-11commission.gov/report/911Report.pdf.

National Conference of State Legislatures. (2003). "Cyberterrorism." http://www.ncsl.org/programs/lis/CIP/cyberterrorism.htm.

National Immigration Forum. (2004). "State and Local Police Enforcement Backgrounder: Immigration Law Enforcement by State and Local Police." National Immigration Forum. http://www.immigrationforum.org/DesktopDefault.aspx?tabid=572.

National Public Radio. (2001). "Liberty vs. Security: An NPR Special Report," December 6. http://www.npr.org/programs/specials/liberties/index.html.

National Strategy for Combating Terrorism. (2006). http://www.whitehouse.gov/nsc/nsct/2006/.

Navarro, J. (2005). *Hunting Terrorists: A Look at the Psychopathology of Terror.* Springfield, IL: Charles C. Thomas.

Navias, M. S. (2002). "Financial Warfare as a Response to International Terrorism." *Political Quarterly* 73 (August): 57–79.

NBC / *Wall Street Journal.* (2004). "War on Terrorism." PollingReport.com, August 23–25. http://www.pollingreport.com/terror.htm.

Nechaev, S. (1987). "Catechism of the Revolutionist." In W. Laqueur and Y. Alexander (eds.), *The Terrorism Reader,* pp. 68–71. New York: Meridian.

Nedelkoff, R. (2002). "Program Brief." Bureau of Justice Assistance. http://www.usaonwatch.org/pdfs/NCJRS/state_local.pdf.

Netanyahu, B. (1997). *Terrorism: How the West Can Win.* New York: Avon.

New Jersey State Police. (2002). Intelligence Service Section. http://www.state.nj.us/lps/njsp/about/intel.html.

New York Times International. (2004). "World Briefing: Middle East." July 29. http://www.nytimes.com/2004/07/29/international/29brie.html?ex=1093752000&en=2ddc52a32376a2a2&ei=5070&pagewanted=all.

New York Times News Service. (1996). "American Terrorist: Just an Average Joe with a Bomb." *Grand Rapids Press*, August 25.

Nice, D. C. (1988). "Abortion Clinic Bombings as Political Violence." *American Journal of Political Science* 32:178–195.

Nilson, C., and T. Burke. (2002). "Environmental Extremists and the Eco-Terrorism Movement." *ACJS Today* 24:1–6.

Nima, R. (1983). *The Wrath of Allah: Islamic Revolution and Reaction in Iran*. London: Pluto.

9/11 Commission Report. *See* National Commission on Terrorist Attacks Upon the United States.

Nordland, R., S. Yousafzi, and B. Dehghanpisheh. (2002). "How al Qaeda Slipped Away." *Newsweek*, August 19, pp. 34–41.

Northern Ireland Office. (2007). "The Agreement." Northern Ireland Office. http://nio.gov.uk/the-agreement.

Novikov, E. (2004). "The Recruiting and Organizational Structure of Hizb ut Tahrir." Jamestown Foundation. *Terrorism Monitor* 2, no. 22 (September 18). http://jamestown.org/terrorism/news/article.php?articleid=2368890.

Nydell, M. K. (2002). *Understanding Arabs: A Guide for Westerners*. Yarmouth, MN: Intercultural Press.

Nzwili, F. (2006). "Leadership Profile: Somalia's Islamic Courts Union." The Jamestown Foundation. June 13. http://jamestown.org/news_details.php?news_id=184.

O Corrain, D. (2000). "Prehistoric and Early Christian Ireland." In R. F. Foster, *The Oxford Illustrated History of Ireland*. New York: Oxford University Press.

O'Conner, T. (2004). "Civil Liberties and Domestic Terrorism." North Carolina Wesleyan College. November 2. http://faculty.ncwc.edu/toconnor/429/429lect19.htm.

———. (2006). "Latin America." http://faculty.ncwc.edu/toconnor/areas/latin.htm.

Office of Homeland Security. (2002). *National Strategy for Homeland Security*. Washington, DC: Office of Homeland Security.

Oliver, H. J. (2002). *The Wahhabi Myth: Dispelling Prevalent Fallacies and the Fictitious Link with bin Laden*. Birmingham, UK: Salafi Publications.

Oliver, M. (2004). "Israel Targeting Entire Hamas Leadership." *The Guardian*, May 23. http://www.guardian.co.uk/israel/Story/0,2763,1175986,00.html.

Organization for the Prohibition of Chemical Weapons. (2000). "Nerve Agents: Lethal Organo-Phosphorus Compounds Inhibiting Cholonest-erase." http://www.opcw.nl/chemhaz/nerve.htm.

Organization of the Islamic Conference. (2002). "Kuala Lumpur Declaration on International Terrorism." http://www.oic-oci.org/english/conf/fm/11_extraordinary/declaration.htm.

Osterholm, M. T., and J. Schwartz. (2000). *Living Terrors*. New York: Delta.

Ostovsky, S., D. Beliakov, and M. Franchetti. (2004). "Death of Mercy." *Sunday Times* (London). Features Section, pp. 14–16.

Outram, D. (1995). *The Enlightenment*. New York: Oxford University Press.

Palestine Monitor. (2004). "Israel Emptying Jerusalem of Palestinians by Bulldozing their Homes." *Palestine Monitor* April 29. http://www.palestinemonitor .org/updates/israel_emptying_jerusalem_of_palestinians.htm.

Palmer, M., and P. Palmer. (2004). *At the Heart of Terror: Islam, Jihadists, and America's War on Terrorism.* Lanham, MD: Rowman & Littlefield.

Pan, E. (2005a). "Europe: Integrating Islam." Council on Foreign Relations. July 13. http://www.cfr.org/publication/8252/.

———. (2005b). "Turkey's EU Bid." Council on Foreign Relations. September 30. http://www.cfr.org/publication/8939/turkeys_eu_bid.html.

Pape, R. A. (2003). "The Strategic Logic of Suicide Bombing." *American Political Science Review* 97 (3): 1–19. www.danieldrezner.com/research/guest/Pape1 .pdf.

———. (2005). *Dying to Win: The Strategic Logic of Suicide Terrorism.* New York: Random House.

Parachini, J. (2003). "Putting WMD Terrorism into Perspective." *Washington Quarterly* 26 (4):37–50. www.mitpressjournals.org/doi/pdf/10.1162/ 016366003322387091.

Parker, L. (2002). "A Frenzied Race for Answers, Antibiotics." *USA Today,* January 23.

Parsons, T. (1951). *The Social System.* Glencoe, IL: Free Press.

Patai, R. (reprint, 2002). *The Arab Mind.* New York. Hetherleigh Press.

Paz, R. (2000). "Hamas's Lesson from Lebanon." Institute for Counter-Terrorism. http://www.ict.org.il/ home.htm.

———. (2004). "Hamas' Solidarity with Muqtada al-Sadr: Does the Movement Fall under the Control of Hizbollah and Iran?" Herzliya, Israel: PRISM Series of Special Dispatches on Global Jihad, no. 4/2.

Peacetalk. (2003). "Politics and Markets." http://www.peaktalk.com/archives/ 2003_07.php.

Pearce, S. (2005). "Religious Rage: A Quantitative Analysis of the Intensity of Religious Conflicts." *Terrorism and Political Violence* 17 (3): 333–352.

Pedahzur, A., A. Perliger, and L. Weinberg. (2003). "Altruism and Fatalism: The Characteristics of Palestinian Suicide Terrorists." *Deviant Behavior* 24 (4): 405–423.

Perl, R. F. (1998). *Terrorism: U.S. Response to Bombings in Kenya and Tanzania: A New Policy Direction?* Congressional Reference Service. CRS Report for Congress. http://usinfo.state.gov/topical/pol/terror/crs96091.htm.

———. (2001). *National Commission on Terrorism: Background and Issues for Congress.* February 6. http://www.maurizioturco.it/National_Security_Achive/ Terrorism_and_US_Policy/crs20010206.pdf.

Peters, R. (1996). *Jihad in Classical and Modern Islam.* Princeton, NJ: Marcus Wiener.

Petraeus, D. H. (2006). "Learning Counterinsurgency: Observations from Soldering in Iraq." *Military Review* (January/February). http://usacac.army.mil/ CAC/milreview/English/JanFeb06/Petraeus1.pdf.

Pew Foundation. (2005). "Pew Global Attitudes Project." http://pewglobal.org/reports/pdf/248.pdf.

Pfau, M., M. Haigh, M. Gettle, M. Donnelly, G. Scott, D. Warr, and E. Wittenberg. (2004). "Embedding Journalists in Military Combat Units: Impact on Newspaper Story Frames and Tone." *Journal of Mass Communication Quarterly* 81 (1): 74–89.

Phillips, K. (1999). *The Cousins' War: Religion, Politics, and the Triumph of Anglo-America.* New York: Basic Books.

Pillar, P. R. (2006). "Intelligence, Policy, and the War in Iraq." *Foreign Affairs* 85 (2): 15–27.

Pipes, D. (2003). *Militant Islam Reaches America.* New York: Norton.

Pisano, V. S. (1987). *The Dynamics of Subversion and Violence in Contemporary Italy.* Stanford, CA: The Hoover Institute.

Pitcavage, M. (1999a). "Anti-Government Extremism: Origins, Ideology, and Tactics." Tallahassee, FL: Institute for Intergovernmental Research.

———. (1999b). "Current Activities and Trends." Tallahassee, FL: Institute for Intergovernmental Research.

———. (1999c). "Old Wine, New Bottles: Paper Terrorism, Paper Scams, and Paper Redemption." *Militia Watch Dog*, November 8. http://www.adl.org/mwd/redemption/asp.

Pizam, A., and A. Fleischer. (2002). "Severity versus Frequency of Acts of Terrorism: Which Has a Larger Impact on Tourism Demand?" *Journal of Travel Research* 40 (3): 337–339. http://jtr.sagepub.com/cgi/content/abstract/40/3/337.

Plet, B. (1999). "World: bin Laden Behind Luxor Massacre." BBC News, May 13. http://news.bbc.co.uk/1/hi/world/middle_east/343207.stm.

Pluchinsky, D. (1982). "Political Terrorism in Western Europe: Some Themes and Variations." In Y. A. and K. A. Myers (eds.), *Terrorism in Europe.* New York: St. Martin's.

———. (1993). "Germany's Red Army Faction: An Obituary." *Studies in Conflict and Terrorism* 16:135–157.

Polack, R. J. (2004). "Social Justice and the Global Economy: New Challenges for Social Work in the 21st Century." *Social Work* 49 (2): 281–291.

Police: The Law Enforcement Magazine. (2002). "Survey." July. http://policemag.com/t_homt.cfm.

Poole, R. (2006). "New Study Calls for Rethinking TSA's Role." *Aviation Security Newsletter* 17 (January). http://www.reason.org/aviationsecurity17.shtml.

Porteous, T. (2006). "The al Qaeda Myth." TomPaine.com. http://www.tompaine.com/articles/2006/04/12/the_al_qaeda_myth.php.

Porzecanski, A. C. (1973). *Uruguay's Tupamaros.* New York: Praeger.

Posner, R. A. (2004). "The 9-11 Report: A Dissent." *New York Times*, August 29. http://www.nytimes.com/2004/08/29/books/review/29POSNERL.html?ex=1094787860&ei=1&en=b755f3ccc383aefd.

Post, J. M. (1984). "Notes on a Psychodynamic Theory of Terrorist Behavior." *Terrorism* 7:241–256.

———. (1987). "Rewarding Fire with Fire: Effects of Retaliation on Terrorist Group Dynamics." *Terrorism* 10:23–36.

Prendergast, J., and C. Thomas-Jensen. (2007). "Blowing the Horn." *Foreign Affairs* 86 (2): 59–74.

Qutb, S. (1965). *Milestones*. Repr., Indianapolis: American Trust Publications, 1990.

Raab, C. P. (2006). "Fighting Terrorism in an Electronic Age: Does the Patriot Act Unduly Compromise our Civil Liberties?" *Duke University Law and Technology Review* 0003. http://www.law.duke.edu/journals/dltr/articles/2006dltr0003 .html.

Rabasa, A., P. Chalk, K. Cragin, S. A. Daly, H. S. Gregg, T. W. Karasik, K. A. O'Brien, and W. Rosenau. (2006). *Beyond al Qaeda: Part II—The Outer Rings of the Terrorist Universe*. Santa Monica, CA: RAND.

Radelet, L., and D. Carter. (2000). *Police and the Community* (7th ed.). New York: Macmillan.

Raman, B. (2002). "Islamic Terrorism in India: The Hydra-Headed Monster." South Asia Analysis Group. http://www.saag.org/papers6/paper526.html.

———. (2003). "Istanbul: The Enemy Within." *Asia Times*. http://www.atimes .com/atimes/Middle_East/EK22Ak01.html.

———. (Mar. 3, 2004). "Massacres of Shias in Iraq and Pakistan—The Background." South Asia Analysis Group. http://www.saag.org/papers10/ paper941.html.

Randal, J. (2004). *Osama: The Making of a Terrorist*. New York: Andrew A. Knopf.

Ranstorp, M. (1994). "Hizbollah's Command Leadership: Its Structure, Decision-Making Relationship with Iranian Clergy and Institutions." *Terrorism and Political Violence* (6) Autumn. http://www.st-andrews.ac.uk/academic/intrel/ research/cstpv/pages/terrorism.html.

———. (1996). *Hizb'Allah in Lebanon: The Politics of the Western Hostage Crisis*. New York: St. Martin's Press.

———. (1998). "Interpreting the Broader Context and Meaning of Bin-Laden's Fatwa." *Studies in Conflict and Terrorism* 21:321–330.

Rapoport, D. (1984). "Fear and Trembling: Terrorism in Three Religious Traditions." *American Political Science Review* 78 (3): 658–677.

———. (1988). *Inside Terrorist Organizations*. New York: Columbia University Press.

Rashid, A. (2002). *Jihad: The Rise of Militant Islam in Central Asia*. New Haven, CT: Yale University Press.

Rasler, K. (1996). "Concessions, Repression, and Political Protest in the Iranian Revolution." *American Sociological Review* 61 (February): 132–152.

Rauf, F. A. (2004). *What's Right with Islam: A New Vision for Muslims*. San Francisco: Harper.

Raufer, X. (1993). "The Red Brigades: Farewell to Arms." *Studies in Conflict and Terrorism* 16:313–325.

Raymond, C. Z. (2006). "The Threat of Maritime Terrorism in the Malacca Straits." *Terrorism Monitor* 4 no. 3 (February 9). http://jamestown.org/terrorism/ news/article.php?issue_id=3614.

Read, C. (1996). *From Tsar to Soviets: The Russian People and their Revolution, 1917–21*. New York: Oxford University Press.

———. (1996). *From Tsar to Soviets: The Russian People and Their Revolution*. London: University College London Press.

Reese, S. (1999). *The New Jackals: Ramzi Youseff, Osama bin Laden, and the Future of Terrorism*. Boston: Northeastern University Press.

———. (2007). "State and Urban Homeland Security Plans and Exercises: Issues for the 110th Congress." Congressional Reference Service. http://www.fas.org/sgp/crs/homesec/RS22393.pdf.

Regan, T. (2004). "New Skirmishes in the Patriot Act Battle." *Christian Science Monitor*, July 14. http://www.csmonitor.com/2004/0714/dailyUpdate.html.

Reuters. (1996). "Israel Arch Foe Hizbollah Tough Nut to Crack." April 12. http://www.nando.net/newsroom/nt/412/r/whoiz.html.

———. (2004). "Paper Says al Qaeda Has Nukes." http://www.reuters.co.uk/newsPackageArticle.jhtml?type=topNews&storyID=454465&section=news. February 8.

Ricks, T. E. (2006). *Fiasco: The American Military Adventure in Iraq*. New York: Penguin.

Riley, K. J., and B. Hoffman. (1995). *Domestic Terrorism*. Santa Monica, CA: RAND. http://www.rand.org/publications/MR/MR505/MR505.pdf.

Riordan, R. J., and A. B. Zegart. (2002). "City Hall Goes to War." *New York Times*, July 5. http://www.nytimes.com/2002/07/05/opinion/05RIOR.html.

Risen, J., and J. L. Thomas. (1998). "Pro-Life Turns Deadly: The Impact of Violence on America's Anti-Abortion Movement." January 26. http://www.rickross.com/reference/a-abortion/a-abortion2.html.

Rivera, M. (n.d.). "Welcome to Puerto Rico: History." http://welcometopuertorico.org/history6.shtml (accessed 2005).

Roberts, A. (2002). "The Changing Faces of Terrorism." BBC, August 27. http://www.bbc.co.uk/history/war/sept_11/changing_faces_01.shtml.

Roberts, D. E. (1999). "Race, Vagueness, and the Social Meaning of Order-Maintenance Policing." *Journal of Criminal Law and Criminology* 89 (3): 775–836.

Rohlinger, D. A. (2002). "Framing the Abortion Debate: Organizational Resources, Media Strategies, and Movement-Countermovement Dynamics." *The Sociological Quarterly* 43 (4): 479–507.

Rojahn, C. (1998). "Left-Wing Terrorism in Germany: The Aftermath of Ideological Violence." *Conflict Studies* (October).

Rood, J. (2004). "Memo to New DHS Secretary: With Intel, Smaller Is Better." *Page Fifteen: Congressional Quarterly*. http://page15.com/2004/12/memo-to-new-dhs-secretary-with-intel.html.

Ross, J. I. (1999). "Beyond the Conceptualization of Terrorism: A Psychological-Structural Model of the Causes of This Activity." In Craig Summers and Eric Markusen (eds.), *Collective Violence: Harmful Behavior in Groups and Governments*. New York: Rowman & Littlefield.

Rotar, I. (2004a). "Hizb ut Tahrir in Central Asia." Jamestown Foundation. *Terrorism Monitor* 2, no. 4 (February 26). http://jamestown.org/terrorism/news/article.php?articleid=23567.

———. (2004b). "Hizb ut Tahrir Today." Jamestown Foundation. *Terrorism Monitor* 2, no. 5 (March 11). http://www.jamestown.org/terrorism/news/article.php?articleid=23608.

Rothem, D. (2002). "In the Spotlight: al-Asqa Martyrs Brigades." Center for Defense Information. http://www.cdi.org/terrorism/asqa.cfm.

Rubenstein, R. E. (1987). *Alchemists of Revolution*. New York: Basic Books.

Rubin, B. (2003). "Lessons from Iran." *Washington Quarterly* 26 (3): 105–115.

Rubin, B., and J. C. Rubin. (2002). *Anti-American Terrorism and the Middle East: A Documentary Reader*. New York: Oxford University Press.

Rubin, J. (2003). "Stumbling Into War." *Foreign Affairs* 82 (September/October): 46–66.

Russell, C. A. and B. H. Miller. (1983). "Profile of a Terrorist" in L. Z. Freedman and Y. Alexander (eds.), *Perspectives on Terrorism*. Wilmington, DE: Scholarly Resources.

Ruthven, M. (2000). *Islam in the World*. New York: Oxford University Press.

Sachs, J. D., J. W. MacArthur, G. Schmidt-Truab, M. Kruk, C. Bahadar, M. Faye, and G. McCord. (2004). "Ending Africa's Poverty Trap." The Brookings Institute. http://www.sociologia.unimib.it/wcms/file/materiali/2635.pdf.

Saeed, A., and H. Saeed. (2004). *Freedom of Religion, Apostasy, and Islam*. Aldershot, UK: Ashgate.

Sageman, M. (2004). *Understanding Terror Networks*. Philadelphia: University of Pennsylvania.

Said, E., and C. Hitchens. (1989). *Blaming the Victims: Spurious Scholarship and the Palestinian Question*. London: Verso.

Said, E. W., and C. Hitchens. (1990). *Blaming the Victims: Spurious Scholarship and the Palestinian Question*. New York: Verso.

Salem, P. (2006). "The Future of Lebanon." *Foreign Affairs* 85 (6).

Saradzhyan, S. (2004). "Cult of the Black Widows." *Moscow Times*. http://www.themoscowtimes.com/stories/2004/02/04/011.html. February 4.

Savage, C. (2006). "Hail to the Chief: Dick Cheney's Mission to Expand—or Restore—the Power of the Presidency." *The Boston Globe*, September 26. http://www.boston.com/news/globe/ideas/articles/2006/11/26/hail_to_the_chief/.

Scarman, L. (1972). *Violence and Civil Disturbance in Northern Ireland in 1969*. London: Her Majesty's Stationary Office.

Scaruffi, P. (2007). "A Time Line of the Indian Subcontinent." http://www.scaruffi.com/politics/indian.html.

Schabner, D. (2004). "ELF Making Good on Threat." ABCNews.com, January 30. http://abcnews.go.com/sections/us/DailyNews/elf010130.html.

Scheuer, M. (2006). *Through Our Enemies' Eyes: Osama bin Laden, Radical Islam, and the Future of America*. Washington, DC: Potomac Books.

Schmaus, W. (1999). "Functionalism and the Meaning of Social Facts." *Philosophy of Science* 66: S314–S323.

Schmid, A., and J. deGraaf. (1982). *Violence as Communication*. Newbury Park, CA: Sage.

Schmid, A. P. (1992). "The Response Problem as A Definition Problem." *Terrorism and Political Violence* 4 (4) (Winter): 7–25.

Schmid, A. P., and A. J. Jongman. (2005). *Political Terrorism: A New Guide to Actors, Authors, Concepts, Data Bases, Theories, and Literature*. Somerset, NJ: Transaction Books.

Schmitt, E. (2002). "Administration Split on Local Role in Terror Fight." *New York Times*. http://www.nytimes.com/2002/04/29/politics/29IMMI.html. April 29.

Schneider, F. (2002). "Money Supply for Terrorism—The Hidden Financial Flows of Islamic Terrorist Organisations: Some Preliminary Results from an Economic Perspective." The Economic Consequences of Global Terrorism. Berlin, June.

Schoof, M., and G. Fields. (2002). "Anthrax Attack Summary." *Wall Street Journal.* March 25.

Schramm, M., and M. Taube. (2002). "The Institution Foundations of al Qaida's Global Financial System." Related papers not presented at The Economic Consequences of Global Terrorism. Berlin conference. June.

Schuster, H. (2006). "In Pakistan, Signs of al Qaida all Around." CNN.com, September 7. http://edition.cnn.com/2006/WORLD/asiapcf/09/05/tracking.terror/index.html.

Schutz, A. (1967). *The Phenomenology of the Social World*. Evanston, IL: Northwestern University Press.

Schweitzer, Y. (2000). "Suicide Terrorism: Development and Characteristics." Institute for Counter-Terrorism. http://www.ict.org.il/_home.htm.

Scott-Joynt, Jeremy. (2003). "Charities in Terror Fund Spotlight." BBC News, October 15. http://news.bbc.co.uk/2/hi/business/3186840.

Seale, P. (1992). *Abu Nidal: A Gun for Hire*. New York: Random House.

Seelye, K. Q. (2002). "War on Terror Makes for Odd Twists in Justice System." *New York Times*, June 23. http://www.nytimes.com/2002/06/29/national/23SUSP.html.

Segaller, S. (1987). *Invisible Armies: Terrorism into the 1990s*. San Diego: Harcourt Brace Jovanovich.

Seghetti, L. M., S. R. Vina, and K. Ester. (2005). "Enforcing Immigration Law: The Role of State and Local Law Enforcement." Congressional Reference Service. http://www.ilw.com/immigdaily/news/2005,1026-crs.pdf.

Semati, M. (2002). "Imagine the Terror Television." *New Media* 13 (May): 213–218.

Serafino, N. M. (2002). "Combating Terrorism: Are There Lessons to Be Learned from Foreign Experiences?" Congressional Reference Service. http://fpc.state.gov/documents/organization/7957.pdf.

Service, R. (1995). *Lenin: A Political Life: Volume 3: The Iron Ring*. Bloomington: Indiana University Press.

———. (2005). *A History of Modern Russia: From Nicholas II to Vladmir Putin*. Cambridge, MA: Harvard University Press.

Shahar, Y. (1997). "Information Warfare." Institute for Counter-Terrorism. http://www.ict.org.il/_articles/articledet.cfm?articleid=13.

———. (1998). "Osama bin Ladin: Marketing Terrorism." Institute for Counter-Terrorism. http://www.ict.org.il/articles/articledet.cfm?articleid=42.

———. (2002). "The al-Asqa Martyrs Brigades: A Political Tool with an Edge." Institute for Counter-Terrorism. http://www.ict.org.il/articles/articledef .cfm?articleid=430.

Shahid, L. (2002). "The Sabra and Shatila Massacres: Eye-Witness Reports." *Journal of Palestine Studies* 3 (1): 36–58. http://links.jstor.org/sici?sici=0377-9 19X%28200223%2932%3A1%3C36%3ATSASME%3E2.0.CO%3B2-5&size =LARGE&origin=JSTOR-enlargePage.

Sharma, D. (2006). "Historical Traces of Hundi, Sociocultural Understanding, and Criminal Abuses of Hawala." *International Criminal Justice Review* 16 (12): 99–121. http://icj.sagepub.com/cgi/reprint/16/2/99.pdf.

Shay, S. (2002). *The Endless Jihad: The Mujahidin, the Taliban, and Bin Laden*. Herzliya, Israel: Institute for Counter-Terrorism.

Sherman, L. (1978). *The Quality of Police Education*. San Francisco: Jossey-Bass.

Shlaim, A. (2001). *The Iron Wall: Israel and the Arab World*. New York: Norton.

Shpiro, S. (2002). "Conflict Media Strategies and the Politics of Counter-Terrorism." *Politics* 22 (2): 76–85.

Shumway, J. (2005). "A Strategic Analysis of the Maneuver Enhancement Brigade." Carlyle, PA: U.S. Army War College. http://www.strategicstudiesin stitute.army.mil/pdffiles/ksil213.pdf.

Silke, A. (2001). "The Devil You Know: Continuing Problems with Research on Terrorism." *Terrorism and Political Violence* 13 (4): 1–14.

Simms, K. (2000). "The Norman Invasion and Gaelic Recovery." In R. F. Foster (ed.), *The Oxford Illustrated History of Ireland*. New York: Oxford University Press.

Simon, S., and J. Stevenson. (2004). "The Road to Damascus." *Foreign Affairs* 83 (May/June): 110–119.

Simpson, G. R., D. Crawford, and K. Johnson. (2004). "Crime Pays, Terrorist Finds." *Wall Street Journal*, April 14.

Singer, P. W. (2001). "Caution: Children at War." *Parameters* 31 (Winter). http:// www.brookings.edu/views/articles/fellows/20011203singer.pdf.

Singh, P. (1999). *The Sikhs*. New York: Knopf.

Slisli, F. (2000). "The Western Media and the Algerian Crisis." *Race and Class* 41 (3): 43–57.

Smith, B. L. (1994). *Terrorism in America: Pipe Bombs and Pipe Dreams*. Albany: State University of New York Press.

Smith, B. L., and K. R. Damphousse. (1998). "Terrorism, Politics, and Punishment: A Test of Structural Contextual Theory and the Liberation Hypothesis." *Criminology* 36 (1): 67–92.

———. (2002). *American Terrorism Study: Patterns of Behavior, Investigation, and Prosecution of American Terrorists, Final Report*. US Department of Justice. http://www.ncjrs.gov/pdffiles1/nij/grants/193420.pdf.

Smith, B. L., K. R. Damphousse, F. Jackson, and A. Sellers. (2002). "The Prosecution and Punishment of International Terrorists in Federal Courts: 1980–1998." *Criminology & Public Policy* 1 (3): 311–338.

Smith, B. L., and P. Roberts. (2005). "Pre-Incident Indicators of Terrorist Activities: The Identification of Behavioral, Geographic, and Temporal Patterns of Preparatory Conduct." National Institute of Justice. http://www.ojp.usdoj.gov/nij/maps/savannah2005/papers/Smith.ppt#397.

Snow, N. (2006). "Terrorism, Public Relations, and Propaganda." In A. P. Kavoori and T. Fraley, *Media, Terrorism, and Theory: A Reader.* Lanham, MD: Rowman & Littlefield.

Solomon, J. (2007). "FBI Finds it Frequently Overstepped in Collecting Data." *Washington Post*, June 14. http://www.washingtonpost.com/wp-dyn/content/article/2007/06/13/AR2007061302453_pf.html.

Sonmez, S. F., and Graefe, A. R. (1998). "Influence of Terrorism Risk on Foreign Tourism Decisions." *Annals of Tourism Research* 25 (1): 112–144.

Soussi, A. (2004). "The Enigma that is Lebanon's Hezbollah." *World Press Review Online*, June 14. http://www.worldpress.org/Mideast/1873.cfm.

Spechard, A., N. Tarabrina, V. Krasnov, and K. Akhmedova. (2004). "Research Note: Observations of Suicidal Terrorists in Action." *Terrorism and Political Violence* 16:305–327.

Stanton, B. (1991). *Klanwatch: Bringing the Ku Klux Klan to Justice.* New York: Grove Weidenfeld.

Sterling, C. (1986). *The Terror Net work.* New York: Dell.

Stern, J. (1999). *The Ultimate Terrorists.* Cambridge, MA: Harvard University Press.

———. (2003a). "When Bombers Are Women." Original *Washington Post*, December 18. Repr. Harvard University, John F. Kennedy School of Government. http://www.ksg.harvard.edu/news/opeds/2003/stern_women_bombers_wp1121803.htm.

———. (2003b). *Terror in the Name of God: Why Religious Militants Kill.* New York: Harper Collins.

Stern, K. S. (1996). *A Force on the Plain: The American Militia Movement and the Politics of Hate.* New York: Simon & Schuster.

Stevenson, J. (2003). "How Europe and America Defend Themselves." *Foreign Affairs* 82 (March/April): 75–90.

Storey, I. (2007). "Malaysia's Role in Thailand's Southern Insurgency." The Jamestown Foundation. *Terrorism Monitor* 5, no. 5 (May 15). http://www.jamestown.org/terrorism/news/article.php?articleid=2370279.

Straub, N. (2002). "USA Patriot Act Powers Prompt Second Look." *The Hill*, May 1. http://www.thehill.com/050102/patriot.shtm.

Strieff, D. (2006). "Inside Islam's Insurgency in Europe." MSNBC, April 10. http://www.msnbc.msn.com/id/11989895/.

Sud, H. (2004). "End Muslim Terrorism by Ending Wahhabi Influence in Saudi Arabia." South Asia Analysis Group. January 26. http://www.saag.org/papers10/paper903.html.

Sugg, J. F. (1999). "Steven Emerson's Crusade: Why Is a Journalist Pushing Questionable Sources Behind the Scene?" *Extra!* http://www.fair.org/extra/9901/emerson.html.

Sutter, D. (2001). "Can the Media Be So Liberal? The Economics of Media Bias." *The Cato Journal.* http://cato.org/pubs/journal/cj20n3/cj20n3-7.pdf.

Swanson, C. R., L. Territo, and R. W. Taylor. (2001). *Police Administration: Structures, Processes, and Behavior* (5th ed.). Upper Saddle River, NJ: Prentice-Hall.

Taber, R. (2002). *The War of the Flea: The Classic Study of Guerilla Warfare.* Dulles, VA: Potomac Books.

Taheri, A. (1987). *Holy Terror.* Bethesda, MD: Adler & Allen.

Talkleft. (2003). "Victory Act: Redefining Drug Crimes as Terrorism." August 20. http://www.w3c.org/TR1999/REC-html1401-19991224/loose.dtd.

Tamas, G. M. (2001). "The Decay of Terrorism." *East European Constitutional Review* 10 (4). http://www.law.nyu.edu/vol10num4/features/tamas.html.

Tamborini, R., J. Stiff, and C. Heidl. (1990). "Reacting to Graphic Horror: A Model of Empathy and Emotional Behavior." *Communication Research* 17:616–640. http://crx.sagepub.com/cgi/content/abstract/17/5/616.

Tamil Eelam. (n.d.). "Tamil Eelam Homepage." http://www.eelam.com/ (accessed 2005).

Taubman, P. (1984). "U.S. Said to Know Little About Group Despite Intelligence Efforts." *New York Times,* September 21, p. A13.

Taylor, R. W. (1987). "Terrorism and Intelligence." *Defense Analysis* 3:165–175.

Tenet, G. (2007). *At the Center of the Storm: My Years at the CIA.* New York: Harper Collins.

Tetlock, P. E. (2002). "Social Functionalist Frameworks for Judgment and Choice: Intuitive Politicians, Theologians, and Prosecutors." *Psychological Review* 100 (1): 451–471.

Thompson, D. (2003). "Target: Zarqawi," ABC News, October 16. http://abcnews.go.com/sections/world/WorldNewsTonight/zarqawi_030224.html.

Thorpe, T. (1996). "Black Hebrew Israelites." http://www.blackomahaonline.com/blkheb.htm.

Thussu, D. (2006). "Televising 'The War on Terrorism': The Myths of Morality." In A.P. Kavoori and T. Fraley (eds.), *Media, Terrorism, and Theory: A Reader.* Lanham, MD: Rowman & Littlefield.

Tilly, C. (2004). "Terror, Terrorism, and Terrorists." *Sociological Theory* 22 (1): 5–13.

Time. (1995). "Interview with a Fanatic—Fathi Shekaki." February 6.

Time Europe. (2004). "Defenseless Targets." September 5. http://www.time.com/time/europe/html/040913/story.html.

Times of India. (2003). "Dawood, Osama Share Smuggling Routes." http://timesofindia.indiatimes.com/cms.dll/html/uncomp/articleshow?msid=291478. November 19.

Tota, A. L. (2005). "Terrorism and Collective Memories: Comparing Bologna, Naples, and Madrid 11 March." *International Journal of Com-*

parative Sociology 46 (1–2): 55–78. http://cos.sagepub.com.ezproxy.gvsu
.edu:2048/cgi/reprint/46/1-2/55.

Trojanowicz, R. C., B. Busqueroux, V. E. Kappeler, and L. K. Ganines. (1998).
Community Policing: A Contemporary Perspective. Cincinnati, OH: Anderson.

Trundle, R. C., Jr. (1996). "Has Global Ethnic Conflict Superseded Cold War Ideology?" *Studies in Conflict and Terrorism* 19:93–107.

Turks.US. (2004). "Chechnya's Fighting Not Terror: U.S. Ambassador." February
29. http://www.turks.us/article.php?story=20040229232835832.

Turvey, B. E., D. Tamlyn, and W. J. Chisum. (1999). *Criminal Profiling: An Introduction to Behavioral Evidence Analysis.* San Diego: Academic Press.

U.S. Army. (2003). "Cultural Guide to Iraq." Fort Riley, KS: United States Army,
First Infantry Division.

U.S. Bureau of Justice Assistance. (2005). *National Criminal Intelligence Sharing
Plan.* http://www.it.ojp.gov/documents/National_Criminal_Intelligence
_Sharing_Plan.pdf.

U.S. Congress. (2004). "Intelligence Reform and Prevention of Terrorism Act
of 2004." December. http://www.congress.org/congressorg/webreturn/
?url=http://thomas.loc.gov/cgi-bin/query/z?c108:S.2845.

U.S. Congress, Office of Technology Assessment. (1995). *Environmental Monitoring for Nuclear Safeguards.* Washington, DC: Government Printing Office.

U.S. Court of Appeals. (1996). Eleventh Circuit, No. 92-4473. *United States of
America, Plaintiff-Appellee v. Robert Louis Beasley et al.* http://www.law.emory
.edu.11circuit/jan96/92-4773.man.html.

U.S. Department of Defense. (2001). "DOD USS *Cole* Commission Report." January 9. http://www.defenselink.mil/pubs/cole20010109.html.

———. (2005). *Homeland Security.* United States Joint Chiefs of Staff. http://
www.dtic.mil/doctrine/jel/new_pubs/jp3_26.pdf.

U.S. Department of Homeland Security. (2004a). "Homeland Security and
the National Academies Highlight the Role of the Media in Terrorism
Response." http://www.dhs.gov/dhspublic/display?theme=43&content=354
9&print=true.

———. (2004b). *Securing Our Homeland.* http://www.dhs.gov/interweb/assetli
brary/DHS_StratPlan_FINAL_spread.pdf.

———. (2004c). "Homeland Security and the National Academies Highlight
the Role of the Media in Terrorism Response." May 11. http://www.dhs
.gov/dhspublic/display?theme=43&content=3549&print=true.

———. (2005). "Border and Transportation Security: Securing Our Borders."
http://www.dhs.gov/dhspublic/display?theme=50&content=875.

———. (2006). "Homeland Security Information Network." http://www.dhs
.gov/xinfoshare/programs/gc_1156888108137.shtm.

U.S. Department of Justice. (2003). "Members of the Palestinian Islamic Jihad
Arrested, Charged with Racketeering and Conspiracy to Provide Support for
Terrorists." Press Release. February 20. http://www.usdoj.gov/opa/pr/2003/
February/03_crm_099.htm.

———. (n.d.). "Preserving Life and Liberty." http://www.lifeandliberty.gov/
(accessed 2005).

———. (2006). "Combat Terrorism." http://www.usdoj.gov/whatwedo/whatwedo _ct.html.

———. (2007). "United States Attorneys." http://www.usdoj.gov/usao/index .html.

U.S. Department of Justice, Office of Justice Programs. (2006). *Fusion Center Guidelines.* http://it.ojp.gov/documents/fusion_center_guidelines_law_en forcement.pdf.

U.S. Department of State. (1996). *Patterns of Global Terrorism 1995.* Washington, DC: Government Printing Office.

———. (1999). *Patterns of Global Terrorism: 1999.* http://www.state.gov/www/ global/terrorism/1999report/appb.html.

———. (2004a). "The Washington File—MIDEAST." http://usinfo.state.gov/ usinfo/products/washfile.html.

———. (2004b). *Patterns of Global Terrorism 2003."* http://www.state.gov/s/ct/rls/ pgtrpt/2003/.

———. (2004c). "Helsinki Groups Issue Three Reports on Human Rights Vi-olations in Russia." August 4. http://usinfo.state.gov/xarchives/display .html?p=washfile-english&y=2004&m=August&x=200408041344401CJsam ohT0.2353632&t=livefeeds/wf-latest.html.

———. (2007). *Country Reports on Terrorism.* http://www.state.gov/s/ct/rls/crt/ 2006/.

U.S. Department of State, Overseas Security Advisory Council. (2006). "U.S. Embassy Damascus Attack, September 12, update number 1." Unpublished briefing.

U.S. Department of the Treasury. (2003). "Informal Value Transfer Systems." http://www.fincen.gov/advis33.pdf.

U.S. Immigration and Customs Enforcement. (2005). "Two Dearborn Residents Plead Guilty to Document and Visa Fraud." http://www.ice.gov/pi/news/ newsreleases/articles/050714detroit.htm.

U.S. Marshals Service. (2005). *Monitor.* http://www.usdoj.gov/marshals/monitor/ autumn05.pdf.

U.S. Office of the Director of National Intelligence. (2007). "An Overview of the United States Intelligence Community." http://www.dni.gov/who _what/061222_DNIHandbook_Final.pdf.

Ulph, S. (2004). "Top Egyptian Terrorist Under Pressure." The Jamestown Foundation. December 9. http://www.jamestown.org/publications_details .php?volume_id=403&issue_id=3171&article_id=2368986.

———. (2006a). "Internet Mujahadeen Intensify Research on U.S. Economic Targets." *Terrorism Focus* 3 (2). http://www.jamestown.org/terrorism/news/ article.php?issue_id=3588.

———. (2006b). Internet Mujahideen Refine Electronic Warfare Tactics." *Ter-rorism Focus* 3 (5). http://www.jamestown.org/terrorism/news/article .php?issue_id=3611.

United Kingdom, House of Commons. (2001). *Operation Enduring Freedom and the Conflict in Afghanistan: An Update.* House of Commons. http://www .parliament.uk/commons/lib/research/rp2001/rp01-081.pdf.

———. (2006). "Report of the Official Account of the Bombings in London on 7 July 2005." House of Commons. http://news.bbc.co.uk/1/shared/bsp/hi/pdfs/11_05_06_narrative.pdf.

United Kingdom, Intelligence and Security Committee. (2006). "Report into the London Terrorist Attacks on 7 July 2005." Report for Parliament. http://news.bbc.co.uk/1/shared/bsp/hi/pdfs/11_05_06_isc_london_attacks_report.pdf.

United Nations. (1948). "Universal Declaration of Human Rights." http://www.un.org/Overview/rights.html.

United States of America v. Mohamad Youseff Hammoud, et al. (March 2002). United States District Court, Western District of North Carolina., Charlotte Division. Docket No. 3:00CR147-MU.

United States of America v. Mousa Mohammed Abu Marzook, et al. (2003). U.S. District Court, Northern District of Illinois, Eastern Division. Docket No. 03 CR 978.

University of Singapore. (2007). "Contemporary Post-Colonial and Post-Imperial Literature in English—Frantz Fanon." http://www.scholars.nus.edu.sg/post/poldiscourse/fanon/fanonov.html.

Uris, L. (1977). *Trinity.* New York: Bantam Books.

Valburn, M. (2002). "Air Marshal Program Drains Other Agencies." *Wall Street Journal*, February 4, A18.

Van Natta, D., Jr. (2002). "Government Will Ease Limits on Domestic Spying." *New York Times*, March 30. http://www.nytimes.com/2002/03/30.html.

Vasilenko, V. I. (2004). "The Concept and Typology of Terrorism." *Statutes and Decisions* 40 (5): 46–56. http://mesharpe.metapress.com/link.asp?id=rj98031ck9y4b41h.

Vatis, M. A. (1999). *Emergency Law Enforcement Services Vulnerability Survey.* Quantico, VA: Federal Bureau of Investigation.

———. (2001). *Cyber Attacks during the War on Terrorism: A Predictive Analysis.* Hanover, NH: Institute for Security Technology Studies, Dartmouth College.

Vest, G. (2007). "Ohio Local Law Enforcement Information Sharing Network: Policy Issues in Data Exchange." *The Police Chief* 72 (6). http://policechiefmagazine.org/magazine/index.cfm?fuseaction=display_arch&article_id=612&issue_id=62005.

Vice President's Task Force on Terrorism. (1986). *The Public Report of the Vice President's Task Force on Terrorism.* http://www.population-security.org/bush_report_on_terrorism/bush_report_on_terrorism.htm.

Victoroff, J. (2005). "The Mind of a Terrorist." *Journal of Conflict Resolution* 49 (1): 3–42.

von Hippel, K. (2002). "The Roots of Terrorism: Probing the Myths." *The Political Quarterly.* www.blackwell-synergy.com/doi/pdf/10.1111/1467-923X.73.s1.4.

Waldmann, P. (1986). "Guerrilla Movements in Argentina, Guatemala, Nicaragua, and Uruguay." In P. Merkle (ed.), *Political Violence and Terror.* Berkeley: University of California Press.

Walker, E. W. (2001). "Roots of Rage: Militant Islam in Central Asia." University of California, Berkeley. http://ist-socrates.berkeley.edu/~bsp/caucasus/articles/walker_2001-1029.pdf.

Walker, S. (1985). *Sense and Nonsense about Crime: A Policy Guide*. Pacific Grove, CA: Brooks/Cole.

———. (1992). *The Police in America*. New York: McGraw-Hill.

Wallach, J., and J. Wallach. (1992). *Arafat in the Eyes of the Beholder*. Rocklin, CA: Prima.

Wall Street Journal Research Staff. (2005). "A Chronology of Violence." *Wall Street Journal*, p. A16. November 11.

Walter, J. (1995). *Every Knee Shall Bow: The Truth and Tragedy of Ruby Ridge and the Randy Weaver Family*. New York: HarperCollins.

Walter, J. P. (2002). "National Drug Control Strategy: Combating Narcoterrorism." May 2. http://fpc.state.gov/9908.htm.

Ward, R., and S. Hill. (2002). Institute for the Study of Violent Groups. Sam Houston State University, College of Criminal Justice. http://www.isgv.org/index.php?option=com_content&task=view&id=29&Itemid=61 (accessed December 21, 2006).

Wardlaw, G. (1982). *Political Terrorism: Theory, Tactics, and Counter-Measures*. London: Cambridge University Press.

Warwick, D. P. (1975). *A Theory of Public Bureaucracy: Politics, Personality, and Organization in the State Department*. Cambridge, MA: Harvard University Press.

Watson, D. L. (2002). *The Terrorist Threat Confronting the United States*. Washington, DC: Federal Bureau of Investigation, www.fbi.gov.

Waxman, D. (1998a). "The Islamic Republic of Iran: Between Revolution and Realpolitik." *Conflict Studies* (April).

Weatherston, D., and J. Moran (2003). "Terrorism and Mental Illness: Is There a Relationship?" *International Journal of Offender Therapy and Comparative Criminology* 47 (6): 698–713. http://ijo.sagepub.com.ezproxy.gvsu.edu:2048/cgi/content/abstract/47/6/698.

Weber, M. (1947). *The Theory of Social and Economic Organization*. New York: Free Press.

Wedgwood, R. (2002). "The Enemy Within." *Wall Street Journal*, June 14, A12.

Wege, C. A. (1991). "The Abu Nidal Organization." *Terrorism* 14:59–66.

———. (1994). "Hizbollah Organization. *Studies in Conflict and Terrorism* (17): 151–164.

Weinberg, L., A. Pedhahzur, and S. Hirsh-Hoefler. (2004). "The Challenges of Conceptualizing Terrorism." *Terrorism and Political Violence* 16, no. 4 (Winter): 777–794.

Weitz, R. (2004). "Storm Clouds over Central Asia: Revival of the Islamic Movement of Uzbekistan (IMU)?" *Studies in Conflict and Terrorism* 27 (6): 505–530.

West, D. L. (2005). "Combatting Terrorism in the Horn of Africa." Harvard University, Belfer Center for Science and International Relations. http://bcsia.ksg.harvard.edu/BCSIA_content/documents/Yemen%20Report%20BCSIA.pdf.

Westcott, K. (2000). "Who Are Hamas?" BBC News Online, October 19. http://news.bbc.co.uk/1/hi/world/middle_east/978626.stm.

Westphal, K. (2003). "Steganography Revealed." http://www.securityfocus.com/infocus/1684.

Wheeler, W. (2003). "Second End to Major Hostilities." Center for Defense Information. December 20. http://www.cdi.org/program/document.cfm?DocumentID=1967&StartRow=1&ListRows=10&appendURL=&Orderby=D.DateLastUpdated&ProgramID=39&from_page=index.cfm.

Whine, M. (1999). "Cyberspace: A New Medium for Communication, Command, and Control by Extremists." Institute for Counter-Terrorism. http://www.ict.org.il/articles/articledet.cfm?articleid=76.

White House. (2003). "Progress Report on the Global War on Terrorism." September 11. http://usinfo.state.gov/xarchives/display.html?p=washfile-english&y=2003&m=September&x=20030911,84825ynnedd0.9592859&t=usinfo/wf-latest.html.

White, J. R. (1986). *Holy War: Terrorism as a Theological Construct.* Gaithersburg, MD: International Association of Chiefs of Police.

———. (1997). "Militia Madness: Extremist Interpretations of Christian Doctrine." *Perspectives: A Journal of Reformed Thought* 12:8–12.

———. (2000). "The Religious Roots of Criminal Behavior." Tallahassee, FL: Institute for Intergovernmental Research.

———. (2001). "Political Eschatology: A Theology of Antigovernment Extremism." *American Behavioral Scientist* 44:937–956.

———. (2002). *Political Violence.* Tallahassee, FL: Institute for Intergovernmental Research.

———. (2004a). *Defending the Homeland: Domestic Intelligence, Law Enforcement, and Security.* Belmont, CA: Wadsworth/Thomson Learning.

———. (2004b). "International Terrorism in Transition." Institute of Intergovernmental Research, Tallahassee, FL.

———. (2007). "Networks and Netwars." First National Fusion Center Conference, Destin, FL. February. Unpublished.

White, R. W. (1989). "From Peaceful Protest to Guerrilla War: Micromobilization of the Provisional Irish Republican Army." *The American Journal of Sociology* 94 (6): 1277–1302.

———. (1993). *Provisional Irish Republicans: An Oral and Interpretative History.* Westport, CT: Greenwood Press.

Wickham-Crowley, T. P. (1992). *Guerrillas and Revolution in Latin America: A Comparative Study of Insurgents and Regimes Since 1956.* Princeton, NJ: Princeton University Press.

Wieviorka, M. (1993). *The Making of Terrorism.* Chicago: University of Chicago Press.

Wikas, Seth. (2002). "The Hamas Ceasefire: Historical Background, Future Foretold?" Peacewatch. http://www.washingtoninstitute.org/watch/Peacewatch/peacewatch2002/357.htm.

Wilkinson, P. (1974). *Political Terrorism.* New York: Wiley.

————. (1997). "The Media and Terrorism: A Reassessment." *Terrorism and Political Violence* 9 (Summer): 51–64.

Williams, B. G., and F. Altindag. (2004). "El Kaide Turka: Tracing an al-Qaeda Splinter Cell." The Jamestown Foundation. *Terrorism Monitor* 2, no. 22 (November 18). http://www.jamestown.org/print_friendly.php?volume_id =400&issue_id=3148&article_id=2368888.

Willis, C. (2005). *The I Hate Ann Coulter, Bill O'Reilly, Rush Limbaugh, Michael Savage, Sean Hannity . . . Reader.* New York: Thunder's Mouth Press.

Wilson, E. O. (1999). *Consilience: The Utility of the Unknown.* New York: Vintage Press.

Winchester, S. (1974). *Northern Ireland in Crisis.* New York: Holmes & Meier.

Windrem, R., and C. Gubash. (2004). "Many Signs Point to al-Qaida." MSNBC News, March 11. http://msnbc.msn.com/id/4507855/.

Wingate, J. E. (2006). "Steganography: Threat or Hype?" *Homeland Security Report*, 167. http://www.terrorisminfo.mipt.org/pdf/hsr167.pdf.

Wise, C. R., and R. Nadar. (2002). "Organizing the Federal System for Homeland Security: Problems, Issues, and Dilemmas." *Public Administration Review* 62 (s1): 44–57.

Wise, D. (2002). "Spy Game: Changing the Rules So the Good Guys Win." *New York Times*, June 2. http://www.nytimes.com/2002/06/02/weekinreview/ 02WISEhtml.

Wolf, J. B. (1981). *Fear of Fear.* New York: Plenum.

Wolfowitz, P. (2004). "Ask the White House." The White House. http://www .whitehouse.gov/ask/20040625.html.

Wolfsfeld, G. (2001). "The News Media and the Second Intifada: Some Initial Lessons." *Press/Politics* 6 (4): 113–118.

Woodcock, G. (2004). *Anarchism: A History of Libertarian Ideas and Movements.* Peterborough, Ontario: Broadview Press, Broadview Encore Editions.

Woodham-Smith, C. (1962). *The Great Hunger.* New York: Harper & Row.

Wright, J., and K. Bryett. (2000). *Policing and Conflict in Northern Ireland.* New York: Palgrave Macmillan.

Wright, L. (2006). *The Looming Tower: Al Qaeda and the Road to 9-11.* New York: Knopf.

Wright, R. (1986). *Sacred Rage.* New York: Touchstone.

————. (1989). *In the Name of God: The Khomeini Decade.* New York: Simon & Schuster.

————. (2000). *The Last Great Revolution: Turmoil and Transformation in Iran.* New York: Knopf.

Young, J. A. T., and J. Collier. (2002). "Attacking Anthrax." *Scientific American* (March): 48–59.

Zassoursky, Y. N. (2002). "Media and Communications as the Vehicle of the Open Society." *The International Journal for Communication Studies* 64 (5): 425–432.

Zissis, C. (2006). "The Sri Lankan Conflict." Council on Foreign Relations. September 11. http://www.cfr.org/publication/11407/sri_lankan_conflict.html?breadcrumb=%2Fregion%2F289%2Fsri_lanka.

———. (2007). "Terror Groups in India." Council on Foreign Relations. March 5. http://www.cfr.org/publication/12773/terror_groups_in_india.html#4.

Index

Italic page numbers indicate material in tables, figures, maps, or expanded text.

TO THE OWNER OF THIS BOOK:

I hope that you have found *Terrorism and Homeland Security,* Sixth Edition useful. So that this book can be improved in a future edition, would you take the time to complete this sheet and return it? Thank you.

School and address:_____

Department:_____

Instructor's name:_____

1. What I like most about this book is:_____

_____

_____

2. What I like least about this book is:

_____

_____

3. My general reaction to this book is:

_____

_____

4. The name of the course in which I used this book is:

_____

5. Were all of the chapters of the book assigned for you to read?_____

    If not, which ones weren't?_____

6. In the space below, or on a separate sheet of paper, please write specific suggestions for improving this book and anything else you'd care to share about your experience in using this book.

_____

_____

_____

DO NOT STAPLE   PLEASE SEAL WITH TAPE

FOLD HERE

WADSWORTH
CENGAGE Learning

BUSINESS REPLY MAIL
FIRST-CLASS MAIL   PERMIT NO. 34   BELMONT CA

POSTAGE WILL BE PAID BY ADDRESSEE

Attn: Carolyn Henderson Meier, Criminal Justice
Editor
Wadsworth Cengage Learning
10 Davis Drive
Belmont, CA   94002-9801

FOLD HERE

OPTIONAL:

Your name:_____ Date: _____

May we quote you, either in promotion for *Terrorism and Homeland Security,* Sixth
Edition, or in future publishing ventures?

Yes: _____ No:_____

Sincerely yours,

Jonathan R. White